THE LANGUAGE OF
SPORT

THE LANGUAGE OF
SPORT

BY TIM CONSIDINE

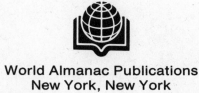

World Almanac Publications
New York, New York

Illustrations: Ed Murawinski
Interior design: Cris Graña
Cover design: Tom Ruis
Cover painting: Tommy Soloski

First published in paperback in 1983.

Paperback edition distributed in the United States by Ballantine Books, a division of Random House, Inc. and in Canada by Random House of Canada, Ltd.

Library of Congress Catalog Card Number 82-61797
Newspaper Enterprise Association, Inc. ISBN 0-911818-25-1
Ballantine Books ISBN 0-345-30398-9

A hardcover edition of this book was originally published by Facts On File, Inc.

Printed in the United States of America

Newspaper Enterprise Association, Inc.
World Almanac Publications
200 Park Avenue
New York, NY 10166

This book is dedicated to the late Bob Considine, whose kindness
and hospitality I'm afraid I tested at the beginning of my professional involvement
with sports, and to all the other great writers and broadcasters,
past and present, who have added so much to our
enjoyment and understanding of athletics by enriching,
popularizing, and, in many cases,
creating the language of sport.

For Willie and Chris

CONTENTS

PREFACE

When man first conceived the notion of sports, that is the codifying of contests into repeatable games and competitions, a new language was born. This volume is a dictionary of that language some three thousand years later in this, the age of sports medicine, sports law, sports science, and twenty-four-hour satellite coverage by sports-only cable television networks. In the 1980s, more people than ever before participate in, watch, follow, and talk sports.

Sports language is so universal and its imagery so strong that some of it finds its way into non-sports use. Something is said to have come "out of left field" or a good looking person is called a "knockout." "Heavyweight," "can't get to first base," and "throw in the towel," are other popular examples. The expression "to start from scratch" dates back to 776 B.C. and the first Olympic Games, where the starting point for a jumping contest or a footrace was a line scratched in the sand. There are more obscure examples as well. The word "agony" is derived from the Greek word *agon,* which means athletic contest. "Ascetic" is also Greek derived, meaning an athlete in full training. Even the Bible contains sports language and imagery. In the Authorized Version of the New Testament, Acts 20:24, St. Paul sums up his life, "I have fought the good fight. I have finished my course. I have kept the faith. Henceforth there is laid up for me a crown of righteousness." Mostly, though, the language is used to enhance the enjoyment of the sports it describes—whether accurately, colorfully, passionately, or humorously.

Because of the constant state of flux of all languages, even as this work is being prepared, new words and expressions are being formed which will eventually find acceptance and popular use. The over-5,000 entries defined herein represent a comprehensive collection of traditional and contemporary terminology, jargon, and slang from nine of the most popular sports.

Each chapter begins with a history tracing the growth and development of the sport from its origins to the present day, with emphasis on the formulation of rules, important firsts, and famous or noteworthy players and contributors. An alphabetical listing of terms follows, using the most common spelling. Whenever possible, specific origins, anecdotes, and related records accompany the term definitions. Broadened or secondary uses, and those removed from the original sports usage, are also included.

i

ACKNOWLEDGMENTS

The author would like to thank the many people who have helped to make this book possible, including Editorial Assistant and Research Coordinator Ellen Baskin; Researchers David Aust, Bob Borgen, Roger Cossack, Tom Craig, Geoffrey Dean-Smith, LeeAn Lowe, Joe McDonnell, Bob Rodgers, and Carl Wilson; Patricia Fisher, Assistant Editor, World Almanac Publications; and the coaches, athletes, officials, administrators, writers, broadcasters, and sports afficianados who provided invaluable assistance, information, and encouragement in the preparation of this volume, among them Joe Axelson (General Manager and President, Kansas City Kings), Jim Campbell (Research Editor, NFL Properties), Sam Foulds (USSF Historian), Hadassa Gilbert (USSF referee), Herbert Goldman (Managing Editor, *The Ring*), Gail Goodrich (former Los Angeles Laker All-Star player), Richard D. Haskell (Executive Director, Massachusetts Golf Association), Mike Holder (Vice President, Los Angeles Bowling Association), Toros Kibritjian (FIFA and senior NASL referee), Patrick Leahy (USGA Press Relations Manager), Mario Machado (radio and television broadcaster), Prof. Julio Mazzei (coach, New York Cosmos), Pete Newell (Basketball Hall of Fame coach and general manager), Carlos Palomino (former World Welterweight Champion), Chuck Pezzano (Bowling Hall of Famer and author), Don Sawyer (international amateur, college, and high school basketball referee), Norm Schacter (NFL Rule Book Co-editor and League Observer), Bob Sibbald (NASL player and coach), Dr. Edward S. Steitz (President ABAUSA, Editor USA rules, member FIBA Technical Committee), June Steitz (Librarian, Basketball Hall of Fame), Burt Randolph Suger (Editor and Publisher, *The Ring*), and Gary Wiren (PGA Director of Club Relations).

The author would also like to thank the following organizations for information and materials provided: the Amateur Athletic Union (AAU), the Amateur Basketball Association of the United States of America (ABAUSA), the Amateur Hockey Association of the United States (AHAUS), the American Bowling Congress (ABC), the American League (AL), the American Soccer League (ASL), the American Youth Soccer Organization (AYSO), the Association of Tennis Professionals (ATP), the Basketball Hall of Fame, the Canadian Football League (CFL), the Consulate General of the People's Republic of China in San Francisco, the International Ice Hockey Federation (IIHF), the International Tennis Federation (ITF), the Ladies Professional Golf

Association (LPGA), the Major Indoor Soccer League (MISL), the National Collegiate Athletic Association (NCAA), the National Football League (NFL), the National Football League Players Association (NFLPA), the National Golf Foundation, the National Hockey League (NHL), the National League (NL), the North American Soccer League (NASL), Pop Warner Football, the Professional Bowlers Association (PBA), the Professional Golfer's Association (PGA), *Soccer America*, Team Tennis, *The Ring*, the United States Golf Association (USGA), the United States Soccer Federation (USSF), the United States Tennis Association (USTA), the Women's Sports Foundation, and the Women's Tennis Association (WTA).

INTRODUCTION

There are those who think that the world of sport is inhabited by monosyllabic mastodons whose longest sentence is, "I hit it real good."

This volume makes it clear that sport does, in fact, have a language of its own. It is a language that is often crisp and to the point, sometimes witty and seldom obscure.

In fact, many of its words and phrases are so clearly descriptive of situations that they are heard as often in the board room as the locker room. Negotiators throw "ballpark figures" at each other (to indicate whether one man's proposal is even "in the ballpark" as far as the other man's expectations are concerned) and even change the noun into a verb ("we had a ballparking session before getting down to the hard negotiating").

Politicans and businessmen who engage in tough infighting are said to be "playing hardball." Political campaigns are "in the homestretch" some months after the candidates "burst from the starting gate." Pollsters often expect a "photo finish."

Any company that begins the fiscal year without a "game plan" is liable to find itself "behind the eight ball" twelve months later.

Sometimes the phrases suffer in translation to everyday life. For example, a person feeling "under par" is not feeling well, whereas a golfer who is under par is in excellent shape.

The language of sport is a lively, changing language. Last year's "pass rush" becomes next year's "Red Dog," by a "blitzing" linebacker in an attempt to "sack" the quarterback. In time, the verb "sack" becomes a noun in the statistics column: "number of QB sacks."

It is time, then, that the whole business be put into an orderly and authoritative volume that can be used for reference or recreation. This is what Tim Considine has done.

I suspect it will be used to settle many a bar bet. I recommend it to wives of hardened sports viewers. If you can't fight them and don't want to join them, you at least can understand what they are talking about if you read this book in small, steady doses.

It is much more than a sports dictionary. In reading it, I was struck by the abrupt, staccato sound of modern sports expressions compared to the soft, reminiscent expressions of the old days.

In the baseball section, for example, there are expressions like Iron Mike (the automatic pitching machine), flake (an odd personality), DH (for designated hitter), and AstroTurf, which hardly evokes the smells and memories associated with the phrase "freshly-mowed green grass." These, however, are the sports words of the eighties.

But the older words and phrases—they are like a childhood thrill re-lived; an old book re-discovered; summer evenings talking baseball with your cousin on the back porch to the accompaniment of crickets and the taste of fresh peach ice cream.

Consider a few:

The Baltimore chop, that high bouncing hit used by the fast-running original Orioles of the Gay Nineties.

The Chicago slide, the original hook slide made famous by King Kelly of the 1880s' Chicago White Stockings, They wrote a song about him: "Slide, Kelly, Slide."

A high fly ball is called a "can of corn," because grocers at the turn of the century kept corn on the top shelf, easy to catch.

Black Betsy—the favorite bat of Shoeless Joe Jackson, that great hitter later disgraced in the Black Sox Scandal. It was he to whom the little boy is supposed to have said, "Say it ain't so, Joe."

Joe McGinnity was the first player called "Iron Man," originally because he had worked in an iron foundry. But he lived up to the name, once pitching five wins in six days, pitching and winning both ends of a doubleheader many times, and playing the game until he was fifty-four.

Is it nostalgia that makes the players and expressions of Ring Lardner's baseball world seem more colorful, appealing, and touching than the wealthy star of today who finds no contradiction in being called "hard-nosed" while doing men's cosmetic commercials?

Or has something been lost along the way?

You can make your own decision while browsing through this book.

In a day when it sometimes seems we read more about free agentry, compensation and three-tiered playoffs than we do about the games themselves, it is fascinating to find a book that in its simple alphabetical listings often takes us back to a time when writers as good as Ring Lardner wrote poems about the heroes of the day.

Under the letter "F" you'll find "Fadeaway," a pitch made famous by Christy Mathewson of the Giants, who pitched so well and died so young. You'll find there the final lines of Lardner's tribute to Mathewson:

> *"May the flowers ne'er wither, Matty*
> *On your grave in Cincinnati*
> *Which you've chosen for your final fadeaway."*

Corny?
Well, it beats the heck out of reading about lawyers.

Jim McKay

BASEBALL

Bat and ball games have been played throughout history by many different cultures, but baseball is most closely related to cricket, the earliest form of which dates back to England in 1300 and the reign of Edward I, and another English sport, rounders. In 1744, the first published reference to rounders, a woodcut of children playing the game with an accompanying verse titled, "Base Ball," appeared in *A Little Pretty Pocket Book*.

It was rounders, a more impromptu game than cricket, that the sons of early American settlers most frequently played. Numerous variations emerged, but all drew on the basic ideas and equipment of rounders. Two teams of nine players took turns hitting a thrown ball with a bat in order to score by running around a set of four posts without being put out by fielders catching the ball or touching it to a post before the batter arrived. Eventually, the posts became bases, the bowler (thrower) a pitcher, and the bowler's square a pitcher's mound. By the 1840s, a new game was evolving that resembled rounders and utilized much of its terminology, but reflected the active, freewheeling American personality. The oblong bat was made round and lengthened, allowing more powerful hits, and it became necessary to anchor the bases to withstand the headlong lunges of runners trying to avoid being "plugged" (a popular innovation which allowed a base runner to be put out between bases by being hit with a thrown ball). Exact rules and playing field configurations varied from town to town, and the game was known by a variety of names including "one old cat" and "two old cat," or simply "town ball."

Though a once popular legend held that Abner Doubleday, a U.S. Army general, laid out the first baseball diamond in 1839 at Cooperstown, New York (present site of the Baseball Hall of Fame and Museum), most historians now agree that the first real baseball game took place at the Elysian Fields in Hoboken, New Jersey on June 19, 1846. In that historic contest, played under rules established by Alexander Cartwright, who umpired the game, the New York Nine defeated the Knickerbockers by a score of 23-1. Soon amateur teams throughout the East and Midwest were playing versions of Cartwright's "New York Game." In 1859, Amherst played Williams in the first college level game, with Amherst winning 66-32.

After the Civil War, during which Southerners picked up the game from Union prisoners, baseball's popularity spread rapidly. Amateur teams representing cities went on barnstorming tours to play the local favorites. As a result of a humiliating defeat administered by one of these traveling teams, the Washington Nationals, some angry citizens of Cincinnati decided to do something radical. In 1869, the Cincinnati Red Stockings became the first professional baseball team. That year, on an 11,000 mile tour of their own, the Red Stockings compiled a record of fifty-six wins and one tie, attracting interest wherever they played.

The economic potential of the sport was becoming more and more evident. In 1871 the National Association of Professional Baseball Players, the first attempt at a professional league, was formed with nine teams competing. The Philadelphia Athletics won the first championship. Though plagued by erratic scheduling and a lack of strong leadership, the league continued on, managing to struggle through the 1875 season before the taint of gambling and bribery finally caused its failure.

In February of 1876, a group of businessmen and club representatives led by Chicago White Stockings owner, William Hulbert, drew up a constitution for a new federation, and on April 22, 1876, with the strongest organizations and the best players of the old Association in tow, the National League opened its first season with a game in Philadelphia. On that day, Boston defeated the home team 6-5 in front of 3,000 spectators.

By 1881, the National League had demonstrated enough success to inspire a new rival league, the American Association. Armed with players lured away from National League teams and with innovations like Sunday baseball games, an admission price of twenty-five cents (as opposed to fifty cents in the National League), and the sale of beer in the ballparks, the American Association soon became a formidable competitor. In 1883, the two leagues signed a mutually protective document called the National Agreement to prevent further harm to either from player raids. The uneasy truce lasted until 1890 when a number of the best players from both leagues, frustrated at being treated as chattel by the owners and united since 1885 in the Brotherhood of Professional Ballplayers, broke off and started their own league, the Players' League. Their venture lasted only one season and ultimately few concessions were won, but the added competition had managed to deal a crippling blow to the struggling American Association. Further weakened when some of the best Players' League personnel were reassigned to the National League, the American Association went under in 1891, no longer able to meet rising operating expenses with the twenty-five cent admission.

In one year, major league baseball went from twenty-four teams to twelve. With just the strongest pitchers remaining, batters suddenly found themselves struggling (only eleven batters hit over .300 in 1892, as compared to twenty-three the previous year). Fearing that interest in the game might dwindle, the baseball owners moved the pitcher's rubber back from 50 feet to 60 feet, 6 inches for the 1893 season. After forty-seven years of constant change, the measurements and configuration of the baseball diamond, as well as most of the rules of the game, had finally stabilized (and remain substantially the same to this day).

In 1901, the National League was again threatened. Ban Johnson, who for seven years had been carefully grooming a successful minor league recently renamed the American League, moved four well-financed franchises into Eastern cities, withdrew from the National Agreement, and proclaimed the new eight-team American League a full-fledged major league. With rosters made up of former National League players, including future Hall of Famers Cy Young, "Iron Man" Joe McGinnity, John McGraw, and Nap Lojoie (who jumped from the National League Phildelphia Phillies to the American League Philadelphia Athletics), the new league was a credible competitor the first season, even managing to outdraw the senior circuit in two long-time National League strongholds, Boston and Chicago. Within two years the National League was forced to recognize the new league as an equal, and the first World Series was played at the end of the 1903 season and won by the American League Boston Pilgrims over the Pittsburgh Pirates. The modern era of baseball had begun.

Thereafter, nothing, including scandal (the shocking discovery that some key Chicago White Sox players had thrown the 1919 World Series with Cincinnati) or war, could come between the American people and the sport embraced as the "National Pastime." Chronicled with skill and care by some of America's keenest observers, from Ring Lardner, Damon Runyon and Grantland Rice to Red Smith, no other sport has made more colorful or numerous contributions to the history and lore of American sport or to everyday language than baseball. Ty Cobb, Christy Mathewson, the legendary Babe Ruth, Lou Gehrig, Dizzy Dean, Joe DiMaggio, Bob Feller, Ted Williams, Jackie Robinson, Stan Musial, Willie Mays, Mickey Mantle, Sandy Koufax, Roberto Clemente, Hank Aaron, Carl Yastrzemski, and Pete Rose are just some of the heroes the game has created. Today, baseball, long the most popular sport in America, has spread far beyond the North American continent, thrilling fans across the seas as far away as Japan and China.

aboard: On base. (two away with one aboard and the tying run at the plate)

ace: A very good pitcher, usually a team's best. In 1869 the first professional baseball club, the Cincinnati Red Stockings, won fifty-six out of fifty-seven games (one tie), incredibly using only one pitcher, Asa Brainard. The following year, any pitcher who put together a string of victories or pitched a particularly impressive game was likened to Brainard and called an "Asa," which eventually became ace. also *stopper*.

••One who excels in any field. (ace reporter)

air it out: To hit the ball a long distance.

alley: The area of the outfield between the players in center field and left field or center field and right field.

All-Star break: The three-day suspension of regular season games by both the American League and the National League to provide for the annual All-Star Game.

All-Star Game: The annual July exhibition game between the best players of the American League and the National League, as chosen by baseball fans through ballots. At the suggestion of *Chicago Tribune* sports editor Arch Ward, the first All-Star Game was played at Comiskey Park in Chicago on July 6, 1933 and was won by the American League.

aluminum bat: A round, one-piece tubular metal bat used in softball (maximum length: 34 inches; maximum barrel diameter: 2-1/4 inches), welded at the knob end and plugged at the barrel end with a contoured hard rubber insert. A grip-improving wrap or material is mandatory for softball (maximum length: 10 inches, and extending no more than 15 inches from the end of the handle) and optional for amateur baseball (extending no more than 18 inches from the end of the handle).

American League: One of the two major professional baseball leagues in the United States. Created in 1900 by Byron "Ban" Johnson, the American League played its first game on April 24, 1901. At that time, there were teams in Chicago, Boston, Detroit, Philadelphia, Baltimore, Washington, Cleveland, and Milwaukee. Although even today the American League is sometimes referred to as the "junior circuit" by members of the older National League, the American League has been considered an equal competitor since the first World Series competition between the two leagues in 1903. The American League Boston Pilgrims won that first best-of-nine series five games to three against the National League Pittsburgh Pirates. The American League is now split into two divisions. In the Western Division, the teams are California, Chicago, Kansas City, Minnesota, Oakland, Seattle, and Texas. In the Eastern Division, the teams are Baltimore, Boston, Cleveland, Detroit, Milwaukee, New York, and Toronto. Abbreviated AL.

American Legion Baseball: A league sponsored by the American Legion since 1926 providing a program of summer baseball for fifteen to eighteen-year-olds. Headquartered in Indianapolis, Indiana, American Legion Baseball conducts an annual World Series tournament for the eight regional United States champions in the month of August.

angel: A cloud that shields the sun from the

eyes of an outfielder preparing to catch a high fly ball. also *guardian angel*.

Annie Oakley: 1. A free ticket to a baseball game. Named by American League president Ban Johnson, because of the resemblance of complimentary baseball tickets (punched with holes) to the playing cards the legendary Annie Oakley shot holes through at Buffalo Bill's Wild West shows in the late 1800s. 2. A base on balls. A walk is considered a free pass, or free ticket, or free trip to first base.

appeal: The official notification to an umpire of a rules infraction such as batting out of order, or a baserunning infraction, or an official request to consult a base umpire in the case of a half swing that has been called a ball. see *appeal play, batting out of order, half swing.*

appeal play: A play made in conjunction with an appeal when a base runner fails to tag up after a fly ball is caught or fails to touch a base when advancing or when returning to his original base. If a member of the defensive team tags the runner or touches the missed base while holding the ball and makes an appeal to the umpire before the next pitch, the runner is out.

apple: A slang word for ball, popularized in the 1920s by players and sportswriters. also *horsehide.*

arbiter: An umpire.

arm: 1. The ability to make a strong, accurate throw, particularly a long throw from the outfield. 2. A player known for the ability to make strong, accurate throws from the outfield. A list of the great arms in baseball history would have to include Al Kaline of the Detroit Tigers, Bob Kennedy, who played both infield and outfield, Carl "The Reading (Pa.) Rifle" Furillo, and Hall of Famers Chick Hafey, Joe DiMaggio, Mickey Mantle, Roberto Clemente, and Willie Mays. California Angels outfielder Ellis Valentine is among those most frequently mentioned as the best arm in contemporary baseball.

around the horn: 1. The ritual of throwing the ball around the infield after an out (when there are no base runners). 2. A double play in which the third baseman fields the ball and throws to the second baseman, who throws to first base. From the old nautical expression, comparing the flight of the ball to the only route between the Atlantic and Pacific before the Panama Canal was built: all the way around South America, with second base representing Cape Horn, the halfway mark.

artificial turf: A synthetic grass substitute used in some ballparks and sold under a variety of trade names.

aspirin: A fastball. see *fastball.*

assist: A throw or deflection of a batted or thrown ball to a teammate, resulting in a putout, or one that would have resulted in a putout except for a subsequent error by a teammate.

AstroTurf: A brand of artificial turf.

at bat: 1. Now batting or about to bat. Part of the expression "at bat, on deck, in the hole," a corruption of the original "at bat, on deck, in the hold," first uttered in 1872 at a game between a local team and the Boston Red Stockings in the small coastal city of Belfast, Maine. This nautical imagery was chosen to inform the watching crowd of seamen and their families who was batting, who was next, and who was waiting to follow. also *at the plate, up.* 2. A turn as a batter that is charged to a player in statistical records and considered in calculating the player's batting average, slugging average, and home run percentage. An "at bat" is not charged when a player hits a sacrifice bunt or fly, receives a base on balls, is hit by a pitched ball, or is interfered with or obstructed by a defensive player.

atom ball: A ball hit right to a defensive player, or "at 'im."

at the plate: see *at bat.*

automatic take: A situation in which the batter is virtually certain to take the next pitch because of the favorable chances of receiving a base on balls, as with a count of three balls and no strikes.

away: Out. (one man on and two away)

Babe Ruth Baseball: A nonprofit educational organization that sponsors summer baseball leagues for youths aged nine through twelve, thirteen through fifteen, and sixteen through eighteen in cities throughout the United States and Canada, and in Guam. Founded in 1951, Babe Ruth Baseball is headquartered in Trenton, New Jersey.

1. backhand: To catch or field a ball by

reaching across the body with the glove hand turned so that the thumb is down.

2. backhand: A backhand catch.

backstop: 1. A screen or barrier behind home plate for the protection of spectators. 2. A catcher. An old term that dates back to the eighteenth century game of rounders and describes a player positioned to field balls missed by the batsman.

back up: To position oneself behind a teammate to be able to assist if the teammate should misfield a hit ball or a throw.

bad head: Players' slang for an ugly teammate or opponent. (such a bad head, he should always wear a catcher's mask)

bad hop: The sudden and unlikely bounce or carom of a hit ball off a flaw in the turf.

bag: A base. So called because canvas bags are used as bases. see *base.*

bail out: To suddenly move out of the way of a pitch while at bat to avoid being hit by the ball. (had to bail out from a head-high wild pitch) also *hit the dirt.*

balk: An illegal act by the pitcher that allows one-base advance by all runners. A balk is called if, in the judgment of the umpire, a pitcher does not make the pitch after initiating the normal delivery motion; stands in the pitching position near or on the pitcher's rubber without the ball; makes a throw to a base in order to take out a runner but neglects to step directly toward that base; fails to come to a set position and stop before pitching but instead pitches directly from a stretch; pitches when the catcher is not in position in the catcher's box; makes any kind of an illegal pitch, including a quick pitch; feints a throw to first base, homeplate, or any unoccupied base; or winds up for the pitch using more than two pumps. If, in the judgment of the umpire, the pitcher commits one of these actions when the bases are empty, a ball is called. The balk rule was adopted in 1899.

ball: 1. A baseball (hardball or softball). see *baseball, softball.* 2. A pitched ball that misses the strike zone and at which the batter does not swing. If the count reaches four balls in one turn at bat, the batter is awarded first base.

••To "be on the ball" or to "have something on the ball" means to be clever or intelligent. To "drop the ball" is to make an error or lose an opportunity.

ball boy, ball girl: A young person who fields foul balls throughout the game and keeps the plate umpire supplied with new balls.

ballgame: A baseball game.

••Just as a pivotal offensive or defensive play or other factors can suddenly make a game in progress "a new ballgame," the introduction of a new factor can be said to figuratively make a new ballgame out of any circumstance. (after the results of the election, it's a whole new ballgame in Congress)

ball hawk: An outfielder skilled at fielding fly balls. (that ball hawk can catch anything that doesn't clear the fence)

ballpark: A stadium or stadium-type area designed for the playing of baseball.

••Although a ballpark is large, it is enclosed by fences or walls. Therefore, anything said to be within it cannot be too far distant. (still an unacceptable offer, but at least within the ballpark) (a ballpark estimate)

ballplayer: A baseball player.

Baltimore chop: A fair ball that is topped so it will bounce on the ground just in front of home plate and high into the air, often allowing time for the batter to reach first base without a play. Originated as a deliberate tactic by the Baltimore Orioles in 1896.

banana stick: see *morning journal.*

band box: A small ballpark. Players' slang dating from the turn of the century, a comparison to the outdoor bandstands or band boxes then prevalent in the parks of American cities.

bang-bang play: 1. A very close play, such as when the ball barely beats the runner to a base. 2. A defensive play (often a double play) completed with machinelike ease and speed.

banjo hit: An accidental ground ball (such as one hit on a check swing), named in 1924 by Jersey City second baseman, Ray "Snooks" Dowd, for the way the ball "plunks" off the bat. also *bleeder, nubber.*

barber: 1. A pitcher with the reputation of throwing "Gillettes," pitches thrown close to the batter's head that deliver "close shaves." also *headhunter.* 2. A pitcher with enough control to be able to "shave the corners," or throw strikes that pass barely within the strike zone corners. Sal "The Barber" Maglie was known for throwing Gillettes, as well as for his ability to "shave the corners" when he got his nickname pitching for the New York Giants in the early 1950s. **3.** A talkative player. From a comparison to constantly talking barbers. First associated with Waite Hoyt, a talky young pitcher who came to the New York Yankees in the 1920s, but popularized later when Red Barber, a master of colorful description, began to broadcast the Brooklyn Dodgers games.

base: One of four objects set at each corner of a baseball diamond and which the runner must contact in sequence in order to score a run. First, second, and third bases are stuffed, 15-inch-square white canvas bags attached to the ground. First and third bases butt up against the infield sides of their baselines. Second base is positioned at the perpendicular angle formed by the baselines which extend from the outfield sides of first and third bases. Home base (almost always referred to as home plate, home, or the plate) is the last base with which the runner must make contact in order to score. It is a flat piece of white rubber with five sides, set into the ground directly opposite second base. The leading edge, which faces the pitcher, is 17 inches wide. Two perpendicular sides extend 8-1/2 inches back from the leading edge, and then taper to meet in a point 8-1/2 inches farther back. This endpoint is placed on the intersection of the first and third baselines. The distance between bases is 90 feet (50 to 80 feet for youths). The distance between softball bases is 60 feet. Originally the bases were 4-foot-high vertical stakes from the game of rounders. In the late 1830s, in order to prevent injuries from collisions, these were replaced by large flat stones for a time, then by sand-filled sacks similar to modern bases. also *bag, sack.*

●●To "touch base" means to figuratively make contact. (should touch base with her office before leaving) Just as it is a mistake for a base runner to be caught off base by the defending team, the expression "off base" connotes a deviation from what is correct or true. (an off base premise)

baseball: 1. A game played on a fan-shaped field, with a ball and bat, by two teams of nine players each. The field is divided into the infield at the small end, a 90-foot (sometimes less for youths) square called a diamond with a base at each corner; and the outfield, the remaining area beyond the diamond at the larger end. From home plate, which is located at the corner of the diamond at the small end of the field, the other three bases (in the counterclockwise order they must be touched by an offensive player on the way back to home plate to score) are first base, second base, and third base. Teams alternate playing on offense and defense. The defensive team has three players in the outfield who are responsible for catching or fielding balls hit to their respective zones: a right fielder, a center fielder, and a left fielder. The infielders assume the following positions: a first baseman near first base, a second baseman between first and second base, a shortstop between second and third base, and a third baseman near third base. A catcher stands behind home plate, facing a pitcher who stands 60 feet, 6 inches away from him (sometimes less for youths) on a direct line through the diamond toward second base. A batter from the opposing team tries to hit a ball thrown by the pitcher into the playing area, but between or away from any fielders so that, without being thrown or tagged out, he may run to at least one base. Offensive players may be put out by striking out (any combination totaling three of missed swings, good pitches thrown within the strike zone not swung at, or balls hit foul—although a foul ball is not applicable for the third strike), hitting a fly ball that is caught in the air, having a fielded ball thrown to a defensive player touching first base (or any base one is forced to run to) before the offensive player can get to the base, or by being tagged with the ball while off base. If a batter receives four pitched balls not in the strike zone and does not swing at them, or if the batter is hit by a pitched ball, the batter is allowed to proceed to first base. When the base runner has successfully reached all the bases as well as home plate in succession and has not been put out, a run is earned for the offensive team. The offensive team's players continue to bat in order (according to the batting sequence established before the game) until three players have been declared out. When three players have been put out, the offensive team switches positions with the team in the field, which then takes its turn at bat. Each cycle (both teams bat until three putouts are made) is an inning. Whichever team has scored more runs at the end of nine innings (sometimes less for youths) is the winner of the game. If the home team (which always bats in the second half of each inning) is leading after eight and one-half innings, the game is over. If the home team scores the winning run during the ninth inning, the game is over. At any time during its turn at bat in the ninth inning, the home team can score the winning run and end the game, no matter how many outs have been made. A margin of only one run is needed to win the game. However, if a home run causes a win, the final score will include runs driven in by it. If, at the end of nine innings, the score remains tied, extra innings are played until one team leads after a complete inning. When rain or darkness force a game to end prematurely, it is regarded as a complete game after five innings. The umpire-in-chief, under whose control the game is played, decides whether or not a game can be called off on account of darkness or rain. Positioned behind home plate, the umpire calls balls and strikes, judges whether a hit ball is fair or foul, and rules on plays at home plate. The umpire-in-chief initiates play with the call "play ball" and has the authority to call time out, eject a manager, player, or coach, or forfeit a game. In professional baseball, there are field umpires at each base to call plays there, and, during the World Series, on the foul lines to help rule on balls hit down the lines. 2. A ball with which the game of baseball is played. A sphere wrapped in white leather, the seams of which are in raised relief, it is 9 to 9-1/4 inches in circumference and weighs 5 to 5-1/4 ounces. Its center is cork, which is then wound in twine.

Baseball Annie: A woman or girl, sometimes known as a baseball groupie, who actively pursues the company of mem-

bers of a professional baseball team. also *green fly.*

baseball mud: A special composition of fine earth used by major league umpires to rub up new baseballs before a game to insure proper and uniform gripping characteristics.

base hit: A batted ball hit within the playing area, enabling the batter to successfully reach a base, unaided by a defensive error, a force play, or an attempt to put out the preceding base runner. also *hit, safe hit, safety.*

baseline: Either of the lines extending at right angles from the rear of home plate through the outer edges of first base and third base respectively to the far boundary of the outfield. Within these lines, also called foul lines, is fair territory. Baselines were first marked with whitewash in 1860.

base on balls: A free passage to first base given to a batter who does not swing at four "balls," pitches thrown outside the strike zone, during one turn at bat. Abbreviated bb. Before 1880, a batter had to receive nine balls in order to be awarded a base on balls. The number of balls required changed to eight in 1880, to seven in 1882, to six in 1884, back to seven in 1886, to five in 1887, and finally, in 1889, to the present four balls. Babe Ruth holds both the single season (170 in 1923) and lifetime (2,056) records for bases on balls. also *Annie Oakley, free pass, free ticket, free trip, pass, walk.*

base path: The lane or path on which base runners travel from base to base. Base runners may deviate from a straight line in order to turn less severe (therefore faster) corners around the bases or to stay out of the way of a defensive player fielding a batted ball, but are restricted from running more than three feet from that line in attempting to evade a tag.

base runner: A member of the offensive team who has taken a turn at bat and subsequently is on base or running toward a base. also *runner.*

bases empty: No member of the team at bat is on base.

bases full: see *bases loaded.*

bases loaded: Base runners on first, second, and third base. also *bases full, ducks on the pond, the table is set.*

basket catch: The fielding of a fly ball

holding the glove at waist height with the palm facing up. A difficult technique first popularized by then-New York Giants player, Willie Mays.

1. **bat:** A tapering, cylindrical hardwood (or, optionally in amateur baseball and softball, metal of the same shape) stick with which the batter tries to hit the ball. The maximum diameter for the larger end is 2-3/4 inches (2-1/4 inches for softball and Little League). The end of the bat that is held is approximately 1 inch in diameter, and is wrapped up in tape or a composition material up to a maximum of 18 inches from the end. This wrapping allows for easier gripping. (The maximum for softball is 15 inches, with an option of a cork-covered grip.) The length of the average baseball bat is 36 to 37 inches, but the maximum is 42 inches (34 inches for softball, 33 inches for Little League). also *hickory, lumber, mace, stick, wand, willow.*

••The expression "right off the bat" is used to mean initially or immediately. (liked her right off the bat)

2. **bat:** To take a turn as a batter.

BATTER

••To figuratively "go to bat for" is to speak or argue on behalf of. (promised to go to bat for lower taxes)

bat around: To have, in one inning, a team's entire lineup come to bat in rotation.

bat boy, bat girl: The boy or girl who is responsible for returning bats to the bat rack after use and for assisting with the preparation and maintenance of the team's equipment.

bat rack: The grating or frame in which a team's bats are arranged and placed.

batsman: A batter. Originally from the sport of cricket, later rounders. see *batter.*

batter: The player at bat. During a turn at bat, the player takes his position in the batter's box and tries to hit the ball pitched by the opposing pitcher.

batter's box: One of two rectangles appropriately placed for the batting position, measuring 6 feet by 4 feet, indicated on the ground parallel to and 6 inches away from each side of home plate (5-1/2 feet by 3 feet and 4 inches from home plate for Little League).

batter up: The umpire's notification to the player whose turn it is to bat, to step into the batter's box so that play can commence.

battery: The pitcher and the catcher. From the mid-nineteenth century military description of the components of an artillery unit.

batting average: A statistic expressing the batting efficiency of a player or team. It is calculated by dividing the number of base hits by the number of official at bats and carrying the quotient three decimal places. Abbreviated ba. In 1894, Hugh Duffy of the Boston Beaneaters (later Braves) set the all-time record for the highest batting average in a single season, .438. The last major league player to bat over .400 was Ted Williams, who batted .406 in 1941. The record for the highest lifetime batting average is held by Ty Cobb at .367.

••A record of success or failure. To "bat a thousand" is to enjoy a perfect record or unqualified success. (the neighborhood grocer is batting a thousand with this week's special)

batting cage: A cagelike apparatus, constructed with wire fencing, and portable in spite of its large size. It provides a space for the batter during batting practice and serves as a collection area for fouled or missed pitches.

batting helmet: A caplike plastic protective helmet, the latest examples of which extend down to cover the ear and temple area. Helmets were first used in 1941 by Brooklyn Dodgers batters and are now mandatory, not only in youth leagues, but in both major leagues.

batting order: The specific sequence in which turns at bat are taken by the players of a team. Established and submitted to the umpire on a lineup card prior to every game, the order is strictly maintained. A substitute player must assume the place held by the replaced player in his team's batting order.

batting out of order: Taking a turn at bat contrary to the fixed batting order on the lineup card submitted to the umpire before the game. If appealed by the defensive team at any time before the first pitch is made to the next batter, the proper batter is declared out, and any advance or score made by or because of the improper batter is nullified.

bat weight: A warm-up device, shaped like a doughnut and heavily weighted, which players slide onto the bat to warm up with just before batting (instead of swinging multiple bats). When the weight is discarded, the player's bat seems particularly light and manageable. also _doughnut._

bb: Abbreviation for base on balls.

BB: A fastball. see _fastball._

bean: To pitch a ball so that it strikes the batter on the head. also _skull._ see _beanball._

••To hit someone in the head, especially with a thrown object. (beaned by a cushion thrown from the bleachers)

beanball: A pitched ball that is intentionally thrown at or strikes a batter's head. The combination of bean (slang for head) with ball is thought to be the creation of sportswriter Charlie Dryden in 1906. Major league baseball's only fatality occurred in 1920, when a beanball thrown by Yankees pitcher Carl Mays struck and killed Ray Chapman, shortstop for the Cleveland Indians. also _beaner, chin music._ compare _brushback, duster, Gillette, knockdown pitch, purpose pitch._

beaner: see _beanball._

beat out: To arrive at first base ahead of an infielder's throw, enabling what

would ordinarily be a ground out to be a base hit. (the batter beat out his grounder to third)

behind: To be at a disadvantage because of the count. When a pitcher gets behind, the batter knows the pitcher must now throw strikes or risk a base on balls. also _in the hole._

belt buckle ball: A ball that is illegally scratched or cut on the pitcher's belt buckle in order to make it curve in an unnatural way when pitched.

1. bench: 1. The long seat in the dugout where reserve players and players waiting to bat sit. 2. Players a team has on reserve, ready to substitute for the current players. (went to his bench for a pinch hitter against the left-hander) 3. The dugout.

••A figurative place for nonparticipants. (relegated to the bench while his wife attempted to paint over his mistakes)

2. bench: To take a player out of the lineup either before or during a game, for the duration or remainder of the game.

bench jockey: 1. A substitute player who seldom plays. One who "rides" the bench. also _bench warmer._ 2. A player who harasses or "rides" opponents from the bench.

bench warmer: A substitute player who seldom plays. One who "warms" the bench by sitting on it. In use since the 1920s. also _bench jockey._

between the lines: Players' slang for being engaged in a baseball game. The term refers to being between the foul lines.

big inning: An important inning for a team because of the number of runs scored. (turned the game around with a big inning in the ninth)

big league: 1. Either or both of, or pertaining to either or both of the two existing major professional baseball leagues: the National League and the American League. 2. Any or all of, or pertaining to any or all of, the six major professional leagues in the history of organized baseball: the National League (1876 to the present), the American League (1901 to the present), the American Association (1882 to 1891), the Union Association (1884), the Players' League (1890), and the Federal League (1914 to 1915). also _major league._

••The highest level of any enterprise or endeavor. (when the limousine called, the new vice president knew she'd made the big league)

bigs: The big leagues, or major leagues. also *majors.*

bingle: A hit, usually a single. Probably a combination of "bingo" (an early term for a hit) or "bing" with single, dating from the early 1900s.

bird dog: see *ivory hunter.*

black: The areas just inside and outside the strike zone, above the side sections of the thin black border around the plate. see *paint the black.*

Black Betsy: A large or strong bat. Originally the nickname for a large dark bat used by Cleveland and Chicago slugger, Shoeless Joe Jackson. Jackson's professional career ended when he was banished from baseball for being one of the eight White Sox players responsible for the infamous Black Sox scandal, in which the 1919 World Series was fixed.

blank: To prevent an opposing team from scoring any runs in a game. also *shut out.*

bleachers: Seats which are usually located beyond the outfield walls or fences and in the open with no roof; not reserved and less expensive than regular grandstand seats. Called bleaching boards or bleachers from the late 1800s because of the sun exposure.

●●Outdoor, or simply inexpensive, seating at any kind of spectator event.

bleeder: see *banjo hit.*

block the plate: To try to tag out the base runner by standing between him and home plate. Only legal when the catcher is in possession of the ball.

bloop: To hit a short fly ball that falls between the infielders and outfielders. (blooped a single to right field)

blooper: 1. see *Texas leaguer.* 2. A slow pitch lobbed in a high arc to the batter that, if not hit or caught, bounces just behind the plate. Originated in 1941 by Pittsburgh Pirates pitcher Rip Sewell (the "ephus pitch"), the blooper was revived in the mid to late 1960s by New York Yankees relief pitcher Steve Hamilton (the "Folly Floater"), and in the 1980s by Yankees reliever Dave LaRoche (the "La Lob").

bloop single: see *Texas leaguer.*

blow smoke: To throw a fastball, or fastballs. (no curveballs, he was just blowing smoke)

blue darter: A low line drive. An allusion to the speed of such a hit, the term dates back to the 1890s. also *darter.* see *line drive.*

1. bobble: To drop or lose control of a ball instead of fielding or throwing it effectively. compare *boot.*

2. bobble: The bobbling of a ball while attempting to field or throw it.

boot: To make an error fielding a ground ball, sometimes by actually kicking it. compare *bobble.*

●●To err or figuratively mishandle. (got careless and booted the decision)

bottom of the inning: The last half of an inning, when the home team has the opportunity to bat.

box: To awkwardly field a ground ball.

box score: A condensed report of a baseball game which lists the lineup and batting order of both teams and basic offensive and defensive information on the performances of all the participating players, including the number of times at bat, runs batted in, etc.

Boys Baseball: A summer program of amateur baseball for boys aged thirteen and fourteen, formerly the Pony League.

boys in blue: The umpires in a baseball game. also *men in blue.* see *umpire.*

1. break: The rise, dip, or curving motion of a pitched ball. (a sidearm pitch that breaks over the plate)

2. break, break off: To pitch a ball so that it breaks. (broke off a roundhouse curve)

breaking ball: A pitched ball that breaks or changes direction, such as a curveball. see *curveball.*

break the wrists: To bring the action of the wrists into play when swinging the bat at a pitched ball. If the wrists are not "broken" or moved, then the batter is said to have checked the swing (or to have made a half swing) and is not charged with a strike if the pitched ball is out of the strike zone.

break up the double play: To, while in the course of sliding into a base, physically contact or obstruct a defensive player at the base in such a way as to delay or prevent the player from throwing the ball to another base for a second out. (upended the second baseman and broke up the double play)

bring it: To throw a fastball with great velocity. (lull the batter with a slow curve and then really bring it)

broken bat single: A safe hit in which the bat breaks at the moment of contact with the ball.

Bronx cheer: A sound expressing derision or contempt, made by extending the tongue between the lips and forcibly expelling air. Some claim that the Bronx cheer, long popular among New York baseball fans, originated in the National Theater in the Bronx. also *razz, razzberry.*

brush back: To throw a high, inside pitch that forces the batter to move away from the plate. also *dust, dust off.*

brushback: A high, inside pitch thrown to move the batter away from the plate, or to intimidate the batter. also *duster, Gillette, knockdown pitch, purpose pitch.* compare *beanball, beaner, chin music.*

bullet: A hard hit line drive. see *line drive.*

bullpen: 1. The part of a field used throughout the game by relief pitchers warming up. Often a fenced in area just beyond the outfield boundary of the playing field. Originally a low-cost spectator area in some ballparks which came to be shared by warming-up relievers, the bullpen got its name around the 1880s for the way spectators were "herded" in. The term was further popularized by Bull Durham tobacco advertisements on outfield walls. 2. A team's group of relief pitchers. (only two good starters, but a great bullpen)

1. bunt: A slow-rolling infield ground ball propelled by a bat which the batter has held virtually still. Although introduced ten years earlier by Brooklyn Atlantics shortstop Dickey Pearce, the bunt achieved popularity in 1876 because of Boston's Tim Murnane, who used a special bat with one flat side to "butt" the ball. "Bunt" is a corruption of "butt."

2. bunt: To execute a bunt. (bunt one down the third base line)

bush, bush league: A derogatory term meaning small-time or amateur. Originally an unflattering reference to backwoods minor league towns and their crude playing grounds. also *high school.*

••Small-time or unworthy. (has no class, strictly bush league)

bushel basket: A larger than usual, scooplike fielder's glove with a deep pocket. compare *pancake.*

busher: 1. A minor league player. 2. A

player who, because of a lack of ability or unprofessional behavior, is undeserving of major league status.

cactus league: The unofficial name for the major league teams that conduct spring training and play preseason exhibition games in the Southwest. compare *grapefruit league.*

cage: 1. A spacious, often glass-roofed facility for foul weather and winter baseball (and track and field practice), offering a floor of dirt or artificial turf and a running track. 2. see *batting cage.*

called strike: A pitch that is neither hit nor swung at by the batter, but is judged by the umpire to have passed through the strike zone.

cannon: see *rifle.*

can of corn: An easily played fly ball. Reported to have originated with the grocers' practice in the early 1900s of storing cans of corn on a high shelf. When a grocer needed one, he'd simply tip it forward with a rod or a broom handle so that it would tumble easily into his waiting hands.

carpet: see *artificial turf.*

1. catch: 1. To halt the flight of a thrown or hit ball by grasping and controlling it. (catch a fly ball) 2. To play the catcher's position.

2. catch: 1. The act of catching a thrown or batted ball. (a diving catch to end the inning) 2. An unstructured recreation, practice, or game, in which two or more people throw a ball back and forth. (playing catch)

catcher: The defensive player behind home plate who catches pitched balls that the batter does not hit. Equipped with a face mask, chest protector, and shin guards to protect against foul balls, the catcher also wears a mitt or glove with extra padding. Until the ball is pitched, the catcher must stay inside the catcher's box, after which he may move out to retrieve a passed ball, to attempt to catch a pop foul, to field a ground ball hit toward the pitcher's mound or first or third base, to back up the first or third baseman on a routine putout, to throw to or feint throwing to a teammate to prevent a base runner from stealing a base, or to receive a throw from a teammate and tag a runner attempting to score. The catcher also, by means of hand signals, calls for certain pitches and prearranged defensive shifts and strategies. also *backstop, receiver.*

catcher's box: A rectangular area behind home plate, 4 feet wide and extending 6 feet behind the rear edge of the batter's box. The catcher must remain within this area until the pitcher releases the pitch.

catcher's mask: A padded metal grating that covers and protects the face of the catcher. The catcher's mask was invented in 1875 by Fred Thayer and first worn by Harvard catcher, James Tyng. Professional catchers began using them two years later. also *face mask, mask.*

catcher's mitt: A special glove with two sections, one for the thumb and one for the four fingers. It is round in shape, with heavy padding in front of the thumb, the heel of the hand, and the four fingers, but little or no padding in the central area, or pocket. A heavy leather web connects the thumb and fingers sections. Special padded catcher's mitts were introduced in 1891.

caught leaning: Picked off by a quick throw from the catcher or pitcher, made as the base runner takes a lead off and "leans" toward the next base.

cellar: The lowest standing in a league. (a poor team that finished in the cellar)

CATCHER

center field: 1. The outfield's central area, between right and left field and reaching behind second base. 2. The position of the player in the central outfield. (to play center field)

center fielder: The defensive player responsible for fielding balls hit to center field. also *middle gardener.*

chance: The opportunity to put out a base runner by either fielding a batted ball or making a play on a base runner, which then is computed in determining the fielding average as an error, assist, or putout.

change of pace: see *changeup.*

changeup: A slow pitch, identical in motion to the fastball, thrown to deceive the batter. also *change of pace, letup.*

charley horse: A pain or stiffness in the leg muscles, particularly the thigh. Often in the 1800s, old workhorses kept on the grounds of ballparks were called Charley. The movements of injured, stiff-legged ballplayers were likened to the labored plodding of these old horses, and the injury itself eventually became known as a "charley" or "charley horse."

1. chart: see *pitching chart.*

2. chart: To record pitches for a pitching chart.

chase: 1. To force the removal of a pitcher by rallying with a number of hits. also *knock out of the box.* 2. To officially throw a player, coach, or manager out of a game. (chased by the umpire)

check swing: see *half swing.*

chest pad: see *chest protector.*

chest protector: 1. A protective pad worn by a catcher or plate umpire covering the area from shoulders to waist or crotch. Padded chest protectors for catchers were introduced in 1885. 2. A foam rubber or inflated shield held, rather than worn, by some plate umpires. also *chest pad.*

Chicago slide: The original hook slide. Originated in the 1880s by Hall of Famer Mike "King" Kelly (about whom the song "Slide, Kelly, Slide" was written), then catcher for the Chicago White Stockings; thus, the name Chicago slide. see *hook slide.*

Chinese homer: A short or "cheap" home run, as one hit out of a small ballpark or down a particularly short foul line. Though there are conflicting claims from the East and West coasts as to the exact origin of the term, it is very probably an allusion to the low wages paid in the 1880s to immigrant Chinese laborers.

chin music: A beanball. see *beanball.*

1. choke: To become incapable of good performance because of tension or fear. also *choke up.* (choked under pressure)

2. choke: A poor performance because of tension or fear.

choke up: see *1. choke.*

choke up on the bat: To assume a shortened or raised grip on the handle of a bat resulting in better control, if slightly less power.

chop: To top, or swing the bat downward at a pitched ball, to make the ball hit the ground and bounce.

chopper: A ball batted down to the ground so it will bounce high in the air.

circus catch, circus play: 1. A seemingly impossible catch or play. also *Jawn Titus.* 2. A simple play made to appear exceptional in order to impress onlookers. Believed to be originated by Chicago sportswriter Charlie Seymour in 1885.

clean the bases: To render all bases empty or "clean" by virtue of a home run that enables all base runners to score. also *clear the bases.*

cleanup: The fourth position in the lineup, usually filled by a player with a strong hitting record, who can possibly score any of the first three batters who may be on base.

●●The final and strongest, or most skillful. (cleanup witness for the defense)

clear the bases: see *clean the bases.*

closed stance: A batting stance in which the front foot is positioned closer to the inside of the batter's box than the rear foot. compare *open stance.*

clothesline, clothesliner: A line drive. see *line drive.*

clout: A ball hit with power.

clubhouse lawyer: A player who habitually complains or makes excuses.

clutch hitter: A player known for the ability to get a hit in crucial game situations.

coach's box: One of two rectangular areas located 8 feet behind first and third bases, extending 20 feet toward home plate (6 feet outside the bases, extending 15 feet for softball). While the ball is in play, first and third base coaches are required to remain in their respective boxes.

cockeye: Left-handed. also *corkscrew arm, crooked arm, twirly-thumb.*

comebacker: A ground ball batted straight back to the pitcher.

come in: To pitch so the ball passes directly over the plate. (to come in with his curve)

complete game: A game that is finished by the same pitcher who started. The all-time single season record for complete games (50) was set in 1893 by New York Giants pitcher Amos Rusie. Cy Young holds the lifetime record with 753 complete games in his twenty-two-year career.

connect: 1. To successfully hit a pitched ball. (connected for a double off the left field wall) 2. To hit a home run.

contact hitter: A batter who is known less for power hitting than for the ability to collect base hits by making good contact with the ball.

control: A pitcher's skill at changing the speed, trajectory, and placement of a pitched ball.

corked bat: see *doctored bat.*

corkscrew arm: see *cockeye.*

count: A tally of balls and strikes, expressed in that order, charged to a batter at any point during a turn at bat. (a full count of 3 and 2)

country-fair hitter: A good hitter. Originally an allusion to the big strong farmers who played baseball at country fairs. Later, the expression evolved into a "pretty fair country hitter," or "pretty fair country player."

●●A person, object, or endeavor deserving merit. (served a pretty fair country chili)

country-fair player: 1. see *country-fair hitter.* 2. A show-off player. also *grandstander.*

courtesy runner: A player allowed to run the bases for a teammate without forcing that player out of the game. Used in some informal and nonprofessional games only.

cousin: An easy opponent (whether a particular batter, pitcher, or team). The term was first used in the 1920s by New York Yankees pitcher Waite Hoyt who likened some of his perennial victims at the plate to cooperating family members or "cousins." Later, the meaning was expanded to include any easy-to-defeat pitchers or teams.

cover: To protect a base by positioning oneself at or on it, ready to make a

13

putout. (moved in to cover second base)

cripple: To put the pitcher into a situation where he must throw a strike because he is behind the batter in the count. With a count such as three balls and no strikes, or three balls and one strike, a pitcher is considered crippled without the normal options of deception, placement, and delivery.

crooked arm: see *cockeye.*

crossfire: A sidearm pitch that seems to cross the plate on a diagonal.

cross-handed grip: A reverse hold on the bat, with the hands crossed, as opposed to the usual grip.

crowd the plate: To assume a batting stance at the inner edge of the batter's box.

crush: To hit a pitched ball with great power. (can really crush the ball) also *hammer.*

Cuban forkball: A spitball. also *drooler, spitter.*

cunning thumb, cunning thumber: A player who is a poor thrower.

cup of coffee: A short stint on the roster of a major league club by a minor league player, just long enough to be observed by the parent club before the end of the season, or long enough to "drink a cup of coffee."

1. curve: A curveball. see *curveball.*

●●A surprise or something unexpected. (the last question on the test threw me a curve)

2. curve: To throw a curveball. (threw two fast balls, and then curved him)

curveball: A pitch thrown in such a way as to impart a spin that causes the ball to break or veer downward and to the side. A right-hander's curve breaks to the left, a left-hander's to the right. Although others had thrown the pitch before, the first person to study and understand the mechanics of the curveball and intentionally use it was William A. "Candy" Cummings in the early 1860s. Cummings introduced the pitch to the major leagues in 1872. also *breaking ball, curve, dipsy-do, fish, fish hook, hook, jug handle curve, mackerel, number two, pretzel, rainbow, roundhouse curve, snake.* compare *fastball, knuckleball, screwball, slider.*

cut: A swing with the bat. An attempt to hit the ball. (took a cut at the slow curve)

cut ball: A ball that is surreptitiously slit,

scratched, or cut so as to make it break or swerve in an unnatural way when pitched. see *doctored ball.*

cut down: To throw out a base runner. (cut down at the plate) also *gun down.*

1. cut off: The interception of an outfielder's throw toward home plate by an infielder, who then may relay the throw to the plate, or make a play at another base.

2. cut off: To cut off a throw from the outfield.

cutoff man: The player who cuts off a throw from the outfield.

Cy Young Award: An award made annually to the pitcher who demonstrates the most outstanding performance in the major leagues as voted by the Baseball Writers Association of America. Named in honor of the legendary Cy Young, who from 1889 to 1911 won a record 511 games pitching for the Cleveland Spiders, St. Louis Cardinals, and the Boston Pilgrims. The award was first given in 1956 to Brooklyn Dodgers pitcher Don Newcombe. Since 1967, a Cy Young Award has been given to a pitcher from each major league. In 1982, Steve Carlton of the Philadelphia Phillies became the only four-time Cy Young Award winner.

daisy clipper, daisy cutter: A low ground ball hit through to the outfield. also *grass clipper, grass cutter, lawn mower.*

Daniel Webster: A player known for debating or arguing with the umpires. Named after the U.S. statesman and great orator of the 1800s, Daniel Webster.

darter: A line drive. see *line drive.*

delayed steal: A steal in which the base runner does not go on the pitch, but waits for the catcher to return the ball to the pitcher or for the defensive team to make a play on another player.

delivery: 1. The act of throwing a pitch. (impatient slugger waiting for the delivery) 2. The manner in which a pitch is thrown. (changed the delivery for the knuckleball)

designated hitter: A player who bats in the lineup but does not play in the field. Technically, the designated hitter takes the pitcher's batting turn throughout the game. The designated hitter rule was introduced by the American League in 1973 and applies to the All-Star Game (as long as both leagues agree) and every other year to the World Series. Although a designated hitter is still not permitted in the National League, the first to suggest an official batter for the pitcher was National League president John H. Heydler in 1928. The always controversial Charles O. Finley, then owner of the American League Oakland A's, led the movement to adopt the designated hitter rule. also *dh*.

dh: see *designated hitter.*

diamond: 1. That part of the playing field which is comprised of the infield. When seen from home plate, this square area looks like a diamond. 2. The entire playing field.

Dick Smith: A nondescript name for a player who does not fraternize with teammates, a loner.

die: To be stranded on base at the end of an inning or half inning.

dig in: To dig one's spikes into the dirt in order to get a better footing from which to push off with the rear foot for a particularly powerful swing.

dig out a throw: To grasp and control a low, bouncing throw. (first baseman digs out the throw in time for the third out)

dinger: A home run. see *home run.*

dipsy-do: A curveball. see *curveball.*

disabled list: A team list of players who are unable to play several games on account of severe injuries. A player whose name appears on the disabled list is still included on the team's roster, but for a term of either fifteen or twenty-one days, he may not play. A team may add a player to the roster to substitute for a disabled player until such time as he comes off the disabled list.

dish: Home plate. see *home plate.*

doctor: 1. To surreptitiously change or modify the playing field or equipment in order to gain an advantage. (the doctored base paths were so soft, it was impossible to steal) 2. A pitcher who doctors the ball.

doctored ball: A ball that has been illegally modified to make it break or swerve in an unnatural way. This can be accomplished by adding a foreign substance to the surface of the ball (greaseball, jellyball, mud ball, pine tar ball, powder puff ball, and spitball), or by scratching, scuffing, or in any other

way marking the surface of a ball (belt buckle ball, cut ball, emery ball, marked ball, sandpaper ball, scuffer, and shine ball).

doctored bat: A bat that has been illegally modified, generally to make it lighter or more lively. The most often used method is to drill a 1/2-inch to 3/4-inch-diameter hole approximately one foot into the large end of the bat. This cavity is either left hollow or filled with a light material such as cork, then capped with a mixture of wood shavings and glue. The cap is then blended in and disguised by careful sanding. The result is a lighter, livelier bat with the mass of a heavy bat. also *corked bat, hollow bat, plugged bat.*

doctored grounds: Areas of the playing field, boundaries, or boundary markers that have been modified (sometimes to an illegal extent) in order to gain an advantage for the home team. In the major leagues, groundskeepers regularly adjust the condition of the playing field according to the relative strengths and weaknesses of the home and visiting teams. Quick teams with speedy base runners prefer the fast surface provided by short, unwatered grass and dry, hard base paths, while slow teams favor the opposite. A particularly wet or soft area near first base can prevent a base-stealer from getting a quick start. (A flagrant and notorious example would be the crucial season-ending series at Candlestick Park in 1962, when the San Francisco Giants successfully employed this trick against baserunning sensation Maury Wills and the Los Angeles Dodgers. The Giants swept the series and eventually went on to the World Series.) Foul lines can be graded to tilt inward or outward in order to influence whether bunts will roll fair or foul. The pitching mound can be raised over the legal 10-inch maximum height in order to give overhand pitchers an advantage over the batter. Even the mound in the visitors' bullpen can be tilted slightly to throw off relief pitchers. To help or hinder a certain hitter, the batter's box can be illegally extended, shortened, or slightly moved in relation to home plate. One of the most spectacular examples of doctored grounds was onetime Cleveland Indians owner Bill Veeck's moveable fence in Cleveland Municipal Stadium. Depending on the hitting strength of the visiting team relative to the weak-hitting Indians, the outfield fence could be moved in or out the night before a game. Six sets of sleeves were installed in the outfield for the fence posts, each set a different distance from home plate.

donkey: A rookie. see *rookie*.

1. **double:** A hit that allows the batter to safely arrive at second base. also *two-bagger, two-base hit*.

2. **double:** 1. To hit a double. (doubled off the left field wall) 2. To advance a base runner by hitting a double. (doubled him to third) 3. To score another runner by hitting a double. (doubled in the tying run)

doubleheader: Two consecutive games on the same day. A ticket holder for that day needs only one admission ticket for both games. Doubleheaders are frequently scheduled to play games postponed earlier in the season. also *twin bill*.

●●Two consecutive events. (attended both the wedding and the reception—a doubleheader)

double play: A putout of two runners or the batter and a runner on one pitch. Two runners may be forced out on a quickly fielded grounder and relay to two bases; the batter may hit a fly ball that is caught for the first out and the

base runner thrown out before tagging up or while running to the next base; or the runner may be caught stealing while the batter strikes out. Hall of Famer George Wright, shortstop for the Cincinnati Red Stockings, is credited with making baseball's first recorded double play, using the "hidden ball" trick. also *twin killing*.

●●Two simultaneous accomplishments. (not only won the case, but established an important legal precedent—a double play)

double play ball: A ball hit to or near a defensive player, virtually assuring the completion of an easy double play.

1. **double pump:** The double swinging of the arms back and then forward over the head during a pitcher's windup.

2. **double pump:** To swing the arms back and forward over the head twice during a windup.

double steal: A single play whereby two runners both advance by stealing. Often a delayed steal with men on first and third base. The base runner on first breaks for second base to draw a throw from the catcher. When the catcher makes the long throw to second base, the base runner on third breaks for home.

double up: To put out a base runner as the second out in a double play.

doughnut: see *bat weight*.

down: Out. (hit a homer in the top of the ninth with one down) also *away, gone*. see *out*.

●●Finished, dispensed with, or out of the way. (starting my senior year—three down and one to go)

downtown: A home run, particularly one hit especially far. (hit one downtown to win the game) also *gone*.

drag: To execute a drag bunt.

drag bunt: A surprise bunt made to get on base (as opposed to a sacrifice bunt) in which the batter bunts the ball without squaring around to face the pitcher. Left-handers are able to turn the body and start for first base, actually leaving the bat to trail or "drag" behind them just before the bunt is made.

1. **drive:** To hit a pitched ball with great power. (drove a fastball into the hole)

2. **drive:** A pitched ball hit with great power. (a drive to deep centerfield)

drive in a run: To hit a ball that allows a base runner to score.

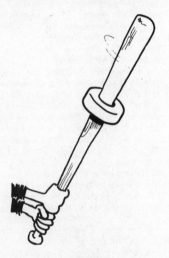

DOUGHNUT

drooler: see *spitball*.

dropball: A fast pitch softball pitch in which the ball drops as it nears the plate.

ducks on the pond: 1. Bases loaded. also *bases full, the table is set*. 2. Runners on base.

dugout: One of two enclosures housing the players' benches and located on each side of the infield, usually sunken slightly beneath ground level so as not to interfere with the view of the spectators. The dugouts are usually directly linked to the dressing room areas.

dust, dust off: see *brush back*.

duster: see *brushback*.

dying quail: An apparently playable routine fly ball that unexpectedly drops in for a base hit, often due to wind.

early bloomer: A rookie who looks particularly promising in spring training, but fades and eventually fails before the start of the regular season. also *morning glory*.

earned run: A run scored before the third putout in an inning that is not the result of an error, and that is charged to the pitcher in computing the pitcher's earned run average.

earned run average: A statistic that reflects the average number of earned runs allowed by a pitcher for every nine innings. The earned run average, or ERA, of a pitcher is calculated by dividing the total of earned runs by the total number of innings pitched and multiplying by nine. (A pitcher charged with sixty-eight runs in 340 innings has an earned run average of 1.80) The single season record for the lowest ERA (1.01) was set in 1914 by Boston Red Sox pitcher Dutch Leonard. The record for the lowest lifetime earned run average is held by spitballer "Big Ed" Walsh who, in his fourteen-year career, won 194 games with an ERA of 1.82.

easy out: A batter who is easily retired, posing little or no threat to the defensive team or pitcher. (like most pitchers, an easy out) also *out man*. compare *hard out*.

emery ball: An illegally altered baseball. When pitched, the ball will swerve or dip abnormally because it has been scratched on one side with emery cloth or powder. also *sandpaper ball*.

error: A fumble or misplay made by a player in the field on a batted or thrown ball, preventing what would normally have been a putout or allowing a base runner to advance. If a player throws a wild ball, misses or fumbles a playable fly, or cannot field a playable gound ball, the scorer records an error against that player and team.

errorless: No errors charged against a player or team. (eighteen consecutive errorless games)

extra-base hit: A hit that allows a batter to advance further than first base, such as a double, triple, or home run.

extra innings: Innings played beyond the ninth inning in order to break a tie.

face: 1. To bat opposite a pitcher. (goes hitless every time he faces a knuckleballer) 2. To pitch to a batter. (on a good day, could strike out every batter he faced)

face mask: A cagelike protective mask worn by the catcher and plate umpire. also *mask*. see *catcher's mask*.

fadeaway: The original screwball, a reverse curve. Pioneered and named in 1900 by the New York Giants' charismatic pitcher Christy Mathewson (though some claim that New York sportswriter Bozeman Bulger coined the name). The last lines of a Ring Lardner memorial for "Matty" in 1925 read: "may the flowers ne'er wither, Matty/on your grave in Cincinnati/which you've chosen for your final fadeaway." see *screwball*.

fadeaway slide: Old name for a hook slide, perfected in the early 1900s by Ty Cobb of the Detroit Tigers. see *hook slide*.

fair: In fair territory.

fair ball: A batted ball that hits the ground within fair territory (between the foul lines), or lands and remains within the foul lines until it passes first or third base, or, on a home run, remains within the foul lines until it clears the outfield fence or wall.

fair territory: The playing area within the foul lines.

fallaway slide: see *hook slide*.

fall classic: The World Series.

fan: 1. To strike out a batter. (fanned the last three batters to retire the side) also *K, whiff*. 2. To swing and miss. (fanned on a letter-high fastball)

●●To swing at an object and miss. (with the goalie on the ice and an open net, he fanned on the shot)

farm, farm club, farm team: A minor league team that is subsidized by or linked with a parent club in the major leagues. Most young major league prospects break into professional baseball and receive training as well as game experience with a farm club. Minor league teams were known as "farms" even before the farm system existed, because of the rural towns in which they often played. see *farm system.*

farm out: To send a player to an associated minor league club. see *farm system.*

●●To send away. (made so much trouble he was farmed out to a boarding school) To subcontract work or part of a job. (the parts are factory-made, but all the assembling and finishing is farmed out)

farm system: The system pioneered and made popular by St. Louis Cardinals manager-executive, Branch Rickey, in the early 1900s in which individual major league teams (parent clubs) operate or subsidize their own minor league teams (farm clubs) to train and season promising new players.

fastball: A powerfully pitched ball that travels extremely fast (up to 100-plus m.p.h.) and can dip or rise somewhat upon approaching the plate. Colorful synonyms for a fastball refer to the sound or high temperature of its "blazing" speed (hummer, heat, smoke, smoker), or to the difficulty in seeing it (fog), particularly because of its apparent small size when trying to hit it (aspirin, BB, pea). compare *changeup, curveball, knuckleball, palmball, screwball, sinker, slider.*

fast hook: A manager's inclination to remove and replace a pitcher at the first sign of trouble.

fast pitch softball: A variety of softball in which the pitcher is allowed to use a full-power underhand pitch. As in baseball, there are nine players on a side. Bunting is allowed as is stealing, but the runners are not permitted to leave the base before the pitcher lets go of the ball. compare *slow pitch softball.*

fat pitch: A pitch that is easily hit.

fence buster: An strong hitter known for regularly hitting the ball to the outfield boundaries or fences.

field: 1. The playing area for a baseball game. 2. To grasp and control a fly ball

or ground ball. (goes to his left to field a high bouncer)

●●To control or handle. (fielded some difficult questions from persistent reporters)

fielder: 1. One who is called upon to field a batted ball. (good fielder, good arm, and can hit) 2. A player in a defensive position other than the pitcher or catcher.

fielder's choice: A scorekeeper's ruling reflecting the opportunity for a fielder to choose between two possible putouts, and in which he decides to throw to a base other than first in order to throw out a preceding base runner instead of the batter. When a fielder's choice ruling is made, the batter is charged with a turn at bat, but does not earn a base hit.

fielding: Catching or stopping and controlling a batted ball with the aim of getting a base runner or batter out.

fielding average: The statistic used to measure the fielding effectiveness of a player or team, determined by dividing the total number of putouts and assists by the total number of chances and rounding off the answer to three decimal places. A player credited with 400 putouts and assists in 425 chances has a fielding average of .941.

field umpire: An umpire positioned on the playing field (as opposed to behind home plate). In the major leagues, there are field umpires positioned at each base. Two umpires are added during the World Series to help with foul rulings from the outfield foul lines. see *umpire, umpire-in-chief.*

find the handle: To keep a solid grip on the ball when both catching and throwing. (plenty of time to throw out the runner, but the fielder couldn't find the handle)

fireballer: An excellent fastball pitcher. One who consistently throws fastballs. also *flamethrower.*

fireman: 1. A relief pitcher who can "put out the fire" when the opponent gets "hot" and appears ready for a big inning. John Murphy, a New York Yankees relief pitcher in the thirties and forties, was the first to be called a fireman. also *ice man.* 2. One who is known for showering, dressing, and leaving the dressing room quickly after a game.

first: First base. (rounding first and headed for second base)

first base: 1. The base located on the baseline on the right side of the diamond when facing the field from home plate. When rounding the bases, this is the first base reached by the runner. also *first, gateway.* 2. The position played by the first baseman. (to play first base) also *first.*

•• The preliminary step in a relationship or endeavor. (couldn't get to first base with her)

first base coach: The coach or member of the team at bat who stands in the marked coach's box adjacent to first base to direct base runners and, through prearranged signals, to relay special batting and baserunning instructions from the manager in the dugout.

first baseman: The defensive player stationed just left of first base who is expected to field the balls hit to the surrounding area and to receive throws from other infielders in order to put out the base runner. also *first sacker.*

first baseman's mitt: A special thinly padded glove, generally with two sections, one for the thumb and one for the four fingers, connected by a web that may not exceed 5 inches from its top to the base, 4 inches in width at the top, and 3-1/2 inches at the base. Some mitts are made in three equal sections (one for the thumb and two for the fingers) laced together to form a scooplike glove. Neither kind may exceed 12 inches in length, top to bottom, or 8 inches in width across the palm.

first leg of a double play: The first out in a double play.

first sacker: The first baseman. see *first baseman.*

fish, fish hook: A curveball.

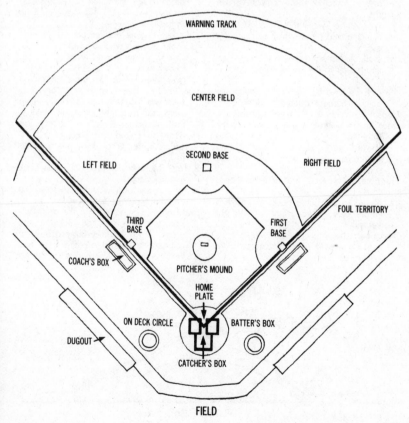

FIELD

fist: To hit a pitched ball with the small end of the bat right next to the hands. (fists an inside pitch right back to the mound)

flag: To catch, or stop and control, a thrown or batted ball.

flake: A peculiar or eccentric player. A noun form created in the 1960s from the adjective "flakey." see *flakey*.

●●An odd or irresponsible person. (can't depend on that flake)

flakey: Off-beat, peculiar, or eccentric. San Francisco Giants outfielder Jackie Brandt is thought to be the first ever to be described as flakey when he was given the nickname in the 1950s.

●●Strange or irresponsible. (so flakey he's probably forgotten where to go)

flamethrower: see *fireballer*.

flutterball: A knuckleball. see *knuckleball*.

1. fly: 1. A fly ball. (hits a high fly to short right field) see *fly ball*. 2. A bothersome fan, an insectlike pest. compare *green fly*.

2. fly: To hit a fly ball that is caught. (flied to centerfield for the third out) also *fly out*.

fly ball: A batted ball which soars high into the air to the outfield. (misjudged a fly ball)

fly out: To hit a fly ball that is caught for an out. (flied out to the left fielder)

fog: A fastball or fastballs. see *fastball*.

foot in the bucket: The movement of the front foot away from the plate (and toward the dugout water bucket) during the batter's stride into a swing, usually a detriment to good hitting.

1. force: A force-out. (out at second on a force)

2. force: To put out a base runner on a force play. (forced the runner at second)

force-out: The instance of throwing a base runner out as a result of a force play. also *force*.

force play: An automatic putout arising from the circumstance of a base runner being required to vacate his base and reach the next base because the batter has hit a fair ball and is running to first base. When the batter reaches first base, the base runner previously there is forced to advance. Regardless of the base, any runner on a base that the runner behind him is attempting to reach must also advance. A fielder is not required to tag the runner on a force play in order to make a putout; the runner is out at the moment a fielder in possession of the ball touches the base the runner is trying to reach. If the batter or any runner behind a given base runner is put out, the force play is no longer in effect.

1. forfeit: To lose a game due to an inability or refusal to play or because of a serious rules infraction. The opposing team is awarded a 9-0 victory (7-0 in softball).

2. forfeit: A game that has been forfeited.

forkball: A somewhat unpredictable, but usually downward-breaking pitch, thrown with the index and middle fingers spread wide like the prongs of a pitchfork. Though the exact origin is unknown (pitches with a similar grip were used near the turn of the century), Boston Red Sox pitcher "Bullet" Joe Bush popularized the forkball in 1920.

1. foul: Outside the foul lines. (the ball rolls foul)

2. foul: To hit a ball foul. (fouls one back into the stands)

3. foul: A foul ball. (a long foul down the right field line) see *foul ball*.

foul ball: A ball batted into the area outside the foul lines, or that hits the ground in fair territory but proceeds to roll behind the first or third base foul lines before reaching one of those

FIRST BASEMAN

bases. If a fly ball is caught in foul territory, the batter is called out, but the base runners may try to advance after tagging up. A foul ball not caught on the fly is charged as a strike unless the batter already has two strikes charged against him. also *foul.*

••An undesirable person. (finally asked the uninvited guest, a real foul ball, to leave)

foul line: One of the two lines that mark the boundaries of fair territory, and which run at right angles from home plate through the outer edges of first and third bases and end at the outfield boundary. Also called baselines.

foul out: To hit a fly ball that is caught in foul territory and results in an out. (fouled out to the third baseman)

foul pole: One of two upright poles marking the foul lines at the outfield boundary. These poles enable the umpire to determine fair and foul balls hit to the outfield. If a long drive hits the foul pole, it is a home run.

foul territory: The entire portion of the field outside the foul lines.

foul tip: A batted ball that travels directly back to be caught by the catcher. The ball is declared in play and the batter is charged with a strike. If the batter hits a foul tip after two strikes, he is called out. If, however, the catcher fails to directly catch the ball, drops it, or traps it, a foul ball is not charged and the batter is not out.

four-bagger: A home run.

frame: An inning. The term dates back to the days when there were no mechanical or electronic scoreboards. Numbers painted on rectangular pieces of wood were set by hand into frames for each inning. also *stanza.*

free agent: Not under contract, free to negotiate with any team.

free pass, free ticket, free trip: A base on balls. see *base on balls.*

frozen rope: A line drive. see *line drive.*

full count: Three balls and two strikes.

fungo: A fielding drill in which a player or coach tosses balls in the air and hits grounders and fly balls to fielders with a special fungo bat. Fungo hitting dates back to the late 1860s, but the exact origin of the term is unknown. Some believe it comes from the rhyme allegedly recited in early versions of the game just as a ball was to be hit.

Others claim that fungo is from "fungus," an allusion to the soft wood used in the strange fungo bats. Yet another theory holds that the term comes from an old Scottish verb, *fung,* meaning "to toss," since the ball is tossed up before hitting fungos.

fungo bat: A bat with a long thin handle and a short thick head specially designed for fungo hitting.

gamer: A "game" ballplayer who plays in spite of injuries. compare *jake.*

••A courageous and persistent individual, as one who continues in an endeavor in spite of great difficulty.

garden: The outfield. also *orchard, pasture.*

gardener: An outfielder. also *orchardman, pastureworker.*

gateway: First base. So-called because it is the "gateway" to a batter's journey around the bases.

get all of the ball: To connect with a pitched ball, hitting it perfectly and with full power.

get a piece of the ball: To hit or make contact with a pitched ball even if just to foul it off when two strikes are charged against the batter.

get around on a fastball: To be able to execute a complete swing of the bat with full wrist action and power before a fastball is already in the catcher's mitt. Requires great quickness and anticipation, but when a batter connects with a fastball on such a swing, the result is a particularly powerful drive. (gets around on a fastball, and goodbye, that ball is gone)

get hold of the ball: To connect with or hit a pitched ball. (got hold of a fastball for a double)

get the thumb: To be ejected from a game by the umpire.

Gillette: A brushback pitch near the batter's head. A "close shave." see *brushback.*

glass arm: 1. A pitching arm that is susceptible to soreness or injury. 2. A throwing arm susceptible to injury or weakness. Although the exact origin is unknown, the term has been in use since the 1800s.

1. glove: 1. A padded leather covering worn on one hand by all defensive players to aid in catching and controlling a batted, thrown, or pitched ball. 2. A padded leather covering usually having a separate section for each finger (as opposed to a catcher's or first baseman's mitt), worn by fielders to aid in catching and controlling batted or thrown balls. It may not exceed 12 inches in length or 8 inches in width. Padding protects the thumb, heel, and finger sections, which are generally laced together at the top. A leather webbing that may not exceed 4-1/2 inches at the top, and 3-1/2 inches at the base, connects the space between the thumb and forefinger sections. The middle, or palm area, of the glove is unpadded and known as the pocket. compare *mitt*.

2. **glove:** Skill as a fielder. (can't hit, but he's got a great glove)

3. **glove:** To catch or grasp and control a batted or thrown ball. (gloved a pop fly for the third out)

glove man: 1. A good fielder. also *leather man*. 2. A poor hitter who plays only because of his skill with a glove; primarily a defensive player. also *leather man*.

goat: A derisive name for a player who makes a critical or game-losing mistake or error. (went from the hero who scored the winning run to the goat when he missed third base)

go down looking: To take a called third strike for an out. compare *go down swinging*.

go down swinging: To swing and miss for the third strike and an out.

go for the fences: To swing with full power and attempt to hit a home run. (jump on the first pitch and go for the fences)

Golden Glove Award: The annual award given by both major leagues to the player voted the best fielder at each position.

gone: 1. Over the outfield boundary, a home run. Popularized by former New York Yankees broadcaster Mel Allen with his famous phrase, "going, going, gone!" also *downtown*. 2. Out. (with two gone in the bottom of the eighth) also *away, down*. 3. Ejected from the game by the umpire. (the ump is motioning, he's gone)

good wood on the ball: To connect and hit the ball well. (got good wood on the

ball and gave it a ride to center field)

go on the pitch: To try to steal a base the moment the pitcher throws the ball toward the plate.

goose egg: An inning with no runs scored, represented on the scoreboard by an egglike zero.

gopher ball: A pitched ball hit for a home run. New York Yankees pitcher, Vernon "Lefty" Gomez coined the term, saying that such pitches "go fer" home runs.

go-sign: 1. A coded signal from the manager or coach telling the base runner to attempt to steal a base. 2. A signal from a coach to a moving base runner to continue to the next base or to home plate. also *green light*.

go the distance, go the route: Pitch an entire game. (went the distance, giving up only one run and five hits)

go with the pitch: To hit an outside pitch toward the outfield on the opposite side of the plate as the batter stands. A right-handed batter goes with the pitch into right field; a left-handed batter into left field. compare *pull*.

grand slam, grand slammer: A home run with the bases full.

grapefruit league: The unofficial name for the major league teams that conduct spring training and play preseason exhibition games in the citrus-growing state of Florida. compare *cactus league*.

grass clipper, grass cutter: see *daisy clipper*.

greaseball: An illegal pitch in which a greasy foreign substance, such as petroleum jelly or hair oil, is surreptitiously rubbed on one part of the ball, so as to make it break or swerve unpredictably when thrown. Tommy Bond, pitcher for the National League Hartford Blues, may have been the first to use a greaseball when he experimented with the application of glycerine in 1876. also *jellyball*. see *doctored ball*.

green fly: A girl or woman who persistently seeks to be in the company of professional baseball players. A baseball groupie. Named after the supposedly most persistent variety of fly, the green fly. also *Baseball Annie*. compare *fly*.

green light: 1. see *go-sign.* 2. A coded signal from the manager or coach freeing the batter to swing if he gets a good pitch instead of taking, as with a 3 and 0 or 3 and 1 count.

1. groove: The central strike zone directly over home plate, where the batter is most likely to get a solid hit.

2. groove: To throw a pitch directly over home plate where it can most easily be hit with power.

ground: To hit a ground ball. (grounded right back to the pitcher for an easy out)

ground ball: A batted ball that rolls or bounces on the ground. also *grounder.* compare *fly ball.*

grounder: A ground ball.

ground out: To hit a ground ball that is fielded and thrown to first base in time for an out. (grounded out to the shortstop)

ground rule: A special regulation applying to a specific ballpark that considers the abnormal conditions of a playing field (field obstructions or unusual outfield fences, for example) and makes appropriate changes in game procedure. Although some ground rules designate certain home runs as automatic, most specify conditions under which a ball is considered dead, in which case base runners are permitted to advance a certain number of bases.

●●A basic rule of procedure. (must establish ground rules for the debate)

ground rule double: A two-base hit automatically given to the batter whose ball lands in fair territory, but bounces over an outfield fence.

groundskeeper: The person in charge of the preparation, maintenance, and marking of the playing field. A job of critical and often strategic importance in professional baseball. also *manicurist.* see *doctored grounds.*

guardian angel: see *angel.*

guarding the lines: A defensive strategy in which the first and third basemen position themselves almost on the foul lines to prevent an extra-base hit down the lines. Often used in the late innings of a close game.

guard the bag: To take a position near a base so as to be ready to receive the throw and make a putout on a base runner.

guess hitter: A batter who attempts to determine what type of pitch he can expect in a given circumstance.

gun: see *rifle.*

gun down: To throw out a base runner. also *cut down.*

half swing: An interrupted swing of the bat in which the wrists are not allowed to "break" or move. Not considered a strike unless the ball passes through the strike zone, or is fouled off accidentally. If the plate umpire calls a "ball" on a half swing, the manager or catcher may request the plate umpire to ask a field umpire on first or third base for help. If the base umpire calls the pitch a "strike," the strike call prevails. also *check swing.*

Hall of Fame: Baseball's most prestigious award, honoring outstanding individuals and their career achievements in the game. In 1936, the first five men were enshrined in the Hall of Fame. They were, in the order of votes received from the Special Committee appointed by Commissioner Kenesaw Mountain Landis: Ty Cobb, Babe Ruth, Honus Wagner, Christy Mathewson, and Walter Johnson. In 1939, the National Baseball Hall of Fame was established in Cooperstown, New York, and several years later, the annual voting was turned over to the Baseball Writers Association of America. In order to qualify for induction into the Hall of Fame, a player must have had ten years of major league experience, must have been retired for a minimum of five years, and must receive votes from 75 percent of those polled.

Hall of Famer: One who has been inducted into the Hall of Fame.

hammer: To hit a pitched ball with great power. (hammers a line drive up the middle) also *crush.*

handcuff: 1. To render the ball unplayable, difficult, or almost impossible to control. (ripped a ball up the line, handcuffing the third baseman) 2. To allow a batter or team few or no hits.

hang a curve: To throw a curveball that fails to break, or "hangs" in the air. The result is an easy-to-hit, high, relatively slow pitch. (lost the shut-out when he hung a curveball that was belted into the right field bleachers)

hardball: 1. The ball used in the game of baseball. Smaller in size (though not much harder) than a softball, and consequently more difficult to hit and field. see *baseball.* compare *softball.* 2. The game of baseball. Considered more difficult (and dangerous) to play than the game of softball, because of the size of the ball used. see *baseball.* compare *softball.*

••To "play hardball" means to hold nothing back, to mean business, no holds barred. (evident that the prosecutor is playing hardball in that case)

hard out: A batter who is hard to retire. A good hitter who poses a threat to the pitcher and the defensive team every time at bat. compare *easy out.*

hat trick: To hit in one game a single, double, triple, and home run. Originally from the sport of cricket, where in the 1800s teams began to award a new hat to a bowler who took three wickets with three balls consecutively. also *hit for the cycle.*

••In horseracing, three wins in three consecutive races by a jockey, or the winning of an annual race for three successive years. In hockey and soccer, three goals scored in one game by a single player.

headfirst slide: The attempt by a base runner to reach or return to a base (and sometimes to avoid a tag) by diving headfirst and skidding along the ground with the arms outstretched to touch the base. see *slide.*

heat: A fastball, or fastballs. (not throwing anything fancy, just heat) see *fastball.*

heavy pitch: A pitch that breaks downward near the plate.

hesitation pitch: A pitch in which the pitcher slows or stops momentarily after the windup and before throwing.

hickory: A baseball bat.

high: Above the strike zone.

high and tight: Above the strike zone and inside, or close to the batter.

high-five: A congratulatory hand slap made high in the air, and usually exchanged between one or more players and a teammate who has just made an important play (home run, putout, etc.), or among teammates after an important or gratifying win. The high-five was originated in 1977 by Los Angeles Dodgers outfielder Glenn Burke.

••The high-five is now used in many sports as well as in nonsports activities.

high school: Amateur, small-time. also *bush, bush league.*

hill: The pitcher's mound. also *mound.*

1. hit: A batted ball hit into fair territory that enables the batter to safely reach a base, unaided by a defensive error, a force play, or an attempt to put out the preceding base runner. In 1920, George Sisler, then of the American League St. Louis Browns, set the all-time record for the most hits in a single season (257). Ty Cobb holds the lifetime record (4,191), although Pete Rose is

HEADFIRST SLIDE

closing in, having overtaken Stan Musial (3,630) in 1981 and Hank Aaron (3,771) in 1982. also *base hit, safe hit, safety.*

••A success. (new show is sure to be a hit)

2. hit: 1. To bat or take a turn at bat. (came in to hit for the pitcher) 2. To get a base hit. In 1941, New York Yankee Joe DiMaggio hit safely in fifty-six consecutive games, considered one of the greatest records in sports. 3. To have the ability to bat successfully. (good fielder, but can't hit)

l. hit and run: An offensive strategy for advancing a base runner. On the pitch, a base runner at first runs toward second base while the batter tries to hit the ball, ideally to the space left open by the infielder who must now cover second base (between first and second, if the second baseman covers; between second and third, if the shortstop covers). In a hit and run play, it is important that the batter makes contact with the ball to protect the runner. If the ball is successfully hit through the vacant spot in the infield, the base runner can often take an extra base and sometimes even score. If the ball is hit to an infielder, the base runner is most often able to reach second base safely because of the early start, though the batter may be thrown out at first. If the ball is hit foul, the base runner must return to first but is in no danger. If the batter misses the ball, there is the chance that the catcher can throw the runner out at second base. compare *run and hit.*

2. hit and run: To execute a hit and run play. compare *run and hit.*

hit away: To use a full swing and attempt to hit the ball with power. (with two out and the tying run on third, look for the batter to hit away) also *swing away.*

hit batsman, hit batter: A batter hit by a pitch and walked.

hit behind the runner: To hit a pitched ball between first and second base, behind a base runner already moving to second (as in the case of a hit and run play).

hitch: A slight dropping or pulling back of the bat immediately prior to swinging. Usually considered a bad habit and detrimental to a good swing.

hit for the cycle: To hit a single, double, triple, and home run in one game. also *hat trick.*

hit into a double play: To hit a ball to or

near a defensive player that can be fielded and relayed from base to base in time to force or tag out two base runners, or can be caught on the fly and thrown to a base before an advancing base runner can return.

hitless: Without a base hit. (held them hitless for the last two innings to hold on for the win)

hitter: 1. A batter. 2. Used with an appropriate number to describe the number of hits given up by a pitcher during a game or part of a game, as in two-hitter, three-hitter, etc. (pitched a two-hitter)

hit the corners: To throw pitches for strikes that pass barely within the strike zone corners. Often taken for a called strike by the batter because they appear to be outside the strike zone. (fooled him with a curveball that hit the corner) also *shave the corners.*

hit the dirt: 1. see *bail out.* 2. To slide into a base to avoid being tagged out. see *slide.*

hold the runner: 1. To prevent a base runner from taking a big lead. Accomplished by frequent looks from the pitcher and occasional throws to the base. 2. To prevent a base runner (one not forced to run) from advancing while a play is being made on another base runner or the batter. Accomplished by a momentary feint toward the unforced base runner by the defensive player fielding the ball before the throw is made to force another base runner or the batter. (stops the ball on one bounce, looks toward second to hold the runner, then throws to first for the out)

hole: 1.The open space between the shortstop and the third baseman. (base hit into the hole) 2. The open space between any two infielders.

holler guy: A team member who loudly encourages fellow players on a regular basis during games.

••A person noted for enthusiasm and encouragement. (the captain of their bowling team is a real holler guy)

hollow bat: see *doctored bat.*

home: 1. Home plate. 2. Across home plate to score. (drove the runner home) also *in.*

home base: see *home plate.*

home plate: A flat piece of white rubber with five sides placed in the dirt at the opposite corner of the diamond from second base, and the last base a runner must contact when scoring a run. The leading edge, which faces the pitcher, is 17 inches wide. Two perpendicular sides (the lateral boundaries of the strike zone) extend 8-1/2 inches back from the leading edge, and then taper to meet at a point 8-1/2 inches further back. This point rests on the intersection of the first and third base lines. also *dish, home, home base, plate.*

1. **homer:** 1. A home run. (hit a homer to clean the bases) 2. An umpire who favors the home team.

2. **homer:** To hit a home run. (homered over the left field wall)

home run: A hit that travels so far or in such a manner that the batter can round the bases and reach home plate before any opposing player can make a putout. Most home runs are hit over the outfield boundaries, but sometimes, with a fast runner, a home run is possible when the ball stays in fair territory. In 1961, Roger Maris of the New York Yankees set the all-time record for the most home runs in a single season, 61. Hank Aaron holds the lifetime record with 755 home runs, followed by Babe Ruth (714), Willie Mays (660), and Frank Robinson (586). also *dinger, four-bagger, homer, round tripper, tater.*

home stand: A number of successive games played at a team's home ballpark.

hook: 1. The removal of a pitcher in trouble from the game. (got the hook after only two innings) 2. A curveball.

hook slide: A method of avoiding the tag when approaching a base, in which the base runner, instead of sliding feetfirst straight into the bag, drops to the side and bends one leg back, which hooks the bag as the player slides by. Though an early version of the technique, the Chicago slide, was practiced in the 1880s by Chicago White Stockings catcher Mike "King" Kelly (of the song, "Slide, Kelly, Slide"), the modern hook slide was first perfected as the fadeaway slide after 1905 by Ty Cobb of the Detroit Tigers. also *fallaway slide.*

hopper: A batted ball that bounces. (a high hopper to the hole)

horse-and-buggy league: A minor league. An allusion to the horse and buggy transportation which was common in

traveling between many rural minor league towns in baseball's early days. also *minors.*

horsecollar: No hits, likening the resulting zero in the box score to the thick collars worn by workhorses. To "wear the horsecollar" is to go without a hit for a game.

horsehide: A baseball. A reference to the material with which a baseball is covered. also *apple.*

hot corner: Third base. Coined by Cincinnati writer Ren Mulford in 1889 in reference to a particular game in which Redlegs' third baseman Hick Carpenter was peppered with repeated powerful drives.

●●An either busy or difficult location. (complaint department is the hot corner)

hot dog: A show-off player.

●●A show off. Also can be complimentary, meaning an outstanding performer, such as in motor racing. (qualified right up there with the hot dogs in the first row)

hot stove league: Off-season conversations among rabid baseball fans (such as might be carried on around a hot stove in winter) during which past games are rehashed. The term is believed to have been coined by Cincinnati writer Ren Mulford around the turn of the century. also *winter league.*

●●The rehashing of past events.

hummer: A fastball. see *fastball.*

hung up: A situation in which a player is caught in a rundown between bases. (hung up between second and third)

hurl: To pitch in a game. (hurled a strong two innings)

hurler: A pitcher.

ice man: A relief pitcher who can "cool" a suddenly "hot" opponent's rally. also *fireman.*

in: Across home plate to score. (drove in two runs to tie the score) also *home.*

infield: 1. The area of the playing field enclosed within the 90-foot square (60-foot or 75-foot for youths) made by home plate and the three bases. 2. The area of the playing field bounded on the sides by the baselines and extending from home plate to the outside edge of the dirt area in which the bases are set. On playing fields with artificial surfaces, this perimeter is marked with a painted white line that arcs from baseline to baseline. 3. The players who play infield positions. (not much of a hitting team, but they have a great infield)

infielder: A defensive player who plays in the infield.

infield fly rule: A special rule in effect only in the case of a fair infield fly ball judged catchable with less than two out and base runners at first and second, or loaded bases. In this circumstance, the batter is automatically called out whether or not the ball is actually caught, thus removing the force on the base runners should the fly not be caught. This prevents an infielder from choosing not to catch the fly so he can make a double play on the other runners (who must stay near their bases so they won't be trapped off base in the event of a fielded fly).

infield hit: A base hit in which the ball does not pass through the infield.

infield out: A batted ball resulting in a putout by an infielder.

inning: 1. A division of a game in which each team gets a turn at bat. also *frame.* 2. One team's turn at bat, ending when three players have been put out. From the cricket term "innings," which signifies a turn at bat for either a single batsman or a side.

●●A turn or period of play in badminton, billiards, bowling, croquet, curling, handball, horseshoes, and trapshooting.

in play: Able to affect or be acted upon by the batter, base runners, or defensive players. While the ball is in play, the batter and base runners can be put out, and runs can be scored. The ball is in play until it leaves the playing area, the umpire calls time out, or the third out of an inning is made. The expression originated in the sport of cricket in the eighteenth century.

inside: Between home plate and the batter. (the pitch is high and inside for a ball)

inside-out swing: A swing of the bat in which the hands are ahead of the barrel of the bat at the moment of contact with the ball, usually sending the ball to the opposite field.

inside-out the ball: To hit a pitched ball to the opposite field with an inside-out swing. compare *pull.*

inside-the-park home run: A fair hit that remains within the boundaries of the playing field, but provides enough time for the batter to round the bases and score before a play can be made.

instructional league: A winter league sponsored by major league baseball to provide instruction for prospective players and special or recuperative training for injured veterans.

intentional pass: see *intentional walk.*

intentional walk: A base on balls deliberately given to an opposing batter, usually either to avoid a strong batter or to set up a possible force play if first base (or sometimes first and second) is unoccupied. also *intentional pass.*

in the hole: 1. Due to bat after the player who is on deck. Part of the expression, "at bat, on deck, in the hole," a corruption of the original nautical form, "at bat, on deck, in the hold." see *at bat.* 2. At a disadvantage to the batter with a count of more balls than strikes. also *behind.* 3. At a disadvantage to the pitcher with two strikes in the count.

iron man: 1. A durable ballplayer who seldom, if ever, misses a game because of illness or injury, or one who accumulates a record of consecutive games played over a period of time. Baltimore Orioles and New York Giants pitcher Joe "Iron Man" McGinnity (actually a former iron foundry worker) was among the first to popularize the term. In 1903, pitching for the Giants, McGinnity won both games of a doubleheader three times in one month. He also once won five games in six days and continued to play in the minors until he was fifty-four years old. Certainly the most famous Iron Man in modern baseball was New York Yankees immortal Lou Gehrig, who in his fourteen-year career (1925-1939) played in 2,130 consecutive games before removing himself from the lineup, already suffering from amyotrophic lateral sclerosis, the incurable disease that killed him two years later. 2. A baseball announcer, presumably because of the iron microphones used by early announcers. 3. An archaic name for the price of admission to a ballgame. From the days when a general admission ticket could be bought with a single silver dollar, once known as an "iron man."

Iron Mike: An automated pitching machine used by hitters taking batting practice.

ivory: A rookie. Though the exact origin is unknown, the term likens a rookie's potential worth to precious ivory. see *rookie.*

ivory hunter: A baseball scout. One who

tracks down or "hunts" for valuable prospects. also *bird dog.*

jake, jaker: A player who makes excuses (such as illness or injury) to keep from playing. The term is associated with Boston Red Sox player-manager Jake Stahl (early 1900s), although whether its present use stems from a particular incident of not wanting to play or simply to the association of the name Jake (Stahl) with a player who would "stall" rather than play is a matter of question. compare *gamer.*

jam the batter: To pitch inside to a batter in order to prevent a full and powerful swing.

Jawn Titus: A exceptional or spectacular catch; a circus catch. A corruption of the name John Titus, a Philadelphia Phillies and later Boston Braves outfielder, who was known for his heroic fielding in the early 1900s.

jellyball: see *greaseball.*

John Anderson: A rare and embarrassing baserunning mistake in which an over-anxious player attempts to steal a base that is already occupied by a teammate. Named after "Honest" John Anderson, a utility player for the New York Highlanders, who in 1904 attempted to steal second with the bases loaded.

Judy: see *punch hitter.*

jughandle curve: A curveball that travels in a broad arc. also *rainbow curve, roundhouse curve.*

jump all over: To quickly hit and score runs against the opposing pitcher. (jumped all over the starting pitcher for three runs in the first inning)

jump on: To swing at and connect with a pitch. (jumps on a fastball and drives it all the way to the right field wall)

junior circuit: The American League. Although still sometimes referred to in this way, the American League has been considered an equal competitor to the National League since 1903, when the American League Boston Pilgrims won the first World Series against the National League Pittsburgh Pirates.

junk, junk pitch: A slow pitch, such as a forkball, knuckleball, or other pitch, that requires an unorthodox grip and delivery. Though regarded as "junk" by some in comparison to the classic fastball and curveball, these deceptive pitches are nonetheless effective when well thrown. (just waiting for a fastball, but saw nothing but junk)

junk man: A pitcher who relies heavily on junk pitches rather than the more orthodox fastball and curve. In the late 1940s, New York Yankee pitcher Ed Lopat became the first pitcher to be called a junk man.

1. K: 1. The symbol used by scorers to indicate a strikeout. Originated in the 1860s by *New York Herald* sportswriter M.J. Kelly, who chose the last letter of "struck" (out) to differentiate between a strikeout and a sacrifice, indicated by the symbol "S." 2. A strikeout.

2. K: see *strike out.*

keystone: Second base. So called because second base is of "key" importance and halfway around the bases (like the keystone in an arch).

keystone sacker: Second baseman.

knob: The end of the bat handle, which has slightly raised rounded edges.

knockdown pitch: A pitch deliberately thrown at or near the batter, forcing him to bail out, or drop to the ground, in order to avoid being hit. Although against the rules, a knockdown pitch is sometimes thrown as a warning against or retaliation for other unsportsmanlike behavior. also *brushback, duster, Gillette, purpose pitch.* compare *beanball, beaner, chin music.*

knock out, knock out of the box: To force the opposing pitcher out of the game with a number of consecutive hits. also *chase.*

●●To render ineffective, to defeat. (her rebuttal knocked my argument right out of the box)

Knothole Club: Special blocks of seats reserved in most ballparks for use by youth groups at nominal or no cost. Cardinals manager-executive Branch Rickey originated the practice in St. Louis in the 1920s with the idea of encouraging future paying customers. The name came from the knotholes in the outfield fences of most early ballparks, through which many neighborhood children watched their first baseball games.

knuckleball: A pitch in which the ball is gripped with the thumb and the tips or fingernails of the first two fingers and released in such a way as to impart little or no spin. The result is a relatively slow pitch that dips, hops, or breaks in an unorthodox and unpredictable manner as it nears home plate. Often the catcher must use a larger than normal mitt when working with a knuckleball pitcher. also *flutterball, knuckler.*

knuckleballer: A pitcher known for his knuckleball.

knuckle curve: A curveball that is thrown with the grip used for a knuckleball.

knuckler: see *knuckleball.*

lawn mower: see *daisy clipper.*

lead: The position away from a base in the direction of the next base which a runner takes in order to gain an advantage by shortening the distance to the next base. The runner must, however, remain near to the base so he can run back in the event of a pickoff attempt by the pitcher or the catcher.

lead off: To be the first batter in a team's or inning's lineup.

leadoff: 1. The first to bat in a team's or inning's lineup. (leadoff batter) 2. Of, by, or made by the first to bat in a team's or inning's lineup. (leadoff bunt single)

leather man: see *glove man.*

leave: To have or strand a specified number of base runners on base at the end of the inning. (still can't seem to score a run as they leave two men on in the eighth) also *strand.*

left field: 1. The left (as viewed from home plate) side of the outfield past third base. 2. The player position in left field. (to play left field)

••Because of the relative vastness of the outfield and its distance from home plate, something said to have come out of left field carries the connotation of something remote or unexpected. (that question came out of left field)

left fielder: The defensive player responsible for fielding balls hit to left field.

leg hit: A bouncer or ground ball that the batter beats out for a base hit.

letter high: The same height (distance from the ground) as the team initials or name generally printed on the chest portion of a uniform. (letter high fastball)

letup: see *changeup.*

line: 1. Baseline or foul line. (hits one down the line toward left field) 2. To hit a line drive. (lines a single through the hole)

line drive: A sharply hit ball that travels close to the ground in a fairly direct path. also *blue darter, clothesliner, darter, frozen rope, liner, rope.*

line out: To hit a line drive straight to a

fielder who catches the ball for an out. (lined out to the shortstop)

liner: A line drive. see *line drive.*

line score: A summary of the results of a game that lists team totals of runs, hits, and errors. A line score may also list each team's lineup and the names of the game's home run hitters. compare *box score.*

lineup: 1. All the players participating in a game. (injured and out of the lineup) 2. A list of the players participating in a game.

••A list of participants or activities in an event. (a star-studded lineup for tonight's program)

lineup card: A prepared list of participating players and the order in which they bat, presented to the plate umpire by a representative from each team before the start of a game.

Little League: An international organization (twenty-nine countries participated in 1981) of baseball leagues in individual towns and cities for youths between the ages of nine and twelve years old who play on a diamond two-thirds the size of a regulation field. The first Little League was founded by Carl E. Stotz in 1939 in Williamsport, Pennsylvania, the present international headquarters and site of the annual Little League World Series.

live bat: Currently hitting well. (has a live bat in this series, so they will walk him)

live fastball: A fastball that moves around, rising (or occasionally dropping) as it nears homeplate.

load the bases: 1. To allow the opposing team to get base runners on all three bases at one time. (pitcher is in trouble again as he loads the bases with only one out) 2. To get base runners on all three bases at one time. (Yankees load the bases in the bottom of the ninth)

load up the ball: To surreptitiously apply saliva or some foreign substance to a baseball so as to make it break or swerve in an unnatural way when pitched. An illegal practice, which, if proved, results in ejection from the game and disciplinary action from the league.

long ball: A ball batted near or over an outfield wall or fence. (known as a long ball hitter)

long man: see *long reliever.*

long relief, long relief man: see *long reliever.*

long reliever: A relief pitcher who is able to pitch five or more innings, and can therefore relieve a starting pitcher early in a game. also *long man, long relief, long relief man.* compare *short reliever.*

1. look: The visual check of a base runner taken by a pitcher in the set position, just before delivering a pitch. (gives the look, and the pitch)

2. look: To hold, with a hit or thrown ball in hand, a base runner with a visual check before making a play on the batter or another base runner. (fields the ball on one hop, looks toward third to hold the runner, and throws to first for the out)

look at: To not swing at a pitch. (looks at a fastball inside for ball four) also *take.*

look for: To expect a certain type of pitch. (with a count of three balls and no strikes, looking for a fastball over the plate)

loop: 1. A league. (best pitching staff in the loop) 2. To hit a pitched ball in a high arc. (loops a single into center field)

losing pitcher: The pitcher charged with the loss of a game. A starting pitcher gets the loss if he pitches a complete game or his team is losing when he is taken out of the game and subsequently never gains the lead. A relief pitcher brought in when the team is leading or tied can be charged with the loss if he gives up the winning run (pitches the ball that puts the runner on base who subsequently scores the winning run). compare *winning pitcher.*

Lowdermilk: A pitcher with control problems, prone to wildness. Named after early 1900s pitcher Grover Cleveland Lowdermilk, a journeyman who was notorious for his lack of control.

lumber: A bat, or bats. see *bat.*

mace: A bat. see *bat.*

mackerel: A curveball. From the old saying "dead as a mackerel," which is how a curveball appears when compared to a fastball.

magic number: The total number of games the leading team in a division, conference, or league must win and/or the second place team must lose in order to mathematically guarantee the championship title for the leading team. (With five games left on the schedule, if the leading team has a two-game lead over the second place team, the magic num-

ber for the leader is four. Four wins by the leader, four losses by the second place team, or any combination of wins and losses by the first and second place teams respectively that total four, mathematically guarantee that the leading team will finish with a better record than the second place team.)

major league: 1. Either or both of, or pertaining to either or both of, the two existing top level professional baseball leagues, the American League and the National League. 2. Any or all of, or pertaining to any or all of, the six top level professional leagues in the history of organized baseball; the National League (1876 to the present), the American League (1901 to the present), the American Association (1882 to 1891), the Union Association (1884), the Players' League (1890), and the Federal League (1914 to 1915). (a major league baseball player) also *big league.*

●●The top level of a sports endeavor, enterprise, or competition. The highest degree. (a major league personality problem)

Major League Baseball Players Association: The union that represents major league baseball players in collective bargaining. Founded in 1953, the union has national headquarters in New York City. The first labor organization in major league baseball was the National Brotherhood of Professional Baseball Players founded in 1885. In 1890, led by Hall of Fame pitcher and shortstop Monte Ward, Brotherhood members seceded from organized baseball and formed the Players League with teams in most of the National League cities. Although the new league was successful and competitive, after a year the players allowed themselves to be talked back into the fold and ultimately won few concessions from the powerful National League owners.

major leagues: The two top level professional baseball leagues in the United States: the American League and the National League. also *big leagues, bigs, majors.*

●●The top level of any sport, enterprise, or endeavor.

majors: see *major leagues.*

manicurist: see *groundskeeper.*

marked ball: A ball that has been surreptitiously cut, scratched, or scuffed in order to make it break or swerve in an unnatural way when pitched. see *doctored ball.*

mark the ball: To surreptitiously cut, scratch, or scuff the surface of a ball in order to make it break or swerve in an unnatural way when pitched.

mask: see *catcher's mask.*

matador: An infielder who goes through toreadorlike motions to move his body out of the way when fielding a batted ball.

McGrawism: Roughhouse, hard-hitting baseball as epitomized by John "Muggsy" McGraw, third baseman for the Baltimore Orioles in the 1890s (later Orioles and New York Giants manager). McGraw practiced and preached a brutal, anything goes style of play in which opposing infielders were bumped and spiked on the base paths, while their base runners would be tripped, held, or hit as they ran by.

meal ticket: A consistently excellent player, particularly a pitcher. The legendary New York Giants pitcher Carl Hubbell of the 1930s was a classic example. Known as "King Carl, the Meal Ticket," Hubbell was said to be the man who "kept the groceries on his manager's table."
●●Any person, object, or quality that guarantees success. (admirable combination of intelligence and integrity will continue to be her meal ticket)

men in blue: The umpires. also *boys in blue.*

middle: 1. The center or middle of the strike zone. (didn't try to hit the corners, just blew a fastball by him right down the middle) 2. Over or near second base, between the normal fielding positions of the second baseman and the shortstop. (a base hit up the middle)

middle gardener: A center fielder.

minor league: Any, or pertaining to any, professional baseball league other than the two major leagues. Often minor league teams are owned and operated by, or affiliated with major league teams. also *minors.*
●●Of small importance or little prestige. (just a pushy minor league bureaucrat)

minors: see *minor league.*

mitt: A padded leather covering worn in place of a normal glove by a catcher or first baseman, generally consisting of two sections, one for the thumb and one for the four fingers (some first baseman's mitts have three sections). compare *glove.*

money player: A player who performs best under pressure or when the stakes are high (as in playoff or championship games).

morning glory: see *early bloomer.*

morning journal: A bat made of poor or soft wood, of no more use than a rolled-up newspaper. also *banana stick.*

motion: The movement of a pitcher's arms and body during the windup for a pitch. Often used to distract or deceive a batter by establishing a false or misleading rhythm.

mound: see *pitcher's mound.*

move: The throw used by a pitcher to pick off a runner caught off base. (picked off the runner with a great move to first)

moxie: A slang expression similar to "guts," meaning a combination of strength and courage or nerve. Moxie was a popular soft drink hawked in East Coast ballparks in the 1880s. The familiar call, "ice-cold moxie" in the stands during a game was eventually associated with the "ice-cold nerves" of courageous players.
●●Spirit, courage, or resolution.

mud ball: An illegal pitch in which mud is applied to (or packed in the seams of) a ball in order to make it break or curve unnaturally when thrown.

muff: To fumble or misplay the ball; to bungle a play. In use since the late 1860s and derived from the early baseball term "muffin," an unskilled or casual player.
●●To make a mistake or bungle something. (muffed his first line in the second act)

MVP: Most valuable player. An annual award given by the Baseball Writers Association of America (since 1931) to the most outstanding player in each league. The American League's first Most Valuable Player was George Sisler of the St. Louis Browns, selected by a special committee in 1922. In 1924, a special committee selected Dazzy Vance of the Brooklyn Dodgers as the National League's first Most Valuable Player. Frank Robinson is the only player ever to be selected MVP in both major leagues (National League MVP in 1961 with the Cincinnati Reds, American League MVP in 1966 with the

Baltimore Orioles). An MVP award is also given to one player (or occasionally more than one) in each World Series.

••An actual or figurative award to the best or most valuable player or person in any sport, event, or circumstance. (whoever remembered to fill the canteen gets my vote for MVP)

National Baseball Hall of Fame and Museum: The official museum of baseball, where historic photos and memorabilia are on display, located in Cooperstown, New York, at the site where popular legend says General Abner Doubleday laid out the first baseball diamond in 1839. One section of the museum, the Baseball Hall of Fame, houses a permanent display of plaques honoring outstanding individuals in the sport of baseball, as selected in an annual balloting of the Baseball Writers Association of America. also *Hall of Fame.*

National League: The older of the two major professional baseball leagues in the United States. Created in 1876 by William A. Hulbert, the National League played its first game on April 22, 1876. At the time, there were teams in Boston, Chicago, Cincinnati, St. Louis, Hartford, New York, Philadelphia, and Louisville. The National League is now split into two divisions. In the Western Division, there are teams in Los Angeles, Cincinnati, Atlanta, San Francisco, Houston, and San Diego. In the Eastern Division, there are teams in St. Louis, Montreal, Philadelphia, Pittsburgh, New York, and Chicago. abbreviated NL.

National Pastime: The nickname the game of baseball came to be known by in the early twentieth century, especially after World War I.

nightcap: The second game of a doubleheader, often played in the evening.

nine: A baseball team.

no-hit: Pertaining to a game or part of a game during which a pitcher allows no base hits. (came in to pitch three no-hit innings)

no-hitter: A game in which a pitcher or pitchers give up no base hits to the opposing team. The first professional no-hitter was pitched in 1875 by Joe Borden on the Boston Red Stockings, then in the old National Association. In 1876, Borden pitched the first ever no-hitter in the National League. In 1981,

Nolan Ryan of the Houston Astros became the first pitcher in major league history to have pitched five no-hitters.

nubber: see *banjo hit.*

number two: A curveball, usually called for by the catcher with a hand signal of two fingers.

obstruction: Contact with a runner deliberately made by a defensive player neither in possession nor trying to obtain possession of the ball, illegally interfering with the progress of the runner. If the umpire rules that the base runner would have safely made the base without the obstruction, the base runner is awarded the base.

off-field hit: A base hit to the field on the opposite side of the plate as the batter stands. also *wrong-field hit.*

official scorer: The person officially designated scorekeeper and who makes decisions as to whether a defensive player is to be charged with an error.

off-speed pitch: A slower than normal pitch, particularly deceptive when mixed with fastballs.

on, on base: Occupying a base as a runner. (with one man on, and the winning run at the plate)

on-base percentage: The statistic used to measure the effectiveness of a batter at getting on base, obtained by dividing the number of times the batter reaches a base by the number of plate appearances (at bats, walks, hit batters, catcher's interference) and carrying the quotient three decimal places.

on deck: Next to take a turn at bat. Part of the expression, "at bat, on deck, in the hole," a corruption of the original nautical form, "at bat, on deck, in the hold." see *at bat.*

••Due, or next on the agenda. (weather bureau reports we have clear skies on deck today)

on-deck circle: Either of two circles marked on each side of the field between the dugout and home plate, in which the batter due to bat next waits.

one-bagger, one-base hit, one-baser: A single.

one-cushion shot: A batted ball that caroms off an outfield wall.

one o'clock hitter: see *two o'clock hitter.*

on the fists: An inside pitch that passes close to the batter's hands, effectively jamming the batter. If contact is made with the ball, it is with the less powerful handle end of the bat. see *jam the batter.*

on the fly: In mid-air. (catches it on the fly for the third out)

open stance: A batting stance in which the front foot is positioned further away from the plate than the rear foot. compare *closed stance.*

opposite field: The field on the opposite side of the plate as the batter stands. (all caught off guard as he lined one to the opposite field)

orchard: 1. A ballpark. 2. The outfield. also *garden, pasture.*

orchardman: An outfielder. also *gardener, pastureworker.*

1. out: The termination of a player's turn as a batter or base runner. Three strikes put a batter out, as do the following: fouling off an attempted bunt with two strikes on the count (an automatic third strike); hitting a fly ball (fair or foul) that is caught in the air; being tagged with the ball after hitting a fair ball and before reaching base; hitting a fair ball and reaching base after a defensive player has touched the base while holding the ball; hitting an infield fly; interfering with the catcher while he attempts to play the ball; batting out of order. A base runner is called out upon being tagged with the ball while off base; reaching a base on a force play after a defensive player in possession of the ball touches that base; being hit by a batted ball before it travels past an infielder; interfering with a fielder's attempt to play the ball; running runs outside the base path to avoid a putout. Originally from the eighteenth century British game rounders. also *away, down, gone.*

2. out: 1. The putting, throwing, or calling out of a player from the opposing team. (got the out that ended the game) also *putout.* 2. The act of being put out or making an out. (made an out his last time at bat) 3. A player who has been put out. (he was caught stealing and became the third out)

outfield: 1. The area of the playing field that is beyond the perimeter of the infield (the grass or turf line behind the bases) and is bounded by the foul lines. The outfield is divided into three general areas, which are, as viewed from home plate, left field, center field, and right field. (to take the relayed throw

from the outfield) 2. The players who play the outfield positions. (a strong throwing outfield)

outfielder: A defensive player who plays in the outfield. also *gardener, orchardman, pastureworker.*

out in front of: Swinging or beginning to swing at a pitch too soon, especially a changeup or slow curve when a fastball is anticipated.

out looking: Out on a pitch that is taken for a called third strike. compare *out swinging.*

out man: see *easy out.*

out of play: Unable to affect or be acted upon by the batter, base runners, or defensive players.

out pitch: One's best or most reliable pitch, the one that most often results in an out. (uses the fastball as his out pitch)

out swinging: Out on a swing and a miss for the third strike. compare *out looking.*

overhand: A type of throw or delivery in which the hand is swung down from over the shoulder in a forward arc. compare *sidearm, underhand.*

overslide: To slide past (instead of safely into) a base. (overslides the base and is tagged out)

1. overthrow: To throw the ball beyond the desired destination. (overthrows the cutoff man and the base runners advance)

2. overthrow: A throw that goes past its desired destination. (takes second base on the overthrow)

paint the black: To throw pitches in the black. Pitchers who are able to paint the black often get these pitches called as strikes or entice batters to swing at them. see *black.*

palm ball: An off-speed pitch in which the ball is gripped between the thumb and the palm (instead of the fingertips) and released in such a way as to impart little or no spin. The result is a pitch that breaks in an unorthodox and unpredictable manner as it nears home plate.

pancake: A thinly padded, rather flat glove preferred by some infielders. The shallow pocket in such a glove allows a fielded ball to be quickly grasped and thrown, particularly important in a double play situation. compare *bushel basket.*

1. pass: A base on balls.

2. pass: To walk, or give a base on balls to a batter.

passed ball: A normally catchable pitch, untouched by the batter, which the catcher misses, enabling base runners to advance. The ruling of passed ball is made by the official scorer. compare *wild pitch*.

pasture: The outfield. also *garden, orchard*.

pastureworker: An outfielder. also *gardener, orchardman*.

pebble picker: An infielder who uses the alibi of a "bad hop" when a ground ball gets by, sometimes picking through the turf for the guilty pebble.

1. peg: To throw a ball. (can really peg the ball)

2. peg: A throw. (out at the plate on a great peg from left field)

pennant: A league championship. The Brooklyn Bridegrooms (later nicknamed the Dodgers) are the only professional team to have won pennants in two different major leagues in successive years: in the old American Association in 1889, and in the National League in 1890. also *flag*.

pennant race: The competition for a league championship, especially near the end of a season.

pepper: A warm-up drill in which a batter hits a series of ground balls in rapid succession to several players a short distance away, who field them and throw them briskly among themselves before returning them to the batter. The term is probably an allusion to the fast or "peppy" quality of the drill.

perfect game: A no-hitter in which all opposing batters are retired in succession, without reaching first base. Since the first major league perfect game by Worcester pitcher John Richman in 1880, only ten more occured in the next 101 years. The most famous may have been New York Yankees pitcher Don Larsen's perfect game against the Brooklyn Dodgers in the 1956 World Series, the first no-hitter ever pitched in a World Series.

pickle: A rundown. From the colloquialism "in a pickle," meaning caught in an embarrassing or dangerous predicament. see *rundown*.

pick off: To put out a base runner who is off base by quickly throwing the ball to a fielder at the base who tags the runner before he can return. The throw to pick off a runner can be made by the pitcher or catcher.

pickoff: The act or an instance of picking off a base runner.

piece of iron: A particularly good bat. From the early days of baseball, when players would sometimes plug bats with nails or bits of metal in the hopes of making them more powerful.

pinch: Made with a pinch-hit. (a pinch double) also *pinch-hit*.

pinch hit: 1. To replace another player at bat. Legal since the baseball rule permitting substitutions was passed in 1892. (will pinch hit for the pitcher) 2. To make a base hit while pinch hitting for another player. (pinch hit a single to start off the inning)

●●To take another's place. (will pinch hit behind the counter until the salesman returns)

1. pinch-hit: A base hit made while pinch hitting for another player. Los Angeles Dodger Manny Mota (retired in 1980) holds the major league lifetime record of 150 pinch-hits.

2. pinch-hit: Made by a pinch hitter. (a pinch-hit double) also *pinch*.

pinch hitter: A player who is sent in to take another player's turn at bat, and who is usually himself replaced by another player who continues in the position vacated by the player whose batting turn was taken. A pinch hitter is generally used at a critical juncture, often to bat for the pitcher or a poor hitter, to face a particular pitcher because of previous success, or to bat from the opposite side of the plate as the player being replaced. Cleveland Spiders player John "Dirty Jack" Doyle became the first pinch hitter in baseball history when he hit successfully in his only attempt in 1892. In the same year, sportswriter Charlie Dryden coined the term "pinch hitter" because the player who came into the game to bat was in a "tight spot," or "in a pinch." compare *designated hitter*.

pinch-run: To act as a pinch runner. (putting in a speedster to pinch run for him)

pinch runner: A player who is sent in to run for a teammate on base, and who is usually himself replaced by another player who continues in the fielding position vacated by the player removed for the pinch runner. In 1974, then Oakland A's owner Charles O. Finley hired Herb Washington, a sprinter with no previous professional baseball experience, to use purely as a pinch runner (Finley called him his "designated runner"). compare *courtesy runner*.

pine tar ball: An illegal pitch in which pine tar (normally rubbed on the handle of a bat to make it sticky) is surreptitiously rubbed on one part of the ball so as to make it break or swerve unpredictably when thrown.

pine tar towel: A pine tar-soaked cloth that is rubbed on the handle of a bat to make it sticky, providing a better grip.

1. pitch: 1. To throw the ball to the batter. To be legal, a pitch must be thrown with an overhand or sidearm delivery (underhand for softball), must not be interrupted or stopped in any way (except when the stretch or set position is used), and must be made with the pitcher's foot touching the rubber until the ball is released. (In slow pitch softball, the ball must travel in an arc between three feet and ten feet high on its way to the batter.) (pitched more fastballs than curveballs) 2. To play the position of the pitcher. (pitched three innings before giving up a hit) also *twirl*. 3. To throw in a specific manner. (pitched him high and inside to move him away from the plate) 4. To start a certain pitcher in a given game. (pitched his two left-handers in the first two games of the series)

●●To be "in there pitching" means to be trying or making an effort.

2. pitch: The ball delivered by the pitcher. (first pitch was a hummer)

pitch around: 1. To pitch so carefully as to risk a base on balls in order to prevent the batter from getting a hit. 2. To intentionally walk a batter.

pitcher: 1. The player who delivers the ball to the batter. Originally "bowler" from cricket, and later, rounders. also *hurler, soupbone*. 2. The player position of the pitcher.

pitcher of record: 1. The pitcher credited with the victory or charged with the loss at the end of a game. 2. The pitcher who would be credited with the victory or charged with the loss if the score remains unchanged when the game is ended.

pitchers' duel: A close game in which both pitchers allow the opposite side few, if any, scoring opportunities. A low scoring game. Any low scoring game or contest, usually featuring defense rather

than offense. Also often used facetiously to refer to a wide-open high scoring game. (the final score was 14-12—a real pitchers' duel)

pitcher's mound: The slightly elevated portion of the playing field in the middle of a diamond on which the pitcher stands to pitch the ball. Eighteen feet in diameter, the mound rises gradually to a maximum height of 10 inches at the leveled-off central area, which contains a 24-inch-long by 6-inch-wide white rubber slab. The front edge (long side) of this slab, called the pitcher's rubber, lies exactly 60 feet 6 inches from the rear corner of home plate. Before the late 1880s, the pitcher's mound was called the pitcher's box, which was taken from the bowler's box in the game of rounders. also *hill, mound*.

pitcher's plate: see *rubber*.

pitcher's rubber: see *rubber*.

pitch from the stretch: To pitch with the special abbreviated motion used instead of a full windup when runners are on base. see *stretch*.

pitching chart: A written log of every pitch made by a particular pitcher to every opposing batter and the subsequent results. The pitching chart, usually kept by a coach or teammate, can help the

PITCHER

pitcher and his manager assess the effectiveness of certain pitches to certain batters, improving his future performance.

pitching coach: A coach (often an ex-pitcher) whose sole responsibility is to teach, train, and console the pitchers on a team.

pitching machine: see *Iron Mike.*

pitching staff: The pitchers on a team. (strongest pitching staff in the league)

pitchout: A pitch that is intentionally thrown wide of the plate and away from the batter to enable the catcher to throw out a base runner who is stealing a base or to prevent one from stealing a base.

plate: Home plate.

plate umpire: The umpire-in-chief, positioned behind home plate. see *umpire, umpire-in-chief.*

play ball: The traditional signal for play to begin or restart after a time-out, called out by the umpire.

••To "play the (ball) game" or cooperate. (if the two sides will play ball, the case will be settled in no time)

play-by-play: A running description of the action of a game for a radio or television broadcast. On August 5, 1921, station KDKA of Pittsburgh broadcast the first major league baseball game on the radio, between the Pittsburgh Pirates and the Philadelphia Phillies. Harold Arlin was the play-by-play announcer. On August 26, 1939, Red Barber did the play-by-play on the first major league telecast, a doubleheader between the Brooklyn Dodgers and the Cincinnati Reds.

••A running commentary on or point-by-point reconstruction of an event. (gave us a play-by-play description of her vacation along with a slide show)

playoff: 1. One of a series of extra games at the end of a season (as between division leaders) to decide the league champion. 2. An extra game or contest or series of games or contests to decide a winner or championship in case of a tie at the end of regular play. 3. Of or pertaining to a playoff or playoffs.

plugged bat: see *doctored bat.*

pocket: The deep central area of a glove or mitt, optimum and most secure for catching or fielding a ball.

1. pop: A pop fly. also *popper, pop-up.*

2. pop: To hit a pop-up. (popped to the shortstop)

pop fly: A short, high fly ball. also *pop, popper, pop-up.*

pop foul: A pop fly that goes foul.

pop out: To hit a pop fly that is caught for an out.

pop-out: A pop fly that is caught for an out.

popper: A pop fly. also *pop, pop-up.*

pop up: To hit a short, high fly ball, usually for an out. (popped up to the second baseman) also *pop.*

pop-up: A short, high fly ball, usually an out. (hits a little pop-up to the pitcher) also *pop, pop fly, popper.*

pop-up slide: A feetfirst slide into a base in which a base runner "pops up" into a standing position on the base, ready to advance to the next base.

powder puff ball: An illegal pitch in which the ball is coated with resin powder (which some claim is mixed with white flour), accumulated in the pitcher's hand from the rosin bag. When the ball is thrown, it arrives at the plate amid a cloud of white dust. Veteran pitcher Gaylord Perry invented the powder puff ball. also *puff ball.* see *doctored ball.*

power alley: Either of two hypothetical lanes in the outfield between the center field and right field and between center field and left field, through which home runs are frequently hit.

pretzel: A curveball. Two derivations: one from the curved shape of a pretzel, and the other from the fact that a curveball can "tie a batter up in a knot" like a pretzel.

protect the plate: To avoid being called out on strikes by attempting to foul off all pitches which might be called strikes if not swung at, while waiting for a hittable pitch.

protect the runner: To give a base runner an opportunity to steal by swinging at any pitch (even a bad one), and thus either hitting the ball or delaying the catcher's attempt to throw out the runner. 2. To attempt to hit the ball during a hit-and-run play.

puff ball: see *powder puff ball.*

pull, pull the ball: To hit the ball to the outfield on the same side of the plate as the batter stands when at bat. A left-handed batter pulls the ball to right field.

pulled off the bag: Made to lose contact with the base in order to catch an errant throw, resulting in the loss of a force play unless contact can be reestablished before the runner reaches the base.

pull hitter: A batter who usually tends to pull the ball.

pull the string: To throw a changeup after a fastball or a series of fastballs, often causing the batter to begin to swing too soon, as though the pitcher had pulled a string attached to the ball before it reached the plate.

1. pump: The part of a pitcher's windup in which he swings his arms back and forward over his head.

2. pump: The raising and swinging of the arms back and then forward over the head in the windup.

Punch and Judy hitter: see *punch hitter.*

punch hitter: A batter who gets hits by punching at the ball (in contrast to using a full swing). also *Judy, Punch and Judy hitter.*

purpose pitch: see *knockdown pitch.*

put out: To cause a player on the opposing team to be out. The expression comes from the game of cricket, and later, rounders.

putout: The putting out of a player, officially credited to the player who completes the putout. To be credited with a putout, a player can tag a base runner, touch a base and force out a runner, or catch a fly ball. If the batter strikes out, hits a foul bunt after two strikes, or is thrown out for obstructing the catcher or batting improperly or in the wrong order, the putout is credited to the catcher. If the runner is put out because of being struck with a batted ball or interfering with a defensive player, the closest player, or the player who would have made the play if unobstructed, is credited with the putout. compare *assist.*

quick hook: 1. The tendency of a manager or coach to immediately remove and replace a pitcher in trouble. 2. The quick or early removal of a pitcher from a game.

quick pitch: 1. An illegal pitch in which the pitcher throws the ball before the batter is ready. If the bases are empty, the quick pitch is called a ball (unless the batter otherwise reaches first base on the pitch, in which case the illegal pitch

is disregarded). If there are runners on base, the quick pitch is ruled a balk and all runners advance one base (unless the batter otherwise reaches first base, causing the runners to advance normally). also *quick return pitch.* 2. A legal pitch made without a windup, but with a simple pivot on the rubber.

quick-pitch: To make a quick pitch.

quick return pitch: see *quick pitch.*

rabbit: The bounce or liveliness of a baseball. (more rabbit in the modern-day baseball)

rabbit ball: The lively ball used in modern baseball, first adopted in 1920 by the American League and one year later by the National League. The rabbit ball (it bounces or jumps like a rabbit) was introduced to take advantage of the box office potential of slugger Babe Ruth (in 1920, Ruth hit fifty-four home runs, his batting average soared fifty-four points to .376, and the American League's collective batting average was twenty-five points higher than the year before).

race to the bag: A footrace between a base runner and a fielder in possession of the ball who will force the runner out if he reaches the base first. (to the pitcher who wins the race to the bag for the third out)

rainbow, rainbow curve: A curveball that travels in a wide sweeping arc. also *jughandle curve, roundhouse curve.*

rain check: The part of the ticket which can be used for admission to another, usually specified, game if a game is rained out. The practice of giving rain checks originated in baseball in the 1880s.

●●When one cannot attend or participate in some activitiy, it is common to ask for a "rain check," another invitation or opportunity at some future time. (already have plans tonight, but I hope you'll give me a rain check)

rain out: To rain hard enough to cause the postponement of a game. (if it continues, the game might be rained out)

●●To rain hard enough to cause the postponement of any event. Also, to be "rained out" connotes a lack of success or the opportunity for success at any endeavor due to circumstances beyond one's control. ("you win some, you lose some, and you'll get rained out of a few")

rainout: A game that is suspended or post-poned because of rain.

1. razz: see *razzberry*.

2. razz: To heckle or deride. Derived from *razzberry*.

••To tease or heckle. (got razzed because of his mismatched socks)

razzberry: A sound expressing derision or contempt, made by extending the tongue between the lips and forcibly expelling air. Some believe that the proper and original spelling of the present term, "raspberry," was a play on the word "rasp," meaning to make a coarse or abrasive sound. also *Bronx cheer, razz*.

••An expression of derision or contempt.

RBI: Run(s) batted in. also *ribby*.

receiver: A catcher. see *catcher*.

relief: A relief pitcher's work in a given game. (pitched two innings in relief)

reliefer: see *relief pitcher*.

relief man: see *relief pitcher*.

relief pitcher: A pitcher who does not start, but who is used to relieve another pitcher, particularly one who is used consistently in this capacity. In 1981, Rollie Fingers of the Milwaukee Brewers became the first relief pitcher ever to win both the MVP award and Cy Young Award in the same year. also *reliefer, relief man, reliever*. compare *starting pitcher*.

relieve: To replace or take over for another pitcher during a game.

reliever: see *relief pitcher*.

resin bag: see *rosin bag*.

retire: To put out a batter, batters, or a side. Originally from the sport of cricket, then later, rounders. (retired the last six men in a row) also *set down*.

retire the side: To put out three batters, ending the opposing team's turn at bat until the next inning.

rhubarb: A noisy argument or heated discussion on the field. The expression was first popularized by Brooklyn Dodgers play-by-play man Red Barber. He first broadcast the term at a game in Cincinnati in 1938, after hearing New York writer Garry Schumacher exclaim "What a rhubarb!" during a game-stopping fracas. Though it was common for film, theater, and radio actors to repeat the word "rhubarb" over and over again to simulate an angry and excited mob, Schumacher explained that his use of the expression probably came out of the subconscious memory of boyhood fights with unpopular rhubarb sandwiches (provided as a mild laxative) in the streets of Brooklyn.

••An argument, sometimes with comic results. (small disagreement that turned into a real rhubarb)

ribby: Run batted in. A pronunciation of the abbreviation for runs batted in, RBI. (the ribby king of the team) also *RBI, run batted in*.

1. rifle: A great throwing arm, especially from the outfield. also *cannon, gun*.

2. rifle: To make a long accurate throw. (rifles the ball home in time for the tag)

right field: 1. The right (as viewed from home plate) side of the outfield past first base. 2. The player position in right field. (to play right field)

right fielder: The defensive player responsible for fielding balls hit to right field.

riseball, riser: A softball pitch that rises as it nears the plate.

rook: Short for rookie.

1. rookie: An inexperienced player. Army slang for, and probably an alteration of, the word recruit. also *donkey, ivory, rook, yan, yannigan*.

••An inexperienced or unskilled person. (drives a car like a rookie)

2. rookie: First year. (won eight games in his rookie season)

Rookie of the Year: An annual award given by the Baseball Writers Association of America to the outstanding first year player in each league. The first Rookie of the Year Award was given to Jackie Robinson of the Brooklyn Dodgers in 1947 (the first two years, only one player was selected from both leagues combined).

root: To cheer or encourage a player or team. The term has been popular in baseball since the late 1800s and derives from the notion that a partisan fan is almost "rooted" to his or her team. (root for the home team)

••To encourage, cheer for, wish the success of, or lend support to someone or something.

rooter: A fan who roots for a player or team. The first recorded use of the expression in print appeared in the July 8, 1890 edition of the *New York Press*.

rope: A line drive. Short for frozen rope. see *line drive*.

rosin bag: A cloth bag of powdered rosin that, when handled by a pitcher, leaves enough rosin in the hand to give him a good grip on the ball. also *resin bag*.

rotation: The regular order in which starting pitchers are used. (trying to work his way into the pitching rotation)

roundhouse curve: A curveball that travels in a wide sweeping arc somewhat like the circular revolving floor of a railroad roundhouse. also *jughandle curve, rainbow curve*.

round-tripper: A home run. A round trip around all the bases and back to home plate. see *home run*.

rubber: A 6-inch by 24-inch rectangular slab of white rubber set into the ground atop the pitcher's mound. The front edge (long side) is 60 feet, 6 inches (46 feet for softball) from the rear corner of home plate. Although he must be in contact with the rubber while making a pitch, the pitcher must leave the rubber before attempting to pick off a base runner. The original regulation distance between the rubber and home plate was 45 feet. In 1881, the rubber was moved back to 50 feet. In 1891, the old American Association failed, cutting the number of major league baseball teams from twenty-four to twelve in one year. With just the strongest pitchers remaining, suddenly batters found themselves struggling (only eleven batters hit over .300 in 1892, as compared to twenty-three the previous year). Fearing that interest in the game might dwindle, the baseball owners moved the rubber back to its present distance for the 1893 season. The move had the desired effect, with no less than forty-three batters exceeding the .300 mark that year. also *pitcher's plate, pitcher's rubber*.

rubber arm: A durable pitching arm. Said of a pitcher who is able to pitch often and/or for long periods without soreness or stiffness.

run: 1. A point scored, accomplished each time a member of the offensive team touches all the bases and home plate in succession without being put out. A run is credited to both the player and the team in statistical records. The term comes from the game of cricket. In 1894, Philadelphia Phillies outfielder "Sliding Billy" Hamilton scored 192 runs, the all-time single season record.

Ty Cobb holds the lifetime record for the most runs scored, 2,244. 2. To eject, or throw a player out of a game. (said something he shouldn't have, so the umpire ran him)

run and hit: A prearranged play in which the runner on first starts for second base on the pitch, while the batter, under no obligation to protect the runner, chooses whether or not to swing at the pitch. If the ball is successfully hit through the infield, the base runner can often take an extra base and sometimes even score. If the ball is hit to an infielder, the base runner is most often able to reach second base safely and prevent a double play. If the ball is not swung at or is swung at and missed, the base runner may be thrown out or come up with a stolen base, depending upon the speed and accuracy of the catcher's throw. compare *hit and run*.

run batted in: A run caused by and credited as a run batted in to a particular batter. A batter is credited with a run batted in when he causes a runner to score by getting a base hit or base on balls, by being hit by a pitch, by making a sacrifice or sacrifice fly, or because of an error when there are fewer than two outs and a runner on third who could have scored had the error not occurred. In 1930, Hack Wilson of the Chicago Cubs set the all-time single season record of 190 runs batted in. Hank Aaron holds the lifetime record of 2,297 runs batted in. also *RBI, ribby*.

run down: To put out a base runner in a rundown.

rundown: A situation in which a base runner is trapped off base between two fielders in the base path who toss the ball back and forth and move closer until the runner can be tagged out. Usually the result of an error on the part of the base runner, but occasionally a strategic ploy in a double steal to take the attention of the defensive team while another base runner breaks for home plate. also *pickle*.

runner: A base runner.

runners at the corners: Base runners at first and third bases.

run out a fly ball: To run, after hitting what appears to be a routine fly ball, as hard as possible until the ball is actually caught. This kind of effort can result in a base hit or even extra bases if the fly ball is misjudged or dropped.

rush seats: Unreserved or bleacher seats. The term dates back to the early days of baseball and the custom of opening the gates and allowing the crowd to pour in all at once to fill up the unreserved seats on a first-come-first-served basis.

sack: Base. Named for the stuffed 15-inch-square white canvas bag or "sack" that is attached to the ground for use as a base. also *bag.*

1. sacrifice: A bunt on which a batter is put out, but which allows a base runner to advance. However, if the putout of the batter is the third out, the inning is ended and a sacrifice is not credited. If the batter is not put out because of an error, but would have been without the error, the sacrifice is credited and the base runner advances. In statistical records, a sacrifice does not count as a time at bat and so does not affect the batting average of the batter. If a run scores as a result of a sacrifice, the batter is credited with an RBI. also *sacrifice hit.*

2. sacrifice: To make a sacrifice or sacrifice fly.

sacrifice fly: A fly ball (fair or foul) caught for the first or second out, but hit far enough to enable a base runner to tag up and reach home plate without being put out. In statistical records, a sacrifice fly does not count as a time at bat and so does not affect the batting average of the batter. Since a run is scored on a sacrifice fly, the batter is credited with an RBI.

sacrifice hit: see *sacrifice.*

safe: Successful in reaching a base without being put out. (slides under the tag and is safe)

safety: A base hit.

safety squeeze: see *squeeze play.*

sandlot baseball: 1. Crude, unorganized baseball games played in vacant lots in or near urban areas, historically the place where many youths are first exposed to the game. 2. Crude or unskilled baseball. An uncomplimentary comparison to the rudimentary game played by youths in sandlots.

save: The credit awarded to a relief pitcher who enters a game with his team in the lead and preserves that lead for the remainder of the game. If a relief pitcher does not finish the game, he cannot be credited with a save unless he is removed for a pinch hitter or a pinch runner. If more than one relief pitcher qualifies for a save, the official scorer will credit the save to the relief pitcher judged to have been the most effective. Only one save can be credited in any game. In 1973, Detroit Tiger reliever John Hiller set the all-time record for the most saves in a single season, thirty-eight. also *vultch.*

scoring position: Either second or third base. So called because a base runner can be expected to score on a base hit when he is on one of these bases. (pitched himself into a jam, with only one out and a man in scoring position)

scratch hit, scratch single: A weak hit that enables a batter to reach first, but would not normally be expected to do so.

screen: The wire protective barrier behind home plate, between the playing field and the spectators. (fouls one back into the screen)

screwball: A breaking ball that breaks the opposite way as a curveball (away from a right-handed batter when thrown by a left-hander), a reverse curve. A difficult pitch to throw, the ball is delivered with an elongated arc with the arm extended almost over the head, and released out of the back of the hand with a snap of the wrist. The earliest version of the screwball (the fadeaway) was pioneered in 1900 by the New York Giants' charismatic pitcher, Christy Mathewson. In 1928, another legendary Giants pitcher, Carl Hubbell, popularized the modern screwball, which he had perfected and renamed three years earlier as a minor league player in Oklahoma City. also *scroogie.*

scroogie: see *screwball.*

scuffer: A ball that is illegally scuffed or scratched in order to make it curve in an unnatural way when pitched.

second: Second base. (will hold up at second with a stand-up double)

second base: 1. The base located on the corner of the diamond diagonally opposite home plate, which must be touched second by a base runner. 2. The name of the position played by the second baseman. (to play second base) also *keystone, second.*

second baseman: The defensive player

positioned usually to the right of second base who makes plays at second base and fields balls hit to the area between second base and first base. also *keystone sacker, second sacker*.

second sacker: Second baseman.

seeing-eye single: A base hit that seems to "find" its way through a narrow gap between infielders, as though led by a seeing-eye dog. also *tweener*.

senior circuit: The National League. So called because the National League is older than the American League, sometimes referred to as the junior circuit.

set down: To cause a batter, batters, or a lineup to be put out. (set down the first three batters in the second inning) also *retire*.

set position: The position a pitcher assumes for the momentary pause that must follow the abbreviated windup or "stretch," during which the pitcher checks a base runner before throwing to a base, delivering the ball to the batter, or stepping off the rubber with the pivot foot. While in the set position, the pitcher stands with one foot (the pivot foot) on the rubber and the other foot in front of the rubber, holding the ball with both hands in front of his body. If the pitcher does not come to a complete stop in the set position, a balk is charged and the runner or runners advance.

seventh-inning stretch: The tradition of standing and stretching for a brief period before one's favorite team comes to bat in the seventh inning. The custom was practiced as far back as 1869 by the fans of the first professional team in baseball, the Cincinnati Red Stockings, and is believed to be related to the age-old superstition about the lucky number seven.

shade: To take up defensive positions slightly to the left or slightly to the right of normal, because of the tendency of a certain batter to hit to one side or the other. (outfield shading to the left) also *shift*.

shag flies: To catch fly balls in practice.
●●To "shag" is to catch, or to run after and retrieve.

shake off a sign: To reject a catcher's sign or signal calling for a certain pitch, usually by shaking the head negatively or flicking the glove.

shave the corners: see *hit the corners*.

shift: see *shade*.

shine ball: An illegal pitch in which one part of the ball is rubbed or polished smooth (in the glove or against some part of the pitcher's uniform) to make it break or swerve unnaturally when pitched. see *doctored ball*.

shin guard: The protective covering worn by the catcher over each shin. Invented and first used in 1907 by New York Giants catcher Roger Bresnahan.

shoestring catch: A catch of a fly or line drive made by a running fielder just before it lands. To make a shoestring catch, the player must lean forward with his glove extended forward almost to the ground.

short: Shortstop.

short fielder: 1. In slow pitch softball, an additional player who is placed just outside the infield. 2. The player position of a short fielder.

short-hop: To catch a ball (especially a batted ball) close to the ground immediately after it bounces. (short-hops the ball and makes the throw to first in time for the out)

short hop: Immediately after the bounce of a ball. (catches it on the short hop)

short man: see *short reliever*.

short relief, short relief man: see *short reliever*.

short reliever: A reliever routinely used for only a few innings, such as during the last couple of innings to protect a close lead. also *short man, short relief, short relief man.* compare *long reliever*.

shortstop: 1. The defensive player positioned usually to the left of second base who is responsible for making plays at second base and for fielding balls hit to the area between second and third base. 2. The position played by the shortstop. (to play shortstop)

shut out: To prevent the opposing team from scoring. Originally from the sport of horse racing in the 1870s and still in use. A bettor who reaches the window too late is shut out and prevented from placing a bet. (the starting pitcher shut them out for the first four innings) also *whitewash*.

shutout: A game (either completed or in progress) in which the opponent is prevented from scoring. Hall of Fame Washington pitcher Walter Johnson pitched a record 110 shutouts in his twenty-one-year career. In 1916,

Grover Cleveland Alexander of the Philadelphia Phillies set the record for the most shutouts pitched in one season, sixteen. also *whitewash*.

•• Any contest or situation where an opponent is prevented from scoring (literally, comparatively, or figuratively), or where a team, group, or individual is particularly successful or dominant. (the prosecutor is pitching a shutout so far)

sidearm: A type of throw or delivery made with the hand and wrist brought forward almost parallel to the ground. compare *overhand, underhand*.

sign: A signal determined prior to the game (a word, gesture, or number of fingers) that managers, coaches, and players use to secretly convey information and instructions. Catchers may ask for particular pitches by giving their pitchers a sign. Coaches in the boxes at first base and third base give signs to the batter and to base runners.

1. single: A base hit enabling the batter to reach first base. (a single up the middle) The term originates from the game of cricket. also *bingle, one-bagger, one-base hit, one baser, singleton*.

2. single: 1. To make a single. (singled up the middle to start the inning) 2. To hit a single that allows a base runner to advance. (singled him to third) 3. To hit a single that causes a run to score. (singled in the tying run in the eighth)

singleton: A single.

sinker: A pitch that drops suddenly (usually without curving) as it nears the plate. also *sinker ball*.

sinker ball: A sinker.

skull: see *bean*.

sleeper rabbit play: A prearranged play with base runners on second and third, wherein the runner on second gets the attention of the catcher by being slow to return to the base after the first pitch. In the hopes of drawing a throw from the catcher, the base runner repeats his "careless" return after the next pitch. When and if the catcher does throw, the runners break for home and third the moment the ball leaves his hand. The sleeper rabbit play was invented by Detroit Tigers third baseman George Moriarty in the early 1900s. In recent years, the play has been revived and used with some success by the Montreal Expos.

1. slide: To leap or dive feetfirst or head-

first when approaching a base, then skid along the ground (away from or under a tag) until the base is safely contacted with an outstretched foot or hand.

2. slide: The action or an instance of sliding feetfirst or headfirst into a base.

slider: 1. A pitch thrown with the speed of a fastball that breaks in the same direction as a curve, just as it crosses the plate. Although the exact origin is unknown, George "The Bull" Uhle of the Detroit Tigers and George Blaeholder of the St. Louis Browns were among the first to throw it in the 1930s. 2. An abrasion from sliding into a base. also *strawberry*.

slip pitch: An off-speed pitch that drops just before it reaches the plate. To deliver the pitch, the ball is held between the thumb and palm, not touched by the fingertips, and released in such a way as to impart little or no forward spin.

slo pitch: Slow pitch softball.

slow pitch: Slow pitch softball.

slow pitch softball: A variety of softball in which pitches are thrown at a moderate speed and must arc higher than the batter's head (a minimum of three feet and a maximum of ten feet above the point of release) on the way to the plate. Each side consists of ten players, with the extra player (short fielder) usually playing in a shallow outfield position. Bunting and base stealing are illegal (base runners must remain on base until the ball reaches the batter). A batter who is hit by a pitch does not walk to first base. also *slo pitch, slow pitch*. compare *fast pitch softball*.

slugfest: A high-scoring game with many hits.

slugger: A batter who is known for hitting extra base hits and home runs. With nine home runs and sixty-two runs batted in, Boston left fielder Charley Jones became baseball's first real slugger in 1879. A list of the greatest sluggers of the game would include Babe Ruth, Lou Gehrig, Stan Musial, Ted Williams, Joe DiMaggio, Willie Mays, Mickey Mantle, and Hank Aaron, who hit more home runs in his career (755) than any man in the history of major league baseball.

slugging average: An official statistic that measures the ability of a batter to hit for extra bases, determined by dividing the total bases reached safely on hits by the total times at bat and carrying the quotient three decimal places. Babe Ruth holds both the all-time single season record slugging average, .847, set in 1920, and the lifetime slugging average, .690.

slurve: A pitch that is faster than a curve, but curves more than a normal slider.

1. smoke: A fastball, or fastballs. (reaching back and throwing smoke) see *fastball*.

2. smoke: To throw hard. (smoked one by him)

snake: A curveball.

sno-cone: A catch in which the ball is barely caught in the top part, or webbing, of the glove and protrudes from the top of the glove like the top of a sno-cone.

softball: 1. A game similar to and derived from baseball, played on a field with the same configurations but smaller dimensions (pitching distance 46 feet, bases 60 feet apart), and using a ball slightly larger than a baseball, which is pitched underhand. Invented in the 1880s, softball was originally intended as an indoor game, known as indoor baseball. There are two varieties of softball: fast pitch softball, in which a great deal of emphasis is put on the speed of the pitching (about equal to hardball, given the shorter pitching distance), and slow pitch softball, which prohibits fast pitching and places more emphasis on the hitting and fielding aspects of the game. see *fast pitch softball, slow pitch softball*. 2. The ball used to play the game of softball. A white horsehide or cowhide-covered sphere sewn together with flat seams, 11-7/8 to 12-1/8 inches in circumference, weighing 6-1/4 to 7 ounces. The center of a softball is kapok, or a mixture of cork and rubber, wound with yarn.

solo home run: A home run with the bases empty, scoring only the batter.

soupbone: 1. A pitcher's arm. 2. A pitcher. The term dates back to the early 1900s, comparing the value of a pitcher or his arm to the team with the value of a soupbone to a soup.

soupboning: Pitching.

southpaw: A left-handed pitcher. From the early practice of orienting baseball parks with home plate towards the west, so that the batter would not have

to look into the afternoon sun (nor would the people in the expensive seats behind home plate). When a left-handed pitcher faces west (home plate), his pitching arm is to the south. The exact origin of the term is unknown, but *Chicago Inter-Ocean* sportswriter Charlie Seymour and humorist Finley Peter Dunne both used the term in baseball stories written in the 1880s.

spear: To make a lunging catch with the glove hand extended. (diving to his right to spear a line drive)

speed: 1. The baserunning ability or speed of a team. 2. The ability of a pitcher to throw a fastball. (his speed is a little off but the curveball is really breaking)

speed gun: A radarlike apparatus used to measure the velocity of pitches. A novelty at first, the speed gun is now often used by coaches to aid in evaluating new prospects or in judging any pitcher's speed and effectiveness on a given day.

1. spike: A metal projection on the sole of a baseball shoe to provide traction.

2. spike: To cut or scrape a player with the spikes of a baseball shoe.

spikes: Baseball shoes with spikes on the soles.

spitball: An illegal pitch in which saliva is surreptitiously applied to one part of the ball, so as to make it break or swerve unpredictably when thrown. It is possible that "Smiling Al" Orth, "The Curveless Wonder," threw the first real spitball in 1892, when pitches were delivered underhand from a distance of 50 feet. Pitcher Elmer Stricklett is generally given credit for reintroducing the overhand version of a spitball to the major leagues in 1904 when he came up to play for the Chicago White Sox. He had learned the pitch in the minors two years before from outfielder George Hildebrand (later an umpire) who had been working on a pitch he called a "wet ball." In his one season with Chicago, Stricklett taught the pitch to "Big Ed" Walsh. Walsh went on to become arguably the greatest spitballer in all of baseball, winning 194 games over a fourteen-year period with the lowest lifetime earned run average in the history of the game, 1.82. The term "spitball" has been in use since 1905. In 1920, the spitball was banned—except for seventeen pitchers (each team could select two) who were allowed to continue to use the pitch until they retired, the last of these being Hall of Famer Burleigh Grimes, who retired in 1934. Though the pitch was illegal, many players and managers accused such pitchers as Preacher Roe, Lew Burdette, Whitey Ford, and Don Drysdale of throwing the spitball regularly in the 1950s and 1960s (only Ford admits it). In 1968, regulations were tightened to prohibit any contact whatsoever between a pitcher's throwing hand and his mouth while he is on the mound. Through the seventies and going into the eighties, veterans Tommy John, Don Sutton, and Gaylord Perry have acquired the reputation of throwing the unpredictable pitch. Aware of the psychological advantage of his reputation, Perry (who became a 300-game winner in 1982) has even encouraged it by writing a book called *Me and the Spitter.* also *Cuban forkball, drooler, spitter.*

spitter: A spitball. The term "spitter" has been in use since 1908.

split a doubleheader: To win one game and lose one game of a doubleheader.

spot pitcher: A pitcher who has enough control to be able to pitch the ball to certain spots, areas in and around the strike zone where individual batters are known to have a problem hitting the ball.

spot reliever: A relief pitcher who is occasionally brought into games to pitch for a short period of time, such as to one or two batters, or to finish an inning.

spray hitter: An unpredictable batter who hits to all fields.

spring training: The time during which annual training and conditioning camps are held by major league teams, also used to play exhibition games and try out rookies. Spring training traditionally starts around the beginning of March and ends just before the start of the regular season.

square around: To move the batting stance from the normal position to one facing the pitcher with the feet side by side, as to bunt. (the runners go as the batter squares around to bunt)

1. squeeze: To make a squeeze play that enables a runner on third to come home. (will try to squeeze in the winning run)

2. squeeze: A squeeze play. (the infield is up, expecting the squeeze)

squeeze bunt: A bunt made in a squeeze play.

squeeze play: A prearranged play (with less than two out) in which a runner at third breaks for home on the pitch and the batter attempts to bunt the ball. The play is called a suicide squeeze if the runner does not wait to see if the batter makes contact with the ball but commits himself as the ball leaves the pitcher's hand, and a safety squeeze if the runner waits until the batter makes contact with the ball before running toward the plate at top speed. also *squeeze.*

stand-up double: A two-base hit in which the batter is able to reach second base without having to slide.

stand-up triple: A three-base hit in which the batter is able to reach third base without having to slide.

stanza: An inning. also *frame.*

Statue of Liberty: A derogatory name for a player who takes a called third strike, originally called a "statue stunt." also *wooden Indian.*

1. steal: 1. To suddenly run for the next base in an attempt to reach it safely before the opposing team can get the ball to a defensive player at the base in position to make a tag. (out stealing on a perfect throw from the catcher) 2. To break for and reach safely the next base, taking advantage of the opposing team's momentary inattention to the runner, rather than because of a teammate's hit or a defensive misplay. (stole home to tie the score) also *steal a base.*

2. steal: The action or an instance of stealing. (got to third on a steal)

steal a base: see *steal.*

steal a sign: To intercept and decipher a signal meant for the opposing team, such as the opposing catcher's sign to the pitcher calling for a certain pitch, or a coach's sign to a batter or base runner.

step off the rubber: To disengage the pivot foot from the pitcher's rubber. Before initiating the windup for a pitch, the pitcher must have the pivot foot in contact with the pitcher's rubber.

stick: A bat.

stickball: A crude form of baseball played by youths in confined areas such as city streets with a broomstick and a lightweight ball. Ground rules vary greatly with the condition of the playing area.

stolen base: A successful steal credited to a base runner in official records. Abbreviated sb. Lou Brock of the St. Louis Cardinals holds the lifetime major record for stolen bases with 938 in his nineteen-year career. Brock's single season record (118 in 1974) was broken by Oakland A's baserunning sensation Ricky Henderson, who stole 130 bases in 1982.

stopper: A team's best pitcher, one who can regularly "stop" the opponents. also *ace.*

strand: 1. To have or leave a base runner or base runners on base at the end of an inning. (goes down swinging, stranding the tying run at third) 2. To retire a batter for the third out in an inning, preventing a base runner or base runners from being able to advance or score. (struck him out on a fastball, stranding the tying run at third)

strawberry: An abrasion from sliding into a base. also *slider.*

stretch: An abbreviated windup. In the stretch, the pitcher lifts his hands to head level, then lowers them both in front of the body to a complete stop in the set position prior to throwing to a base, delivering the ball to the batter, or stepping off the rubber. Usually used when there are runners on base.

strike: A pitched ball at which the batter swings at and misses, does not swing at even though it passes through the strike zone, or hits foul for the first or second strike. When there are two strikes in the count, a ball hit foul and not caught is not charged as a strike, except in the case of an attempted bunt. A batter is out when three strikes are charged against him during one time at bat.

●●A perfectly thrown object. (threw a strike into the wastebasket) Also a flawless performance. (author was throwing strikes until the last chapter, which must be rewritten) A strike can figuratively be charged against one, as it is literally to a batter. (his appearance and manners are two strikes against him)

strike out: 1. To be out as a result of being charged with three strikes. (struck out looking) also *K.* 2. To put a batter out by throwing or causing three strikes. (struck him out to retire the side) also *fan, K, whiff.*

●●To fail. (struck out in her attempt to renegotiate the contract)

strikeout: The out made by a batter by getting three strikes. A pitcher's record is credited with the number of strikeouts he has made. In 1972, Nolan Ryan, then with the California Angels, set the all-time record for the most strikeouts in a single season, 383. In 1983, Nolan Ryan (Houston Astros) and Steve Carlton (Philadelphia Phillies) both surpassed Hall of Famer Walter Johnson's lifetime record of 3,508 strikeouts. also *K.*

strike zone: The area through which a ball must pass in order to be ruled a strike; that is, between the batter's armpits and the top of his knees when he is in his usual batting position, and over home plate.

stuff: The movement or liveliness of a pitch or pitches on the way to the batter. (has the best stuff since he pitched the no-hitter last season)

1. **submarine:** A pitching delivery in which the arm is brought forward in a low arc with the hand at or just below waist level.

2. **submarine:** To pitch the ball using a submarine delivery.

submariner: A pitcher who uses a submarine delivery.

suicide squeeze: see *squeeze play.*

suspended game: A called game that is to be completed at a later date.

1. **swat:** A long hit, especially an extra-base hit or home run. One of the nicknames given by the press to New York Yankees slugger Babe Ruth was "The Sultan of Swat."

2. **swat:** To hit a long ball, especially an extra-base hit or home run.

sweetheart: A great player whose quiet, consistent style of play, game after game, season after season, is the kind most respected by professional ballplayers, as compared to the more visible "heroics" of glory hogs and headline hunters. Lifetime home run king Hank Aaron was a classic example of a sweetheart player.

sweet spot: The optimum part of a bat with which to hit the ball.

1. **swing:** To move the bat through an arc in order to hit a pitched ball. (swung at the first pitch and hit a line drive to left field)

2. **swing:** The movement of a bat in an arc in an attempt to hit a pitched ball. (took

a swing at a fastball and missed for strike three)

●●To "take a swing at" is to make an attempt. (took a swing at playing quarterback in high school)

swing away: see *hit away*.

swing for the fences: To swing as hard as possible in order to hit the ball to or over the outfield wall or fence. also *swing from the heels*.

●●To make an all-out effort. (decided to swing for the fences rather than play it safe)

swing from the heels: To swing as hard as possible in an attempt to hit a pitched ball with full power. also *swing for the fences*.

●●To go all-out or to hold nothing back. (the debate ended with both candidates swinging from the heels)

swinging bunt: A ball that is swung at normally, but topped so that it dribbles slowly along the ground like a bunt.

switch-hit: To bat or be able to bat both left-handed and right-handed.

switch hitter: A batter who is able to bat left-handed and right-handed.

1. tag: 1. To put out a runner who is off base by touching the runner with the ball or with the hand or glove that is securely holding the ball. (tags the runner going by and throws to first for the double play) also *tag out*. 2. To, while holding the ball securely, touch a base a runner must attain because of a force, before the runner arrives. (tags second for the force) 3. To get a hit or a run, or hits or runs, off a pitcher. (was tagged for three runs in the second inning)

2. tag: 1. The act or an instance of tagging a runner out. (makes the tag on the runner at third and the inning is over) 2. The act or an instance of tagging a base for a force-out.

tag out: see *tag*.

tag up: To return to and touch, or stay in contact with a base until after a fly ball is caught, so as to be able to advance to the next base. (tagged up and beat the long throw home to score)

take: To let a pitch go by without swinging. (takes a strike to even the count at two and two) also *look at*.

take sign: A prearranged (and coded) signal from a coach, instructing the batter to take the next pitch.

take something off a pitch: To throw a

changeup after a fastball or fastballs. (took something off the pitch and caused the batter to be way out in front)

tape-measure shot: A particularly long home run. In 1953, New York Yankees slugger Mickey Mantle hit a booming home run off of Chuck Stobbs of the Washington Senators. Red Patterson, then public relations director for the Yankees immediately left the ballpark and found a witness who showed him the spot where the ball hit the ground. Patterson measured the total distance at 565 feet (among the longest in baseball history) and reported his findings to the press, and the expression tape-measure shot was born.

Tartan Turf: A brand of artificial turf used in some baseball stadiums.

tater: A home run. Originally derived from the use of the word "potato," then "tater" as synonyms for "ball" in the 1920s. A home run came to be known as a "long tater," shortened subsequently to "tater."

Texas leaguer: A short fly ball that falls between the infielders and outfielders. In 1890, a Toledo sportswriter described a hit that was the specialty of Toledo ballplayer Art Sunday, a veteran of the old Texas League, as a "Texas League hit." Shortened to "Texas leaguer," the expression soon became popular and is in use throughout baseball today. also *blooper*.

The Sporting News: A national sports weekly founded in 1886. Although now expanded in format to include seasonal coverage of football, basketball, hockey, and other sports, *The Sporting News* has throughout the years served as a chronicle of the sport of baseball with comprehensive statistical information and analysis.

the table is set: Bases loaded.

third: Third base.

third base: 1. The base located on the baseline on the left side of the field, which must be touched third by a base runner. (rounds third base, heading for home) 2. The position played by the third baseman. (to play third base) also *hot corner, third*.

third base coach: The coach or member of the team at bat who stands in the marked coach's box adjacent to third base to direct base runners, and, through prearranged signals, to relay special batting and baserunning instructions from the manager in the dugout.

third baseman: The defensive player who normally stands to the right side of third base who makes plays at third base and fields balls hit to the infield between shortstop and third base. also *third sacker*.

third sacker: Third baseman.

three-bagger: A triple. also *three-base hit*.

three-base hit: see *three-bagger*.

three up, three down: An inning in which three batters come to bat and are retired in succession.

through the wickets: A batted ball that goes through the pitcher's legs, as a croquet ball is knocked through wire wickets.

throw ground balls: To be known for throwing the kind of pitch (a low ball, especially a sinker) that usually results in ground balls when it can be hit.

throw out: To cause a batter or base runner to be put out with a good throw of a fielded or pitched (in the case of a catcher) ball or a ball relayed from another defensive player.

tools of ignorance: The equipment of a catcher: catcher's mask, chest protector, shin guards, and catcher's mitt. Unlike modern-day catchers, who must constantly make strategic decisions and who, in subtle ways, affect many aspects of a game, catchers in the late 1800s and early 1900s were known mostly for their brawn, not their brains. The man who first called the equipment of a catcher "the tools of ignorance" was an obvious exception. Muddy Ruel, who caught 1,422 games in a nineteen-year career, and played in the World Series for Washington in 1924 and 1925, was a practicing attorney between baseball seasons.

top of the inning: The first half of an inning, when the visiting team has the opportunity to bat.

top of the order: The first batter or batters in the batting order. (will come in to face the top of the order)

total bases: The total number of bases (single equals one base, double equals two bases, triple equals three bases, home run equals four bases) reached on hits by and credited in official records to batters and teams. In 1921, Babe Ruth set the all-time single season record for total bases, 457. Hank Aaron holds the lifetime record for total bases, 6,856.

1. trap: To seemingly catch a fly or line drive, but in reality stopping it or picking it up just as or moments after it first touches the ground. A ball that is trapped is often difficult to distinguish from one caught on the fly.

2. trap: The action or an instance of trapping a ball.

1. triple: A hit that allows the batter to reach third base safely. also *three-bagger, three base hit*.

2. triple: 1. To hit a triple. (tripled off the wall in center field) 2. To advance a base runner by hitting a triple. (tripled in the tying run)

Triple Crown: The distinction of leading a league at the end of a season in the three major batting categories in official records: batting average, home runs, and runs batted in. The first Triple Crown winner in major league history was Providence Gray center fielder Paul Hines, who in 1878 led the National League with a batting average of .358, four home runs, and fifty runs batted in.

triple play: A play in which three players are put out.

turn a double play: To execute a double play. (able to turn a double play and end the inning)

turn around a fastball: To hit a fastball, thereby changing its direction, or "turning it around."

turned away: Out, retired without scoring. (home team was turned away in the ninth, losing 3-0)

turn the ball over: To throw a screwball. Because a screwball comes out from the back of the hand, the pitcher must turn the hand (and the ball) over just before the release.

tweener: A base hit through a narrow gap between infielders. also *seeing-eye*.

twin bill: A doubleheader.

twi-night doubleheader: A doubleheader with the first game scheduled in late afternoon, followed by an evening game. also *twi-nighter*.

twi-nighter: A twi-night doubleheader.

twin killing: A double play.

twirl: To pitch in a baseball game. (twirled the first game of the doubleheader)

twirly-thumb: see *cockeye*.

two-bagger: A double.

two o'clock hitter: A player who hits

impressively in batting practice, but not in a game. When the term was originated, day games began at 3:00 p.m. with batting practice at 2:00 p.m. Now that games (and batting practice) start earlier, the expression "one o'clock hitter" has also come into use.

ump: An umpire.

1. umpire: The official or one of the officials responsible for the conduct of a game and for interpreting and enforcing the rules. Umpires make decisions regarding proper playing conditions, when to begin, end, suspend, or forfeit a game, when the ball is in play, when time is to be called, whether a pitch is a ball or a strike, whether a ball is hit fair or foul, whether a base runner is out or safe at a base, and whether a player or coach has committed an infraction of the rules. If there is only one umpire, he or she will usually take a position behind the plate (or sometimes behind the pitcher with runners on base). If there are two or more umpires, one, the plate umpire, is designated umpire-in-chief and the others field umpires. In major league baseball, four umpires are usually used: the umpire-in-chief behind the plate, who presides, calling balls and strikes and ruling on plays at home plate, and field umpires at each base, who assist the plate umpire, calling plays at their respective bases. During the World Series, two additional field umpires are positioned in the outfield on the foul lines to help rule on foul balls. Originally from the sport of cricket, then later, rounders. also *arbiter, ump.* see *field umpire, umpire-in-chief.*

2. umpire: To be or act as umpire in a game.

umpire-in-chief: The presiding umpire, positioned behind the plate when there are two or more umpires. The umpire-in-chief is in full charge of and responsible for the proper conduct of the game and has authority to call and count balls and strikes, call and declare fair balls and fouls (except those commonly called by field umpires because of better position), to make decisions about the procedures and play of the batter, the pitcher, the catcher, infielders, and base runners (except those commonly made by field umpires because of better position), to make decisions about

plays around home plate or in the infield (except those commonly made by field umpires because of better position), to call field umpires into consultation (when different decisions are made on a play by two umpires) and determine which decision shall prevail, to announce special time limits or ground rules, to inform the official scorer of the batting order and any changes in the lineups and batting order, to (concurrent with the jurisdiction of field umpires) call time out, to enforce the rules of baseball, to eject a player or coach from a game if necessary, and to start, suspend, or forfeit a game. also *plate umpire.*

unearned run: Any run scored because of an error or interference by the catcher, or following an error on an earlier play that would have ended the inning. An unearned run is not charged against a pitcher in computing his ERA. compare *earned run.*

up: At bat, or due to bat. (will pinch hit for the pitcher, who is due up next)

●●**Ready,** or next to take a turn. (the quartet is up after this number)

voodoo ball: A baseball sewn together in Haiti, but with parts made in the United States.

vultch: A save by a relief pitcher. From the word "vulture." In the 1960s, pitchers likened relievers, who came into well pitched games in the late innings and got credit for saves and sometimes wins, to vultures, figuratively picking over the bones of starting pitchers. Los Angeles Dodgers reliever Phil "The Vulture" Regan was so-named in 1966 by Dodgers pitcher Claude Osteen.

1. walk: A base on balls. (gave up a walk, and then struck out the next three men in order) also *Annie Oakley, free pass, free ticket, free trip, pass.*

2. walk: 1. To be awarded first base on four balls. (walked his first time at bat) 2. To pitch four balls to a batter during one turn at bat, allowing him a free passage to first base. (walked the first two men he faced) 3. To allow a run by giving up a base on balls with loaded bases. (walked in the tying run)

Wally Pipp: An instance of taking a day off from one's regular starting position in the lineup. Wally Pipp, who had played first base for the New York Yankees for ten years, elected not to play on June 1, 1925. He had been beaned in a previous game and was still suffering from a headache. Pipp never regained his job, for the twenty-one-year-old player who replaced him on that day was the legendary Lou Gehrig, who would go on to play first base for the Yankees for the next fourteen years and a record 2,130 consecutive games. Because of Pipp's experience, regular players who want a day off (and risk a similar fate) are said to be doing a Wally Pipp.

wand: A bat.

warning path, warning track: The area bordering the outer edge of the outfield, consisting of a dirt or cinder track in many ballparks. So called because it warns a fielder that he is nearing the wall as he backs up to make a catch.

wave on: To signal a base runner to continue on to the next base without stopping.

web, webbing: The leather panel or lacing in the crotch between the thumb and finger sections of a glove or mitt.

wheelhouse: The part of the strike zone (approximately chest high) in which the ball can most easily be hit with full power.

1. whiff: 1. To strike out. (whiffed his first time at bat) also *K.* 2. To strike out a batter. (whiffed the last two batters to end the inning) also *fan, K.*

2. whiff: A strikeout.

whip: A lightweight bat.

1. whitewash: To hold an opposing team scoreless. The term has been used since the mid-1800s. also *shut out.*

2. whitewash: A shutout.

••A contest or situation in which an opponent is held literally or figuratively scoreless.

wide: 1. Outside, or out of the strike zone on the side of the plate opposite the batter. (the pitch is wide for ball three) 2. To either side of a base, or a defensive player waiting for a throw. (throw is wide, and the runners keep going)

wild: 1. Lacking control. (a little wild in the first inning, but throwing nothing but strikes now) 2. Away from, and beyond the grasp of the intended receiver. (the pitch is wild, and the runner at third will score) (the throw is wild, and the runner is safe)

wild pitch: A pitched ball not touched by

the batter that is so high, so wide, or so low that it is unable to be stopped and controlled by the catcher (and could not be expected to be stopped and controlled by ordinary effort in the judgment of the official scorer) and enables a runner or runners to advance. compare *passed ball.*

wild-pitch: 1. To pitch a wild ball. (threw two strikes and then wild-pitched) 2. To throw a wild pitch which results in a run scored. (wild-pitched in the tying run)

willow: A bat.

wind up: To go into a windup before delivering a pitch to a batter.

windup: The motion of a pitcher prior to delivering a pitch in which, with the pivot foot on the rubber, the pitcher swings both arms back over the head, turns the body away and then back as he steps toward the plate and brings the ball forward to release it. Once initiated, the windup must be completed and the ball delivered to the plate or a balk is called. When there are runners on base, an abbreviated windup, the stretch, is used in order to give the runner less time to steal a base.

windmill, windmill pitch: An underhand delivery of a pitch in softball in which the pitching arm makes a 360 degree vertical revolution before the ball is delivered to the plate.

wing: To throw with strength and accuracy. (one of the best arms in the league who can really wing it)

winning pitcher: The pitcher on the winning team who is given credit in official records for a victory. To be credited with a win, a starting pitcher must have pitched five complete innings (four in a five-inning game) and be leading when the game ends or when replaced. If a starting pitcher has completed less than the required innings and is leading when replaced, the relief pitcher who maintains the lead until the game ends (or, if there is more than one, the relief pitcher judged by the official scorer to be the most effective) is credited with the win. If, while a relief pitcher is pitching, his team assumes a lead that he maintains until the game ends, the relief pitcher is credited with the win. compare *losing pitcher.*

winter ball: Organized baseball played by major league and minor league players during the off season, often in instructional leagues or in organized leagues in foreign countries.

winter league: see *hot stove league*.

wolves: Abusive baseball fans who persistently harass and heckle players.

wooden Indian: A derogatory name for a player who takes a called third strike. The term originated in the 1900s when cigar-store Indians were common. also *Statue of Liberty*.

wood man: 1. A good hitter. 2. A poor fielder who plays only because of hitting ability.

World Series: A championship series played at the end of the season between the National League and American League pennant winners. In 1903, in order to prevent further destructive player raids and territorial competition, the National League was forced to recognize and grant equal status to the fledgling American League and agreed to the first "World's Championship Games" or "World's Championship Series," a best-of-nine series to be played in the fall. Much to the embarrassment and anger of the National League, the American League representative, the Boston Pilgrims behind the pitching of Cy Young and "Big Bill" Dinneen, won that first series five games to three over the Pittsburgh Pirates. The following year, the New York Giants refused to play the American League repeat pennant winner, Boston, but from 1905 on, pennant winners from both leagues have met annually. The World Series is now a best-of-seven series. also *fall classic*.

●●The championship or highest level, literally or figuratively.

worm burner: A hit ball that skims along the ground.

wrong-field hit: see *off-field hit*.

yan, yannigan: A rookie. It is reported that Jerry Denny, third baseman for the National League Providence Grays in the early 1880s, was the first to reserve the names "yan" and "yannigan" for rookies. Derived from the "yannigan bag," a kind of carpetbag used by prospectors and traveling performers, the term originally applied to all ballplayers, because of their similar lifestyle and low social status. see *rookie*.

Basketball is unique among major sports. It did not evolve from other games over a period of years, but rather was invented by one man to fill a particular need.

In the fall of 1890, faced with the annual drop in membership during the winter, leaders at the International YMCA Training School in Springfield, Massachusetts (now Springfield College), concluded that there should be a game that could be played indoors in the winter months. Dr. James Naismith, a Presbyterian minister at the institution's School for Christian Workers was given the assignment to create such a game.

Naismith observed that all team games used some kind of ball, but concluded that a method would have to be found to take the speed and physical contact out of the new game if it was to be popular and able to be played in a confined area. Noting that much of the roughness of football came from the physical contact between the ballcarrier and tacklers, Naismith decided that one fundamental principle in his game would be that the offense should not be able to run while holding the ball, thereby eliminating the need for tackling. Next he had to devise a goal for the ball to pass through in a manner so that the player did not benefit from speed or power. A horizontal goal placed above the reach of the players was the answer. It made it necessary to curve or lob the ball rather than drive it, and its height and configuration made it difficult for players to block off the goal or interfere with the ball once it was shot. It was forbidden to play the ball with anything but the hands and all rough physical contact was specifically banned. To start play, the ball was to be thrown up between two players in the middle of the court.

Naismith drew up a set of thirteen rules and in December of 1891, the first game was played between teams of nine players inside the gymnasium at the Springfield YMCA Training School, using a soccer ball as the ball and peach baskets attached to the gymnasium balconies as goals—the source of the name "basket ball," changed to one word after 1921.

The game was an immediate success, and in little time was being played in school gymnasiums all around Springfield, though the exact rules often varied from the first printed rules that appeared in the "Triangle," a paper at the School for Christian Workers, on January 15, 1892. Within a year, baskets with iron rims and braided cord netting were introduced, eliminating the need to retrieve the ball after each field goal (by a person on a ladder in the first games, and then by pulling on a chain when the peach basket was replaced shortly thereafter by cylindrical baskets of heavy woven wire).

Another major rule change was introduced in 1893. Overenthusiastic fans in the balcony seats in gymnasiums had begun to interfere with shots at the baskets, using their hands, umbrellas, and sticks to "help" their team's shots into the goal and block the other team's. To counter this, it was required that 12-foot by 6-foot barriers be erected behind the basket, wire mesh at first, and later, wood. These early backboards suddenly made it possible to bank shots in and rebound. Real basketballs replaced soccer balls the following year, and free throws were introduced (until 1924, any teammate, not just the fouled player, could shoot them).

The first intercollegiate game was played in 1895 between Hamline of St. Paul, Minnesota and the Minnesota State School of Agriculture. In 1896, the University of Chicago defeated the University of Iowa in Iowa City in the first college game with five players on a side (accepted by most within a year).

In 1898, a professional league was formed, the National Basketball League, comprised of six teams: Trenton, New Jersey; Camden; Millville, Pennsylvania; Bicycle Club; Hancock Athletic Club; and Germantown Club. The professionals played a version of basketball known as the "cage game." In it, a heavy wire mesh fence, 11 feet high, enclosed the entire court, both to keep the ball in play and to prevent spectator interference. The result was a fast, relentless, and sometimes rough style of play. Players of this kind of basketball came to be known as "cagers," a name that remains popular even today, though the wire fences were eliminated from basketball by regulation in 1929. The National Basketball League lasted only two seasons, and other attempts to operate a professional league in the next few years were even less successful.

The first college conferences were formed in 1901 and 1902; the Triangular League (Yale, Trinity, and Wesleyan), the New England League (Amherst, Williams, Dartmouth, Trinity, and Holy Cross), and the Ivy League. A "national" college tournament was held as an exhibition at the 1904 Olympic Games in St. Louis, and won by Hiram College, but true national intercollegiate competition was not to come until regional variations in game rules and interpretation were reconciled. In 1908, the Intercollegiate Athletic Association (two years later renamed the National Collegiate Athletic Association, or NCAA) took charge of college rules. Still, there remained numerous variations around the country until the rules were finally standardized in 1934. The same year, in the first of what was to become a great attraction in New York, NYU defeated Notre Dame 25-18 in front of 16,188 spectators in a Madison Square Garden collegiate doubleheader suggested by sportswriter Ned Irish.

Basketball had gone out of the country as early as 1892, when it was introduced in Mexico, but the first international basketball tournament was the Inter-Allied Games in Paris in 1919, won by the United States team comprised of players from the U.S. Armed Forces. The final game (U.S.A. 93-France 8) was witnessed by Dr. James Naismith and General John Pershing, who presented the championship trophy to Basketball Hall of Famer Max "Marty" Friedman.

In 1931, a three-night tournament in Peking (then Peiping) drew 70,000 spectators. The following year in Geneva, Switzerland, the Federation of International Basketball Amateur (FIBA) was formed as the governing body of international amateur basketball. The sport became an Olympic event in 1936 at the Berlin Olympics, where the United States defeated Canada 19-8 in the final, which was played outdoors on an earthen "floor" in a driving rain. It was estimated that before the outbreak of World War II, between 18 and 20 million people were playing basketball in seventy-five countries.

In 1937, a rule change eliminating the center jump after each field goal revolutionized the game. The center and guards, formerly involved in the tipoff and defensive play only, now became part of the offense. This innovation, together with the introduction of the quick one-handed shot soon after by three-time Stanford All-American Hank Luisetti forever changed basketball from a low-scoring defensive struggle to the exciting modern game.

In 1939, the NCAA held the first National Collegiate Basketball Championship Tournament, won by Oregon, with Ohio State the runner-up. The following year, basketball made its first appearance on television, a doubleheader from Madison Square Garden in which Pittsburgh defeated Fordham, 57-37, and NYU defeated Georgetown, 50-27. The popularity of college basketball continued to grow until the sport was rocked by a major scandal in 1951, when it was discovered that some college players had taken bribes from professional gamblers to "shave" points in league and tournament games. Thirty-one arrests were made in 1951, and in the New York Grand Jury's 1953 report, it was revealed that forty-nine games had been fixed in twenty-three cities in seventeen states.

From the mid-fifties on, the college game was again on the rise with such outstanding players as Frank Selvy, who in 1954, scored a major college record: 100 points in a game for Furman against Newberry; Tom Gola of LaSalle; Bill Russell of the University of San Francisco; and Cincinnati's Oscar Robertson.

Professional basketball, after some lean early years, was also healthy, with the National Basketball Association beginning to stabilize. Formed in 1946 under the name of the Basketball Association of America, the NBA adopted its present name in 1949, after absorbing its older rival, the National Basketball League. Weighted down at first by several weak franchises, the league and individual teams struggled to find an audience, often scheduling exhibition and preliminary games with the Harlem Globetrotters to bring new people into the arenas. The Globetrotters, an all-black touring team founded in 1927 by Abe Saperstein, had become a great box office draw with a unique blend of dazzling skills and comedic showmanship. In 1951, a record crowd of 75,000 people saw the Globetrotters play in Berlin's Olympic Stadium.

In 1954, the NBA adopted a rule requiring the offensive team to shoot at the basket within twenty-four seconds of gaining possession of the ball. The change was an immediate success, speeding up the game and placing more emphasis on scoring than the slow-tempo ball control style of play that had evolved, as well as eliminating dull "slowdown" tactics used to freeze the ball and protect a lead.

Beginning with the 1956-57 season, one team, the Boston Celtics, led by the sharpshooting and playmaking of Bob Cousy and the intimidating defense of Bill Russell, dominated basketball as no professional team has dominated a sport in modern history. In ten years, the Celtics won the NBA championship nine out of ten times, losing only in the 1957-58 season to the St. Louis Hawks.

No less impressive, however, was UCLA's record in college play from the mid-sixties through the mid-seventies. From 1964 to 1975, UCLA was NCAA champion nine out of eleven times, losing only to Texas-El Paso in 1966 and to North Carolina State in 1975. Unbeaten for an entire season four times, UCLA also set the NCAA record for the most consecutive victories, eighty-eight, from January 30, 1971, through January 17, 1974 (both the last loss before the streak and the streak-ending loss came at Notre Dame).

Another long winning streak came to an end at the 1972 Munich Olympics. Undefeated in sixty-three games dating back to 1936 (the first year basketball was an Olympic event), the United States stumbled in a controversial loss to the USSR. A dispute between officials and an improperly set game clock caused the final three seconds to be replayed twice. The Russians scored during the second replay, winning the game 51-50.

Although tested by the rival American Basketball Association from 1967 through 1976, the NBA has remained the premiere basketball league in the world since the Boston Celtics "dynasty" of the 1950s and 1960s, showcasing the greatest players in the game, such as all-time scoring leader Wilt Chamberlain, Elgin Baylor, John Havlicek, Oscar Robertson, Jerry West, Kareem Abdul-Jabbar, Bill Walton, Moses Malone, Julius Erving, Larry Bird, and Earvin "Magic" Johnson.

ABAUSA: The Amateur Basketball Association of the United States of America.

air ball: A missed shot that touches neither the rim, backboard, nor the net. The expression was coined by Los Angeles Lakers broadcaster Chick Hearn in the early 1970s. compare *glass ball.*

air dribble: An archaic technique, once allowed in conjunction with a bouncing dribble, in which a player could throw the ball in the air, run, and handle it again before it hit the floor or was touched by any other player. In modern basketball, an air dribble would be considered a traveling violation, resulting in the loss of the ball and a throw-in by the opposing team from the sideline.

alley-oop shot: 1. A shot in which the ball travels in a high arc. The expression was coined in the late 1960s by Los Angeles Lakers broadcaster Chick Hearn to describe a shot used by Lakers guard John Egan when he had to shoot over taller players. 2. A leaping tip-in of a high lobbed pass near the basket.

Amateur Basketball Association of the United States of America: The governing body of amateur basketball in the United States, responsible for the preparation and supervision of national teams to participate in international and Olympic competition. Founded in 1975, the Amateur Basketball Association of the United States is an affiliate member of the Federation of International Basketball Amateur, and is headquartered in Colorado Springs, Colorado. also *ABAUSA.*

around the world: An informal game for two or more players in which contestants take turns shooting, and try to move through seven stations placed outside of and around the free throw area (three on each side, and one at the top of the key), advancing to the next station only when a shot has been successfully made. The first player to move around all seven stations (after all have had the same number of turns) wins the game. Sometimes a variation is played in which a player who misses a shot moves back one station. Around the world is a game that emphasizes pure shooting skill, rather than the trick shots that often characterize the game of H.O.R.S.E. compare *H.O.R.S.E.*

assist: A pass that leads directly to a score, such as one to a teammate who shoots immediately and scores, or drives to the basket and scores. No assist is given if the receiver stops, holds the ball, or dribbles back and forth for position before shooting. The all-time NBA record for the most assists in a single game is held by Kevin Porter, who, while playing for the New Jersey Nets, was credited with twenty-nine assists in a game against the Houston Rockets on February 24, 1978. Porter also holds the NBA single season record of 1,099 assists, set in the 1978-79 season when he played for the Detroit Pistons. Oscar Robertson, credited with 9,887 assists in his career, holds the NBA lifetime record.

back: To guard an opponent by playing behind him (between the guarded player and the basket). compare *front*.

backboard: Either of two opaque or transparent flat 4-foot by 6-foot-wide rectangular (or 35-inch by 54-inch-wide, with a 29-inch radius, fan-shaped) surfaces, suspended above and perpendicular to the floor, 4 feet inside and parallel to the boundary line at each end of the court, to which the basket rings are fastened. NBA regulations call for a transparent rectangular backboard. A small rectangle (18 inches by 24 inches wide) centered behind the ring, is marked on the surface by a 2-inch-wide white line. Players bank shots off the backboards, which also serve to keep the ball in play if a shot is missed. The first backboards were 6 feet by 12 feet wide, and made of wire mesh (then later, wood). They were put behind the baskets in 1893 as a barrier to keep overenthusiastic fans from interfering with shots at the basket from the balcony seats behind each goal. Rectangular backboards were reduced to the present dimensions in 1895, and fan-shaped backboards were approved in 1940. also *board, boards, glass*.

backcourt: 1. The half of a court a team defends, and which contains the basket at which the opposing team shoots. (across the center line from the backcourt) 2. The guards. (their backcourt can really move the ball around)

backcourtman: A guard.

backcourt violation: 1. A violation of the ten-second rule (in continuous control of a ball in the backcourt for more then ten consecutive seconds), which results in the loss of the ball to the opposing team for a throw-in from out of bounds near where play stopped. see *ten-second rule*. 2. A violation resulting from the return of the ball to the backcourt from the frontcourt by dribbling, passing, or tapping the ball across the division line. This results in the loss of the ball to the opposing team for a throw-in from the sideline at the center of the court. also *over and back*.

backdoor: Next to the end line, under the basket. (came through the backdoor and scored on a reverse lay-up)

backdoor play: A play in which an offensive player momentarily slips in behind the defense along the end line to receive a pass under the basket for a lay-up.

ball control: 1. The ability to dribble, pass, and maintain possession of the ball. (not much of a shooter, but an expert at ball control) 2. A strategy used in amateur, college, and high school basketball, in which a team attempts to maintain possession of the ball. Ball control is used offensively to encourage the opposing team to make defensive mistakes, or vary from a game plan or customary style of play, or as a ploy to maneuver players into certain positions for a set play, or defensively to deny the opposing team a chance to score (as in the case of a stall or freeze), or simply to protect a lead near the end of a game. also *stall ball*.

ball fake: A fake pass or shot by the player with the ball in order to momentarily deceive a defender.

ball handler: 1. The player in possession of the ball. 2. A player with good ball control, adept at dribbling and passing.

BACKBOARD AND BASKET

bang the boards, bang the glass: To rebound aggressively under the backboards. (got the opportunity for the second shot because he bangs the boards) also *crash the boards, hammer the boards, pound the boards, pound the glass.*

bank: To bounce the ball off the backboard toward the basket. To make a bank shot. (banks one in from the side of the key)

bank shot: A shot in which the ball is made to bounce off the backboard towards the basket.

baseball pass: A one-arm overhand pass (often long) in which the ball is thrown like a baseball.

baseline: 1. The boundary line at each end of the court, 50 feet long and marked with a 2-inch-wide line. also *end line.* 2. The area of the court just inside the end line. (a 15-foot jump shot from the baseline)

basket: 1. Either of the goals at the ends of a court, consisting of a metal ring, 18 inches in inside diameter, with a 15 to 18-inch-long sleeve, made of white cord net, suspended below. The basket ring is attached to the backboard with its upper edge 10 feet above and parallel to the floor, and equidistant from the vertical edges of the board. For regulation play, the basket ring is painted orange, and mounted so that the nearest point of the inside edge of the ring is 6 inches from the front surface of the backboard. The term "basket" originated from the use of a peach basket as a goal when the game was invented in 1891 (the ball had to be retrieved with the aid of a ladder after each goal). Within a year, the peach basket was replaced by a cylindrical basket made of heavy woven wire, with a pull chain attached to drop the ball. Baskets with iron rims and braided cord netting were introduced in 1893. also *bucket, hoop.* 2. A field goal. also *bucket, deuce.*

basketball: 1. A game played between two teams of five players on a 94-foot-long by 50-foot-wide court (84 feet by 50 feet for high school play), with a horizontal 18-inch metal ring mounted 10 feet above the floor on a vertical backboard suspended over each end of the court. Points are scored by tossing an inflated ball (leather or rubber, 9-1/2 inches in diameter) through the metal ring, or basket, defended by the opposing team. A player with the ball may shoot or pass to a teammate at any time, but may not walk or run without dribbling the ball (bouncing the ball off the floor with successive taps of the hand). A player who stops dribbling may not start again, but must pass or shoot. If a player takes steps without dribbling the ball, or resumes a dribble after stopping, possession of the ball is awarded to the opposing team, to be thrown in from the sideline. In an attempt to prevent an opponent from advancing the ball or scoring, a player may bat away, intercept, or block a ball being dribbled, passed, or shot by the opposing team, but may not hit, push, hold, or trip an opponent. These actions are considered fouls, and result in the loss of possession of the ball to the opponent (to be thrown in from the sideline), or in the fouled player being awarded one or mcre free throws (an undefended shot at the basket from a line drawn 15 feet away). If, during the course of a game, a player is charged with a specified number of fouls (five fouls in high school, collegiate, women's, and international amateur basketball, six fouls in the NBA), the player is put out of the game. A player charged with a dangerous or violent foul is immediately ejected from the game. A team is made up of a center (usually the tallest on the team), who often takes a position in the middle of the frontcourt near the basket to receive and relay passes, shoot, and rebound; two guards, good ball handlers who usually bring the ball out of the backcourt, start plays, and distribute the ball to teammates closer to the basket; and two forwards, usually positioned to the side of the basket near the baseline, from where they may shoot or break in toward the basket to shoot or rebound. A referee is in charge of the game, assisted by another (or by two others in some college conferences). Both have the authority to call fouls and violations. In the NBA, a game consists of four twelve-minute quarters. College and international amateur games are divided into two twenty-minute halves. High school games consist of four eight-minute quarters. A game (and each period in international amateur and high school games) is started by a jump ball (the ball is thrown up between two opponents to be tapped to a teammate) in the center of the court, and play continues to the end of the period, except for fouls, violations, or time outs. When a team scores, the ball is given to the opposing team for a throw-in from outside the end lines under the basket. If a ball goes out of bounds, the ball is given to the team opposing the player who last touched it, for a throw-in from the sideline. Each field goal is two points. In the NBA, a field goal made from outside an area marked by parallel lines 3 feet inside the sidelines, extending from the baseline to intersect with a line drawn in an arc of 23 feet, 9 inches from the middle of the basket, is three points (a provision that was adopted experimentally by some college conferences in the early 1980s and may ultimately be universally adopted). A free throw is one point. If, at the end of regulation play, the score is tied, overtime periods (five minutes in NBA, international amateur, and college games; three minutes in high school games) are played until one team is leading at the end of a period. Basketball (written "basket ball" before 1921) was also known as "roundball." 2. The ball used in a basketball game: an inflated bladder with a leather, rubber, or synthetic covering, 9-1/2 inches in diameter, weighing 20 to 22 ounces. The first specially designed basketball was introduced in 1894 to replace the soccer balls originally used.

Basketball Hall of Fame: The Naismith Memorial Basketball Hall of Fame. The institute that honors the achievements of the outstanding figures of basketball, located on the campus of Springfield College in Springfield, Massachusetts, where Dr. Naismith invented the game of basketball. The first members of the Hall of Fame were elected in 1959, fifteen individuals and two teams: Dr. Naismith's original team and the original Celtics, a pioneer barnstorming professional team of the 1920s. The permanent headquarters and museum opened in 1968. Nominations for the Hall of Fame are voted on annually by an anonymous Honors Committee. also *Hall of Fame.*

basket-hanger: A player who leaves the backcourt early or remains in the frontcourt near the basket when play is at the other end of the court, waiting for a long pass in order to take an undefended shot at the basket. also *cherry picker, hanger.*

basket interference: see *goaltending.*

big man: The center on a basketball team, usually the tallest player.

blind screen: A screen that is established out of the line of sight of an opponent (as to the side of or behind).

1. block: 1. To legally obstruct or deflect an opponent's shot with the hands. Elmore "The Rejector" Smith of the Los Angeles Lakers holds the NBA record for the most blocked shots in one season (393, 1973-74). Smith also holds the single game record (17, vs. Portland, October 28, 1973). also *reject.* 2. To legally obstruct or deflect an opponent's pass with the hands. 3. To cause physical contact by stepping into the path of an opponent. A personal foul. see *blocking.* compare *charge.*

2. block: 1. The act or an instance of blocking an opponent's shot or pass with the hands. 2. The act or an instance of physical contact as a result of stepping into the path of an opponent. A personal foul. see *blocking.* compare *charge.*

blocking: A personal foul in which physical contact occurs as a result of illegally impeding the progress of an opponent, such as by stepping or extending an arm, shoulder, hip, or leg into the path of a moving opponent. see *personal foul.* compare *charging.*

block out: see *box out.*

board: 1. Backboard. (banks a shot off the board) 2. A rebound. (he's got eleven boards in the game so far)

boards: Backboard.

bomb: A long distance low percentage shot.

bonus, bonus free throw: An additional free throw awarded to a fouled player when the opposing team has reached a specified number of team fouls during a period of play (five fouls in one quarter in NBA games, seven fouls in one half in college and women's games, nine fouls, including technical fouls, during a half in international amateur games, and five fouls during a half in high school games). In college and high school games, the bonus applies only to one-shot fouls and is not given if the first free throw is missed (called a one-and-one situation). In the NBA, a bonus free throw is called a penalty free throw.

bonus situation: A situation in which a team has reached a specified number of team fouls for a period of play (five fouls in one quarter in NBA games, seven fouls in one half in college and women's games, nine fouls, including technical fouls, in international amateur games, and five fouls during a half in high school games), and each foul thereafter yields a bonus free throw to the opposing team. In the NBA, a bonus situation is called a penalty situation or penalty stage.

bounce pass: A pass in which the ball is bounced off the floor between the passer and the receiver. A bounce pass is easy to handle at full speed and difficult to intercept.

box, box-and-one: A defensive strategy which employs a four-man zone, with players deployed in a "box" around the free throw lane (two on each side) leaving one defender to play man-to-man against the most dangerous scorer on the opposing team. compare *diamond-and-one*.

box out: To take a position between an opponent and the basket, to prevent the opponent from having access to a rebound or tip-in. also *block out, screen out*.

brush-off: To maneuver so that a defending opponent is blocked by the screen or pick of a teammate and left behind.

bucket: 1. A field goal. also *basket, deuce*. 2. The basket ring and net. also *basket, hoop*.

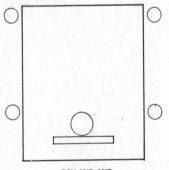

BOX-AND-ONE

buzzer shot: A shot made just as a period is ending, with the ball in the air at the buzzer.

cager: A basketball player. In the 1890s, one version of basketball, the "cage game," used a heavy wire-mesh fence, 11 feet high, to enclose the entire court, both to keep the ball in play and to prevent spectator interference. Players of this fast and sometimes rough kind of basketball came to be known as cagers, a name that remains popular today, though wire fences were eliminated by regulation in 1929.

carry: see *palm the ball*.

center: 1. The player on a team (usually the tallest) responsible for the tipoff or center jump, for defending against the opposing center, and for playing the "pivot" in the middle of the frontcourt near the basket, from where he can set screens, receive and relay passes, shoot, and position himself for rebounds. Called "center" because, prior to the 1937 rule change, the jump ball after each field goal in the center circle was the main responsibility of the center. also *frontcourtman*. 2. The position played by a center.

center circle: 1. The 12-foot restraining circle for jump balls in the center of the court, divided by the center or division line, with (except in international amateur play) a 4-foot jumping circle marked in the middle. also *circle, restraining circle*. see *jump ball*.

center line: see *division line*.

1. charge: To run into a defensive player who has established position. A personal foul. see *charging*. compare *block*.

2. charge: The act or an instance of running into a defensive player who has established position. A personal foul. see *charging*. compare *block*.

charging: A personal foul in which an offensive player runs into a defensive player who has established position. also *charge*. see *personal foul*. compare *blocking*.

charity line: The free throw line. also *charity stripe, foul line, line*.

charity shot: A free throw.

charity stripe: The free throw line. also *charity line, foul line, line*.

check: 1. see *hand check*. 2. To guard an opponent.

cherry-pick: To leave the backcourt early, or to remain in the frontcourt near the basket when play is at the other end of the court, waiting for a long pass in order to take an undefended shot at the basket.

cherry picker: One who cherry-picks. also *basket-hanger, hanger.*

chest pass: A two-handed pass in which the ball is pushed away from the body by a quick extension of the arms and released with a snap of the wrists.

chippie: see *cripple.*

chucker: see *gunner.*

circle: see *center circle.*

clutch shooter: A player who can be counted upon to make a basket or baskets in crucial, game-deciding situations. Los Angeles Lakers guard Jerry West, "Mr. Clutch," who played from 1960 to 1974, is thought to have been one of the all-time great clutch shooters in the NBA.

coast to coast: From one end of the court to the other, as in a court-length pass.

cold: Temporarily unable to score. (gone cold in the second quarter)

collapse: To, with two or more defenders, converge on the opposing center the moment the ball comes into him at the pivot, in order to pressure him and deny the easy pass or shot.

common foul: A personal foul that is neither flagrant nor intentional, nor a part of a double or multiple foul (and, in the NBA only, that is not committed against a player in the act of shooting). When a player commits a common foul, the result is a loss of the ball to the opposing team for a throw-in from out of bounds, except in the case of a bonus situation, when the fouled player is awarded a bonus free throw.

continuation: A shot, or the follow through or consequences of a shot attempt committed to by the fouled player at the moment of, or just prior to, the foul. Though the actual shot may not be made until after the foul, in the NBA, if the shot goes in, the field goal counts in addition to the free throw awarded for the foul.

conversion: A successful free throw. (if he makes the conversion, it's a three-point play)

convert: To make a successful free throw.

cord: The net. (his shot hit nothing but the cord)

corner: Any of the four areas of the court where the sidelines and baselines intersect.

cornerman: A forward.

court: The rectangular playing area for a basketball game (94 feet long by 50 feet wide for NBA and college play, 84 feet long by 50 feet wide for high school play), divided by a line across the middle between the sidelines, the center or division line. At each end of the court, a 10-foot-high, horizontal 18-inch metal ring is attached to a flat rectangular (6 feet wide by 4 feet high) or fan-shaped (54 inches wide by 35 inches high, with a 29-inch radius) white or transparent surface, which is suspended above and perpendicular to the floor 4 feet inside the end line. A 12-foot circle, the restraining circle, is marked in the middle of the court, and divided into equal parts by the center or division line (an additional 4-foot concentric circle is marked for NBA, college, and high school play). Nineteen feet in from and parallel to each end line, and centered on the middle of the basket, the 2-inch-wide, 12-foot (16-foot in the NBA) free throw line is marked. The free throw line bisects a marked 12-foot circle. Two lines extend from the end line to the ends of the free throw line to enclose the free throw lane in the rectangle formed (in international amateur play, the lines form a trapezoid, with a 19-foot, 8-1/4-inch base on the end line). In the NBA, the three-point field goal area is marked by lines extending from the end line 3 feet from and parallel to the sidelines, intersecting an arc of 23 feet, 9 inches from the middle of the basket. (The three-point field goal and similar markings were adopted experimentally by some college conferences in the early 1980s and may ultimately be universally adopted.) In addition, two 2-inch-wide, 3-foot-long "hashmarks" extend inward from and perpendicular to each sideline, 28 feet from the end lines. Although informal games can be played outdoors on asphalt or dirt courts, regulation basketball is played indoors on a hardwood court.

crash the boards: see *bang the boards.*

cripple: An easy, unhindered shot, made from close to the basket. also *chippie.*

1. cut: To suddenly move at an angle, or change directions to leave a defender behind, receive a pass, or move toward the basket. (faked a shot, then cut in to the basket)

2. cut: The act or an instance of cutting.

defensive boards: The backboard of the basket a team is defending. (took charge of the game by controlling the defensive boards)

defensive rebound: A rebound from an opponent's shot at the basket a team is defending.

deuce: A field goal. (hit the jumper for a deuce) also *basket, bucket.*

diamond-and-one: A defensive strategy which employs a four-man zone, with players deployed in a "diamond" around the free throw lane (one at each end of the free throw line and one at high and low post positions), leaving one defender to play man-to-man against the most dangerous scorer on the opposing team. compare *box.*

disqualification: The suspension of a player for the remainder of a game for "fouling out" or committing a specified number of fouls during a game (five fouls in high school, college, women's, and international amateur basketball; six fouls in the NBA). Don Meineke of the Ft. Wayne Pistons holds the NBA record of twenty-six disqualifications in one season (1952-53). Vern Mikkelsen of the Minneapolis Lakers holds the all-time career mark of 127 disqualifications in his ten-year NBA career (1949-59).

division line: A line parallel to the end lines that divides a basketball court in half. The division line, which separates a team's backcourt from the frontcourt, is

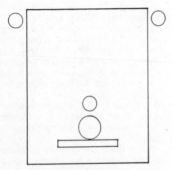

DIAMOND-AND-ONE

used to enforce the ten-second rule and determine backcourt violations. also *center line, midcourt line, ten-second line, time line.*

double-cover: see *double-team.*

1. double dribble: To resume dribbling after a dribble has been stopped, or to dribble with both hands simultaneously. A violation that results in the loss of the ball to the opposing team for a throw-in from a spot out of bounds near the violation.

2. double dribble: A violation that occurs when a player resumes dribbling after a dribble has been stopped, or dribbles the ball with both hands simultaneously. This results in a loss of the ball to the opposing team for a throw-in from a spot out of bounds near the violation.

double figures: Ten or more points, rebounds, or assists in a game. also *doubles.*

double foul: Approximately simultaneous fouls committed by opponents against each other. Penalties are cancelled out, and play resumes with a jump ball between the two players involved at the center circle (except in college, where the ball is awarded to the teams on an alternate basis), unless the foul was committed away from the ball, in which case play resumes where it was interrupted (and in the NBA the twenty-four-second clock is reset to twenty-four). compare *multiple foul.*

1. double pump: To fake a shot at the basket twice in rapid succession in order to momentarily deceive a defender (especially to make him leave his feet) before a real shot, a pass, or a dribble. (double pumps, then scores with a thirteen-foot jumper)

2. double pump: The act or an instance of double pumping.

doubles: Double figures in points, rebounds, or assists in a game.

double-team: To guard or defend against an opponent with two players at the same time. (double-team the center, and force him to pass) also *double-cover, two-time.*

downcourt: To or toward the end of the court containing the basket at which a team is shooting. also *upcourt.*

draw a foul: 1. To deliberately maneuver in such a way as to be fouled. 2. To be fouled.

draw iron: To hit the rim of the basket on a shot. Chick Hearn, broadcaster for the Los Angeles Lakers, popularized the expression in the late 1960s. (a poor shot that didn't even draw iron)

1. dribble: 1. To bounce the ball off the floor, giving impetus with successive taps of the hand. A player with the ball may not walk or run without dribbling. Once a dribble has ended (when the ball is allowed to come to rest in one or both hands), the player may not resume dribbling until after control of the ball has been lost and regained (the ball is shot and recovered, passed and returned, batted away by an opponent and recovered). 2. To move or maneuver while bouncing the ball. (dribbles into the frontcourt)

2. dribble: The act or an instance of dribbling the ball.

dribble drive: A determined advance with the ball, especially toward the basket or baseline. Los Angeles Lakers broadcaster Chick Hearn originated the expression in the mid-1960s to describe the penetrating drives of Hall of Famer Laker Elgin Baylor. also *drive.*

dribbler: 1. The player who is dribbling the ball at a given time during a game. 2. A player who is skilled at, or known for dribbling. (not much of a shooter, but a great playmaker and dribbler)

1. drive: To make a determined advance with the ball, especially toward the basket or baseline. (drives into the lane and shoots)

2. drive: A determined advance with the ball, especially toward the basket or baseline. also *dribble drive.*

drive the lane: To make a determined advance with the ball through the key or lane toward the basket.

drop pass: A pass in which the dribbler leaves the ball for, or pushes it back to a trailing teammate. The passer often continues forward to momentarily draw away a defender.

drop step: A technique in which a player with the ball, positioned at the post with his back to the basket, takes a step back, just to the side of a defender behind him, before turning and driving around him in that direction.

1. dunk: To leap up and push the ball down into the basket from above. Though the exact origin is unclear, the expression stems from "dunking a doughnut." also *jam, stuff.* compare *slam dunk.*

2. dunk: A field goal made by leaping up and pushing the ball down through the basket from above. also *jam, stuff, stuff shot.* compare *slam dunk.*

elbowing: The illegal use of an elbow to hit an opponent, a personal foul. see *personal foul.*

end line: see *baseline.*

fadeaway, fadeaway jumper: see *fallaway.*

fallaway, fallaway jumper: A shot taken while moving back, or "falling away" from the basket. The expression "fallaway jumper" was coined by Los Angeles Lakers broadcaster Chick Hearn in the early 1960s to describe a particular shot favored by Laker guard Dick Barnett. Hearn also applied the expression to all-time NBA scoring leader Wilt Chamberlain's "fallaway bank shot." also *fadeaway, fadeaway jumper.*

false multiple foul: A situation in which two fouls are committed in succession (rather than simultaneously) by teammates against a single opponent, the second foul occurring before the clock is started following the first foul. A free throw is awarded for each foul if the fouled player was in the act of shooting, if the foul was flagrant, or if the bonus situation applies.

fast break: An offensive strategy and concept of play in which a team breaks toward the frontcourt immediately after gaining possession of the ball or putting it in play, in order to constantly pressure the opponents and deny them the

DRIBBLER

time to organize defensively. Ward "Piggy" Lambert, coach of Purdue University (1917, 1919-45) was an early exponent of the fast break or "firewagon basketball," popularized further after the center jump was eliminated in 1937. One of Lambert's star players, three-time All-American John Wooden, later coached UCLA to ten NCAA championships in the 1960s and 1970s using the fast break.

Federation International Basketball Amateur: The international governing body of amateur basketball. Founded in Geneva, Switzerland, in 1932, the Federation International Basketball Amateur is headquartered in Munich, Germany. also *FIBA*.

1. feed: To pass to a teammate near the basket. (feeds to the big man, who turns and dunks for two points)

2. feed: A pass to a teammate near the basket.

FIBA: The Federation International Basketball Amateur.

field goal: A two-point score made by throwing the ball through the basket (three points in the NBA and some college conferences, if shot from outside the three-point field goal area, approxi-

DUNK

mately 23 feet from the basket). Before the mid-1890s, all field goals were three points. NBA superstar Wilt Chamberlain holds the all-time record for the most field goals scored in a single game (36 for the Philadelphia Warriors on March 2, 1962) and one season (1,597 for the Philadelphia Warriors, 1961-62). Chamberlain also holds the lifetime record, making 12,681 field goals in his fourteen-year NBA career (1959-1973). also *basket, bucket, deuce*.

fill the lane: To run toward the opponent's basket in one of the imaginary alleys or lanes near the sidelines on a fast break, thereby spreading the attack and increasing the difficulty for the defense.

finger roll: A shot from close range in which the ball rolls gently off the fingertips into the basket. The expression was coined by broadcaster Chick Hearn to describe a shot often made by Wilt Chamberlain.

five: A basketball team. also *quintet*.

five-second rule: 1. A rule in college and high school play that requires a closely guarded player holding or dribbling the ball in the frontcourt, or holding and/or dribbling in the midcourt, to shoot or pass within five seconds. A violation (held ball) results in the ball being awarded to the opposing team for a throw-in. 2. A rule in women's and international amateur play that requires a closely guarded player holding the ball to shoot, pass, or dribble within five seconds. A violation (held ball) results in a jump ball.

flagrant foul: A foul in which a player deliberately attempts to hurt an opponent by violent contact, such as kicking, kneeing, or running under a player who is in the air. A flagrant foul is charged as a personal foul and a team foul, and carries a penalty of two free throws. The offending player is ejected (and, in the NBA, may be subject to suspension and/or a fine).

floor: 1. The playing surface of a basketball court. 2. The playing area of a basketball court. (will put the five best men on the floor to finish the game)

forecourt: The area of a team's frontcourt between the hashmarks (midcourt area markers) and the end line. see *five-second rule*.

forward: 1. Either of two players who operate from a position near the baseline, on either side of and close to the basket. The two general types of forwards are the "power forward," usually large and strong and an aggressive rebounder, and the "small forward," usually noted for quickness and mobility, and often a particularly good shooter. Before the center jump after each field goal was abandoned in 1937, the offensive players often remained in the frontcourt, in a "forward" position. also *frontcourtman.* 2. The position played by a forward. (can play forward or center)

1. **foul:** An infraction of the rules that prohibit illegal physical contact (personal fouls such as pushing, charging, etc.), actions that violate game regulations (technical fouls such as too many players on the court, delay of game, etc.), or those which call for sportsmanlike conduct (technical fouls such as disrespect of officials, profanity, etc.). A foul is charged to the player who commits it (and sometimes toward the number of team fouls allowed before the bonus situation applies), and (depending upon the nature and gravity of the foul, whether it is committed by an offensive or defensive player, and whether the bonus situation applies) is penalized by awarding the opposing team possession of the ball, or by awarding one or more free throws. see *bonus situation, personal foul, technical foul.* compare *violation.*

2. **foul:** 1. To commit a foul. 2. To commit a foul against a specific player. (fouled him in the act of shooting)

foul lane: see *free throw lane.*

foul line: see *free throw line.*

foul out: To be put out of a game for committing a specified number of fouls during a game (five fouls in high school, college, women's, and international amateur basketball; six fouls in the NBA). see *disqualification.*

foul shot: A free throw.

four-corner offense: A ball control strategy in high school and college basketball in which offensive players form a large box, with one player near each of the four corners in the frontcourt and the fifth player near the center circle. Used as a control type offense to spread the defense, or as a stalling tactic employed to prevent the opposing team from gaining possession of the ball, such

as at the end of a game to protect a lead. Extensive use of the four-corner offense usually results in a low-scoring game. The four-corner offense was developed by University of North Carolina coach Dean Smith in the mid-1960s.

four-point play: 1. A situation in an NBA game (or a college game in a conference where the three-point field goal is used) in which a player is fouled as he shoots and makes a field goal from outside the three-point area (approximately 23 feet away from the basket). The basket counts, and if the free throw is made, the total is a four-point play. 2. A situation in a college, women's, or high school game in which a player is fouled flagrantly or intentionally as he or she shoots and makes a field goal. The basket counts, and two free throws are awarded. If both are made, the total is a four-point play. 3. A situation in a college, women's, or high school game in which a player is fouled after shooting a field goal (or his or her teammate is fouled). The basket counts and a one-and-one free throw is awarded. If both are made, the total is a four-point play. 4. A situation in a women's game in which a player is fouled flagrantly as she shoots and misses. Four free throws are awarded to the fouled player. If all are made, the result is a four-point play.

free ball: see *loose ball.*

free throw: An uncontested shot at the basket from behind the free throw line (15 feet from the basket) awarded to the fouled player when an opponent has committed a personal foul, or to any player chosen by the coach when an opponent has committed a technical foul. After a personal foul, players from the two teams line up in alternate positions along both sides of the free throw lane, with two players from the fouling team closest to the basket. If a free throw attempt is unsuccessful, the ball is in play as soon as it makes contact with the backboard, rim, or net, and players may then enter the lane to contend for it (if more than one free throw is awarded, the ball is not in play until the second attempt). If the free throw is successful, the ball is dead until put into play by the opposing team with a throw-in from outside the baseline under the basket. After a technical foul, the ball is dead and is put into play (usually by the team shooting the foul) with a throw-in from the sideline. Each successful free throw scores one point. Free throws were introduced in 1894 and were valued at three points each until 1895. NBA scoring champion Wilt Chamberlain set the all-time record for the most free throws in a single game on March 2, 1962, when he made 28 free throws for the Philadelphia Warriors. Jerry West of the Los Angeles Lakers set the record for the most free throws in one season, 840, in 1965-66. Houston Rockets guard Calvin Murphy holds the record for the highest free throw percentage in one season (95.8 percent in 1980-81, including a record 78 consecutive free throws made). Rick Barry owns the highest career percentage, making 90 percent of his attempted free throws during his ten year NBA career (1965-1967 and 1972-1980). Oscar Robertson holds the NBA lifetime record of 7,694 free throws in his fourteen-year career (1960-1974). also *charity shot, foul shot.*

free throw area: 1. The free throw lane. 2. The free throw lane and the free throw circle. also *key, keyhole.*

free throw circle: Either of the two 12-foot restraining circles that form the top of the key at both ends of the court and are bisected by the free throw lines. The free throw circle is sometimes used for jump ball situations.

free throw lane: The rectangular (19 feet long by 12 feet for college and high school play, 19 feet long by 16 feet in the NBA) or trapezoidal area (19 feet long by 12 feet wide at the free throw line and 19 feet, 8-1/4 inches wide at the end line for international amateur play) marked at each end of the court between the free throw line and the end line. No player may remain within his offensive free throw lane for more than three consecutive seconds while his team has possession of the ball in the frontcourt. No player may enter the lane on a free throw until the ball has made contact with the backboard, the rim, or the net. also *foul lane, free throw area, key, keyhole, lane, paint, three-second area, three-second lane.*

free throw line: Either of two 2-inch-wide, 12-foot-long lines (16 feet in the NBA) marked 19 feet from and parallel to the end line (15 feet from the basket) at both ends of the court. A player attempting a free throw must stand behind the free throw line and within the 12-foot free throw circle it bisects. The free throw lines were moved from 20 feet to 15 feet from the basket shortly after free throws were introduced in 1894. also *charity line, charity stripe, foul line, line.*

1. freeze: To stall. see *stall.*

2. freeze: The act or an instance of stalling.

front: To guard an opponent (especially a taller opposing center or pivot) by playing in front of him in the passing lane (between him and the ball), instead of between him and the basket. compare *back.*

frontcourt: 1. The offensive half of a court, which contains the basket at which a team shoots. (bring the ball into the frontcourt) 2. The center and forwards. (overmatched if you try to go man-to-man on their frontcourt) also *front line.* 3. The positions played by the center and forward.

frontcourtman: A center or forward; one who plays in the frontcourt.

front lay-in: see *front lay-up.*

front lay-up: A lay-up made while in front of and facing the basket. also *front lay-in.* see *lay-up.* compare *reverse lay-up.*

front line: see *frontcourt.*

full-court press: A defensive tactic in which opponents are closely guarded man-to-man the full length of the court, from the moment the ball is put in play after a basket. Used to disrupt an

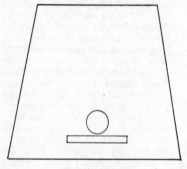

FREE THROW LANE

opposing team's normal offensive flow, to apply intense pressure and force mistakes, or as a part of a concerted effort to steal the ball for a quick score. compare *half-court press, zone press*.

game clock: The clock that indicates the remaining time to be played in a period. compare *shooting clock*.

garbage: 1. An easy or uncontested basket, or of or pertaining to an easy or uncontested basket, made from close range. (grabbed the rebound for a garbage two points) 2. The closing minutes of a game in which one team has such a commanding lead that the outcome has been decided, and substitutes are sent in to finish up. also *garbage time*.

garbage time: see *garbage*.

give and go: To execute a give-and-go.

give-and-go: A play in which the ball handler passes to a teammate, then breaks past a defender or defenders to receive a return pass in the clear. In the early 1930s, Nat Holman, coach of City College of New York, helped to refine the give-and-go into a system of play that eventually was adopted and practiced by many East Coast colleges. (worked the give-and-go into the lane)

glass ball: A missed shot that touches only the glass backboard and rebounds. compare *air ball*.

Globetrotters: see *Harlem Globetrotters*.

goaltending: Interference with a shot by touching the ball or the basket while the ball is on, over, or within the rim, touching the ball on its downward flight to the basket before it hits the rim, touching the ball on its upward flight to the basket after it has touched the backboard (as on a lay-up), or trapping the ball against the backboard. A violation, resulting in the loss of the ball to the opposing team for a throw-in from the sideline even with the free throw line if committed by an offensive player, or by the awarding of two points (three points in the NBA and some college conferences if the shot was taken from outside the three-point line) to the shooter. The ball is then inbounded in the normal manner after a field goal. The first goaltending rule was introduced in 1944. also *basket interference*.

guard: 1. Either of two players (often smaller and better ball handlers than the forward) who usually bring the ball out of the backcourt, start plays, and dis-

tribute the ball to teammates closer to the basket. Before the center jump was abandoned in 1937, the main responsibility of the two guards was to play defense and to "guard" the opposing forwards. (best outside-shooting guard in the league) also *backcourtman*. 2. The position played by the guards. 3. To prevent an opponent from being able to maneuver, pass, or receive a pass, or shoot effectively.

gunner: A player who shoots at every opportunity, even when teammates are more open or in a better position to score. also *chucker, pump*.

1. hack: To hit an opponent on the arm with the hand or forearm, in an attempt to knock the ball away; a personal foul. see *hacking*.

2. hack: The act or an instance of hacking.

hacking: A personal foul in which a player hits an opponent's arm with his hand or forearm. see *personal foul*.

half-court press: A defensive strategy in which the opponents are closely guarded man-to-man as soon as they enter a team's backcourt. compare *full-court press, zone press*.

Hall of Fame: see *Basketball Hall of Fame*.

hammer the boards: see *bang the boards*.

hand check: To maintain intermittent or continuous physical contact with the hand while guarding an offensive player, especially the ball handler. A personal foul. also *check*. see *personal foul*.

hanger: see *basket hanger*.

hardship case: A situation in which a college basketball player, not yet in his senior year, claims eligibility for a special NBA draft before graduating, under the "hardship" rule. NBA regulations originally forbade the playing or drafting of any college player before his class graduated. A court decision in the early 1970s ruled in favor of Seattle SuperSonics owner Sam Sullivan's attempt to hire Spencer Haywood, who had left the University of Detroit to play in the rival ABA. Ruling that the NBA regulation denying his right to play would work a hardship on Haywood, the court opened the way for other underclassmen to be drafted if they claim a hardship.

Harlem Globetrotters: A touring all-black

team that travels all over the world to play exhibition games that feature a unique blend of dazzling basketball skills and comedic showmanship. Founded in 1927 by Abe Saperstein, the Globetrotters have introduced the game of basketball to millions of fans and have become one of the all-time great attractions in sports. Some credit the Trotters with saving professional basketball when they played prior to some NBA games in the 1950s and drew many new fans to the arenas. Superstar Wilt Chamberlain, the greatest scorer in NBA history, played with the Harlem Globetrotters before his NBA days. also *Globetrotters, Trotters.*

hashmark: see *midcourt area marker.*

held ball: 1. A situation in which two or more opponents have their hands so firmly on the ball that neither can gain sole possession without undue roughness. This results in a jump ball at the circle nearest the spot where the held ball occurs (except in college games, where the ball is given alternately to the teams). also *tie ball.* 2. A violation of the five-second rule in college and high school play in which a closely guarded player holds or dribbles the ball in the frontcourt, or holds and/or

HOOK SHOT

dribbles the ball in the midcourt for five seconds without shooting or passing, resulting in the opposing team being awarded the ball for a throw-in. 3. A violation of the five-second rule in women's and international amateur play in which a closely guarded player holds the ball for five seconds without shooting, passing, or dribbling, resulting in a jump ball.

high post: A position just outside the lane near the free throw line in the frontcourt where a team's center often plays, and around which the offense maneuvers as he sets screens, receives and relays passes, and shoots. compare *low post.*

holding: A personal foul in which a player uses the hands to interfere with the movement or impede the progress of an opposing player. see *personal foul.*

1. hook: 1. A one-handed overhead shot made with the back arm when the body is turned sideways to the basket. With the shooting arm extended, the ball is lifted in an arc, then released with a flick of the wrist. Because the ball is released high, out of reach, and because it is further protected from defenders by the width of the shooter's body, an accurate hook is almost unstoppable. also *hook shot.* 2. An illegal, but common tactic in which a player with the ball, positioned with his back to a defender close behind, subtly moves a hand or elbow back to hold or "hook" the defender just before wheeling around him in that direction on a drive. If the infraction is detected, a personal foul results. see *personal foul.*

2. hook: 1. To execute a hook shot. (hooked right over the big man for two points) 2. To use an illegal hook to turn and dribble around an opponent.

hook pass: A pass made with the overhead motion of a hook shot.

hook shot: see *hook.*

hoop: The basket. also *bucket.*

H.O.R.S.E.: An informal game for two or more players in which contestants take turns making various kinds of shots from different locations around the court. When a shot is made, all players must then duplicate that shot. Each time a player fails to duplicate another player's shot, the unsuccessful player is assigned one letter of the word "horse" (other longer or shorter words are sometimes substituted). When a player misses enough times to spell out the word "horse" (or the substitute word), that player is eliminated from the game. The last player left in a game is the winner. Because of the requirement to duplicate the style of a shot, as well as the distance and type, and because there is usually no penalty to a player who misses an original shot (the next player makes his original shot attempt), low-percentage trick-shots are often employed in the game of H.O.R.S.E. compare _around the world._

hot hand: A temporary heightened ability to make baskets, lasting for an indeterminate period of time. (had a hot hand for the three games he's played since coming off the bench)

●●A temporary heightened ability to accomplish or perform a task or activity. (got the hot hand at picking winners today)

inbound: To put the ball in play by a throw-in from out of bounds. If the ball is not inbounded within the five-second time limit, the opposing team is awarded the ball for a throw-in. (will inbound the ball from the sideline)

inbound pass: A throw-in from out of bounds. (takes the inbound pass and immediately moves the ball upcourt)

in bounds: Within the boundary lines of the playing court. (the ball is still in bounds)

inbounds: Of or pertaining to putting the ball in play with a throw-in from out of bounds. (broke up the inbounds play with a steal)

incidental contact: Legal physical contact with an opponent that is incidental to an effort by a player to perform normal defensive or offensive movement or to reach a loose ball.

in one's face: Disrespectfully, disdainfully, in spite of one's best efforts to oppose, as of a direct and deliberate challenge. (drove the lane right at their big man and scored two points in his face)

1. inside: The area in and around the free throw lane, close to the basket. (dominate the boards with the big man on the inside)

2. inside: To or toward the area in and around the free throw lane, close to the basket.

inside game: The ability of an individual or team to maneuver, shoot, and rebound

close to the basket. (can't shoot from the outside, but his inside game is great)

intentional foul: A deliberate foul to stop the clock by a defensive player whose team is behind late in a game, conceding one or two free throws (which might be missed) for possession of the ball and the opportunity to score. Two free throws are awarded to the opposing team, except in the NBA in the final two minutes of play or an overtime period if the foul is committed against someone other than the ball handler. In such a case, one free throw is awarded to the opposing team.

in-your-face: Aggressively challenging, disrespectful, or disdainful. (scored with an in-your-face slam dunk)

isolate a defender: To maneuver a defender into a situation in which an offensive player is able to go one-on-one against him.

jab step: A technique in which the player with the ball takes a sudden step (without lifting the pivot foot) to fake a drive and momentarily deceive a defender, as before a shot, pass, or a drive in another direction. (backed the defender off with a jab step just long enough to shoot)

1. jam: To dunk the ball. also _stuff._

2. jam: A dunk. also _stuff, stuff shot._

jump ball: 1. A method of putting the ball in play in which two opponents within one of the three restraining circles jump up to try to tap a ball thrown in the air between them by the referee to a teammate outside the circle. A jump ball occurs in the center circle at the beginning of a game or overtime period (and at the beginning of every period in international amateur, women's, and high school play), and (except in college play) when a double foul on the ball is called. Except in college play, a jump ball occurs in the nearest circle in the case of a held ball, an out of bounds ball caused by both teams, a double-free throw violation, a ball lodged in a basket support, or a dead ball that neither team controls when no goal or infraction is involved. Jumpers must remain within, and teammates may not enter, the restraining circle before the ball is tapped. When a jump ball occurs in the center circle, jumpers must have at least one foot within a 4-foot jumping circle marked in a middle of the 12-

foot restraining circle (except in international amateur play). also *toss-up*. 2. A held ball.

●●A conflict in which there is no winner, or an even choice between options; a toss-up. (by train or by car, it's a jump ball)

jumper: A jump shot. (sinks a 15-foot jumper)

jumping circle: A 4-foot circle marked in the middle of the center circle in high school, college, and NBA play, inside which each jumper must have at least one foot before a jump ball.

jump pass: A pass made while jumping, often disguised as a jump shot.

jump shot: A shot in which the ball is released over the head at the peak of a jump. Difficult for a defender to block because of the height of the release. Though a two-handed jump shot was used as early as 1939 and 1940 by University of Arkansas forward Johnny Adams, and Minneapolis Laker Jim Pollard showed an unorthodox jump shot in the NBA in 1948, one of the earliest to use the modern jump shot was Universi-

JUMP SHOT

ty of San Francisco All-America forward Don Lofgran. After seeing him in a 1949 tournament, New York sportswriters dubbed his shot the "kangaroo shot." also *jumper*.

key, keyhole: The free throw area (including the restraining circle) or the free throw lane. The terms date from the early days of basketball and refer to the keyholelike appearance of the pre-1950s free throw area, with a 6-foot-wide lane extending from one end of the 12-foot restraining circle. (misses a jump shot from the top of the key)

lane: 1. The free throw lane. 2. Either of two imaginary alleys near the sidelines that offensive players attempt to fill during a fast break in order to spread the attack and increase the difficulty for the defense.

lay-in: A lay-up.

lay-up: A relatively easy shot made usually off the backboard from close to the basket at the peak of a jump. (steals the ball in the backcourt and scores with an easy lay-up) also *lay-in*.

lead official, leading official: The official who precedes play down the court and takes a position off the court near the basket. On a fast break, the lead and trail officials usually switch roles. compare *trail official*.

line: The free throw line.

loose ball: A ball that is in play but not in the possession of any player (such as a ball in the air on a pass or rebound, or rolling on the floor uncontrolled), and recoverable by either team. also *free ball*.

loose ball foul: In the NBA, a personal foul committed while the ball is in the air for a shot or a rebound, or otherwise in possession of neither team. The offending player and the team are charged with a foul, and the ball is awarded to the opposing team for a throw-in from out of bounds near where the foul occurred. If a loose ball foul occurs during a penalty situation, the number of free throws that normally applies on the personal foul are awarded.

lowbridge: To knock the legs out from under an opponent who is in the air to make a play (such as a shot, rebound, or pass). A personal foul that results in the awarding of two free throws to the fouled player. also *submarine, undercut*.

low post: A position close to the basket just outside the free throw lane in the frontcourt where a team's center often plays, and around which the offense maneuvers as he sets screens, receives and relays passes, shoots, and rebounds. compare *high post.*

makeup foul: A dubious or questionable foul that is called to "make up" for an earlier dubious or questionable foul called against the other team.

man defense: Man-to-man. also *man-for-man, man-on-man.*

man-for-man, man-on-man: Man-to-man. also *man defense.*

man-to-man: A defense in which each player guards a specific opponent. also *man defense, man-for-man, man-on-man.*

midcourt: The area of a team's frontcourt between the center line and the hash-marks (midcourt area markers). see *five-second rule.*

midcourt area marker: Either of two 2-inch-wide lines extending 3 feet in from each side boundary line 28 feet from and parallel to the end line. also *hash-mark.*

midcourt line: see *division line.*

moving pick: An illegal maneuver in which an offensive player fails to come to a stop or remain stationary in an attempt to screen an opponent. If physical contact results, a personal foul is charged against the guilty player. see *personal foul.*

multiple foul: A situation in which two or more players on a team foul the same player at approximately the same time. A multiple foul results in the fouled player being awarded one free throw for each foul. compare *double foul.*

muscle player: A player who uses physical strength to maneuver for or maintain position, and rebound.

National Basketball Association: The major professional basketball league in the United States, founded in 1946 under the name of the Basketball Association of America. When the first games were played on November 1, 1946, there were eleven charter member teams. The league adopted its present name in 1949, after absorbing the rival National Basketball League. Today there are twenty-four franchises in the National Basketball Association in two conferences, each with two divisions. In the Eastern Conference, the Atlantic Division is made up of the Boston Celtics, the New Jersey Nets, the New York Knicks, the Philadelphia 76ers, and the Washington Bullets, and the Central Division is made up of the Atlanta Hawks, the Chicago Bulls, the Cleveland Cavaliers, the Detroit Pistons, the Indiana Pacers, and the Milwaukee Bucks. In the Western Conference, the Midwest Division is made up of the Dallas Mavericks, the Denver Nuggets, the Houston Rockets, the Kansas City Kings, the San Antonio Spurs, and the Utah Jazz, and the Pacific Division is made up of the Golden State Warriors, the Los Angeles Lakers, the Phoenix Suns, the Portland Trail Blazers, the San Diego Clippers, and the Seattle Super-Sonics. Abbreviated NBA.

NBA: The National Basketball Association.

net: The white mesh cord sleeve (15 to 18 inches in length) attached beneath the 18-inch metal rim to slow the ball momentarily as it passes through the basket. also *cord.*

no harm, no foul: The guiding philosophy of professional basketball officiating. If a foul is inconsequential, and no harm is done nor advantage gained, play is usually allowed to continue. "No harm, no foul" was coined by Los Angeles Lakers broadcaster Chick Hearn.

●●The expression is now used in sports other than basketball, as well as figuratively in nonsports circumstances where the same sentiment applies. (though his car did tap my bumper, no harm, no foul)

offensive boards: The backboard of the basket at which a team is shooting. (always got a second shot because they controlled the offensive boards)

offensive foul: A personal foul committed by a player of the team in control of the ball in NBA, international amateur, and women's play. When an offensive foul is committed, the guilty player and (except in the NBA) the team are charged with the foul, and the ball is awarded to the opposing team for a throw-in from out of bounds near where the foul occurred. In college and high school play, an offensive foul committed by a player other than the ball handler is a common foul and results in the ball being awarded to the opposing team for a throw-in (except in a bonus situation, when a one-and-one free throw is awarded to the fouled team). compare *player control foul.*

offensive rebound: A rebound taken off the backboard of the basket at which a team is shooting. (got the offensive rebound for his own shot)

official: Either of the two referees (or any of the three in some college conferences) who administer the rules of the game, or any of the individuals responsible for the timing and scoring of a game (in the NBA there is a lead official, a referee, a timer to operate the game clock, a timer to operate the twenty-four-second clock, and a scorer to compile game statistics). see *lead official, trail official.*

one-and-one: A situation in college, women's, and high school play in which a bonus free throw is awarded to a fouled player if the first free throw is successful during a bonus situation. A bonus situation applies when the opposing team has committed a specified number of team fouls during a period of play (seven fouls in one half in college and women's games, five fouls during one half in high school games). also *one-plus-one.*

one-handed push: see *one-hand set.*

one-hand set: A shot in which the ball is held shoulder high in the palm of one hand (knuckles toward the basket), and pushed toward the basket by the fingertips of the other hand with a snap of the wrist. Three-time Stanford All-American Hank Luisetti is credited with popularizing the one-handed set shot in the late 1930s, a major contribution to the modern high-scoring game. With his quick, hard to defend against one-hand shot, Luisetti once managed to score fifty points against Duquesne University, at a time when it was not uncommon for the winning team to score less than twenty points. The introduction of the one-hand set shot (out of which later came the jump shot) and the abolishing of the center jump after each field goal in 1937 (which integrated the center and guards into the offense and allowed the fast break to be developed) were the two most revolutionary changes in the game of basketball. also *one-handed push.*

one-on-one: 1. A situation in which a player offensively or defensively confronts

or is confronted by a single opponent. Often a team with the ball will maneuver to create a situation where a good ball handler and shooter can go "one-on-one" against a defender. 2. An informal basketball game between two players.

●●Any contest or situation (athletic or nonathletic) that pits one individual against another. (broke through the secondary to be one-on-one with the free safety on the 10-yard line) Also a situation that allows one individual to talk or interact with another individual, unbothered by other people. (a productive one-on-one discussion after everybody left)

one-plus-one: see *one-and-one.*

open: Unguarded by or away from any opponent. (fed the open man under the basket for an easy two points)

OT: see *overtime.*

outlet: To start a fast break after a defensive rebound with a pass to a teammate. (outlets the ball right up the middle, and the fast break is on)

outlet pass: A pass to a teammate to start a fast break, made by a player who pulls down a rebound from the defensive boards.

out of bounds: Beyond the boundaries of the playing area and out of play. A player is out of bounds when he touches the floor, a person, or any object on or outside a boundary. A player in the air who takes off from in bounds is not out of bounds until he touches the floor, a person, or any object on or outside a boundary. The ball is out of bounds when it touches the floor, a person, or any object on, above, or outside of a boundary, or the supports or back of the backboard. When a ball goes out of bounds, the ball is awarded to the team opposing the player who last touched it for a throw-in.

out of bounds play: A special play used by a team awarded a throw-in in the frontcourt, in which players maneuver so that one, or more than one, designated teammate will be open to receive the throw-in. Often players crowd into a line perpendicular to the boundary line in front of the thrower-in, then break suddenly in different prearranged directions for the inbound pass.

1. **outside:** The area near the sides and back of the frontcourt, away from the

basket and free throw lane. (good shooters from the outside)

2. outside: To or toward the area near the sides and back of the frontcourt, away from the basket and free throw lane, near the division line or sidelines.

outside shooter: A player who can make shots from far away from the basket.

over and back: see *backcourt violation.*

overhead pass: A two-hand pass in which the ball is released over the head by snapping the hands forward. Often used to feed the post, over the defense.

overload the zone: To send more offensive players into an area than there are defenders.

overplay: To bias one's defense toward the strongest or favorite side of an opponent to make him go the other way.

over the top: 1. A situation in which a player leaps, or extends arms or part of the body over a player who has established position. A personal foul if physical contact results. see *personal foul.* 2. A shot from the outside, over the defense.

overtime: An extra five-minute period of play (three minutes in high school games) to decide a game tied at the end of regulation play. Overtime periods continue to be played until one team wins. also *OT.*

paint: The free throw lane. The expression was coined by Al McGuire, coach of Marquette University from 1965 to 1977. (into the big man on the paint) see *free throw lane.*

palm the ball: 1. To hold the ball in the palm of the hand momentarily while dribbling, or "catch" the ball between bounces. A violation, resulting in the loss of the ball to the opposing team for a throw-in from the sideline. also *carry.* 2. To hold a ball in one hand, with the palm facing down. (could palm a regulation ball by the time he was sixteen)

passing lane: A safe path or channel for a pass to a teammate.

penalty situation: A situation in NBA games in which a team has reached five team fouls, and each foul thereafter yields an additional free throw to the opposing team. also *bonus situation, penalty stage.*

penalty stage: see *penalty situation.*

personal foul: A foul in which there is physical contact with an opponent

(holding, pushing, charging, hacking, elbowing, blocking, etc.). If a personal foul is committed by an offensive player, the player and (except in the NBA) the team are charged with a foul, and the ball is awarded to the opposing team for a throw-in. Free throws are awarded instead in international amateur play (two free throws) and college, women's, and high school play (one-and-one) if the foul occurs during or causes a bonus situation. If a personal foul is committed by a defensive player, the player and the team are charged with a foul, and the fouled team is awarded a throw-in. Free throws are awarded (two in NBA, international amateur, and high school play, one-and-one in college and women's play) if the foul occurs during or causes a bonus situation (penalty situation in the NBA). If the foul is flagrant (an automatic disqualification for the guilty player) or intentional (or, in the NBA, if it is committed before the ball is inbounded), two free throws are awarded. If the foul is committed against a shooter who misses or is prevented from shooting, two free throws are awarded (three-to-make-two in international amateur play). One free throw is awarded if the foul is committed against a shooter who scores. see *flagrant foul, intentional foul.* compare *technical foul, violation.*

pick: see *screen.*

pick and roll: A play in which an offensive player sets a screen, then wheels towards the basket in order to receive a pass.

1. pivot: 1. The post position. see *post.* 2. The player who plays the pivot or post position. (their pivot can play in a high post or low post position) also *pivotman, post, post man.* 3. The act of, while holding the ball, stepping forward, backward, or to the side with one foot while the other foot (pivot foot) remains in contact with the floor in one place. see *pivot foot.*

2. pivot: To execute a pivot. see *pivot foot.*

pivot foot: The foot on which a player pivots, and which must remain in contact with the floor in one place while the player holds the ball. As long as the pivot foot remains in one place, any number of steps taken with the other foot count as the one step a player is permitted to take while holding the ball. If the pivot foot is moved from its original point of contact (except in the case of a jump pass or jump shot), or if a player, in attempting to make a jump pass or jump shot, touches the floor with either foot before the ball leaves his hands, the player is guilty of traveling. A traveling violation results in the loss of the ball to the opposing team for a throw-in from out of bounds near where the violation occurred. Either foot may be used as the pivot foot if a player receives the ball while standing still, or receives the ball while in the air and lands on both feet. If a moving player stops a dribble or receives a pass, the pivot foot is the first foot to touch the floor after the dribble stops or the ball is caught. If a moving player receives a pass while both feet are in the air, the pivot foot is the first foot to touch the floor after the ball is caught.

pivotman: The player (usually the center) who plays in the pivot or post position. also *pivot, post, post man.*

player control foul: A personal foul committed by the player in control of the ball in college and high school basketball. When a player control foul is committed, the guilty player and the team are charged with a foul, and the ball is awarded to the opposing team for a throw-in from out of bounds near where the foul occurred. compare *offensive foul.*

play for one: To play for one shot only, to maintain control of the ball near the end of the period or game so that when a shot is taken, there will not be enough time remaining for the opposing team to score.

point: 1. The basic scoring unit in basketball. A field goal counts for two points (in the NBA and some college conferences, a field goal made from outside the three-point line, approximately 23 feet from the basket, counts for three points). A successful free throw counts for one point. 2. The area toward the back of the frontcourt from where the point guard runs the offense.

point guard: The guard who runs the offense from a position near the back of the frontcourt.

point shaving: The deliberate (and illegal) limiting of the amount of points scored in a game by a team by one or more

players to conform to the interests of gamblers.

post: 1. A position in the frontcourt, just outside the free throw lane, either close to the basket (low post), or near the free throw line (high post), occupied by the player (usually the center) around which the offense maneuvers as he sets screens, receives and relays passes, and shoots. Some teams use a two-post offense, with one player at the high post, and another at the low post. also *pivot.* 2. The player who plays the post position. also *pivot, pivotman, post man.*

post man: The player who plays the post position. also *pivot, pivotman, post.*

post-up: To establish a post position close to the basket.

pound the boards, pound the glass: see *bang the boards.*

power forward: A strong forward, usually large, primarily responsible for establishing and maintaining good position in front of the basket in order to be able to rebound aggressively, and to inhibit drives toward the basket by players on the opposing team. Minneapolis Lakers forward Vern Mikkelson, a six-time NBA All-Star in the 1950s, was the prototype for the modern power forward.

1. press: A defensive tactic in which opponents are closely guarded man-to-man either from the moment the ball is put into play after a basket (full-court press), or as soon as they enter a team's backcourt (half-court press), or when they enter specific zones defended by individual players (zone press). Used to disrupt an opposing team's normal offensive flow, to apply intense pressure and force mistakes, or as a part of a concerted effort to steal the ball for a quick score.

2. press: To execute a press against the opposing team. (press them and try to come up with a steal)

1. pump: To fake a shot at the basket in order to momentarily deceive a defender before a real shot, a pass, or a dribble. (pumps, then drives into the lane)

2. pump: 1. The act or an instance of pumping. (fakes with a pump, then sinks a 15-foot jump shot) 2. A gunner. see *gunner.*

pure shooter: A player with the ability to consistently make baskets, a very good shooter.

quintet: A basketball team. also *five.*

racehorse: see *run-and-gun.*

1. rebound: 1. The carom off the rim or backboard of a missed shot at the basket. (goes up for the rebound) 2. The act or an instance of gaining control of a ball that caroms off the rim or backboard from a missed shot at the basket. Wilt Chamberlain set the all-time NBA records for the most rebounds in a single game (55 on November 24, 1960) and in one season (2,149 in 1960-61) when he played for the Philadelphia Warriors. Chamberlain also holds the lifetime record, with 23,924 rebounds in his fourteen-year NBA career. also *board.*

2. rebound: To gain possession of a rebound. (rebounds and immediately outlets the ball)

ref: A referee.

referee: One of two officials (called the "umpire" and "referee" in high school and college play, and "lead official" and "referee" in the NBA, though all are commonly referred to as "referees") responsible for administering the rules of the game. Some college conferences require three officials, one "referee" and two "umpires." All call violations and fouls, and indicate successful goals. also *ref.*

reject: To block a shot at the basket. (rejected by the big man) see *block.*

release: To leave one assignment, such as guarding an opponent, for another (such as to double-team the player with the ball).

release early: To leave the backcourt early, as to start a fast break or to cherry-pick.

restraining circle: Any of three 12-foot circles (one in the middle of the court, bisected by the division line, and one at each end of the court, bisected by the free throw lines) within which a jump ball may be held, and inside which no other player may step until a jump ball has been tapped.

reverse dunk: A dunk shot made back over the head from underneath the basket, with the player facing out.

reverse lay-in: A reverse lay-up.

reverse lay-up: A lay-up made back over the head from underneath the basket. also *reverse lay-in.* see *lay-up.* compare *front lay-up.*

rim: Either of the 18-inch metal rings attached to the backboards at both ends of the court, from which a white cord net is suspended, and through which the ball must pass to make a basket. The most advanced model rims are designed with a hinge that allows the rim to give way under a certain amount of weight, and snap back when the pressure is released. This is to prevent injuries from shattered glass backboards that can result from hanging on the rim or from a particularly powerful slam dunk. These spring-loaded rims were adopted by the NBA (and approved for college use) in 1981-82.

rim shot: A shot that is banked in off the rim.

rocker step: A technique in which a player with the ball fakes a drive by taking a step (without lifting the pivot foot), then pulls back to shoot (or sometimes, to fake a shot before actually driving), appearing to "rock" back and forth.

roll: To suddenly wheel around from a stationary position (such as from a pick) and break toward the basket.

run-and-gun: A wide-open offensive style of play, characterized by a fast break and relentless attacks on the offensive basket rather than deliberate or complicated offensive and defensive strategies. also *racehorse, run-and-shoot.*

run and gun: To employ a run-and-gun offense. (will be forced to run and gun now to cut down the lead) also *run and shoot.*

run-and-shoot: see *run-and-gun.*

run and shoot: see *run and gun.*

run the break: To play the key part in and direct a team's fast break offense. (a great ball handling guard who runs the break)

sag: see *slough off.*

scoop, scoop lay-up: A lay-up in which the ball is brought up to the basket with an underhand motion.

scorer: The official responsible for keeping a record of field goals made, free throws made and missed, and a running summary of points scored. Scorers also record the personal and technical fouls called on each player and the time-outs charged to each team, and notify the nearest official when the maximum number of fouls permitted a player, or time-outs permitted a team is reached. Scorers record the names, numbers, and positions of all starting players and substitutes, as well as the time of any substitutions. When a player is disqualified from the game, or when a penalty shot is being awarded, a buzzer, siren, or some other audible sound is used by the scorer (or sometimes the timer) to notify the game officials.

1. **screen:** A maneuver in which an offensive player without the ball takes a stationary position in back of, to the side of, or in front of a defensive player in order to momentarily obstruct his path and free the ball handler. Legal only if the offensive player remains stationary, and leaves enough room for the defensive player to avoid a collision. also *pick.*

2. **screen:** To take a stationary position in back of, to the side of, or in front of a defensive player in order to momentarily obstruct his path and free the ball handler. (screened the defender off the ball handler) also *set a pick.*

screen out: see *box out.*

set a pick: To screen a defensive player or to execute a screen.

set offense: An offense that utilizes practiced patterns of movement in order to maneuver for a good shot at the basket.

set play: An offensive play in which specific patterns of movement are used to maneuver for a good shot at the basket.

set shot: A shot that is taken with both feet on the floor, as opposed to a jump shot. see *one-hand set shot, two-hand set shot.*

shave points: To deliberately (and illegally) limit the amount of points scored in a game by one's team to conform to the interest of gamblers.

shoot: To make an attempt to throw the ball through the basket. (shoots from the top of the key)

shootaround: A short, midday practice session consisting of stretching and skill and shooting drills designed to promote "muscle memory" and reinforce specific tactics between closely scheduled games. Basketball Hall of Fame coach Bill Sharman introduced the now widely used shootaround in 1961 with the ABL Los Angeles Jets, bringing it to the NBA San Francisco Warriors in 1966, and then to his 1971-72 NBA champion Los Angeles Lakers.

shooting clock: A clock that tells the amount of time a team has left to make a shot at the basket under the thirty-

second rule (women's and international amateur play) or twenty-four-second rule (in the NBA). A shooting clock was adopted experimentally in the early 1980s by some college conferences and may ultimately be universally adopted. also *shot clock, thirty-second clock, twenty-four-second clock.*

shoot over the zone: To make shots from the outside in order to force a team to abandon a zone defense and play man-to-man instead.

shot: An attempt to throw the ball through the basket for a score.

shot clock: see *shooting clock.*

shovel pass: An underhand pass used occasionally for short distances.

1. **simulcast:** To simultaneously broadcast a game on radio and television. Chick Hearn, play-by-play announcer for the Los Angeles Lakers began to regularly simulcast Lakers games in 1966, an idea credited to then Laker owner Jack Kent Cooke and subsequently adopted by others.

2. **simulcast:** The simultaneous broadcast of a game on radio and television.

sink: To make a successful shot.

sixth man: The player who normally substitutes first when a starting player must be rested or is in foul trouble, or when a team needs a change of pace.

sky: To jump high and almost sail through the air. (can really sky) also *talk to God.*

skyhook: A high hook shot, released above the level of the basket. The expression was coined by Milwaukee Bucks broadcaster Eddie Doucette in 1969 to describe a shot perfected by NBA superstar Kareem Abdul-Jabbar (then Lew Alcindor) in his first year with the Bucks.

1. **slam dunk:** A particularly forceful dunk shot. The expression was coined by Los Angeles Lakers broadcaster Chick Hearn to describe the technique first popularized by all-time NBA scoring champion Wilt Chamberlain. Because of the increasing incidence of shattered glass backboards, usually the result of a violent slam dunk, in the 1981-82 season the NBA (and some colleges) began to use a hinged, spring-loaded rim, which is designed to give way under a certain amount of pressure, and return when the pressure is released. compare *dunk.*

2. **slam dunk:** To execute a slam dunk.

(gets the rebound and slam dunks for two points) compare *dunk.*

slough off: To leave the opponent one is guarding in order to play a passing lane, double-team, double-team another opponent, or get a good position under the basket for a rebound. also *sag.*

small forward: A forward who is known more for quickness, mobility, and shooting rather than rebounding, unlike the usually larger "power forward."

spread-court offense, spread offense: A control-type offense in which the team with the ball attempts to spread the defense (leaving the middle open for scoring opportunities) by keeping the ball outside or near the perimeters of the frontcourt until the defensive team abandons zone coverage and moves out to cover man-to-man.

stack: An offensive alignment in which the two forwards (or the center and one forward) begin play in the frontcourt from a low post position on one side of the lane with the center (or other forward) at a low post position on the other side of the lane. Occasionally a variation is used with all three players beginning from a low post position on one side of the lane.

1. stall: To attempt to maintain possession of the ball, not for the purpose of scoring, but to prevent the opposing team from gaining possession and having the opportunity to score. Most often a team will stall the ball to protect a lead near the end of a game, but occasionally, when faced with a particularly strong, high-scoring opponent, a team will stall the ball for an entire game in order to keep the score low, and an upset victory within reach. also *freeze.*

2. stall: The act or an instance of stalling the ball. also *freeze.*

stall ball: see *ball control*

1. steal: To take possession of the ball from an opponent by batting it away, or intercepting a pass.

2. steal: The act or an instance of stealing the ball. (makes a steal, and the fast break is on)

steps: see *traveling.*

1. stuff: see *dunk.*

2. stuff: A field goal made by dunking the ball. see *dunk.*

stuff shot: see *stuff.*

stutter step: A momentary change in rhythm or pace (and sometimes direc-

tion) while moving, or a feint in one direction with a quick step and return, in order to "freeze" or confuse an opponent for an instant.

stutter-step: To execute a stutter step. (stutter-stepped, then drove to the baseline)

submarine: see *lowbridge.*

swing: To play or be able to play in two different positions, usually guard and forward. To be a swingman.

swingman: A player who is able to play two different positions on a team. (a swingman who can play at guard or forward)

1. swish: A shot that travels through the basket without hitting the backboard or rim. also *swisher.*

2. swish: To shoot a swish, or swisher. (swished a 10-footer).

swisher: see *swish.*

1. switch: To momentarily change defensive assignments with a teammate or to pick up an open or free man.

2. switch: The act or an instance of switching, or switching off.

T: A technical foul. (picked up a T for unsportsmanlike conduct)

talk to God: To jump high and almost sail through the air. also *sky.*

tap: A tipoff. also *tapoff, tip.*

tapoff: A tipoff. also *tap, tip.*

team foul: Any personal foul (except an offensive foul in the NBA) charged toward the specified number of fouls a team is allowed within a certain period of play before a bonus or penalty situation exists (four in one quarter or three in an overtime period in NBA games, eight, including technical fouls, in one half in international amateur games, six in one half in college and women's games, and four in one half in high school games.

technical foul: A foul committed by a player, coach, or bench personnel that does not involve contact with an opponent, or that involves intentional or flagrant contact with an opponent (such as punching or fighting) when the ball is dead and the clock has stopped, unsportsmanlike conduct (such as profanity, disrespect for an official, illegal substitutions), or (in the NBA only) the use of a zone defense. When a player commits a technical foul in high school, women's, or college play, the opposing team is awarded one free throw, or two free throws if the foul is flagrant or intentional, or if committed by a coach or bench personnel (one free throw for coach or bench personnel in women's basketball). The player or coach is automatically ejected from the game if the foul is flagrant, or if it is his third technical foul. When a player or coach commits a technical foul in the NBA, the opposing team is awarded one free throw, and the ball is returned to the team having possession at the time the foul was called for a throw-in from out of bounds near where play ended. The player or coach is automatically ejected from the game if the infraction is his second technical foul. When a player commits a technical foul in international amateur play, the foul is charged against the player and the team, and the opposing team is awarded two free throws (one free throw if the foul was committed by a coach). Play resumes with a jump ball. In college basketball, the ball is awarded alternately to the teams after a technical foul. also *T.* compare *personal foul, violation.*

ten-second line: The division line when used in conjunction with the ten-second rule. also *time line.*

ten-second rule: A rule that states that a team may not be in continuous control of a ball in its backcourt for more than ten consecutive seconds. If, within ten seconds of inbounding or gaining possession of the ball in the backcourt, a team fails to bring the ball across the division line, a violation occurs, resulting in the loss of the ball to the opposing team for a throw-in from out of bounds near where play stopped. The ten-second rule was introduced in 1937.

thirty-second clock: A clock that tells the amount of time a team has left to make a shot at the basket under the thirty-second rule used in international amateur and women's basketball. When a shot is attempted, or when the opposing team gains possession of the ball, the clock is reset for another thirty seconds. also *shooting clock, shot clock.*

thirty-second rule: A rule in international amateur and women's basketball that requires a team to attempt a shot at the basket within thirty seconds of gaining possession of the ball or putting it in play. see *thirty-second violation.*

thirty-second violation: A violation of the thirty-second rule, resulting in the loss of the ball to the opposing team for a throw-in.

three-point field goal: A field goal made from outside the three-point line, an arc drawn from each baseline, approximately 23 feet from the basket. The three-point field goal was first used by Abe Saperstein (founder of the Harlem Globetrotters) in 1961 in his short-lived professional league, the American Basketball League. The three-point field goal was reintroduced in 1967 by the American Basketball Association, adopted by the NBA in 1978, and tried on an experimental basis by some college conferences in the early 1980s. In time, it may be universally adopted.

three-point line: A 2-inch-wide semi-circular line marked at each end of the court, in games where the three-point field goal is used, by lines extending from the end line 3 feet from and parallel to the sidelines, intersecting an arc of 23 feet, 9 inches from the middle of the basket (23 feet from the basket). Any field goal made from outside the three-point line counts three points. see *three-point field goal.*

three-point play: A situation in which a foul is committed against a player as he shoots and scores. The basket counts, and if the awarded free throw is made, the total is a three-point play.

three-second area, three-second lane: The free throw lane when used in conjunction with the three-second rule.

three-second rule: A rule that states that no offensive player may remain within the free throw lane (between the end line and the outer edge of the free throw line) in the frontcourt for more than three consecutive seconds while his team is in possession of the ball.

three-second violation: A violation of the three-second rule, resulting in the loss of the ball to the opposing team for a throw-in from out of bounds.

thrower-in: The player who inbounds the ball on a throw-in.

throw-in: A method of putting the ball in play from out of bounds (as after a score, a violation, a foul for which no free throws are awarded, or when the ball goes out of bounds) in which a player is given five seconds to pass, roll, or bounce the ball to a teammate from out of bounds. A throw-in begins when the ball is at the disposal of the team or player entitled to it, and ends when the passed ball touches or is touched by an inbounds player other than the thrower-in. If a player is unable to inbound the ball within five seconds, a violation occurs, resulting in the loss of the ball to the opposing team for a throw-in from out of bounds at the point of the infraction.

ticky-tack foul: A questionable or inconsequential foul which could (or should) go uncalled by an official. Los Angeles Lakers broadcaster Chick Hearn coined the expression.

tie ball: A held ball.

time line: see *ten-second line.*

timer: Either of two officials responsible for the operation of game clocks (and shot clocks in international amateur and NBA play), recording and timing time outs, and signaling the beginning and end of a period.

tip: A tipoff. also *tap, tapoff.*

tip in, tip-in: A field goal made from close to the basket by tapping in a rebound or a high-arcing pass or shot.

tipoff: The jump ball at the beginning of a game or a period of play. (wins the tipoff) also *tap, tapoff, tip.*

top of the key: The area behind the free throw line just inside or outside the restraining circle. (the ball goes into the high post at the top of the key)

toss-up: A jump ball.

●●A conflict in which there is no winner, or an even choice between options. (either the apple pie or the chocolate cake, it's a toss-up)

trail official: The official or referee who follows play down the court and takes a position near the division line, with the primary responsibility of signaling if a field goal counts. The trail official shares the responsibility of calling fouls and violations with the lead official. On a fast break, the lead and trail officials usually switch roles. compare *lead official.*

transition: The change from defense to offense after a team gains possession of the ball in its backcourt.

transition game: The ability of a team to change from defense to offense after gaining possession of the ball in the backcourt.

1. trap: 1. To suddenly double-team and

pressure the ball handler in the hopes of forcing a mistake. 2. To pin the ball against the backboard, a violation. see *goaltending.*

2. trap: 1. The act or an instance of trapping the ball handler. 2. The act or an instance of pinning the ball against the backboard, a violation. see *goaltending.*

travel: To take more than the allowed number of steps while holding the ball or at the end of a dribble, or to lift or drag the pivot foot. A traveling violation. see *traveling.*

traveling: A violation in which a player with the ball takes more steps than allowed without dribbling, or at the end of a dribble, or lifts or drags the pivot foot. A traveling violation results in the loss of the ball to the opposing team for a throw-in from out of bounds near where the violation occurred. also *steps, walking.*

triple doubles: Double figures in points, rebounds, and assists in a game by a player. Incredibly, Hall of Famer Oscar "The Big O" Robertson averaged triple doubles for five consecutive seasons for the Cincinnati Royals (30.3 points, 10.4 rebounds, and 10.6 assists per game from 1960-61 through 1964-65).

triple-team: To guard an opponent with three players at the same time.

Trotters: The Harlem Globetrotters.

turnaround jumper: A turnaround jump shot.

turnaround jump shot: A jump shot that a player facing away from the goal pivots toward the basket, jumps, and shoots. also *turnaround jumper.*

turnover: The loss of possession of the ball, whether because of a mistake, a steal, or as a result of a violation.

twenty-four-second clock: A clock that tells the amount of time a team has left to make a shot under the twenty-four-second rule in NBA play. When a shot is attempted, or when the opposing team gains possession of the ball, the clock is set for another twenty-four seconds. also *shooting clock, shot clock.*

twenty-four-second rule: A rule in the NBA that requires a team to attempt a shot at the basket within twenty-four seconds of gaining possession of the ball or putting it in play. The twenty-four-second rule was first adopted by the NBA for the 1954-55 season to combat the slowdown tactics used to freeze the ball and protect a lead. Bitterly opposed at first by some owners, the change proved to be a great success, providing an immediate speed-up in play and placing more emphasis on scoring. see *twenty-four-second violation.*

twenty-four-second violation: A violation of the twenty-four-second rule, resulting in the loss of the ball to the opposing team for a throw-in.

two-handed push: A two-handed shot in which the ball is held above the head and pushed toward the basket with a flick of the wrists. Occasionally used for a short to mid-range jump shot. Nicknamed the "Illinois kiss" around the 1930s (because of the proximity of the ball to the shooter's face), the two-handed push was a specialty of New York Knicks guard (late 1940s to early 1960s) Carl Braun.

two-hand set shot: A shot in which the ball is held with the fingertips of both hands about neck-high with the body slightly crouched, then pushed up and out and released over the head as the legs and body spring straight. Seldom used in modern basketball, except from the outside against a zone defense, when there is sufficient time to get set.

two-shot foul: A personal or technical foul that carries a penalty of two free throws. see *personal foul, technical foul.*

two-time: see *double-team.*

umpire: One of the two officials in international amateur play (one called the "referee" and one called the "umpire" but both commonly referred to as referees) equally responsible for the conduct of a game, and calling fouls and violations.

undercut: see *lowbridge.*

unsportsmanlike conduct: Unfair, unethical, dishonorable, or violent behavior, such as using profanity or abusive language, unfairly distracting or blocking the vision of an opponent, fighting, striking, or physically contacting an official (by a coach or player), etc. Unsportsmanlike conduct is penalized by a technical foul, and, depending upon the nature and severity of the infraction, ejection from the game and possible further disciplinary action by

the league or conference under whose auspices the game is played.

upcourt: To or toward the end of the court containing the basket at which a team is shooting. also *downcourt.*

violation: An infraction of the rules by the team in control of the ball (traveling, stepping out of bounds with the ball, etc.) that results in the opposing team being awarded the ball for a throw-in. compare *personal foul.*

walking: see *traveling.*

1. weave: An offensive strategy in which players move laterally in the frontcourt between the division line and the top of the key in a figure-eight pattern, passing and handing the ball off as they move past each other and edge closer to the basket until a player who is momentarily left unguarded can shoot or drive in toward the basket. A popular strategy in college play in the 1950s, but less effective against modern zone or switching man-to-man defenses.

2. weave: To execute a weave.

white legs: see *white man's disease.*

white man's disease: Locker room humor for a player's lack of speed or jumping ability, originating from vulgar racial stereotyping of athletic or intellectual superiority or inferiority. (a great ball handler, but he has white man's disease) also *white legs.*

wing: 1. A position played by a forward in the frontcourt near the baseline on either side of the lane. 2. A player who plays in the wing position.

yo-yoing: Dribbling the ball continuously in one spot, as one might play with a yo-yo. Coined by broadcaster Chick Hearn.

zone: 1. A specific area of the court a defender is responsible for in a zone defense. 2. A zone defense.

zone defense: A defensive strategy in which each player defends a specific area of the court, rather than an opponent. A defender guards an opponent only when the opponent moves into the area of the zone the defender is assigned to cover. A zone defense is not permitted in NBA games, and its use results in a technical foul. also *zone.*

zone press: A defensive strategy in which close, man-to-man coverage is applied only when the ball or ball handler enters a specific area or zone that a defensive player is assigned to cover. compare *full-court press, half-court press.*

The earliest known evidence of bowling was found in the late 1800s by Sir Flinders Petrie in the tomb of an Egyptian child buried in 5200 B.C. Among the objects unearthed were nine pieces of stone, the "pins," at which a stone "ball" was rolled through an archway made from three pieces of marble.

In the South Sea Islands, an ancient game called *ula maika* was played by the Polynesians, also utilizing balls and pins made of stone. Ironically, the stone targets were placed 60 feet away, the length of a modern bowling alley.

Bowling at pins, as we know it today, originated in ancient Germany, where a pinlike club or *kegel* was carried by men as an all-purpose tool. The kegel was taken everywhere and used as a hammer, a grip and wrist strengthening aid, a cudgel in combat, and as the means by which the piety of religious Germans was periodically tested.

In a Christian ritual practiced in Germany until the fifth century, the kegel was made a symbol of a godless heathen (*heide*) and was stood upright at one end of a church passageway. Then, in front of the faithful, each man was required to knock down his kegel from the other end, by throwing or rolling a small stone.

The pastime of knocking over a kegel—and later, a group of kegels—with a stone evolved within the walls of German monasteries from this ancient rite of "striking down the heathen." By the early Middle Ages, however, the practice had been adopted by laymen all across the country, and gamelike rules developed city by city as the stone was replaced by a round wooden ball, and the kegel by special uniformly shaped pins.

Gradually, a single set of rules evolved, and the number of pins used, which had previously varied greatly, was finally standardized at nine in the early 1500s by Martin Luther, an avid bowler himself.

Bowling at pins had already spread throughout Europe and into England (where it was called kayles or keels) and Scotland (where it was known as kyles). Henry IV had an outdoor alley built in London in the early 1400s. At the time, most alleys were located outdoors and made of beds of clay and mashed cinders. The first specially constructed indoor bowling alley on record was built in 1445 in London.

Lawn bowling was brought to the United States in the early seventeenth century by Dutch settlers and was featured at Old Bowling Green in the Dutch colony of New Amsterdam (now downtown Manhattan). It is believed that the Dutch also introduced pin bowling, though the exact year is not known. The first reference in American literature to bowling at pins was in Washington Irving's *Rip Van Winkle*, published in 1819.

The game of ninepins became popular in the mid-1800s, first in cities with large German populations like New York, Syracuse, Buffalo, Cincinnati, Chicago, and Milwaukee, later spreading throughout New England. Before long, gamblers moved in on the game, and with them came toughs, hustlers, and other shady characters. Finally, the game of "bowling at ninepins" was banned by the Connecticut legislature.

Illegal in one state and generally discredited, the sport began to die out until some anonymous enthusiast led a move to change the number of pins used to ten, thereby creating a "new" game, not in conflict with any state laws.

In 1875, the first attempt to form a national rule-making organization had failed because of differences between regional factions, but on September 9, 1895, delegates from all over the country met in New York City and organized the American Bowling Congress. Within a short time, uniform game rules, alley specifications, and equipment dimensions were agreed upon and established for the game of "tenpins." New materials have been introduced that changed the equipment, but, essentially, the same rules govern the sport to this day.

The first ABC National Championship Tournament was held in Chicago in 1901. It remains the oldest and largest bowling event in the United States.

Though photographs have documented scenes of women bowling as early as the 1880s, the first women's league was formed in 1907 in St. Louis, Missouri, by bowling proprietor and sportswriter Dennis J. Sweeney.

In 1916, Sweeney helped Mrs. Ellen Kelly organize the first women's national tournament, with eight teams entered and championships decided in team, doubles, singles, and all events. The total prize money was $222. Following the tournament, forty women from eleven cities met and created the national organization that, after several name changes, became the Women's International Bowling Congress.

Under the guidance of these two bodies, the sport of bowling once again began to grow in popularity, becoming America's number one indoor sport by the 1940s. By the 1950s, almost 20 million people were bowling in the United States alone.

During the fifties and sixties, television shows like *Make That Spare* and *Jackpot Bowling* brought the sport into the home. New enthusiasts all over the country began to bowl and become aware of the exploits of bowling's superstars, such as Hall of Famers Don Carter (voted Bowler of the Year by the Bowling Writers Association of America in 1953, 1954, 1957, 1958, 1960, and 1962, and named Greatest Bowler of All Time by the writers of *Bowling Magazine* in 1970) and Dick Weber (winner of twenty-six PBA titles, second leading tournament money winner of all time, and voted BWAA Bowler of the Year in 1961, 1963, and 1965).

Founded in 1958, the Professional Bowlers Association (PBA) initiated a professional tournament and championship series, which has provided top-level competition between the best bowlers in the world since 1960. Network television coverage of these events has enabled millions to witness the machinelike precision of bowling "stylists" such as 1973, 1974, 1975, and 1981 PBA National Champion Earl Anthony, the all-time leader in tournament earnings, as well as the "power bowlers" and "big crankers" who have risen to prominence since the mid to late seventies, such as Mark Roth (BWAA Bowler of the Year in 1977, 1978, and 1979), Mike Aulby (PBA National Champion in 1979), Wayne Webb (Bowler of the Year in 1980), Marshal Holman, Kyle Shedd, and Steve Cook.

Because of the number of people who participate in the sport, the language of bowling is colorful, but there are more regional differences and contradictions in the use and meaning of bowling terms than in any other major sport.

action: The rebounding of a pin or pins off the sideboards to hit a pin or pins still standing. (got the last pin with action)

AJBC: see *American Junior Bowling Congress.*

all events: 1. The total score of games bowled by an individual in a tournament, usually three games in the team event, three in doubles, and three in singles matches. The ABC individual tournament record for all events was set in 1974 by Jim Godman of Lorain, Ohio, with a total score of 2,184 (731, 749, 704). 2. The total for the three events by the five members of a team. The Chadwick Studio team of Houston, Texas, set the ABC team all events record in 1980 with a total score of 9,628.

alley: 1. A bowling lane. (rolled down the alley) also *lane.* 2. A building that contains bowling lanes. see *bowling alley.*

American Bowling Congress: The sanctioning body that oversees the playing rules and sets equipment standards for the sport of bowling. Founded in New York in 1895, the American Bowling Congress is now headquartered in Greendale, Wisconsin, and is the world's largest nonprofit membership service organization, with more than 4.8 million members. also *ABC.*

American Junior Bowling Congress: The sanctioning body and service organization for bowlers under the age of twenty-one, co-sponsored by the ABC and the WIBC. Headquartered in Greendale, Wisconsin, with a membership of 800,000. also *AJBC.*

anchor man: The player who bowls last in a team's lineup, usually the best bowler on the team.

apple: 1. The ball. 2. Short for sour apple. see *sour apple.*

approach: 1. The portion of the lane a minimum of 15 feet behind the foul line that the bowler uses to move up in preparation for releasing the ball. also *runway.* 2. The number of steps taken and type of movement a bowler uses preparatory to releasing the ball. The four-step approach is used most frequently, although some bowlers prefer three-step and five-step approaches.

area bowling: A method of aiming a ball in which a three-board wide area surrounding a selected target point (such as the second arrow from the right gutter) is used as a visual guide over which the ball is rolled to reach a desired point of impact (such as the 1-3 pocket). compare *line bowling, pin bowling, spot bowling.*

arrows: The seven triangular sighting targets imbedded in the lane near the foul line, often used to line up the exact point where the ball is released. also *range finders.*

baby split: A split in which the 2 and 7 pins or the 3 and 10 pins are left standing.

backswing: The path of the arm behind the body during the next to last step in a bowler's delivery.

backup, backup ball: A ball that curves in the opposite direction from a hook (that is, toward the delivering hand), thus hitting the pins from the opposite side. also *fade ball, reverse, reverse hook.*

1. balk: To fail to deliver the ball after making an approach.

2. balk: The act or an instance of balking.

ball cushion: The padded back wall of the pit that prevents pins or a ball from bouncing back onto the lane.

ball rack: The raised area beside the approach at the end of the ball return where the ball rests between deliveries.

ball return, ball-return track: The channel alongside (and sometimes under) the lane, inside which (or on, if not enclosed) the ball is returned to the bowler. also *return.*

barmaid: see *one in the dark.*

basket: see *bucket.*

bed: The wood surface of the lane between the foul line and the pit.

bedposts: see *goalposts.*

belly: 1. To roll the ball in a wide-curving

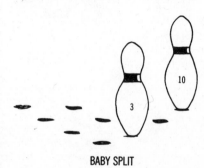

BABY SPLIT

arc. 2. The fat middle part of a bowling pin.

big ball: see *strong ball*.

big cranker: see *cranker*.

big fill: A good pinfall made on the roll immediately after a spare.

big four: A 4-6-7-10 split. also *double pinochle, golden gate*.

big hook: A powerfully delivered ball that breaks sharply toward the pocket with great force. (a power bowler who could deliver a big hook)

blank: A bowling ball that has not yet had finger holes drilled into it.

blind, blind score: The number of points added to a team's score to make up for the absence or disqualification of a team member. The blind is usually the absent player's average minus ten. also *vacancy points, vacancy score*.

block: 1. An oil buildup in the lane (often in the center) that illegally helps guide the ball to the pocket, the result of lane blocking or tampering. 2. One of several series bowled in a tournament or match.

blow: see *miss*.

blow a rack: To roll a strike that clears the deck, leaving no dead wood. (can blow a rack anytime his big hook hits)

board: One of the (usually thirty-nine) wood panels that make up the width of a bowling lane. A bowler may use a particular board as an aiming target in the delivery. A bowler "playing the tenth board" attempts to roll the ball over a designated point on the tenth board from the gutter.

bocci, boccie: A type of bowling game originated and played in Italy between two teams of two players each. Two opposing players face each other at the opposite ends of a dirt court 75 feet in length and 8 feet across, bounded on all sides by vertical boards. The game is begun when one player, chosen by lot, rolls or tosses a small target ball (called a *pallino*) to the opposite end of the court. Then, taking turns with his opponent, the player proceeds to deliver four larger balls at the pallino in an effort to place them nearer to it than the opponent's balls, or to displace the opponent's balls, since points are scored for each ball a team places closer to the pallino than the opponents. When all eight balls have been played from one end, the teammates play from the other end. The game continues in this manner until a designated score is reached (usually twelve points).

body English: Instinctive body contortions made by a bowler after he releases the ball, in an effort to direct the ball toward its intended target.

bonus: Points added to a bowler's score for making a strike or spare. The bonus for a spare is the pinfall from the first ball in the next frame. The bonus for a strike is the pinfall from both the first and second balls in the next frame. The bonus is added to the score for the previous frame's spare or strike, as well as to the score for the frame in which it is rolled.

1. bowl: The delivery of a ball down the

BACKSWING

DELIVERY

lane. (a beautiful bowl for another strike)

2. bowl: 1. To deliver a ball down the alley. (bowled a perfect hook to pick up a spare) 2. To score a particular number of points. (once bowled a 230) 3. To play a game of bowling. (bowls every Saturday night)

•• To be "bowled over" is to be literally or figuratively knocked over or overwhelmed. (bowled over by her generosity)

bowl a line: To participate in one game of ten frames or in a string of games. (haven't bowled a line in over a week)

bowler: A person who bowls.

bowler's thumb: A strained thumb muscle caused by twisting the thumb when removing it from the thumb hole during a delivery.

bowling: A sport in which individuals or teams compete by rolling a hard rubber or plastic ball (weighing up to 16 pounds, with a circumference of up to 27.002 inches) down a 60-foot-long alley in order to knock down ten wooden pins arranged in a triangular setup. The individual or team that accumulates the highest score (knocks down the most pins) wins the game. A game consists of ten periods of play called frames. In each frame the bowler may make two attempts to fell the pins. If the first ball rolled in a frame knocks down all ten pins (a strike), the bowler receives a bonus of the number of pins downed with the next two balls which is added to the score of the frame in which the strike occurred. If all ten pins are knocked down with two balls (a spare), a bonus of the number of pins downed with the first ball of the next frame is added to the score of the frame in which the spare occurred. If a strike or spare occurs in the tenth or final frame, a bonus of the number of pins downed by two extra balls (in the case of a strike) or one extra ball (in the case of a spare) is added to the bowler's score. The maximum score per game (one strike in each frame plus two final bonus strikes) is 300. If a bowler steps over the foul line, or touches anything beyond it during a delivery, the delivery is counted as one of those allowed, but the pins knocked down are not counted in the bowler's score (and are replaced if the foul is commit-

ted on the first ball of the frame). also *kegling, tenpins.* see *bocci, Canadian*

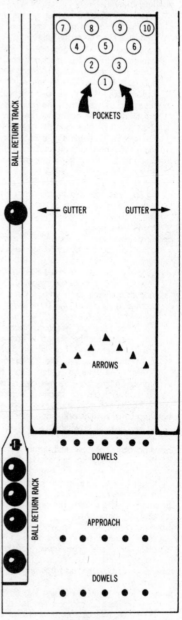

BOWLING ALLEY

fivepins, candlepins, duckpins, lawn bowling.

bowling alley: 1. A long, narrow wooden surface on which a bowler at one end rolls the ball at ten pins arranged in the form of a triangle at the other end. It is comprised of an approach, which extends 15 to 16 feet from one end to a foul line, and a 41 to 42-inch-wide lane, which extends from the foul line 62 feet, 10-3/16 inches to a pit at the other end (60 feet from the foul line to the middle of the headpin). The lane is constructed of pine boards, except for the first 16 feet and the area directly under the pins, which are constructed of maple boards. A gutter runs along each side of the lane to guide errant balls into the pit. also *alley, lane.* 2. A building, or area inside a building that contains one or more lanes for bowling. The first indoor bowling alley was built in 1445 in London.

bowling average: A bowler's average score, calculated by dividing the total number of downed pins (including bonuses) by the number of games bowled over a particular span of time, such as a week or a year. (A bowler scoring a total of 4,300 pins in 20 games has a 215 average.) Nelson Burton Jr. of St. Louis, Missouri, holds the ABC record for the highest tournament bowling average (207.51 in 548 games in twenty-one years). The Professional Bowlers Association record for the highest lifetime bowling average is held by Earl Anthony of Dublin, California (217.56 in 548 games in eleven years).

bowling bag: A small bag made specifically to carry a bowling ball and other equipment.

bowling ball: The ball used in the sport of bowling, weighing up to 16 pounds (minimum 8 pounds), with a 27-inch circumference, and made of plastic or hard composition rubber.

bowling on the green: The game of lawn bowling. also *bowls.*

bowling pin: One of the wooden objects to be knocked down by a bowling ball. also *pin.* see *candlepin, duckpin, tenpin.*

bowls: Lawn bowling. also *bowling on the green.*

box: The space on a bowling score sheet in which to record the score for a single frame. also *double box, frame.* see *score sheet.*

bread basket: see *bucket.*

bread line: A 1-2-4-7 or 1-3-6-10 leave. The name derives from the "line" of pins left standing.

bridge: The distance between the finger holes in a bowling ball, measured from inside edge to inside edge. compare *span.*

Brooklyn: 1. A hit into the pocket opposite the bowler's delivering hand. A ball rolled by a right-handed bowler hits the 1-2 pocket, and a ball rolled by a left-handed bowler hits the 1-3 pocket. also *crossover, Jersey.* 2. A 1-2 pocket hit (on the left side of the pins, with New York and Jersey being on the right side).

bucket: A 2-4-5-8 or 3-5-6-9 leave. also *basket, bread basket, dinner bucket.*

bury: To deliver a perfectly placed ball into the 1-3 pocket (1-2 pocket for left-handed bowlers), most often resulting in a strike. also *pack, pack the pocket.*

Canadian fivepins: A bowling game in which individuals or teams compete against each other by rolling a 5-inch-diameter hard rubber ball with no finger holes down a 3-1/2-foot-wide, 60-foot-long alley in an attempt to knock down five pins (12-1/2 inches high with a strip of rubber around the middle to deaden the force of the ball) arranged in the form of a "V." A player is entitled to three deliveries (if a strike or a spare is not scored before) for each of the ten frames in a game. The bonus for a strike or a spare is the same as in tenpins. In Canadian fivepins, the bowler gets points according to the scoring value of the pins knocked down. The headpin is worth five points, the next two pins are worth three points each, and the rear pins are worth two points each. If a player delivers a ball and commits a foul (touching the foul line or anything beyond the foul line), the pins knocked down are counted, but a penalty of fifteen points is deducted from the final score.

candlepin: A small, almost cylindrical wooden pin (2-3/4 inches in diameter at the middle, tapering to 2 inches in diameter at each end, and 15-3/4 inches high) used in the game of candlepins.

candlepins, candlepin bowling: A bowling game in which players roll a small ball without finger holes (4-1/2 inches in diameter, weighing no more than 2 pounds, 7 ounces) at ten tall, slender pins arranged in the form of a triangle, with a 9-inch space between each pin. The game is played and scored like tenpins, except that a player is allowed up to three deliveries in each of the ten frames in a game, and dead wood is not cleared, but left on the deck to be played. A spare made on the third delivery is worth ten points, and no bonus applies.

carry, carry a rack: To make a strike. (a big hook that is sure to carry)

channel: see *gutter.*

channel ball: see *gutter ball.*

cheesecake: see *pie alley.*

cherry: An error in which the front pin is "chopped" off, or driven back or to the side in such a way that it misses the other pins of a relatively simple leave.

chop: To hit the front pin in such a way that it is driven back or to the side, missing the other pins of a relatively simple leave. also *leave a cherry, pick a cherry.*

Christmas tree: A 3-7-10 split by a right-handed bowler, or a 2-7-10 split by a left-handed bowler. A 1-7-10 leave can also be called a Christmas tree.

Cincinnati: An 8-10 split.

clean game: A game without a miss or a split.

composite average: A bowling average computed for an individual who participates in two or more leagues by dividing the total pinfall in all leagues by the total number of games bowled in all leagues.

conditioner: The special oil applied to the surface of the lane to prepare the lane for play.

conventional, conventional grip: A grip for holding a bowling ball in which the thumb and fingers are inserted into the thumb and finger holes up to the second joint. The conventional is the grip most often used by beginning bowlers because it provides a firm hold and the feeling of a secure release. compare *fingertip grip, semi-fingertip grip.*

convert, convert a spare: To knock down all remaining pins with the second ball to make a spare. also *pick up.*

converted split: A spare made by knocking down the remaining pins of a split with the second ball. see *split.*

count: 1. The pins downed by the first ball of a frame after the frame in which a spare or a strike has been scored. The count determines the bonus points for the previous frame. 2. The failure to knock down all ten pins in any frame. 3. Any frame in which all ten pins have not been knocked down.

cover: To knock down a pin or pins with the second ball in order to convert a spare.

crank: To apply a lot of lift or rotation to a delivery in order to make it hook or curve. see *finger.*

cranker: A power bowler who applies a lot of lift or rotation to deliveries. also *big cranker.*

creeper: A ball that is rolled slowly.

cross alley, cross lane: Across the lane diagonally, at the corner pin at the side of the lane opposite the side on which the ball was delivered. (rolled a perfect cross lane shot at the 7 pin for a spare)

crossover: see *Brooklyn.*

1. curve: A ball rolled in a wide-sweeping arc, an exaggerated (and less controllable) hook. compare *hook.*

2. curve: To roll a curve.

dead ball: 1. A poorly rolled ball that knocks down only a few pins. also *flat apple, flat ball.* 2. A ball which has left the lane at some point before reaching the end and with which no points may be scored, even if pins are knocked down (should the ball bounce out of the gutter).

dead mark: A tenth-frame strike or a spare rolled with the last ball allowed.

dead wood: Overturned pins left on the pin deck after a roll. In tenpins, dead

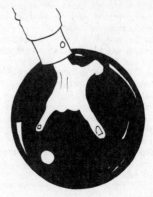

CONVENTIONAL GRIP

wood is removed by the automatic pin spotter, while in candlepins, it is left on the deck and in play.

deck: see *pin deck.*

deliver: To roll a ball toward the pins. also *bowl, roll.*

delivery: 1. The act or action of bowling a ball, including the stance, approach, backswing, and release of the ball. (classic form in his delivery) 2. A bowled ball. (her first delivery yielded a strike) also *roll.*

deuce: 1. A game score of 200. 2. A bowling average of 200.

dinner bucket: see *bucket.*

division boards: The part of the lane where dark and light boards touch.

dodo, dodo ball: An illegally balanced or weighted ball.

dodo split: A 1-7 or 1-10 leave.

dog: The lowest scoring player in a team game and/or a series.

dots: see *dowels.*

double: A pair of consecutive strikes.

double box: see *box.*

double pinochle: see *big four.*

doubles: Two players paired against two other players.

double wood: A leave in which two pins remain standing, one behind the other.

dowels: Wooden pegs imbedded in the approach (usually two sets of five dowels at the rear of the approach, and a set of seven dowels about two inches from the foul line) sometimes used as sighting guides for the delivery. also *dots, spots.*

downswing: The part of the delivery motion after the pushaway, when the ball is brought down with a pendulum swing on the way to the backswing. also *pendulum swing.*

dress the lane: To apply oil or conditioner to the surface of a lane to prepare it for play.

drive: The power or momentum of a ball. (well placed, but not enough drive)

drives: Bowling lanes. (last three drives are all good hooking lanes) also *planks.*

driving ball: A rolled ball that slams into the pocket with power and momentum, causing vigorous pin action.

duckpin: The pin used in duckpins, shaped like a tenpin, but shorter (9-13/32 inches tall, 4-1/8 inches in diameter at the belly, tapering to 1-3/8 inches at the base).

duckpins: A bowling game played with small balls with no finger holes (4-3/4 inches to 5 inches in diameter, weighing from 3 pounds to 3 pounds, 12 ounces, and made of hard composition rubber) and ten duckpins arranged in the tenpin triangle, on a regulation bowling lane. A game consists of ten frames, and each bowler is allowed a maximum of three deliveries in each frame. Tenpins rules govern play, except that no bonus points are added if a spare is made in the third attempt. The game of duckpins was introduced in 1900 by Baseball Hall of Famers John J. McGraw and Wilbert Robinson, co-owners of a bowling alley in Baltimore, Maryland. Baltimore Morning Sun sportswriter Bill Clarke coined the name ''duck pins'' (later duckpins) after McGraw and Robinson, both duck hunters, mused that the pins scattered and flew around like a flock of flying ducks.

dump: To let go of the ball with the thumb and fingers at the same time (instead of with the thumb first) so that the ball does not hook.

Dutch, Dutch 200: A game in which the bowler rolls alternating strikes and spares. The score of a game of Dutch is 200. also *Dutchman.*

Dutchman: see *Dutch.*

English: The spin (around the vertical axis) given a bowling ball by twisting the hand just as the bowler releases the ball.

error: see *miss.*

fade ball: A backup ball.

fast alley, fast lane: 1. A lane whose surface allows the ball to skid more than usual and delays and diminishes hooking action. (West Coast usage) see *holding alley.* 2. A lane that allows a wide hook. (East Coast usage) see *hooking lane.*

Federation Internationale des Quilleurs, FIQ: The sanctioning body for international bowling competition. Divided into three zones (American, Asian, and European), the FIQ has sponsored World Championship tournaments since 1954, and Zone Championship tournaments since 1961. World Championship tournaments for both individual and team competition are scheduled every four years (175 men and 146 women from thirty nations competed at the ninth Championships at Manila, the Philippines, in 1979). The United States has been participating in FIQ World and American Zone Tournaments since 1963.

fence: A row of pins standing after the first roll of a frame.

fenceposts: see *goalposts*.

field goal: A ball rolled between the pins of a split without touching a pin, as a football travels between the uprights in a field goal. also *three points*.

fill: The pinfall of the first ball after a spare, used to compute the bonus for the spare.

fill the woodbox: To make a strike on the final ball of a game. also *load the boat*.

finger: To snap the fingers up at the moment the ball is released in order to impart ''lift,'' a spin or rotation on the ball that will cause it to hook or curve. (fingered the ball for a big hook) also *crank, turn*.

finger holes: The two holes drilled into a bowling ball for the middle and third finger, used in conjunction with the thumb hole to grip the ball.

fingers: see *lift*.

fingertip grip: A grip for holding a bowling ball in which the thumb is inserted all the way into the ball and the middle and third fingers just to the first joint. The fingertip grip provides an experienced bowler the greatest leverage at the point of release, allowing maximum lift and/or turn. compare *conventional grip, semi-fingertip grip*.

five-step approach: A delivery in which an extra shuffle or step is taken (with the foot opposite the side from which the ball is delivered) before the normal four steps that accompany the pushaway, the downswing, the backswing, and the swing forward and release. When the normal starting position is used, the ball is kept stationary during the additional shuffle or step, but some bowlers prefer to start with the ball away from the body, and pull the ball back to the normal position during the shuffle or step. compare *four-step approach, three-step approach*.

flat apple, flat ball: A poorly rolled ball that knocks down only a few pins. also *dead ball*.

flat box: A box on a scoresheet for a frame in which neither a strike nor a spare is scored after two deliveries.

1. foul: The act of stepping on or over or touching the foul line or anything past the foul line during a delivery. When a foul is committed, any points scored are not counted.

2. foul: To commit a foul.

foul line: A 3/8 to 1-inch-wide line across the alley that is 60 feet away from the headpin and separates the lane from the approach.

foundation: A ninth-frame strike.

four horsemen: A 1-2-4-7 or 1-3-6-10 leave.

four-step approach: A delivery in which the first step or shuffle (by the foot on the side from which the ball is delivered) accompanies the pushaway; the second, the downswing; the third, the backswing; and the fourth step or shuffle, the swing forward and release. The four-step approach is the most common

FIVE-STEP APPROACH

form of delivery, and the most preferred by new bowlers.

frame: 1. One of the ten periods of play in a game. also *inning.* 2. A box indicating one period of play on a score sheet. also *box, double box.* see *score sheet.*

fudge shot: A ball that is poorly delivered because of a last moment attempt to make an adjustment when releasing the ball.

full count: A strike on the last ball of a game.

full hit: A ball that hits more of the headpin and less, if any, of the 3 pin (or 2 pin for left-handers) than a perfect pocket hit. compare *light, light hit.*

full roller: A delivery in which the ball is released in such a way (thumb out first,

FOUR-STEP APPROACH

fingers lifted straight up) as to impart a rotation that is almost perpendicular to the direction in which the ball is traveling, causing it to "hook" sharply into the pocket as it nears the pins. compare *full spinner, semi-roller.*

full spinner: A delivery in which the ball is given an undesirable toplike spin as a result of the thumb and fingers being improperly positioned when the wrist is snapped at the point of release. compare *full roller, semi-roller.*

goal posts, goalposts: A 7-10 split. also *bedposts, fenceposts.*

golden gate: see *big four.*

grandma's teeth: A 7-8-10 or 7-9-10 split.

graveyard: 1. A lane that consistently yields low scores. 2. A bowling establishment with lanes that consistently yield low scores.

Greek church: A 4-6-7-8-10 or 4-6-7-9-10 split.

grinder: A rolled ball that hooks or curves powerfully.

grip: The manner in which a bowling ball is held, usually with the thumb, middle, and third finger (some bowlers use only the thumb and middle finger). The three principal grips used are the conventional grip, the fingertip grip, and the semifingertip grip. see *conventional grip, fingertip grip, semi-fingertip grip.*

groove: A slight rut worn into the lane that tends to lead the ball into the pocket.

gutter: A shallow channel that runs along each side of a lane to catch poorly aimed balls and guide them past the pins into the pit. also *channel.*

gutter ball: A poorly aimed ball that rolls into the gutter and past the pins. A gutter ball counts as a turn for the bowler, but scores no points. also *channel ball, dead ball.*

gutter bum: A poor bowler whose deliveries often end up in a gutter.

gutter shot: A delivery that is released at the edge of the lane and rolls parallel to the gutter before veering into the pocket.

half Worcester: A 3-9 or 2-8 split.

handicap: A mutually agreed-upon number of points added to an individual's or team's score in order to permit balanced competition with an opponent or opposing team possessing a greater degree of skill.

hang a pin: To miss an apparent strike, leaving one pin standing.

headpin: The number one pin. also *king-pin*.

heads: The maple planks making up the first 16 feet of a lane forward of the foul line.

high board: A loose or slightly raised board in a lane that can change the direction of a rolled ball.

high hit: A perfectly rolled ball that hits the pocket.

high-low-jack: A 1-7-10 split.

high 30: A series of three ten-frame games.

holding alley, holding lane: A lane whose surface finish allows a ball to skid more than usual and delays and diminishes hooking action. also *fast alley, fast lane* (West Coast usage), *slow alley, slow lane* (East Coast usage), *stiff alley, stiff lane*. compare *fast alley, fast lane* (East Coast usage), *hooking lane, running lane, slow alley, slow lane* (West Coast usage).

hole: see *pocket*.

1. hook: A ball delivered with a cross-lane rotation, which causes it to break sharply towards the pocket as it nears the pins. compare *curve*.

2. hook: 1. To break sharply toward the pocket. (hooks into the pocket) 2. To deliver a hook. (hooks the first ball for a strike)

hooking lane: A lane that allows the ball to break into the pocket. also *fast alley, fast lane* (East Coast usage), *running lane, slow alley, slow lane* (West Coast usage). compare *fast alley, fast lane* (West Coast usage), *holding alley, holding lane, slow alley, slow lane* (East Coast usage), *stiff alley, stiff lane*.

house ball: One of an assortment of balls of various weights and grips at bowling alleys that are available to bowlers who don't own their own balls.

inning: A frame.

inside angle: The path of a ball aimed away from the pocket (to the side) from a starting point left of center (right of center for a left-handed bowler), and that hooks or curves back into the pocket. also *out and in*. compare *outside angle*.

in the bucket: A hit that converts a 2-4-5-8 or 3-5-6-9 pin "basket" or "bucket" leave. (put one in the bucket to pick up a spare in the last frame)

Jersey, Jersey hit: 1. A hit on the side of the headpin opposite the hand that delivers the ball. see *Brooklyn*. 2. A 1-3 pocket hit (on the right side of the pins with Brooklyn being on the left side). also *New York*.

junior ball: A special smaller ball made for young bowlers, weighing between 8

HOOK

and 12 pounds, with the finger holes drilled closer together to fit a small hand.

kegler: A bowler. see *kegling.*

kegling: The sport of bowling. A *kegel* was a club carried by men in ancient Germany. An all-purpose tool, the kegel was taken everywhere and used as a hammer, a grip and wrist strengthening aid, and as a weapon in combat. The kegel assumed a new role when at some point, a priest probably used a parishoner's kegel to dramatically symbolize a heathen and invited him and others to cast stones at it and "strike down the heathen." Soon this ritual was formalized and made a test of the piety of German Christians, and at certain times, each worshiper was required to place his kegel at the end of the long alleylike church passageways and knock it down with a rolled or thrown stone. The ritual was abandoned before the beginning of the Middle Ages, but the practice of rolling a stone at a kegel or group of kegels had already become popular as the earliest form of pin bowling.

kickbacks, kickboards: The side walls that divide the lanes at the pit end.

kingpin: 1. The central or number 5 pin. Originally the central pin in the game of ninepins. 2. The headpin or foremost pin in an arranged set.

●●The central or most important person in a group, or part in an object. (the kingpin of the organization)

lane: The 41 to 42-inch-wide, 60-foot-long area between the foul line and the pit. see *bowling alley.* also *alley.*

lane blocking: Illegally tampering with a lane by building up oil in one place (often near the middle) in order to guide the ball into the pocket.

lawn bowling: A bowling game played by two individuals or two teams of up to four players on a rectangular grass playing area (rink), 33 to 44 yards long by 14 to 19 feet wide. To start the game, one player, chosen by lot, rolls a small target ball (jack) to the opposite end of the rink. Opponents then alternate turns rolling four larger balls (bowls) each (three each in triples, four each in fours matches) in an effort to place them nearer to the jack than the opponents' balls, or to displace the opponents' balls. Points are scored for each ball a team places closer to the jack than the opponents. Rather than being perfectly round, the bowls are biased so they follow a curved path. When each player has rolled the allowed number of bowls, a period of play (end) is concluded, and play begins from the other end. The game continues in this manner until a designated number of points or ends (usually twenty-one) has been played. also *bowling on the green, bowls.*

leadoff: The first player to bowl on a team.

leave: The pins that remain standing after the first ball is delivered. (an easy leave to convert)

leave a cherry: see *chop.*

lift: The spin or rotation imparted to a ball by snapping the fingers up at the moment of release, in order to make the ball curve or hook. (a straight ball with no lift) also *fingers, turn.*

light, light hit: A ball that hits less of the headpin and more of the 3 pin (or 2 pin for left-handers) than a perfect pocket hit. also *thin, thin hit.* compare *full hit.*

lily: see *sour apple.*

line: A ten-frame game. also *string.*

line ball: A ball aimed along an imaginary line. see *line bowling.*

line bowling: A method of aiming a ball in which several target points are sighted along an imaginary line drawn from the starting point to the desired point of impact (such as the 1-3 pocket) during a delivery. compare *area bowling, pin bowling, spot bowling.*

load: The low scorer on a team. (their best bowler, who can more than compensate for the load)

load the boat: see *fill the woodbox.*

loft: To drop or bounce the ball over the foul line. (a beginner who lofted his first two deliveries)

maples: 1. Bowling pins. also *wood.* 2. Bowling lanes.

mark: A ten-point strike or spare.

match play: Direct competition between two bowlers.

miss: The failure to knock down the remaining pins of any leave that is not a split to make a spare. also *blow, error.*

mixer: A delivery with a lot of action, causing the pins to fly around and strike other pins and often resulting in a strike. also *schleifer, sweeper, swisher.*

mother-in-law: The number 7 pin.

move in: To start from or near a center position on the approach. compare *move out.*

move out: To start from or near a corner position on the approach. compare *move in.*

National Bowling Hall of Fame and Museum: The institution honoring the most outstanding individuals in the game of bowling and housing displays that detail the evolution of the sport. The ABC Hall of Fame was founded in 1941. That year ten charter members were inducted: Joseph Bodis, Cleveland, Ohio; Adolph Carlson, Chicago, Illinois; Charlie Daw, Milwaukee, Wisconsin; John Koster, Nyack, New York; Herbert Lange, Watertown, Wisconsin; Mort Lindsey, Stamford, Connecticut; Hank Marino, Milwaukee, Wisconsin; James Smith, Buffalo, New York; Harry Steers, Chicago, Illinois; and Gilbert Zunker, Milwaukee, Wisconsin. Peter Howley of Chicago, Illinois was also elected in 1941, and then later moved to the Meritorious Service section when it was founded in 1963. Inductees for the ABC Hall of Fame are selected annually by ballots voted on by American Bowling Congress officials, bowling sportswriters, and Hall of Fame members. Women are selected for the WIBC Hall of Fame by the WIBC Board of Directors. The Women's International Bowling Congress Hall of Fame was established in 1953. That year the first four inductees were selected: Emma Jeager, Toledo, Ohio; Grace Garwood Hatch, Cleveland, Ohio; Goldie Greenwald, Cleveland, Ohio; and Louise Stockdale, Los Angeles, California. Presently at ABC headquarters in Greendale, Wisconsin, the National Bowling Hall of Fame and Museum is scheduled to move in 1983 to a new location now under construction in St. Louis, Missouri.

New York: A 1-3 pocket hit (on the right side of the pins with Brooklyn on the left side). also *Jersey.*

ninepins: An early German bowling game played much like tenpins without a headpin. It is reported that Martin Luther standardized the number of pins at nine for the game of ninepins.

nose hit: A ball that hits the middle of the headpin.

on a limb: The expression for an anchorman's turn after all teammates have rolled strikes.

one in the dark: A pin that is hidden behind another standing pin. also *barmaid, sleeper.*

open frame: A frame in which a bowler fails to make a strike or spare. (three games in a row without an open frame)

out and in: see *inside angle.*

outroll: To score more pins than an opponent. (outrolled him in the last two games to win the series)

outside angle: The path of a ball released from a point about halfway between the center of the lane and the gutter that stays "outside" until it hooks or curves into the pocket. compare *inside angle, out and in.*

pacer: A noncompeting bowler who takes turns bowling in a tournament with a competitor. This allows the competing bowler to take a normal break between frames and complete his string simultaneously with the other competitors. A pacer's score is not counted in the tournament.

pack, pack the pocket: see *bury.*

part of the building: An expression for a stubborn pin that does not fall.

PBA: see *Professional Bowlers Association.*

pendulum swing: see *downswing.*

perfect game: see *300 game.*

pick a cherry: see *chop.*

picket fence: A 1-2-4-7 or 1-3-6-10 leave.

pick up: To convert a leave.

pie alley: A lane on which strikes and high scores can be made with minimum effort or skill. also *cheesecake, soft alley.*

pin: One of the wooden objects to be knocked down by a bowling ball; a bowling pin, candlepin, duckpin, or tenpin. see *candlepin, duckpin, tenpin.*

pin bowling: A method of aiming a ball in which the desired point of impact (such

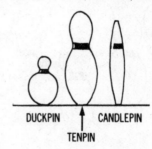

DUCKPIN   CANDLEPIN

TENPIN

as the 1-3 pocket) is sighted during the delivery. Used less frequently than other methods using closer sighting targets because of the difficulty of making accurate adjustments on a target 60 feet away. compare *area bowling, line bowling, spot bowling.*

pinch: To grip the ball hard enough to cause an unnatural delivery.

pin deck: The part of the lane on which the pins rest, made of maple. also *deck.*

pinfall: 1. The pins overturned by one ball or in one frame. 2. The total number of pins knocked down by a bowler in a game or series.

pinsetter, pinspotter: The machine or person responsible for arranging the pins on the deck.

pit: The sunken area at the end of an alley into which the bowling ball and pins fall. Before the days of automatic pinspotters, pinboys would sit and wait atop the rear and side walls of the pit, pulling their legs up to avoid being hit by pins and the ball.

pitch: The angle at which a finger hole is bored into a bowling ball.

planks: Bowling lanes. also *drives.*

play the lane: To adjust the delivery and release point according to the characteristics of the lane (such as a fast lane or slow lane).

pocket: The space between the headpin and the number 3 pin (or number 2 pin for a left-handed bowler). The pocket is the place where a ball can most easily make a strike. also *hole, strike pocket.*

pocket split: A split resulting from a pocket hit, often including the number 5 pin (such as a 5-4, 5-7, or 5-9 split). A pocket split can occur because of not enough turn or drive on the ball or because one or more pins are set slightly off-spot.

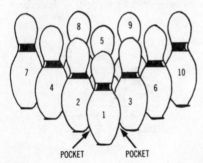

POCKET   POCKET

point the ball: To turn the hand at the moment the ball is released in an effort to aim or "steer" the ball toward the pocket, instead of letting it roll naturally.

powerhouse: see *strong ball.*

power player: A bowler whose deliveries consistently have enough drive and/or lift to produce vigorous pin action.

Professional Bowlers Association, PBA: The sanctioning body that oversees tournament play for professional bowlers, headquartered in Akron, Ohio. Founded in 1958 by Eddie Elias, the PBA considers for membership only bowlers with an average of 190 or better for two years in tournament play. All-time earnings leader and four-time PBA National Champion (1973, 1974, 1975, and 1981) Earl Anthony was the first professional bowler to win thirty PBA titles and earn more than $100,000 in one year (1974). Anthony was also voted Bowler of the Year in 1974, 1975, 1976, and 1981, as well as Bowler of the Decade for the 1970s.

provisional ball: A ball rolled because of an unresolved protest or foul claim on a previous delivery.

provisional frame: A frame rolled because of an unresolved protest on the results of a previous frame.

pull a shot, pull the ball: To unintentionally roll the ball toward the side of the lane opposite the hand that releases it. This occurs when the ball is brought slightly across the body on the swing forward and release, instead of straight ahead.

pumpkin: A weakly delivered ball with little or no hook, usually resulting in a meager pinfall.

punch out: To finish a game with three straight strikes. also *strike out.*

pushaway: The initial hand motion in most deliveries in which the ball is pushed away and forward from the starting position close to the body, just prior to the downswing.

rack: The triangular arrangement of the ten pins. also *setup, triangle.*

railroad split: A difficult split of usually parallel pins, such as a 4-6, 7-9, 8-10, or 7-10 split, or, if not parallel, such as a 4-10 or 6-7 split.

range finders: see *arrows.*

rap: A single pin left standing on a pocket hit, such as a "solid 10" or "ringing 8."

read a lane: To judge, by means of practice rolls, whether a lane is a running lane or holding lane so that adjustments can be made in the delivery.

return: see *ball return.*

reverse, reverse hook: see *backup.*

ringing 8: The 8 pin, left standing on a pocket hit.

rob the cradle: To overturn only one pin of a baby split.

rocking 4: A number 4 pin that wobbles but won't fall over for a strike. The expression is sometimes used for other pins in the same circumstance.

1. roll: To deliver a bowling ball. (rolled a strike in the first two frames) also *bowl.*

2. roll: A delivery. (found the groove with her last two rolls)

rolloff: 1. A match between competing individuals or teams to decide a championship or finishing position. 2. The tenth frame in a game.

roundhouse: A broad curve.

rubberband duckpins: 1. A variation of the game of duckpins in which the pins are encased in rubber, causing them to react differently from hard pins when struck by the ball. 2. The rubber encased duckpins used in the game of rubberband duckpins.

running lane: see *hooking lane.*

runway: see *approach.*

rush the foul line: To reach the foul line too quickly, with the arm and ball still in the backswing. A common fault, particularly with beginning bowlers.

sanctioned competition: Any bowling competition conducted in accordance with ABC or WIBC rules, on lanes and with equipment manufactured and installed to ABC specifications and, in the case of tournaments, handling and disbursing prize funds according to the ABC or WIBC tournament prize formula.

schleifer: see *mixer.*

score sheet: A written record of a bowling game, using the double box system of scoring (in compliance with ABC and WIBC rules), with a large box for each frame and two smaller boxes within (the tenth frame box contains three smaller boxes). The symbols for a strike (an "X"), a spare (a diagonal line), an error (a horizontal line), a split (a circle), and a foul (an "F"), and the number of pins knocked down in any delivery in which one of the symbols is not used (and inside the split symbol) are marked inside the small boxes. A running tally of the bowler's score (including any bonus points for the next one or two deliveries) is marked inside the large box.

scratch: A bowler's actual score, without any handicap.

semi-fingertip grip: A grip for holding a bowling ball in which the thumb is inserted all the way into the ball and the middle and third fingers somewhere between the first and second joint. Since the depth of the fingers can vary in a semi-fingertip grip, a slightly different feel and release occasionally results. compare *conventional grip, fingertip grip.*

semi-roller, semi-spinner: A delivery in which the ball is released in such a way (thumb out first, fingers rotated counterclockwise) as to impart a cross-lane rotation, causing it to "hook" into the pocket as it nears the pins. compare *full roller, full spinner.*

settee: The area where bowlers sit and await their turn.

setup: The triangular arrangement of the ten pins. also *rack, triangle.*

short pin: A pin that falls and rolls, but overturns no other pins.

sidearm: An incorrect delivery in which the ball is brought forward to the point of release too far away from the body

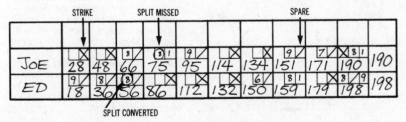

SCORING

instead of with the normal underhand motion. The result is usually an inaccurate delivery.

skittle: One of nine various shaped wooden pins, 14-1/2 inches high, 3 inches in diameter at the base, and 6-3/4 inches in diameter at the widest point, used in the game of skittles.

skittles: A bowling game in which an even number of individual players up to twenty-four, or two teams of up to five players each, take turns tossing or bowling a 4-1/2 to 5-inch wood or molded rubber ball, or a thick, flat hardwood disk (cheese) weighing between 10 and 12 pounds, at nine wooden skittles of various shapes positioned so as to form a diamond at the other end of an alley 21 feet long and 3 feet wide. One point is scored for each skittle knocked over. Each player has a turn of three throws (a chalk), and if a player knocks down all nine skittles before the third throw, they are set up again. Three chalks from each player constitute a "leg." At the end of a leg, scores are compared and the side with the higher total wins that leg. A match is the best of three legs.

sleeper: see *one in the dark.*

slow alley, slow lane: 1. (West Coast usage) A lane that allows the ball to hook into the pocket. see *hooking lane.* 2. (East Coast usage) A lane whose surface allows the ball to skid more than usual, and delays and diminishes hooking action. see *holding alley.*

small ball: A ball that will only cause a strike if it hits straight into the pocket, since it has little rotation or turn. also *squash.*

soft alley: see *pie alley.*

solid: 1. A resounding hit in the strike

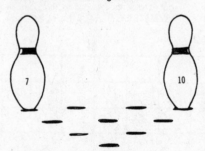

7-10 SPLIT

pocket that, nevertheless, occasionally leaves a corner pin standing. (a solid pocket hit) 2. A corner pin (7 or 10) left standing on a resounding hit in the strike pocket. (looked like a strike all the way, but hung a solid 10 pin)

sour apple: A 5-7-10 split. also *apple, lily.*

span: The distance between the thumb hole and a point halfway between the finger holes in a bowling ball. compare *bridge.*

spare: A total pinfall of ten pins made with both balls rolled in one frame. When a bowler scores a spare, a bonus equal to the pinfall of the first ball of the next frame is added to the bowler's score in the frame in which the spare occurred.

spare break: A leave (such as 1-3, 1-2, 5-8, 5-9, etc.) that can easily be converted.

spiller: A lucky strike that results from a less than ideal delivery.

1. split: One of numerous combinations of pins left standing after the first delivery (not including the headpin), with a pin down immediately ahead of or between them.

2. split: To roll a ball that results in a split.

spot bowling: A method of aiming a ball in which a specific target point (such as a certain arrow or another spot closer or farther away) is used as a visual guide over which the ball is rolled to reach a desired point of impact (such as the 1-3 pocket). compare *area bowling, line bowling, pin bowling.*

spots: see *dowels.*

spread eagle: A split in which the 2, 3, 4, 6, 7, and 10 pins remain standing.

squash: see *small ball.*

steal: A lucky and unexpected pinfall after a poor delivery.

stepladder: A series in which a bowler improves his score by one pin in each game or by ten pins in each game.

stick, stick at the line: To falter or stumble on the last step in a delivery because of unwanted traction during the shuffle or slide forward. When a bowler "sticks," he or she will most often "pull the ball" on the release and miss the desired impact area.

stiff alley, stiff lane: see *holding alley.*

straight ball: A ball delivered with little or no hook, rarely resulting in a strike unless perfectly placed and often producing a difficult split.

1. strike: The knocking down of all ten pins on the first delivery. If a bowler rolls a strike, a bonus of the number of pins downed with the next two balls is added to the bowler's score in the frame in which the strike occurred.

2. strike: To roll a strike. also *carry, carry a rack.*

strike artist: A bowler who often scores strikes.

strike out: To score three consecutive strikes in the tenth frame of a game. also *punch out.*

strike pocket: see *pocket.*

string: 1. Ten frames, a game. In some areas, three strings constitute a series. 2. Three or more consecutive strikes.

stroke: The swing forward and follow through in a delivery.

strong ball: A powerful delivery that produces enough action to accomplish a strike virtually anywhere it hits the pins. also *big ball, powerhouse.*

stuff ball: A well-placed delivery that has a great deal of spin or turn.

sweep: 1. The sweep bar. 2. Three straight victories against an opponent in a three-game series. 3. A total score higher than the opposing team's in a three-game series.

sweep bar: The part of an automatic pin setting device that removes fallen pins from the deck after the first ball and remaining pins after the second ball. also *sweep.*

sweeper: 1. see *mixer.* 2. A tournament for individual bowlers, often of short duration. (a weekend sweeper)

swisher: see *mixer.*

tandem: A two pin leave, one behind the other.

tap: An seemingly strong pocket hit that knocks down all pins but one.

tenpin: The pin used in the game of tenpins, 15 inches high, and shaped like a bottle with a diameter of 2 inches at the base and approximately 4-3/4 inches at the thickest point where the ball strikes (4-1/2 inches above the base). Approved pins are made of laminated hard maple, covered with a plastic coating, and fitted with a plastic base or one of synthetic or non-wood materials. Plastic coated woodcore pins weigh from 3 pounds, 2 ounces to 3 pounds, 10 ounces. Synthetic or non-wood pins weigh from 3 pounds, 4 ounces to 3 pounds, 6 ounces.

tenpins: The modern game of bowling. see *bowling.*

thin, thin hit: see *light.*

300 game: A game in which twelve consecutive strikes are rolled, scoring 300 points. The first ABC award for a 300 game was made to A.C. Jellison of St. Louis, Missouri, for a game rolled on December 15, 1908. In 1913, William Knox of Philadelphia, Pennsylvania, became the first bowler to roll 300 in an ABC championship. Elvin Mesger of Sullivan, Missouri, holds the all-time record for ABC sanctioned 300 games (twenty-seven), as well as the record for the most ABC sanctioned 300 games in one season (eight in the 1966-67 season). also *perfect game.*

three points: see *field goal.*

three-step approach: A delivery in which the pushaway and downswing are combined as the first step is taken (with the foot opposite the side from which the ball is delivered), the backswing is completed during the second step, and the ball is brought forward and released as

THREE-STEP APPROACH

the third (sliding) step is taken. The three-step approach demands a quick movement with the pushaway and downswing (creating the possibility of a physical strain on the hand) and speeds up the tempo of the swing and steps, but provides one less chance for a physical or mental error than the more common four-step approach. compare *five-step approach, four-step approach.*

1. track: 1. A path on a lane to the pins, created by many balls previously rolled in the same area. 2. A worn area on the surface of a ball from many repetitions of the same release and spin.

2. track: To roll down a track.

triangle: 1. The triangular arrangement of the ten pins. also *rack, setup.* 2. A three-pin leave that forms a triangle, such as the 1-2-3, the 2-4-5, the 3-5-6, etc.

trip 4: A late falling 4 pin on a strike, often resulting from the 2 pin rebounding off the kickback.

triple, triple header: see *turkey.*

turkey: Three consecutive strikes. The expression originated in the late 1800s, when scoring was more difficult and to get three strikes in a row was a remarkable accomplishment. Around Christmas and Thanksgiving, bowling alley proprietors began to offer a live turkey to the first man on a bowling team to score three consecutive strikes. also *triple, triple header.*

1. turn: see *lift.*

2. turn: To apply lift or rotation to the ball at the moment of release. see *finger.*

twenty board: The center of the lane or approach area, approximately twenty boards from the side.

two teen: A 200 game in which the score is between 213 and 219.

up the hill: Into the strike pocket. The expression is used by bowlers to "coax" a ball into the pocket.

vacancy points, vacancy score: see *blind.*

wallshot: A roll that benefits from a pin or pins rebounding off the kickbacks to knock down more pins.

washout: A difficult leave of the 1, 2, and 10 pins, or 1, 2, 4, and 10 pins (1, 3, and 7 pins, or 1, 3, 6, and 7 pins for left-handed bowlers). Not a split.

WIBC: The Women's International Bowling Congress.

Women's International Bowling Congress: The sanctioning body and service organization that conducts tournaments and oversees playing rules for women's bowling. Founded in St. Louis in 1916, the Women's International Bowling Congress is now headquartered in Greendale, Wisconsin, and is the world's largest sports organization for women, with a membership of 4.2 million. The Women's International Bowling Congress Championship tournament is now the largest women's sports event in the world. also *WIBC.*

wood: Bowling pins. (a big ball that sent a lot of wood flying) also *maples.*

Woolworth: A split that leaves the 5 and 10 pins standing.

Worcester: A split leaving all but the 1 and 5 pins.

working ball: A ball rolled into the pocket with enough turn and drive to produce a strike. (won the game with a working ball on his last roll)

The earliest record of boxing as a sport was found in a temple in Khafaja near Baghdad, Iraq. There, a stone slab dating back to the fifth millennium B.C. clearly shows two fighters boxing, their hands wrapped with pieces of leather: the first crude boxing gloves.

Ancient Mycenaean and Minoan civilizations enjoyed the sport, the latter evidenced beautifully by a vase discovered at Hagia Triada on the island of Crete. Minoan boxers are portrayed on the vase, which dates back to 1600 B.C.

It was the Greeks of later years, however, who took the greatest interest in boxing. Homer's *Iliad* tells of a famous boxing contest between Epeus and Euryalas at the funeral games of Patroclus, killed in the final days of the siege of Troy, now thought to have occurred in the fourteenth century B.C. Greek boxers, from this period until the end of the fifth century B.C., had their hands and forearms wrapped with "soft gloves," 10 to 12-foot-long thongs of ox-hide, sometimes dressed with fat to make them supple. Greek boxers resembled their modern counterparts to a surprising degree. They fought two-handed, cocking the right hand high with the left slightly extended, and trained with meal or sand-filled leather punching bags. References to knockouts and cauliflower ears by both Homer and Plato attest to the punching power of the Greeks, presumed to be mostly heavyweights in the absence of actual weight divisions. Some historians believe the word "boxing" comes from the Greeks' comparison of the clenched fist with a box (*pyxis*).

The rules for Olympian boxing were drawn up in 688 B.C. by Onomastus of Smyrna, the first boxing champion at Olympia. According to Diogenes Laertius, the first scientific boxer was Pythagoras of Samos, who was champion at the Olympia games in 588 B.C. and possibly an uncle of the mathematician-philosopher Pythagoras.

The greatest Greek boxer of them all was Theogenes of Thasos. After winning at Olympia in 480 B.C., it is claimed that Theogenes remained undefeated for twenty-two years, winning over 1,400 matches. With his awesome record and reputation, undoubtedly some of Theogenes' victories were barely contested. Greek jargon for such a walkover was *akoniti*, a "victory without dust."

Early in the fourth century B.C., boxers began to use "sharp gloves" (*sphairi*), still made of leather thongs, but with a hard leather ring with sharp edges over the knuckles. The sport took a turn toward violence, a trend that would continue when the conquering Romans introduced the *caestus* (cestus), a thong handwrapping that included bits of lead and sharp pieces of metal projecting from the knuckles.

Soon the sporting aspect of boxing gave way to the bloody gladiatorial spectacles favored by the Romans. By the first century B.C., first the cestus, then boxing itself were prohibited, and the sport would not surface again in history or literature for some seventeen hundred years, except, ironically, in one report which raises the possibility of a link between boxing and a canonized saint of the Catholic church.

In Siena, Italy, in the early thirteenth century, a priest (later St. Bernardine) is alleged to have taught his male parishoners the art of fisticuffs as an alternative to dueling and served as the referee for these contests of honor. Some believe that Bernardine's special instructions for "boxing up" (blocking with the hands and arms) an opponent's punches were the origin of the word "boxing."

In the seventeenth century, English men began to settle differences with fists as well as knives and cudgels, some even betting on the outcome. Eventually, as many of these crude anything-goes contests were fought for "purses" as for anger, honor, or ego. Thus, England, and particularly London, soon became the center of "prize fighting."

By 1719, one young man had begun to emerge as England's best fighter. At the age of twenty-four, James Figg had won fifteen consecutive fights. Though handy with weapons and a good wrestler, it was Figg's devastating punches that won fights and a reputation for him. All of London began to hear of the pugilist James Figg and his "Figg Fighting."

Because of his following, Figg was able to open a boxing academy, called Figg's Amphitheater, where he staged fights and taught wrestling and boxing, and was always prepared to accommodate any challenger. James Figg, the first heavyweight champion, retired undefeated at the age of thirty-five and died ten years later, in 1740, of pneumonia.

Three years later, another famous English fighter and teacher, Jack Broughton, framed the first set of rules to civilize the sport. Broughton's rules forbade hitting below the waist, hair pulling, and hitting a downed man, and they allowed a fighter thirty seconds of rest before having to return to the square drawn in the center of the fighting area to "toe the line." Regarded as the father of boxing, Broughton also invented padded leather boxing gloves, which he allowed his young noblemen students to wear while sparring.

In 1838, Broughton's code formed the basis of the London Prize Ring Rules, which, with revisions, were to regulate prize fighting until its final evolution from bareknuckles to boxing fifty years later. London Prize Ring Rules called for a 24-foot-square ring, specified the end of a "round" to be whenever a fighter hit the floor, and replaced Broughton's chalked square with a line drawn at the center of the ring (the scratch line). To avoid defeat by being "knocked out of time," a downed fighter had eight seconds after the thirty-second rest allowed, to come "up to scratch" unassisted.

The first recorded bareknuckle fight in the United States was in New York in 1816. In that contest, Jacob Hyer defeated Tom Beasly, who was forced to retire in the second round with a broken arm. The first big international fight took place in 1860 at Farnborough, Hampshire in England. American "champion" John Carmel Heenan and English champion Tom Sayers fought forty-two grueling rounds before the match ended controversially as a draw because of crowd interference.

In 1865, John Sholto Douglas, the ninth Marquis of Queensberry, sponsored a set of rules framed by John Graham Chambers, which were to become the basic rules for modern boxing. They called for a 20-foot-square ring, three-minute rounds with a one-minute rest in between, padded gloves, a ten-second count for a downed boxer, and outlawed wrestling, gouging, and clinching.

In England, bareknuckle fights, though often illegal, had gained a wide following, particularly among the gentry, who were called the "fancy" (later shortened to form the word "fan"). However, the sport was largely ignored in America, and the few who did attend early matches spent as much time looking out for the police as they did watching the fights.

When John L. Sullivan became the bareknuckle world heavyweight champion in 1882 by knocking out Paddy Ryan in nine rounds, his victory went almost unnoticed. But Sullivan had the answer. In a bold and clever move with far-reaching consequences for the sport of boxing, he began to tour the country with a theatrical troupe, performing boxing exhibitions on stage with gloves and under Queensberry Rules (thereby, neatly sidestepping the police, who were more tolerant of gloved matches and the new rules).

The public responded, and Sullivan's reputation grew, especially after he abandoned his regular sparring partners and began challenging all comers in each city. Across the country, people flocked to theaters to see Sullivan flatten the local bruisers, who were offered $500 if they could last four rounds with him. Though still officially banned in most states, boxing was becoming popular, and "The Great" John L. Sullivan was its biggest attraction.

By 1885, Sullivan not only held the bareknuckle title, but claimed the first Queensberry heavyweight championship, after defeating Dominick McCaffrey in six rounds. In 1889, in the last bareknuckle championship fight, John L. Sullivan defeated Jake Kilrain by a knockout when Kilrain was unable to answer the bell for the seventy-sixth round.

In 1892, Sullivan lost the heavyweight title (Queensberry) to James J. Corbett in New Orleans, by a knockout in the twenty-first round.

In 1896, New York became the first state to sanction boxing matches, followed shortly thereafter by Nevada. But the New York law was changed and revoked. For years, bouts could be held, but for ten rounds only, and no decision could be rendered. Until the Walker Law (sponsored by Speaker of the New York Senate James J. Walker) legalized boxing in 1920, all decisions in fights not ending by a knockout were made by boxing writers.

In 1904, boxing was included in the Olympics at St. Louis, though there were few foreign entries, and the United States boxers won all eight gold medals. The year before, Englishman Bob Fitzsimmons, who had won the heavyweight title from Corbett in 1897 (the first title fight ever filmed), and lost it in 1899 to James J. Jefferies, won the world light heavyweight championship to become the first boxer ever to win titles in three divisions (he had won the middleweight championship in 1891).

George "Little Chocolate" Dixon had become the first black world champion when he claimed the bantamweight title in 1890. In 1908, Jack Johnson became the first black heavyweight champion, knocking out Tommy Burns in fourteen rounds. A superb defensive fighter, Johnson was the subject of controversy during his seven-year reign. His arrogance, womanizing, and well-publicized trouble with the law only served to infuriate those who raised the racial cry for a "white hope" to topple him. Finally, in 1915 in Havana, Cuba, 6-foot, 6-1/4-inch, 240-pound Jess Willard knocked out Johnson in the twenty-sixth round to win the heavyweight championship and a reputation as the "great white hope."

In 1921, heavyweight champion Jack Dempsey (he had taken the title from Willard in 1919) knocked out Georges Carpentier in four rounds. It was the first title fight ever broadcast on the radio and the first fight ever to gross over one million dollars. Boxing was becoming big business, and by the middle twenties, most states had legalized the sport and banded their commissions together under the National Boxing Association for the purpose of jointly recognizing weight divisions, suspensions, and champions. The New York State Athletic Commission continued to act independently and, consequently, there was often more than one champion in some of the weight divisions. This unfortunate condition exists even today with the two rival professional sanctioning bodies, the World Boxing Association, an outgrowth of the old NBA, and the World Boxing Congress, set up in 1963 as an opposing voice to the WBA.

In spite of political maneuvering and occasional scandals, boxing's popularity grew, and by 1937, Joe Louis had become heavyweight champion. He would hold the title until 1949, longer than any other man. Late in 1937, Henry Armstrong won the featherweight championship. It was the first of three titles he would win within a year (welterweight, May, 1938, and lightweight, August, 1938), becoming the only man in the history of boxing to hold three world championships simultaneously.

After retiring undefeated in 1949, Joe Louis tried unsuccessfully to take back the heavyweight crown from Ezzard Charles in 1950. It was the first fight shown on closed-circuit television, a medium that, in the 1970s and 1980s, would make millionaires out of boxers and promoters.

In the late 1940s and early 1950s, great champions like welterweight and middleweight king Sugar Ray Robinson (some say the all-time greatest "pound-for-pound", an expression coined to describe him) and undefeated heavyweight champion Rocky Marciano dominated the sport.

In 1964, boxing fans greeted a new champion who would single-handedly raise boxing to new heights and would ultimately become one of the two most popular athletes in the world, challenged only by soccer's legendary Pele. The 1960 Olympic Light Heavyweight Champion, Cassius Clay, knocked out the seemingly invincible Sonny Liston to become World Heavyweight Champion at the age of twenty-two.

Brash and controversial, Clay adopted the Muslim name Muhammad Ali and refused to fight in the Vietnam War on religious and moral grounds, braving a possible jail sentence. Though ultimately he would emerge a hero, Ali's position was a courageous and unpopular stand at the time. At the physical prime of his life, Ali was prevented from fighting in 1968 and 1969. In 1971, Ali lost a fifteen-round decision to the new heavyweight champion, Joe Frazier. In 1973, he became only the second man in boxing history to regain the heavyweight title when he knocked out George Foreman in eight rounds. (In 1960, Floyd Patterson had regained the title he lost the previous year to Ingemar Johansson.) Then, incredibly, in 1978 at the age of thirty-six, Ali became the only man ever to regain the heavyweight championship twice when he lost and regained the title from 1976 Olympic light heavyweight champion Leon Spinks.

In the early 1980s, another Olympic gold medalist (1976), with the help of closed-circuit television, emerged as the greatest money-winner of all time, out-earning even Ali who set all previous records. Bright, charismatic, and able Sugar Ray Leonard took the world welterweight championship from Wilfred Benitez in 1979 and lost and regained it in 1980 from seven-year lightweight title holder Roberto Duran. Leonard won the junior middleweight championship from Ayub Kalule in 1981, and then unified the welterweight title by defeating WBA welterweight champion Thomas Hearns, before retiring in 1982.

As one of the oldest sports in the history of mankind, it is fitting that boxing has made one of the largest and most colorful contributions to our spoken language.

AIBA: The Association Internationale de Boxe Ameteur.

Ali shuffle: A rapid series of changes in the lead foot of the boxing stance. The invention of three-time heavyweight champion Muhammad Ali in the mid-seventies. Ali used the showy technique more to gain a psychological advantage than a physical or tactical advantage.

answer the bell: To resume fighting when the bell rings for the next round. If a boxer is unable to answer the bell, he is declared the loser by a knockout in that round. (took so many punches in the eighth round, he couldn't answer the bell for the ninth)

●●To resume or continue an activity. (won't be able to answer the bell tomorrow if he stays out too late)

apron: The section of the ring floor that extends approximately 2 feet outside the ropes.

arm puncher: A boxer who uses only the

strength of the arms rather than the whole body in his punches.

arm weary: Fatigued in the arms from throwing punches, no longer able to punch or defend properly. also *punched out.*

Association Internationale de Boxe Ameteur: The sanctioning body formed in 1946 to control and oversee international amateur boxing.

babyweight: 1. Any weight division below lightweight. (a card of babyweight fights) 2. A boxer whose weight classes him below the lightweight division.

backpedal: To retreat or back up in the ring. (backpedalled after taking a straight right to the chin)

●●To literally or figuratively retreat or back up from someone or something. (backpedalled until he could think of an answer)

bag: A punching bag. Either a heavy bag, speed bag, or double-end bag.

bagged fight: A fight that is fixed, the outcome illegally decided before the match takes place. also *tank job.*

bandage: To apply the protective gauze bandages to a boxer's hands. also *wrap.*

bandages: The 1-1/2 to 2-inch protective gauze wrappings that are placed over a boxer's hands and taped at the wrist. also *wrapping.*

bang: To punch hard. (not much of a boxer, but he can really bang) also *belt, bomb, slug.*

banger: see *slugger.*

bantam: Bantamweight. also *banty.*

bantamweight: 1. The 118 pound weight division (119 pounds in amateur boxing. also *bantam, banty.* 2. A boxer who fights in the bantamweight division. Originally the smallest weight division (105 pounds, then 112, 115, and finally 118 pounds), bantamweight boxers were called "bantams" or "little chickens." Early records are incomplete, but in 1856, American Charlie Lynch claimed the world bantamweight title after defeating British boxer Simon Finighty in forty-three rounds. Lynch retired undefeated in 1861 and the division was inactive until 1887. Though several fighters claimed supremacy, no clear champion emerged until 1890 when George "Little Chocolate" Dixon claimed the title. Dixon, the first black world champion, held onto the title until

1892 when he outgrew the division. He was elected to the Boxing Hall of Fame in 1956. also *bantam, banty.*

banty: Bantamweight. also *bantam.*

beat a tattoo: To pummel an opponent or score repeated hits. also *pepper, tattoo.*

●●To hit repeatedly. (beat a tattoo on the conga drum)

beat the count: To get up before being counted out.

●●To recover from a serious problem or illness. (broke his back, but he beat the count and is walking today)

beat to the punch: To score with a punch faster than or before an opponent can land one of his own. (making use of his great hand speed and consistently beating the challenger to the punch)

●●To act faster than another. (was well qualified for the work, but someone beat him to the punch and got the job)

bell: A bell that is rung to mark the beginning and end of each round.

●●The beginning or end of an activity or period of time. (may seem confused now, but when the bell rings, she'll be ready to present her case)

belly jab: A straight jab to the abdomen.

below the belt: Below an imaginary line drawn across the body at the top of the hipbones. A punch delivered below this line is a foul, resulting in the loss of points, the round, or disqualification if repeated, depending upon the sanctioning body of the match. also *south of the border.* see *low blow.*

●●Unfair or cowardly. (tried to influence the vote with below the belt smear tactics)

belt: 1. To deliver a powerful punch. also *bang, bomb, connect, nail, slug, tag.* 2. see *championship belt.*

big: Particularly powerful. (ended the fight with a big right hand in the ninth round)

big bag: see *heavy bag.*

bleeder: A boxer who cuts easily.

bob and weave: To move the head and upper part of the body back and forth and up and down, becoming a moving target that is difficult to hit.

body punch: A punch delivered to the abdomen or ribs. Effective body punches tend to weaken an opponent and/or cause an opponent to lower his guard, leaving the chin unprotected.

body puncher: A boxer who specializes in body punches.

bolo, bolo punch: An uppercut that is delivered from a point below the hip with an exaggerated pendulum swing and the arm extended. The bolo punch was popularized by Boxing Hall of Fame member and World Middleweight Champion (1939, 1940) Ceferino Garcia, who compared its sweeping underhand delivery with the path of a bolo knife used to cut through the jungles of his native country, the Philippines. Cuban sensation Kid Gavilan, World Welterweight Champion in 1952, 1953, and 1954, also frequently made use of the bolo punch.

1. bomb: A powerful punch. also *haymaker, Sunday punch*.

2. bomb: To throw a bomb. see *belt*.

bomber: see *slugger*.

bout: A boxing match that consists of a specified number of three-minute rounds (usually three to fifteen) and ends in a decision by the referee and/or the judges, or by a knockout or technical knockout. also *fight, prizefight*.

box: 1. To engage in the sport of boxing. also *fight*. 2. To practice the skills of boxing, defensive as well as offensive, instead of just slugging.

boxer: 1. One who engages in the sport of boxing. also *fighter, gladiator, prizefighter, pug, pugilist*. 2. One who possesses the offensive and defensive skills of boxing as opposed to just being a slugger. (just a fair puncher, but a skillful boxer)

boxing: A sport in which two opponents fight each other with fists (covered with protective gloves) for a specified number of three-minute rounds (three to fifteen, with one-minute rest periods in between) inside a usually elevated "ring" (a square canvas-covered mat enclosed by ropes strung from posts in each corner). Boxers attempt to score points by hitting the opponent above the waist on the front or the sides of the body and the head with the knuckle part of the gloved hands. One referee in the ring presides over a boxing match making sure that all blows are fair, separating the boxers when they clinch, giving the count in case of a knockdown, and sometimes (depending on the sanctioning body and location of the match) assisting the judges in scoring the match. A boxing match can be won by a decision (the winner of a round being awarded a specified maximum number of points depending upon the sanctioning body and location of the match, and the loser a fewer number of points), by a technical knockout (when the referee stops a match because the opponent is injured or unable to continue), or by a knockout (when an opponent is unable to get up after being knocked down before a count of ten, measured by a timekeeper and given out loud by the referee). To insure fair competition, boxing matches are conducted in weight divisions, the parameters of which vary according to the sanctioning body. Some historians believe the term "boxing" came from the Greeks (some of the earliest practitioners of the sport) and their comparison of the clenched fist with a box (*pyxis*). Others attribute the origin to a priest in Siena, Italy, who was later canonized as St. Bernardine. Early in the thirteenth century, Bernardine is alleged to have taught his male parishoners to fight with their fists rather than deadly weapons, emphasizing special techniques to "box up" (block) an

BOLO PUNCH

opponent's punches with the hands and arms.

boxing gloves: Padded leather-covered mitts (having one section for the thumb and another for the four fingers) with laces on the inside of the wrist, worn to somewhat cushion the blows to an opponent, as well as to protect a boxer's hands. "Thumbless" gloves, which considerably lessen the chances for eye injuries, were introduced in 1981. British boxing pioneer Jack Broughton invented modern boxing gloves in the mid-1700s. For training and sparring, Broughton fitted padded leather gloves ("mufflers") on the hands of the young noblemen to whom he taught the science of pugilism. Eight-ounce gloves are now used in amateur bouts. In professional boxing, six, eight, and ten-ounce gloves are used, depending upon the sanctioning body, the weight division, and the location of the boxing match. also *gloves*.

breadbasket: The belly or abdomen.

1. break: To withdraw from a clinch when so ordered by a referee.

2. break: The withdrawal from a clinch when so ordered by a referee.

break clean: To separate from a clinch without throwing a punch. It is a foul to throw a punch after being ordered to break from a clinch, resulting in a loss of points or disqualification.

brittle chin: see *glass chin*.

bum: An unskilled or no longer skilled boxer. also *chump, ham, ham-and-egger, palooka, stiff, tomato can*.

bust up: A slang expression meaning to inflict or suffer cuts on the face during a boxing match. (got the decision, although he was all busted up)

busy fighter: A boxer who moves constantly and throws a lot of punches.

1. butt: To use the top of the head for striking an opponent. To butt an opponent intentionally is a foul that can result in a loss of points or disqualification.

2. butt: The act or an instance of butting an opponent. also *head butt*.

button: The point of the chin. In use since the 1920s. (took a straight right to the button)

●●The expression "on the button" means in the exact spot or at the exact moment in time. (called at seven o'clock on the button)

can't break an egg: Has no power in his punches; can't punch.

●●Has no power or strength. (looks big, but he can't break an egg)

can't lay a glove on: Unable to connect due to an opponent's boxing skill.

●●Unable to harm. (tried to discredit the witness, but couldn't lay a glove on him because his record was clean)

canvas: The floor of a boxing ring, a canvas covering stretched over a mat. (a left hook sent him to the canvas for the third time)

●●To "get up off the canvas" is to recover from a defeat or setback. (after his misfortune, he got up off the canvas to become a success)

canvasback: A fighter who gets knocked down or knocked out often.

card: see *fight card*.

carry: To hold back in order to make a weaker opponent look good. (carried him for a couple of rounds before taking him out in the third)

carry the fight: To dominate in a boxing match.

catcher: A boxer who takes a lot of punches during the course of a fight. also *punching bag*.

cauliflower ear: A deformity of the ear caused by repeated blows, and the resulting growth of excess scar tissue.

cement chin: The ability to take a punch on the chin without fear of a knockout. also *granite chin*. compare *brittle chin, china chin, glass chin, glass jaw, round heels*.

challenger: A boxer who fights a champion for the title.

champ: A champion. also *titleholder, titlist*.

●●The best, of superior quality. (when the chips were down, she came through like a champ)

championship: The title held by a champion; the highest accomplishment in boxing. also *crown, title*.

●●The highest level of any competition or endeavor. (will compete tomorrow in the pie-baking championship)

championship belt: The ornamental belt awarded to the champion of a weight division. also *belt*.

championship fight: A boxing match to decide a championship, as in a title defense. also *title fight*.

china chin: see *glass chin*.

chump: see *bum*.

class: see *weight division*.

clean break: The separation from a clinch

on the orders of the referee, with no illegal punches thrown by either fighter while disengaging.

clean up: To score with repeated unanswered blows against an opponent.

1. clinch: To hold an opponent with one or both arms so that no effective punches can be thrown, usually for the purpose of resting or for recovering after being hurt. When boxers clinch, the referee may order them to break or step back in order to keep the action going. also *tie up*.

2. clinch: The act or an instance of clinching.

close the distance: To maneuver closer to an opponent. also *cut the distance*.

clubber: Clubfighter.

clubfighter: 1. The product of a neighborhood boxing club, often noted for the ability to absorb punishment and keep punching. 2. A small-time boxer with modest skills. also *clubber*.

coldcock: To knock an opponent unconscious with a single blow. also *lower the boom*.

combination: Two or more different punches delivered quickly and in sequence, most often in a pattern planned and practiced before the fight. (floored by a left-right combination)

combination puncher: A boxer who throws punches in combinations.

connect: 1. To successfully hit an opponent; to land a punch. (has found the range and is beginning to connect with the jab) also *land*. 2. To land a particularly strong punch. (when the champ really connected, the challenger went down for the count) also *bang, belt, bomb, land, nail, slug, tag*.

●●To be particularly successful. (really connected with her last two songs)

contender: A boxer good enough to fight for the championship.

●●A prospect with sufficient qualities for success or the attainment of a particular goal or level of achievement. (definitely a contender for MVP)

cool: To knock out an opponent. see *knock out*.

cop a Sunday: To land a Sunday punch. (trying to cop a Sunday and knock him out)

corner: 1. Any of the four corners of a boxing ring. (had to fight his way out of the corner) 2. One of the two assigned corners (opposite each other) where the

boxers rest between rounds and are attended by seconds. (held on and looked to his corner for help)

●●To be "in one's corner" is to be for that person or on that person's side. (with most of the legislators in his corner, the Governor felt confident that his bill would pass)

cornerman: One of the seconds allowed inside the ring between rounds to attend to and advise the boxer.

count: 1. The calling off of the ten seconds allowed a boxer who has been knocked down. The ten seconds (timed by the timekeeper and called out by the referee) begin as soon as the boxer goes down and the opponent retires to a neutral corner. If the downed boxer is unable to get up before the count of ten, he is "counted out," and the opponent is declared the winner by a knockout. 2. The number of seconds counted against a downed boxer. (got up at the count of nine)

1. counter: To counterpunch. (countered with a left hook)

●●To respond to an action, argument, or proposal with an opposing action, argument, or proposal. (countered with her own list of complaints)

2. counter: A counterpunch. (knocked out by a right-hand counter)

●●An opposing response to an action, argument, or proposal. (silenced the critic with a witty counter)

1. counterpunch: To parry or block an opponent's lead and answer with a punch. (likes to counterpunch over a jab) also *counter*.

2. counterpunch: A punch that is a response to an opponent's lead. (never saw the counterpunch) also *counter*.

counterpuncher: A boxer with the ability to counterpunch, or one who prefers to counterpunch. (an effective counterpuncher)

count out: To complete an audible count of ten seconds before a downed boxer can get up, the result being a knockout. (went down three times before being counted out)

●●To be "counted out" is to be finished or defeated. (don't count her out yet, she's full of surprises) .

cover up: To abandon all offense and protect one's head and body as much as possible with the arms. (ran into a right hand near the end of the round and had to cover up until the bell sounded)

crazy bag: A double-end bag.

1. cross: A punch thrown over and across an opponent's lead. (dropped him with a right cross)

2. cross: To throw a cross. (crossed him to counter the jab)

crown: A championship. also *title*.

cruiserweight: 1. The 190 pound (maximum) weight division. Of the two major professional sanctioning bodies, only the WBC recognizes the cruiserweight division. 2. A boxer who fights in the cruiserweight division.

cutie: A clever boxer with deceptive moves.

cut man: The second who is responsible for stopping the bleeding of cuts a boxer may receive during a fight. Television boxing commentator Angelo Dundee, trainer and cornerman for nine world champions (among them three-time heavyweight champion Muhammad Ali and welterweight champion Sugar Ray Leonard) is regarded as one of the premier cut men in boxing.

cut off the ring: To move laterally in such a way as to limit the part of the ring an opponent can maneuver in. (the strategy will be to cut off the ring and keep the challenger in front of him)

cutter: A boxer whose punches spin and tend to open cuts on opponents.

cut the distance: see *close the distance*.

cut the tree: To throw body punches, or direct punches at the "trunk" of an opponent. also *go to the body*.

dance: To use footwork to maneuver and present a moving target to an opponent. (a cutie who will just dance and counterpunch until he sees an opening)

●●To stall, evade, or avoid. (just danced around the issue and never gave a straight answer)

dancer: 1. A fighter who uses footwork and movement as a strategic tactic. also *mover*. 2. A fighter who is not aggressive but fights defensively, always moving away.

●●An individual who is skilled at stalling, avoiding, or evading. (hard to pin down, a real dancer)

1. decision: The awarding of a win to a boxer on the basis of the number of points scored or rounds won in a match in which there is no knockout or technical knockout. A decision can be a unanimous decision (all three officials cast their votes for one boxer), a major-

ity decision (two officials vote for one boxer and the third votes for a draw), or a split decision (two officials vote for one boxer and the third votes for his opponent).

●●A less than conclusive victory. (won the argument by a decision)

2. decision: To win a fight by a decision. (won the first fight by a knockout and decisioned him in the rematch)

deck: To knock an opponent down. (decked the challenger in the third round) also *drop, flatten, floor*.

distance: The total number of rounds scheduled for a boxing match if there is no knockout or technical knockout. see *go the distance*.

division: see *weight division*.

double-end bag: A small inflated leather punching bag suspended about head-height between ceiling and floor mounts with elastic cords. Used to improve a boxer's timing and accuracy. also *crazy bag*. compare *heavy bag, speed bag*.

double up: To throw two consecutive punches with the same hand or with alternate hands. (found he could double up on the jab after the first round)

down: 1. Touching the canvas with any part of the body except the feet (or outside the ropes) and subject to the ten second count. 2. Knocked down. (down twice in the eighth round but came back to score a knockout in the ninth)

down and out: Knocked out, unable to rise before the count of ten. also *down for the count*.

●●Poor, desolate, in a hopeless or miserable state. (down and out, and living on charity) To be "down but not out" means to be in a bad state, but not defeated. (we were down but not out, and eventually came back to win the game)

down for the count: Knocked out, unable to rise before the count of ten. (finally went down for the count in the seventh round)

●●Defeated, finished, dying, or dead. (finally went down for the count after a long illness)

downstairs: The abdomen and/or ribs or to the abdomen and/or ribs. (can't take a good punch downstairs) compare *upstairs*.

1. draw: A boxing match that ends in a tie.

2. draw: To gain a tie in a boxing match.

dreadnought: A boxer in the heavyweight division. also *heavy, heavyweight.*

drop: To knock an opponent down. (dropped him in the fourth round) also *deck, flatten, floor.*

drop one's guard: To lower the hand that guards one's chin (right hand for a right-handed boxer, left hand for a left-handed boxer), leaving it unprotected. (got nailed with a left hook when he dropped his guard)

●●To relax, leaving oneself unprotected. (presiding judge dropped her guard long enough to reveal a wry sense of humor)

dukes: The fists. Short for "Duke of Yorks," the original Cockney rhyming slang for "forks," which stood for fingers or hands, and later, fists.

●●To "put up one's dukes" means to raise the hands or fists to prepare for a fight. To "duke it out" means to fight.

elimination bout, elimination match: One of a series of matches in which winners advance and are matched against each other until a champion emerges.

Enswell: A smooth, slightly convex stainless steel rectangular device (approximately 2 inches by 1 inch, by 1/4 inch thick) with a small flat-ironlike handle, designed specifically to remove swelling from the area under a fighter's eyes. Developed by sports physician and New Jersey State Boxing Commission member Dr. Michael Sabin, the Enswell is kept on ice, then applied with pressure directly against the swollen area between rounds and drawn sideways toward the ear. First tried on middleweight Bobby Czyz by veteran handler Ace Marotta, the device proved to be a convenient and effective replacement for the ice bags and cold fifty-cent pieces previously used. The Enswell received national attention in welterweight champion Sugar Ray Leonard's celebrated 1981 victory over Thomas Hearns, when handlers Angelo Dundee (Leonard) and Emanuel Stewart (Hearns) used the device on their fighters.

even: Tied, no winner. (finally took charge in the third after two even rounds)

1. **exchange:** To trade punches with an opponent. (got the worst of it when they exchanged right hands)

2. **exchange:** Two or more punches traded between opponents. (both fighters scored in the exchange)

face fighter: A boxer who is willing to take punches to the head in order to score his own punches; one who "leads with his face."

fan: An enthusiast or devotee. Though the word "fanatic" was abbreviated and used similarly as early as the 1600s, "fan" was applied to sports independantly, early in the nineteenth century. At that time in London, bareknuckle prize fighting was popular among the gentry, who could be seen dressed up and parading through the streets in their carriages on the way to matches. They were called the "fancy," corrupted to the "fance," then shortened to "fans," from whence came the singular "fan."

featherweight: The 126 pound weight division (125 pounds in amateur boxing). 2. A boxer who fights in the featherweight division. In the late 1800s, a number of boxers laid claim to the championship of the featherweight division (originally 118 pounds, then 122, and finally 126 pounds). New Zealander "Torpedo" Billy Murphy (1890) and Australian Young Griffo (1890, 1891) are both now recognized as worthy early claimants, but when American featherweight titleholder George "Little Chocolate" Dixon knocked out English featherweight champion Abe Willis on July 28, 1891, he became the accepted World Featherweight Champion. Elected to the Boxing Hall of Fame in 1956, Dixon had already become the first black world champion when he claimed the bantamweight title in 1890.

1. **feint:** To quickly move the head, hand, or body in such a way as to momentarily deceive an opponent. A boxer often feints with one hand, then throws a punch with the other.

2. **feint:** A quick movement of the head, hand, or body in order to momentarily deceive an opponent.

1. **fight:** To take part in a boxing match. also *box.*

2. **fight:** A boxing match. also *bout, prizefight.*

fight card: A program of boxing matches. also *card.*

fighter: A boxer. see *boxer.*

finish: To follow up when an advantage is gained and the opponent is stunned or hurt in order to end a match by a knockout.

fistic: Having to do with boxing. (a fistic attraction)

five point must system: A method of scoring a bout in which the winner of a round is awarded five points, and the loser a fewer number (usually the difference is less than one point). In the case of an even round, both boxers are awarded five points. compare *five point system.*

five point system: A method of scoring a bout in which the winner of a round is awarded from one to five points, and the loser a number fewer than those awarded to the winner (usually the difference is less than one point). In the case of an even round, neither boxer is awarded points. compare *five point must system.*

flatten: 1. To knock an opponent down. also *deck, drop, floor.* 2. To knock out an opponent. see *knock out.*

float: To evade an opponent's punches by a combination of footwork and movement of the head and body. Popularized by three-time Heavyweight Champion Muhammad Ali, who fulfilled his friend and cornerman Drew Bundini Brown's prediction that Ali (then Cassius Clay) would "float like a butterfly and sting like a bee" in his 1964 title fight with Sonny Liston. Ali won by a knockout when Liston failed to answer the bell for the seventh round.

floor: To knock down an opponent. also *deck, drop, flatten.*

●●Overwhelm, or surprise. (floored by the warm welcome she got)

flyweight: 1. The 112 pound (maximum) weight division. 2. A boxer who fights in the flyweight division. The flyweight class was created in England in 1910 at 108 pounds, with America following suit in the same year. At that weight (later raised to 112 pounds), Welshman Jimmy Wilde became the first generally accepted World Flyweight Champion in December of 1916 when he knocked out American flyweight Young Zulu Kid in eleven rounds. Wilde was elected to the Boxing Hall of Fame in 1959.

footwork: The movement of the feet in the boxing stance, not only to maneuver in relation to an opponent but to insure maximum balance and leverage for the punches thrown.

●●The term "fancy footwork" can be applied to dancing, or to a quick movement of the feet to recover balance or avoid a collision (some fancy footwork saved him from a terrible fall), or to take "steps" to stall, avoid, or evade. (had to do some fancy footwork to avoid giving away the surprise)

1. foul: An illegal blow or action that generally results in a warning first, followed by a loss of points or disqualification if repeated. This can be a blow below the belt, in back of the head or neck, during a break from a clinch, while an opponent is down or outside the ring, or one delivered with any part of the glove other than that which covers the knuckles, wrestling or butting with the head.

2. foul: To commit a foul. (ahead on points until he fouled twice in the tenth round)

get off: To properly execute one's punches. (tight for the first few rounds and couldn't get off)

gladiator: A boxer. see *boxer.*

glass chin, glass jaw: Easily knocked out. also *brittle chin, china chin, round heels.* compare *cement chin, granite chin.*

gloves: see *boxing gloves.*

●●To "put on the gloves" is to literally or figuratively fight. (seemed ready to put on the gloves if the bill was vetoed) To "hang up the gloves" is to retire. (after forty years with the company, he decided it was time to hang up the gloves)

go into the tank: To intentionally lose a fight. also *swoon, take a dive, throw a fight.*

Golden Gloves: A program of amateur elimination tournaments that take place in many larger United States cities, culminating in an annual Golden Gloves National Championship Tournament in which national titles are awarded in the various weight divisions. In 1926, Arch Ward, sports editor for the Chicago Tribune, got his newspaper to sponsor the first Golden Gloves tournament. A year later, at the urging of sports editor Paul Gallico, the New York Daily News sponsored its own Golden Gloves tournament in New York. In response to a challenge from Gallico, winners from the two cities' tournaments met on March 4, 1928, in Chicago Stadium for the first Golden Gloves Inter-City Championship Tournament. Two youngsters who fought in that first tournament went on to become professional titleholders, Bob Olin, World Light Heavyweight Champion in 1934 and 1935, and National Boxing Association Middleweight Champion (in 1938 and 1939) Solly Krieger. Among other world champions who fought in Golden Gloves tournaments were Barney Ross, Joe Louis, Tony Zale, Sugar Ray Robinson, Rocky Marciano, and Muhammad Ali.

go the distance: 1. To last or be able to last or complete all of the rounds scheduled for a particular bout before tiring or before losing on a knockout or technical knockout. (in good enough shape to go the distance) 2. To last the scheduled amount of rounds without a knockout or technical knockout. (don't expect the fight to go the distance)

●●To last, or go all the way. (finished medical school, surprising all those who thought he'd never go the distance)

go to the body: To punch to the abdomen and ribs of an opponent, or throw body punches. also *cut the tree.*

1. gouge: see *thumb.*

2. gouge: The act or an instance of thumbing an opponent. see *thumb.*

granite chin: see *cement chin.*

guard: The hand held high and close to the head to protect the chin (right hand for right-handed boxers, left hand for left-handed boxers). see *drop one's guard.*

gumshield: see *mouthpiece.*

gym fighter: A boxer who looks good in training but fails in a real bout.

ham: see *bum.*

ham-and-egger: see *bum.*

HEADGEAR

handle: To train and act as a second for a boxer.

handler: Someone who trains and acts as a second for a boxer. (his handlers have taught him to pace himself in the early rounds)

hand speed: The speed with which a boxer can throw punches, parry, and block.

hang on: To clinch or tie up an opponent, especially when tired or hurt, or to last until the end of a round.

●●To keep trying; to refuse to give up or give in. (hung on somehow until help arrived)

hard to find: Difficult to hit. Adept at slipping punches and movement. (has good footwork and he's hard to find)

haymaker: A powerful punch, or crushing blow. (landed a haymaker that ended the fight) also *bomb, Sunday punch.*

●●A devastating "blow." (the news of his wrecked car came as a haymaker)

●●An individual's or entertainment event's best song, joke, piece, or performance. (closed the show with a haymaker that brought the crowd to its feet)

head butt: see *butt.*

head feint: A quick movement of the head in order to momentarily confuse or deceive an opponent. (gives a little head feint before he throws the right)

headgear, headguard: A padded protective covering for a boxer's head, worn while sparring and in some amateur bouts. Headgear padding protects the forehead, temples, ears, and cheeks.

headhunter: A boxer who punches mainly to the head and rarely throws a body punch.

heavy: A heavyweight. also *dreadnought.*

●●Important (a Congressional heavy) or meaningful. (made a heavy point)

heavy artillery: Powerful punches. (an even fight until the eighth round when the champ started throwing his heavy artillery)

heavy bag: A large stuffed canvas or leather bag (approximately 3 feet high and 1 to 1-1/2 feet in diameter), suspended about 3 feet off the ground for the purpose of hitting. A boxer uses a heavy bag to develop power and strength. also *big bag.* compare *double-end bag, speed bag.*

heavy hitter: see *slugger.*

heavyweight: 1. The weight division for boxers over 175 pounds (between 179 and 200 pounds for amateur bouts). also *dreadnought*. 2. A boxer who fights in the heavyweight division. The first ever heavyweight champion (under London Prize Ring Rules) was English bareknuckler James Figg, who held the crown from 1719 to 1734. Figg was elected to the Boxing Hall of Fame in 1954. The first modern heavyweight champion (under Marquis of Queensberry Rules) was John L. Sullivan, who won the title in 1885 and held it until he was knocked out in the twenty-first round by James J. Corbett in 1892. Sullivan was elected to the Boxing Hall of Fame in 1954. also *dreadnought, heavy*.

●●Particularly important (a heavyweight in the corporation) or meaningful. (we were all affected by the heavyweight message in the lyric)

1. heel: To shove an opponent or deliver a blow with the part of a glove that covers the heel of the hand. A foul that can result in the loss of points or disqualification. (heeled him as they clinched)

2. heel: The act or an instance of heeling an opponent.

hit on the break: To illegally punch an opponent while in the process of breaking from a clinch as ordered by the referee. A foul that can result in the loss of points or disqualification.

1. hook: A usually short circular blow by the lead hand (left hand for a right-handed boxer, right hand for a left-handed boxer), delivered with the elbow bent and rigid. The hook can be a powerful punch and is used to attack both the body and the head. (hurts him with a hook to the body)

2. hook: To throw or deliver a hook. (hooks twice to the body, then throws an overhand right)

hook off a jab: To immediately follow a jab with a hook, circling the hand into the hook instead of pulling it back after the jab.

hungry: Desperately in need of or desirous of a win. The expression originally applied only to monetarily poor boxers who needed to win in order to eat, but now includes any boxer who has yet to attain success, recognition, or a desperately wanted goal, such as a championship. (no longer trains like a hungry fighter since he won the championship)

●●Desirous, desperately wanting or needing. (artists and athletes alike are told to "stay hungry")

ice: To knock out an opponent. (iced him in the seventh) see *knock out.*

in and out: A maneuver in which a boxer moves close to an opponent in order to deliver one or more blows, then quickly away to avoid being hit. (moved in and out with a beautiful combination to the head)

infighter: A boxer who moves inside and fights at close quarters. (a punishing infighter)

●●A figuratively tough individual, willing and able to take care of oneself in personal/political conflicts. (an adept infighter who quickly rose to a leadership position)

infighting: Fighting inside, close to the opponent.

●●The personal/political struggles between members of a group. (finally left the company, a victim of vicious infighting)

inside: At close quarters with an opponent. (not a pretty boxer, but dangerous inside)

in the bag: Fixed, the outcome decided before the match takes place.

●●A virtual certainty, a sure thing (though not necessarily because of a fix). (with three minutes to go in the final quarter and a three-touchdown lead, he knew the game was in the bag)

in the tank: Throwing a fight, taking a dive. (lost his boxing license when it

HEAVY BAG

was discovered he'd gone in the tank)

in trouble: Stunned and hurt by blows, ready to be knocked down or out. see *on queer street.*

1. jab: A rapid and direct punch (often aimed at the opponent's head) made by suddenly extending the arm of the lead hand (left hand for right-handed boxers, right hand for left-handed boxers). Though not always the most powerful punch, a jab can be used to bother or keep an opponent off balance and as a lead punch for another blow or a combination. (likes to hook off the jab)

2. jab: To throw a jab. (jabs twice, then crosses with the right) also *shoot the jab, stick.*

jab bag: A stuffed teardrop-shaped leather punching bag, suspended at head height similar to a speed bag, for the purpose of practicing a jab. Used less frequently than the speed bag, double-end bag, and heavy bag.

junior bantamweight: 1. The 115 pound (maximum) weight division. also *super flyweight.* 2. A boxer who fights in the junior bantamweight division. also *super flyweight.*

junior featherweight: 1. The 122 pound (maximum) weight division. also *super bantamweight.* 2. A boxer who fights in the junior featherweight division. also *super bantamweight.*

junior flyweight: 1. The WBA 108 pound (maximum) weight division. also *light flyweight* (WBC). 2. A boxer who fights in the junior flyweight division. also *light flyweight* (WBC).

junior lightweight: 1. The WBA 130 pound weight division (132 pounds in amateur boxing). also *super featherweight* (WBC). 2. A boxer who fights in the junior lightweight division. Artie O'Leary (real name Arthur Lieberman) was the first to claim the title in the junior lightweight division, from 1917 through 1919, but the first generally accepted junior lightweight champion was Italian born Johnny Dundee (real name Joseph Corrara), who won the title in 1921 and held it until 1923. Dundee was elected to the Boxing Hall of Fame in 1957. also *super featherweight* (WBC).

junior middleweight: 1. The WBA 154 pound weight division (156 pounds in amateur boxing). also *super welterweight* (WBC). 2. A boxer who fights in the junior middleweight divi-

sion. The first champion in the junior middleweight class was Dennis Moyer, who held the title in 1962 and 1963. also *super welterweight* (WBC).

junior welterweight: 1. The WBA 140 pound (maximum) weight division. also *super lightweight* (WBC). 2. A boxer who fights in the junior welterweight division. Myron "Pinkey" Mitchell became the first junior welterweight champion in 1922, holding the title until 1926. also *super lightweight* (WBC).

1. kayo: To knock out an opponent. see *knock out.*

●●To literally or figuratively knock out, or defeat decisively. (kayoed the opposition with a brilliant proposal)

2. kayo: A knockout. see *knockout.*

kidney punch: An illegal blow to the kidneys. A foul that can result in the loss of points or disqualification.

killer instinct: The ability to follow up an advantage, to finish or knock out a stunned or weakened opponent.

kill the body, the head will die: A favorite boxing axiom attesting to the sure result (a knockout) of an effective body attack. First associated with black heavyweight Sam Langford who, in 1906, lost in fifteen rounds to then Negro Heavyweight Champion Jack Johnson, two years before he became World Heavyweight Champion.

kiss the canvas: To be knocked down. (kissed the canvas twice in the sixth round before being knocked out)

knock down: To punch an opponent and cause him to fall to the floor. also *deck, drop, flatten, floor.*

knockdown: The act or an instance of one of the contestants in a bout being knocked down. When a knockdown occurs, a ten second count (timed by the timekeeper and called out by the referee) begins as soon as the standing opponent retires to a neutral corner. If the downed boxer is unable to get up before the count of ten, he is "counted out," and the opponent is declared the winner by a knockout.

knock out: 1. To knock an opponent unconscious. 2. To win a boxing match by a knockout. also *cool, flatten, ice, kayo, KO, put away, put out the lights, starch, stop, stretch, take out.*

●●To be figuratively "knocked out" is to be overwhelmed. (knocked out by the view from the edge of the canyon)

knockout: 1. The act of knocking out an opponent. 2. The termination of a bout when one boxer is knocked unconscious or is knocked down or out of the ring and is unable to resume fighting before the ten-second count has elapsed. also *kayo, KO.* compare *technical knockout.*

●●"Stunningly" attractive (she's an absolute knockout) or good (a knockout finish for the third act).

●●A "knockout blow" describes a decisive or defeating action. (another touchdown in the fourth quarter, which proved to be the knockout blow)

1. KO: To knock out an opponent. see *knock out.*

●●To literally or figuratively knock out, or decisively defeat. (enough votes to KO the motion)

2. KO: A knockout. see *knockout.* compare *TKO.*

lace: To illegally rub the laces of a boxing glove against the opponent's face or head. A foul that can result in the loss of points or disqualification. (laced him and opened up a cut above the eye)

laces: The string or cord used to fasten boxing gloves, located on the inside of the wrist.

land: 1. To successfully hit an opponent; to connect with a punch. (beginning to land the hook) also *connect.* 2. To connect with a particularly strong punch. (really landed that time, and the challenger is hurt) also *bang, belt, bomb, connect, nail, slug, tag.*

lay a glove on: To land or be able to land a punch. (couldn't lay a glove on him for the first three rounds)

●●To literally or figuratively touch, or effect. (in spite of all the money spent and the smear tactics employed, the special interest group couldn't lay a glove on the veteran senator)

1. lead: To start a combination or series of punches, usually used in reference to starting with a particular punch or hand. Most often, a right-handed boxer will lead with a left jab.

●●To "lead with one's chin" is to leave oneself completely unprotected or vulnerable, to invite disaster. (the thief was leading with his chin when he challenged the priest's honesty)

2. lead: 1. The first in a series of punches. 2. The jab or jabbing hand. (occasionally changes to a right-hand lead to confuse his opponent)

left: A punch with the left hand. (lands with two lefts, then throws a right cross)

light flyweight: 1. The WBC 108 pound (maximum) weight division. also *junior flyweight* (WBA). 2. A boxer who fights in the light flyweight division. also *junior flyweight* (WBA).

light heavyweight: 1. The 175 pound weight division (178 pounds in amateur boxing). 2. A boxer who fights in the light heavyweight division. Chicago newsman and boxing promoter Lou Houseman urged the formation of the light heavyweight class just after the turn of the century. A boxer he managed, Jack Root, who could no longer make the weight for the middleweight division but was too light to be a heavyweight, became the first light heavyweight champion in 1903. Root was elected to the Boxing Hall of Fame in 1961.

lightweight: 1. The 135 pound weight division (139 pounds in amateur boxing). 2. A boxer who fights in the lightweight division. Though John Moneghan, an Irishman from Liverpool, England claimed the lightweight title (bare-knuckle rules) as early as 1855, the first recognized World Lightweight Champion (Marquis of Queensberry Rules) was George "Kid" Lavigne, who won the title by knocking out Dick Burge in London, England in seventeen rounds. Lavigne was elected to the Boxing Hall of Fame in 1959.

●●Small-time, not important. (paid no attention to what he said, because he was a real lightweight)

load up: To make sure all one's power is behind a punch. (loading up and throwing bombs)

long count: A count that takes more than the prescribed ten seconds. The most famous long count incident took place

LEFT JAB

in the second Jack Dempsey-Gene Tunney World Heavyweight Championship fight in Chicago in 1927. Tunney survived what many have alleged to be a long count in the seventh round to come back and win a unanimous decision in ten rounds and retain the heavyweight title. Jack Dempsey was elected to the Boxing Hall of Fame in 1954 and Gene Tunney, in 1955.

low blow: A blow delivered below the belt of the opponent, or below an imaginary line drawn across the body at the hipbones. A low blow is a foul for which the boxer may be warned, lose points, lose the round, or be disqualified.

●●An unfair or cowardly act. (spreading the lie about his opponent was a low blow)

lower the boom: To knock an opponent unconscious, especially with a single blow. (the challenger dropped when the champ lowered the boom in the fourth round) also *coldcock.*

main event: The most important bout on a fight card, the principal attraction.

●●The principal or most important. (a seven-course gourmet dinner on the last night of the holiday weekend was definitely the main event)

majority decision: A decision in which two of the three officials vote for one boxer and the third votes for a draw. compare *split decision, unanimous decision.*

make him pay: A popular boxing exhortation that urges a fighter to take advantage of a mistake or mistakes made by an opponent.

make the weight: To be able to be within the weight parameters of a particular division at the time of the official weigh-in for a fight (usually by reducing from a higher weight). (called off the bout when the challenger couldn't make the weight)

mandatory eight count: A rule that states that in the case of a knockdown, the count must reach eight before the fight can begin again, whether or not the downed boxer has already reached his feet. The mandatory eight count is a safety measure to protect boxers and is in force in most bouts.

Marquis of Queensberry Rules: The basic rules under which boxing has been conducted since they began to be gener-

ally accepted in 1885, when John L. Sullivan, the Bareknuckle World Heavyweight Champion, defeated Dominick McCaffrey in six rounds to become the first World Heavyweight Champion under Queensberry Rules. There were few rules for the earliest pugilistic contests in seventeenth and eighteenth century England. These were free-for-alls in which contestants kicked, butted, wrestled, gouged, and bit each other with no rest periods until one contestant could not go on. Fists became predominant only when the legendary fighter and boxing pioneer, Boxing Hall of Famer James Figg, demonstrated what a formidable weapon they could be in the early 1700s in London. In 1743, another Boxing Hall of Fame member, Jack Broughton (called the "Father of Boxing") framed the first set of rules to civilize prize fighting. These formed the basis for the London Prize Ring Rules, which were formally adopted in 1838 to govern bareknuckle fighting. The London Prize Ring Rules called for a 24-foot square ring, the end of a round when either fighter was downed, and a 30-second rest period at the end of each round (if a fighter was not ready to resume the contest in thirty seconds, he was declared the loser). The rules forbade grappling, low blows, butting, kicking, and biting. In the mid-1860s, John Sholto Douglas, the ninth Marquis of Queensberry, sponsored a set of boxing rules framed by John Graham Chambers, which eventually came to be accepted as the basic rules of modern boxing. The Queensberry Rules outlawed wrestling or clinching and called for a 20-foot square ring, three-minute rounds with a one-minute rest interval, padded gloves for the fists of the boxers, a ten-second count for a downed boxer, and the withdrawal of the standing boxer to a neutral corner during the count.

measure: To leave the lead hand propped against a stunned opponent to use as a "guide" for a big punch. (got the challenger in trouble and is just measuring and bombing at will)

mechanic: A boxer with good technical skills.

middleweight: 1. The 160 pound weight division (165 pounds in amateur boxing).

2. A boxer who fights in the middleweight division. Irishman Jack "The Nonpareil" Dempsey (not to be confused with heavyweight Jack Dempsey) became the first World Middleweight Champion in 1884 when he knocked out George Fulljames in twenty-two rounds. Dempsey was elected to the Boxing Hall of Fame in 1954.

mini flyweight: The 106 pound (maximum) weight division in amateur boxing. 2. A boxer who fights in the mini flyweight division.

mix it up: 1. To fight, or exchange blows. (felt each other out in the first two rounds but began to mix it up in the third) also *trade, trade punches.* 2. An exhortation advising a boxer to throw a combination, or a series of different kinds of punches.

●●To fight. (shoved each other after the whistle, but the linesman skated between them before they could drop their gloves and mix it up)

mouse: A swelling and discoloration around the eye, the result of a blow. (a left hook, which raised a pretty good mouse under the challenger's eye)

●●A black eye, or swelling around the eye from a collision or blow. (suffered only a mouse under one eye from the fall)

mouthpiece: A rubberized protector worn inside the mouth to protect the teeth and lips of a boxer. Invented in the early 1900s by London dentist Jack Marks. Popularized (after considerable resistance) in 1913 by British fighter, two-time Welterweight Champion Ted "Kid" Lewis, who introduced the device in the United States on November 19, 1914, at Madison Square Garden, when he fought a ten round no-decision bout against Phil Bloom. Lewis was elected to the Boxing Hall of Fame in 1964. also *gumshield.*

mover: see *dancer.*

nail: To deliver a powerful punch. (got nailed with a haymaker and went down for the count) also *bang, belt, bomb, slug, tag.*

neutral corner: Either of the two corners not assigned to a boxer that face each other diagonally across the ring. After a knockdown, the standing boxer must retire to a neutral corner for the duration of the ten-second count.

no contest: The termination of an inconclusive boxing match by the referee before the scheduled number of rounds is completed, due to a lack of action, disqualifications, or uncontrollable circumstances (such as a sudden downpour, a structural failure of the ring or other equipment, etc.).

no decision: A boxing match in which the scheduled number of rounds is completed, but no official decision is reached. A rare occurence in modern boxing, a no decision ruling can result from the invalidation of a bout's scoring by the sanctioning body under whose authority the match is made. In the early 1900s, many bouts that were not ended by a knockout were called "no decision" because of rules in various states and countries that forbade the rendering of a decision in a prize fight. In such cases, boxing writers would often later declare a winner, but officially the fight was ruled "no decision."

no foul rule: A rule that prohibits the automatic awarding of a bout to the victim of a low blow. Before the no foul rule, many fights were won and lost on fouls. It was not uncommon for a fighter who knew he was overmatched to intentionally hit his opponent with a low blow and lose on a foul. Since all bets were off in such a situation, a fighter could not only save himself discomfort and a more serious blemish on his record, but could save some money for himself and his backers as well. A fed-up ringside telegraph operator for the newspapers, Stan Taylor, finally did something about the problem. Taylor invented a device that would come to be known as a "protective cup," now mandatory equipment for all boxers. So effective was his invention (he actually wore it to the fights and had people kick him and hit him below the belt to demonstrate its worth), that Commissioner James J. Farley of the New York State Athletic Commission amended the boxing regulations in 1930 with the no foul rule.

no knockdown: A judgment and declaration by the referee that an instance of a boxer dropping to the canvas was due to a slip or a push and is not to be scored a knockdown.

on a bicycle, on one's bicycle: Using footwork to stay away from an opponent. (been on his bicycle since he got tagged in the second round)

one-hand fighter: A boxer who can or does punch with one hand only, rarely using the other.

one-two: A two-punch combination, consisting of a short left jab followed immediately by a hard right cross, usually to the jaw of an opponent. Left-handed boxers use a right jab followed by a left cross. (connects with a good one-two)

••A two-step or two-phase action or program. (a good one-two combination of sales and service)

on one's toes: Dancing, moving. In order to move quickly and maneuver properly, a fighter must be up on his toes, rather than flat-footed. (fresh, up on his toes, and moving as though it were the first round)

••To "stay on one's toes" means to stay alert, ready to act or react quickly. (had to stay on her toes backstage, or she would have missed her cue)

on queer street: Stunned and hurt by blows, ready to be knocked down or out. (caught with a big right hand, and all of a sudden, the champion was on queer street) also *in trouble, on the ropes, out on one's feet, ready to go, walking on one's heels.*

••Dazed, confused, not in possession of one's senses. (was on queer street for about an hour after the accident)

on the button: Directly on the chin. (took a left hook on the button)

••Exact, precisely correct. (her directions were right on the button)

on the ropes: Leaning helplessly against the ropes, stunned and hurt by blows, ready to be knocked down or out. see *on queer street.*

••Close to ruin or failure. (the company is on the ropes because of years of mismanagement)

open hook: A hook that is thrown alone, rather than following a jab or in a series. (went down when he walked into an open hook)

open up: To throw a number of punches with little or no thought of defense. (began to open up in the second round)

out: Knocked out, unconscious. (out before he hit the floor)

••Unconscious, asleep. (so tired he was out just after dinner)

out on one's feet: Stunned, almost unconscious, ready to be knocked down or out. see *on queer street.*

••Dazed, sleepy, barely conscious. (hadn't slept for two days and was out on his feet)

outpoint: To win a boxing match by a decision. (got outpointed in the rematch)

over and under: A punch to the head followed by a body punch, often both hooks.

overhand punch: A punch made with the fist brought forward and down from above shoulder level, such as a straight right or cross (or left for a left-handed boxer).

paint job: An instance of scoring repeated blows against an opponent, "covering" an opponent with blows. (did a paint job on the challenger after stunning him with a big right hand)

palooka: An unskilled, or sometimes no longer skilled boxer. Coined in the 1920s by journalist Jack Conway. see *bum.*

••A lout or lummox. (two big palookas blocking the doorway)

peanut bag: A small speed bag, 4 to 5 inches in diameter. Because of its size and quick bounce, the peanut bag is difficult to hit, and is used to develop hand speed and timing.

peek-a-boo: A relatively unorthodox boxing stance, in which both hands are held high to protect the front and sides of the face. The name comes from the appearance of "peeking" over the boxing gloves. Boxing Hall of Famer Floyd Patterson, World Heavyweight Champion in 1956, 1957, 1958, 1959, 1960 (after losing in 1959, then becoming the first man ever to regain the Heavyweight Title), 1961, and 1962, popularized the peek-a-boo defense.

pepper: see *beat a tattoo.*

pick off: To block an opponent's punch. (seems to be able to pick off the left jab)

preliminary bout: An opening bout before the main event that most often involves boxers of less skill and experience.

prizefight: 1. A professional boxing match. 2. A boxing match. also *bout, fight.*

prizefighter: 1. A professional boxer. 2. A boxer. also *fighter, gladiator, pug, pugilist.*

prize ring: A boxing ring. also *square circle.*

pug: A boxer. Short for pugilist.

pugilism: The art of boxing. From the Latin words *pugunus* (fist) and *pugil* (boxer).

pugilist: A boxer. also *fighter, gladiator, prizefighter, pug.*

pull a punch: To punch with less than full strength; to hold back.

••To hold back. (up before a tough judge who pulls no punches)

pumper: A bad cut that bleeds profusely.

1. punch: To strike a blow or blows with the fist or fists. also *stick, throw a punch, throw leather.*

2. punch: A blow with the fist. also *shot.*

••Vitality, force. (a thought-provoking editorial with a lot of punch)

punch-drunk: Suffering the long term effects of repeated blows to the head, slow in movement and speech. also *punchy.*

••Dazed, or confused. (still punch-drunk from sitting next to the speaker at the rock concert)

punched out: Arm weary, exhausted from throwing punches.

punching bag: 1. One of several kinds of suspended stuffed or inflated bags used for training in boxing. see *heavy bag, double-end bag, speed bag.* 2. see *catcher.*

punchy: Punch-drunk.

••Dazed, groggy. (punchy from lack of sleep)

put away: To knock out an opponent. (finally put him away in the eleventh round) see *knock out.*

••To destroy or defeat (put him away with three straight service aces) or to captivate, delight, or spellbind. (her closing number put me away)

put out the lights: To knock out an opponent. see *knock out.*

quick count: An unfair count that takes less than the allotted ten seconds.

rabbit punch: An illegal clubbing blow to the back of the neck. A foul that results in the loss of points or disqualification.

reach: A measurement of the arm fully extended. A boxer must sometimes alter his strategy due to a reach advantage held by himself or his opponent.

ready to go: Stunned and hurt by blows, ready to be knocked down or out. see *on queer street.*

ref: Short for referee.

referee: The official in the ring who presides over a boxing match. A referee makes judgments about rules infractions and fouls, issues warnings and removes points when he or she deems it necessary, separates the boxers when they clinch, gives the count when a boxer is knocked down, and has the authority to stop the bout if a boxer is injured or unable to continue. Referees also sometimes assist the judges in scoring the bout, depending on the sanctioning body and location of the match. also *ref, third man in the ring.*

rematch: A bout in which two boxers who have fought each other previously meet again. In most cases, a clause in the contract for a championship fight guarantees the champion a rematch should he lose the title.

right: A punch with the right hand. (decked by a straight right)

right lead: 1. A straight right or right cross that is not preceded by a jab or combination. A surprise, and somewhat risky, maneuver. 2. A right jab for a left-handed boxer.

ring: A usually elevated 18 to 20-foot-square area surrounded by three (and sometimes four) 1 to 2-inch cloth-wrapped ropes attached to padded turnbuckles on the posts in each corner, and in which a boxing match is conducted. The ring floor, a canvas-covered rubber or felt mat, usually extends an additional 2 feet outside the ropes on all four sides of the ring. also *prize ring, square circle.*

••To "toss one's hat into the ring" is to enter into a competition.

Ring Magazine; see *The Ring.*

ring post: One of the four posts at the corners of a boxing ring, to which the ropes are attached that surround the ring.

ring rust: The inability to time punches or maneuver properly due to an absence from the ring. (showed some ring rust in his first comeback fight)

ring savvy: Knowledge and understanding of the techniques and tricks used in a boxing ring. (up against a veteran with a lot of ring savvy)

ringside: Next to or close to the ring. (saw it all from ringside seats)

••A good or close vantage point. (ringside seats for the whole performance)

roadwork: The part of a boxer's training program that involves long-distance running, often on public roads.

••Long-distance running as part of an athlete's training.

roll with a punch: To move the head or body in the same direction of an opponent's blow in order to diminish its effect. (would have been a sure knockout if he hadn't rolled with the punch)

•• To take a setback in stride; to be resilient. (can survive corporation politics because he knows how to roll with a punch)

rope: One of the three (or four) parallel ropes surrounding a boxing ring, attached by means of padded turnbuckles to the four posts at the corners of the ring. The ropes are strung at 2, 3, and 4-foot heights measured from the floor of the ring (international amateur boxing requires 40, 80, and 130 centimeters). Four ropes, when used, are strung 18, 30, 42, and 54 inches high.

rope-a-dope: An unorthodox strategy devised by three-time World Heavyweight Champion Muhammad Ali in which a boxer leans back against the ropes in a defensive shell, in the hopes that an opponent will tire himself out by throwing punches that can be blocked with the arms. Ali named the technique after using it in his successful bid to regain the heavyweight title from then champion George Foreman in 1974, knocking out Foreman in the eighth round.

round: The three-minute periods into which a bout is divided (two minutes in some amateur competitions), with a one-min-

ute rest period after each round. The idea of a time-limited round was first introduced in the Marquis of Queensberry Rules in 1865. In bareknuckle contests prior to that time, a round had ended only when one of the combatants slipped to or was knocked or pushed to the ground. One fight under such rules, between Mike Madden and Bill Hays in England in 1849, was contested for 185 rounds over a period of six hours and three minutes. The longest fight under Marquis of Queensberry Rules was in 1893 between Andy Bowen and Jack Burke, who both were unable to continue after fighting 110 three-minute rounds, taking a total of seven hours and nineteen minutes. The match was called "no contest." also *stanza.*

rounder: A bout lasting a specific number of rounds. (decisioned him in a grueling fourteen-rounder)

round heels: see *glass chin.*

1. roundhouse: A punch delivered with a wide-sweeping arc. Named after the circular revolving floor of a railroad roundhouse. (got tagged with a roundhouse)

2. roundhouse: Of or pertaining to a punch delivered with a wide-sweeping arc.

saved by the bell: About to be counted

RING

out when the bell rings, ending the round. Sanctioning bodies in some locations do not allow a fighter to be saved by the bell but require that the count be continued. In this case, a fighter who is not able to rise unassisted by the count of ten is counted out, and the match is ended. Regardless of the sanctioning body, no fighter may be saved by the bell in the final round of a match.

●●To be saved just in time from something bad or unpleasant. (saved by the bell when his wallet was found just before the plane left)

scar tissue: Layers of new skin that remain after healing in and over wounds or cuts, especially over an area that has been wounded or bruised repeatedly.

scorecard: A card on which an official keeps a tally of rounds or points awarded to the boxers in a bout.

second: One of the cornermen allowed inside the ring between rounds to attend to and advise a boxer.

shadow box: To spar with an imaginary opponent as a training exercise.

shadow boxing: A training exercise in which a boxer spars with an imaginary opponent.

shake the cobwebs: To attempt to clear one's head after being dazed by a blow or blows. (backing up now and just trying to stay out of range of the champion until he can shake the cobwebs)

●●To clear one's head; to wake up. (takes her about fifteen minutes to shake the cobwebs after the alarm goes off in the morning)

shoot the jab: To quickly throw a jab. (shoots the jab, then crosses with the right) also *jab, stick.*

shop fighter: A journeyman, experienced but less than first class.

shot: A punch. (scored with some good shots in the first two rounds)

slide rule decision: A close decision.

slip: 1. To dodge a punch by moving the head sideways. 2. An instance in which a boxer falls to the canvas as a result of a loss of footing rather than a punch. In such a case, there is no knockdown and no count.

slug: To punch hard. (a banger who can slug with anybody) also *bang, belt, bomb.*

slugfest: A boxing match between two sluggers, with each swinging from the heels to score a knockout. also *war.*

●●A literal or figurative brawl. (a disagreement that quickly turned into a verbal slugfest)

slugger: 1. A fighter who prefers to slug, rather than rely on boxing skill or style. 2. A powerful puncher. also *banger, bomber, stiff puncher.*

smoking: Relentless punching. "Smoking" Joe Frazier, Heavyweight Champion in 1968, 1969, 1970, 1971, 1972, and 1973, got his nickname for just such a style. Frazier was elected to the Boxing Hall of Fame in 1980.

south of the border: Below the belt. see *below the belt, low blow.*

spar: To box in a practice or exhibition bout.

●●To argue, or bandy words. (the judge looked on as the two attorneys sparred with each other)

sparmate: A sparring partner.

●●A humorous name for one's mate or spouse.

sparring partner: An individual who spars with a boxer in training. Sparring partners are often young up-and-coming boxers. also *sparmate.*

●●A humorous name for one's mate or spouse.

speed bag: A leather punching bag that hangs at head level from the middle of a round, horizontal board or frame so that when the bag is hit, it bounces back rapidly. The inflated, pear-shaped speed bag is used in training to develop speed and timing. compare *double-end bag, heavy bag.*

split decision: A decision in which two officials vote for one boxer, and the third votes for his opponent. compare *majority decision, unanimous decision.*

SLIP

square circle: A boxing ring. also *prize ring.*

standing eight count: A count of eight given, at the discretion of the referee, when a boxer has been stunned or hurt. In professional boxing, a standing eight count is scored as a knockdown.

stanza: A round.

starch: To knock out an opponent. (starched him in the third round) see *knock out.*

stay there: To stay in front of and close to an opponent; to remain inside. (has to stop dancing and stay there)

steal a round: To flurry and step up one's performance in the closing minute of a round, impressing and influencing the judges' scoring. An acknowledged master at this technique was three-time heavyweight champion Muhammad Ali.

step back: To break from a clinch. When fighters clinch, a referee will order them to "break" or "step back."

stick: 1. To throw a jab. (he would stick, stick, then hook) also *jab, shoot the jab.* 2. To punch.

stick and move: 1. To jab and immediately move, in order to present a more elusive target for an opponent. 2. To throw a punch and immediately move, in order to present a more elusive target to an opponent.

stiff: see *bum.*

stiff jab: A strong, stinging jab.

stiff puncher: see *slugger.*

stop: To knock an opponent unconscious. see *knock out.*

stop a fight: To officially end a boxing match before the completion of all the rounds scheduled. A referee has the authority to stop a fight by declaring a technical knockout if one of the contestants is injured or unable to continue, to disqualify one of the contestants, or to declare a bout "no contest."

straight punch: A right-hand or left-hand punch that travels in a direct line to the opponent, as opposed to hooking, crossing, or traveling upward or downward. (dropped him with a straight right)

straight-up fighter: A boxer who does not crouch, bob, or weave, but stands erect.

stretch: To knock out an opponent. (took him only two rounds to stretch his last opponent) see *knock out.*

1. sucker punch: An unexpected or deceptive punch, as one thrown before an opponent is ready.

2. sucker punch: To throw a sucker punch. (tried to sucker punch him as he reached to touch gloves)

Sunday punch: One's best or most powerful punch. also *bomb, haymaker.*

●●A powerful "blow." (opened the negotiations with his Sunday punch)

super heavyweight: 1. The amateur weight division for boxers over 200 pounds. 2. An amateur boxer who fights in the super heavyweight division.

super lightweight: 1. The WBC 140 pound (maximum) weight division. also *junior welterweight* (WBA). 2. A boxer who fights in the super lightweight division. also *junior welterweight* (WBA).

swing from the heels: To put all one's power behind a punch or punches. (both fighters stood toe-to-toe, swinging from the heels) also *tee off, unload.*

●●To make one's best effort, holding nothing back. (it was obvious from the opening statement that the committee intended to swing from the heels)

1. swoon: 1. To intentionally lose a fight, especially by a faked knockout. also *go into the tank, take a dive, throw a fight.* 2. To be knocked out. (after being hurt in the second and third, he finally swooned at two minutes and twelve seconds into the fourth round)

2. swoon: The act or an instance of intentionally losing a fight, especially by a faked knockout.

take a dive: To intentionally lose a fight, especially by faking a knockout. (lost his boxing license for taking a dive) also

SPEED BAG

go into the tank, swoon, throw a fight.

●●To intentionally lose a contest.

take a punch: To withstand or be able to withstand a blow or blows from an opponent. (proved he could take a punch in his first two fights)

take out: To knock out an opponent. (took him out with a vicious left hook) also *cool, flatten, ice, kayo, KO, put away, put out the lights, starch, stop, stretch.*

take the count: 1. To allow oneself to be counted out after being knocked down. A fighter who has been badly beaten and is exhausted is sometimes told to take the count by his corner in order to prevent an injury.

tale of the tape: The weight and measurements of a boxer, or of two boxers who are about to meet in a boxing match. The exact origin of the expression is unclear, but television sports commentator Howard Cosell did much to popularize it in the 1970s.

tank job: see *bagged fight.*

tattoo: see *beat a tattoo.*

technical draw: The termination of a boxing match due to an injury incurred accidentally (most often a cut from an accidental butt) by one or both boxers. If neither boxer is ahead on points at the time of the injury, or if the injured boxer is behind on points at the time the match is stopped, a technical draw is declared under the rules of some sanctioning bodies.

technical knockout: The termination of a boxing match by the referee when one of the contestants is injured, unwilling to continue, or, in the referee's judgment, unable to defend himself. also *TKO.* compare *knockout.*

tee off: To put all one's power behind a punch or punches. Originally from golf, meaning to strike the ball off of a golf tee, starting play. (just standing in the middle of the ring, teeing off on each other)

●●To hit something with all one's power (tees off on the first pitch and sends it to deep center field) To severely reprimand or openly express anger. (teed off on her son for disrupting the picnic)

telegraph a punch: To unintentionally communicate to an opponent (as by a glance or some movement) the blow

that one intends to deliver next. (he drops his shoulder and telegraphs the punch)

●●To "telegraph" a word or an action is to involuntarily signal one's intention. (clumsily telegraphed his next move and quickly found his king in check)

ten point must system: A method of scoring a bout by awarding ten points to the winner of a round and a lesser number to the loser (usually the difference is less than two points). Both boxers are awarded ten points in the case of an even round.

The Ring: A national sports magazine, published monthly since 1922. Founded by boxing authority Nat Fleisher, *The Ring* is the oldest sports magazine in the United States and has, since 1924, issued ratings that have served as a practical, if not official, measure of the ascension of challengers to championships in the various weight divisions. Writers such as Paul Gallico, Dan Daniel, Ed Sullivan, Bud Schulberg, Red Smith, Damon Runyon, and others have contributed to *The Ring,* known as "The Bible of Boxing." also *Ring Magazine.*

third man in the ring: The referee. also *ref.*

three knockdown rule: A rule in effect in some locations that requires a bout to be stopped automatically if one boxer is knocked down three times in any round. In such a case, the opponent of the downed boxer is awarded a victory by a knockout in the round the bout is stopped.

throw a fight: To intentionally lose a fight. also *go into the tank, swoon, take a dive.*

throw a punch: To punch, or attempt to hit an opponent. also *stick.*

throw in the towel: To concede defeat for a boxer by throwing a towel into the ring from the boxer's corner. To prevent a serious injury, a boxer's seconds may throw in the towel even if the boxer himself wants to continue. The act of throwing in the towel is not recognized by some sanctioning bodies, but in practice, if the cause is obvious, the referee will usually stop the match and award a victory by a technical knockout to the opponent.

●●To give up, to concede defeat. (finally threw in the towel and went along with the majority opinion)

throw leather: To deliver punches, especially flurries of hard punches. (backs up the champion as he begins to throw leather)

1. thumb: To illegally stick the thumb of a boxing glove in an opponent's eye. A foul that can result in the loss of points or disqualification. (a dirty fighter who would thumb and lace his opponents) also *gouge.*

2. thumb: The act or an instance of thumbing an opponent. also *gouge.*

tie up: see *clinch.*

timekeeper: The official at ringside responsible for timing rounds, the interval between rounds, and the ten-second count in case of a knockdown.

title: A championship. (held the middleweight title for two years) also *crown.*

●●The highest level of any competition or endeavor. (will compete in the final race to decide the national title)

title defense: see *championship fight.*

title fight: see *championship fight.*

TKO: A technical knockout. (won in the eighth round on a TKO)

toe-to-toe: A furious exchange of punches in which opponents face each other and slug with no effort made to move or defend. (went toe-to-toe in the last round of the fight)

●●An open and heated argument or confrontation. (an unproductive session, with union and management negotiators going toe-to-toe)

tomato can: see *bum.*

TIMEKEEPER

trade, trade punches: To exchange punches with an opponent. (stick and move, don't trade with him) also *mix it up, punch.*

twenty point must system: A method of scoring a bout in which the winner of a round is awarded twenty points, and the loser a lesser number. In the case of an even round, both boxers are awarded twenty points.

unanimous decision: A decision in which all officials cast their votes for one boxer. compare *majority decision, split decision.*

under and over: A punch to the body followed by a punch to the head, often both hooks.

undercard: Preliminary bouts before the main event.

unload: To deliver a hard punch or hard punches. (unloaded and knocked the champion off his feet)

1. uppercut: A punch of fairly short extension delivered up toward the head or upper body with either hand from the waist and with a bent elbow.

2. uppercut: The act or an instance of delivering an uppercut. (step in and uppercut him)

upstairs: The head or to the head. (hit him in the gut, then go upstairs) compare *downstairs.*

walk away: To take several steps to the right of an opponent (away from a right-handed boxer's right hand). A boxer usually walks away to take a safe breather, but Boxing Hall of Famer Jersey Joe Walcott, World Heavyweight Champion in 1951 and 1952, used the technique to momentarily lull an opponent before an attack.

walking on one's heels: Stunned, off balance, ready to be knocked down or out. (he's up, but still walking on his heels) see *on queer street.*

waltz: A boxing match characterized by dancing and fancy movement, but little punching.

war: An action-packed and/or brutal boxing match, in which the combatants pummel each other from the opening bell. also *slugfest.*

warning: An official notification to a boxer from the referee that points will be subtracted from the boxer's score if an observed foul is repeated.

WBA: The World Boxing Association.

WBC: The World Boxing Council.

weigh-in: The official weighing of boxers before a match to insure that the weights of both contestants are within the specified limits of their weight division. see *weight division*.

weigh in: To have one's weight measured and recorded at the official weigh-in before a boxing match. (weighed in at 209 pounds)

weight division: The class or category into which boxers are grouped according to weight. also *class, division*.

welter: A boxer in the welterweight division.

welterweight: 1. The 147 pound (maximum) weight division. also *welter*. 2. A boxer who fights in the welterweight division. "Welter" was a weight term used in English horse racing (a weight of 28 pounds sometimes added to a horse's weight for age). In 1792, 145-pound Tom Jones became the first champion of the "welters," a name which had been adopted by a number of small English fighters of the same weight. There was little interest in the division until 1888, when American-born Paddy Duffy claimed the first World Welterweight Championship holding the title through 1889 and 1890. also *welter*.

white hope: A white boxer who is a contender for a title held by a black boxer. A racial expression that originated in the early 1900s, when Boxing Hall of Famer Jack Johnson, the first black World Heavyweight Champion, domi-nated the heavyweight ranks for seven years (1908-1915). Johnson's arrogance, womanizing, and public scrapes with the law only served to fuel those who clamored for a "white hope." Finally, on April 15, 1915, in Havana, Cuba, 6 foot 6-1/4-inch, 240-pound Boxing Hall of Famer Jess Willard knocked out the controversial Johnson in the twenty-sixth round of their championship fight to win the heavyweight crown and the title of the "Great White Hope."

wing: To deliver big, looping punches. (winging punches in the hopes of connecting)

win on points: To win a boxing match by a decision.

●●To just barely win. (she won the argument on points this time, but next time, it won't even be close)

work the corner: To act as a second or cornerman for a boxer.

World Boxing Association: One of the two major sanctioning bodies of professional boxing. An outgrowth of the old National Boxing Association in the United States, the World Boxing Association is headquartered in the Republic of Panama. also *WBA*.

World Boxing Council: One of the two major sanctioning bodies of professional boxing. Formed in 1963, the World Boxing Council is headquartered in Mexico. also *WBC*.

wrap: see *bandage*.

wrapping: see *bandages*.

UPPER CUT

The ancestor of all football games is soccer, but rugby, an offshoot of soccer, served as both the inspiration and departure point for American football.

Rugby was invented in 1823 at Rugby School in England when William Webb Ellis suddenly picked up the ball in frustration during a soccer game and ran with it to the goal line. Though Ellis was soundly criticized, the idea of carrying the ball as well as kicking it was soon accepted and identified with the school.

Popular with players and spectators alike, the "Rugby game" was soon adopted by students at other schools and, by the late 1850s, had been taken up by some of the playing clubs formed by the newly emerging middle class. In 1863, English football (soccer) purists were alarmed enough to form the Football Association and adopt rules that separated their game, "association football," from "rugby football."

When Princeton and Rutgers pioneered intercollegiate "football" in the United States in 1869, the game played was soccer, albeit with twenty-five players on a side. Soon Yale, Cornell, Columbia, and Michigan organized football teams. In 1873, Yale convened a meeting to form the Intercollegiate Football Association. However, Harvard did not join the Association, having over a period of years developed its own conflicting "Boston game" in which it was permitted to catch, handle, and run with the inflated rubber ball.

Unable to compete with other American schools, Harvard scheduled a series of games with McGill University of Montreal. The initial contest was played by Harvard's rules, but the following day, May 15, 1874, McGill introduced the game of rugby in the United States. Thus began America's fascination for the odd egg-shaped ball and for a game which would soon begin to undergo great changes, although always retaining the running and tackling of rugby. Within two years, a slightly modified form of rugby had been adopted officially by Harvard, Yale, Princeton, Columbia, and Rutgers under a new Inter-collegiate Football Association.

The first changes which would separate the American game from rugby occurred in 1880. Led by a twenty-year-old Yale halfback, Walter Camp, the rules committee agreed to a reduction of players from fifteen to eleven players per side, the naming of team positions, and the substitution of scrimmage for the rugby scrum. The scrimmage line, giving unhindered possession of the ball to one team until the ball was "snapped" back by the center to the quarterback, is considered the most important rule of football, allowing variable strategies to be implemented with prearranged plays. Camp also persuaded the committee to change the standard field size from the original 140 by 70 yards to 110 by 53-1/3 yards (the maximum width which could be accommodated in Harvard's stadium). In 1882, the rules committee introduced "downs," compelling the offensive team to advance the ball 5 yards within three consecutive downs or lose possession to the opponent. In the same year, new scoring values were assigned. For the first time, a total of four touchdowns was given precedence over a goal from the field (field goal) and two safeties were made equal to one touchdown. Changes would continue to be made until 1912, when the present field dimensions and scoring values were codified.

In 1887, Pennsylvania and Rutgers played the first indoor football game in Madison Square Garden. In 1889, Walter Camp chose the first All-America team for Caspar Whitney's magazine, *Week's Sport*. Among his selections was Yale end Amos Alonzo Stagg, a future legendary coach, whose all-time record of 314 victories wasn't surpassed until 1981 by Alabama coach Paul "Bear" Bryant. Also selected from Yale was guard William "Pudge" Heffelfinger, who in 1892 was paid $500 to play for the Allegheny Athletic Association in a game against the Pittsburgh Athletic Club, becoming the first known professional football player.

The same year, Harvard coach L.H. Deland opened the second half of the Yale-Harvard game with the devastating flying wedge. With the quarterback at his own 40-yard line with the ball, his teammates were arranged in two groups, about 20 yards back and wide to either side. On a signal, both groups of players ran toward the quarterback, who put the ball in play (touched it to his foot) just as they passed and overlapped in front of him. The ball was handed off to a halfback who fell in behind the steam-rolling wedge. On that first occasion, the play went 50 yards before Yale could down the ballcarrier, and the era of the flying wedge had begun. Already criticized for being too rough (Harvard had once banned the sport for a year in 1885), football was becoming even more violent, and injuries abounded. At the line of scrimmage, opposing linemen stood toe-to-toe, grappling, punching, and kicking at each other throughout a game. The introduction in 1903 of the neutral zone separating the two lines helped this somewhat, but rules to protect the ballcarrier were largely ignored. The player with the ball was often the object of a violent tug-of-war between the offense and defense, and, to preserve flesh and hair, would have leather handles attached to his uniform.

In 1905, eighteen fatalities and 159 serious injuries were reported. "Dead and wounded of the football battlefields," read the headline of a December feature in *The World*, a New York paper. The story called football "the most brutal, perilous, and unnecessary sport sanctioned by any country in the world." All across America, educators, clergymen, and parents clamored for an end to football. Finally, horrified by a newspaper photograph of 250-pound Swarthmore lineman Bob Maxwell (for whom the Maxwell Trophy was later named), bloodied and beaten after a game, President Theodore Roosevelt summoned college athletic leaders to the White House and threatened to ban the sport by executive order if the violence wasn't curbed.

In December of 1905, New York University Chancellor Henry M. MacCracken called a special meeting of the football-playing colleges of the nation, at which it was decided to completely reform the sport. In a second meeting the same month, with representatives of sixty-two institutions in attendance, a new Football Rules Committee was appointed and the Intercollegiate Athletic Association of the United States was formed (in 1910, renamed the National Collegiate Athletic Association).

Sweeping rules changes followed for the 1906 season, the most important of which prohibited almost all mass formations and plays, upped the yards to gain in a series of downs to ten, and legalized the forward pass. Both Wesleyan (vs. Yale) and Yale (vs.

Harvard) are said to have been among the first to have used a pass in 1906, but it would be many years before the potential of the forward pass was fully realized.

In 1913, a team from a Catholic university in Indiana traveled to West Point to play what was considered little more than a tune-up game for powerhouse Army. Instead, Notre Dame stunned their hosts 39-13. Quarterback Gus Dorns repeatedly dumbfounded the hulking Army players with pinpoint passes to end Knute Rockne. It was, of course, just the beginning of the legendary exploits of Rockne and Notre Dame, but it was also a turning point in the history of college football. Notre Dame's astonishing feat proved that smaller colleges with relatively modest football programs and normal-sized players could compete with the football juggernauts, by the use of clever strategy and the forward pass.

The first "professional" football game was the one in which Pudge Heffelfinger played in 1892. Subsequent attempts to form a professional league were unsuccessful. Because of competition from the college game, real and imagined scandals, and a lack of finances, only a few individual clubs were able to survive, such as the team founded in 1898 in Chicago by the Morgan Athletic Club (ultimately becoming the St. Louis Cardinals, the oldest continuing operation in professional football).

In 1902, the Philadelphia Athletics, organized by Connie Mack as a football counterpart to his champion baseball team, played in the first night football game with baseball pitcher Rube Waddell in the lineup, but the Athletics only lasted two seasons. After a betting scandal in 1906 ended an earlier effort in Ohio, the Canton Bulldogs were revived in 1915, with the signing of college star and 1912 Olympic hero Jim Thorpe. Making use of Thorpe's extraordinary ability, Canton won ten straight games in 1916.

Finally, in 1920, twelve teams from five states formed the American Professional Football Association, with Jim Thorpe as league president. Among the teams represented were Thorpe's Canton Bulldogs, the Racine Cardinals of Chicago (later St. Louis), the Decatur Staleys (later the Chicago Bears) with player-coach George Halas, and a year later, the Green Bay Packers. In 1922, the APFA changed its name to the National Football League, but had little success until 1925, when University of Illinois three-time All-American Harold E. "Red" Grange left school at the end of the season to play for the Chicago Bears.

Grange, "The Galloping Ghost," was at the time the most spectacular player ever. In his three years at Illinois, he rushed for 3,637 yards, once scoring four touchdowns in the first ten minutes of a game against Michigan in 1924. His enormous popularity made his signing the turning point for professional football and the NFL. Thirty-eight thousand fans watched his first game against the Cardinals, and the Bears immediately launched a barnstorming tour, playing seven games in eleven days. A record crowd of 70,000 saw Grange and the Bears at the Polo Grounds against the New York Giants, 5,000 more than were at the Army-Navy game the week before.

A parade of college stars followed Grange's example and turned pro. Though many weak franchises were forced to drop out, professional football was beginning to attract crowds with well-known college players like Stanford's Ernie Nevers, Michigan's Benny Friedman, the famed Four Horsemen of Notre Dame, and Minnesota's Bronko Nagurski.

Rule changes which slimmed the football in 1929 and 1933 virtually eliminated the drop kick because of the untrue bounce of the more pointed ends, but they also made the ball easier to throw and control. Ten-yard inbounds lines were adopted in 1933 and increased to 15 yards in 1935 (1938 in college play).

In 1934, the NFL legalized the forward pass from anywhere behind the line of scrimmage. The same year, the first College All-Star game was played in Chicago before 79,432 fans, with the collegians holding the Chicago Bears to a scoreless tie. In 1936, the first college draft was held, with the team finishing last in the standings having first choice on each round of the draft. A far-reaching idea, the draft was designed to equalize the strengths of teams throughout the league, and to prevent any one team from dominating the game. This same principle was eventually adopted by other professional sports.

In 1939, a game at Ebbets Field between the Philadelphia Eagles and Brooklyn Dodgers was broadcast live by NBC, becoming the first NFL game ever to be televised. Only two cameras were used for that game (one at ground level and one in the stands), which was announced by Allan "Skip" Walz.

The following year, the modern T formation, as developed by Stanford coach Clark Shaughnessy and George Halas and coach Ralph Jones of the Chicago Bears (with Shaughnessy as a special advisor), revolutionized football offense with its counterplays, players in motion, and forward pass options. In the first championship carried on network radio, the Bears used the T formation to defeat Washington 73-0 to become the 1940 NFL champions, with sportscaster Red Barber doing the play-by-play for 120 stations of the Mutual Broadcasting System.

In 1946, the Cleveland franchise was transferred to Los Angeles to become the Los Angeles Rams, making the NFL a coast-to-coast league for the first time. An eight-team rival league, the All-America Football Conference, was formed the same year. The two leagues agreed to merge in 1950, with three AAFC teams being added to the NFL: the Cleveland Browns, the San Francisco 49ers, and the Baltimore Colts.

In the 1950s, professional football was to emerge as the most popular spectator sport in America. The 1951 NFL championship game, in which Los Angeles defeated Cleveland 24-17, was televised coast-to-coast for the first time. Wisely, NFL Commissioner Bert Bell formulated a league policy of televising away games, blacking out only the city where the game was being played. Millions who had never seen a game in person now watched on television just at the time football was being made even more exciting by explosive passing attacks by quarterbacks such as Otto Graham of Paul Brown's Cleveland Browns, Bobby Layne of the Detroit Lions, and Johnny Unitas of the Baltimore Colts.

In 1960, an eight-team professional league began to operate as the American Football League. Fueled by generous contracts from television networks, the two leagues battled fiercely for college talent, while on the field, professional football came under the domination of one team, the Green Bay Packers, led by the legendary Vince Lombardi. In last place when he came to coach them in 1959, the Packers were Western Conference Champions by 1960, and NFL Champions by 1961. Though individual stars like Cleveland Brown running back Jim Brown continued to set records (many of which stand even today), and new lights emerged like Chicago Bears middle linebacker Dick Butkus and running back Gale Sayers, defensive linemen Merlin Olsen of the Los Angeles Rams, Bob Lilly of the Dallas Cowboys, and New York Jets quarterback Joe Namath, the 1960s will always be remembered for the dynasty of Vince Lombardi's Green Bay Packers (a total of five NFL championships).

The AFL-NFL war reached its peak in 1966, with the leagues spending a combined total of $7 million to sign their draft choices that year. Later in 1966, a merger was announced, with the leagues agreeing to play separate schedules until 1970, but meeting in a world championship game (the Super Bowl) beginning in 1967.

Lombardi's Green Bay Packers defeated the AFL Kansas City Chiefs in Super Bowl I in 1967 and the AFL Oakland Raiders in Super Bowl II in 1968. In 1969, Joe Namath led the AFL New York Jets to victory over the NFL's Baltimore Colts in Super Bowl III.

Though briefly challenged by the would-be rival World Football League in 1974 and 1975, the NFL became even stronger in the 1970s, with record network television contracts (and ABC's innovative Monday Night Football starting in 1970), new expansion franchises in Tampa and Seattle, rule changes adopted in 1978 to stimulate offense by opening up the passing game, and exciting players such as Fran Tarkenton, Bob Griese, Ken Stabler, Roger Staubach, O.J. Simpson, Walter Payton, and Franco Harris.

Though a combination of escalating operating budgets, injuries, and resulting insurance problems began to cause a dropoff in youth and high school-level football programs in the late 1970s, football's place as America's most popular spectator sport seems secure for the 1980s. In 1982, the twelve-team professional United States Football League (USFL) was formed to conduct an eighteen-week schedule from March through June, normally football's off season. Undoubtedly, football fans young and old will continue to be thrilled by the gridiron exploits of college and professional players like Tony Dorsett, Earl Campbell, Billy Sims, George Rogers, Marcus Allen, Herschell Walker, and others following in the footsteps of Jim Thorpe, Red Grange, and Ernie Nevers.

ace formation: see *one-back formation.*

aerial: A pass or pertaining to a pass. (won with an inspired aerial attack)

AFC: The American Football Conference.

A formation: see *one-back formation.*

against the grain: Toward the sideline opposite the direction most players are moving.

air: Pass plays or pertaining to pass plays. (went to the air in the second half)

air it out: To pass or attempt to pass, especially a long pass. (will air it out on third-and-long) also *put it up.*

All-America: A national honor given annually to outstanding college football players at each of the positions on a team. Yale player, coach, and football innovator Walter Camp chose the first All-America team in 1889 for Casper Whitney's magazine, *Week's Sports.* The honor and title of All-America is now also given to athletes who participate in other sports at both the college and high school level.

All-American: A player named to an All-America team.

●●Excellent, or exemplary. (a clean-cut All-American boy)

alley: A gap between players in the offensive line through which a defensive player attempts to rush into the offensive backfield.

All-Pro: 1. An honor and title given annually to outstanding professional football players at each of the positions of an all-star team, as selected by a national news service, or by the Professional Football Writers Association. Among the players selected for the first All-Pro team in 1920 (then called All-League) were Jim Thorpe of the Canton Bulldogs, and George Halas of the Decatur Staleys, later to become the Chicago Bears. 2. A player named to an All-Pro team.

all the way: The remaining yards for a touchdown. (to the forty, to the thirty, he's going all the way)

American Football Conference: One of the two conferences of the National Football League, the championship teams of which compete annually for the national championship in the Super Bowl, and from which individual players are selected to compete in the annual AFC-NFC Pro Bowl. The AFC is made up of three divisions: the Eastern Division, which is comprised of the Baltimore Colts, Buffalo Bills, the Miami Dolphins, the New England Patriots, and the New York Jets; the Central Division, which is comprised of the Cincinnati Bengals, the Cleveland Browns, the Houston Oilers, and the Pittsburgh Steelers; and the Western Division, which is comprised of the Denver Broncos, the Kansas City Chiefs, the Los Angeles Raiders, the San Diego Chargers, and the Seattle Seahawks. also *AFC.*

angle block: A block in which contact is made diagonally, as when an opponent is lined up just to the left or right of the blocker.

approved ruling: An official ruling for a given set of circumstances.

area blocking: A blocking strategy in which specific areas or zones are assigned to offensive players to protect, and any opponent entering the zone is blocked (as opposed to individual blocking of designated players). also *zone blocking.*

armchair quarterback: One who criticizes or second-guesses a team's play, though neither personally concerned nor necessarily well informed. compare *curbstone coach, grandstand quarterback, Monday morning quarterback.*

●●A kibbitzer, one who second-guesses or offers advice about matters with which he is not concerned.

1. arm tackle: To tackle a ballcarrier using just one or both arms, without the shoulder or body. (a powerful runner who is almost impossible to arm tackle)

2. arm tackle: The act or an instance of arm tackling a ballcarrier.

artificial turf: A synthetic surface used as a substitute for grass in some stadiums.

AstroTurf: A brand of artifical turf developed by Monsanto for use inside the Houston Astrodome in 1965.

audibilize: To call an audible at the line of scrimmage. also *check off.*

audible: A verbal change of the intended offensive play or defensive alignment made in code at the line of scrimmage, as to adjust to a particular deployment of players or anticipated action by the opposing team. An audible is usually called by the quarterback on offense, or the middle linebacker on defense. also *automatic.*

automatic: see *audible.*

back: One who plays in the offensive or

ANGLE BLOCK

defensive backfield. see *defensive back, offensive back.*

backer-up: see *linebacker.*

backfield: 1. The offensive and defensive backs. see *offensive back, defensive back.* 2. The positions played by the offensive and defensive backs. 3. The area behind the line of scrimmage.

backfield in motion: see *illegal motion.*

backfield line: The imaginary vertical plane 1 yard behind and parallel to the line of scrimmage in the offensive backfield (or in high school play, even with the waistline of an offensive lineman). No offensive back except the player "under the center" (usually the quarterback) is permitted to line up in front of the backfield line.

back judge: A football official who, at the snap, is positioned approximately 17 yards downfield on the same side of the field as the line judge, and who is responsible for judging when and where the ball or the ballcarrier go out of bounds downfield on his side, watching for clips and pass interference on his side behind the area covered by the umpire, counting the number of defensive players on each play, ruling with the field judge on conversions and field goals, and recording all time-outs.

backpedal: To run backwards while facing an opponent or a play in progress. Often defensive backs must backpedal while guarding the receivers of the opposing team.

backward pass: see *lateral.*

bait the hole: To fake a pass, pitchout, or handoff in order to lure a rusher through a gap in the offensive line so that he can be trap blocked away from the intended path of the ballcarrier.

balanced line: An offensive alignment with an equal number of players on either side of the center.

ball: see *football.*

ballcarrier: The player (usually a halfback or fullback) who carries the ball on a running play, whether directly from the snap or on a handoff or pitchout. also *runner.* compare *receiver.*

ball control: An offensive strategy in which a team attempts to maintain possession of the ball for as long as possible while advancing methodically toward the opposing team's goal line. A ball control offense usually features a strong running game and conservative short

127

passes to maximize the chances of consecutive first downs. also *possession football*.

ball hawk: A defensive player who often gains possession of the ball; one who is particularly adept at intercepting passes and recovering fumbles and loose balls.

1. bat: The intentional striking of a loose ball or a ball in player possession with the hand, fist, elbow, or forearm. A bat is illegal if used to punch a loose ball in the field of play toward the opponent's goal line, a loose ball in any direction if it is in either end zone, a ball in the possession of a player, or a pass in flight forward toward the opponent's goal line. An illegal bat results in a 10-yard penalty.

2. bat: To punch or strike the ball with the hand, fist, elbow, or forearm.

beat the line: see *beat the spread*.

beat the price: see *beat the spread*.

beat the spread: 1. Betting parlance meaning to win a wager, either by betting on a favored team which wins by more than the point spread or by betting on an underdog which wins, or loses by less than the point spread. If the favored team wins by the same number of points indicated in the point spread, the bet is considered a "push" and is usually cancelled. also *beat the line, beat the price*. see *point spread*. 2. To win a game one's team is favored to win by more than the point spread, or to defeat a favored opponent or lose by less than the point spread. (managed to beat the spread only once in their last three games) also *beat the line, beat the price*. see *point spread*.

belly back: To momentarily carry the ball away from the line of scrimmage on a sweep in order to get around blockers and rushing linemen.

belly series: A series of offensive running and passing plays which begin in the same manner, with a handoff or fake handoff to the midsection of a running back.

1. bench: 1. The long seat adjacent to the sideline, where players sit during a game. Usually, team benches are centered on the 50-yard line on opposite sides of the field. 2. Players not on the first string, but held in reserve as substitutes. 3. The area in front of and immediately around the bench, from where the coach and coaching staff observe

and send plays into a game. (scored with a trick play from the bench) also *sideline*.

2. bench: 1. To take a player out of a game, or to prevent a player from taking part in one or more games. 2. To cause a player to be unable to play. (benched by a pulled hamstring) also *hamstring*.

bench warmer: A reserve player. One who "warms" the bench by sitting on it for long periods of time.

Big Ben: A Hail Mary pass play used in desperation (such as when trailing in the closing moments of a game) in which the ball is passed into a group of receivers in or near the end zone in the hopes that one receiver will be able to leap up over covering defenders and tip the ball to an eligible teammate. Most professional teams now use a version of the Big Ben play, popularized by the Minnesota Vikings in 1980, when a pass from Viking quarterback Tommy Kramer was successfully tipped to receiver Ahmad Rashad to defeat the Cleveland Browns 28-23 in a critical, late-season game.

betting line: The point spread set by oddsmakers for a particular game. also *line, point line, price*.

big play: An important or consequential play, especially one that changes the momentum of a game or insures a victory. A big play can be a spectacular kickoff return or run, the completion of a "bomb," a pivotal goal line stand, or a timely interception or fumble recovery.

birdcage: A cagelike metal face mask attached to the front of a helmet, consisting of several horizontal bars bisected by a central vertical bar. see *face mask*.

black out: To ban or withhold the local telecast of a home game.

blackout: The banning of a local telecast for a home game. First adopted as NFL policy in the early 1950s and modified in 1973 to permit a local telecast if a sellout is declared seventy-two hours before game time.

1. blind side: The side a quarterback cannot see once in position to throw (the left side for a right-handed quarterback). When a quarterback is sacked or injured, it is often the result of a blind side hit.

2. blind side: To hit or tackle a quarterback on his blind side. (blind sided and thrown for a 5-yard loss)

1. blitz: A defensive play used in passing situations in which one or more defensive backs rush the quarterback at the snap in an attempt to sack him, or to block or hurry his throw. In common usage, the meaning of the term is often broadened to include rushing linebackers. The blitz can be an effective tactic against the pass, but if the blitzers are unable to reach the quarterback before he passes, the deep backs are then left to cover receivers man-for-man, and are, therefore, vulnerable. In addition, if detected or anticipated by the quarterback, a blitz can be taken advantage of by a run or a short pass, particularly to the area vacated by the blitzers. compare *red dog*.

2. blitz: 1. To execute a blitz. 2. To have one or more defensive backs or linebackers execute a blitz.

blitzer: A linebacker or defensive back who takes part in a blitz.

1. block: To legally use the shoulders or body (but not the hands) to delay or obstruct a defensive player from the front or side, or to knock him down or move him out of the way in order to protect or clear a path for the ballcarrier or passer.

2. block: The act or an instance of blocking.

blocking back: An offensive back (often the fullback) whose primary responsibility is to block in front of a running back, or block for the quarterback during a pass attempt.

blow a coverage: 1. To miss or poorly execute a defensive assignment to cover a receiver or zone, often resulting in the completion of a pass. 2. To misread a defensive coverage and throw a pass to a well-defended receiver, often resulting in an interception.

blow dead: To signal by blowing a whistle that the ball is no longer in play. The ball is blown dead by an official if it is downed or travels out of bounds, if a time out is called, or because of a rules infraction.

blow in: To break through the offensive line into the backfield. (blew in on a blitz and sacked the quarterback)

body block: A block in which the side of the body is used to hit the opponent instead of the shoulders. Football coach Glenn S. "Pop" Warner is credited with inventing the body block. also *crab block, cross-body block*. compare *shoulder block*.

1. bomb: A long pass, especially a touchdown pass. First used to describe the "aerial bombardment" of the 1951 Los

BOX AND CHAIN CREW

Angeles Rams, with quarterbacks Bob Waterfield and Norm Van Brocklin and receivers Tom Fears and Elroy "Crazylegs" Hirsch, all Pro Football Hall of Famers.

2. bomb: To throw a long pass, or long passes.

bomb squad: see *suicide squad.*

1. bootleg: An offensive play in which the quarterback attempts to deceive the defense by faking a handoff in one direction, then moving toward the opposite sideline (as though finished with the play) with the ball hidden behind his hip, before running or passing. The term "bootleg" derives from the quarterback's "smuggling" action with the ball.

2. bootleg: 1. To execute a bootleg. 2. To gain yardage with a bootleg play. (bootlegged 3 yards for the score)

bowl game: An annual post-season exhibition game between teams invited on the basis of performance during the regular season or all-star teams. The first such annual game was the Tournament of Roses, played in Pasadena, California in 1902. Michigan defeated Stanford that year 49-0. In 1923, the game was moved to the newly completed Rose Bowl stadium, taking its name thereafter to become the first bowl game.

box and chain crew: A group of workers who, under the supervision of the linesman, operate the 10-yard measuring chain and the down box on one sideline of the field. also *chain crew, chain gang.*

boxman: The member of the box and chain crew responsible for operating the down box.

break a tackle: To break out of the grasp of a tackler and continue running with the ball. (not only has good speed, but enough power to break tackles)

breakaway runner, breakaway threat: A runner with the agility and speed to be able to get through or around tacklers for a long gain.

break off a run: To successfully execute a running play, especially for a long gain. (finally managed to break off a long run and score)

bring down: To tackle the ballcarrier.

broken field: The sparsely defended area of the field beyond the line of scrimmage, or away from the point of origin of a play. also *open field.*

broken-field runner: A player who is adept at broken-field running.

broken-field running: Eluding tacklers in an open field, often without the aid of blockers running interference.

broken play: A play that does not go according to plan, usually due to a mix-up between the quarterback and the running backs or receivers. In such a case, the quarterback is forced to improvise to avoid being thrown for a loss. also *busted play.*

brush block: A block that is intended only to momentarily obstruct or delay an opponent rather than knock him down, often used by a receiver.

bubble: The potentially weak and vulnerable spot in an "over" or "under" defense covered only by the middle linebacker who has changed places with the shifted defensive tackle. Because the linebacker is usually physically smaller than the shifted defensive tackle, and because he must play off the line in case of a pass, a quarterback will often call a running play directly at the bubble. see *over, under.*

bullet: A hard straight pass.

bump and go: see *bump and run.*

bump and run: A defensive technique first popularized in the 1960s in the AFL, in which a cornerback covering a wide receiver chucks or makes contact with the receiver as he comes off the line to momentarily delay him and disturb his concentration, then runs with him to defend man-for-man against a pass. Contact on a bump and run is limited to one chuck and may be made only within 5 yards of the line of scrimmage. also *bump and go.*

burner: A particularly fast runner, usually a receiver or running back.

busted play: see *broken play.*

butt-blocking: An illegal technique in which the face mask, front, or top of the helmet is driven directly into an opponent as the primary point of contact either in close line play or in the open field. Dangerous to both the blocker and opponent, butt-blocking results in a 15-yard penalty.

buttonhook: see *comeback.*

cab squad: see *taxi squad.*

cadence: see *signals.*

cage: see *birdcage.*

1. call: 1. A ruling by an official (such as on an infraction, a question of whether or not the ball or a player was out of bounds, etc.). 2. The choice or selection of a play.

2. call: 1. To make an official ruling. 2. To select a team's plays. (too inexperienced to call his own plays)

Canadian football: A game similar to American football with the following rule differences. In Canadian football there are twelve players on a team instead of eleven (the extra man is a backfield player). The playing field is 110 yards long between goal lines and 65 yards wide, with 25-yard end zones (goal posts on the goal lines). A team is allowed three downs, instead of four, to make 10 yards, and any number of backfield players may be in motion in any direction at the snap, instead of just one back moving backwards or laterally. The offensive line of scrimmage is at the forward point of the football, and the defensive linemen may line up no closer than 1 yard beyond. One point is awarded for a PAT (called a "convert") if it is kicked through the uprights, two points if it is run or passed into the end zone. If a player is unable to run a punted ball out of his end zone, or if a punted ball travels through the end zone and across the end boundary (called the "deadline") or sideline, a "rouge" or "single" is scored, for which one point is awarded. All other scoring is the same as in American football. There is no fair catch on a punt, but tacklers must remain outside a 5-yard area around the receiver until he has touched the ball. Blocking above the waist is permitted on punt returns. The ball is kicked off from the 45-yard line at the start of each half and after a touchdown. After a field goal, the team scored against may take a first down or kick off from its own 35-yard line, or elect to receive a kickoff. After a "rouge," the team scored against gets a first down on its own 35-yard line. Only one time-out per team is permitted, and then, only in the last three minutes of each half. There are 5, 10, 15, and 25-yard penalties (disqualification accompanies the 25-yard foul for rough play or fighting), and no yardage difference between offensive and defensive penalties. A game is played in four quarters of fifteen minutes each. The attacking team is given twenty seconds

to put the ball into play, but the referee allows "reasonable" time for teams to line up and make substitutions, before starting the time count. If even one second of a period remains after the previous play ends, one complete play must be permitted.

Canadian Football League: The major professional football league in Canada. Established in 1958, the Canadian Football League is split into two geographic divisions. The Western Division is comprised of the British Columbia Lions, the Calgary Stampeders, the Edmonton Eskimos, the Saskatchewan Roughriders, and the Winnipeg Blue Bombers, and the Eastern Division is comprised of the Hamilton Tiger-Cats, the Montreal Concordes, the Ottawa Rough Riders, and the Toronto Argonauts. Division winners meet annually in late November to play for the national championship and the Grey Cup, put up in 1909 by Earl Grey, then governor general, for "the rugby-football championship of Canada." also *CFL*.

1. carry: To run with the ball. also *run, rush.*

2. carry: The act of running with the ball. (gained 75 yards in fifteen carries) also *run, rush.*

1. center: 1. The player positioned in the middle of the offensive line who snaps the ball between his legs to a back (usually the quarterback) to begin play on each down. The center and quarterback positions were created in 1880 when the intercollegiate rules committee adopted the scrimmage concept with a center snap urged by Walter Camp, a twenty-year-old Yale halfback who is now called the primary architect of American football. also *snapper*. 2. The position played by the center. (at center, a two-time All-Pro)

2. center: To snap the ball to a back to begin play on a down. also *hike, snap.*

center snap: see *snap.*

CFA: The Canadian Football Association.

CFL: The Canadian Football League.

chain: The 10-yard long chain (with a rod attached at each end) used to measure the distance the ball must be advanced by the offensive team in a series of four downs in order to maintain possession of the ball for a new series of downs (first-and-ten). If the ball has been advanced close to the 10 yards necessary for a first down, the referee may request, or be asked by a team captain to request, that the chain be brought out onto the field for an exact measurement. also *measuring sticks, sticks, yardage chain.*

chain crew, chain gang: see *box and chain crew.*

chalk talk: A team meeting in which tactics and specific plays are diagrammed (such as on a chalkboard) and discussed. also *skull session, skull practice.*

●●A meeting or session in which a blackboard is used for diagrams or illustrations.

cheat: To bias one's defensive position toward one side in anticipation of a play in that direction.

check: To execute a brush block, momentarily obstructing or delaying an opponent (as opposed to knocking him down).

check off: see *audibilize.*

chicken-fight: To stand an opponent up and block him from an upright position (sometimes several times in succession while slowly backing up) in order to protect the passer.

chop block: An illegal delayed block at or below the knees against an opponent who is in contact with a teammate of the blocker in the free-blocking zone (a rectangular area extending 4 yards on either side of the point from which the ball is centered, and 3 yards behind

each scrimmage line). In high school play, a chop block results in a 15-yard penalty.

1. chuck: To bump a receiver with the hands, arms, or body as he comes off the line in order to momentarily delay his pass route. Legal one time within 5 yards of the line of scrimmage. also *jam.*

2. chuck: The act of chucking.

1. circle: see *circle pattern.*

2. circle: 1. To run a circle pattern or route. 2. To call a circle pattern for a receiver. (circles the left end and hits him over the middle)

circle pass: A pass thrown to a receiver in a circle pattern or route.

circle pattern, circle route: A pass route in which a receiver circles in toward the middle. also *circle.*

circus catch: An extraordinary or spectacular catch. Originally a baseball expression, first used in the late 1800s.

1. cleat: One of a number of cone-shaped 1/2-inch long projections that extend from the bottom of a football shoe. A cleat may be no less than 3/4-inches in diameter at the free end and must be constructed of a material that does not chip or develop a cutting edge (usually hard rubber or nylon). also *stud.*

2. cleat: To kick or scrape a player with the cleats of a football shoe.

cleats: Football shoes with cleats on the soles.

1. clip: To illegally block or charge into an

CIRCUS CATCH

opponent who is not the ballcarrier below the waist from behind. It is not considered clipping if the opponent is hit within a specified clipping zone or free-blocking zone around the point from which the ball is snapped, as long as the blocker was in the zone at the snap. To clip is a foul that results in a 15-yard penalty.

2. clip: The act of clipping. also *clipping*.

clipping: The act of clipping an opponent, a foul that results in a 15-yard penalty. also *clip*.

clipping zone: A specified rectangular area around the line of scrimmage (extending laterally 4 yards on either side of the spot from which the ball is snapped and 3 yards behind each scrimmage line, or in the NFL, extending laterally to the position occupied by the offensive tackles at the snap and 3 yards back from each line of scrimmage). A player positioned inside the clipping zone at the snap may legally block an opponent below the waist from behind within the zone. also *free-blocking zone*.

clock play: An offensive play used to stop the clock near the end of a period of play, usually a pass thrown to a receiver near the sideline. If the pass is incomplete, or if the pass is complete and the receiver steps out of bounds, the clock automatically stops.

1. clothesline: A dangerous and illegal tackle in which an arm is swung or extended to deliberately catch a ballcarrier by the head, much like an unseen clothesline might. A foul that results in a 15-yard penalty.

2. clothesline: To execute a clothesline tackle.

coffin corner: Any of the four corners of a field where the sidelines and goal lines intersect. Punters aim for a coffin corner in the hopes that the ball will go out of bounds just short of the opponent's goal line, thereby preventing a return and insuring that the opponents will have to put the ball in play dangerously close to their own goal line.

College Football Association: An association within the NCAA of large schools with extensive football programs. Formed in 1976 to lobby for a stronger voice in the determination of NCAA bylaws and policies governing football, the College Football Association came into open conflict with the NCAA in 1981 by offering to negotiate independently with the major networks for the right to televise football games of its members. also *CFA*.

College Football Hall of Fame: The national institution that honors outstanding college football players. The Hall of Fame was opened in 1978 at Kings Island, Ohio (near Cincinnati).

color: Commentary and incidental information that makes the radio or television broadcast of a game more interesting and/or informative, usually provided by someone other than the play-by-play announcer.

color commentator: The member of a radio or television broadcast team who provides commentary or incidental information to augment the play-by-play account of a game. also *color man*.

color man: see *color commentator*.

combination coverage: A defensive strategy that employs double coverage for a receiver on one side of the field, and man-for-man coverage for the receiver on the other side of the field.

comeback, comebacker: A pass pattern in which the receiver runs straight ahead, then abruptly turns back toward the passer. also *buttonhook, hook*.

come off the ball: To react quickly and

CLIPPING

133

spring forward from a set position the moment the ball is snapped. Play at the line of scrimmage is often dictated by the team that has the ability to come off the ball quickly, or "fire out." also *move off the ball.*

compensation: Money and/or future draft choices given to a team to compensate for the loss of the services of a high-quality veteran player who has played out his option, by the team signing the player at the end of the option year. see *option.*

1. complete: To throw a pass that is caught by the intended receiver. (completes a short pass over the middle to the tight end)

2. complete: Caught by the intended receiver. (a long pass, complete at the 2-yard line)

completion: A completed forward pass. A completion is credited to the passer in statistical records. Fran Tarkenton of the Minnesota Vikings and New York Giants holds the NFL career record for completions, 3,686. San Diego Chargers quarterback Dan Fouts holds the NFL record for the most completions in a season, 348 in 1980. Richard Todd of the New York Jets set the NFL one-game record for completions on September 21, 1980, against the San Francisco 49ers, 42.

conversion: The scoring of one or two extra points on a try for point after a touchdown. see *convert.*

convert: To score on a try for point after a touchdown, either by kicking the ball over the crossbar between the goal posts, or running or passing the ball over the goal line. In college and high school play, two points are awarded for running or passing the ball over the goal line.

corner: see *cornerback.*

cornerback: 1. One of two defensive backs who line up behind and outside the linebackers (usually opposite the wide receivers), and whose primary responsibilities are to prevent the opponents from turning the corner on sweeps and to cover the wide receivers on pass plays. also *corner, cornerman.* 2. The position played by a cornerback. also *corner, cornerman.*

corner blitz: A blitz by one or both cornerbacks. see *blitz.*

cornerman: A cornerback. also *corner.*

corner route: see *flag.*

cough up the ball: To fumble and lose possession of the ball. (coughed up the ball on their own 3-yard line)

count: see *signals.*

counter, counter play: An offensive play in which the ballcarrier runs "against the grain," toward the sideline opposite the direction most players are moving.

cover: 1. To guard a receiver in order to prevent him from catching a forward pass. 2. To defend in a particular area or zone. (the safety covered deep)

coverage: The covering of a receiver or receivers, or the manner in which a receiver or receivers are covered (man-for-man, zone, etc.).

crab block: see *body block.*

crackback block: An illegal block in which a flanking player (2 yards or more outside the tackle) turns in and blocks a defensive player from the side or back within an area 5 yards on either side of the line of scrimmage. A foul that results in a 15-yard penalty.

crawling: An attempt by a runner to advance the ball on the ground after he has been downed, or after the ball has been blown dead. A foul that results in a 5-yard penalty.

cross: A pass pattern in which receivers on opposite sides of the field run downfield and turn inward so that their routes cross. also *crossing pattern.*

1. cross block: A side block made on a defensive lineman positioned to one side of (as opposed to directly across the line from) the blocker, either to move the defensive player laterally to clear a path for a particular play, or to vary from normal blocking patterns by switching assignments with another blocker. Invented by pioneer football coach Amos Alonzo Stagg.

2. cross block: To execute a cross block.

cross-body block: see *body block.*

cross buck: An offensive play in which the quarterback hands the ball off to one of two running backs (faking to the other) who run past him toward the line on diagonally crossing paths. Invention of the cross buck credited to Amos Alonzo Stagg.

crossing pattern: see *cross.*

curbstone coach: see *grandstand quarterback.*

1. curl: A pass pattern in which the receiver runs straight ahead, then turns inside or outside and curls back toward the line of scrimmage. also *curl-in, curl-out.*

2. curl: To run a curl pattern.

curl-in: see *curl.*

curl-out: see *curl.*

1. cut: 1. To suddenly change direction, often with a burst of acceleration or after a fake in the opposite direction. 2. To eliminate from a team. (cut five men in the final week of practice)

2. cut: 1. A sudden change of direction. (eludes the tackle with a quick cut inside) 2. The elimination of a player from a team. (survived the last cut) see *make the cut.*

cut back: To suddenly almost reverse direction with a cut, such as back into the middle after running wide.

cutback: The act of cutting back.

cut block: A low block (below the knees) made by interior linemen to trip defensive linemen. also *cutoff block.*

cutoff block: see *cut block.*

D: Defense. (the D has held again)

daylight: A gap or open space between defensive players. (moves laterally, looking for some daylight) also *hole.*

D back: A defensive back.

dead ball: A ball that is out of play. A ball is dead if it is downed or travels out of bounds, if a fair catch is made, if a time out is called, or if an official blows a whistle to indicate a rules infraction.

dead man play: see *hideout play.*

decline a penalty: To exercise the option given to the captain of the offended team on most fouls and refuse a penalty, in which case play proceeds with the next down as though no foul had been committed. The captain of the offended team will decline a penalty if the existing field position and down favor his team.

deep: 1. Far away from either side of the line of scrimmage. (sends his receivers deep, looking for the bomb) 2. Close to either team's goal line. (will be forced to put the ball in play deep in their own territory) 3. Having an ample number of players available for or capable of playing a position or positions. (deep in receivers) see *depth.*

deep drop: The movement of the quarterback to a position far back from the line of scrimmage in order to throw a pass. A deep drop is taken to avoid a pass rush and to provide a quarterback with an extra measure of time to find an open receiver.

1. defense: 1. The endeavor to stop the opposing team from advancing the ball or scoring, and whenever possible, to get possession of the ball for one's own team. (a conservative, defense-oriented team) also *D.* 2. The specific plan or alignment used to defend. (use the nickel defense against the pass) 3. The defensive team or its members. also *D, defensive team, defensive unit.*

2. defense: To defend against an opposing player, team, or play. (made some adjustments to defense the pass effectively)

defensive: Pertaining to defense, or the playing of defense. (defensive play) (defensive game plan)

defensive back: 1. One of the players (usually two cornerbacks and two safeties) positioned behind (and outside in the case of cornerbacks) the linebackers in the defensive backfield, and who are primarily responsible for defending against passes, and for preventing long gains on running plays which get through or around the defensive line. For special defensive coverages, extra defensive backs replace one or more linebackers. also *back, D back.* 2. The position played by a defensive back. also *back, D back.*

defensive end: 1. One of the usually two defensive players positioned outside the defensive tackles on the line of scrimmage, and who are primarily responsible for defending against sweeps and other wide running plays, and for rushing the passer. also *end.* 2. The position played by a defensive end. also *end.*

defensive tackle: 1. One of the two defensive players who are positioned on the line of scrimmage between the defensive ends, and who are primarily responsible for defending against inside running plays, and for rushing the passer. 2. The position played by a defensive tackle.

defensive team, defensive unit: The players on a team who regularly play as a unit on defense. also *D, defense.*

1. delay: A deception play on offense or a deceptive part of an offensive play in which a player disguises his actual assignment (to run a pass route, take a handoff, or make a key block) by hesitating long enough to appear to be doing something else.

2. delay: To disguise one's actual assignment on a play with a delay.

delay of game: An infraction of the rules that involves any action or inaction by either team that delays play or the progress of a game, such as, the failure to put the ball in play within the allotted time (twenty-five seconds in high school and college play, thirty seconds in the NFL), remaining on a dead ball or on a downed runner, taking and/or advancing a dead ball, or advancing the ball of a fair catch. Delay of game results in a 5-yard penalty.

depth: An ample number of players available for or capable of playing a position or positions. A team with depth is less vulnerable to an injury to (or a poor performance) by one or more key players.

depth chart: A coach's chart that lists and ranks the available players for each position on a team.

diamond defense: The center part of a 3-4 defense, consisting of the nose guard, the two interior linebackers, and the free safety.

dime defense: A prevent defense that employs six defensive backs. A nickel defense uses one extra back, a dime, two extra backs.

dive: An offensive play in which the ballcarrier lunges headfirst into, under, or over the line in order to gain a short distance (as when lacking a yard or less to make a first down or score a touchdown).

diveback: The fullback or up back in the I formation.

dog: see *red dog*.

1. double: To double-cover.

2. double: Double coverage.

double-cover: 1. To cover a receiver with two defensive players, either simultaneously or using zones. In the latter case, when a receiver is double-covered, the field is divided into two defensive zones, with the cornerback responsible for preventing a short pass, and the safety for preventing a long pass. also *double*. 2. To join with a teammate in guarding a receiver. also *double*.

double coverage: The covering of a receiver by two defensive players. also *double*. see *double-cover*.

double-double zone defense: Double zone coverage on both sides of the field. see *double-cover*.

double motion: 1. A change or reverse in

direction by a man in motion. 2. An obsolete offensive formation with two men in motion. Now an infraction of the rules, illegal motion, resulting in a 5-yard penalty.

double reverse: An offensive play in which a back running laterally toward one sideline hands off to a teammate running in the opposite direction, who in turn hands off to another teammate running laterally in the original direction of the play.

double-slot formation: An offensive formation that employs two slotbacks, one lined up in the slot between (and behind) the tackle and tight end, and the other lined up in the slot between (and behind) the other tackle and split end.

double-team: 1. To block an opponent with two players. 2. To join with a teammate in blocking an opponent.

double wing: An offensive formation employing an unbalanced line in which the ball is snapped directly to the tailback, positioned 4 to 5 yards behind the center, with the fullback about a yard in front and just to the side of him on the strong side. The remaining backs (the quarterback and a halfback) are positioned as wingbacks, just behind and outside of the two ends, with the quarterback playing on the weak side. Though tried as early as 1911 at Carlisle Indian School by Glenn S. "Pop" Warner, the double wing was not popular until Warner's Stanford team used the formation to defeat Army in 1928. The double wing was the basis for modern spread formations such as the shotgun.

1. down: 1. No longer in play, not able to be advanced, dead. (nullified the runback, and marked the ball down at the 20-yard line) 2. No longer able to advance the ball because of having touched the ground with a part of the body other than hands or feet after being touched by an opponent. (he is down at the 2-yard line)

2. down: 1. To cause the ball to be dead intentionally by touching it or one knee to the ground. 2. To tackle the ballcarrier. (caught from behind and downed at the 12-yard line)

3. down: 1. A play or period of action that starts when the ball is put into play with a snap (for a scrimmage down) or a free kick (for a free kick down), and that ends when the ball is dead. see *dead ball*. 2. One of a series of four chances allotted to the offensive team to score or to advance the ball 10 yards in order to retain possession. Downs were introduced in 1882 and originally called for the offense to gain 5 yards in three downs to retain possession. Rules increasing the distance to gain to 10 yards and the number of downs to four were introduced in 1906 and 1912.

down-and-in: see *in*.

down-and-out: see *out*.

down box: A 5 to 6-foot rod, atop which is fastened a set of numbered cards (1 through 4) to indicate the down being played. At the start of each down, a member of the box and chain crew displays the appropriate numbered card and places the rod at the point indicated by the linesman along the sideline to mark the spot of the ball. also *down indicator, down marker, downs box*.

downfield: Toward the opposing team's goal line. also *upfield*.

downfield blocker: An offensive player, usually accompanying the ballcarrier, who makes blocks downfield away from the line of scrimmage or the start of a play.

downfield blocking: Blocking in an open field, away from the line of scrimmage or the start of a play. (got some good downfield blocking and went all the way for a touchdown)

down indicator: see *down box*.

down lineman: An interior lineman, one who normally assumes a crouching stance.

down marker: see *down box*.

downs box: see *down box*.

draw, draw play: An offensive play in which a quarterback, anticipating a pass rush, drops back as though passing to draw a rush, then hands off to a back who runs straight forward through the gap left by the onrushing defensive players. The first draw play was an accident, the result of a broken play involving Pro Football Hall of Famers Otto Graham and Marion Motley of the Cleveland Browns. In a pre-NFL merger game in the late 1940s, quarterback Graham, seeing that he was trapped by onrushing linemen on a pass play, in desperation handed off to full-

back Motley, who ran right by the rushers for a big gain. In the game films, coach Paul Brown noticed the alley up the middle through which Motley ran, and decided to employ the tactic as a designed play, dubbing it the "draw play."

drive: A series of plays which produces an advance toward the opposing team's goal line.

drive-block: To block an opponent in such a way as to drive him back, thereby clearing a space or path for the runner.

drop: 1. A quarterback's move back from the line of scrimmage to set up before throwing a pass. 2. A defensive player's move back from the line of scrimmage into a zone to defend against a pass. (would sometimes fake a blitz before making his drop to cover the zone)

drop back: To move straight back from the line of scrimmage with the ball to set up before throwing a pass. also *fade back*.

1. drop kick: A kick made by dropping the ball and kicking it just as or immediately after it touches the ground. In football's early days, the drop kick was a powerful weapon. The legendary Jim Thorpe could score a field goal with it from the 50-yard line. Though still legal for field goals, extra points, and free kicks, the technique virtually disappeared from football after the 1930s, when the shape of the ball was made less rounded. The pointed ends of a modern football make it difficult to get a true bounce. Among the last players to be known for the drop kick were 1939 Heisman Trophy winner Nile Kinnick of Iowa and Pro Football Hall of Famer Dutch Clark, who played for the Detroit Lions from 1934 to 1938. Ray "Scooter" MacLean made what is believed to be the last NFL drop kick in the 1941 championship game, scoring the final point for the Chicago Bears in their 37-9 victory over the New York Giants.

2. drop kick: To make a drop kick.

duck, duck ball: A poorly thrown pass that seems to hang in the air or float, making it easy to intercept. also *dying quail, floater*.

dump: 1. see *sack*. 2. see *dump off*.

dump off: To throw a short pass to a back when all primary receivers are covered, or to take advantage of an undefended area vacated by blitzing linebackers or defensive backs. also *dump*.

dying quail: see *duck, duck ball*.

eat the ball: To be tackled behind the line of scrimmage when an open receiver cannot be found for a pass. There are times when a quarterback must "eat the ball" rather than risk an interception.

eleven: A football team.

eligible receiver: Any player who is permitted by the rules to catch a forward pass. On the offensive team, only the backs and two ends are eligible receivers, unless a member of the defensive team touches or tips the ball, in which case, any member of the offensive team may legally catch it. All players on the defensive team are eligible receivers. A pass caught by an ineligible receiver behind the line of scrimmage results in the loss of a down. A pass caught by an ineligible receiver on or beyond the line of scrimmage results in the loss of 10 yards, or the loss of the down.

encroaching, encroachment: The illegal entry into the neutral zone (having a part of one's body on or over the line of scrimmage or free kick line) after the ball is ready for play up to the time it is put into play (snapped or kicked). The center on a scrimmage down and the holder and kicker on a free kick down are the only players permitted to be partially in the neutral zone before the ball is put into play. Encroachment results in a 5-yard penalty. compare *offside*.

end: 1. Either of two players positioned at the extremities of the offensive or defensive line. see *offensive end, defensive end*. 2. The position played by an end.

end around: A reverse in which a wide receiver or tight end turns back through the offensive backfield for a handoff, and continues running around the opposite side of the line. Invented by Amos Alonzo Stagg.

end line: Either of two 160-foot lines, between and perpendicular to the sidelines, that mark the end boundaries of the playing area.

end run: An offensive play in which the ballcarrier runs around one end of the line.

••An attempt to avoid someone or something. (did an end run around the autograph seekers by slipping out a side exit)

end zone: The 160-foot-wide by 30-foot-deep area at either end of the field bounded by the goal line, the end line, and the sidelines.

enforcement spot: see *spot of enforcement*.

exchange: see *snap*.

extra point: 1. A point scored by successfully placekicking or drop kicking the ball through the uprights, or by successfully running or passing the ball into the end zone on a "try for point" following a touchdown. From 1884 until 1897, when it was given its present one-point value, the extra point (then called the "goal from touchdown" or "goal after") counted for two points. Before 1884, it had been valued at four points, more than a touchdown, which then counted for two points. 2. Two points scored by running or passing the ball into the end zone on a "try for point" following a touchdown (an option in USFL, college, and high school play). also *PAT, point after, point after touchdown*.

face guard: see *face mask*.

face-guarding: The illegal obstruction or hindrance of a pass receiver by a defensive player who, turning his back to the ball, waves his arms in the receiver's face to interfere with his vision. Face-guarding is pass interference and results in a first down for the offensive team at the spot of the foul.

face mask: 1. A steel bumper or cage attached to the front of a helmet to protect the face, consisting of one or more horizontal bars around the front (and for linemen, one vertical bar in the middle). Invented in the 1950s by Cleveland Browns' coach Paul Brown. also *birdcage, cage, face guard, face protector*. 2. An infraction of the rules in which an opponent's face mask is grabbed, resulting in a 5-yard penalty, or a 15-yard penalty if the face mask is twisted or pulled.

face protector: see *face mask*.

fade back: see *drop back*.

1. **fair catch:** An unhindered catch of a ball kicked by the opposing team made by a player of the receiving team who signals his intention to the officials (by extending one arm at full length above the head and waving while the kick is in flight), and does not attempt to advance the ball after making the catch. In signalling for a fair catch, a receiver

forfeits his right to advance the ball in return for protection against being blocked or tackled immediately after catching the ball by an onrushing opponent, which could cause a fumble. The ball becomes dead when a fair catch is made, and is put into play at that spot by a scrimmage down or, optionally, by a free kick. If a fair catch is muffed, it is considered a loose ball as soon as it touches the ground, and may be recovered by either team.

2. fair catch: To make a fair catch of a kick. (a short kick that he will fair catch around the 40-yard line)

1. fake: 1. To feign an action (such as a move in a certain direction, pass, hand off, etc.) in order to momentarily deceive an opponent. (fakes a handoff, then completes a short pass to the tight end) also *juke.* 2. To momentarily deceive an opponent by a feigned move or action. (faked the free safety and went all the way for a touchdown). also *fake out, juke.*

2. fake: A feigned move or action that is intended to momentarily deceive an opponent. (got the cornerback going the wrong way with a fake to the outside) also *juke.*

fake out: To deceive an opponent with a fake. also *fake, juke.*

●●To deceive or fool someone. (faked her out by disguising his voice when he called)

false start: A rules infraction in which one or more offensive players move after assuming a set position before the ball is snapped, resulting in a 5-yard penalty. Any defensive encroachment or offside caused by a false start is nullified.

false trap: An influence, or deception play, in which a blocker pulls as though on a sweep or trap in order to cause the opposing defensive lineman to misread the play and follow the blockers, leaving his position vacant to be run through by the ballcarrier. also *sucker trap.*

field general: The quarterback.

field goal: A three-point score made by drop kicking or placekicking the ball between the goalposts over the crossbar from behind the line of scrimmage. In the late 1800s, a field goal was worth five points, and was assigned its present three-point value only after a rule change in 1909. The

all-time record for the longest field goal in college play is 67 yards, set in 1977 by Texas kicker Russell Erxleben, equalled in the same year by Steve Little of Arkansas, and by Joe Williams of Wichita State in 1978. The all-time NFL record for the longest field goal is 63 yards, set in 1970 by then-New Orleans Saints kicker Tom Dempsey.

field judge: A football official who, at the snap, is positioned approximately 25 yards downfield near the middle of the field, and who is responsible for the ball, the tee, and the kicker on all free kicks, covering scrimmage kicks, passes, and runs into his area, timing the thirty-second count (twenty-five-seconds in college play) and the two-minute intermissions following the first and third quarters, and ruling with the back judge on conversions and field goals.

field position: The area where the ball is put into play by the offensive team, and its relative proximity to the goal line toward which the ball is being advanced. The closer the offensive team is to the opponent's goal line when the ball is put into play, the better the field position. (the interception and runback have given them good field position)

find: To complete a pass to a receiver. (found the tight end with a bullet over the middle) also *hit.*

fire out: To move off the line of scrimmage explosively the moment the ball is snapped. (the offensive line is really firing out and controlling play at the line of scrimmage)

first-and-ten: A first down.

first down: The first of a series of four downs in which the offensive team must attempt to score, or to advance ten yards in order to maintain possession of the ball for a new series of downs. also *first-and-ten.*

first string, first team: The players, or of and pertaining to the players, who regularly start or play in games, as opposed to those held in reserve or as substitutes. (made the first string in his rookie year)

●●The best or highest rated, or of or pertaining to the best or highest rated, of a team or group. (sent in the first string negotiators for the final round of talks)

first stringer: One who regularly plays on the first string or first team.

1. **flag:** 1. see *penalty flag.* 2. A pass pattern in which a receiver runs downfield then cuts diagonally toward the goal line marker or ''flag'' at the corner of the field. also *corner route.*

2. **flag:** To call a foul or infraction on a player. (nullified the runback when he was flagged for clipping)

flag football: A variation of football played between teams of usually six to nine players, and in which the ballcarrier can be ''tackled'' only by removing a flag or handkerchief hung from the waist or hip pocket. In flag football, all players are eligible to catch a forward pass, and the offensive team must score within four downs or lose possession of the ball. also *tail football.*

flag on the play: An instance of a flag being thrown because of a rules infraction or foul, a penalty.

●●An unforeseen problem which causes a change in plans. (right on schedule until a flat tire caused a flag on the play)

flagrant foul: A vicious act such as a slug or kick, a vicious clip, or a vicious grasping of the face mask, resulting in a 15-yard penalty, and often, the disqualification of the guilty player.

flak jacket: Special lightweight padding worn like a vest to protect the ribs. Adapted by designer Byron Donziz from the flak jackets worn by combat helicopter crews, the flak jacket was first used to protect the injured ribs of then-Houston Oilers quarterback Dan Pastorini.

1. **flank:** Either side or end of a formation. (a receiver out on the flank)

2. **flank:** To position oneself on the flank. (flanking on the strong side)

flanker: An old name for a wide receiver or an offensive player positioned wide of a formation, either on the line of scrimmage or a yard or more back (a flankerback). Amos Alonzo Stagg is believed to have introduced the use of a flanker (later called a split end) and a flankerback (a halfback positioned wide). In modern football, wide receivers line up in either position, depending on the play called.

flankerback: see *flanker.*

1. **flare:** A short pass to a back moving out toward the sideline in the backfield. Used as a safety valve when the quarterback is under pressure from a pass rush or blitz. also *swing, swing pass.*

2. **flare:** To release from a pass blocking assignment in the backfield and move toward the sideline for a pass. also *swing.*

flat: The area of the field to either side of a formation.

flat ball: A ball placed on its side (ends pointed toward the sidelines) for a placekick, instead of on one end, as on a tee.

flat pass: A pass made to a backfield player in the flat.

flea-flicker: A trick play that usually consists of a lateral followed by a pass, a handoff followed by a pass, or a pass followed by a lateral. Innovative 1920s Illinois coach Bob Zuppke is given credit for developing the first flea-flicker play (a pass followed by a lateral).

flex defense: A defensive strategy in which varying sets of two linemen drop back slightly just before the snap to protect against a run. The flex defense was developed in 1977 by Dallas Cowboys coach Tom Landry.

1. **flip:** A quick short pass.

2. **flip:** To make a quick short pass.

flip-flop: To exchange the positions of the safeties and/or linebackers before the ball is snapped in order to get the better tacklers on the strong side of the offensive formation. also *flop.*

floater: see *duck.*

flood a zone: To send more receivers into a zone than there are defenders to cover.

flop: see *flip-flop.*

fly, fly pattern: A pass pattern in which the receiver runs straight downfield at full speed. also *go.*

flying wedge: An early offensive formation in which blockers converged at full speed (from about 20 yards back) to form a moving wedge behind which the ballcarrier would follow, or be pulled or dragged along by his belt or special handles sewn onto his uniform. Invented in 1892 by Harvard coach L.H. Deland, the flying wedge and similar mass-momentum plays were soon in wide use, causing a number of deaths and serious injuries until they were finally outlawed in 1906.

football: 1. A game played between two teams of eleven players on a rectangular field 53-1/3 yards wide and 120 yards long (including a 10-yard deep end zone at each end of the field).

Points are scored by running with or passing an inflated ball (oval with pointed ends) into the opponent's end zone (a touchdown, six points), kicking the ball over a 10-foot-high, 23-foot, 4-inch- long horizontal bar (18 feet, 6 inches in the NFL) and between the 20-foot-high uprights (40 feet in the NFL) that together form a goal on the end boundary line of each end zone (if after a touchdown, an extra point, one point, any other time, a field goal, three points), running or passing the ball into the opponent's end zone on a try for point after a touchdown, two points (one point in the NFL), or tackling an opponent with the ball in his own end zone (a safety, two points). Defensive players are permitted to tackle the ballcarrier or the passer. Offensive players are permitted to protect the ballcarrier or the passer by using the body (not the hands) to block their opponents. Play starts (at the beginning of each half, and after each score) with one team kicking the ball to the other. The team in possession of the ball or offensive team (usually there are separate eleven-man offensive and defensive units on a team) has four scrimmage downs to score, or to advance the ball ten yards in order to maintain possession with another series of downs. Play on a scrimmage down is started from the line of scrimmage (the point at which the ballcarrier was tackled or went out of bounds) by one player (of the minimum seven offensive players positioned at the line of scrimmage) passing the ball back between his legs to a backfield player (usually the quarterback) who may run with the ball, pass it to another backfield player or to one of the two ends (players at either end of the offensive line), or hand the ball off to a teammate. Any player is permitted to run with the ball, but most often the ballcarrier is one of the four backfield players positioned 1 yard or more behind the line (usually a quarterback, fullback, and two halfbacks), and the linemen do the blocking. Defensive alignments vary, but most often there are four or five linemen (two ends, two tackles, and sometimes a middle guard), two or three linebackers positioned a yard or so behind the line, and four backfield players (two cornerbacks and two safeties). If the offensive team is unable to score or advance the ball 10 yards in the allotted four downs, or if a fumble is recovered or a pass intercepted by the opposing team, possession of the ball is lost, and the opposing team becomes the offensive team. When it seems unlikely that the ball can be advanced the necessary 10 yards in the allotted four downs, the offensive team may voluntarily give up possession of the ball by kicking or punting the ball (as far from its own goal line as possible). Rules infractions or fouls result in a loss of 5, 10, or 15 yards, or the loss or replay of the down. The game is divided into four fifteen-minute quarters (twelve-minute quarters in high school play) and the team with the highest score at the end of the fourth quarter wins. In the NFL, ties are decided in one or more fifteen-minute sudden-death overtime periods. 2. An inflated rubber bladder enclosed in a pebble-grained, leather case without corrugations of any kind. In the shape of a prolate spheroid (an oval with pointed ends), the ball is 11 to 11-1/4 inches long, and 21-1/4 to 21-1/2 inches in circumference around the middle, and weighs 14 to 15 ounces. Before the 1920s, when rule changes slimmed and streamlined it, the football was a blunt-nosed rugby-type ball. also *ball, pigskin.*

●●A "political football" is an issue that is figuratively tossed back and forth, and with which each side attempts to score points.

football knee: Cartilage and/or ligament damage to the knee that can result from the physical contact in football.

FOOTBALL

force: To turn a running play into the middle, or prevent it from getting outside.

force man: The defensive player (linebacker, cornerback, or strong safety) who is responsible for turning a sweep (or any running play to the outside) inside. (got outside after the lead blocker took out the force man)

formation: A specific offensive or defensive alignment at the beginning of a play, with players deployed in prearranged positions. also *set*.

40, forty: A 40-yard sprint used to measure the acceleration and speed of football players. (a lineman who can do a 4.5 forty)

forward lateral: An illegal lateral made in a forward direction beyond the line of scrimmage. A forward lateral is considered a forward pass from beyond the line of scrimmage, and results in a 5-yard penalty from the spot of the pass and the loss of the down.

forward pass: An offensive play in which the ball is thrown forward from behind the line of scrimmage to an eligible receiver (any backfield player or either of the two ends). Only one forward pass can be thrown on a down, and if the pass is incomplete, the ball is dead, and put into play for the next down at the previous line of scrimmage. The forward pass was made legal in 1906 as a part of a general movement to open up the game of football and cut down on the number of injuries. Both Wesleyan (vs. Yale) and Yale (vs. Harvard) are believed to have been among the first to use a forward pass in 1906. The pass came into national prominence in 1913 when Notre Dame upset a powerful Army team at West Point, 39-13, with quarterback Gus Dorais throwing to end Knute Rockne.

four-three defense: A defensive alignment that uses a four-man line (two tackles and two ends) and three linebackers. The four-three defense emerged in the NFL in the 1950s, and remained the standard defense for fifteen years, until the three-four began to gain popularity.

fourth down: The last of a series of four opportunities given to the offensive team to advance the ball a total of 10 yards.

free ball: see *loose ball*.

free-blocking zone: see *clipping zone*.

free kick: An unhindered kick (drop kick, placekick, or punt) made from or behind a restraining line (free kick line) beyond which no member of the kicking team may advance until the ball is kicked. The opposing team is under the same restriction at its own free kick line, located 10 yards in advance of the kicking team's line. The ball is put into play with a free kick (kickoff) made from the kicking team's 40-yard line (35-yard line in the NFL) at the start of each half, after a try for point, and after a successful field goal. A kickoff is usually made with a placekick. Punts are prohibited. When a safety is scored, the team scored upon puts the ball in play from the 20-yard line with a free kick (usually a punt). In the NFL, after a fair catch, the receiving team may elect to put the ball in play with a free kick from or behind the point where the free catch was made, as for a field goal.

free kick down: A down during which a free kick is made, as at the start of each half, after a try for point, after a successful field goal, after a safety, and, optionally in the NFL, after a fair catch. compare *scrimmage down*.

free kick line: Either of two imaginary restraining lines used during a free kick 10 yards apart, between and perpendicular to the sidelines, and beyond which the kicking and receiving teams may not advance until the ball is kicked. The kicking team's free kick line (from which the receiving team's line is measured) is set at the kicking team's 40-yard line (35-yard line in the NFL) for kickoffs, and at the 20-yard line after a safety (and for a free kick after a fair catch in the NFL, on or behind the spot of the catch).

free safety, free safetyman: 1. A defensive back usually positioned about 10 yards behind the line of scrimmage on the weak side. Normally the deepest

FOUR-THREE DEFENSE

playing defender, the free safety covers the central area of the field against a long run or pass and is "free" to assist other defensive backs assigned to cover specific receivers. also *weak safety*. 2. The position played by a free safety. also *weak safety*.

front: The defensive line.

front four: The four defensive linemen in a four-man front.

front line: The players positioned on the line of scrimmage. also *line*.

fullback: 1. An offensive back usually positioned behind the quarterback (directly, in the T and I formations), and primarily responsible for blocking and carrying the ball, especially in short yardage situations. Fullbacks tend to be more powerful, if less elusive than other running backs. also *diveback, upback*. 2. The position played by a fullback. also *diveback, upback*.

full house: 1. Any offensive formation with all four backs in the backfield. 2. A full house T formation.

full house T formation: The basic T formation, utilizing all four backs. also *T, T formation, tight T*.

1. fumble: To drop or lose control and possession of the ball (as opposed to failing to gain control and possession of the ball on a pass or a kick). also *cough up the ball*. compare *muff*.

2. fumble: 1. The act of fumbling the ball. When the ball is fumbled, it becomes a loose or free ball, and any player recovering it may advance the ball. (the fumble in the first quarter was one of three critical turnovers) compare *muff*. 2. A ball that has been fumbled. (lunges to recover the fumble)

gadget, gadget play: A trick play, one that is deceptive and/or unusual. also *razzle-dazzle play*.

1. gain: To advance the ball a specified distance. (gained six yards with a run off tackle)

2. gain: The advancement of the ball or the distance a ball is advanced on a play. (ran a reverse for a long gain)

game ball: 1. One of the balls approved by the referee for use in a game. 2. A game ball that is awarded by the players to a teammate or coach for his contribution to a winning effort.

●●A figurative award given for excellence or a superior performance in some endeavor. (the chef should be voted the game ball for a feast like this)

game films: Sixteen-millimeter films of a game studied on special stop-motion and reversing projectors by the coaching staff and players of a team. To insure fairness, the NFL has strict rules governing the exchange of film by teams. Pro Football Hall of Fame coach Sid Gillman pioneered the use of game films in the late 1930s, when he was assistant coach of Denison College. Another Pro Football Hall of Fame coach, Paul Brown, was among the first to stress the use of game films in professional football.

game plan: The specific strategy and tactical schemes (both offensive and defensive) planned for a particular game or opponent.

●●A scheme or plan to achieve a particular goal.

gamer: A player whose performance in actual games always exceeds the ability he shows in practice.

games: The apparent changes (jitterbugging) and actual changes in alignments and rushing patterns (stunts, stacks, slants, etc.) employed by a defensive team on different plays to confuse the offense.

gang-tackle: To tackle a ballcarrier with two or more tacklers.

gap: An open space between linemen. also *daylight, hole*.

giveaway football: Sloppy play, characterized by fumbles, pass interceptions, and other mistakes.

go: see *fly*.

goal: 1. A wooden or metal structure centered on each end line consistng of a 23-foot, 4-inch (or in the NFL, 18-foot, 6-inch) long horizontal crossbar whose top face is 10 feet above the ground, with uprights at each end that extend vertically 10 feet above the crossbar (or 10 yards in the NFL). High school and college goals are usually H-shaped, with a two-post base. NFL goals are supported by a single standard, padded and slightly recessed from the plane of the goal and end line. also *uprights*. 2. The vertical plane extending indefinitely above the crossbar, between the goalposts or uprights. 3. Goal-to-go. (first and goal on the 3-yard line)

goal line: A line extending from sideline

to sideline 10 yards from and parallel to each end line, separating the end zone from the field of play, and over which the ball must be carried or passed to score a touchdown or a two-point conversion after a touchdown.

goal-line defense: The personnel and alignment used by the defensive team in a goal-line stand.

goal-line stand: An attempt by the defense to prevent, or an instance of preventing, the opposing team from scoring from near the goal line. also *goal stand.*

goal post, goalpost: Either of the two uprights that extend vertically from both sides of the crossbar, and mark the sides of the goal.

goal stand: A goal-line stand.

goal-to-go: A situation in which the opponent's goal line is closer than 10 yards from the line of scrimmage, the distance the ball would have to be

advanced for a first down. (finally brought down at the 4-yard line, where it will be first down and goal-to-go) also *goal.*

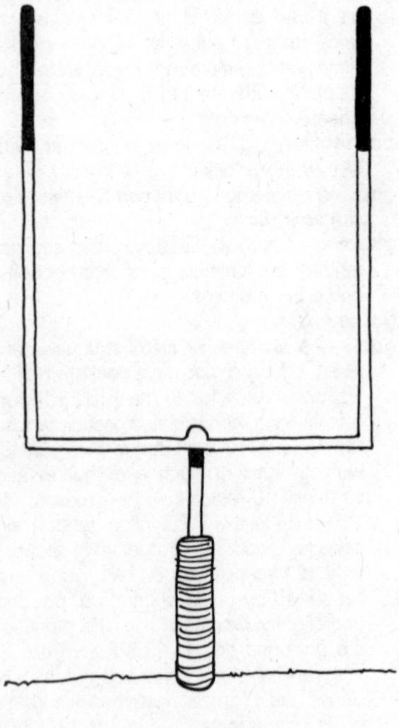

go for it: To gamble and attempt to make the necessary yards for a first down instead of kicking the ball to the opposing team on fourth down. If the attempt is unsuccessful, the opposing team takes over possession of the ball in a usually more advantageous field position than if the ball had been kicked.

●●To pursue a desired goal or activity, regardless of the risk or consequences. (decided to go for it and quit her job to write full time)

go long: 1. To throw a long pass. (going long, looking for the bomb) 2. To run a deep pass pattern. (fakes to the inside and goes long)

grandstand quarterback: One who second-guesses the quarterback from the grandstands. also *curbstone coach.* compare *armchair quarterback, Monday morning quarterback.*

●●One who constantly second-guesses or offers advice about matters with which he is not concerned.

grasp and control rule: An NFL rule that empowers the referee to blow the ball dead and rule a sack when, in his judgment, the quarterback is within the "grasp and control" of a defensive player. The grasp and control rule was initiated in 1979 to help protect the quarterback from injury.

Green Gripper towel: A specially treated cloth (similar to baseball's pine tar towel) that is rubbed on players' hands to increase adhesion and make the ball stick to the hands of a receiver or defensive back. In 1981, the NFL outlawed the use of the Green Gripper towel, "stickum," and any other substance having qualities of slipperiness or adhesiveness.

grid: see *gridiron.*

gridder: A football player.

gridiron: 1. A football field. When the forward pass was legalized in 1906, the quarterback was required to be 5 yards behind the line of scrimmage and could move no more than 5 yards laterally in either direction before the

GOAL POST

pass was thrown. To facilitate this and help the officials watch for infractions, lines were marked the length of the field at 5-yard intervals between and parallel to the sidelines. These, combined with the yard lines at 5-yard intervals, gave the football field the appearance of a "grid" or gridiron. also *grid*. 2. The game or pertaining to the game of football. also *grid*.

grind out: To methodically gain short yardage with running plays through the line. (able to grind out another first down at the 35-yard line)

1. ground: Running plays or pertaining to running plays. (make up for their weakness in the air with a formidable ground attack)

2. ground: To deliberately throw the ball to the ground or out of bounds (away from any possible receiver) rather than be thrown for a loss behind the line of scrimmage. Intentional grounding is a foul that results in a penalty. also *unload*. see *intentional grounding*.

ground-gainer: A skilled ballcarrier, one who gains yards rushing.

guard: 1. Either of two offensive linemen usually positioned next to and on either side of the center, primarily responsible for pass blocking, drive-blocking to open holes for runs through the line, and pulling, whether for a trap or to lead a sweep. also *offensive guard*. compare *middle guard*, *nose guard*. 2. The position played by a guard.

Hail Mary: A low-percentage pass, one that would require a great deal of luck or the intercession of a "higher power" for completion. (won the game in the closing seconds with a spectacular end zone catch of a real Hail Mary) also *prayer*.

halfback: 1. An offensive backfield player who functions primarily as a receiver or ballcarrier. The number of halfbacks (more commonly called running backs) and their exact position varies with different offensive formations. 2. A cornerback. 3. The position played by a halfback.

halfback option: An offensive play in which a halfback with the ball has the option of carrying it, pitching it out to a teammate, or passing.

Hall of Fame: see *College Football Hall of Fame, Professional Football Hall of Fame*.

hand off: To give (hand-to-hand) the ball to a teammate. (hands off to the fullback on a draw play)

handoff: The act or an instance of giving or handing the ball to a teammate.

hang: 1. To stay up in the air a long time, as a kicked football. (gets off a booming punt that should hang long enough to be easily covered) 2. To kick a ball high enough so that it remains in the air for a long time. (hangs another towering punt)

hang time: The number of seconds between the time the ball is kicked and caught on a kickoff or punt. Along with accuracy and distance, hang time is used to evaluate the effectiveness of a kicker. A kick with a long hang time gives the defense an opportunity to get downfield in position to tackle the receiver, thereby narrowing the chances for a runback. The best punters try for a hang time of about five seconds.

hard-out: see *out*.

hashmarks: The field markings that indicate the inbounds lines at the yard lines. see *inbounds line*.

headhunter: A player known for excessive roughness or violence.

head linesman: see *linesman*.

head slap: An intentional clubbing blow to the side of an opponent's helmet. A personal foul that results in a 15-yard penalty and, if judged to be flagrant or vicious, the disqualification of the offending player. Legal throughout the 1970s, the head slap was an effective technique used by rushing defensive linemen.

hear footsteps: To anticipate and be momentarily distracted by an imminent hit or tackle by an approaching opponent. Often the cause of a hurried throw by the quarterback or a dropped catch by a receiver. (took his eye off the ball when he heard footsteps)

●●To be distracted from one's course of action by the fear of imminent danger. (might have invaded the smaller country had he not heard the footsteps of the international community)

heavy hitter: A player with the reputation of being a punishing blocker or tackler.

Heisman Trophy: The Heisman Memorial Trophy, an annual award given to the outstanding college football player of the year, as voted by sportswriters and former Heisman Trophy winners. The award for the player of the year was originated in 1935 by the Downtown Athletic Club of New York and given first to Chicago University halfback Jay Berwanger. The trophy received its present name in 1936, after the death of John Heisman, a College Hall of Famer who played at Brown University and Pennsylvania in the 1890s, before beginning a distinguished thirty-six-year coaching career. The first recipient of the Heisman Memorial Trophy was Yale All-America end Larry Kelley in 1936.

helmet: The protective covering for a player's head, comprised of a hard plastic outer shell with foam rubber and inflatable vinyl air cushions (connected by tubes to spread the load of an impact) individually fitted to conform to the size and shape of a player's head. The first leather helmets or "head harnesses" were worn around the turn of the century, primarily to protect the ears. In the mid-1930s, hard fiber composition crowns were introduced, and for the first time, players were able to use the helmet as a weapon. Plastic helmets were introduced in the late 1930s and used sporadically throughout the 1940s. After a number of injuries due to shattered plastic, leather and composition helmets regained popularity during the 1950s until new stronger plastic shells finally replaced them. Among the last holdouts, Chicago Bears end Dick Plasman was playing without a helmet as late as 1940. The NFL made helmets mandatory in 1943. In 1947, Los Angeles Ram halfback Fred Gehrke painted ram's horns on the team helmets, the first emblem or design ever to appear on a helmet in professional football.

hen's team: 1. A derogatory expression for a team with no blockers, or poor blocking. 2. An onside prevent defensive team, in which normal blockers are replaced by quicker backs and receivers, who have a better chance of reaching an onsides kick.

hideout play: Any of a number of variations of an outlawed play in which an offensive player who appears to be leaving the field (as with other players for whom substitutes have entered the game) lingers at the sidelines until the ball is snapped, then runs downfield for a pass. The Los Angeles Rams used a hideout play with some success until it was outlawed by the NFL in the early 1950s. also *dead man play, sleeper play.*

hike: To snap the ball to a back to begin play on a down. (will take on the nose guard the moment he hikes the ball) also *center, snap.*

1. hit: 1. To make contact with an opponent in blocking, especially by tackling. 2. To complete a pass to a receiver. (got on the scoreboard when he hit his wide receiver with a bomb) also *find.*

2. hit: The act or an instance of hitting. (stopped at the line of scrimmage with a tremendous hit by the middle linebacker)

hitch: A pass pattern in which the receiver runs straight downfield for a short distance, then abruptly turns to the outside for a quick pass.

hitch and go: A pass pattern in which the receiver runs straight downfield a short distance, fakes a hitch to the outside, then continues downfield at full speed.

hit the hole: To lunge into an open space in the line momentarily created by blockers.

hold: 1. To illegally grab, hook, grasp, or obstruct an opponent with the hands or

HELMET

arms. see *holding*. 2. To limit the yards gained by an opponent or opposing team. 3. To stop the opposing team from advancing or scoring. (could not hold them once they reached the 10-yard line)

holding: The act or an instance of illegally grabbing, hooking, grasping, or obstructing an opponent (other than the ballcarrier) with the hands or arms. Offensive holding results in a 15-yard penalty (10-yard penalty in the NFL). Defensive holding results in a 15-yard penalty (5-yard penalty in the NFL).

hole: A momentary gap or open space in the line cleared by blockers. also *daylight*.

1. hook: 1. To run a buttonhook pass pattern. 2. To move a defensive player to the side with a hook block.

2. hook: see *comeback*.

hook block: A block in which an offensive lineman steps to the side of a defensive player, then turns back to block him laterally, away from the ballcarrier.

hospital ball: A short pass lofted over the middle that forces a receiver to leap and catch it, leaving himself unprotected and vulnerable to injury from a hit by a defensive back.

1. huddle: A brief grouping of players between downs (usually in a small circle behind the line of scrimmage) in which signals and specific instructions for the next down are given by the quarterback or defensive captain. Amos Alonzo Stagg is credited with inventing the huddle.

●●A meeting to discuss a specific situation or plan of action. (should have a huddle before the next bargaining session)

2. huddle: To gather in a huddle with teammates before the next play in order to receive signals and instructions.

●●To meet in order to discuss a specific situation or plan of action. (huddled with her attorney to devise a strategy)

hurry-up offense: see *two-minute drill*.

I: The I formation.

I back: The tailback in an I formation.

I formation: An offensive formation in which the fullback and the tailback (running backs) are positioned in line behind the quarterback with the remaining back playing wide as a receiver. Coach Tom Nugent of Virginia Military Institute is credited with developing the I formation in the 1950s. see *power I, stack I*.

illegal motion: An infraction in which an offensive player other than one "man in motion" fails to come to a complete stop in a set position and remain motionless for one full second before the snap, or in the case of "backfield in motion," a backfield player is moving forward or more than one is moving laterally or backward at the snap. Illegal motion results in a 5-yard penalty. see *man in motion*.

in: 1. Into the end zone for a score. also *over*. 2. A pass pattern in which a receiver runs straight downfield, then cuts sharply to the inside (parallel to the line of scrimmage) for a pass. If the cut is made just a short distance from the scrimmage line, the pattern is sometimes called a short in. also *down-and-in, square-in*. compare *out*.

inbounds: Within the playing area, inside and not touching the boundary lines.

inbounds line, inbounds marker: Either of two imaginary lines extending the length of the playing field, 53 feet, 4 inches (or 70 feet, 9 inches in the NFL) in from and parallel to each sideline, and marked on the field at the yard lines by the hashmarks. When a ballcarrier is tackled in a side zone (the area of the field between the inbounds line and the nearest sideline) or a ballcarrier goes out of bounds over a sideline, or the ball is punted or fumbled out of bounds over a sideline, the ball is put into play at the intersection of the inbounds line and the yard line where the ball was dead or out of bounds. Inbounds lines (30 feet from each sideline) were experimented with in the first NFL playoff game in 1932, played indoors because of blizzard conditions (Chicago Bears 9, Portsmouth, Ohio, Spartans, 0). In 1933, the 30-foot inbounds lines were adopted for use in the NFL and in college play. Current specifications were

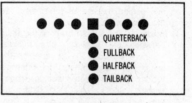

QUARTERBACK
FULLBACK
HALFBACK
TAILBACK

I FORMATION

adopted in 1947 and 1972 by the NCAA and NFL respectively. also *hashmarks.*

inbounds spot: The point at which the ball is put into play for a scrimmage down after it has been blown dead in a side zone or gone out of bounds, determined by the intersection of the inbounds line and the yard line where the ball was dead or out of bounds.

incomplete: Not caught or intercepted (as of a pass), and resulting in a dead ball. After an incomplete pass, the ball is put into play for the next down at the previous spot (the point from which the ball was put into play on the previous down).

incompletion: An instance of an incomplete pass.

ineligible receiver: An offensive player (any lineman between the two ends) who is not permitted to catch a forward pass, or to advance beyond the point where physical contact is broken with the opponent blocked from the initial line charge until the ball is thrown. If an ineligible receiver advances beyond this point before a pass is thrown (ineligible receiver downfield), the offensive team is charged with a 15-yard (10-yard in the NFL) penalty.

influence: An offensive tactic in which the linemen move at the snap in such a way as to deceive the defensive team, such as a blocker pulling as though on a sweep (causing the defensive lineman to misread the play and follow the blocker, leaving a gap through which the play is run), or dropping back as if pass blocking (so as to lure the defensive player across the line where he can be trapped).

in motion: Legally moving laterally or backward behind the line of scrimmage at the snap. After assuming a set position for one full second after the huddle or a shift, a single player may move or be in motion in a lateral or backward direction behind the line of scrimmage. see *man in motion.*

1. inside: 1. The middle area of the field, between the sidelines. also *middle.* compare *outside.* 2. The area of the line of scrimmage between the offensive tackles. Army's 1945 Heisman Trophy winning fullback, Felix "Doc" Blanchard, was nicknamed "Mr. Inside" (to halfback Glen Davis's "Mr. Outside") for

his ability to run through the inside. compare *outside.*

2. inside: To or toward the inside. (cut back inside for a gain of 4 yards) compare *outside.*

inside handoff: A handoff given to a running back who passes between the quarterback and the line of scrimmage.

instant replay: The televised repetition of a particular play or incident immediately after its completion by means of videotape. Often the replay is from several different angles and utilizes slow-motion. Using computers and advanced electronics, some stadiums and arenas are equipped to reproduce instant replays on scoreboard-sized screens. Although ABC Television pioneered the concept of replaying during a time out or break in the action, the instant replay was first used by CBS director Tony Verna on December 7, 1963, immediately after quarterback Rollie Stichweh plunged 2 yards for an Army touchdown against Navy. Ironically, it remained for NBC to give the technique its name. also *replay.*

●●Any kind of repetition or near duplication. (he is like an instant replay of his older brother)

intentional grounding: An infraction in which the passer, under a rush and unable to find an open receiver, deliberately throws the ball to the ground, into a player behind the line, or out of bounds to avoid being thrown for a loss. Intentional grounding results in a 5-yard penalty and the loss of the down. In the NFL, intentional grounding results in a 10-yard penalty and the loss of the down, or if the foul occurs more than 10 yards behind the line of scrimmage, the loss of the down at the spot of the foul, or a safety if the passer is in his end zone when he grounds the ball.

intercept: 1. To catch and control a pass meant for an opponent. 2. To have a pass one has thrown intercepted. (was intercepted only twice in the season)

interception: The act or an instance of a pass being intercepted, charged against the passer and credited to the defensive player making the interception in statistical records. Paul Krause of the Washington Redskins (1964-67) and the Minnesota Vikings (1968-69) holds the NFL career record for interceptions, eighty-one. The NFL record for the most interceptions in one season, four-teen, was set in 1952 by Dick "Night Train" Lane of the Los Angeles Rams. In 1943, Sammy Baugh of the Washington Redskins became the first NFL player to make four interceptions in one game.

interference: 1. The illegal obstruction or hindrance of an opponent who is trying to catch a pass or a kick. On a for-ward pass, receivers and defensive players have an equal right to the ball, and neither may interfere with the other's attempt to catch it. Offensive pass interference results in a 15-yard penalty from the "previous spot" and the loss of the down (or a 10-yard pen-alty in the NFL and USFL). Defensive pass interference results in an automatic first down at the spot of the foul (or in the USFL, a first down 15 yards ahead of the "previous spot" if unintentional, and a first down at the spot of the foul with a minimum 15-yard advance if intentional). On a kickoff, the kicking and receiving teams have an equal right to the ball after it travels 10 yards, but, as on a punt, no member of the receiv-ing team may be prevented from catch-ing it. Interference on a kick results in a 15-yard penalty from the spot of the foul. 2. Legal blocking or blockers, as in front of the ballcarrier. The first block-ing rules permitting legal interference for the runner were sponsored by Wal-ter Camp in 1884.

interior line: The part of an offensive or defensive line between the ends.

interior lineman: The center, guards, tackles, and middle or nose guard, all players positioned in the interior line.

iso: see *isolated camera*.

isolated camera: A television camera used to record the actions of one player (such as a receiver) on a particular play, for possible use on an instant replay. also *iso*.

isolation block: A delayed block by a back on a defensive lineman left "isolat-ed" or unblocked by an offensive line-man.

jam: 1. see *chuck*. 2. To use acts or words designed to distract, disconcert, or confuse the offensive team at the snap. Jamming is considered unsportsmanlike conduct and results in a 15-yard penalty.

jitterbug: To jump in and out of the defen-sive line or exchange places with another defensive player just before the ball is snapped in order to confuse the offense and disguise actual rushing plans.

juice: see *vigorish*.

1. juke: 1. To fake a motion or movement in a certain direction in order to momentarily deceive an opponent. (tried to juke his way out of trouble just before he was hit) also *fake*. 2. To momentarily deceive an opponent by a fake. also *fake, fake out*.

2. juke: A simulated move or faked action that is intended to momentarily deceive an opponent. (got past the cornerback with a little juke after he turned the corner) also *fake*.

jump pass: A pass thrown at the peak of a jump.

kamikaze corps, kamikaze squad: see *suicide squad*.

keeper: An offensive play in which the quarterback keeps the ball and runs with it, often after faking a handoff. Pioneer football coach Amos Alonzo Stagg is credited with inventing the keeper.

1. key: A tipoff or indication of the oppos-ing team's intentions (offensive or defen-sive) on a particular play.

2. key: To watch a particular opponent (where he looks, his position, or move-ment) as a clue to the intentions of the opposing team. (keys on the free safety to read the coverage)

key block: An important or pivotal block for a particular play, one without which the play would fail.

1. kick: 1. To propel the ball by hitting it with the foot. 2. To score by kicking. (kicked the extra point to tie the score) 3. To execute a kickout block on a defensive player, moving him to the outside, away from an inside run.

2. kick: The act or an instance of kicking the ball, as for a kickoff, a punt, a field goal, or a try for an extra point.

kicker: The player who kicks the ball.

kicking game: The execution and perform-ance of a team's kickers (for kickoffs, punts, field goals, and extra points) and the players who make up the kicking team or teams.

kicking team: The members of a team who regularly play in kickoff, punt, field goal, and extra point situations.

kicking tee: A small, flexible plastic or rub-ber device used to prop up the ball on

149

one end for a placekick. Legalized in 1948 (though solely for kickoffs in the NFL). also *tee*.

kick off: To put the ball in play with a kickoff.

●● To begin something. (Will kick off the festivities with a song

kickoff: A free kick (placekick) made from the kicking team's 40-yard line (or 35-yard line in the NFL) to put the ball in play at the start of each half, after an extra point attempt, and after a field goal. The kicking team may not advance past their free kick line (the line from where the kick is taken), nor may the receiving team advance past their free kick line 10 yards away, until the ball is kicked. On a kickoff, either team may recover the ball after it travels 10 yards, as long as no member of the receiving team is prevented from catching or recovering it.

kickoff return: The runback of a kickoff. Three players share the NFL record for the longest kickoff return, 106 yards; Al Carmichael of the Green Bay Packers (1956), Noland Smith of the Kansas City Chiefs (1967), and Roy Green of the St. Louis Cardinals (1979). The NFL career record for the highest average yardage on kickoff returns (30.56 yards) is held by Gale Sayers of the Chicago Bears (1965-71). The NFL record for the highest kickoff return average for a season (41.06 yards) was set in 1967 by Travis Williams of the Green Bay Packers. Williams also shares the NFL record for the most touchdowns scored in a season on kickoff returns (four, 1967) with Cecil Turner of the Chicago Bears (four, 1970).

kickout block: An offensive technique in which a defensive lineman is blocked toward the outside, as to clear a path for an inside run.

kill the clock: see *run out the clock*.

late hit: The act or an instance of diving or running into an opponent after he is down or out of play, or after the ball is dead. A late hit is considered unnecessary roughness and results in a 15-yard penalty.

1. lateral: A pass thrown (underhand or overhand) in any direction other than forward. Any player is eligible to catch a lateral, and more than one lateral may be thrown on a single down, but if a lateral is not caught, the ball remains

in play and may be recovered by either team. Amos Alonzo Stagg is credited with inventing the lateral. also *backward pass, lateral pass*.

2. lateral: To make a lateral pass.

lateral pass: see *lateral*.

lead block: A block executed by a player who leads the ballcarrier or a play.

leg whip: To, while on the ground or falling, move or extend one's legs in order to trip an opponent. Leg whipping is a tripping foul and results in a 10-yard penalty.

1. letter: A school monogram to be worn on a sweater or jacket, awarded to students who are members of the school football team. Amos Alonzo Stagg invented the letter award, which is now given for participation in other sports and school activities.

●●A figurative award, often given in jest. (has earned a letter in communication as captain of the gossip team)

2. letter: To earn a school letter in football, or another sport or school activity. (lettered in football and track in his senior year)

●●To earn a figurative award, often in jest. (a fraternity man who lettered in beer-drinking and partying)

letterman: A student who is awarded a student letter for participation in athletic or other school activities.

line: 1. Short for the line of scrimmage. 2. The offensive or defensive linemen positioned at the line of scrimmage. At least seven players (usually a center, two guards, two tackles, and two ends) must line up on the offensive line. There are normally three to five players in a defensive line (defensive tackles and ends in a 4-man line, and a middle guard or nose guard for a 3- or 5-man line). also *front line*. 3. The positions played by linemen.

linebacker: 1. One of several defensive players usually positioned a yard or so behind the line, who are primarily responsible for backing up the defensive linemen on running plays, protecting against a short pass (as to a running back), or rushing the passer (as in a red dog blitz). also *backer-up*. 2. The position played by a linebacker. also *backer-up*.

line judge: A football official who, at the snap, is positioned even with the line of scrimmage on the opposite side of the field from the linesman, and who is responsible for the timing of the game and halftime intermission, for watching for encroachment or offsides, illegal motion or illegal shifts, an illegal pass from beyond the line of scrimmage, and for signalling the end of each quarter.

lineman: An offensive or defensive player who plays on the line.

line of scrimmage: An imaginary vertical plane (between and perpendicular to the sidelines) passing through the end of the ball nearest a team's own goal line when the ball is spotted for a down. Neither team may cross the line of scrimmage until the ball is snapped. The concept of the line of scrimmage or scrimmage line, guaranteeing unhindered possession of the ball to one team until the snap, is considered the single most important rule of football, making possible the use of prearranged plays and variable strategies. It was adopted by the intercollegiate rules committee in 1880 at the urging of Yale halfback Walter Camp, now regarded as the primary architect of American football. also *scrimmage line.*

linesman: A football official who, at the snap, is positioned even with the line of scrimmage on a sideline (switching to the other sideline for the second half), and who is responsible for supervising the box and chain crew, watching for encroachment and offsides and other action in and around the line, watching for the forward progress of the ball on his sideline, aiding the umpire in checking for ineligible linemen going downfield, and counting the offensive players on every play. also *head linesman.*

line surge: The forward movement of the offensive line at the snap of the ball on a running play. (easily made the first down behind a good line surge)

line-to-gain: see *necessary line.*

live ball: A ball that has been snapped or kicked and is in play, either under the control of a player or team, or "loose" or "free" and recoverable by either team. see *dead ball.*

locomotive: A mass cheer that, like a steam locomotive, starts slowly and increases in tempo. The locomotive was the first deliberate, rhythmic college cheer, and originated at a Princeton football game in 1871.

Lombardi Award: The Vince Lombardi Rotary Award, an annual award given to the outstanding college lineman of the year by the Rotary Club of Houston, Texas. Named after Pro Football Hall of Fame coach Vince Lombardi, whose Green Bay Packers won five NFL championships in the 1960s. The Lombardi Award was first given in 1970 to Ohio State All-American middle guard Jim Stillwagon.

long gainer: A play that makes a long gain.

look: The appearance of a certain alignment or the positioning of a key player or key players, used to determine (or to mask) a team's intentions on a play. (a sophisticated defense that moves constantly and gives the opposing quarterback a lot of different looks)

look-in: An offensive play in which the receiver runs diagonally across the middle for a quick pass.

look off: To deceive a defender or the defense by looking one way before throwing a pass to a different location. (looks off the linebacker, then completes a short pass over the middle)

loop: To circle around an adjacent defensive lineman at or just before the snap, as for a stunt. see *stunt.*

loose ball: A live ball that is not in the possession of any player, and that can be recovered by either team.

loss of down: The loss of the opportunity to repeat a down as a penalty or part of a penalty assessed for rules infractions such as intentional grounding, a second forward pass during a down, or a pass touched or caught by an ineligible receiver.

make the cut: To survive a cut or the elimination of unneeded or unsuitable players from a team or roster.

●●To be chosen, especially when others have been eliminated. (elated as she had made the cut and been offered a part in the play)

man, man coverage: see *man-for-man.*

man-for-man: A defensive coverage in which each receiver is guarded by one defensive player. also *man, man coverage, man-to-man.*

man in motion: The act or an instance of a single offensive backfield player, after assuming a set position for one full second after the huddle or a shift, moving in a lateral or backward direction behind the line of scrimmage at the snap. Putting a "man in motion" is one of the innovations of Amos Alonzo Stagg.

man-to-man: see *man-for-man.*

match-up: The confrontation between two specific opposing players who guard or play against each other in a game. (our wide receiver against their All-Pro cornerback is one of the most interesting match-ups in the game)

Maxwell Trophy: An annual award given to an outstanding college football player. Named after All-American lineman Robert Maxwell of Swarthmore, the award, originated by the Maxwell Football Club of Philadelphia, was first given in 1938 to Texas Christian quarterback Davey O'Brien.

measuring sticks: see *chain.*

middle: 1. The central area of the field, between the sidelines. also *inside.* 2. The middle of the line. (followed the big guard through the middle)

middle guard: A defensive lineman usually positioned in the middle of the line, opposite the offensive center, and between the defensive tackles, as on a three or five-man front. also *nose guard, nose man, nose tackle.* compare *guard.*

middle linebacker: The linebacker positioned behind the middle of the defensive line, often the defensive captain.

midfield stripe: The 50-yard line.

misdirection: An offensive tactic in which backfield players move in a particular direction at the snap in order to mislead or deceive the defense.

Monday morning quarterback: A football fan who criticizes or second-guesses a team's play after the fact. compare *armchair quarterback, grandstand quarterback.*

••One who criticizes or second-guesses with the advantage of hindsight.

mousetrap: A trap block.

move list: A list containing the names of players taken off a team's active roster.

move off the ball: see *come off the ball.*

1. **muff:** To touch and fail to gain possession of a loose ball (such as a kick, pass, or fumble). compare *fumble.*

2. **muff:** The act or an instance of muffing a loose ball. compare *fumble.*

multiple foul: A situation in which two or more fouls are committed by the same team during the same down. If a multi-

ple foul occurs, only one penalty may be enforced. The captain of the offended team makes the choice.

multiple offense: An offense in which different kinds of plays are run from a single formation. Michigan State coach Biggie Munn, named Coach of the Year in 1952 by the American Football Coaches Association, is credited with popularizing the multiple offense.

naked reverse: A reverse in which all the blockers move in the original direction of the play (ideally, drawing the defense with them), leaving the ultimate ballcarrier (after the handoff) without blockers, but with an open field if the play is successful.

National Collegiate Athletic Association: The national organization that oversees, administers, and publishes rules for intercollegiate athletics. Formed in 1905 at a conference of colleges called by New York University Chancellor Henry MacCracken to decide whether to reform or abolish the game of football, the association was originally called the Intercollegiate Athletic Association of the United States. Renamed in 1910, the National Collegiate Athletic Association is headquartered in Shawnee Mission, Kansas, and presently oversees fifty-three national championships in twenty sports. also *NCAA.*

National Football Conference: One of the two conferences of the National Football League, the championship teams of which compete annually for the national championship in the Super Bowl, and from which individual players are selected to compete in the annual AFC-NFC Pro Bowl. The NFC is made up of three divisions: the Eastern Division, which is comprised of the Philadelphia Eagles, the Dallas Cowboys, the Washington Redskins, the St. Louis Cardinals, and the New York Giants, the Central Division, which is comprised of the Minnesota Vikings, the Detroit Lions, the Chicago Bears, the Tampa Bay Buccaneers, and the Green Bay Packers, and the Western Division, which is comprised of the Atlanta Falcons, the Los Angeles Rams, the San Francisco 49ers, and the New Orleans Saints. also *NFC.*

National Football League: The oldest and largest major professional football league in the United States. Established in 1920 as the American Professional Football Association, the National Football League (the name adopted in 1922) is comprised of two conferences, the American Football Conference and the National Football Conference, each of which is comprised of fourteen teams divided into three geographic divisions (Eastern Division, Central Division, and Western Division). Conference champions (determined by divisional playoffs) meet annually for the league championship in the Super Bowl. also *NFL*. see *American Football Conference, National Football Conference*.

National Football League Players Association: The sole and exclusive collective bargaining agent for players in the NFL. The present association was formed in 1970 by the combination of the American Football League Players Association and the old NFL Players Association, originated in 1956. also *NFLPA*.

NCAA: The National Collegiate Athletic Association.

necessary line: The yard line to which the offensive team must advance the ball within four downs in order to score or maintain possession of the ball for a new series of downs. Unless there is a penalty, the necessary line is ten yards in advance of the foremost point of the ball at the beginning of a series of downs. If the ten yards extend into the end zone, the goal line is the necessary line. also *line-to-gain*.

neutral zone: An imaginary area between the lines of scrimmage (one at either end of the football) on a scrimmage down or the free kick lines (10 yards apart) on a free kick down, extending from sideline to sideline parallel to the goal lines. Once the ball is spotted and the referee whistles play begin, no player from either team, except the snapper on a scrimmage down and the holder and kicker on a free kick down may enter the neutral zone until the ball has been snapped or kicked. The neutral zone was introduced in 1903 by former Harvard team captain Bert Walters. Previously, opposing linemen were separated only by an imaginary line through the center of the ball. The neutral zone virtually eliminated the time-consuming arguments on every down about who crossed the imaginary line.

NFC: The National Football Conference.

NFL: The National Football League.

NFLPA: The National Football League Players Association.

nickel back: The defensive back who replaces a linebacker when a nickel defense is employed.

nickel defense: A prevent defense in which five defensive backs are used, the extra back replacing a linebacker. The term nickel defense was coined by Pro Football Hall of Fame coach Clark Shaughnessy.

North-South runner: A ballcarrier who tends to run straight toward the opponent's goal line, rather than zigzagging back and forth across the field.

nose guard: see *middle guard*.

nose man: see *middle guard*.

nose tackle: see *middle guard*.

nutcracker: A contact drill in which ballcarriers are subjected to game-type hits, sometimes simultaneously or alternately by more than one player.

odd front, odd line: A four-man defensive line in an "over" or "under" shift, with one defensive tackle directly opposite the center. also *odd man front*. see *over, under*.

odd man front: see *odd front, odd line*.

off: Outside of a specified offensive lineman. (ran a slant off tackle)

offense: 1. The endeavor to advance the ball or score against the opposing team. (a great defensive team, but mediocre on offense) 2. The specific plan or formation used to advance the ball or score. 3. The offensive team or its members. also *offensive team, offensive unit*.

offensive: Pertaining to offense, or the playing of offense. (offensive play) (offensive game plan)

offensive end: 1. One of the two offensive players positioned at the ends of the offensive line, who are primarily responsible for blocking and receiving passes. In a typical unbalanced line, one offensive end (tight end) lines up just outside the offensive tackle, and the other (split end), is positioned on the line of scrimmage, ten yards or more wide of the other offensive tackle. also *end*. 2. The position played by an offensive end. also *end*.

offensive guard: see *guard*.

offensive tackle: 1. Either of two offensive

players positioned on the line of scrimmage outside of the offensive guards, and who are primarily responsible for pass blocking, drive-blocking to open holes for runs through the line, and pulling, whether for a trap or to lead a sweep. also *tackle*. 2. The position played by an offensive tackle. also *tackle*.

offensive team, offensive unit: The players on a team who regularly play offense. also *offense*.

official: Any of the four to seven officials who administer the rules of the game, and who are responsible for the timing and scoring of a football game. They are the referee, the umpire, the linesman, and the field judge (and in seven-man crews, also the line judge, back judge, and side judge).

official's time out: A time out called by the referee (and charged against neither team) when the ball is dead for the measurement of a possible first down, the repair of game or player equipment, an injury to a player or official, a conference for a rules interpretation, a change of team possession, and the notification of two minutes remaining for a half. also *referee's time out*.

offside, offsides: Illegally being beyond the line of scrimmage on a scrimmage down or the free kick line on a free kick down at the moment the ball is put into play (snapped or kicked). The center on a scrimmage down and the holder and kicker on a free kick down are the only players permitted to be partially in the neutral zone when the ball is put into play. Offsides results in a 5-yard penalty. compare *encroaching, encroachment*.

Oklahoma drill: see *nutcracker*.

old leather: One or more older or seasoned veteran players. An allusion to the old leather helmets and pads worn in earlier days. (a blend of talented rookies and old leather made them a championship team)

one-back formation, one-back offense: A T formation derivative in which only one back lines up behind the quarterback, with the others positioned as tight ends and/or wide receivers. also *ace formation, A formation, single-back offense*.

one-on-one: A situation in which a player is covering or covered by a single opponent.

••Any situation in which one individual is

pitted against another, or interacts directly with another. (the principals resolved the misunderstanding in a one-on-one meeting)

on scholarship: Given under-the-table payments or placed on a team's official injured reserve list, though not injured. An illegal practice by a professional team in order to "protect" (keep other teams from signing) a player of potential future value while carrying the maximum number of players allotted on the active roster list. A team guilty of this practice ("stashing") is subject to a fine and further league disciplinary action.

onside: Legally positioned behind the line of scrimmage or free kick line when the ball is snapped or kicked.

onside kick: A kickoff in which the kicking team attempts to maintain possession of the ball by recovering the kick after it travels the required 10 yards. Because of the chance that the receiving team will recover the ball and have excellent field position, an onside kick is usually attempted only by a team that is behind near the end of a game. The onside kick was invented by pioneer coach Amos Alonzo Stagg. also *onsides kick*.

onside prevent defense: A tactic employed by the receiving team in anticipation of an onside kick on a kickoff, in which blockers who normally play on or close to the receiving team's free kick line are replaced by quicker backs and receivers, who have a better chance of reaching and recovering an onside kick. also *hen's team*.

onsides kick: see *onside kick*.

on the numbers: Chest-high, or on the chest. Numbers (first used on football jerseys by Washington and Jefferson College in 1908) make a good target for a tackle, a block, or a well-placed pass. (hit his wide receiver on the numbers with a perfect pass)

open: Unguarded by an opponent. (looking for an open receiver)

open field: The sparsely defended area of the field beyond the line of scrimmage, or away from the point of origin of a play. also *broken field*.

open field tackle: A tackle made in a sparsely defended area of the field.

option: 1. An offensive play in which the ballcarrier, after the play begins, has the option to run with the ball or pass. also *option play*. 2. Short for option clause. 3. Short for option year. see *option clause*.

option clause: A clause in professional players' contracts which gives a team the option for the services of a player for one additional year (option year) with an automatic raise (as per the NFL/NFLPA agreement) over the expired contract terms. The player may choose to play or to sit out during the option year, after which he becomes a free agent, or free to negotiate with other teams. also *option.*

option play: see *option.*

option year: see *option clause.*

out: A pass pattern in which a receiver runs straight downfield, then abruptly cuts to the outside (parallel to the line of scrimmage) for a pass. If the cut is made just a short distance from the scrimmage line, the pattern is sometimes called a quick out, hardout, or short out. also *down-and-out, square-out.* compare *in.*

Outland Trophy: An annual award given to the outstanding college interior lineman of the year as voted by the Football Writers Association of America. Named after All-American tackle John B. Outland, who played at Pennsylvania in the late 1890s, the Outland Trophy was first awarded to Notre Dame tackle George O'Connor in 1946.

outlet man: A receiver to whom a pass can be thrown if the primary receiver or receivers are covered and the quarterback is in danger from a pass rush.

out of bounds: Out of the playing area, on or over either of the sidelines or end lines, or touching someone (other than another player or an official) or something on or over the boundary lines.

1. outside: The area of the playing field near the sidelines, wide of the flanks of an offensive formation. Army's 1946 Heisman Trophy winning halfback, Glen Davis, was nicknamed "Mr. Outside" (to fullback Felix "Doc" Blanchard's "Mr. Inside") for his ability to run outside. compare *inside.*

2. outside: To or toward the outside. (trying to get outside and turn the corner) compare *inside.*

over: 1. Over the goal line for a score. (went over from the two-yard line) also *in.* 2. Short for overshift. compare *under.*

overshift: A defensive alignment in which all or some of the defensive linemen shift one position over toward the strong side of an unbalanced line (placing one tackle head-on the center) to disrupt blocking patterns, or to move big linemen to the expected point of attack. also *over.* compare *under, undershift.*

overtime: An extra fifteen-minute period of play to decide a game tied at the end of regulation play in the NFL. The period begins with a kickoff (decided by coin toss) and ends when one team scores, or when time runs out. In a regular season game, if neither team is able to score during the overtime period, the game ends as a tie. In a playoff or championship game, if neither team is able to score in the overtime period, fifteen-minute periods continue to be played (with two-minute intermissions in between) until one team scores. also *sudden death.*

pads: The various pieces of protective equipment worn to protect a player's shoulders, ribs, elbows, hips, thighs, and knees. Pads are usually constructed in layers, with a hard surface (such as molded plastic or combat-derived composite materials) on the outside and a foam or inflatable cushion layer underneath.

1. pass: The act or an instance of throwing the ball to a teammate. (scored with a short pass to the tight end) see *forward pass, lateral.*

2. pass: To throw the ball to a teammate, as in a forward pass, or a backward or lateral pass.

pass block: To protect the passer by blocking on a pass play.

passer: A player who attempts to throw a forward pass to a teammate.

passing down: A down in which the circumstances indicate the use of a pass to gain the yards necessary for a score of a first down (such as third and eight).

passing game: The use of the forward pass on offense. (hard to defense their passing game)

pass interference: see *interference.*

pass pattern: A planned route run by a pass receiver to be in a predetermined area or at a predetermined spot for a pass. also *pattern, route.*

pass play: A play in which a forward pass is attempted.

pass protection: Pass blocking, blocking to protect the passer. also *protection.*

pass receiver: An eligible receiver. One to

whom a pass is thrown, or for whom a pass is intended.

pass rush: An attempt to rush the passer by the defensive team. (had to hurry his throw to avoid the pass rush)

PAT: The point after touchdown. see *extra point.*

pattern: see *pass pattern.*

penalize: To charge or enforce a penalty against a team.

penalty: The loss of 5, 10, or 15 yards and/or the loss of a down (depending upon the nature and severity of the offense), imposed against a team guilty of a rules infraction or foul. Certain flagrant or violent fouls result in a disqualification penalty.

penalty flag, penalty marker: A weighted red or gold handerchief carried by football officials and thrown on the ground to signal an infraction or a foul. also *flag.*

penetration: 1. The movement by rushers through or past the opposing team's offensive line. 2. The advancement of the ball through the opposing team's defenses and to or toward its goal line.

personal foul: A foul in which a player strikes, kicks, knees, spears, trips, clips, charges into (as a kicker or passer), piles on, or grabs the face mask of an opponent, or commits other acts of unnecessary roughness or unsportsmanlike conduct, resulting in a 15-yard penalty and, if the foul is considered fla-

grant or violent, the disqualification of the guilty player.

picket, picket fence: A wall of blockers behind which the ballcarrier runs on a punt or kickoff return.

pick off: To intercept a pass intended for an opposing receiver. (picked off and run back to the 35-yard line)

pick up the blitz: To anticipate and adjust for a blitz by the defensive team.

pigskin: 1. A football. Actually a misnomer, as the only time a football was ever really close to a "pigskin" was back in the earliest days of soccer (from which American football is derived), when an inflated animal bladder was used as the ball. also *ball, football.* 2. Of or pertaining to football. (a pigskin festival)

piling on: The act of illegally jumping on a downed ballcarrier, or onto a "pile" of defensive players on a downed ballcarrier. Piling on results in a 15-yard penalty.

1. **pinch:** A defensive tactic in which a lineman positioned in the gap between two offensive blockers joins with an adjacent teammate in a charge against one offensive player in order to take that blocker out of the play and disrupt normal blocking plans. When big defensive tackles work a pinch on the center, the offensive guards and tackles are forced to move in, thereby shortening the pass rushing routes for the defensive ends. First tried by Pittsburgh Steelers defensive tackles "Mean" Joe Greene and Ernie Holmes in 1974, the technique was adopted as part of the Steelers' defensive strategy and soon copied by other teams in the NFL.

2. **pinch:** To execute a pinch against an offensive lineman. also *squeeze.*

pit: see *trenches.*

pitch out: To pass laterally toward the outside to a teammate behind the line of scrimmage.

pitchout: A lateral pass toward the outside made to a teammate behind the line of scrimmage.

1. **placekick:** A kick made while the ball is in a fixed position on the ground, on a kicking tee or held in position by a teammate. A placekick is normally used for kickoffs (at the start of each half, after an extra point attempt, and after a field goal) and for field goal and extra point attempts (a kicking tee may not be used for a field goal or extra point

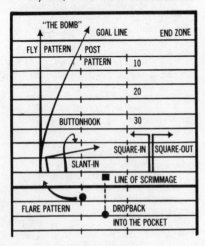

PASS PATTERNS

attempt in the NFL). Invented by Amos Alonzo Stagg.

2. placekick: 1. To execute a place-kick. 2. To score a field goal or extra point with a placekick.

placekicker: A placekicking specialist, or one who kicks a placekick.

platoon: Players who are put into and taken out of a game as a group or unit to play offense or defense. see *two-platoon system.*

play: 1. A specific and practiced plan of action for a down. (have gone into a prevent defense in anticipation of long pass play) 2. A down or the action that occurs during a down, from the moment the ball is snapped or kicked until the ball is dead. (will have time for one more play from scrimmage before the end of the quarter)

play-action fake: A fake handoff to a running back on a play-action pass. (freezes the linebacker with a play-action fake, then throws) also *play fake.*

play-action pass: An offensive pass play that is disguised to look like a running play, with a running back taking a fake handoff and following blockers as though carrying the ball. An effective tactic for deceiving linebackers (whose roles differ critically for a run and pass), the play-action pass was popularized in the NFL in the early 1950s (quarterback Bobby Layne and the Detroit Lions were among the foremost exponents of the tactic). It was originally called a "play number pass," the "number" being that of the specific running play the pass was to resemble. Later, this was shortened to "play pass" (still in use), and eventually became play-action pass. also *play pass.*

playbook: A player study guide that contains diagrams and notes regarding a team's plays and strategies.

play fake: see *play-action fake.*

play out one's option: To play for a team during an option year. see *option clause.*

play pass: see *play-action pass.*

pocket: An area several yards back from the line of scrimmage from which the quarterback passes, protected by blockers who drop back from the line of scrimmage to form a cuplike barrier. As rushing defenders are forced out and around the blockers, the quarterback is able to step up into the pocket to pass.

pocket passer: A quarterback who passes from a pocket, rather than rolling out or scrambling to pass.

point after, point after touchdown: see *extra point.*

point line: see *point spread.*

point spread: Betting parlance for an estimation by oddsmakers of the number of points by which one team is favored to beat another, given to provide a fair basis for wagering on teams of uneven strength. One who bets on the favored team collects and is said to "beat the spread" if the favored team wins by more than the point spread. One who bets on the underdog collects and beats the spread if the underdog wins, or loses by less than the point spread. The bet is considered a "push" and usually cancelled if the favored team wins by the same number of points indicated in the point spread. also *betting line, line, point line, price, spread.*

pop: 1. A hit, as a block or tackle. (the quarterback took a pretty good pop just as he was letting the ball go) 2. A short pass.

Pop Warner Football: A national organization that charters and oversees commercially sponsored football leagues for boys between the ages of seven and fifteen who compete in seven different divisions on the basis of age and weight. Founded as the Junior Football Conference in 1929 by Joseph J. Tomlin, the organization was renamed in 1934 after legendary coach and football innovator Glenn Scobey "Pop" Warner. Two-time Kansas All-American and Pro Football Hall of Famer Gale Sayers of the Chicago Bears is among the famous graduates of Pop Warner Football. National headquarters are located in Philadelphia, Pennsylvania.

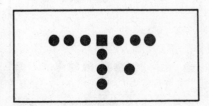

POWER I

possession: Control of the ball by a player or team.

possession football: see *ball control*.

post pattern: A pass pattern in which a receiver runs downfield near the sideline, then cuts inside toward the goalpost.

pour it on: To augment or concentrate a team's efforts in order to take advantage of a weak opponent, especially to run up a high score. Ironically, the man remembered as the greatest pour it on coach in the history of college football was John Heisman (of the Heisman Trophy), who once ran up a score of 222-0 against an overmatched opponent, still an American record.

power block: The act or an instance of drive-blocking, in which a defensive player is driven straight back or to the side to clear a path for a runner.

power I: A version of the I formation in which the fourth back lines up in the backfield beside the fullback rather than as a wide receiver. Developed and popularized by coach John McKay at the University of Southern California in the 1960s. see *I formation, stack I*.

power sweep: A running play in which both guards pull out of the line at the snap to lead a sweep around one end.

prayer: A low-percentage pass, one that would require a great deal of luck or the intercession of a "higher power" for completion. (in desperation sent up a prayer into the end zone) also *Hail Mary*.

prevent defense: A defensive formation that utilizes extra defensive backs (and/or extra linebackers) in order to protect against a long pass. Because of its vulnerability to a running play or

short pass, a prevent defense is generally used only when the offensive team needs long yardage for a first down or for a score.

previous spot: The spot at which the ball was last put into play on a scrimmage down or a free kick down. Many penalties are enforced at (measured from) the previous spot. compare *succeeding spot*.

price: see *point spread*.

primary receiver: The first or intended receiver for a pass on a particular play.

Pro Bowl: An annual post-season exhibition game between all-star teams from the American Football Conference and the National Football Conference of the NFL. The original Pro Bowl was played in 1939 at Los Angeles between the NFL Champion New York Giants and a team of professional all-stars (won by the Giants 13-10). Suspended in 1942, the Pro Bowl was revived under a new format in 1951, matching the all-stars of the old American Conference and National Conference. The first AFC-NFC Pro Bowl was played in Los Angeles, California in 1971, and won by the NFC by a score of 27-6.

Pro Football Hall of Fame: The national institution that honors outstanding players, coaches, and contributors (administrators, owners, etc.) in professional football, located in Canton, Ohio, the site of the 1920 organizational meeting from which the National Football League evolved. A charter class of seventeen enshrinees was elected in 1963, the year the original complex was dedicated. New members of the Pro Football Hall of Fame are elected annually from the nominations of fans by a twenty-nine-member National Board of Selectors, made up of media representatives from each league city and the president of the Pro Football Writers Association. An affirmative vote of approximately 80 percent is needed for election.

pro set: Any of several variations of the T formation used in the NFL in which one back lines up as a wide receiver on one side of the formation, and the end on the other side is positioned as a split end. also *pro T*.

pro T: see *pro set*.

protection: see *pass protection*.

pull: see *pull out*.

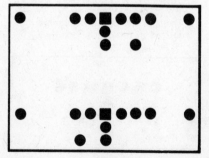

PRO SETS

pulling guard: An offensive guard who pulls back out of the line to lead the blocking for a running play toward the outside.

pull out: To pull back out of the line of scrimmage at the snap in order to lead a running play to the outside, or to trap block a defender. also *pull.*

1. pump: To fake a forward pass by cocking the arm and starting it forward, without releasing the ball. The quarterback will often "pump" the ball to freeze a defensive player, or make him commit in one direction before throwing elsewhere to the intended receiver.

2. pump: The act or an instance of faking a pass by pumping the passing arm. (freezes the linebackers with a little pump, then goes long to the wide receiver)

punishing runner: A powerful and bruising runner, one who takes a physical toll on tacklers throughout the course of a game. also *sledgehammer runner.*

1. punt: A kick in which the ball is held in front of the body, dropped, and kicked with the instep before it hits the ground. The longest punt in NFL history was 98 yards, made in 1969 by New York Jets kicker Steve O'Neal. Washington Redskins quarterback (1937-1952) Sammy Baugh holds the NFL career record for punting yardage, averaging 45.10 yards per punt. Baugh also holds the NFL one-season record, averaging 51.40 yards per punt in 1940.

2. punt: To make a punt. When a team is forced to relinquish possession of the ball (because of an inability to score or make the 10 yards necessary for a first down), the ball is punted to the opposing team, ideally, high in the air (to give the kicking team time to get downfield to tackle the receiver and prevent a runback) and as deep as possible in the opponent's position.

●●To give up, to literally or figuratively retreat so as to cut one's losses in the face of an impossible situation. (decided he had better punt after his third motorcycle accident, and find a less risky hobby)

punter: A player who specializes in punting, or one who kicks a punt.

punt formation: An offensive formation from which the ball is punted. In a punt formation, the punter lines up 10 to 15 yards behind the line of scrimmage (or shifts into this position before the ball is snapped).

punt return: The runback of a punt. The NFL career record for the highest punt return average (13.16 yards) is held by Billy "White Shoes" Johnson of the Houston Oilers (1974-1980). The NFL record for the highest punt return average for a season (23 yards) was set in 1950 by Herb Rich of the Baltimore Colts. Jack Christiansen of the Detroit Lions (1951-58) holds the NFL career record for the most touchdowns scored on punt returns (eight). Christiansen also holds the one-season record (four, in 1951). Three NFL players have scored two touchdowns on punt returns in a game: Jack Christiansen of the Detroit Lions (twice in 1951), Dick Christy of the New York Titans (1961), and Rick Upchurch of the Denver Broncos (1976).

punt return specialist: A special teams player whose job it is to receive and run back punts, usually an evasive runner with great speed.

pursuit: The persistent movement of a defensive player toward the passer or ballcarrier, as from the opposite side of the formation, or after being delayed by a blocker.

push: Betting parlance for a bet that is neither won nor lost, but usually cancelled. When a favored team wins by the exact number of the point spread, the bet is considered a push.

put it up: To pass. (will have to put it up on third-and-eight) also *air it out.*

quarter: Any of four fifteen-minute time periods (twelve minutes in high school play) that make up a game. At the end of the first, second, and third quarters, the competing teams change goals. also *stanza.*

1. quarterback: 1. An offensive back usually positioned directly behind the center to receive the snap. The quarter-

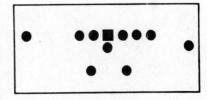

PRO OFFENSE

back runs a team's offense on the field, calling the signals to put the ball in play, then passing, running, or handing the ball off to a teammate. The quarterback was one of two positions created in 1880 (the other being the center) when the intercollegiate rules committee adopted the scrimmage concept with a center snap, urged by Yale halfback Walter Camp. The quarterback was not permitted to run with the ball until another rule change in 1910. also *field general, signal caller*. 2. The position played by a quarterback. also *field general, signal caller*.

●●A leader. (acted as quarterback on the outing because of his camping experience)

2. quarterback: To play the quarterback position.

●●To lead or direct an activity or group. (needed a strong President to quarterback the country)

quarterback draw: A draw play in which the quarterback, after dropping back as though to pass, runs straight forward through the onrushing defenders.

quarterback sneak: An offensive play for short yardage, in which the quarterback takes the snap and immediately runs over center. also *sneak*.

quick count: A shorter-than-usual sequence of signals called by the quarterback at the line of scrimmage to catch the defense off guard.

quick hitter: see *quick opener*.

quick kick: A surprise punt made on a down before fourth down and from a normal appearing pass or run formation. A quick kick is intended to catch the opposing team off guard, and to pin them deep in their own territory with little chance of a runback (because of the usual absence of a receiver in position to return the kick).

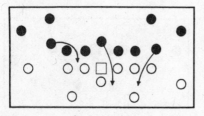

RED DOG

quick opener: An offensive play for short yardage in which a running back takes a quick handoff from the quarterback and plunges into a momentary hole in the line "opened" by blockers. also *quick hitter*.

quick out: see *out*.

quick release: The ability to set up and throw a pass quickly. (an accurate passer with a quick release)

quick slant: A quick opener in which the running back approaches the line from an angle.

razzle-dazzle play: A tricky and unconventional play (such as a double or triple reverse or a reverse and pass) intended to deceive or confuse the opposing team. also *gadget*.

read: To determine the intentions of an opposing player or team by observing keys such as the position or movement of an opponent or opponents. (read the blitz perfectly and dumped off to his running back for a first down)

receive: 1. To catch a pass or a punt. 2. To be the team to whom the ball is kicked. (won the toss and elected to receive)

receiver: 1. An offensive player who is eligible to catch a pass, to whom a pass is thrown, or who catches a pass. Don Hutson of the Green Bay Packers (1935-1945) was the first great receiver in the NFL, and the prototype for all those that followed. In only his second game as a professional, against the Chicago Bears, Hutson scored on an 83-yard touchdown pass from Arnie Herber. It was the first of ninety-nine touchdowns Hutson would score in his career, an NFL record. Hutson also scored a record seventeen touchdowns in 1942, a mark that was equalled in 1951 by Elroy "Crazylegs" Hirsch of the Los Angeles Rams and in 1961 by Bill Groman of the Houston Oilers. 2. A player who receives a kick, or who is designated to receive a kick.

receiving team: The team to whom the ball is kicked on a kickoff or a punt.

reception: 1. The act or an instance of catching a forward pass. 2. A caught pass, credited to a receiver's statistical records. Charley Taylor of the Washington Redskins (1964-1975, 1977) holds the NFL career record for the most pass receptions, 649. Charley Hennigan of the Houston Oilers set the one-season record in 1964, with 101 receptions.

The one-game record was set by Los Angeles Rams receiver Tom Fears in 1950, when he made 18 receptions in a game against the Packers.

red dog: A pass rush or blitz by linebackers. During the 1949 season, New York Giants player Don "Red" Ettinger, normally an offensive guard, had to fill in at linebacker for a game. On third-and-long for the opposing team, Ettinger bolted from his position to rush the quarterback. The result was a sack and a loss of yards on the play. Asked about the manuever later, the red-headed Ettinger claimed he was "just doggin' the quarterback a little." Thus, the expression "red dog" was born. also *dog.* compare *blitz.*

red-dog: To rush the passer from a linebacker position. also *blitz.*

1. redshirt: A college student who practices but does not play with the school football team, either to rehabilitate an injury or to gain experience at a position without losing a season of playing time. The major sanctioning body for college athletics, the NCAA, permits an athlete to play any four seasons in a five-year span of eligibility. The name redshirt comes from the fact that such athletes historically wear red shirts on the practice field.

●●The term is now also used in major college sports other than football.

2. redshirt: To practice, or have an athlete practice, as a redshirt while remaining off the varsity roster.

1. ref: The referee.

2. ref: To referee a game.

1. referee: The crew chief of all game officials, charged with the general oversight and control of a game. He is the final authority on the score, the number of a down, and on all matters not specifically delegated to other officials. On a scrimmage down, the referee is initially positioned behind the offensive backfield, to the right of a right-handed quarterback (or to the left of a left-handed quarterback). The referee is responsible for conducting the coin toss prior to the opening kickoff, explaining all fouls and their options to the team captains and indicating choices by the proper signal, administering all penalties, notifying the coach of a disqualified player, notifying the captain and

head coach when all allowable time outs have been used and at the two-minute warning, and raising and dropping one arm while sounding the whistle to signify the start of the twenty-five-second count (thirty seconds in the NFL) when the ball is ready for play.

2. referee: To act as the referee in a game.

referee's time out: see *official's time out.*

release: 1. The action of throwing a pass. see *quick release.* 2. To break off from one assignment (such as a block) to perform another.

remaining back: Either of the set backs who "remain" in the T formation while the other back is in motion or is positioned as a flanker.

replay: see *instant replay.*

1. return: To advance the ball after receiving a kick or intercepting a pass. also *run back.*

2. return: The advance of the ball by the player who receives a kick or intercepts a pass. (got to the outside for a 35-yard return on the kickoff) also *runback.*

reverse: An offensive play in which a back running laterally toward one sideline hands off to a teammate going the opposite way. The reverse was invented by Amos Alonzo Stagg and was used by him at Springfield College in Massachusetts as early as the 1890s.

ride the bench: To spend a lot of time on the bench rather than as a starter or regular player.

●●To be unneeded or unused, particularly because of an inability to perform or function relative to others. (when the female lead recovered, the understudy went back to riding the bench)

ring one's bell: To stun, to cause one's ears to ring because of a blow or collision, as during a block or tackle. (got the pass away, but took a pop that rang his bell)

●●To stun by a blow or collision.

roll out: To move laterally behind the line of scrimmage after receiving the snap before passing, pitching out, or running with the ball. (rolls out to his right, fakes a pitchout, and cuts downfield to the 40-yard line for a first down) also *sprint out.*

rollout: An offensive maneuver in which the quarterback takes the snap and moves laterally behind the line of scrimmage before passing or running with the ball. also *sprintout.*

rotate: To move back into an adjacent zone according to a prearranged scheme of coverage to defend against a pass. see *rotation.*

rotation: The simultaneous movement of linebackers and defensive backs into adjacent zones to cover against a pass. In a rotation, linebackers retreat in one direction, the defensive backs in the other, thus appearing to "rotate" into position.

roughing the kicker: A personal foul in which a defensive player charges into the kicker on a punt, field goal, or extra point attempt (quick kicks and kicks following a fumble or an attempted pass or run are exempted). It is not roughing the kicker if the contact is incidental to and after blocking or deflecting the kick, the result of being blocked into the kicker, or the result of the kicker's momentum. Roughing the kicker results in a 15-yard penalty from the previous spot. In the NFL, a player can be charged with the less serious foul of running into (as opposed to roughing) the kicker, which results in a 5-yard penalty from the previous spot.

roughing the passer: A personal foul in which a defensive player charges into, blocks, or tackles the passer after it is clear that the ball has been thrown. Roughing the passer results in a 15-yard penalty from the previous spot.

route: see *pass pattern.*

roverback: A defensive back who also functions like a linebacker. Often in college football, the increased responsibilities of a roverback are assigned to a particularly skilled athlete in order to maximize his effect on defense.

Rozelle Rule: The original NFL rule governing compensation for free agents, in effect from 1962 to 1977. Named for NFL Commissioner Pete Rozelle, the controversial rule entitled a team losing the services of a player (a free agent who had played out his option) to another team mutually agreeable compensation (or compensation set by the commissioner) from the team signing the player. In 1977, the Rozelle Rule was replaced by a provision in the Basic Agreement between the NFL and the

NFLPA limiting free agent compensation.

rule blocking: The use of predetermined blocking assignments ("rules") for various contingencies. When a defensive alignment or shift precludes the normal blocking patterns for the play called, each blocker has rules to follow. Football innovator and coach Sid Gilman was among the first to develop a system of rule blocking, introducing it to the NFL in the mid-1950s.

1. run: To advance the ball by carrying it rather than passing. (a big, strong team that likes to run right at you) also *carry, rush.*

2. run: An offensive play in which the ball is carried rather than passed. (not much success defending against the run) also *carry, running play, rush.*

run back: To return a kick or an intercepted pass.

runback: The return of a kick or an intercepted pass.

runner: The ballcarrier.

running back: An offensive back (halfback or fullback) who is used as a ballcarrier, blocker, and receiver. The term first came into use in the 1960s because of the different positions played by backs in pro football's multiple offensive sets, and, in 1970, replaced the more specific "halfback" and "fullback" as a matter of NFL policy.

running game: The use of the run on offense. (good blockers for a strong running game)

running play: A play in which the ball is advanced by running rather than passing. also *run, rush.*

run out the clock: To protect a lead near the end of a game by maintaining possession of the ball with conservative, time-consuming play, thereby denying the opposing team the opportunity to score and overcome the advantage. also *kill the clock.*

1. rush: 1. To advance the ball by running rather than passing; to run with the ball. Yardage gained by rushing is credited to the player and the team in statistical records. Jim Brown, running back from the Cleveland Browns (1957-1965) is the all-time NFL rushing champion, with a career record of 12,312 yards, averaging a record 5.22 yards per carry. Brown led the league in rushing for a record eight seasons, gaining 100 or more yards rushing in fifty-eight games, and scoring 106 touchdowns in his career (both NFL records). O.J. Simpson of the Buffalo Bills set the NFL record for the most yards gained by rushing in a single season in 1973, 2003 yards. Walter Payton of the Chicago Bears set the NFL record for a single game, rushing for 275 yards in a game against the Minnesota Vikings in 1977. also *carry, run*. 2. To attempt to get through or past the offensive line to tackle the passer, kicker, or the ballcarrier, or to block a pass or kick.

2. rush: 1. The act or an instance of running with the ball. Rushes are credited to the player and the team in statistical records. also *carry, run*. 2. The act or an instance of attempting to get through or past the offensive line to tackle the passer, kicker, or the ballcarrier or to block a pass or kick.

rusher: A defensive player who rushes.

1. sack: To break through or past the blockers and tackle the opposing quarterback in the offensive backfield before he can pass the ball. also *dump*.

2. sack: The act or an instance of sacking the opposing quarterback.

safety: 1. A two-point score awarded to the defensive team when an offensive player in control of the ball is downed or goes out of bounds on or behind his own goal line, or loses control of a ball which is downed or goes out of bounds on or behind the goal line (unless impetus to the player or ball comes from the defensive team), or when a foul is committed or an illegal pass is made behind the goal line by the offensive team. No safety is awarded if a player who receives a kick or intercepts a pass behind his goal line is downed or goes out of bounds, or downs the ball or fumbles it out of bounds, or if the momentum of the player intercepting the ball carries him back over the goal line and he is then tackled or driven out of bounds. After a safety, the ball is put into play with a free kick (usually a punt) by the team scored upon from their 20-yard line. compare *touchback*. 2. Either of two defensive backs usually positioned behind all other players, and primarily responsible for protecting against a

long run or pass. also *safetyman*. 3. A player on the receiving team positioned deep to receive a kick. also *safetyman*. 4. A safety blitz.

safety blitz: A blitz by one (usually the free safety) or both safeties. The safety blitz was first used by St. Louis Cardinals coach Frank "Pop" Ivy and free safety Larry Wilson in 1961. In the early 1960s, the Boston Patriots began to blitz not only the free safety, but the strong safety, an innovation that was soon copied and in wide use throughout football. also *safety*.

safetyman: see *safety*.

safety sack: A sack made by a blitzing safety.

safety valve: A short pass dumped off to a back in the flat when a quarterback cannot find an open receiver and is under pressure from a pass rush.

scatback: A tricky and elusive running back.

scissors: see *cross block*.

1. scramble: To move around behind the line of scrimmage eluding pass rushers when the pocket has been penetrated before passing or running. Some quarterbacks who are fast and mobile, and who have the ability to throw on the run, prefer to scramble rather than remain in the pocket. One of the most successful quarterbacks in football, Fran Tarkenton of the Minnesota Vikings and the New York Giants, was known for his inclination and ability to scramble. Tarkenton holds the NFL career records for the most passes completed (3686), the most yards gained (47,003), and the most touchdown passes (342).

2. scramble: The act or an instance of a quarterback scrambling.

scrambler: A quarterback who is known for his inclination and/or ability to scramble.

1. scrape: To "scrape off" or move from behind a defensive lineman at the snap in order to charge through a gap in the line. To stunt, as from a stacked position.

2. scrape: A linebacker's stunt around a lineman, often from a stacked position.

1. screen: A screen pass.

2. screen: To execute a screen pass.

screen pass: A pass thrown to a receiver in the flat (either a running back or a wide receiver who steps back) with a wall of blockers in front of him. Dis guised to look like a long pass, screen pass is particularly effectiv against a blitz or strong rush. also *screen.*

1. **scrimmage:** 1. An unofficial or practice game. 2. Pertaining to a scrimmage down. (pulled a muscle on the next play from scrimmage, and had to leave the game)

2. **scrimmage:** To engage in a scrimmage.

scrimmage down: A down that begins when the ball is put into play with a snap from the line of scrimmage and ends when the ball is dead. compare *free kick down.*

scrimmage kick: A kick made during a scrimmage down, such as a punt, field goal, or extra point attempt.

scrimmage line: see *line of scrimmage.*

seam: An undefended area between two zones of a zone defense. (hit him with a perfectly thrown pass in the seam)

secondary: 1. The players in the defensive backfield, the cornerbacks and safeties. 2. The area behind the defensive line and linebackers. (got into the secondary before he was finally brought down)

set: A formation, a specific offensive or defensive alignment at the beginning of a play.

set back: An offensive back positioned behind the quarterback, as in the T formation. also *remaining back.*

set up: To get into position in preparation for a pass.

shank: To miskick the ball on a punt, as with the ankle or off the side of the foot instead of the instep.

1. **shift:** 1. The simultaneous movement or change of position of two or more offensive players after assuming a set position. Legal once on each down as long as the shifting players assume a new set position and are motionless for

required one full second before the ap. A shift is used, often in combinan with a man in motion, to cause fensive imbalances and personnel matches or to distract or deceive the enders. 2. The movement or change position of one or more defensive players in anticipation of a certain kind of offensive play.

2. **shift:** To move to a new position as a part of an offensive or defensive shift.

shiver: A defensive lineman's technique in which the hands and forearms are thrust upward to stun an opposing lineman and deflect his block.

shoestring catch: A running catch (as of a pass) in which a player leans forward with his arms extended, grasping the ball just before it hits the ground.

shoestring tackle: A tackle in which the runner is able to be grasped only by the feet or one foot.

shootout: A high-scoring game.

shoot the gap: To rush through a space between offensive linemen toward the passer or ballcarrier.

short out: see *out.*

short side: The weak side of an unbalanced line, the "shorter" side with fewer linemen.

short yardage offense: A special offensive alignment employing extra players on the front line, used in situations where the ball must be advanced only a short distance in order to score or gain a first down.

shotgun offense: A spread formation primarily for passing in which the quarterback is positioned several yards behind the center to receive the snap, with the other backs lined up as slotbacks and flankers. Though a similar spread formation was used as early as 1920 by player-coach George Halas's Decatur Staleys (later the Chicago Bears), the shotgun was invented in 1960 by San Francisco 49ers' coach Red Hickey, and revived and popularized in 1975 by Tom Landry's Dallas Cowboys.

shoulder block: A block in which the opponent is hit with the shoulder.

shoulder pads: Padding that protects the collarbone and shoulder area of a player. Constructed with a hard outer surface (such as molded plastic or combat-derived composite materials) on top and a foam or inflatable cushion layer underneath.

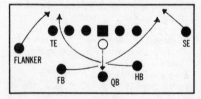

SHOTGUN

shovel pass: An underhand pass (with the arms swung as though "shovelling") often used for a pitchout or lateral.

1. sideline: 1. One of the two boundary lines on each side of the playing area between and perpendicular to the end lines. 2. The players' bench and surrounding area, from where the coach and coaching staff observe and send plays into a game. also *bench*. 3. see *sideline pattern, sideline route*.

2. sideline: To cause a player to be unable to play. (sidelined for three weeks with a pulled hamstring) also *bench*.

●●To prevent or remove one from active participation. (returned to work after being sidelined by the flu)

sideline pattern, sideline route: A pass pattern in which a receiver runs downfield then breaks toward the outside to catch a pass near the sideline. To gain time in the closing minutes of a game or a half, a receiver on a sideline route can step out of bounds to stop the clock. also *sideline*.

sidelines: The area next to either sideline, off the playing field.

●●Away from the action or activity, the point of view of an outsider or nonparticipant. (watched proudly from the sidelines as his son received the award)

sidewinder: see *soccer-style kicker*.

side zone: Either of two areas of the playing field between the inbounds lines and the sidelines. When the ball is blown dead or a ballcarrier is tackled in a side zone, the ball is put into play at the intersection of the inbounds line and the yard line where the ball was dead.

signal caller: A quarterback.

signals: 1. A coded series of words and numbers used in the huddle (or, when there is a change, at the line of scrimmage) by the quarterback or defensive captain to call for a specific play or alignment for the down about to be played. Offensive signals given by the quarterback also specify the precise timing of the snap. Gestures corresponding to the coded words and numbers are "wig-wagged" by coaches to send in signals from the sidelines. The use of signals originated in 1882 with the introduction of downs. Entire sentences at first, signals had, by 1885, been shortened to words and numbers.

2. A prearranged sequence of code words and numbers called out loud by the quarterback at the line of scrimmage to cue formation shifts and the snap from center. also *cadence, count, snap count*.

single-back offense: see *one-back formation*.

single wing: An offensive formation employing an unbalanced line in which the ball is snapped directly to the tailback, positioned 4 to 5 yards behind the center, or to the fullback, about a yard in front and just to the side of him on the strong side. The remaining two backs line up on the strong side, the quarterback as a blocking back behind the guard or tackle, and the other as a wingback behind and just outside the end. Invented by coach Glenn S. "Pop" Warner around 1906, the single wing was still being used successfully in the mid-1950s by UCLA, Arkansas, and the NFL Pittsburgh Steelers.

sit on a lead: To play conservatively so as to maintain possession of the ball and, thereby, protect a scoring advantage held.

six-man football: A variation of football with six players on a side, played, when possible, on a slightly smaller field (80 yards between goal lines, 40 yards wide, with 15-yard side zones) and special goals (crossbar 9 feet high, goalposts 25 feet apart). In six-man football, the offense must advance 15 yards instead of 10 in four downs, unless the ball is kicked or forward passed, it may not be advanced across the line of scrimmage until after a backward pass to a teammate (or "clear pass") is made by the receiver of the snap, all players (except the passer) are eligible to receive a pass, a field goal counts four points, a try for point counts two points if placekicked or drop kicked and one point if made by a pass or run, and the game is ended immedi-

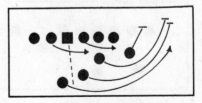

SINGLE WING OFFENSE

ately when one team is forty-five or more points ahead at the end of the first half, or when such a lead is secured during the second half.

sixty-minute player: 1. A player who is known for giving his full effort for an entire game. 2. A two-way player who plays on offense and defense. see *two-way player*.

skull session, skull practice: see *chalk talk*.

1. slant: 1. An offensive play in which the ballcarrier hits the line at an angle, such as off guard or off tackle. 2. A pass pattern in which a receiver runs diagonally across the middle of the field. also *slant-in*. 3. A planned charge at an angle to the left or right by a defensive lineman instead of straight ahead.

2. slant: 1. To angle into the line on a running play. 2. To charge to the left or right when rushing the ballcarrier or passer instead of straight ahead.

slant-in: see *slant*.

slasher: A ballcarrier who is known more for quick, powerful runs through the line than for outside speed or elusiveness.

sled: An apparatus that consists of a steel frame on skids with one or more large vertical pads attached to the front. As a training exercise, players practice blocking by contacting these pads with the arms and shoulders, forcing the sled straight back as it slides along the ground.

sledgehammer runner: see *punishing runner*.

sleeper play: see *hideout play*.

slingshot goalposts: The single-standard goalposts adopted by the NFL in 1967, as opposed to the H-shaped goals often used in high school and college games.

slot: The space or channel between (and extending behind) a tackle and an end in the offensive line.

slotback: A back positioned behind the space between a tackle and an end.

slot formation: A T formation in which one of the halfbacks or running backs is positioned in the slot between the tackle and split end. First popularized in the 1950s. also *slot T*.

slot T: see *slot formation*.

snakehips: An elusive or hard-to-tackle runner, one who "wriggles" away from tackles.

1. snap: 1. The method of putting the ball in play on a scrimmage down, in which the snapper (center), in one quick and continuous motion, passes or hands the ball backward between his legs from its position on the ground to a back behind him. The center snap and the scrimmage concept, football's cardinal and essential features, were adopted in 1880 by the intercollegiate rules committee led by Yale halfback Walter Camp. also *center snap, exchange*. 2. An instance of the center putting the ball in play by passing or handing it back through his legs. also *center snap, exchange*.

2. snap: To pass or hand the ball back between the legs to begin a scrimmage down. also *center, hike*.

snap count: see *signals*.

snapper: The center.

sneak: A quarterback sneak.

soccer-style kicker: A placekicker who uses the instep to propel the ball with a side approach (as one would kick a soccer ball) rather than the toe from straight back. In 1964, Pete Gogolak of Cornell University signed with the Buffalo Bills, becoming the first soccer-style kicker in professional football. Today, the majority of the placekickers in the NFL are soccer-style kickers. also *sidewinder*.

soft: Loose, a distance from the receiver one is guarding, as opposed to tight man-to-man coverage. (such a fast wide receiver that the cornerback has to play him soft)

solid play: A play that has no keys (such as a guard pulling to lead a running play, etc.) to tip off the defense.

1. spear: To deliberately drive the helmet into a player who is down, held by a teammate and going down, or obviously out of the play. A personal foul that results in a 15-yard penalty.

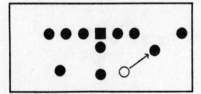

SLOT T FORMATION

2. spear: An instance of spearing. see *spearing*.

spearing: A personal foul in which the helmet is deliberately driven into a player who is down, held by a teammate and going down, or obviously out of the play, resulting in a 15-yard penalty.

special team, specialty team: A squad of players (mainly reserves and substitutes) called into a game for one play in special circumstances. There are special teams for kickoffs, punts, field goals, and extra point attempts. see *suicide squad*.

1. spike: A ritual in which the ball is slammed to the ground and bounced in the end zone after scoring a touchdown, popularized in the 1970s.

2. spike: To slam the ball to the ground and bounce it in the end zone after scoring a touchdown.

spinner play: One of several variations of an offensive play from the single-wing formation in which the ball is snapped to the fullback, who either fakes or hands off to the other backs passing him as he "spins" in a full circle, sometimes keeping and carrying the ball himself.

spiral: 1. The smooth, even spin around the long axis of the ball on a well thrown or kicked pass or punt. Coach and football innovator Glenn S. "Pop" Warner was among the first to develop and teach the spiral pass and punt. 2. A pass or a punt in which the ball spins smoothly and evenly around its long axis.

split end: 1. An offensive player positioned on the line of scrimmage several yards outside the formation as a pass receiver. Originally known as a flanker, the split end is now most often called a wide receiver. also *spread end*. 2. The position played by a split end. also *spread end*.

split T: A variation of the T formation in which the line is spread out, with the tackles and ends lining up wider than usual. Coach Don Faurot of Missouri invented the split T in 1941, which was regularly used successfully by coach Bud Wilkinson's Oklahoma teams. also *spread T*.

split the seam: To pass into the middle of the unguarded area between two zones in a zone defense.

split the uprights: To make good on a field goal or extra point attempt by kicking the ball over the crossbar and between the uprights.

spot: To put the ball down where it is next to be put into play. (the referee spots the ball at the 30-yard line, where it will be first-and-ten)

spot foul: An offense that can (depending on specific circumstances) be penalized from the "spot" of the foul, where the official throws his flag down (as opposed to the "previous spot"). Clipping and defensive pass interference are two examples of spot fouls.

spot of enforcement: The point from which a distance penalty resulting from a foul is measured. Depending on specific circumstances, the spot of enforcement may be at the spot of the foul (such as for clipping or defensive pass interference), the spot from which the previous play began (previous spot), the spot where the ball will next be put into play (succeeding spot), or at the spot where the ball is dead. also *enforcement spot*.

spot pass: A pass that is thrown to a predetermined spot rather than to a receiver.

spotter: One who identifies players for the announcer on a radio or television broadcast of a game.

spread end: see *split end*.

spread formation: An offensive formation in which the backs are spread out (such as the double wing, shotgun, etc.).

spread T: see *split T*.

sprint out: see *roll out*.

sprintout: see *rollout*.

spying: To delay rushing, to hold back long enough to read the play. One of the first to employ the technique of spying was defensive tackle Eugene "Big Daddy" Lipscomb of the Los Angeles Rams (1953-56), Baltimore Colts (1957-1961), and the Pittsburgh Steelers.

square-in: see *in*.

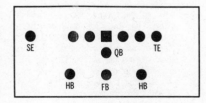

SPLIT T OFFENSE

square-out: see *out*.

squeeze: see *pinch*.

squib kick: A kickoff that is intentionally kicked low so as to bounce erratically along the ground and be difficult for the receiving team to handle.

1. stack: An offensive or defensive tactic in which players line up one behind another to disguise or delay recognition of the direction in which they will move (such as the intended path of a linebacker in a stack behind a lineman).

2. stack: To have one player line up behind another in a stack.

stack I: A variation of the I formation in which both running backs line up behind the fullback, creating a "stack" behind the quarterback.

stack the defense: To specially position defensive players in accordance with an opposing team's tendencies or strength, or to defend against a specific anticipated play.

stand one up: To block or tackle a charging opponent into a standing position, completely stopping his forward progress. (stood him up at the line of scrimmage)

stanza: A quarter.

stashing: An illegal practice in which a professional team "protects" (keeps other teams from signing) a potentially valuable player by under-the-table payments to the player, or by placing the player on the team's official injured reserve list, though not injured. A team found guilty of this practice in the NFL is subject to a fine and disciplinary action.

Statue of Liberty play: An old offensive play in which the back receiving the snap cocks his arm as though passing, but instead, the ball is taken from his hand by another back passing behind.

stick: To hit an opponent hard with a block or tackle.

sticks: see *chain*.

stickum: A once-legal sticky substance applied to the arms and hands of receivers and defensivebacks to increase adhesion and make the ball "stick" to the player. In 1981, the NFL outlawed the use of stickum and any other substance having qualities of slipperiness or adhesiveness.

stiff-arm: see *straight-arm*.

stone hands: An inability to catch a ball in flight, as a pass or a kick. (might have made a good receiver if he hadn't had stone hands)

1. straight-arm: To legally use the palm of the hand to ward off or hold at arms length a would-be tackler. also *stiff-arm*.

2. straight-arm: The act or an instance of straight-arming a would-be tackler. also *stiff-arm*.

stretch a zone: To pass to a receiver at the far edge of a defensive zone (such as deep to a fast receiver, or at the sideline).

stripe: Slang for a yard line. also *yard marker*.

strip the ball: To cause a fumble by knocking or taking the ball out of the ballcarrier's hands.

strong safety, strong safetyman: A defensive back positioned opposite the strong side of the offensive line, and primarily responsible for defending against a long run or pass. In man-for-man pass coverage, the strong safety usually covers the opposing tight end. also *tight safety, tight safetyman*.

strong side: The side of an unbalanced line on which the tight end is positioned.

strongside: Of or pertaining to the strong side. (stopped short of the first down by the strongside linebacker)

student body left: A power sweep to the left. see *student body right*.

student body right: A power sweep to the right. The expressions student body left and student body right came out of the coach John McKay era at the University of Southern California (1960-1975), when the USC offense ran the power sweep so successfully, with great running backs like Mike Garrett, O.J. Simpson, Anthony Davis, and Ricky Bell carrying the ball.

1. stunt: To exchange rushing routes with another defensive lineman by looping around him just before the ball is snapped.

2. stunt: The act or an instance of looping around a defensive lineman just before the ball is snapped to exchange rushing routes with him.

stutter step: A momentary change in rhythm or pace (and some times direction) while moving, or a feint in one direction with a quick step and return, in order to momentarily freeze or confuse an opponent.

stutter-step: To execute a stutter step.

1. submarine: To assume a low stance and duck under the block of an offensive lineman, thereby blunting his initial surge. A defensive tactic used to clog the intended path of the ballcarrier on a short yardage play.

2. submarine: The act or an instance of assuming a low stance and ducking under the block of an offensive lineman.

succeeding spot: The spot from which the ball is next to be put in play for a scrimmage down or free kick down. Some penalties, depending on specific circumstances, are enforced from the succeeding spot.

sucker play: An offensive play that is intended to specifically deceive and take advantage of one or more players on the defensive team.

sucker trap: see *false trap*.

sudden death: An extra fifteen-minute period of play to decide a playoff or championship game tied at the end of regulation play in the NFL. The period begins with a kickoff (decided by coin toss) and ends when one team scores, or when time runs out. If neither team is able to score in the overtime period, fifteen-minute periods continue to be played (with two-minute intermissions in between) until one team scores. Sudden death was first introduced by the NFL in 1941 to decide tied playoff games. Its use was expanded to championship games in 1947.

●●A "sudden death" or tiebreaking period of play is now often used in other sports.

suicide squad: The special team for kickoffs and punts. Because of the higher-than-usual risk of injury from the full-speed head-on collisions that occur on kickoffs and punts, the special teams for these occasions are given names like the bomb squad, kamikaze corps, kamikaze squad, and suicide squad.

suit up: To dress (pads and team uniform) to play in a game. (first time he's suited up since his injury)

●●To dress for a contest or an occasion. (suited up for the senior prom)

Super Bowl: The annual post-season game between AFC and NFC champions for the NFL championship. The first Super Bowl was played at Los Angeles in 1967, one year after the American Football League-National Football League merger was announced. In Super Bowl I, the NFL Green Bay Packers defeated the Kansas City Chiefs of the AFL 35-10 (NFC and AFC conferences weren't formed until 1969).

1. sweep: An offensive play in which the ballcarrier runs outside around one end behind blockers.

2. sweep: To execute a sweep.

1. swing: Short for swing pass. see *flare*.

2. swing: see *flare*.

swing pass: see *flare*.

1. tackle: To seize and stop the forward progress of the ballcarrier, especially by knocking, pulling, or throwing him to the ground. also *bring down*.

2. tackle: 1. The act or an instance of tackling the ballcarrier. 2. Either of the two offensive or defensive tackles positioned on the line of scrimmage. see *offensive tackle, defensive tackle*. 3. The position played by a tackle. 4. A normal game of football in which tackling is permitted, as opposed to a game of touch football. (played his first game of tackle at the age of twelve)

tackling dummy: A heavy stuffed bag suspended from above and used to practice tackling. Pioneer coach Amos Alonzo Stagg invented the tackling dummy in 1889, when he was a student at Yale.

tailback: The deepest positioned offensive back in formations such as the I and the single wing.

tail football: see *flag football*.

Tartan Turf: A brand of artificial turf used in place of grass in some stadiums.

taxi: 1. To play on a team's taxi squad. (taxied for a year before he made the roster) 2. To assign a player to the team's taxi squad.

taxi squad: A squad of salaried reserve players who practice and scrimmage with a team, but do not suit up for games. Though the use of taxi squads was prohibited by the NFL in the early 1970s, the term is now applied to the four extra players allowed on NFL team rosters beginning in 1982 (forty-nine-man rosters with forty-five eligible to play each week). The taxi squad got its name because in the late 1940s, Arthur McBride, the original owner of the Cleveland Browns (then still with the All-American Football Conference, rival to the NFL), used to employ some of his practice players as drivers for a taxi company he owned. also *cab squad.*

team area, team box: A marked area on the sidelines on both sides of the field for team benches, reserve players, coaches and trainers.

tear-away jersey: A special jersey often worn by backs and receivers that is designed to tear loose if grasped by an opponent, thereby freeing the ballcarrier.

TD: A touchdown.

1. tee: A kicking tee.

2. tee: see *tee up.*

tee up: To place the ball on a kicking tee. also *tee.*

T formation: An offensive formation in which the backs are arranged roughly in the shape of a T, with the quarterback positioned just behind the center to take the snap directly, and the fullback several yards straight back, in between and slightly behind the two halfbacks. The modern T formation, which ushered in an era of counter plays, players in motion, and forward passes to widely spaced ends and receivers, was developed in the late 1930s by Ralph Jones, coach of George Halas' Chicago Bears, and college coach Clark Shaughnessy. In 1940, in his first year as Stanford coach, Shaughnessy's team went undefeated employing the T, beating Nebraska 21-13 in the Rose Bowl. That same year, the Bears used the T in a 73-0 rout of the Washington Redskins in the NFL championship game. The T formation and its variations are still widely used in college and professional football. also *tight T.* compare *pro T, slot T, split T, wing T.*

thread the needle: To throw a perfectly placed pass between defenders.

three and out: A defensive team's motto and goal, to stop the opposing offensive team for three downs and force them to punt.

three-end offense: Any of the modern offensive formations which employ a tight end, split end, and a flanking back as a wide receiver, effectively three "ends." Although born in 1931 with Chicago Bears coach Ralph Jones's split end and man-in-motion, the modern three-end offense emerged in the late 1940s with the appearance of the position and role of the tight end.

three-four defense: A defensive alignment that uses a three-man line (a nose guard and two defensive ends) and four linebackers. The three-four defense was reported to have been used in 1922 by Georgetown University coach Maurice Dubofsky, though it was perfected and popularized by coach Bud Wilkinson at Oklahoma in the 1940s. College teams sometimes refer to the three-four as the "Oklahoma." Since Don Shula's Miami Dolphins went undefeated in 1972 using the three-four, the alignment has become a staple in the NFL.

three-man front: A three-man defensive line (a nose guard and two defensive ends), as in the three-four defense.

three-point stance: A crouching stance with the feet set 18 to 24 inches apart and staggered slightly, and the body leaning forward with one hand touching the ground. Linemen and some backs wait for the snap in a three-point stance.

throw a strike: To complete a pass, especially a perfectly thrown or accurately placed pass. (threw a strike into double coverage to make the first down)

throwball: A description of the wide-open passing game in the NFL made possible by rule changes in the late 1970s.

throw for a loss: To tackle the passer or ballcarrier behind the line of scrimmage for a loss of yardage. (couldn't find an open receiver and was thrown for a loss)

throw into traffic: To throw a pass to a receiver in the midst of defenders. Dangerous because of the high risk of an interception.

tight end: 1. An offensive lineman usually positioned at one end of the line of scrimmage within a yard or so of the tackle. The tight end is both a blocker and a pass receiver. 2. The position

THREE-FOUR DEFENSE

played by a tight end. The position and role of the tight end emerged in the NFL in the late 1940s, making possible the modern three-end offense (tight end, split end, and a flanking back as a wide receiver).

tight safety, tight safetyman: see *strong safety*.

tight T: The basic T formation, called "tight" because of the small space between the linemen. compare *split T*.

time out: 1. A one and one-half-minute suspension of play requested by and charged to either team any time the ball is dead. Each team is allowed three time outs in each half. 2. A suspension of play by the referee. see *official's time out*.

●●A pause. (took a time out from his studies to watch the news)

total offense: A statistic which reflects the total net yards gained by rushing and passing by a player or team in a period of play, game, season, or (in a player's individual records) a career.

touch: 1. The end zone. (downed the ball in touch rather than attempt a runback) 2. Touch football.

touchback: A situation in which a ball kicked, punted, or passed by one team travels over the other team's goal line and is deliberately downed there by the other team, or goes out of bounds. After a touchback, the team into whose end zone the ball was kicked, punted, or passed puts the ball in play at its own 20-yard line. compare *safety*.

touchdown: A six-point score made by advancing the ball to a point on or behind the opposing team's goal line, whether by carrying it, passing it to a teammate, or recovering a loose ball there. Originally, a touchdown counted for less than an extra point (then called a "goal from touchdown" or "goal after"). In 1883, a touchdown was valued at two points, in 1884, four points (and the extra point was reduced from four points to two points), in 1897, five points (and the extra point reduced to one point), and finally, six points in 1910.

touch football: A variation of football played without protective pads, in which the ballcarrier is "downed" not by tackling, but by a defensive player touching him with both hands below the

waist (or sometimes anywhere between the shoulders and knees). also *touch*.

1. trap: 1. see *trap block*. 2. see *trap play*.

2. trap: To execute a trap block against an opponent. also *trap block*.

trap block: An offensive blocking technique in which a rushing defender is allowed to charge through the offensive line, then is blocked from the side by a pulling guard or tackle (or occasionally, the center). also *mousetrap, trap*.

trap-block: To execute a trap block against an opponent. also *trap*.

trap play: A running play that depends on a trap block and is directed at the space vacated by the trapped defensive player. also *trap*.

trenches: The area around the line of scrimmage in which the offensive and defensive lines make contact and contend. (have taken control of the

PENALTY FLAG

OFFICIAL—TOUCHDOWN SIGNAL

trenches in the second half) also *pit*.

triple option: An offensive play designed to begin the same way on every down, in which the quarterback has three choices: he can hand off to the fullback for a run through the line, pitch the ball out to a halfback for a run to the outside, or keep the ball to run or pass it himself. Popular in college play, the triple option evolved out of the split T formation popularized in the 1940s.

triple-team: 1. To block or guard an opponent with three players simultaneously. 2. To join with two teammates to block or guard an opponent.

triple threat: A player who is able to run, pass, and kick the ball well.

●●A person who is skilled in three areas of activity. (a triple threat who can sing, dance, and act)

triple wing: An offensive formation similar to the double wing, but with the fullback playing close behind and just outside the tight end, and the halfback on the weak side playing in the slot several yards back. also *trips*.

trips: see *triple wing*.

try: see *try for point*.

try for point: An attempt to score an additional point (or in high school, college, and USFL games, one or two additional points), by the scoring team after a touchdown. On a try for point, the scoring team is allowed one down at the 2-yard line (3-yard line in high school and college games) to successfully placekick or drop kick the ball through the uprights, or successfully run or pass the ball over the goal line for the additional point (or two additional points for a run or a pass in high school, college, and USFL games). also *try*. see *extra point*.

turf toe: A tear in the posterior capsule surrounding the joint that attaches the big toe to the foot (the first metatarsal

pharangeal joint). A painful injury caused by hyper-extending the joint when the back of the heel (of a player on his toes) is forced downward (as by an impact), bending the toe back. Called turf toe because of the frequency of the injury on the unyielding surface of artificial turf.

turn-in: A pass pattern in which the receiver turns in across the middle of the field after running downfield a short distance.

turn-out: A pass pattern in which the receiver turns out toward the sideline after running downfield a short distance.

turn over: To lose possession of the ball because of a misplay or an error.

turnover: The loss of possession of the ball by a team because of a misplay or an error. (fumbled the ball in the second half to give up another turnover)

turn the corner: To turn upfield after running laterally to the outside, as on a sweep or end run. (tackled before he could turn the corner)

two-minute drill: An offensive strategy in which several plays are called in one huddle in order to save time near the end of a half or a game (especially by a team which is tied or behind). Typically, two-minute drill plays feature passes thrown to receivers near a sideline so that the clock is stopped automatically with an incompletion, or by the receiver stepping out of bounds if the pass is complete. The first acknowledged master of the two-minute drill was quarterback Bobby Layne of coach Buddy Parker's Detroit Lions in the early 1950s. also *hurry-up offense, two-minute offense*.

two-minute offense: see *two-minute drill*.

two-minute warning: The referee's notification to the coach of each team that only two minutes remain in a half.

two-platoon system: The common practice of using separate groups or squads of players for offense and defense. Though a rule change made unlimited or free substitution possible in college play in 1941 (and 1943 in the NFL), the two-platoon system was first used by Michigan coach Fritz Crisler against Army in 1945. Its popularity spread until substitutions were severely limited by another rule change in 1953 (the NFL had ended free substitution in 1946). When unlimited substitution was restored by the NFL

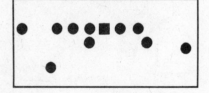

TRIPLE WING

in 1950 and the NCAA in 1958, the two-platoon system once again became popular.

two-way player: One who plays on offense and defense. The last real two-way player was Pro Football Hall of Famer Chuck Bednarik, who played both offense and defense for the Philadelphia Eagles in their 1960 NFL title drive. also *sixty-minute player.*

umpire: A football official who, at the snap, is positioned 4 to 6 yards behind the line of scrimmage in the defensive backfield, and who is responsible for supervising play at the line of scrimmage, assisting the referee in setting up the ball for the next play, and watching for ineligible linemen downfield on a pass play. Before a game, the umpire checks the players' equipment and any special bandages or pads worn.

unbalanced line: An offensive alignment in which there are more linemen on one side of the center than the other. The unbalanced line is credited to Amos Alonzo Stagg.

1. under: 1. Short for undershift. compare *over.* 2. Underneath, or under the coverage. (looped a little pass over the middle, under the coverage)

underneath: Short of an area or zone covered by defensive backs, to an undefended area between the line of scrimmage and the coverage. (will throw underneath to the tight end when his other receivers are double-covered) also *under.*

undershift: A defensive alignment in which all or some of the defensive linemen shift one position over toward the weak side of an unbalanced line (placing one tackle head-on the center) to disrupt blocking patterns, or to move big linemen to the expected point of attack. also *under.* compare *over, overshift.*

under the center: Positioned close to and directly behind the center, with the hands under him, ready to receive the ball.

United States Football League: A major professional football league that conducts an eighteen-week season from March through June, normally off season for football. Formed in 1982, the United States Football League (USFL) scheduled twelve teams to contest in

1983, the inaugural season, with three geographic divisions: the Atlantic Division (the Boston Breakers, the New Jersey Generals, the Philadelphia Stars, and the Washington Federals), the Central Division (the Birmingham Stallions, the Chicago Blitz, the Michigan Panthers, and the Tampa Bay Bandits), and the Pacific Division (the Arizona Wranglers, the Denver Gold, the Los Angeles Express, and the Oakland Invaders).

unload: 1. see *ground, intentional grounding.* 2. To inflict a particularly hard hit on an opponent with a block or tackle. (unloaded on the quarterback from the blind side)

unnecessary roughness: An illegal action such as kicking, striking, butting, or spearing an opponent, tackling or contacting the ballcarrier when he is clearly out of bounds, throwing the ballcarrier to the ground after the ball is dead, contacting a ballcarrier who falls or slips to the ground untouched and makes no attempt to advance (before or after the ball is dead), or running into or throwing the body against or on a player obviously out of the play (before or after the ball is dead). Unnecessary roughness results in a 15-yard penalty, and if the foul is judged to be flagrant,

QUARTERBACK

CENTER

UNDER THE CENTER

the disqualification of the guilty player.

unsportsmanlike conduct: An illegal act that is contrary to the principles of sportsmanship, such as the use of abusive or insulting language or gestures to opponents, teammates, or officials, hiding or substituting something in place of the ball, repeatedly baiting or distracting an opponent, giving unfair assistance to or accepting it from a teammate, or attempting to punch or kick an opponent even though no contact is made. Unsportsmanlike conduct results in a 15-yard penalty, and if the infraction is judged flagrant, the disqualification of the guilty player.

up back: 1. A blocking back positioned just behind the line on kicking plays. 2. The receiver or receivers positioned in front of the deep receivers on a kick. 3. The running back positioned just behind the quarterback in an I formation, sometimes called the diveback.

upfield: 1. Toward the opposing team's goal line. also *downfield.* 2. Back toward the area from which a play originates.

upright: One of the two goalposts that extend vertically from either side of the crossbar, and mark the sides of the goal.

uprights: 1. The two goalposts that extend vertically from either side of the crossbar (10 feet in high school and college, 30 feet in the NFL), and mark the sides of the goal. 2. The goal.

up top: Into the air, as with a pass or a pass play. (will be forced to go up top if he can't get his ground game going)

USFL: The United States Football League.

veer, veer ofense: An offense based on the triple option run from a modern three-end formation (with a tight end, split end, and a flanking back as a wide receiver).

vig: see *vigorish.*

vigorish: Betting parlance for the service

charge paid to a professional betting service or bookie when placing a bet, usually 10 percent of the bet. also *juice, vig.*

weak safety: A defensive back positioned across from the weak side of the offensive line. also *free safety, free safetyman.*

weak side: The side of an unbalanced line having fewer players (opposite the side on which the tight end is positioned). also *short side.*

weakside: Of or pertaining to the weak side.

wedge: A wedge-shaped alignment of blockers who form in front of the ballcarrier on kickoff returns, legal as long as the blockers neither link arms nor hold onto each other.

wide receiver: An offensive player positioned wide of a formation, as a split end or flanker, and who functions primarily as a pass receiver.

wind: Breath or the ability to breathe properly while taking part in a strenuous activity. (will have to train to improve his wind)

winded: Out of breath, unable to take in a sufficient amount of oxygen to sustain a strenuous physical activity.

wind sprint: One of a series of short sprints run at full speed with brief rest periods in between to build up a player's speed, wind, and endurance. Developed by Amos Alonzo Stagg.

wingback: 1. An offensive back positioned just outside and behind the end on the strong side of a single wing formation, and who functions primarily as a ballcarrier, pass receiver, and blocker. 2. Another name for the original flankerbacks. 3. The position played by a flankerback.

wing T formation: A variation of the T formation in which one halfback lines up on the flank as a wingback. Small-college coach Dave Nelson of Delaware is credited with inventing the wing T, popularized later by Forest Evashevski at Iowa.

wishbone, wishbone T: A variation of the T formation which utilizes an unbalanced line (with a split end and tight end), and in which the halfbacks are positioned to either side of and slightly behind the fullback (roughly forming the shape of a wishbone when viewed from

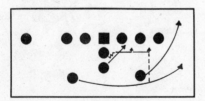

WISHBONE OFFENSE

above). Coach Darrell Royal's 1968 University of Texas team introduced the wishbone formation.

Xs and Os: 1. The two symbols used to represent a team and an opposing team in diagrams of offensive plays and defensive strategies. 2. Basics, the initial stages of teaching or learning offensive plays or defensive strategies. (would have gone back to the Xs and Os had he known they would execute so poorly)

Yale coverage: A defensive strategy against a pass that employs a zone defense deep, with each safety covering one half the field, and man-to-man coverage underneath.

yardage: The number of yards gained by a player or team in one play, a period of play in a game, a game, a season, or (in the case of an individual player) a career.

yardage chain: see *chain.*

yard line, yard marker: A marked or unmarked line and its vertical plane parallel to the end line. Yard lines extend across the field one yard apart and are named by the number of yards to the nearest goal line. also *stripe.*

zebra: An official, usually wearing the regulation black and white striped shirt.

1. zone: 1. An area of the field assigned to be covered by a particular defender or defenders in a zone coverage. 2. Short for zone coverage. (switched from man-to-man to a zone in the second half)

2. zone: To use zone coverage against an opponent. (will cover man-to-man short, and zone deep)

zone blocking: see *area blocking.*

zone coverage: A defensive strategy to protect against a pass in which specific areas or zones are assigned to defensive players, and any opponent entering the zone is guarded (as opposed to individual or man-to-man guarding). The fundamental principles of the zone defense, the rotation of the secondary, appeared in the NFL as early as the 1930s, when Earl "Curly" Lambeau's Green Bay Packers and Gus Dorais's Detroit Lions rotated the secondary toward George Halas's man-in-motion from the Chicago Bears' T formation. By the 1960s and 1970s, zone coverage had become the rule rather than the exception in the NFL. also *zone.*

It is probable that the ancient Roman game *paganica*, in which a stuffed leather ball was knocked about the countryside by mallet-wielding players, was the progenitor of the various ball-and-club games developed in European countries. The basic elements of golf may also be related to the Roman game, but golf itself developed in Scotland.

Scottish shepherds made a game out of using a knotted staff or stick to knock a pebble (and later, a small ball) around on the tough grass between the heathery, wind-swept "links" or ridges of sand along the rugged coasts of Scotland. Friends and passers-by watched, then sampled the new game, and soon, fishermen, farmers, masons, and blacksmiths were also playing.

When St. Andrews University was founded in 1411, the game was already known throughout Scotland. The playing of golf had become so widespread by 1457 that the Scottish Parliament passed laws prohibiting the sport, which was said to be jeopardizing the national defense by seriously interfering with the practice of archery.

These laws were revoked in 1491, and, near the end of the century, King James IV of Scotland himself became a devotee of the game. The Lord High Treasurer's accounts of 1502 and 1503 included payments for the king's "golf clubbis and ballis."

James IV's granddaughter, Mary, Queen of Scots, may have been the first woman golfer. When she returned to Scotland in 1560 from France, several young French boys, or *cadets*, came with her to serve as pages and porters. Whether or not these pages carried the Queen's clubs around when she played golf, golf club porters came to be known as caddies, an anglicized version of the French pronounciation "cahday."

In 1682, while in Edinburgh with the Scottish Parliament for his brother the king, the Duke of York (later James II, King of England, Scotland, and Ireland) and a local shoemaker, John "Far and Sure" Patersone, handily defeated two English noblemen in the first international foursome. The ball was made of leather, stuffed tightly with goose feathers. The players' golf clubs were hand carved from Scottish hardwoods, with crude and somewhat fragile heads and long, sturdy shafts, forcing golfers to play well away from the ball and use a flat or more horizontal swing. Some iron-headed clubs were in use, probably to cut down on breakage.

Though some claim that the Royal Blackheath Club was founded as early as 1608, and the Royal Burgess Golfing Society of Edinburgh in 1735, the first documented golf club was the Honorable Company of Edinburgh Golfers, founded in 1744. In 1745, a tournament was played in Edinburgh for a silver club donated by the City Council, and won by John Rattray, an Edinburgh surgeon. Thirteen playing rules were drafted for the tournament. The same rules were adopted nine years later when the Royal and Ancient Golf Club of St. Andrews was founded in 1754. This organization, with its course in St. Andrews, was soon to become the governing body and the center of the sport of golf, as keeper of the official rules. Since 1952, that responsibility has been shared with the United States Golf Association.

The 1800s brought important changes in golf equipment. By 1810, varnish was being applied to wooden clubs to protect them from weather. In 1848, the revolutionary gutta-percha or "guttie" ball was introduced. Heavier and more perfectly round than the old feather-stuffed ball, the guttie could be driven farther (over 200 yards, vs. 175 yards maximum for the old ball), and could be bounced and actually rolled toward the hole. This quality when combined with the practice of mowing the greens closer around the hole, made the modern putt possible.

In 1860, the first tournament was staged at the Prestwick Course in Scotland, and won by pioneer professional, Willie Park, Sr. This competition would eventually be known as the British Open, not because both professionals and amateurs could compete, as they did from the second year on, but because after 1865, the tournament was "open" to any golfer who wanted to play, whether or not from around Prestwick.

The English were equally enamored of the game. In 1869, the Royal Liverpool Club was formed and a course laid out over a rabbit warren in Hoylake. It was at Hoylake that the first British Amateur Championship was played in 1885, won by A.F. MacFie. The Royal and Ancient Golf Club of St. Andrews accepted the management of both the British Open and Amateur Championships in 1919.

It is believed that golf may have first been brought to America by Scottish soldiers who took part in the Revolutionary War (1775-1783). Several golf clubs survived the war in parts of Georgia and South Carolina, though there is little evidence that they were any more than social clubs. One advertisement appearing in a New York newspaper, James Rivington's *Gazette*, in 1779, does mention the sport: "To the golf players: The season for this pleasant and healthy exercise now advancing, gentlemen may be furnished with excellent clubs and the veritable Caledonian (Scottish) balls by enquiring at the Printers."

Though there is evidence of informal courses in Burlington, Iowa (1883), and Oakhurst, West Virginia (1884), the Dorset (Vermont) Golf Links (later the Dorset Field Club), founded in 1886, is probably the oldest golf club and course in the United States, followed by the Foxburg (Pennsylvania) Golf Club (later the Foxburg Country Club) in 1887.

On Washington's Birthday in 1888, John Reid, a Scotsman who had come to the United States as a youth, introduced the game to several neighbors. Using clubs and balls he had asked a friend to bring back from Scotland, Reid and neighbor John B. Upham put on a demonstration of golf over an improvised three-hole course in a cow pasture in Yonkers, New York. By summer, a new six-hole course was laid out on a nearby thirty-acre plot of land. In November, Reid's friends gathered at his home to found the St. Andrews Golf Club of Yonkers, honoring the famous club in Scotland. On March 30, 1889, the first mixed foursome of record was played, with Upham partnered with Mrs. Reid, and Miss Carrie Low partnered with Reid. Upham and Mrs. Reid were the victors.

By 1892, the club boasted thirteen players, and a new six-hole course was laid out where Reid and his friends would become known as the "apple tree gang" for their habit of hanging their coats on the branches of a large apple tree next to the first tee.

The first professionally designed golf course in the United States was laid out in 1891 near the Shinnecock Indian Reservation at Southhampton, Long Island by Scottish pro Willie

Dunn, financed by William K. Vanderbilt and several wealthy friends. With a large and luxurious clubhouse designed by architect Stanford White, the club catered to a wealthy and privileged membership, drawn from American big business and high society. As golf became the preferred game of the wealthy, other clubs were founded, with courses often designed by Dunn or other knowledgeable golfers who had been brought over from Scotland by Dunn. These enterprising young Scotsmen stayed on at the new clubs as home pros, teaching members and their families, maintaining the courses, selling and repairing equipment, training caddies, and arranging competitions. The first American Open was held at St. Andrews in Yonkers in 1894, with Willie Dunn defeating the three other entrants. In the same year, two different clubs held "Amateur Golf Championships," St. Andrews and the Newport (Rhode Island) Country Club. It was evident that a single sanctioning body was needed to prevent such conflicts, and to set uniform standards and administer the game nationally.

On December 22, 1894, the Amateur Golf Association was born in New York, soon renamed the United States Golf Association (USGA) to include professional golf. For the first time, a governing body existed that could establish and enforce uniform rules for everyone, and conduct national amateur and open championships.

By 1895, golf and golf clubs were flourishing throughout the country. Enough Americans were eager to learn the new game to cause the first "how-to" book to be published, James P. Lee's *Golf in America—A Practical Manual*. The USGA held the first U.S. Amateur at the Newport Country Club in October, with thirty-two entries competing at match play. Charles Blair Macdonald, one of the five founding members of the USGA, won handily.

On the day following the Amateur Championship, the first U.S. Open was held on the same course. Ten professionals and one amateur competed in the one-day, thirty-six-hole stroke play tournament, won by Horace Rawlins, the Newport Club's nineteen-year-old assistant professional from England. The Open was the first major U.S. competition to use stroke play, a format that would gain great popularity in future years.

In November of 1895, the USGA held the first Women's Amateur Championship at the Meadow Brook Club in Hempstead, New York. Thirteen entrants competed at stroke play over eighteen holes, won by Mrs. Charles S. Brown of the Shinnecock Hills Golf Club. The first national intercollegiate tournament was played in 1897, with Yale winning the team championship, and L.B. Bayard, Jr., of Princeton emerging as the first individual intercollegiate champion.

In 1899, Coburn Haskell, an American from Cleveland, Ohio, produced the first modern golf ball, comprised of strips of rubber thread wound tightly around a rubber core, with a durable composite rubber covering. It was livelier and could be driven farther than the old guttie ball, and was much more resistant to cuts from iron clubs. Golfers, however, were reluctant to switch until 1901, when Alex "Sandy" Herd won the British Open, and Walter Travis, the U.S. Amateur Championship, with the new ball.

By 1900, over 982 golf courses existed in the United States. The majority were nine holes, but already there were over 90 eighteen-hole courses.

The 1900 U.S. Open was won by British golfing great, Harry Vardon. All athletes who profit by the use of their names to advertise products owe a debt to Vardon. Arguably the best golfer of his era, Vardon made the first-ever player endorsement, when Spalding introduced the Vardon line of golf clubs in 1901.

Harry Vardon, John Henry Taylor, and James Braid, known as the "great triumverate," and golfing great Edward "Ted" Ray epitomized Great Britain's dominance in golf since the late 1800s. When American-born amateur and former caddie Francis Ouimet won the U.S. Open in 1913, defeating Vardon by five strokes, the tide began to turn.

In 1904, a golf competition was made part of the St. Louis Olympics and was won by George S. Lyon of Canada. Though judged to be a less-than-ideal Olympic sport and dropped thereafter, the fact that it was even tried indicated the growing popularity of the sport.

As the British pros had done in 1901, American professionals united in 1916 and formed the Professional Golfers Association (PGA). The first PGA Championship was held that year at the Siwanoy Country Club in Bronxville, New York and was won by James M. Barnes. Home-grown American golf stars such as amateurs Francis Ouimet and Charles Evens, Jr., and professionals such as Walter Hagen and Gene Sarazen began to emerge. Hagen's 1922 victory in the British Open (the first of four) clearly signalled the new prominence of the United States in international competition.

Stylish, witty, and a golfing friend of the Prince of Wales, Hagen raised the social status of the professional golfer and was the first pro to draw galleries of faithful fans. The sudden rise in national popularity of casual slacks and sport coats is attributed to Hagen's fashion influence, first with other golfers, then the general public. The trend is said to have started one day in the mid-1930s, when "The Haig" and the Prince of Wales neglected to change into their normal golf knickers, playing instead in slacks.

In 1922, Glenna Collett (Vare), after whom the LPGA Vare Trophy is named, won the first of a record six Women's Amateur Championships, and the United States team won the first Walker Cup international amateur competition. The following year, a twenty-one-year-old amateur from Georgia, Robert T. Jones, Jr., won the U.S. Open. Bobby Jones would go on to become the game's greatest star. Jones won the British Open in 1926 and 1927, the U.S. Amateur in 1924, 1925, 1927, and 1928, and the U.S. Open again in 1926 and 1929. In 1930, Jones became the only golfer in history to score a Grand Slam, winning in that year the British Amateur Championship, the British Open, the U.S. Amateur Championship, and the U.S. Open. In 1981, Bobby Jones and Olympic champion and pioneer woman professional golfer Mildred "Babe" Didrikson Zaharias became the first athletes honored by the U.S. Postal Service with a commemorative stamp.

The first Ryder Cup international team competition for professionals was held in 1927 at the Worcester Country Club in Massachusetts, with the United States team defeating the team from Great Britain 9-1/2 to 2-1/2.

In 1934, the first Masters Tournament was held at the Augusta National Golf Club, and won by Horton Smith. The Masters was soon considered one of golf's most prestigious tournaments, in which only the best golfers competed.

Entertainer and golfing enthusiast Bing Crosby put on the first-ever Celebrity Pro-Am match in 1937, at Rancho Santa Fe in Southern California. During World War II, Crosby and Bob Hope raised millions of dollars for war bonds, military relief, and recreation organizations by playing exhibition matches with Ben Hogan, Sam Snead, and other professionals all over the country.

After the war, major tournaments resumed, and other events were added to the pro Tour, all with ever-increasing purses. Women professionals, who had first organized in 1944 as the Women's Professional Golfers' Association, reorganized into the Ladies Professional Golfers' Association in 1950, with Patty Berg, Louise Suggs, Babe Didrikson, and others competing. In 1953 the USGA assumed the responsibility of conducting the Women's Open Championship, thereby putting all men's and women's national championships under the control of one sanctioning body. The previous year, the USGA had joined with the Royal and Ancient Golf Club of St. Andrews, Scotland, to issue the uniform code of playing rules observed throughout the world today.

During his administration, President Dwight D. Eisenhower's love for the game brought golf increased recognition. Television turned its spotlight on golf in the late 1950s with a weekly series, Shell's *Wonderful World of Golf*, hosted by Gene Sarazen and Jimmy Demaret. Tour events were televised with increasing frequency. Arnold Palmer was packing the galleries (nicknamed "Arnie's Army") with his spectacular play and became the first professional golfer to have earned more than a million dollars in purses.

New professional stars emerged in the 1960s and 1970s, and the number of tour events increased yearly as golfers like South Africa's Gary Player, Jack "The Golden Bear" Nicklaus, (the all-time money winner as of 1981), Lee Trevino, Johnny Miller, and Tom Watson competed for higher and higher purses.

The Women's Tour also grew, producing players like Mickey Wright, Kathy Whitworth (the all-time money winner as of 1981), Judy T. Rankin (who, in 1976, became the first woman pro to win over $100,000 in a season), JoAnne Carner, Jane Blalock, Amy Alcott, and the popular Nancy Lopez.

By the early 1980's, Spain's Severiano Ballesteros, Isao Aoki and Mashishi and Tateo Ozaki of Japan, and Australia's David Graham had joined Roberto De Vincenzo of Argentina and others in making professional golf an international sport. American players like Jerry Pate, Bruce Lietzke, Tom Kite, Bill Rogers, Craig Stadler, and Calvin Peete added new excitement to the PGA Tour.

In addition to its popularity as a professional event, golf is now a major family participation sport. In 1980, it was estimated that there were more than 13 million golfers in the U.S. who regularly played a minimum of fifteen rounds annually.

The modern trend toward efficient, low-maintenance golf courses should facilitate further growth, especially in places like China and Russia, where the first golf courses were being planned in the early 1980s.

1. ace: see *hole in one.*

2. ace: To make a hole in one. (aced the second hole)

1. address: To position oneself at the tee before hitting the ball. In a "hazard," a player is considered to have addressed the ball when he has taken his stance.

ADDRESS

2. address: 1. The act or action of addressing the ball. 2. The stance or position taken before hitting the ball.

advice: Any counsel or suggestion that could influence a player in determining his play, the choice of a club, or the method of making a stroke. A player may give advice to, or ask for advice from, only his partner or either of their caddies. Information on the Rules or Local Rules is not advice.

air-mail: To hit a long drive or shot.

air shot: see *whiff.*

albatross: see *double eagle.*

all flat: see *all square.*

all square: An even score after finishing a hole or a match. also *all flat, square.*

amateur: A golfer who plays the game as a nonrenumerative or nonprofit sport.

Amateur: see *U.S. Amateur Championship.*

Amateur Championship: see *U.S. Amateur Championship.*

Amateur Public Links Championship: An annual national championship open to individual amateur golfers and teams representing cities, played on a different public or municipal golf course each year. Nineteen-year-old Edmund R. Held of St. Louis won the first Amateur Public Links Championship in 1922. In 1923, the first Amateur Public Links Team Championship was won by Chicago.

American tournament: A match play tournament in which each competitor plays all the others, the winner being the player scoring the most victories. also *round robin tournament.*

angel raper: see *sky ball.*

approach: see *approach shot.*

approach cleek: An early iron-headed club, forerunner to the "mashie iron" or number 4 iron, and popular from the early to mid-1800s.

approach shot: 1. A shot hit onto the green from the fairway. also *approach.* 2. A long putt made with a putter. also *approach.*

apron: The grass encircling the putting green, cut somewhat longer than the green, but shorter than the fairway. also *collar, fringe, froghair.*

Around the World: A round of golf played with a score of eighty, an allusion to Jules Verne's *Around the World in Eighty Days.*

away: 1. The ball lying farthest from the cup on any hole. The player whose ball is away plays first. 2. The player whose ball is farthest from the hole.

baby a shot: To hit a ball (usually an approach shot) so feebly that it stops far short of its intended objective.

back door: The side or back rim of a hole. A ball is said to have gone in by the back door when it drops in at the side or around the back part of the hole.

back nine: The last nine holes on an eighteen-hole course. compare *front nine.*

backspin: A backward rotation given to a ball to make it rise sharply, then stop suddenly or roll backward upon landing. also *bite, stop.*

back stalls: see *back tees.*

backswing: The rotation of the body and backward and upward movement of the hands, arms, and club to a position from which the downward swing is initiated to contact the ball.

back tees: The back area of a teeing ground, usually reserved for expert or professional players. see *blue tees.*

baffing spoon: see *baffy.*

baffy: An obsolete term for a deeply pitched wooden club similar to a mod- ern number 5 wood. So-called because the ground immediately behind the ball was "baffed" or struck. The term was popular until the numerical classifications for clubs were introduced in the 1920s. also *baffing spoon.*

ball: see *golf ball.*

ball at rest: A ball that has been struck during the course of play and has come to a standstill.

ball holed: A ball lying within the circumference of a hole, completely below the level of the lip of the hole.

ball in play: A ball on which a stroke has been made on the teeing ground. A ball remains in play until holed out, except when it is out of bounds, lost or lifted, or another ball has been substituted under an applicable Rule or Local Rule (the substituted ball becomes the ball in play).

ball lost: A ball that cannot be found or identified by the player after a five-minute search. A ball is also considered "lost" if another ball has been put into play under the Rules, or if the player has played a stroke with a provisional ball from a point nearer the hole than the place where the original ball is likely to be (the provisional ball becomes the ball in play).

BACKSWING

ball mark: 1. An identification mark put on a ball. 2. An indentation in the surface of a putting green caused by a ball landing.

ball marker: A small thumbpin-like plastic disc used to mark the spot on a putting green from which a ball is lifted.

banana ball: A ball that is sliced, traveling in a long arc (left-to-right for a right-handed golfer).

bandit: A high-handicap golfer who is able to play much better than his handicap indicates.

bango: see *bingo, bango, bungo.*

bare lie: A grassless patch of ground on which the ball comes to rest.

baseball grip: A grip in which a golf club is held similar to a baseball bat, with the hands meeting but not overlapping. also *ten-finger grip.* compare *interlocking grip, overlapping grip.*

bats: Slang for golf clubs. also *hammers, hickories, shooting irons, sticks, tools, weapons.*

beach: see *sand trap.*

belly it: To hit the ball poorly.

bend: To curve the ball around an object blocking one's passage to the green, as with a long iron or wood shot.

best-ball: A match in which the best individual score is used as a team's score on each hole. A best-ball match may also be a four-ball, or a match between one player and a side consisting of two or three partners.

billy goat course: A course that is laid out with many blind holes.

bingo: see *bingo, bango, bungo.*

bingo, bango, bungo: An informal game in which separate wagers are made on the first ball to reach the green (bingo), the closest ball to the pin (bango), and the first ball in the cup (bungo).

bird: Short for birdie.

bird dog: A particularly good caddie.

1. birdie: One stroke under par for a hole. The use of the expression "bird" for an extraordinary or unusual person or thing dates from the 1800s. There are conflicting accounts of exactly when the term was given its present golf meaning by two claimants, player A.H. "Ab" Smith and noted golf architect and historian A.W. Tillinghast. Both anecdotes place the origin around the turn of the century and tell of a particularly good shot (which led to a one-under-par hole) being called a "bird." Soon, "bird," then "birdie," came to mean a one-under-par hole. also *bird.*

2. birdie: To score a birdie. (birdied the fourth hole to pull even)

bisque: A handicap (of one or more strokes) deducted from a player's score at the player's option on one or more holes a round in match play, as long as the intention to use bisque on a hole is declared before play begins on that hole. A bisque may also be given in tennis and croquet, and was first used in the medieval game of court tennis. The term is of French origin, and connotes an advantage given.

bite: see *backspin.*

blacksmith: A player with a rough touch on the putting green.

bladesman: A particularly good putter. also *pool shark, undertaker.*

1. blast: To hit a ball out of a sand trap using an "explosion shot," in which the club (a sand wedge) digs into the sand behind the ball, driving the ball up and out with "explosive" force.

2. blast: The act or an instance of blasting the ball out of a sand trap. also *explosion shot.*

blaster: An old term for a sand iron or sand wedge.

blind bogey: see *kicker's tournament.*

blind green, blind hole: A hole in which the green or the hole is hidden from view when teeing off or making an approach shot.

block shot: A shot that goes off the club at an angle (to the right for a right-handed golfer), caused by hitting the ball with an open club face.

blow: 1. To suddenly begin to play badly,

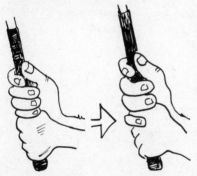

BASEBALL GRIP   OVERLAPPING GRIP

as in a pressure situation. (was under par until he blew on the last three holes) also *blow up*. 2. To suddenly play badly and inflate one's score to a specified number. (blew to a seventy-six and dropped from the lead)

blowup: A sudden collapse in play, as in a pressure situation.

blow up: see *blow*.

blue darter: A ball hit in a straight line, a line drive.

blue plates: see *blue tees*.

blueprint: To execute a perfect shot. (blueprinted his tee shot and arrived at the green in two)

blue tees: The back area of a teeing ground, usually reserved for expert or professional players. The teeing ground is divided into three sections. The rear section, indicated by blue tee markers, is known as the "blue tees" and intended for professional use. The middle section, indicated by white tee markers, is known as the "middle tees" or "white tees" and intended for regulation play. The front section, indicated by red tee markers, is known as the "women's tees," "ladies' tees" or "red tees" and intended for women golfers. also *back stalls, back tees, blue plates, championship tees, tiger tees, tips*.

boge: Slang for *bogey*.

1. bogey: 1. A score of one over par on a hole. In Great Britain in the early 1890s, a "bogey" or "bogeyman" was a ghost or someone to be feared. When it became accepted practice at that time to rate golf holes to be played in a standard number of strokes, the fixed ground score (representing errorless play) became like another opponent. At the United Service Club in southern England, where all members held military rank, this mythical feared opponent was given the name "Colonel Bogey," shortened in popular use to "bogey." When the lively modern golf ball came into use in the late 1800s, the previously established "bogey" for a hole became too easy and soon in the United States the term came to mean one over "par." The British often still use the traditional meaning, referring to a par as a bogey. also *boge*. 2. The score an average golfer should be able to make under normal conditions on a particular course. In the United States, bogey is most frequently figured by taking an average of one stroke above par on each hole.

2. bogey: To score a bogey. (still managed to bogey the last hole after blasting out of the trap)

bogey sickness: An "ailment" caused by a particularly poor round by a professional player.

bold: The choice of a difficult and risky shot rather than a conservative shot. (decided to play bold and attempt to reach the green with one shot straight over the trees)

bolt a putt: To hit a putt so hard that it is still travelling fast when it drops into the hole.

bomb: see *boom*.

boom: To hit a ball exceptionally hard, propelling it like a cannon shot. also *bomb*.

1. borrow: The distance a putt will curve over a sloping section of green. also *break, fall*.

2. borrow: To bias a putt to the left or right to compensate for the slope of a green.

both cheeks in it: Hit with full power. (got both cheeks in it and drove the ball to the edge of the green)

bounce and squeeze course: A short, tightly laid out course where placement is more valuable than long-distance drives.

brag tags: Tournament tags left on a golf bag. also *scare tags*.

brassie: A name for a number 2 wood with a brass plate on the sole, popular until numerical classifications for clubs were introduced in the 1920s.

brassy: see *brassie*.

1. break: The curvature of a putt, as over a sloping section of green. also *borrow, fall*.

2. break: To curve or deviate from a straight line, as of a ball over a sloping section of green.

break par: To finish a round of golf with a score less than the designated par for the course.

brillo: A stubby section of rough near a green.

British Open: An annual seventy-two-hole stroke play competition, open to qualified professionals and amateurs. The first Open was played in 1860 at Prestwick, Scotland, and won by pioneer professional golfer Willie Park. That first contest was thirty-six holes, which remained the format until Harold H. Hilton won the first seventy-two-hole British Open in 1892. The competition was called the "Open" not because both amateurs and professionals could compete, as they did from the second year on, but because after 1865, the tournament was "open" to any golfer who wanted to play, whether or not from around Prestwick. In 1922, Walter Hagen became the first American to win the British Open.

buggy top: A two-over-par seven.

bumpy green: A putting green with an uneven surface. also *peanut brittle.*

bungo: see *bingo, bango, bungo.*

1. bunker: A grassless area causing a "hazard" on a golf course, usually a sand trap. The original bunkers were hollowed-out holes made by sheep to protect them from the wind on the seaside courses of Scotland. see *sand trap.*

2. bunker: To drive a ball into a bunker.

bunkered: To be in a bunker.

bunkering: The configuration of a course's bunkers.

bunker trap: see *bunker.*

1. bunt: To deliberately hit a short shot.

2. bunt: A deliberately hit short shot.

buzzard: Slang for an over par hole for professional players.

bye: 1. The position of a player who, assigned no opponent, automatically advances to the next round of a match. 2. The holes remaining to be played after the winning side has been determined in a round of match play. When a player's lead is greater than the remaining holes (as in the case of ten holes won with eight remaining), the remaining holes are not played. Often, however, the remaining holes are played as a separate match. Holes remaining after this match has been decided (as three remaining after five holes are won by one player) are called a "bye bye." If the three remaining holes of that match are then played as a separate game, and two holes are won by a player, the remaining hole is a "bye bye bye." also *bye hole.*

bye bye: see *bye.*

bye bye bye: see *bye.*

bye hole: see *bye.*

cabbage pounder: A player who spends a lot of time in the rough.

1. caddie: One who carries a golfer's clubs and assists him in accordance with the rules during play. From the French word *cadet,* (pronounced "cahday"), a young military officer, an apprentice. When Mary, Queen of Scots, the first woman golfer, returned to Scotland from France in 1560, several French youths accompanied her to serve as pages and porters. Whether these "cadets" carried the Queen's clubs around when she played, or whether those who did were just likened to the cadets, golf club porters came to be known as "caddies," anglicized from "cahday." The first caddie on record was Andrew Dickson, who carried clubs for the Duke of York (later James II, King of England, Scotland, and Ireland) in Edinburgh in 1681 and 1682. also *caddy, stretcher bearer.*

2. caddie: To act as a caddie. also *caddy.*

caddie cart: A small two-wheel pullcart to which a golfer attaches his bag of clubs. also *cart, golf cart, trolley.*

caddy: see *caddie.*

Callaway System: A method of determining handicaps for unhandicapped players in stroke play, devised by golf pro Lionel F. Callaway in the 1950s. Under the Callaway System, a player's handicap is determined after each round by deducting from his gross score for eighteen holes the scores of the worst individual holes during the first sixteen holes played. A special copyrighted table shows the number of "worst hole" scores to be deducted and the adjustments to be made, based on the player's gross score.

1. can: see *hole.*

2. can: see *hole out.*

1. card: Short for scorecard.

2. card: To make a specific score.

carpet: A particularly smooth putting green.

carry: The distance a ball travels from where it is struck to where it first lands.

cart: see *caddie cart.*

casting: A flaw in a player's swing in which the wrists are released prematurely at the top of the downswing, as though "casting" a fishing line.

casual water: A puddle or other accumulated water that is visible before or after the player takes his stance, and that is temporary in nature and not a regular water hazard. Casual water itself is not considered a "hazard." At a player's option, he may move the ball without penalty within one club-length of a point that is not nearer the hole, not in a hazard or on a putting green, and that avoids interference by the condition.

cat box: see *sand trap.*

championship tees: see *blue tees.*

character builder: A 6-foot putt.

charge: 1. To hit a putt hard at the hole. 2. To play aggressively and well on a given day, with one good score after another.

chief: The number 1 wood. also *driver.*

chili dip: To strike behind the ball, digging up a large piece of turf.

1. chip: see *chip shot.*

2. chip: To make a chip shot. also *pitch and run.*

chipper: The club used to make a chip shot, as a number 5, 6, or 7 iron.

chippie: A chip shot that is holed, especially one that wins a bet for the player in an informal game. compare *greenie, sandie.*

chip shot: A short approach shot in which the ball is lofted in a low arc onto the green and rolls toward the pin. also *chip, pitch and run, run up shot.*

choke down: 1. To play a shot with less than the full power of the club used by lowering the hands down the shaft and narrowing the stance. 2. To grip a club with the hands placed lower than normal on the shaft.

chowder: To play poorly, whether on one shot, a hole, or a round. (might have had a good round if he hadn't chowdered the last two holes)

circuit: A series of scheduled professional tournaments held in different locations throughout the season, and competed in by the same players. also *tour.*

cleek: 1. The number 4 wood (approximately the same loft as the number 1 or number 2 iron). 2. The number 1 iron (the least lofted iron club except for the putter). Gaelic for a bent piece of iron, the term cleek and the other names for different clubs were popular until the introduction of club classification by numbers in the 1920s.

clock: To hit the ball well, with full power.

closed stance: A stance in which the front foot is closer to the line of play of the ball than the rear foot when the ball is addressed. compare *open stance, square stance.*

club: 1. A long thin shaft with a grip at the top and a wooden or steel head at the bottom used to hit a golf ball. The three major types of clubs are woods: long shafts with thick wooden heads, used for shots from the tee and some long shots on the fairway; irons: shorter than woods with thin steel heads, used for fairway and approach shots; and putters: the shortest of the clubs with thin metal heads, used to tap the ball across the putting green and into the cup. Originally, woods and irons were identified by individual names, but since the 1920s, they have been numbered in order of increasing loft (the angle at which the club face is tipped back), woods, 1 through 5, and irons, 2 through 9. The pitching wedge and the sand wedge are usually unnumbered. These two specialty irons have the greatest degree of loft and cause the highest and shortest flight of the ball. A golfer is permitted to carry up to fourteen clubs, usually three or four woods, seven or eight irons, a pitching wedge, a sand wedge, and a putter. also *golf club.* 2. An organization or establishment that provides playing facilities and instructional programs for members and their guests. also *golf club.*

club face: see *face.*

club head: see *head.*

clubhouse: A building on the grounds of a golf club where members and guests can change clothing, relax, and socialize.

club player: A better-than-average weekend player.

club pro, club professional: The resident professional player at a golf club, usually responsible for overseeing all aspects of the club's golf activities, including instructional programs, course scheduling, directing club tournaments, and administering an in-house golf shop. Although club pros cannot spend the time to play regularly on tour, they are qualified to play in local Sectional events and eligible for the annual PGA Club Professional Championship. also *home pro.*

collar: see *apron.*

commercial job: A cautious putt that is holed for a win, as might be featured in a television commercial.

Committee: The group of members or officials in charge of the course or a competition.

concede: To award a holed ball to an opponent whose ball lies close to the hole without requiring him to actually make the shot. The conceded putt is scored as one stroke.

course: see *golf course*.

course rating: The evaluation of the playing difficulty of a course compared with other rated courses, expressed in strokes and decimal fractions of a stroke for the purpose of providing a uniform basis on which to compute handicaps. Performed by a Rating Committee of the golf association having jurisdiction, course rating is based on the "yardage rating" of a course with adjustments for the condition and length of fairway grass, wetness, the overall tightness of the course and width of the fairways, the amount and proximity of rough, out of bounds areas, and hazards, the design, size, and condition of the greens, ground slope, altitude, and prevailing winds. compare *par, yardage rating*.

cowboy: A reckless and erratic player.

cow pasture pool: The game of golf. also *pasture pool*.

cripple: A long slow putt that barely reaches the hole and topples in.

Cuban: A shot in which the ball is sliced, and veers toward the side of the player's dominant hand. also *fade, slice*.

cup: see *hole*.

cuppy lie: Small depressions in the turf where the ball is positioned.

Curtis Cup Match: A biennial international women's amateur competition, hosted alternately by the United States and the British Isles. The match features foursomes and singles competitions at match play between teams of eight players each. Named after Miss Harriet S. Curtis (Women's Amateur Champion in 1906) and Miss Margaret Curtis (Women's Amateur Champion in 1907, 1911, and 1912), who donated the trophy. The first Curtis Cup Match was played in 1932 at the Wentworth Golf Club, Wentworth, England, and was won by the United States team 5-1/2 to 3-1/2.

cut: 1. In tournament competition, the elimination of golfers whose scores exceed a set maximum after a specified period of play (usually two rounds). (only the second time he has not made the thirty-six-hole cut) 2. see *dimple*.

cut shot: A sliced high-arcing shot with strong backspin.

dead: A ball positioned so close to the hole that the next shot is a "dead certainty."

Declaration of Independence: A score of seventy-six for a round. also *play the trombone*.

delicatessen department: A situation that requires a finesse shot.

designated tournament: A tournament determined by a players' association as one required for top-ranked players.

deuce: 1. A score of two strokes on a hole. 2. The number 2 iron.

dew sweeper: 1. The first or among the first players on the course in the morning. 2. The first or among the first professionals to tee off in the morning during a tournament, often a rookie.

dimple: 1. One of the small impressions on the surface of a ball that reduce wind resistance on a ball as it flies through the air. There are approximately 300 dimples on the modern ball. In the 1890s, "pimpled" balls with bumps instead of dimples were tried to help the ball grab when landing, but were discontinued when it was found that they cut air speed. Spalding popularized the dimpled ball in 1907 when the Glory Dimple and Baby Dimple balls were introduced. 2. A crease in the surface of a golf ball made by a misaimed (too high) swing with an iron. also *cut, smile*.

ding-dong: see *ham 'n egg*.

direction post: A marker on the course that indicates the correct line of play to a hidden fairway or blind green.

divot: A piece of turf dislodged by the club during a stroke. also *rug*.

divot repair: The immediate replacement of dug up or displaced turf as per the rules of golf etiquette.

dogleg: A slight but abrupt change of direction in a fairway.

dog license: The British expression for a win in match play by seven and six (seven holes won with six left to play). From the traditional price of a dog license in Great Britain, seven and six (seven shillings and sixpence).

Dolly Parton: see *roller coaster*.

do or die: A "bold" or risky shot, fruitful if successful, but costly if missed.

dormie: Ahead of an opponent or team in match play by as many holes as remain to be played. From the French word *endormi*, meaning asleep, because a dormie player cannot lose even if he goes to sleep. also *dormy*.

dormy: see *dormie*.

double bogey: Two strokes over par for a hole.

double-bogey: To score a double bogey. (double-bogeyed the last hole)

double eagle: Three strokes under par for a hole. also *albatross*.

double press: A press or separate bet on the holes remaining on an initial press. see *press*.

double-press: To initiate a second press, a separate bet on the holes remaining on a press. see *press*.

down: 1. Behind, as by a number of strokes or holes. (started the back nine two holes down) 2. Having holed out. (took another two strokes to get down after hitting the green)

downswing: The downward and forward sweep of the arms, hands, and club, beginning at the top of the backswing and ending when the ball is contacted.

1. drain: see *hole*.

2. drain: To hole the ball. (drained it with one putt) see *hole out*.

1. draw: 1. The method by which pairings and order of play are decided in match play, the results to be published as a draw list or draw sheet. 2. The order of competitors' names as drawn and listed on a draw list or draw sheet. 3. A shot in which the player purposely hooks the ball. see *hook*. compare *Cuban, cut shot, fade, slice*.

2. draw: 1. To randomly pick the names of competitors in match play for a draw list or draw sheet. 2. To be paired with a particular opponent as a result of a draw. (drew a tough opponent for the first round) 3. To purposely hook the ball. (a difficult shot that required him to draw the ball to the left) also *pull*. see *hook*. compare *Cuban, fade, slice*.

draw list, draw sheet: An official roster of match play competitors, match-ups, and playing order based on the results of a draw.

dreadnought: A type of driver popular in the early 1900s, distinguishable by an oversized head.

1. drive: To hit the ball for distance, usually from the tee.

2. drive: A hard stroke hit from the tee toward the green.

drive and a kick: A short par-four hole.

drive for show, putt for dough: A popular axiom among professional golfers that indicates that, while driving may be more spectacular, getting the ball into the hole wins the money.

driver: A number 1 wood, used to drive the ball from the tee. also *chief*.

drive the green: To reach the putting green in one shot from the tee, especially on a hole where the par is more than three.

driving cleek: see *driving iron*.

driving iron: A number 1 iron; called a driving iron until numerical classifications for clubs were introduced in the 1920s. also *driving cleek, knife*.

driving range: A special area featuring marked distances where players can practice driving and other shots and take instruction.

1. drop: 1. To take a replacement for a lost ball or one in a water hazard, or to move a ball from an unplayable lie or ground under repair (under the Rules or Local Rules) by dropping it over one's shoulder while facing the hole so that it comes to rest no closer to the hole than where it originally lay, and within two club-lengths of where it first struck the ground. Dropping a ball often carries a one stroke penalty, depending on specific circumstances. 2. see *hole out*.

2. drop: The act of dropping the ball.

drown it: To hit the ball into water.

1. dub: An unskilled or inept player. Use of the slang term "dub" for a clumsy or bumbling person dates back to the mid-1880s in the United States.

2. dub: To hit the ball poorly. also *duff*.

duck hook: A low, sharply hooking shot.

duck-hook: To hit a low, sharply hooking shot. (duck-hooked his drive into the rough)

1. duff: A misplayed shot. also *fluff, foozle*.

2. duff: To misplay a shot. also *dub*.

duffer: An inexperienced, occasional golfer; one who is not particularly skillful.

dunk: To hole the ball. (dunked a 2-footer to win the hole) also *can, drain, drop, hole out, sink*.

1. eagle: Two strokes under par for a hole.

2. eagle: To make an eagle. (eagled the two last holes to win the round)

Egyptian Bermuda: see *sand trap*.

eight iron: An iron used to make approach shots to the green of 120 to 150 yards.

Known formerly as a lofter, lofting iron, and pitching niblick.

even par: A score of par for a hole or a round.

executive course, executive length course: A short (most often nine holes), less demanding course, usually designed to accommodate older players.

exempt player: A player whose past record makes him eligible to compete in a tournament without first qualifying. The American innovation of exempting proven performers began in 1920, when the first thirty-one PGA players to finish the U.S. Open were declared exempt from having to qualify for the PGA Championship.

explosion shot: see *blast.*

extra hole: see *sudden-death hole.*

face: The flat front surface of the head of a club with which the ball is struck. The angle at which the face is set regulates the amount of loft in a club. The higher the number of the club, the greater the angle and degree of loft. also *club face.*

1. fade: To purposely slice a ball. see *slice.* compare *draw, hook, pull.*

2. fade: A shot in which the ball is purposely sliced. see *slice.* compare *draw, hook.*

fairway: The specially prepared turf between the teeing ground and the green, excluding hazards.

fairway house: A house built close to a fairway on a golf course.

fall: see *borrow.*

fast green: A dry, fast-running green.

fastest foot in the South: Said of a player who often nudges the ball into a better lie in the rough.

1. fat: 1. Striking the ball low, sometimes digging up the turf behind the ball. also *heavy.* 2. Higher and shorter in distance than intended because of the club striking the ground behind the ball on a stroke, or striking the ball low. (hit it fat and ended up short of the green)

2. fat: The wide part of a putting green.

five iron: The iron used for approach shots to the green of approximately 160 yards. Formerly known as a mashie. also *nickel.*

five wood: The most lofted wood, sometimes used for getting out of difficult lies in the rough. Formerly known as a baffy, and a baffing spoon.

flagstick: A thin movable pole that is anchored upright in the cup, circular in cross-section, often bearing a numbered flag. also *pin, pole.*

flat iron, flat stick: A putter, a flat-faced iron with no loft.

flats: The lay-up area in front of the green.

flier: A high-trajectory shot with overspin that usually travels farther than desired.

flippy wrists: An inconsistency or weakness in putting.

fluff: see *duff.*

follow through: The continuation of the

[Diagram labels: TRAP, APRON, TRAP, GREEN, TRAP, ROUGH, TRAP, FAIRWAY, WATER HAZARD, ROUGH, BUNKER, ROUGH, TEE]

swing after the club head makes contact with the ball.

foozle: see *duff.*

fore: The traditional vocal warning to golfers who might be playing ahead that a shot is about to be taken or that a ball is in flight. An Old English word meaning "in front."

forecaddie: A caddie employed by the Committee to be stationed ahead on the fairway in order to be able to indicate to players the position of balls on the course, considered an "outside agency."

forward press: A deliberate or involuntary slight movement of the body in a forward direction just before the backswing. also *press.*

four-ball: A match in which four players compete, with two on each side, and in which the better scorer between the two partners on one side is matched against the better scorer from the other side for each hole. Four-ball can be either match play or stroke play.

four iron: A long-range iron used for distances of approximately 170 to 180 yards. Formerly known as an approach cleek, and a mashie iron.

foursome: 1. A match in which four players compete, two to a side, with each side playing only one ball which the partners take turns hitting. also *Scotch foursome.* 2. A group of four players, two to a side, with each side playing only one ball which the players take turns hitting. In the United States and Canada, the term "foursome" is sometimes used inaccurately to describe a fourball match, or simply to describe a group of four players, each playing his own ball and competing against the others. also *match foursome, Scotch foursome.*

four wood: A wooden club used for fairway shots of approximately 200 yards. Formerly known as a cleek.

free drop: A drop sometimes allowed by Local Rules when a ball lands in an unplayable lie and that does not incur a penalty stroke.

fresh air shot: see *whiff.*

fried egg: A ball that is buried in the sand.

fringe: see *apron.*

frisbee: A low, skulled shot.

froghair: see *apron.*

front nine: The first nine holes on an eight-

een-hole course. also *out nine.* compare *back nine.*

full stroke: A stroke in which the ball is hit "pure," with the sweet spot of the club head making contact with the ball.

fungo: One of a series of practice shots when not engaged in a match. From the baseball term for practice fly balls hit to players before a game with a special bat.

gallery: The fans and spectators at a golf tournament.

gamble hole: A hole laid out in such a way as to invite a bold or risky shot that would bring a considerable advantage if properly executed, but disastrous results if not.

gamesmanship: The science and/or practice of causing an opponent to experience confusion, anxiety, the loss of confidence or concentration by one's words and actions before and during a match. British golfer Steven Potter popularized the notion of gamesmanship in his 1947 book, *The Theory and Practice of Gamesmanship.*

gangsome: Slang for a group of more than four players.

gimme: A short putt that is conceded or given to an opponent.

Ginsberg: 1. A timid but successful putt, one that appears soft but is well-planned. 2. A free shot with a second ball sometimes permitted in informal play when a golfer's original ball is mishit, and that the player may then, at

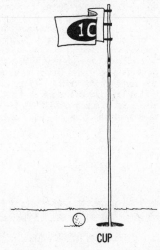

CUP

189

his option, choose to continue play with, rather than the original ball. compare *mulligan, Shapiro.*

gobble: An old name for a fast putt that drops into the hole, one that would have gone a long way past had it not been "gobbled" by the hole.

golf: A game in which one or more players (often groups of two to four), using several different clubs (up to fourteen) try to knock a small resilient ball into nine or eighteen holes in sequence, placed strategically over an outdoor course among hazards of sand, water, trees, and rough in the fewest possible number of strokes. When playing alone, a golfer competes against par (a specified number of strokes an expert golfer would need to complete a particular hole or course, based on the distance of the hole from the tee), or attempts to reduce his handicap (a specified number of strokes an amateur player is permitted to subtract from his score in order to be able to compete fairly against better players, determined by the golfer's past performance on a particular course). When more than one golfer plays, a round (usually eighteen holes) may be scored according to stroke play (the player with the lowest total number of strokes wins) or match play (strokes counted to determine a winner at each hole, with the winner of the most holes winning the round). A player may compete against all other players; against the best score of a partnered pair; with a partner against two other players, each playing a ball, with the lowest score for each hole winning that hole (four-ball); or with a partner against two other players, with each team playing alternate shots with a single ball (a foursome). Rules infractions can result in the addition of penalty strokes to a player's score or the loss of a hole in match play. There is still some question about the origin of the

BALL ON THE FAIRWAY

word golf. It is now thought to be derived from the German *kolbe,* which, like the Dutch *kolf* and French *chole,* means club. All, in their earlier forms (*kolben,* the Icelandic *kolfr,* and Old High German *cholbo*), have been attributed by some etymologists to a hypothetic Gothic word *kulban,* meaning a knobbed stick. also *cow pasture pool, pasture pool.*

golf bag: A large bag designed to carry golf clubs and accessories, first used in the late 1800s. By the 1930s, golf bags had grown large and heavy, necessitating the invention of the two-wheel caddie cart. also *tool chest.*

golf ball: A spherically symmetrical ball consisting of a compressed solid rubber or liquid-filled rubber center wrapped tightly with rubber thread, and covered by a dimpled hard rubber composition, measuring not less than 1.680 inches in diameter and weighing not more than 1.620 ounces (USGA specifications) or measuring not less than 1.620 inches in diameter and weighing not more than 1.620 ounces (Royal and Ancient Golf Club of St. Andrews specifications). Strict guidelines also limit the liveliness, velocity, and distance (USGA only) specifications of a ball. In golf's earliest days, the ball was made of feathers stuffed as tightly as possible into a small bag of thin leather. Of varying quality and liveliness, the early ball could not be driven farther than a maximum of 175 yards. In 1848, the gutta-percha (or guttie) ball was introduced that could be driven over 200 yards. Perfectly round, the guttie, along with closely mowed greens, made the modern rolling putt possible. After noting the improvement in the flight stability of a marked or worn ball, indentations were first hand-hammered, then molded into the ball around 1880. In the 1890s, a pimpled ball was tried (with bumps rather than the normal 300 or more surface dimples on a modern ball) in the hopes that it would better grab the turf on landing. Instead, it was found that the bumps cut air speed. The modern rubber-cored, thread-wound golf ball was invented by American Coburn Haskell in 1899, but became popular only after it was used by Walter Travis to win the 1901 U.S. Amateur Championship, and by Alex "Sandy" Herd to win the 1901 British Open. also *ball*.

golf car: see *golf cart*.

golf cart: 1. A light battery-powered three- or four-wheel vehicle used to ride around the course, usually accommodating two golfers and their clubs. First popularized in the 1950s. also *golf car*. 2. A two-wheel pullcart to which a golf bag is attached. also *caddie cart, cart, trolley*.

golf club: see *club*.

golf course: A specially constructed and maintained course over which the game of golf is played, consisting of nine or eighteen holes, in most cases laid out 300 to 500 yards apart. Each hole consists of a teeing ground where the ball is put into play, a well-kept grass fairway, strategically placed natural or artificial hazards (such as a body of water or a sand trap), uncut areas of rough, and a well-trimmed area of short grass around the hole, a putting green. Most eighteen-hole golf courses are between 6300 and 7000 yards in total length, with an average tee-to-hole distance of 300 to 500 yards, though every hole and every golf course is unique. The most famous golf course in the world is the Old Course at St. Andrews in Scotland, home of the Royal and Ancient Golf Club of St. Andrews, founded in 1754. also *course, golf links, links*.

golf course architect: One who designs and supervises the construction of golf courses. The American Society of Golf Course Architects is headquartered in Chicago, Illinois.

golfdom: The realm and pertaining to the realm of golf and golfers.

golfer: One who plays golf.

golfing: The sport of golf or the action of playing it.

golf links: see *golf course*.

golf shoes: Leather shoes with sharp metal spikes for gripping the turf.

golf widow: The wife of a golfer who devotes most of his spare time to playing golf; one who has "lost" her husband to golf.

grain: The direction in which the grass grows on a putting green. (a short putt, but against the grain)

grand slam: A victory in the four major men's or women's golf tournaments (the United States Open, the British Open, the Masters, and the PGA Champion-

ship for men; the Women's Open Championship, the LPGA Championship, the Peter Jackson Classic, and the Nabisco-Dinah Shore for women) by one player in the same year. Only one player in history has won the men's grand slam, legendary amateur golfer Robert T. "Bobby" Jones of Atlanta, Georgia. Jones accomplished this remarkable feat in 1930, at which time the four major tournaments were the British Amateur, the British Open, the USGA Open, and the USGA Amateur. As professional golf gained dominance over amateur competition after World War II, the two amateur-only events were replaced by the Masters Tournament and PGA Championships as a part of the grand slam.

green: A smooth, closely shorn grass area surrounding the hole toward which the ball is played. Originally, "green" referred to the whole course, a meaning that survives in the term "greenkeeper" and the expression "through the green." also *putting green*.

green fee: A fee paid in order to play on a golf course. In the early days of the sport, golf courses were often located on a village green, and it became common practice to charge a fee to provide for their upkeep. also *greens fee*.

greenie: A shot that reaches the green (as from the tee on a par 3 hole) and lies closest to the pin, frequently the object of a bet in a casual game. compare *chippie, sandie*.

greenkeeper: The individual responsible for the preparation and maintenance of a golf course.

greens fee: see *green fee*.

greenside: At or adjacent to a putting green.

greensome foursome: A type of match in informal play in which all four players in

BALL IN THE ROUGH

191

a foursome drive a ball off the tee before each side selects one ball to continue playing the hole.

grip: 1. The manner in which a golf club is held. The three major grips used in golf are the overlapping grip or Vardon grip, the interlocking grip, and the ten-finger grip or baseball grip, differing mainly in the proximity of and relationship between the little finger of the bottom hand (right hand for a righthanded golfer) and the forefinger of the top hand. 2. The top part of the shaft of the golf club, covered with a rubber, leather, or leatherlike material to facilitate gripping by the hands. Regulations call for a grip to be substantially straight and plain, with channels, furrows, or molding for any part of the hands not permitted.

grooved swing: A well-practiced swing that can be repeated consistently, as though following a "groove."

gross score: The total number of strokes, before subtracting a handicap, taken to play a hole or a round. compare *net score*.

ground one's club: To place the club head on the ground behind the ball when addressing the ball. It is against the rules to ground a club when a ball is being played from a "hazard," resulting in the loss of the hole in match play, or two penalty strokes in stroke play.

gruesome: Slang for a mixed foursome. also *quarrelsome*.

hacker: A poor golfer.

Hall of Fame: see *LPGA Hall of Fame, PGA Hall of Fame, World Golf Hall of Fame*.

halve: To score an identical number of strokes on a hole or round as the opposing player or team in match play. (halved the first two holes before winning the next three)

hammers: Slang for golf clubs. also *bats, hickories, shooting irons, sticks, tools, weapons*.

ham 'n egg: To play well with a partner, either because of complementary skills or offsetting luck. also *ding-dong*.

handicap: A specified number of strokes an amateur player is permitted to subtract from his score in order to be able to compete fairly against better players, determined by the golfer's past performance on a particular course. A golfer's handicap is computed as 96

percent of the average differential between the course rating (not par) and the player's ten lowest rounds in the last twenty rounds played. A golfer's handicap may be subtracted in stroke play from his total score at the end of a round or at specific "stroke holes" noted on the scorecard. In match play, one or more strokes may be subtracted from the score at each hole or at specified holes. compare *plus handicap*.

handicapper: A golfer who has a specified handicap. (rounded out the foursome with a thirteen handicapper)

handicap stroke hole: see *stroke hole*.

hand mashie shot: A thrown ball.

hang: To stop rolling or be situated on sloping ground. (hung a chip shot just above the sand trap)

hanging lie: A ball resting on sloping ground.

hazard: An area of ground covered by sand (bunker) or water (water hazard, lateral water hazard), strategically placed in or adjacent to a fairway in order to present a special challenge to a golfer. A player is not permitted to ground his club behind a ball situated in a hazard. see *bunker, lateral water hazard, water hazard*.

head: The thickened part of a golf club at the end of the shaft, the "face" or front surface of which makes contact with the ball. also *club head*.

head up: A fault in a swing in which the head is raised and the eyes taken off the ball before it is hit, usually resulting in a poor stroke.

heavy: see *fat*.

heel: The part of the club attached to the shaft.

hello God: see *sky ball*.

hickories: Slang for golf clubs. The term comes from the fact that often golf club shafts were made of hickory before steel shafts were made legal in 1929. also *bats, hammers, shooting irons, sticks, tools, weapons*.

hit on the hat: see *top*.

hit on the screws: see *hit pure*.

hit pure: To make perfect contact with the ball, to hit the ball well. also *hit on the screws*.

hit the Chief: To use the number 1 wood or driver.

hit the deuce: To use the number 2 iron.

hit the nickel: To use the number 5 iron.

hockey it in: To sink a fairly good putt.

1. hole: 1. The small cavity into which the ball is played, 4-1/4 inches in diameter and at least 4 inches deep. also *can, cup, drain, pot, puttoon.* 2. A division (usually one of nine or eighteen) of a golf course, comprised of a tee, a fairway, and the putting green on which the hole is located.

2. hole: To drive or knock the ball into a hole. (holed it in three strokes to break par) see *hole out.*

holeable: A putt that appears to be reasonably easy for a golfer to sink.

hole high: A situation in which the ball stops even with the hole on one side or the other, such as in an approach shot. also *pin high.*

1. hole in one: A ball played from the tee into the hole in one stroke. also *ace, solitaire.*

2. hole in one: To hit a ball into the hole in one stroke from the tee. (took the lead on the eighteenth, which he holed in one) also *ace.*

hole out: To sink the ball into the cup. (took him four strokes to hole out) also *can, drain, drop, dunk, hole, sink.*

Hollywood handicap: A handicap that is based more on pride or vanity than on ability.

home hole: The final hole of a course or a round.

home pro: see *club pro.*

honor: The privilege of playing first from the teeing ground, decided by lot or draw on the first hole, and given to the winner of the previous hole thereafter.

hood the club: To lessen the loft of a club by addressing the ball so that it is positioned near the back foot, then diminishing the angle of the club face by advancing the hands so that they are forward of the ball at the moment of contact. also *shut the face.*

1. hook: A shot in which the ball is made to veer to the side opposite the dominant hand of the player. also *draw.* compare *Cuban, fade, slice.*

2. hook: To hit the ball in such a way as to cause it to veer to the side opposite the dominant hand of the player. also *draw, pull.* compare *Cuban, fade, slice.*

hooker: A player with a tendency to hook.

Hoover: A "sweeping" hook.

hosel: The socket in the head of a golf club into which the shaft is fitted.

hospital zone: The practice tee on a golf course.

1. hustle: To make or seek to make an unethical wager on a match, as by hiding one's true skill level or some advantage.

••To unethically take advantage or seek to take advantage of someone by deception.

2. hustle: The act or an instance of hustling.

hustler: A player who makes money or attempts to make money by wagering on his matches, especially one who hides expertise or some advantage in order to attract less skilled opponents. One who seeks to make or win money by deception.

in: The last nine holes of an eighteen-hole course. (made par all the way in)

inchworm: A player who cheats a little bit every time he marks his ball on the green.

in jail: A ball mishit into trees, a bunker, or the rough.

in regulation: On the green in the prescribed number of strokes enabling the player to make par with two putts.

inside the leather: Close enough to the hole to be conceded. A reference to the common practice in informal play of conceding any ball closer to the cup than the length of the leather or rubber grip of a putter. also *in the leather.*

interlocking grip: A method of gripping a golf club in which the little finger of the lower hand (right hand for a right-handed golfer) interlocks with the forefinger of the top hand. compare *baseball grip, ten-finger grip, overlapping grip.*

in the clubhouse: A term used to describe a player who has completed his score.

in the leather: see *inside the leather.*

in to out: A swing in which the club is taken back and the downswing begun inside the line of flight, crossing to the outside of the line of flight as the ball is contacted.

Irish birdie: A score of one stroke under par for a hole, resulting from the use of a "mulligan." see *mulligan.*

iron: A club with a medium-length shaft and a relatively thin steel head, used to make shots from the fairway, the rough, and often from within a hazard. Though a number 1 iron or "driving iron" was once popular, irons are usually numbered from 2 through 9 in order of increasing loft (the angle at which the club face is tipped back). Two special and usually unnumbered irons, the pitching wedge and the sand wedge, have the greatest degree of loft and cause the highest and shortest flight of the ball. Though a putter is usually made of steel, it is not considered an iron.

jigger: A special thin, fin-faced iron club, used in the past for running up shots to the green.

jungle: In the rough. also *tiger country*.

junk man: An unstylish golfer who appears ineffectual off the tee and on the fairway, but always seems to arrive at the green in time to salvage a par or a bogey.

kickers' tournament: A competition for golfers with no established handicap in which participants choose a handicap that they estimate will bring their adjusted score for a round to within established parameters (such as between sixty-five and eighty). At the end of the

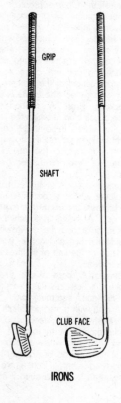

GRIP

SHAFT

CLUB FACE

IRONS

round, the player whose adjusted score matches or is closest to a number drawn by the Committee from within the established parameters wins. also *blind bogey*.

knife: see *one iron*.

knockout competition: An tournament in which players compete in pairs for a round of golf, the loser being eliminated from competition. The winner of each round moves to the next higher level to compete with other winners. At each level of play, the losers are "knocked out" of the tournament.

Ladies Professional Golf Association: The organization responsible for overseeing professional tournament golf for women. Founded in 1950, the Ladies Professional Golf Association is now headquartered in Houston, Texas, and is comprised of a Tournament Division and a Teaching Division. also *LPGA*.

ladies' tees: see *women's tees*.

lag up: see *lay up*.

1. lateral: see *shank*.

2. lateral: A shanked ball.

lateral water hazard: A water hazard running parallel or approximately parallel to the line of play. When a ball is hit into a lateral water hazard and is lost or unplayable, the player may, under penalty of one stroke, drop the ball (or a new ball) behind the hazard on a line formed by the hole and the point where the ball last crossed the margin of the hazard; play the ball (or a new ball) from the point where the original stroke was made; or drop the ball (or a new ball) outside the hazard within two club-lengths of the point where the ball last crossed the margin of the hazard or a point on the opposite margin of the hazard equidistant from the hole, so long as the ball comes to rest no nearer the hole than the point where the ball last crossed the margin of the hazard. Lateral water hazards are marked by short red stakes or by red lines.

lay up: To intentionally hit a ball short (as on a fairway or approach shot) to prevent it from going into a hazard. also *lag up*.

leaderboard: see *scoreboard*.

licorice sticks: Golf clubs with graphite shafts. also *soul poles*.

1. lie: 1. The position of a ball that has come to rest after a stroke. (not allowed to improve the lie) 2. The angle at which the club head is attached to the shaft.

2. lie: To occupy a location. (if hit properly, the ball will lie just outside the trap at the edge of the green)

like as we lie: An old expression indicating that the opposing sides have played the same number of strokes at a hole.

line: The correct direction that a ball should travel toward the green or hole. For every shot, from the longest drive to the shortest putt, there is a correct line.

line up: To "read" or sight the line for one's next shot.

links: A golf course. A Scottish word for the rolling sandy coastal land that was the site of many early golf courses. Possibly derived from the Old English word *hlinc*, meaning a ridge of land. see *golf course.*

linksman: A golfer.

lip: see *rim.*

lip out: see *rim.*

litter box: see *sand trap.*

Local Rules: Official rules that take into consideration temporary and/or abnormal conditions at a particular golf course, published by the Committee.

1. loft: 1. The angle at which the face of a club is slanted back (away from vertical). Since the 1920s, golf clubs have been numbered in order of increasing loft (woods, 1 through 5, and irons, 2 through 9). Two usually unnumbered irons, the pitching wedge and the sand wedge, have the greatest degree of loft and cause the highest and shortest flight of the ball. 2. A stroke that causes the ball to be lofted in an arc. 3. The height of the arc of a lofted ball.

2. loft: To hit a ball in a high arc. (lofted the ball over the water onto the green)

lofter: A number 8 iron, popularly called a lofter until numerical classifications for clubs were introduced in the 1920s. also *lofting iron, pitching niblick.*

lofting iron: see *lofter.*

long game: The longer shots, as those from the tee, or those made with wooden clubs and low-number irons.

long iron: A low-lofted iron (such as a 1, 2, or 3 iron) for making long-distance shots.

long knocker: A player who hits long drives.

long steal: 1. A come-from-behind victory in match play. 2. A long putt.

loop: Caddie slang for an eighteen-hole round.

loose impediment: A natural object around the ball or in the line of play that is loose and movable and does not adhere to the ball, such as a pebble or stone not solidly embedded, an unrooted leaf, twig, or branch, an insect, or dung. Sand and loose soil are loose impediments on the putting green, but not elsewhere on the course. The player may elect whether to consider snow and ice a loose impediment or casual water. Loose impediments may be removed without penalty unless the ball and the impediment are both in a hazard.

lost ball: A ball remaining unlocated or unidentified after a five-minute search; or one given up as "lost" and replaced by a new ball that is played, whether or not a search is made for the original ball; or one replaced by a "provisional ball" that has been played from a point nearer the hole than the place where the original ball is likely to be (provisional ball automatically becomes the ball in play). When a ball is lost outside a water hazard or is hit out of bounds, a new ball may be played as near as possible to the spot from which the original ball was played with the addition of a penalty stroke to the player's score for the hole. see *lateral water hazard, provisional ball, water hazard.*

LPGA:. The Ladies Professional Golf Association.

LPGA Championship: The LPGA's own annual stroke play competition for women professional golfers, one of the four major tournaments that together comprise the women's grand slam. The first LPGA Championship was played in 1955 at the Orchard Ridge Country Club in Fort Wayne, Indiana, and won by Beverly Hanson.

LPGA Hall of Fame: The institution that honors outstanding women professional golfers. Originally a part of the Women's Golf Hall of Fame founded in Augusta, Georgia in 1950, the LPGA Hall of Fame became a separate entity in 1967, moving to one wing of the World Golf Hall of Fame in Pinehurst, North Carolina in 1977, and in 1982, to its present location in Houston, Texas. In order to be selected for membership in the Hall of Fame, a woman must have been a member of the LPGA for ten consecutive years and have won thirty official Tour events including at least two different major championships, or thirty-five official Tour events including at least one major championship, or forty official Tour events. The first women to be elected to the LPGA Hall of Fame in 1951 were Patty Berg, Betty Jameson, Louise Suggs, and all-around athlete and Olympic champion Mildred "Babe" Didrikson Zaharias.

lumber city: A long course that requires many fairway wood shots.

magic wand: A favored club, with which a player experiences success, often a putter.

marker: 1. One who is appointed by the Committee to record a competitor's score in stroke play, sometimes a fellow competitor. 2. A small object (often a coin or a flat disc) left on the green to indicate the position of a golfer's ball when it must be lifted.

mashie: A number 5 iron, which at the end of the nineteenth century was the most lofted club in a normal set. The term "mashie" became less popular when numerical classifications for clubs were introduced in the 1920s. John Henry Taylor, five-time winner of the British Open (1894, 1895, 1900, 1909, 1913) was among the first to popularize the mashie, with which he developed an amazing mastery of the cut shot.

mashie-iron: A number 4 iron, popularly called a mashie-iron until numerical classifications for clubs were introduced in the 1920s. also *approach cleek.*

mashie-niblick: A number 7 iron, popularly called a mashie-niblick until numerical classifications for clubs were introduced in the 1920s.

Masters, Masters Tournament: An invitational open tournament held annually since 1934 (except in World War II years 1943-45) at the Augusta National Golf Club in Georgia. First won in 1934 by Horton Smith, the Masters got its name from the fact that the first competition was restricted to current and past tournament winners, and still ranks as one of the most prestigious events in the sport of golf.

match: A game of golf in which two or more players compete.

match foursome: see *foursome.*

match play: Play based on the number of holes won by an individual or a side in a round. Each hole is either won (fewer strokes), halved (an equal amount of strokes), or lost (more strokes), with the individual or side who wins the most holes winning the round. compare *medal play, stroke play.*

medalist: The low scorer in a stroke play qualifying round of a tournament.

medal play: see *stroke play.*

medium iron: see *mid-iron.*

member's bounce, member's kick: A favorable or lucky bounce.

merry: A British expression meaning too strong or too far, as of a putt. (the crucial putt was a bit merry)

middle iron: see *mid-iron.*

mid-iron: A medium-lofted iron for making medium distance shots, such as a number 4, 5, or 6 iron. also *medium iron, middle iron.*

mid-mashie: A number 3 iron, popularly called a mid-mashie until numerical classifications for clubs were introduced in the 1920s.

miniature golf: An informal putting game played over a small, specially constructed course (usually with a synthetic playing surface), consisting of a number of holes, each containing a series of strategically placed obstacles that the ball must travel through, over, under, or between in order to reach a tunnel, ramp, or channel that then advances the ball to the hole. The object of the game is to complete the course in the fewest number of strokes.

miss the green: To fail to reach the green in regulation. (missed the green, but scrambled to make par)

mixed foursome: A foursome made up of a man and a woman on each side. John Reid, one of the five founding members of the USGA in 1894, took part in the first reported mixed foursome in 1889 in Yonkers, New York. A mixed foursome is sometimes facetiously called a "gruesome" or "quarrelsome."

Mod-Sod: A brand of artificial turf made by Playfield Industries and used for synthetic tees and putting greens. First installed in 1980 at the PGA Tour's "Wee Links," a prototype low-maintenance six-hole course at the Walt Disney World Golf Resort in Florida.

moving day: The day following the thirty-six-hole cut in a professional tournament.

Mr. Aerosol: A name for a player who is a spray hitter.

mug hunter: see *sandbagger.*

mulligan: A free shot to compensate for a mishit ball, sometimes permitted in a casual game. Named after Canadian golfer David Mulligan. In the late 1920s, Mulligan, who provided transportation to the golf course for his regular foursome, was given a second ball after mishitting his drive off the first tee with hands still numb from driving over rough roads and a particularly bumpy bridge at the course entrance. also *Shapiro.*

Nabisco-Dinah Shore: An annual stroke play competition for women professional golfers, designated as one of the four major tournaments that together comprise the women's grand slam. Held at the Mission Hills Country Club in Rancho Mirage, California, the event (formerly the Colgate-Dinah Shore) was first won in 1972 by Jane Blalock.

nap: The physical characteristics of the surface of a putting green, as the length, thickness, and direction of growth.

Nassau, Nassau bet: A basis for betting in a casual game. Players make bets on the outcome of play on the first nine holes, on the second nine holes, and on the complete eighteen holes. Originally from a system of scoring in which one point was awarded to the winner of the first nine holes, one point to the winner of the second nine holes, and one point to the winner of the entire nineteen holes. Invented at the Nassau Country Club in Glen Cove, Long Island in New York at the turn of the century, reportedly to save face for local club members who, thereafter, were spared having to read newspaper accounts about losing team matches by more than three points.

National Golf Foundation: A nonprofit organization supported by the major manufacturers of golf equipment to promote the growth of the sport. Founded in 1936 by golf journal publishers Herb and Joe Graffis, the National Golf Foundation collects and publishes golf records and statistics, instructional programs, and educational materials about the planning and management of golf courses. The Foundation is headquartered in North Palm Beach, Florida.

National Open: The U.S. Open. also *open.*

NC: see *no card.*

neck: The thin part of a club head near the area where the shaft is attached. also *socket.*

net score: The total number of strokes taken to play a hole or a round after a player's handicap is deducted. compare *gross score.*

never up, never in: A golf axiom meaning that a ball that fails to reach the hole cannot possibly go in.

niblick: A number 9 iron. Four-time British Open winner Tom Morris Jr. (1868, 1869, 1870, 1872) popularized the use of the niblick for short pitch shots. The term "niblick" became less popular when numerical classifications for clubs were introduced in the 1920s.

nickel: A number 5 iron.

nine iron: An iron club with a high degree of loft, used for distances of approximately 120 yards. Formerly known as a niblick.

nineteenth hole: 1. The clubhouse bar. 2. An extra or "sudden-death hole" played to decide a match that ends up all square after eighteen holes. In such a case, the first hole is played again as the "nineteenth hole." see *sudden-death hole.*

no card: 1. No score for a round, marked NC on a scorecard. also *NC.* 2. A withdrawal from a tournament. also *NC, North Carolina.*

no deposit: see *out of bounds.*

nonreturnable: see *out of bounds.*

North Carolina: Slang among professional players for no card, or the withdrawal from a tournament. also *NC.*

nudging: The act or an instance of moving a ball to a better lie with the end of one's club, not allowed by the Rules of Golf, but sometimes permitted in informal play by local winter rules.

OB: Out of bounds. see *out of bounds.*

observer: One appointed by the Committee to assist a referee to decide questions of fact and to report to him any breach of a Rule or Local Rule.

obstruction: An artificial object that hinders normal play. Obstructions include anything built, placed, or left on the course, but does not include objects that define out of bounds (walls, fences, stakes, railings, etc.), artificially surfaced banks or beds in water hazards (including bridge supports on such a bank), and any construction declared by the Committee to be an integral part of the course. A movable obstruction may be moved if it interferes with the player's stance or intended area of his swing, or the ball may be lifted and dropped (not closer to the hole) away from an obstruction, without penalty.

odd: 1. One more stroke than used for a hole by one's opponent. 2. A handicap stroke deducted from the hole score of an opponent.

old man par: A slang expression for par, popularized by grand slam winner Bobby Jones, who claimed that during a match, he never played his opponent, but played against "old man par."

one iron: An old iron club with little loft, used to make shots of approximately 190 to 200 yards. Formerly known as a driving cleek or driving iron. also *knife*.

on the amateur side: Having missed a putt by underestimating the borrow or break of a ball over a sloping section of green. compare *on the professional side*.

on the professional side: Having missed a putt because of overestimating the borrow or break of a ball over a sloping section of green. compare *on the amateur side*.

on the dance floor: Having reached or on the putting green. The expression "on the dance floor" was popularized in the 1980s by Australian professional golfer and television commentator Bruce Devlin.

1. open: Enterable by both amateur and professional players.

2. open: A tournament that is open to both amateur and professional players, such as the U.S. Open.

Open: The U.S. Open. also *National Open*.

open stance: A stance in which the rear foot is closer to the line of play of the ball than the front foot when the ball is addressed. compare *closed stance, square stance*.

Oral Roberts: Slang among professionals for a shot mishit with the heel of a club, or a shot that is "well-heeled."

out: The first nine holes of an eighteen-hole course. (held the lead going out) compare *in*.

out nine: see *front nine*.

out of bounds: Ground on which play is prohibited, determined by the Committee, and marked by a fence, stakes, or a line on the ground. When a fence or stakes are used to define out of bounds, the boundary line is determined by the nearest inside edges of the fence posts or stakes. When a line is used to define out of bounds, the line itself is out of bounds. A ball is out of bounds when all of it lies out of bounds. When a ball is hit out of bounds, the stroke is replayed from as near as possible to the spot from which the original ball was played, and a penalty stroke is added to the player's score. also *no deposit, nonreturnable, OB*.

outside agency: Any person, being, or object that is not part of a match, or in stroke play, not part of a competitor's side (including any official appointed by the Committee). When a moving ball is stopped or deflected by an outside agency, it is considered a "rub of the green" and the ball is played as it lies, without penalty. When a ball lodges in a moving or animate outside agency, the player may drop a ball (or on the putting green, place a ball) as near as possible to the spot where the object was when the ball lodged in it, without penalty. A ball that is accidentally stopped or deflected by an opponent, his caddie, or equipment, may be played as it lies or cancelled and replayed from the spot where the ball previously lay.

overlapping grip: A method of gripping a golf club in which the little finger of the lower hand (right hand for a right-handed golfer) rests between the forefinger and middle finger of the top hand. also *Vardon grip*. compare *baseball grip, interlocking grip*.

overspin: see *topspin*.

1. par: 1. The number of strokes it would take an expert golfer to complete a particular hole (or course, when the individual hole pars are added together) under ordinary weather conditions. The par for a hole is computed on the basis of yardage (measuring from the middle of the tee area along the line of play planned by the course architect to the center of the green), allowing two strokes on the putting green. Yardage guidelines are provided by the USGA, who adopted the use of par in 1911. compare *course ratng, yardage rating*. 2. A golfer's score when it equals the par designation for a hole or a round. (finished the match with an even par seventy-four round)

●●Average (not feeling up to par today), or of a normal or expected quality or quantity (missed two questions on her driving test, which is about par for the course).

2. par: To make par, either on a hole or a round. (parred the last two holes of the front nine to take a two-stroke lead)

par in: To make par on the last nine holes of a golf course.

par out: To make par on the first nine holes of a golf course.

peanut brittle: A bumpy, uneven green.

penalty: 1. The assessment of one additional stroke (a penalty stroke) to a player's score for certain infractions, sometimes coupled with the necessity of replaying the ball or playing a new ball from the point where the original stroke was played (stroke and distance). 2. The assessment of two additional strokes (penalty strokes) to a player's score for a hole for a breach of the Rules of Golf in stroke play. 3. The loss of the hole in match play for a breach of the Rules of Golf. see *penalty stroke, stroke and distance.*

penalty stroke: 1. A stroke added to a player's score for a hole for hitting a ball twice during a stroke, improperly moving, lifting, or dropping a ball, for failing to mark a ball lifted from a putting green, for playing a second ball before informing the opponent and marker of the player's intention to hit a provisional ball, for a ball lost or out of bounds, for a ball resting in an unplayable lie, or for a ball resting in a water or lateral water hazard that cannot be played. 2. One or two strokes added to a player's score for a hole in stroke play for a breach of the Rules of Golf. compare *stroke and distance.*

Peter Jackson Classic: An annual Canadian stroke play competition for women professional golfers, one of the four major tournaments that together comprise the women's grand slam. The Peter Jackson Classic (formerly La Canadienne) was first played in 1973 at the Montreal Golf Club in Montreal, Quebec, and won by Jocelyne Bourassa.

PGA: The Professional Golfers' Association.

PGA Championship: An annual tournament sponsored by the PGA for touring professionals and the top twenty-five finishers in the PGA Club Professional Championship tournament. The first PGA Championship was played under match play rules in 1916 at the Siwanoy Country Club in Bronxville, New York, and won by James M. Barnes of England. Five-time winner Walter Hagen became the first American-born player to win the PGA Championship in 1921. Don Finsterwald was the first to win the tournament under stroke play when match play was discontinued in 1958.

PGA Club Professional Championship: An annual stroke play tournament sponsored by the PGA for club professionals (as opposed to touring professionals). The PGA Club Professional Championship was first won by Howell Frazer in 1968, and is now the largest seventy-two-hole stroke play championship in the world. The nine top finishers automatically earn a position on the International PGA Cup Match team, and the top twenty-five finishers are eligible to play in the PGA Championship.

PGA Hall of Fame: The Professional Golfers' Association honor roll of outstanding players (amateur and professional) and contributors to the sport of golf. New members are nominated annually and selected by a special Hall of Fame Selection Committee, which includes golf writers and others closely identified with the game. The PGA Hall of Fame was created in 1940, at which time the first twelve members were selected.

PGA Tour: The competitive arm of the PGA (a separate corporate entity since 1968, comprised of tournament players), directly responsible for the planning and organization of the series of major tournaments that make up the "tour." PGA Tour headquarters is at Ponte Vedra Beach, Florida.

Phillips Oil: Slang for a score of sixty-six for a round.

pick clean: To strike a ball high rather than swinging "down through the ball," imparting overspin, which causes the ball to roll rather than stop on landing (as on an approach shot).

pin: see *flagstick.*

pin high: see *hole high.*

1. pitch: A shot in which the ball is hit (usually with a wedge) in a high arc with backspin to stop it from rolling when it lands on the green. also *pitch and stop, pitch shot.*

2. pitch: To hit the ball (usually with a wedge) in a high arc with backspin to stop it from rolling when it lands on the green.

pitch and putt course: 1. A small course laid out specifically to give a player practice with a wedge and a putter. 2. A short regulation course.

pitch and run: see *chip shot.*

pitch and stop: see *pitch.*

pitching niblick: see *lofter.*

pitching wedge: A high-loft (approximately fifty-five degrees) iron club used to pitch and sometimes chip the ball from close to the putting green. compare *sand wedge.*

pitch out: see *shank.*

pitchout: A shanked ball.

pitch shot: see *pitch.*

Pittsburgh Persimmon: A trade name for a particular steelie or all-metal "wood," facetiously named for the steel capital of the United States. Aerospace engineer John Zebelean is credited with developing the first successful stainless steel "wood," introduced in 1979 by the Taylor Company of California. Said by users to drive the ball farther and straighter than a normal wood, steel-headed clubs have become increasingly popular with professional and amateur golfers (over 12 million clubs were sold in 1982). The name "Pittsburgh Persimmon" was coined by Alan Cook, head professional at the Municipal Golf Course in San Clemente, California, and later patented with permission by the Taylor Company.

play: 1. To hit the ball with a club, to make a stroke. (has the honor and will play his ball first) 2. To direct a ball toward a target. (played a beautiful chip shot just short of the pin) 3. To be a longer or shorter distance from the tee because of a change in the exact location of the cup on the green. (the hole now plays shorter than at the beginning of the summer)

playable: Able to be hit or played, as of a lie.

playing the like: Playing the same stroke as one's opponent. compare *playing the odd.*

playing the odd: Playing one more stroke than one's opponent. compare *playing the like.*

play safe: To deliberately hit the ball short of the green or the hole to avoid possible trouble. (a hole on which all the amateurs play safe)

play the trombone: see *Declaration of Independence.*

play through: To continue play, moving ahead of a single player or a slower-paced match on the course with permission. Golf etiquette calls for a single player or a slow-paced match to stand aside and allow a match to pass or "play through."

plug ball: A ball that makes a small hole or indentation on landing and does not roll.

plus golfer: A better-than-scratch player, one with a plus handicap.

plus handicap: The number of artifical strokes a better-than-scratch player gives to adjust his scoring ability to the common level. compare *handicap.*

pocket the ball: see *rake it in.*

point tournament: see *Stableford.*

pole: see *flagstick.*

pool shark: see *bladesman.*

pot: see *hole.*

pot bunker: A deep, craterlike bunker with steep sides.

practice green: A putting green area constructed usually in close proximity to the clubhouse to allow golfers to practice putting away from the course's putting greens.

practice tee: A teeing area that is not a part of the regular course, used to practice tee shots. also *hospital zone.*

preferred lies: A provision sometimes included in Local Rules that allows a ball to be moved to a more advantageous lie under certain circumstances in informal play. Preferred lies or winter rules are sometimes invoked when severe weather either damages or makes unplayable certain parts of a course, or when other special or temporary conditions interfere with normal play.

1. press: 1. A bet made separate from any other bet on the remaining holes of a round. Once one or more holes of a press have been played, if yet another bet is made on holes that remain from that point, it is called a double press. 2. A forward press.

2. press: 1. To bet separate from any other bet on the remaining holes of a round. 2. To deliberately or involuntarily move a part of the body forward just at the beginning of a swing.

pro-am: A competition or tournament in which amateurs play with professionals.

Professional Golfers' Association: An organization dedicated to the growth and promotion of the sport of golf that tests and licenses local club and teaching professionals, provides three- to eight-year-long training programs for apprentices that emphasize practical business skills as well as playing and teaching, and ongoing educational, service, and junior golf programs. In addition, the Professional Golfers' Association produces some thirty tournaments per year, including the PGA Championships, the International Ryder Cup Matches, and the Club Professional Championship, the largest seventy-two-hole professional competition in the world. It also co-produces the World Series of Golf with the PGA Tour, a separate corporate entity since 1968, comprised of tournament players. Founded in 1916, the Professional Golfers' Association is now the largest working sports organization in the world, and is headquartered in Palm Beach Gardens, Florida. PGA Tour headquarters is at Ponte Vedra Beach, Florida.

provisional ball: A ball played from as near as possible to the spot where an original ball was played when the original ball is assumed to be out of bounds or lost (except for one that might be lost in a water hazard, for which a provisional ball may not be played). If the original ball is found, the provisional ball is abandoned, and play is continued with the original ball without penalty. If the original ball is out of bounds or cannot be found, the provisional ball becomes the ball in play, and one penalty stroke is added to the player's score.

pull: see *draw.*

punch shot: A shot that is deliberately hit low, as to provide additional control when hitting into the wind.

1. push: To hit the ball at an angle to the same side as the dominant hand of the player.

2. push: A stroke in which the ball is hit at an angle to the same side as the dominant hand of the player.

1. putt: A light stroke in which the ball is tapped while on the green or on the edge of the green so as to roll along the surface of the grass toward the hole. The introduction of the perfectly round guttie ball in 1848 together with closely-cut greens made the modern rolling putt possible.

2. putt: To lightly tap the ball so as to make it roll toward the hole.

putter: 1. A short-shafted iron club with a flat face and no loft, used to tap a ball on the putting green toward the hole. When the perfectly round guttie ball replaced the old featherstuffed ball in 1848, Scotsman Allan Robertson, the pioneer professional golfer who reportedly never lost a match, introduced the use of the putting cleek on the green, the forerunner to the modern putter. Previously, wooden putters were used to jump rather than roll the old featherstuffed balls toward the hole. The minimal loft of the putting cleek allowed the ball to be chipped and rolled toward the pin. 2. One who is engaged in or skilled at putting. The first golfer to be known as a deadly putter was Willie Park Sr., four-time winner of the British Open (1860, 1863, 1866, and 1875).

putting green: see *green.*

puttoon: see *hole.*

quail-high: A description of a low drive or shot, resembling the flight of a quail.

quarrelsome: Slang for a mixed foursome. also *gruesome.*

quitting: A pulling back or hesitance on the downswing of a stroke rather than hitting "through the ball," usually resulting in a poor shot.

rabbit: 1. A touring professional not eligible for exempt status, thus having to "hop" from tournament to tournament in order to play in the qualifying rounds for tour events. This usage became archaic in 1983 when the PGA Tour was restricted to exempt players. 2. An uncomplimentary name for an indifferent golfer, alluding to such a player's timid nature and habit of aimlessly dashing around the course.

rake it in: To give up or withdraw from a tournament. also *pocket the ball.*

read the green: To analyze the slope and surface of a putting green before attempting a putt.

recovery: A stroke that successfully plays the ball out of either the rough or a sand trap.

recovery room: Slang among touring professionals for the scorer's tent at a tournament.

Red Grange: A score of seventy-seven for a round, alluding to the jersey number of the legendary football player Red Grange. also *Sunset Strip.*

red tees: see *women's tees.*

1. referee: An official appointed by the Committee to accompany players around the course and decide questions of fact and of golf law, and to act on any breach of a Rule or Local Rule, whether personally observed or reported to him by an official "observer."

2. referee: To act as referee for a match.

relief: The right to move a ball that lies in casual water, ground under repair, or in a hole, cast, or runway made by a burrowing animal, or one that is interfered with by an immovable obstruction without incurring a penalty stroke.

1. rim: The edge of the cup. also *lip.*

2. rim: To hit or roll around the rim of the cup with a ball without sinking it. also *lip, lip out.*

rim out: see *rim.*

roll: see *run.*

roller coaster: A putt over a particularly hilly green. also *Dolly Parton.*

rough: The rough ground or area of uncut grass immediately adjacent to and on either side of the fairway. (played it out of the rough to the edge of the green)

round: A complete circuit of the course, usually eighteen holes. A round was not always comprised of eighteen holes. That number came to be recognized as the standard number for a round because of the preeminence in golf of the St. Andrews course in Scotland. There, after subtracting four of the original holes in 1764, the game was played nine holes out, with the players turning around and playing the same nine holes in, completing one eighteen-hole "round." also *loop.*

roundhouse hook: A sweeping hook shot.

rub of the green: A situation in which a moving ball is accidentally stopped or deflected by an "outside agency." In such a case, the ball is played as it lies without penalty.

●●Luck or fate. (the accident was no one's fault, just a rub of the green)

rug: Slang for a divot.

1. run: The path followed and distance travelled upon landing by a ball hit into the air. also *roll.*

2. run: To hit the ball so that it rolls forward upon landing, as on an approach shot. (unfortunately, ran the ball right past the hole, off the green)

run up shot: see *chip shot.*

Ryder Cup Matches: A biennial competition between professional teams from the United States and Great Britain (for whose team eligibility was expanded in 1979 to include British and European PGA members residing in Europe), featuring foursomes, four-ball, and singles matches, with the United States and Great Britain alternating as hosts. Named after British seed merchant Samuel A. Ryder, who donated the solid gold trophy bearing his name, the Ryder Cup Matches were first played in 1927 in Worcester, Massachusetts, and won by the United States team 9-1/2 to 2-1/2.

sandbagger: A player with an inflated or too-high handicap. also *mug hunter.*

sandblaster: see *sand wedge.*

sand bunker: see *sand trap.*

sandie: The basis for a bet in a casual game in which a player gets out of a sand trap and holes out in a total of two shots. also *sandy.* compare *greenie, chippie.*

sand iron: see *sand wedge.*

sand trap: A hazard consisting of a bare area or a depression filled with loose sand, usually located near or adjacent to the putting green. see *bunker.* also *beach, bunker, bunker trap, cat box, Egyptian Bermuda, litter box, sand bunker, trap, white face.*

sand wedge: A usually unnumbered iron club with pronounced loft (approximately fifty-five degrees), used to hit the ball out of sand. The base of the sand wedge is specially thickened into a flange, which digs into the sand behind and under the ball, and bumps the ball out with a cushion of sand. Clubmaker and golf great Gene Sarazen first produced this effect in the 1930s by altering the sole angle of an old flanged-sole sand club. also *sandblaster, sand iron.* compare *pitching wedge.*

sandy: see *sandie.*

1. sclaff: A misplayed stroke in which the club head bounces off the ground before making contact with the ball.

2. sclaff: To make a sclaff.

scoreboard: A display board, usually hand-operated, on which the current status, position, and scores of tournament leaders are posted during a competition. In 1981, the PGA Tour introduced a modular and portable electronic scoring and information system, consisting of one large leader-information board and up to twenty connected leader-status information boards to be placed at various locations around a course. also *leader-board*.

scorecard: A card on which the score for each hole for one or more golfers is kept, and upon which "stroke holes" are listed where handicap strokes are to be applied. According to the Rules of Golf, in a stroke play competition, it is the responsibility of each player to check his scorecard for errors, and to make sure that both he and the "marker" have signed it before turning it in to the Committee. If a scorecard is not turned in, or if it is not properly signed, or if a lower score than was actually made is turned in, the player is disqualified. If a higher score than was actually made is turned in, the score must stand as returned. 1980 Vardon Trophy winner Lee Trevino was disqualified from the 1980 PGA Championship tournament for accidentally failing to sign his scorecard after the first round. The most famous case of a scorecard mistake occurred in the 1968 Masters Tournament, when Roberto DeVicenzo hurriedly signed an incorrect scorecard—one stroke higher than he actually scored—that cost him a tie and a chance to play off for the title. also *card*.

Scotch foursome: An American expression for a foursome. see *foursome*.

scramble: To recover or attempt to recover after a poor start on a hole, as to make par after failing to reach the green "in regulation."

scrambler: A player who seems always to be able to make a good score on a hole, even after an unimpressive start; one who makes the important or necessary shot under pressure, whether a critical approach shot, a recovery from the rough or a hazard, or a delicate or difficult putt. Walter Hagen, Gene Sarazen, Arnold Palmer, and Gary Player are among the golfing greats who have been known as scramblers.

scratch golfer, scratch player: A golfer with enough skill to play with no handicap.

Seniors: A class of competition for older players (over age fifty-five for amateurs, over age fifty for professionals). The first PGA Seniors' Championship was held in 1937 in Augusta, Georgia, and won by Jock Hutchison. The first USGA-sponsored Senior Amateur Championship was held in 1955 in Nashville, and won by fifty-six-year-old J. Wood Platt of Bethlehem, Pennsylvania.

seven iron: A high-lofted iron club used for approach shots to the green of approximately 140 yards. Formerly known as a mashie niblick.

shaft: The long, thin, cylindrical part of a golf club between the head and the grip.

shank: To mishit the ball with the heel of the club head, making it veer to one side. also *lateral, pitch out, socket*.

Shapiro: A mulligan with a Jewish name, a free shot with a second ball sometimes permitted in informal play when a golfer's original ball is mishit. Similar to a Ginsberg. However, like a mulligan, a Shapiro must continue to be played, even if it is mishit worse than the original ball.

sharpshooter: see *shotmaker*.

shoot: To make a particular score while playing. (shot an even-par seventy-one in the first round)

shooting gallery: Slang among professionals for an easy "birdie" course.

shooting irons: Slang for golf clubs. also *bats, hammers, hickories, sticks, tools, weapons*.

shoot scratch: To play with no handicap as professional players do.

short: Stopping before reaching the intended destination. (a well-aimed drive, right down the fairway, but short of the green)

short game: Of or pertaining to relatively short shots, such as approach shots or putts.

short iron: An iron with high loft and shorter shaft for short approach shots, such as a 7, 8 or 9 iron.

shot: A stroke in which the ball is hit. (a poor shot into the rough)

shotmaker: A player known for the ability to accurately place his shots. Tommy Bolt, winner of the U.S. Open in 1958 and the PGA Seniors' Championship in 1969, and five-time PGA Player of the Year (1967, 1972, 1973, 1975, and

1976) Jack Nicklaus are usually mentioned among the great shotmakers in the game of golf. also *sharpshooter*.

shotmaking: 1. The stroking of the ball to make a shot. 2. The making of accurately placed shots.

shut the face: see *hood the club*.

side: Two or more players who are partnered in a competition.

sidehiller: A putt that rolls or must roll across the face of a sloping green to reach the hole.

silent one: see *whiff*.

singles: A competition between two players.

sink: To hole the ball. (will win the match if she can sink this 6-foot putt) see *hole out*.

six iron: An iron club with medium loft used for approach shots to the green of approximately 150 yards. Formerly known as a spade mashie.

skull: see *top*.

skull shot: A ball that is topped or skulled.

sky: 1. To hit a ball almost straight up; a mishit. (fell behind when he skied his approach shot) 2. To intentionally loft a ball high into the air, as to clear a "hazard" or obstacle.

sky ball: A ball mishit almost straight up into the air. also *angel raper, hello God, up in Minnie's room*.

1. slice: To hit the ball in such a way as to cause it to veer to the side of the player's dominant hand. (sliced one into the rough) also *fade*. compare *draw, hook, pull*.

2. slice: A shot in which the ball is sliced, and veers toward the side of the player's dominant hand. also *Cuban, fade*.

slow green: A putting green with a soft or lush surface that inhibits the bounce or roll of a ball.

smile: see *dimple*.

1. smother: To hit down on the ball, causing it to roll a short distance on the ground.

2. smother: The act or an instance of smothering a ball.

snake: A long putt over a hilly green.

snowman: A score of eighty-eight for a round, because the figure 8 resembles a snowman.

1. socket: The thin part of a club head near the point where it joins the shaft. also *neck*.

2. socket: To shank a ball, hitting it on the socket of the club. see *shank*.

sole: The bottom of a club head.

solitaire: see *hole in one*.

spade mashie: A number 6 iron, popularly called a spade mashie until numerical classifications for clubs were introduced in the 1920s.

spoon: A number 3 wood, although, originally, all lofted clubs were known as spoons. The term "spoon" became less popular when numerical classifications for clubs were introduced in the 1920s.

square: see *all square*.

square stance: A stance in which the front foot and rear foot are positioned parallel to the line of play of the ball when addressed. compare *closed stance, open stance*.

1. stab: A short thrusting putting stroke.

2. stab: To make a short thrusting putting stroke.

Stableford: A type of stroke competition popular in Great Britain, in which play is against a fixed score (such as par) at each hole. Points are awarded in relation to par, with one point for a hole completed in one stroke over par, two

SLICE   HOOK

points for a hole done in par, three points for one under par, four points for two under par, and five points for a hole done in three under par. The winner is the player or side scoring the most points in a round. The scoring system for Stableford competitions, called "point tournaments" in the United States, was invented in 1932 by English surgeon and golfer Dr. Frank B. Stableford.

stadium golf: A concept of golf as a spectator sport, played on courses designed to provide spectators with accessible elevated vantage points for each hole and up-to-the-moment information about what is taking place on other parts of the course. The Tournament Players Club, opened in Jacksonville, Florida in 1981 as PGA Tour headquarters and the permanent site of the Tournament Players Championship, was the first golf course designed specially to accommodate "stadium golf."

steamy putt: A putt that has been hit too hard and rolls well past the hole.

steelie: Slang for a steel-headed "wood." see *Pittsburgh Persimmon.*

sticks: Slang for golf clubs. also *bats, hammers, hickories, shooting irons, tools, weapons.*

stick the pick: To stub the club head on the ground behind the ball before making contact on a chip or wedge shot, resulting in a mishit stroke.

stipulated round: A completed round of usually eighteen holes played in their correct sequence (unless the Committee authorizes fewer holes or a different sequence). To settle a tie in match play, the Committee may extend a stipulated round to as many holes as are required for a match to be won.

stone: To hit a ball that stops right next to the pin. (kept on stoning his putts after getting to the green in regulation)

stone dead: A ball that stops right next to the pin.

stop: see *backspin.*

stretcher bearer: Slang for a caddie.

string of birdies: Birdies (one stroke under par for a hole) on consecutive holes.

1. stroke: A swing or forward movement of the club that is intended to strike the ball, and that is charged to a player's score whether or not the ball is hit. (two strokes behind the leader on the sixteenth hole)

2. stroke: To swing and hit the ball with a club. (stroked one right down the middle of the fairway)

stroke and distance: A penalty in which a player is assessed one penalty stroke, and must play a new ball (or the original ball) from where the last stroke was made. A stroke and distance penalty is applied when a ball is lost or out of bounds, when a second ball is played before informing the opponent and marker of one's intention to play a provisional ball, and as one of the player's options when the ball rests in an unplayable lie, or in a water hazard or lateral water hazard. compare *penalty stroke.*

stroke hole: A hole on which a player applies a handicap stroke to hit gross score. The numerical order in which handicap strokes are allocated to specified holes of the course is usually shown on the scorecard. also *handicap stroke hole.*

stroke play: A competition in which the winner is the player who completes the stipulated round or rounds in the fewest strokes. Golf was always played at match play until the eighteenth century, when stroke play or "medal play" was first used in England for one-day competitions for the prize of a "medal." When the USGA conducted the first U.S. Amateur Championship in 1895, match play was still considered the standard method of play. The first U.S. Open was played the next day with thirty-six holes played in one day, reportedly so that the ten "professionals" who had entered wouldn't be away from their shops for too long. Stroke play flourished in the United States, and today, it is the method of play in most professional tournaments. compare *match play.*

stymie: A situation in which a player's ball rests between the cup and another ball (obstructing its path). The Rules of Golf were changed in 1951 to permit the interfering ball to be lifted in match play, and then replaced after the further ball has been played. In stroke play, the player whose ball is interfering may either lift or play the ball, at his option. There are conflicting ideas about the exact origin of the term, with some suggesting that "stymie" is from the Gaelic *stigh mi*, meaning "inside me," or the Dutch *stuit mij*, meaning "it stops me."

205

Others claim the term is derived from a similar English word, "styme," in use as early as 1300, as in the phrase "not to see a styme," meaning "not able to see at all," or in the golf application, not able to see around the interfering ball.

•• To be "stymied" is to be literally or figuratively blocked, stopped, or stumped. (stymied by the last question on the test)

sudden-death hole: An extension of the stipulated round by the Committee in match play, for the purpose of settling a tie after eighteen holes. Usually, as many sudden-death holes as necessary are played until the round is won by the first player to win a hole. The all-time record for the PGA is eleven sudden-death holes, in the 1949 Motor City Open, when Cary Middlecoff and Lloyd Mangrum were declared co-winners by mutual agreement. When the winner of a round is determined by a single sudden-death hole or "extra hole," the hole is sometimes called the nineteenth hole.

summer rules: A euphemism for normal play under the Rules of Golf, indicating that no preferred lies or winter rules provisions are in effect.

Sunday best: An excellent shot.

Sunset Strip: A score of seventy-seven for a round, an allusion to the 1950s television program, *77 Sunset Strip.* also *Red Grange.*

sweet sixteen: The group or flight of sixteen players who advance from a tour-

TEE MARKER

TEEING AREA

nament qualifying round. (made the sweet sixteen for the big amateur tournament)

sweet spot: The central area of a club's face, optimum for making contact with the ball on a stroke.

swing weight: The characteristics of balance and weight that affect the feel and performance of a club as it is swung.

take away: The first hand movement taking the club back away from the ball at the beginning of the backswing.

take turf: To dig a divot or take a patch of turf when playing a shot.

teaching pro: A professional player who is primarily concerned with teaching golf to other players, as opposed to a touring professional. Most teaching pros are associated with a golf club, and often function as the club or home pro.

1. tee: 1. A small wooden or plastic peg, larger at the top end, upon which the ball is placed for the first shot on each hole. A New Jersey dentist, Dr. William Lowe, worried that his hands would be injured by constantly digging in the turf or sand to build a mound for a ball (the original tee), first marketed a wooden tee in the 1920s. 2. A mound of turf or sand used instead of a plastic or wooden peg, still legal, but not often used. Before the wooden tee became popular, teeing grounds were often equipped with a handy box of sand so that a golfer or caddie could make a small mound. 3. see *teeing ground.*

2. tee: To place a ball on a tee in preparation for a stroke. also *tee up.*

tee box: An old name for a teeing ground.

teeing area: see *teeing ground.*

teeing ground: The area from which the ball is teed and the first stroke is made for the hole to be played, a rectangle two club-lengths in depth, the front and sides of which are defined by the outside limits of two tee markers. A teeing ground is divided into three sections. The rear section, indicated by blue tee markers, is intended for professional use. The middle section, indicated by white tee markers, is intended for regulation play. The front section, indicated by red tee markers, is intended for women golfers. also *tee, tee box, teeing area.*

tee markers: Devices firmly attached to the ground that are used to define the teeing ground from which play begins on each hole. Blue tee markers indicate the championship tees, white tee markers indicate the middle tees for regular play, and red tee markers indicate the ladies' tees.

tee off: To begin the play of a round of golf. (usually the first player to tee off in the morning)

●●To "tee off on" someone or something is to literally or figuratively hit, punch, or attack. (a scathing editorial which teed off on rising white collar crime)

tee peg: see *tee.*

tee shot: A shot played from the teeing ground, the stroke that begins play at each hole.

tee up: To place a ball on a tee in preparation for the first stroke of the hole to be played.

ten-finger grip: see *baseball grip.*

ten iron: A rarely-used special high-lofted iron club, replaced by the modern wedge.

Texas wedge: A putter, when used to play a ball that lies just off the edge of the green.

thread the needle: To make an excellent, straight shot.

three-ball: A match in which three golfers, each with his own ball, play against one another.

three iron: A slightly-lofted iron club used for distance shots of approximately 180 yards. Formerly known as an approach cleek or mid-mashie.

three-putt: To use three putts to hole a ball (rather than the two allowed for par). (three-putted for a bogey on the last hole)

three-putt territory: A difficult lie on the green, far away from the pin.

threesome: A match in which one plays against two, and each side plays one ball. Sometimes, the term "threesome" is inaccurately applied to a group of three golfers playing together.

●●Any group of three.

three wood: A wooden club used for fairway shots of approximately 220 yards. Formerly known as a spoon.

through the green: Any place on the course except the teeing ground and putting green of the hole being played and within a hazard.

throw it at the flag: To play a bold or risky shot at the pin.

throw-up zone: About six feet away from

the pin, close enough to put pressure on a player, but far enough away to be a difficult putt.

tiger: An expert or good player.

tiger country: Slang for the rough. also *jungle.*

tiger tees: see *blue tees.*

timber: A call given in jest when a ball is headed towards the trees.

tips: see *blue tees.*

toe: The tip or outer end of a club head.

tool chest: A golf bag.

tools: Golf clubs. also *bats, hammers, hickories, shooting irons, sticks, weapons.*

top: To strike a ball above the center or too high, causing the ball to roll or bounce along the ground, or imparting overspin, which results in a low flight and causes the ball to roll rather than stop on landing. also *hit on the hat, skull.*

topspin: A forward rotation (as imparted by skulling or topping) that causes the ball to move in a low flight, and to bounce and roll forward upon landing. also *overspin.*

Tour: see *PGA tour.*

Tour golfer, Tour player: A professional player who makes his or her living by playing on the PGA Tour or the LPGA Tour. also *touring pro, touring professional.*

touring pro, touring professional: see *Tour golfer, Tour player.*

Tournament Players Championship: The PGA's own major tournament, open to all designated players, winners of major PGA Tour co-sponsored or approved events during the previous year, the current British Open champion, and leaders in the PGA Tour official standings as necessary to complete the field. The first Tournament Players Championship was played in 1974 at the Atlanta Country Club in Atlanta, Georgia, and won by Jack Nicklaus. In 1981, the Tournament Players Championship moved to the site of its new permanent home (and headquarters of the PGA Tour) at the Tournament Players Club in Ponte Vedra Beach, Florida.

tour swing: A technically good swing, a swing that shows particularly good form, as might be expected from a professional on the Tour.

trap: see *sand trap.*

trapped: Bordered by sand traps. (an almost completely trapped green)

trap shot: A stroke made from inside a sand trap.

triple bogey: A score of three over par on a given hole.

triple-bogey: To score a triple bogey on a hole.

trolley: 1. A straight shot, as though on "rails." 2. British slang for a caddie cart. also *cart, golf cart.*

turn: The half-way point on an eighteen-hole course. From the early days of golf, at the famous St. Andrews course in Scotland, where, after four of the original holes were subtracted in 1764, the game was played nine holes out to the turn, with the same nine holes played in. Prior to 1764, the turn had been at eleven holes. (still leading at the turn)

twitch: A British expression for a "case of nerves" that causes a player to choke under pressure and miss a putt. also *yips.*

two iron: A long-range iron club used for distances of approximately 190 yards. Formerly known as a midiron. also *deuce.*

two wood: A wooden club used for long fairway shots of approximately 220 yards. Formerly known as a brassie.

twosome: Slang for a match between two players.

●●Two people, a couple.

underclub: To use the wrong club (one with too much loft and not enough shaft), resulting in the ball landing short of the intended target. (didn't make the green in regulation because he underclubbed his fairway shot)

undertaker: A good or "lethal" putter, one who can "bury" the ball. also *blades-man, pool shark.*

United States Golf Association: The national governing body of golf in the United States. Formed in 1894 for the purpose of promoting and conserving the best interests and the true spirit of the game of golf, the United States Golf Association, or USGA, began work on a uniform code of rules in the 1920s, and in 1952, joined with the Royal and Ancient Golf Club of St. Andrews, Scotland to issue the Rules of Golf, in use throughout the world today. The USGA also developed and now maintains the national system of handicap-

ping, which allows players of different abilities to compete on relatively equal terms, and is responsible for testing and approving golf equipment and defining and maintaining the distinction between amateur and professional golfers. The USGA conducted its first national competitions in 1895, the U.S. Amateur, the U.S. Open, and Women's Amateur Championships. Today, the USGA conducts nine other national championships as well, including the Women's Open, Junior Amateur, Girls' Junior, Amateur Public Links, Women's Amateur Public Links, Senior Amateur, Senior Women's Amateur, Senior Open and Mid-Amateur Championships. The USGA also conducts international competitions such as the Walker Cup Match with the Royal and Ancient Golf Club of St. Andrews, Scotland, and the Curtis Cup Match with the British Ladies' Golf Union, and selects the U.S. teams for the World Amateur and Women's World Amateur Team Championships.

unplayable lie: A ball positioned so as to be impossible to play. Sometimes in informal play, Local Rules ("preferred lies" and "winter rules") allow a player to move a ball in an unplayable lie.

up: Ahead by a number of holes in match play. (two up at the end of nine holes)

up in Minnie's room: see *sky ball.*

U.S. Amateur Championship: The prestigious annual national tournament for amateur players, sponsored by the USGA. The first U.S. Amateur Championship was held in 1895 at the Newport Golf Club in Newport, Rhode Island, and won by Charles B. Macdonald, of the Chicago Golf Club. Francis Ouimet (1914, 1931), Robert T. "Bobby" Jones, Jr. (1924, 1925, 1927, 1928, 1930), Gene Littler (1953), Arnold Palmer (1954), Jack Nicklaus (1959, 1961), and Deane R. Beman (1960, 1963) are among those who won the Amateur Championship at match play. From 1965 through 1972, the format was changed to stroke play, reverting to match play in 1973. In 1981, Nathaniel Crosby won the U.S. Amateur Championship. Crosby's famous father, Bing Crosby, whose pioneer celebrity pro-amateur tournament did much to heighten the public appeal of golf, and particularly professional golf, is honored in the World Golf Hall of Fame as an outstanding contributor to the sport. also *amateur, amateur championship.*

use all the cup: To roll around the rim of a hole before dropping, as of a putt.

USGA: The United States Golf Association.

U.S. Open: The major annual national competition sponsored by the USGA, open to professionals and amateurs (with handicaps not exceeding two strokes) who are exempt or who have qualified in Local and Sectional Qualifying Championships. The first U.S. Open was held at the Newport (Rhode Island) Golf Club in 1895, and won by twenty-one-year-old Horace Rawlins. It was the first major tournament played at stroke play in the United States and was originally a thirty-six-hole, one-day competition. The Open was extended to seventy-two holes in 1898, played in four eighteen-hole daily rounds since 1965. The first amateur player to win the Open was Francis Ouimet in 1913, defeating British golfing greats Harry Vardon and Edward Ray. The record for the most victories in the U.S. Open is held by four men: Willie Anderson (1901, 1903, 1904, and 1905), Robert T. "Bobby" Jones, Jr. (1923, 1926, 1929, and 1930), Ben Hogan (1948, 1950, 1951, and 1953), and Jack Nicklaus (1962, 1967, 1972, and 1980). also *National Open, Open.*

Van Gogh it: To play an "artistic" round.

Vardon grip: The overlapping grip, first popularized by six-time British Open winner (1896, 1898, 1899, 1903, 1911, and 1914) Harry Vardon. see *overlapping grip.*

Vardon Trophy: The annual award given to the PGA member maintaining the finest playing average in events co-sponsored or designated by the PGA. The PGA Vardon Trophy, named in honor of the internationally famous British golfer, Harry Vardon, was placed in competition among American professionals in 1937 as a successor to the Henry E. Radix Trophy, which, prior to that time, had been awarded annually to the professional having the finest tournament record in play in this country. In 1937, the first winner was Harry Cooper. The Vardon Trophy has been won five times by Lee Trevino (1970, 1971, 1972, 1974, and 1980) and Billy Casper (1960, 1963, 1965, 1966, and 1968), four times by Sam Snead (1938, 1949, 1950, and 1955), and Arnold Palmer (1961, 1962, 1964, and 1967), and three times by Ben Hogan (1940, 1941, and 1948) and Tom Watson (1977, 1978, and 1979).

Vare Trophy: The annual LPGA award given to the woman professional player (with a minimum of seventy official rounds of tournament competition during the year) with the lowest scoring average at the end of each year, computed by dividing a player's total number of strokes in official LPGA tournaments by the number of official rounds she played during the year. The trophy was presented to the LPGA by Betty Jameson in 1952 in honor of the great American player Glenna Collett Vare. The Vare Trophy was first won in 1953 by Patty Berg, who played sixty-five rounds in an average of 75.00 strokes per round.

Volkswagen: An awkward or poor shot that turns out well; an unartistic but successful shot.

1. waggle: An intentional movement of the club back and forth behind the ball just before starting a swing, done to help break down tension in the hands, arms and legs.

2. waggle: The act or an instance of waggling before a stroke is made to relieve tension.

Walker Cup Match: A biennial international competition played between teams of ten male amateur golfers from the United States on the one side and from England, Scotland, Wales, Northern Ireland and Eire on the other, hosted alternately by the United States and Great Britain. The Walker Cup Match, so-dubbed by the press because the trophy (the International Challenge Trophy) was donated by George Herbert Walker (President of the USGA when the tournament was first discussed in 1920), is the oldest international golf competition. It was first played in 1922, with the United States team winning eight to four. Going into the 1980s, teams from Great Britain had won Walker Cup Matches only twice (1938 and 1971), tying once in 1965. The teams, selected by the USGA and the Royal and Ancient Golf Club of St. Andrews, Scotland, play four eighteen-hole foursomes in the morning and eight eighteen-hole singles in the afternoon on each of the two days of the competition.

water hazard: Any sea, lake, pond, river, ditch, surface drainage ditch, or other open water course except a "lateral water hazard" within the boundaries of a golf course, regardless of whether or not it contains water. When a ball is lost or unplayable in a water hazard, the player may, under penalty of one stroke, drop the ball (or a new ball) behind the hazard on a line formed by the hole and the point where the ball entered the hazard, or drop the ball (or a new ball) from the point where the original stroke was made. Water hazards are marked by short yellow stakes or by yellow lines.

weapons: Slang for golf clubs. also *bats, hammers, hickories, shooting irons, sticks, tools.*

weaver: Slang for a shot in which the ball is hit so straight toward the hole that it is said to "hide the flagstick," making it necessary for the player to "weave" from side to side in order to see the pole.

wedge: A usually unnumbered iron club with pronounced loft (approximately fifty-five degrees), used either to pitch and chip the ball from close to the putting green (a pitching wedge) or to hit the ball out of sand (a sand wedge).

Wee Links: A low-maintenance, six-hole course utilizing synthetic "Mod-Sod" tees and putting greens, first installed at the Walt Disney Golf Resort in Florida. The concept of "Wee Links" courses is to provide accessible low-cost training grounds for young players.

1. **whiff:** To swing and miss the ball completely, wasting a stroke. (fell behind at the beginning of the round when he whiffed on his first tee shot)

2. **whiff:** A swing of the club that does not make contact with the ball as intended. Though the ball is missed, the swing counts as a stroke on the golfer's score for the hole. also *air shot, fresh air shot, silent one.*

whiskey jerk, whiskey wrists: An "affliction" said to be suffered by poor putters.

white face: A sand trap, appearing somewhat like a white face amid the surrounding grass. see *sand trap.*

white knuckles: A slang expression for a shot that a player tries to hit with full power. (a long hole, requiring a white knuckles tee shot)

white tees: The middle section of a teeing ground, indicated by white tee markers, and intended for regulation play. also *middle tees.*

wind cheater: A low drive or shot under the wind.

windy: A comment or description of an air shot or whiff.

winter rules: A provision sometimes included in Local Rules that allows a ball to be moved to a more advantageous lie under certain circumstances in informal play. "Winter rules" or "preferred lies" are sometimes invoked when severe weather either damages or makes unplayable certain parts of a course, or when other special or temporary conditions interfere with normal play.

Women's Open Championship: An annual seventy-two-hole, four-day competition sponsored by the USGA that is open to exempt and qualified (in Sectional Qualifying Competitions) women professionals and amateurs with handicaps of not more than four strokes. The Open is one of the four major tournaments that together comprise the women's grand slam. The first Women's Open Championship was played in 1946 at the Spokane (Washington) Country Club, and won by golfing great Patty Berg (in match play that year only). The tournament was originally conducted by the then Women's Professional Golfers' Association from 1946 through 1948, and by the Ladies Professional Golf Association from 1949 through 1952. Two women have won the Women's Open Championship four times, Betsy Rawls (1951, 1953, 1957, and 1960) and Mickey Wright (1958, 1959, 1961, and 1964).

women's tees: The front section of a teeing ground, indicated by red tee markers, and usually reserved for women golfers. also *ladies' tees, red tees.*

Women's World Amateur Team Championship: An international amateur team championship for women, played biennially in conjunction with the World Amateur Team Championship in a different host country from one of three global zones; the Australasian Zone (Asia, Australia, New Zealand, and Oceania), the American Zone (North America, South America and Central America), and the European-African Zone. The Women's World Amateur

Team Championship is sponsored by the World Amateur Golf Council (comprised of representatives of national governing bodies of golf in nearly sixty countries) and is contested by three-woman teams over a four-day period. Competition is at stroke play, with the two best individual scores counted as a team's score each day. The winning team (with the lowest four-day score) is awarded the Espirito Santo Trophy, presented in 1964 by Mrs. Espirito Santo Silva of Portugal. The first Women's World Amateur Team Championship was instituted by the French Golf Federation on a suggestion by the USGA and won in 1964 by the French team at the St. Germain Golf Club, near Paris, France.

wood: 1. A long-shafted club with a large wooden head, for making long shots, as from the tee, fairway, and sometimes, the rough. Woods are numbered from one through five in order of increasing loft (the angle at which the club face is tipped back). In recent years, all-steel "woods" (with metal replacing the hardwood normally used in the heads) have been marketed. see *Pittsburgh Persimmon.* 2. A wood shot.

wood cover: A covering of leather or some other pliable material to protect the club heads of woods from knocking against other clubs. Wood covers were originally invented in 1916 by a Japanese golfer, Seiichi Takahata, later a leading figure in Japanese golf.

wood shot: A shot made with a wood. also *wood.*

workingman's par: A scrambling par, as of a par made after not reaching the green in regulation.

World Amateur Golf Council: An international amateur organization, comprised of representatives of national governing bodies of golf in nearly sixty countries, founded in 1958 to foster friendship and sportsmanship through the conduct of international team competitions. Based in Far Hills, New Jersey, the World Amateur Golf Council sponsors the World Amateur Team Championship and the Women's World Amateur Team Championship.

World Amateur Team Championship: An international amateur team championship for men, played biennially in conjunction with the Women's World Amateur Team Championship in a different host country from one of three global zones: the Australasian Zone (Asia, Australia, New Zealand, and Oceania), the American Zone (North America, South America, and Central America), and the European-African Zone. The World Amateur Team Championship is sponsored by the World Amateur Golf Council (comprised of representatives of national governing bodies of golf in nearly sixty countries) and is contested by four-man teams over four rounds of stroke play competing for the Eisenhower Trophy, named for former United States President and golfing enthusiast Dwight D. Eisenhower. Tied with the United States after four rounds, Australia won a playoff round to win the first World Amateur Team Championship, played in 1958 on the old course at St. Andrews, Scotland.

World Cup: An international competition of over seventy-two holes of stroke play between thirty-two two-man teams of professional players from among over fifty participating nations. Teams compete on the basis of total strokes, with a special award (the International Trophy) going to the player with the lowest individual score. The field is comprised of twenty-two exempt teams (based on five-year performance records) and ten teams that are selected in qualifying events in three geographical zones. Beginning with the 1982 World Cup, five special invitations for the individual competition were also extended to the current PGA Tour leading money-winner, the current British Open, Japanese Open, and Australian Open champions, and the national champion of the host nation. Originally founded by American scholar and industrialist, John Jay Hopkins, in 1953 as the Canada Cup, the competition was renamed the World Cup in 1965, and is sponsored by the commercially funded International Golf Association, headquartered in New York.

World Golf Hall of Fame: An institution that annually honors outstanding players and contributors to golf, and that also serves as a museum and shrine to the sport of golf. Located in Pinehurst, North Carolina, the World Golf Hall of Fame opened in 1974, when the first thirteen inductees were selected. Inductees to the World Golf Hall of Fame are determined in two ways. Selection in the Pre-Modern category is accomplished by a panel of six members of the Golf Writers' Association of America and six members of the Hall of Fame. The Golf Writers' Association membership votes for the candidates in the Modern Era category. The LPGA Hall of Fame is housed within the World Golf Hall of Fame.

World Series of Golf: An international seventy-two-hole stroke play competition, played annually at the Firestone Country Club in Akron, Ohio. First won in 1976 by Jack Nicklaus (prior to 1976, the event was played as a four-man, thirty-six-hole exhibition), the World Series of Golf is open to the winner of the previous World Series, the previous Tournament Players Championship, the previous Masters Tournament, the previous U.S. Open, the previous British Open, the previous PGA Championship, the previous Canadian Open, the previous Western Open, the previous United States Amateur Championship (provided the player is still an amateur), the previous British Amateur Championship (provided the player is still an amateur), the first two finishers in each of the four Season Championships within the PGA Tour, winners of two or more co-sponsored events on the PGA Tour in the previous year, the winner of the PGA National Club Pro Championship, the fifteen leaders on the PGA Tour official money list, and winners or leaders of the Order of Merit rating systems as follows: three each from the European and Japanese Orders of Merit, and two each from the South African, Australian and Asian Golf Circuit Orders of Merit.

yachtsman: A player who "tacks" toward the hole, from one side of the fairway to the other.

yardage marker: A permanent indicator of the starting point from which the length of each hole is measured, firmly attached to the ground at that point on each tee.

yardage rating: The evaluation of the playing difficulty of a course based on yardage alone. compare *course rating, par.*

yip: To mishit a putt, missing the hole as a consequence.

yips: A case of nerves causing a golfer to choke under pressure, missing an easy putt. also *twitch.*

Though rough forms of field hockey date back to 2000 B.C. in Persia, and 500 B.C. in Greece, hockey, or ice hockey, is believed to have originated in eastern Canada in the nineteenth century.

One popular conflicting story tells of a group of French explorers in the St. Lawrence River Valley in 1740 who happened upon a group of Indians chasing a ball over the frozen river. The Indians swung wildly at the ball with curved sticks, yelling, "*ho ghee*" ("it hurts") whenever a player was hit by mistake. Some claim this was the origin of the word "hockey." Others say it is an Anglicized version of the French word *hoquet*, the curved stick or staff of a shepherd.

There is evidence that in 1855, members of an Imperial Army unit, Her Majesty's Royal Canadian Rifles, played a crude kind of hockey game on the ice behind their barracks in Kingston, where "shinny," a sort of field hockey had been played since the 1830s.

In the late 1870s, J.G.A. Creighton, a student at McGill University in Montreal, organized a game he had first tried in his native Halifax. Divided into two teams of thirty players each, Creighton's McGill classmates took part in what is widely regarded as the first rule-structured ice hockey game. It was an immediate success, and soon, students from other schools adopted the new sport, which, unlike tennis, rugby, soccer, or even field hockey, could be played outdoors throughout Canada's long, cold winters. Using folded magazines as shin pads, players clamped skating blades on their shoes and borrowed field hockey sticks to hit a ball, tin can, or other objects between two poles stuck in the ice as goals at each end of the playing area, which was surrounded by one-foot high boards to keep the "puck" in play.

By the 1880s, many colleges had teams, and in 1885, the first league was started in Kingston, including teams from Queen's University (the first league champion) and the Royal Military College, as well as amateur teams from the Kingston Athletics and Kingston Hockey Club. By now, rules specified that each team could have no more than seven players on the ice.

Canadian servicemen spread the game as they were transferred to new posts across Canada, and by the 1890s, hockey rivalled lacrosse as the national sport.

In 1892, at the urging of his aid Lord Killcoursie, Canadian Governor General Frederick Arthur, Lord Stanley of Preston donated a trophy to be given to the best amateur team in Canada. Competition for the "Stanley Cup" (awarded first to the Montreal A.A.A. in 1893) served to unite and strengthen hockey in Canada. The same year, hockey was introduced in the United States in at least two different places.

College tennis stars Malcolm G. Chase and Arthur E. Foote brought the game back to Yale after first trying it while competing in tennis tournaments in Canada. C.S. Shearer, a Johns Hopkins University student from Montreal, arranged the first recorded "international" ice hockey game at the Baltimore, Maryland, campus between Johns Hopkins students and a team from Quebec. By 1896, the first hockey league was formed in the United States: the four-team Amateur Hockey League, organized in New York in November. The first league game was played in December, 1896, between the St. Nicholas and Brooklyn Skating Clubs. One month later, another league was formed in Baltimore, and soon, teams were playing throughout New England and in New York, Chicago, Washington, D.C., Philadelphia, and Pittsburgh.

During the 1880s and 1890s, several amateur hockey leagues were formed in Canada, foremost among them the Amateur Hockey Association (1885), which would become the Canadian Amateur Hockey League (CAHL) in 1899.

The first professional ice hockey team was formed in the United States, albeit with all Canadian players. In 1903, a dentist from Houghton, Michigan, sponsored the first pro team, the Portage Lakers. In their first season, barnstorming from town to town, the Lakers won twenty-four of twenty-six games. To be competitive, other American towns were forced to hire Canadian players, and by 1904, the first professional league was organized, the International Professional Hockey League.

Hockey's first stars (and eventual Hall of Famers) began playing in these early years, including Fred "Cyclone" Taylor, Newsy Lalonde, Sprague Cleghorn, and Art Ross, who later coached the Boston Bruins to three Stanley Cup Championships.

New rules evolved with the professional game, one of the most important of which limited the number of players on the ice to six for each team. Owners struggling to pay the salaries demanded by the best players greeted this rule with enthusiasm, but by 1908, several teams were unable to continue, and the U.S. league was forced to disband. That same year, Canada's first professional league was organized, the Ontario Professional Hockey League.

In 1910, another professional league was formed, the five-team National Hockey Association, including the Montreal Canadiens (the oldest professional hockey team still in existence). With hockey thriving throughout eastern Canada, two enterprising brothers, Frank and Lester Patrick, along with their father, decided to spread professional hockey westward.

Late in 1911, the Patricks formed the Pacific Coast Hockey Association (PCHA), initially with teams in Vancouver, Victoria, and New Westminster. The Patricks added numbers to the backs of players' uniforms, changed the game from two thirty-minute halves to three twenty-minute periods, and introduced blue lines, dividing the rink into three zones.

Since the emergence of professional hockey in Canada in 1910, the Stanley Cup, originally an amateur trophy, had been controlled by the National Hockey Association and had come to be regarded as the symbol of professional hockey supremacy. In 1913, the PCHA champions from Victoria challenged the NHA Quebec Bulldogs to a Stanley Cup championship series. Quebec accepted, and though Victoria, led by Hall of Fame player-coach Joe Malone, won the series, the Bulldogs refused to part with the Stanley Cup.

Both leagues continued to operate through World War I, though their rosters were depleted by players joining the armed forces. In 1917, the PCHA champion Seattle Metropolitans defeated Montreal of the NHA, and the Stanley Cup crossed the U.S.-Canada border for the first time.

By 1917, the NHA had evolved into a viable six-team league, but one owner had become a constant source of problems for the other clubs. To rid themselves of the troublemaker, the other five teams withdrew from the NHA and, in November, 1917, formed the National Hockey League (NHL), naming former NHA secretary Frank Calder as its first president.

The first NHL season featured the Ottawa Senators, the Montreal Canadiens, the Montreal Wanderers, and the Toronto Arenas. The fifth team, the Quebec Bulldogs, did not operate until 1919. Toronto won the NHL's first Stanley Cup in 1918, while Joe Malone, now with the Canadiens, was the first NHL scoring champion, with forty-four goals in the twenty-two-game season. The NHL adopted three-zone blue lines and permitted forward passing in the central zone, and allowed a goaltender to leave his feet to make a save. Previously, a goalie was fined two dollars for making a diving or flopping save.

The International Ice Hockey Federation was formed in 1908, but the first worldwide hockey tournament wasn't held until 1920. Canada won an exhibition ice hockey tournament held that year at the Olympics at Antwerp, Belgium. Hockey was played as an Olympic event in 1924 at the first winter Olympics, held at Chamonix, France. Canada won in 1924 and would win four of the next five Olympic competitions, losing only in 1936 to Great Britain.

By 1924, the NHL had become an international league, adding the Boston Bruins. For the 1925-26 season, two teams in New York, the Americans (formerly the Hamilton Tigers) and the Pittsburgh Pirates, joined the NHL. In 1926, the PCHA was sold to the NHL, which used the players to stock three new franchises in New York (the Rangers), Chicago (the Black Hawks), and Detroit (the Cougars, changed to the Falcons in 1930, and the Red Wings in 1933). The NHL was now a ten-team league, with American and Canadian Divisions, and in sole control of the prized Stanley Cup.

Important rule changes throughout the 1920s and 1930s further opened up the game of ice hockey, including the delayed penalty rule, forward passes within all three zones, penalty shots, passing into the attacking zone (as long as the puck preceded a player across the blue line), and the prohibition of icing.

Among the game's dominant players in the 1930s were Toronto's Charlie Conacher, Howie Morenz, and Toe Blake of the Montreal Canadiens, and Boston's Milt Schmidt. Throughout the 1930s, NHL franchises were moved, added, and dropped, and by 1942, the league had slimmed to six teams, the Montreal Canadiens, Toronto Maple Leafs, Boston Bruins, Chicago Black Hawks, Detroit Red Wings, and the New York Rangers. In 1943, the center or "red" line was introduced in the NHL and forward passing was allowed up to mid-ice, beginning the so-called modern era of ice hockey.

NHL 1940s stars included Montreal's Maurice "Rocket" Richard and Elmer Lach, Bryan Hextall of the New York Rangers, Chicago's Max Bentley, and Ted Lindsay of Detroit. One goaltender, Montreal's Bill Durnan, dominated the decade, winning the NHL's award for goalies, the Vezina Trophy, six out of seven seasons from 1943 through 1950. In 1948, the NCAA held the first National Collegiate Ice Hockey Championship at Colorado Springs, won by Michigan.

Other hockey milestones in the 1940s included the first game televised in the United States (February 25, 1940, station W2XBS in New York, Rangers vs. Canadiens), the first annual NHL All-Star Game (Toronto, 1947), and the rookie season of Detroit's Gordie Howe (1946-47), the first of his NHL record twenty-six seasons played over five decades.

Howe, playing on a line with Sid Abel and Ted Lindsay (nicknamed the "Production Line"), led the Red Wings to Stanley Cup victories in 1949-50, 1951-52, 1953-54, and 1954-55. Backed by the goaltender who developed the protective face mask, Jacques Plante, winner of the Vezina Trophy a record five consecutive times from 1955-56 through

1959-60, and behind the scoring exploits of Jean Beliveau, Bernie "Boom Boom" Geoffrion, Rocket Richard, and Dickie Moore, the Montreal Canadiens took over in 1955-56, winning the Stanley Cup every season for the remainder of the decade. In 1956, Montreal's almost unstoppable power play forced an important rule change, ending a minor penalty as soon as a power play goal was scored.

In 1960, at the Winter Olympics in Squaw Valley, California, the United States hockey team shocked hockey followers around the world by defeating both Canada and Russia to win the Gold Medal. The Russians, after winning at the 1956 Olympics, were becoming the leaders in international amateur hockey, and would win the next four Olympic competitions, employing training methods and a soccer-inspired style of play featuring constant movement and pinpoint passing, which would, years later, find its way into the NHL.

In 1961-62, Bobby Hull became the third player in the history of hockey to score fifty goals in one season (after Rocket Richard in 1944-45 and Boom Boom Geoffrion in 1960-61). Converted to a winger in the 1959 playoffs after two seasons at center, Hull suddenly emerged as hockey's greatest attraction and most feared shooter, with his 110 mph slap shot. Hull's development of the slap shot, made even more dangerous and unpredictable by his use of a curved stick, left a lasting mark on ice hockey.

In 1967, the NHL doubled in size, adding a Western Division with new teams in Los Angeles, Oakland, Minnesota, Philadelphia, Pittsburgh, and St. Louis. The year before, an eighteen-year-old rookie defenseman broke in at Boston who would forever change the game, and, particularly, the role of a defenseman.

Bobby Orr was and remains the greatest defenseman in the history of hockey, and some say, hockey's greatest player. He made the backliner a scoring threat, serving as the prototype of the modern "rushing defenseman." Orr could skate, stickhandle, pass, and shoot better than most forwards, and still get back to check and defend. He undoubtedly would have added to his many NHL records had his career not been interrupted and, in 1978, ended by knee injuries.

Orr was the inspiration behind the Boston Bruins' rise to prominence in the NHL, often scoring the winning goal or making the crucial pass to teammate Phil Esposito, one of the game's great goal scorers. Esposito, who led the league in goals from 1969-70 through the 1974-75 season, became the first NHL player to score over 100 points in a season in 1968-69, and in 1970-71, scored a phenomenal seventy-six goals, a record which would stand in the NHL for eleven years.

In 1972, the NHL expanded to sixteen teams, with new entries in Long Island and Atlanta, and a rival league was born, the World Hockey Association (WHA), with twelve new teams. A bidding war resulted, with some of the NHL stars following Bobby Hull to the new league. Gordie Howe came out of retirement to play with his sons in the WHA, which would operate in twenty-eight cities over a seven-year period.

In 1972 the so-called "Summit Series" between the NHL All-Stars, called "Team Canada," and the national team from the USSR was held. The Russians had dominated every Olympic and international competition since 1962. But those who followed pro hockey discounted the Russians' success, since the best North American players were in the NHL, and thus were ineligible for international "amateur" competition. Most experts predicted that Team Canada would win the series easily, perhaps sweeping all eight games. Instead, the Soviets stunned Team Canada 7-3 in the first game. By the time the series was moved to Russia for the final four games, the NHL players had lost two and tied one of the four games played at home. National disgrace turned to celebration when Team Canada rallied to take the series, winning three of the four Russian games, the last one on a goal by Paul Henderson in the final thirty-four seconds of the third period.

Though their honor had been preserved in the historic series, Canada and the NHL were forced to concede that hockey was now truly a world sport.

Despite losing players to the WHA, the NHL continued to grow, adding new teams in Washington, D.C., and Kansas City (later moved to Colorado, then New Jersey) in 1974 to become an eighteen-team league. With nearly thirty professional teams in North America, the quality of play slipped measurably. New strategies were developed as strong, physically aggressive players were brought into the leagues to supplement the few skilled players. A rough, bruising style of play began to emerge in which physical intimidation played an ever-increasing role. The expansion Philadelphia Flyers earned the nickname "Broad Street Bullies" as they bumped and brawled their way to back-to-back Stanley Cup Championship victories in 1973-74 and 1974-75.

In 1979, the long-awaited merger took place between the WHA and the NHL, with four surviving WHA teams (Edmonton, Hartford, Quebec, and Winnipeg) brought into the NHL, now a twenty-one-team league (the Cleveland team, moved from Oakland in 1976, had merged with Minnesota in 1978). In February, 1979, the Soviet National Team faced an NHL All-Star team for a three-game "Challenge Cup" series. This time, the NHL team was beaten soundly, managing to win only the first game against the fast-skating, sharpshooting Russians. United States owners and coaches began to look more and more to European players to help with the transition to the smoother, quicker style of hockey played by the Soviets.

The 1979-80 season was a milestone, as Gordie Howe, at age fifty-one, played his thirty-second and final year of professional hockey, after a record twenty-six NHL seasons, 801 goals, 1,049 assists, and 1,850 career points. But that year another superstar appeared in hockey, who well may be the first player to surpass Howe's amazing career scoring totals. Edmonton's eighteen-year-old Wayne Gretzky in his first NHL season led the league in assists (86), tied with the Los Angeles Kings' Marcel Dionne in total scoring points (137), and won both the Hart and Lady Byng Trophies. In only his third year, Gretzky would break Phil Esposito's eleven-year-old record for goals in one season, scoring a phenomenal 92 goals in 1981-82, and setting new NHL records for assists (120), and total points (212).

The 1980 Winter Olympics saw a group of young American college players, led by a relatively unknown coach, Herb Brooks, shock the sports world by winning the Gold Medal, defeating the Soviet team that had the year before embarrassed the NHL. Brooks used a style of play that combined the traditional North American checking with European puck control. Eighteen months later, he would bring his Olympic-style hockey to the NHL, as coach of the New York Rangers, and, for the first time, American college players (among them, the Olympians) began to take their place alongside the Canadians and Europeans in the NHL.

With increased interest in collegiate hockey, and a change to a faster, more artistic, and entertaining style of play in the NHL, one that favors superstars like Gretzky, Dionne, Montreal's Guy Lafleur, Buffalo's Gilbert Perreault, and Mike Bossy and Brian Trottier of the New York Islanders, hockey's popularity can only grow.

Adams Division: One of the two divisions in the NHL Prince of Wales Conference, comprised of teams from Boston, Buffalo, Hartford, Montreal, and Quebec. Named in memory of Charles F. Adams, co-founder of the Boston Bruins in 1924. compare *Patrick Division*.

AHAUS: The Amateur Hockey Association of the United States.

All-Star: A player selected to participate in the annual NHL All-Star Game. see *All-Star Game*.

All-Star Game: The annual midseason exhibition game between the best players of the Prince of Wales Conference and the Clarence Campbell Conference, selected by members of the Professional Hockey Writers' Association. Additional players are chosen by the coaches of each team. Prior to the inception in 1947 of an annual All-Star Game, there had been three benefit games in which stars of the NHL teams at the time opposed one regular team (1934, 1937, and 1939). The 1947-1950 format pitted the previous season's All-Star Team against the previous season's Stanley Cup champion. After 1951 and 1952, when the First All-Star Team of the previous season, augmented by members of the four United States teams played against the Second All-Star Team of the previous season, augmented by members of the two Canadian teams, the original format was resumed until the 1968-69 season, when West Division teams opposed players from East Division teams. This lasted until the present format was adopted in 1975. In 1979, the All-Star Game was replaced by a three-game series between the NHL All-Stars and the Soviet Union for the Challenge Cup, won by the Soviet Union, two games to one. The regular All-Star game format was resumed in 1980.

alternate captain: A player who functions as team captain at any time the actual captain is off the ice, identified by the letter "A" on his jersey.

Amateur Hockey Association of the United States: The governing body of amateur hockey in the United States, responsible for the preparation and supervision of national teams to participate in World Championship and Olympic competition. Founded in New York in 1937, the Amateur Hockey Association of the United States is an affiliate member of the International Ice Hockey Federation, and is headquartered in Colorado Springs, Colorado. also *AHAUS.*

Art Ross Trophy: The annual award given to the player who leads the NHL in scoring points (goals plus assists) at the end of the regular season. Named after former manager-coach of the Boston Bruins, Arthur Howie Ross, who presented the trophy to the NHL in 1947. The award was first given in 1948 to Elmer Lach of the Montreal Canadiens.

1. assist: To tip or pass the puck to a teammate who scores a goal, or to a teammate who then tips or passes it to the goal scorer.

2. assist: A scoring point earned by tipping or passing the puck to a teammate who scores a goal, or to a teammate who then tips or passes to the goal scorer. A maximum of two assists can be credited for any goal scored. Gordie Howe holds the all-time NHL career record for assists, 1,049 in 1,767 games played over twenty-six seasons (Detroit Red Wings, Hartford Whalers). Wayne Gretzky of the Edmonton Oilers set the NHL one-season record, scoring 120 in 1981-82.

attacking zone: The area that contains the goal a team is shooting at, extending from the end of the rink (behind the goal) to the nearest blue line. also *attack zone, offensive zone.* compare *defensive zone, neutral zone.*

attack zone: see *attacking zone.*

awarded goal: A point awarded when an attacking player in control of the puck in the offensive zone moves toward an unprotected net (with the goalie off the ice and no defenders in the zone) and is fouled from behind or interfered with by an opponent illegally entering the game, or when the goaltender throws his stick at the puck or at an opponent taking a penalty shot.

backcheck: To check an opponent or opponents in one's own defensive zone. compare *forecheck.*

1. backhand: A shot or pass made with the back side of the blade.

2. backhand: To pass or shoot the puck with a backhand motion. (backhanded the rebound and scored)

backline: 1. The defensemen. (a strong, hard-checking backline) 2. The defensive positions. (playing on the backline)

backliner: see *defenseman.*

banana blade: A stick with a pronounced curve in the blade to give better control of the puck when shooting. The maximum amount of curvature allowed in the blade of a stick is 1/2 inch in NHL and college hockey and 1.5 centimeters in international amateur hockey. A player caught using an illegally curved stick is subject to a minor penalty (and, additionally, a fine in the NHL).

beat: 1. To momentarily take advantage of an opponent, or get past an opponent. (beat the defenseman and took a shot) 2. To score with a shot past the goaltender. (beat the goalie on the stick side)

bench minor, bench minor penalty: A two-minute penalty for various infractions assessed against a coach, manager, trainer, or a player who is not on the ice. Any player except a goaltender may be designated by the coach or the playing captain to serve a bench minor penalty.

between the pipes: 1. In the goal, a goal scored. (put one between the pipes with his slap shot to tie the game) 2. see *in the nets.*

big save: A difficult and/or important save, especially one made at a crucial point in a game. (frustrated the opposing team with one big save after another)

Bill Masterson Memorial Trophy: The annual award given to the NHL player who best exemplifies the qualities of perseverence, sportsmanship, and dedication to hockey, as selected by the Professional Hockey Writers' Association. Named in memory of Minnesota North Stars player William Masterton, who exemplified the qualities for which the award is given (and who became the first NHL player to be fatally injured in a game in 1968), the award was first given to Claude Provost of the Montreal Canadiens in 1968. A $1,500 grant from the Professional Hockey Writers' Association is awarded annually to the Bill Masterton Scholarship Fund, based in Bloomington, Minnesota, in the name of the Bill Masterton Memorial Trophy winner. also *Masterton Trophy.*

blade: 1. The flat part at one end of a hockey stick used to control and shoot the puck. see *hockey stick.* 2. The metal (or hard plastic) strip on the bottom of an ice skate that tracks along the surface of the ice.

blocker: see *blocking glove.*

blocking glove: A large padded leather glove worn by a goaltender on the hand that holds the stick. An extra rectangular pad that may not exceed 16 inches in length nor 8 inches in width is attached to the back of a blocking glove. also *blocker.*

blocking glove save: A save made by a goaltender with the blocking glove. compare *glove save, kick save, pad save, stick save.*

blue line: Either of two 12-inch-wide painted blue lines extending the width of the rink (and continued vertically up the sideboards), 60 feet from and parallel to the goal lines. The blue lines divide the ice into the defensive zone, the neutral zone, and the attacking zone, and are used to determine offside and two-line pass violations. Blue lines were among the innovations introduced in 1911 by the Pacific Coast Hockey Association.

blueliner: see *defenseman.*

board: see *board-check.*

board check: The act of board-checking.

board-check: To body check an opponent by pushing him into the boards and out of the play. If done with violence, or to a player other than the puck carrier, a penalty results. also *board.* see *boarding.*

board-checking: see *boarding.*

boarding: The act of illegally board-checking an opponent, resulting in a major or minor penalty at the discretion of the referee, depending upon the degree of violence of the impact with the boards. also *board-checking.*

boards: The 3-foot, 4-inch to 4-foot-high wooden or fiberglass wall or fence surrounding the surface of the ice. An unbreakable glass or wire screen is mounted on top of the boards to protect spectators. also *dasher boards, fence.*

body check: The act or an instance of bodychecking an opponent.

bodycheck: To, with the upper part of the body, bump or physically contact an opponent above the knees who is in

BOARDING

possession of, contesting for, or approaching the puck. Legal as long as contact is made from the front or side from no more than two strides away and the checker's feet do not leave the ice at the moment of contact.

body checker: A player who is known for his ability to bodycheck. also *checker, hitter.*

box: 1. see *penalty box.* 2. A defensive strategy in which the four remaining players of a shorthanded team form a square in the defensive zone.

breakaway: A momentary scoring opportunity in which an attacking player with the puck skates into the attacking zone toward the opposing goalie with no other defensive player between him and the net. (scored on a breakaway near the end of the second period)

break out: To gain possession of the puck in the defensive end and skate or pass it out to begin an attack. (stuck in their own end, unable to break out)

breakout: A play in which a team gains possession of the puck in its defensive zone and moves it out to begin an attack.

broomball: An informal hockey-type game in which players wear tennis shoes instead of skates and use brooms with taped bristles to maneuver a soccer ball around the ice and shoot at normal hockey goals.

butt: The tip at the top end of a hockey stick.

butt-end: To illegally poke an opposing player with the butt of a stick. see *butt-ending.*

butt-ending: The act of poking or attempting to poke an opposing player with the butt of a stick, incurring a major penalty (and an automatic fine in the NHL).

cage: see *goal.*

Calder Memorial Trophy: The annual award given to the outstanding rookie of the year, as selected by the Professional Hockey Writers' Association. To be eligible, a player must be in his first year of competition, or cannot have played more than five games in any single preceding season nor in six or more games in each of any two preceding seasons in any major professional leagues. Named after Frank Calder, first President of the National Hockey League. From 1936-37 until his death in 1943, Calder bought a trophy each year to be given to the outstanding rookie. After his death, the NHL presented the Calder Memorial Trophy in his memory. The first recipient in 1943 was Gaye Stewart of the Toronto Maple Leafs.

camp by the side of the net: To take a position in front of or just to the side of the opposing net so as to be in position to score on a tip in or rebound, or to screen the goalie while a teammate shoots.

carry the puck: To skate with the puck, controlling it with a hockey stick.

catching glove: A padded leather glove that is worn by a goalie on the hand opposite the hand that holds the stick, and that is used to catch the puck. also *glove.*

caught in a linechange: At a momentary numerical disadvantage due to a linechange at an inopportune time, often the result of an attempt to "change on the fly."

caught up ice: Out of position in the offensive zone while the opposing team is attacking at the other end of the ice, leaving one's defending teammates outnumbered.

1. center: 1. The player between two wings on the forward line, usually responsible for taking faceoffs. Normally playing in the central portion of the ice, the center often leads an attack, moving the puck into the offensive zone and shooting, or passing to a teammate and taking a position near the net to wait for a tip in or rebound, or to screen the goalie while a teammate shoots. also *centerman.* 2. The position played by the center. (will play at center tonight) 3. see *centering pass.*

2. center: 1. To play the position of center. 2. To pass the puck from either side into the central area in front of the goal, to make a centering pass. (centered the puck to a teammate who tipped it in for an easy score)

center circle: The center ice circle.

center faceoff spot: The faceoff spot inside the center ice circle at the center of the ice, 1 foot in diameter and painted blue in the NHL, and 2 feet in diameter and painted red in amateur hockey. also *center ice spot.*

center ice: 1. The center or neutral zone between the blue lines. (cleared the puck to a teammate at center ice) 2. The center ice circle or faceoff spot. (will face off at center ice)

center ice circle: The faceoff circle surrounding the center ice spot in the exact center of the rink, bisected by the center line. also *center circle.*

center ice spot: see *center faceoff spot.*

centering pass: A pass from the side into the central area in front of the goal. also *center.*

center line: see *red line.*

centerman: see *center.*

center zone: see *center ice.*

change on the fly: To substitute players or change lines while play continues, rather than waiting for a stoppage of play.

1. charge: To illegally run or jump into an opponent, such as from behind or more than two strides away. see *charging.*

2. charge: 1. The act or an instance of illegally running or jumping into an opponent. see *charging.* 2. A foul called as a result of illegally running or jumping into an opponent. (will try to draw a charge to get a power play) also *charging.*

charging: A foul in which a player runs or jumps into an opponent from behind or more than two strides away. Charging results in a minor or major penalty, depending upon the severity of the foul. also *charge.*

1. check: To use the upper part of the body (in the case of a body check) or the hip (in the case of a hip check) to legally bump an opponent away from the puck or play, or to use the stick to trap, poke, or sweep the puck away from the puck carrier (as in the case of a hook check, poke check, or sweep check).

2. check: The act or an instance of checking an opponent. also *hit.*

checker: 1. A player in the act of checking an opponent. (slipped away from the checker and scored) 2. A player who is known for his skill at checking. also *body checker, hitter.*

checking line: A line or set of three forwards whose primary role is to prevent the other team from scoring, with offense only a secondary consideration. The checking line is used against the opposing team's highest-scoring line whenever possible.

chest pad: A padded chest protector worn under a goalie's jersey to shield the upper body from the puck.

chippy: Unnecessarily rough or physical, as of one or more fouls, the play of one or more individuals or a team, a period of play, or a game in general. (settled down after a chippy first period)

circle: see *faceoff circle.*

Clarence S. Campbell Bowl: The award presented annually to the team finishing with the most points in the Clarence S. Campbell Conference at the end of the regular championship schedule. Named for Clarence S. Campbell, President of the NHL from 1946 to 1977, the trophy was from 1968 through 1974 awarded to the champions of the then West Division, changing to the present system for the 1974-75 season.

Clarence S. Campbell Conference: One of two NHL conferences, each comprised of two divisions. The Clarence S. Campbell Conference, named after Clarence S. Campbell, President of the NHL from 1946 to 1977, includes teams from the Norris Division and the Smythe Division. see *Norris Division, Smythe Division.* compare *Prince of Wales Conference.*

clear: 1. To knock the puck safely away from one's own goal, or out of the defensive zone. (stopped the puck twice, but his defensemen couldn't clear it before the scoring shot) also *clear the puck.* 2. To push or knock an opponent away from the slot in front of one's goal. also *clear the slot.*

clearing pass: A pass designed to move the puck out of the defensive zone (and danger) to a teammate in the neutral zone.

clear the puck: see *clear.*

clear the slot: see *clear.*

close checking: A style of play that emphasizes constant defensive pressure. also *tight checking.*

coincidental majors: see *coincident major penalties.*

coincidental minors: see *coincident minor penalties.*

coincident major penalties: Simultaneous major penalties assessed against both teams. also *coincidental majors.*

coincident minor penalties: Simultaneous minor penalties assessed against both teams. also *coincidental minors.*

coincident penalties: see *coincident major penalties, coincident minor penalties.*

come up big: 1. To make a particularly difficult, courageous, or crucial play. (came up big with a diving save on a point-blank shot to preserve the win) 2. To play particularly well or courageously. (came up big in the final after two shaky games)

Conn Smythe Trophy: The annual award given to the player selected by the Professional Hockey Writers' Association as the most valuable player for his team in the Stanley Cup playoffs. Named in honor of Conn Smythe, former coach, manager, president, and owner-governor of the Toronto Maple Leafs. The Conn Smythe Trophy was first given in 1965 to Jean Beliveau of the Montreal Canadiens.

corner: The area of the ice adjacent to any of the four rounded corners of a rink where the sideboards and endboards meet. (not afraid to go into the corners for the puck)

cornerman: see *digger.*

crease: see *goal crease.*

crossbar: The 6-foot-long horizontal bar that connects the goal posts 4 feet above the surface of the ice, marking the upper limit of the goal.

1. cross-check: To commit an act of cross-checking. see *cross-checking.*

2. cross-check: The act or an instance of cross-checking. see *cross-checking.*

cross-checking: The act of illegally hitting an opponent with the stick held in both hands, and no part of the stick touching the ice. A player guilty of cross-checking is assessed a minor or major penalty, at the discretion of the referee.

crossover: A skating technique used to gain speed while making a curve, in which the outside foot crosses ahead of the skating foot and is placed down inside. The weight then shifts to that foot for a thrust as the inside leg is moved back around in position to accept the weight and glide at the start of the next cycle.

cut down the angle: To skate out from the crease toward an onrushing puck carrier so that he will be able to see less of the goal.

dasher: The small ledge at the top of the boards.

dasher boards: see *boards.*

defender: see *defenseman.*

defending zone: see *defensive zone.*

defenseman: One of two players (other than the goalie) whose primary responsibility is to prevent the opposing team from scoring and, if possible, to gain possession of the puck. Defensemen are usually positioned behind and closer to their own goal than the forwards, and though often called upon to back up or sustain an attack (by playing the point and keeping the puck inside the offensive zone), must always be ready to get back on defense when the opposing team gains control of the puck. also *backliner, blueliner, defender.*

defensive shell: A strategy in which a team's forwards make little or no effort to score, but concentrate on defense instead, and preventing the opposing team from scoring. A defensive shell is most often employed by a team to protect a lead near the end of the game.

defensive zone: The area that contains the goal a team is defending, extending from the end of the rink (behind the defended goal) to the nearest blue line. compare *attacking zone, neutral zone.*

deflection: A shot, pass, or errant puck which is deflected toward the goal after striking a stick, skate, or player. (picked up his second goal on a deflection off his skate)

1. deke: 1. To fake a motion or a movement in a certain direction in order to momentarily deceive an opponent. (deked to his forehand side before scoring with the backhand) 2. To momentarily deceive an opponent by a fake. (deked the goalie and scored)

2. deke: A simulated move or faked action that is intended to momentarily deceive an opponent. (got past the defenseman with a little deke)

delayed offside: A situation in which a linesman delays blowing the whistle to signal an offside because the puck is intercepted by a defending player at or near the blue line. In such a case, the offside is called only if the defending player loses possession of the puck before skating or passing it out of the defensive zone. also *delayed whistle, slow whistle.*

delayed penalty: 1. A penalty called while the penalized team already has two players in the penalty box, leaving the minimum four players on the ice. In such a case, the penalized player must proceed at once to the penalty box, but may be replaced by a substitute until the penalty time of one of the two previously penalized teammates has elapsed, at which time the official penalty time of the third penalized player commences. A delayed penalty is called to insure that no less than the minimum of four players are on the ice at all times. 2. A penalty called on the defending team while the attacking team controls the puck. In such a case, the referee raises one arm and points to the offending player, but does not blow the whistle or stop play until the attacking team loses control of the puck or a goal is scored. If a goal is scored, the penalty is enforced only if it is a major penalty. also *delayed whistle, slow whistle.*

delayed whistle: 1. see *delayed offside.* 2. see *delayed penalty.*

delaying the game: An infraction in which a player attempts to delay the progress of a game, called most frequently when a player deliberately shoots or bats the puck with his stick outside the playing area (resulting in a minor penalty), freezes the puck against the net or boards without being checked (resulting in a minor penalty), deliberately displaces a goal post from its normal position (resulting in a minor penalty and, if during the course of a breakaway by an opponent, a penalty shot), or if a team stalls or refuses to place the correct number of players on the ice and commence play, makes additional substitutions, or persists in having its players offside after a warning by the referee to the team's captain or designated substitute (resulting in a bench minor penalty).

dig: To contest opposing players for possession of the puck in the corners.

digger: A player who excels at "digging." also *cornerman.*

dive, dive job: A faked or exaggerated fall to call the referee's attention to an alleged foul in the hopes that a penalty will be assessed against an opponent. (an obvious dive job that the referee ignored)

double minor: The assessment of two minor penalties against one player at the same time, for one or two different infractions, each carrying a two-minute penalty.

down a man: Shorthanded, outnumbered by one player because of a penalty. (were down a man for half the third period) also *short a man.*

1. draw: see *faceoff.*

2. draw: 1. To face off against an opponent. (will have to draw against their best faceoff man) 2. To win a faceoff, pulling the puck back toward a teammate. (will try to draw the puck back to the point)

drop pass: A pass in which a moving puck carrier stops the puck, leaving it for or tapping it back to a teammate behind him, and continues without breaking stride in the hopes of deceiving a member of the opposing team.

drop the gloves: To take off one's hockey gloves in preparation for a fight.

dump the puck: To move the puck into the offensive end by knocking it into one of the corners and skating in after it (or in anticipation of a teammate skating after it), rather than trying to stickhandle the puck into the zone.

elbow: To illegally strike an opponent with the elbow. see *elbowing.*

elbowing: The act of illegally striking an opponent with the elbow, resulting in a major or minor penalty at the discretion of the referee.

elbow pad: A padded protective covering for the elbow joint, usually made of a hard plastic or composition material on the outside with soft padding underneath.

empty net: A goal left unguarded by a goaltender, either because he is out of position, or off the ice to enable an extra attacking player to skate, as in the case of a delayed penalty or a desperate attempt to tie or win in the closing minutes of a game. (deked the goalie out of position and flipped the puck into the empty net) also *open net.*

empty net goal: A goal scored into a net left unguarded by the opposing goalie, as in the last minutes of a game when the goalie has been pulled. also *open net goal.*

end: Either of the two zones in which the nets are located. Usually a team's defensive zone is referred to as "their end." (having a lot of trouble getting the puck out of their own end) also *end zone.*

endboards: The section of boards at either end of the rink behind the goals.

end-to-end action: Non-stop play that alternates at both ends of the rink, as the two teams take turns attempting to score.

end zone: see *end.*

enforcer: see *policeman.*

extra attacker: An additional player (usually a forward) who substitutes for the goalie when the goalie is pulled because of a delayed penalty or a desperate attempt to tie or win in the closing minutes of a game. also *sixth attacker.*

face mask: see *goalie mask.*

face off: To participate in a faceoff. (usually assigned to face off against the opposing team's best center) also *draw.*

faceoff: The beginning of play at the start of a period, after a goal, or after any stoppage of play. In a faceoff, the referee or a linesman drops or throws the puck on the ice between two opposing players (usually centers) lined up squarely facing each other (and the goal at which they are shooting) approximately one stick length apart with the blades of their sticks on the ice. Both then attempt to gain control of the puck or tap it to a teammate (or

sometimes, attempt to shoot the puck directly at the opponent's goal). Faceoffs may be held any place on the ice where play is stopped, except within 15 feet of the goal or the sideboards. In this case, and when play is to be resumed in a different zone (as for icing, etc.), a faceoff occurs at one of the nine marked faceoff spots. At the beginning of a period and after a goal, the faceoff is held at the center ice spot. No other players may come within 15 feet of the players participating in a faceoff (or inside the 15-foot circle within which a faceoff occurs) until the puck is dropped and contact is made. also *draw.* see *faceoff circle, faceoff spot.*

faceoff circle: Any of the five 15-foot radius restraining circles marked around the faceoff spots at center ice and in the two end zones. When a faceoff occurs no one but the referee or linesman and the two participating players is permitted inside the faceoff circle until the puck is dropped and contacted. also *circle, restraining circle.*

faceoff spot: Any of nine round spots painted on the ice to mark the site of a faceoff in certain circumstances. A 1-foot-diameter (or 2-foot-diameter in

FACEOFF

college hockey) blue spot is marked in the middle of the center line, the center faceoff spot. This is used primarily at the start of each period and after a goal is scored. Four 2-foot-diameter red faceoff spots are marked in the neutral zone, 5 feet from each blue line and 22 feet on both sides of an imaginary line joining the exact centers of the two goals. These are used primarily when a stoppage of play occurs within 15 feet of the sideboards in the neutral zone, when an offside is called, and when a player draws a penalty or causes a stoppage of play in his attacking zone. Two 2-foot-diameter red faceoff spots are marked in each end zone, 20 feet from the goal lines and 22 feet on both sides of an imaginary line joining the centers of the two goals. These are used most often when a stoppage of play occurs within 15 feet of the goal or the sideboards, when icing is called, and after a penalty shot is missed.

fan: To miss hitting the puck on an attempted pass or shot. (had an open net, but he fanned on the shot)

1. feed: To pass the puck to a teammate in position for a shot on goal.

2. feed: A pass to a teammate in position for a shot on goal.

fence: see *boards*.

finish off a check: To continue the action of a check long enough to insure that the checked opponent is out of the play. (got the puck back and scored because the defenseman didn't finish off the check) also *hold a check*.

flat pass: A pass in which the puck slides along the surface of the ice without lifting or bouncing.

flip pass: A pass made with a quick snap of the wrist to "flip" the puck off the ice, often to clear an opponent's stick or skate.

flip shot: A shot made with a quick snap of the wrist in which the puck is "flipped" toward the goal.

floater: 1. A deceptively slow shot. (fooled the goalie with a floater from the point) 2. A player who stays out in the neutral zone when his goal is under attack to be in position for a quick breakout or a possible breakaway when his team gets possession of the puck. also *hanger, sleeper*.

flop: To drop to the ice in order to make a save. (flopped and made a kick save to stop the breakaway)

flopper: A goaltender known for flopping saves. compare *standup goalie*.

forecheck: To check an opponent or the opposing team in their defensive zone in order to prevent an attack from being started and to gain possession of the puck. compare *backcheck*.

forechecker: A player who forechecks.

forehand: A shot or a pass made with the front face of the blade.

forward: Any of the three players making up the forward line: the left wing, the right wing, and the center. Forwards are primarily offensive players.

forward line: 1. The three forwards: the left wing, the right wing, and the center. 2. A group of three players (a left wing, a right wing, and a center) who play together as a unit. also *line*.

four-pointer: A victory over a rival in the same division. Two points are awarded to a team's point totals (used to determine division standings and playoff participants) for each victory (one point for a tie, none for a loss). A win over a division rival not only yields the two points for the victory, but insures that the rival has lost an opportunity to gain two points within the division, and, thus, is called a four-pointer.

Frank J. Selke Trophy: The annual award given to the NHL forward who best excels in the defensive aspects of the game, as selected by the Professional Hockey Writers' Association. Named in honor of Frank J. Selke, former general manager of the Montreal Canadiens (1952-53 through 1959-60), and one of the great architects of NHL championship teams. The award was first given to Bob Gainey of the Montreal Canadiens in 1978. Gainey also won the award in 1979, 1980, and 1981, becoming the first player in NHL history to win an individual award in each of the award's first four seasons. also *Selke Trophy*.

freeze the goalie: To make a goaltender hesitate momentarily with a deke or fake. (froze the goalie with a little deke to his forehand side, and put the backhand in the net)

freeze the puck: A strategy for forcing a faceoff in which a player stops the puck against the boards or the back of the goal with his stick or skates, thus taking it out of play. If only one player attempts to freeze the puck (with no opponents contending for it), a minor penalty results for delaying the game.

full strength: All six players on the ice, with none in the penalty box. (skating at full strength for most of the third period)

game misconduct: A penalty in which a player is suspended for the balance of the game (and ten penalty minutes are charged in his records) for serious infractions such as being the third man to join in an altercation, or continuing an altercation after being separated by the linesmen. When a game misconduct is given, a substitute is permitted to immediately replace the player removed from the game. compare *gross misconduct, match penalty.*

game timekeeper: The minor official responsible for recording the starting and finishing time of each period (and sounding a buzzer or bell signifying the finish of a period) and all playing time during the game, and causing an announcement to be made at the nineteenth minute in each period that one minute remains to be played in the period.

garbage: see *garbage goal.*

garbage collector: A player (most often a center) who excels at scoring goals from rebounds, deflections, or on tip ins, usually from close to the goal. also *garbage man.* see *garbage goal.*

garbage goal: A goal that is not considered "clean" or "artistic," but rather, an easy or lucky goal, such as an easy rebound with the goalie out of position, or an accidental deflection off another player's body. (won it on a garbage

GOAL CREASE

goal kicked in by the defenseman) also *garbage.*

garbage man: see *garbage collector.*

give and go: To execute a give-and-go.

give-and-go: A play in which the puckhandler passes the puck to a teammate, then skates past one or more defenders to receive a return pass in the clear.

glove: 1. One of a set of two padded leather gloves worn by players to protect the backside of the hands and fingers from injury. 2. see *catching glove.*

glove hand: The hand on which the goaltender wears the catching glove.

glove save: A save made with the goaltender's catching glove. compare *blocking glove save, kick save, pad save, stick save.*

glove side: The side on which a goaltender wears the catching glove. (beat him on his glove side with a little wrist shot) compare *stick side.*

goal: 1. The structure centered on each goal line into which the puck must be played in order to score. A goal consists of a rectangular metal frame with two 4-foot-high goal posts (set over metal rods or pipes affixed in and projecting from the ice on the goal line to hold them in place) connected at the top by a 6-foot-long crossbar, with a metal frame (made up of two curved sections that resemble the figure 3) extending back horizontally at the top and base of the structure, and draped with a nylon mesh net to completely enclose the back of the frame. also *cage, net, nets.* 2. A point scored as a result of the puck being played (from the stick of an attacking player or from a deflection off of any part of an attacking or defending player) completely over the goal line between the goal posts and under the crossbar. A goal is credited in the scoring records (one point) to the player who propels the puck into the opponents' goal (or to the last offensive player to touch it before the goal). The NHL record for the most goals scored in one game was set in 1920, when Joe Malone of the Quebec Bulldogs scored seven goals against the Toronto St. Patricks. In the 1981-82 season, Wayne Gretzky of the Edmonton Oilers broke Phil Esposito's 1970-71 NHL record of 76 goals (in seventy-eight regular season games for the Boston Bruins), scoring 92 goals in eighty regular season games. Hockey Hall of Famer Gordie Howe (Detroit Red Wings, Hartford Whalers) holds the NHL career record for regular season goals, scoring 801 goals in his twenty-six seasons and 1,767 games. In 1979, New York Islanders goalie Billy Smith made history, becoming the first goaltender ever to score a goal in the NHL. Smith was credited with the goal when he was ruled the last Islander to touch the puck (on a save) before an errant pass of the rebound went the length of the ice into the Colorado Rockies' open net. 3. The position played by a goaltender. (must decide who will play goal) see *goaltender*.

goal crease: A rectangular area marked on the ice in front of each goal, 8 feet wide, and extending 4 feet out from the goal line (or, in college play, a semi-circle with a 6-foot radius extending out from the goal line). No attacking player may enter or hold his stick in the goal crease unless the puck is within it. also *crease*.

goaler: 1. A popular Canadian term for a goaltender. 2. The position played by a goaltender.

goalie: 1. see *goaltender*. 2. The position played by a goaltender.

goalie mask: Either of two kinds of protective devices worn by a goalie to shield his face from being hit by a puck, a molded plastic mask with small holes for the eyes and mouth held in place by straps, or a steel cage, padded and held in place by straps, or attached to a helmet. In 1929, Montreal Maroons goaltender Clint Benedict wore a mask briefly, while recovering from a broken nose, but Hall of Fame goalie Jacques Plante of the Montreal Canadiens is credited with developing and popularizing the goalie mask in the NHL. After being struck in the face by a puck during a game in 1959, Plante returned to the ice wearing a plastic mask, but, unlike Benedict, he continued to use a mask for the rest of his career. Andy Brown of the Pittsburgh Penguins (1973-74) was the last NHL goaltender to play without a goalie mask. also *face mask, mask*.

goal judge: Either of two minor officials who decide whether or not the puck has passed between the goal posts and over the goal line for a goal, and who

signify the scoring of a goal by switching on the red light set up behind each goal. The referee may overrule a goal judge's decision to allow or disallow a goal. The goal judges sit in screened cages behind the boards in back of each goal.

goalkeeper: 1. see *goaltender*. 2. The position played by a goaltender.

goalkeeping: see *goaltending*.

goal light: A red light at both ends of the rink behind the goals, activated by the goal judge when a goal has been scored. Goal lights were made mandatory in the NHL in 1945.

goal line: A 2-inch-wide, red-painted line extending the width of the ice (and continued vertically up the sideboards), 10 feet from and parallel to each end of the rink, in the center of which is the goal. A puck that entirely crosses the vertical plane of the goal line between the goal posts and under the crossbar counts for a goal, scoring one point.

goal mouth: The opening at the front of a goal formed by the goal posts and top crossbar. In common usage, the meaning of the term is expanded to include the area immediately in front of the opening of the goal.

GOALIE MASK

CATCHING GLOVE

GOALIE

goal mouth scramble: A scramble between opposing players for control of the puck immediately in front of the goal.

goal post, goalpost: Either of two 4-foot-high posts, 6 feet apart and connected at the top by a crossbar, that constitute the side boundaries of each goal. also *pipe, post.*

goals against: The total number of goals allowed by a goaltender or team within a specified time, such as a period, a game, or a season.

goals against average: The statistic reflecting the average number of goals allowed by a goaltender in one sixty-minute game, computed by multiplying the total number of goals against by sixty, then dividing by the total number of minutes played, usually carried two decimal places (a goaltender who has played a total of 1,777 minutes and given up 71 goals has a goals against average of 2.40).

goaltender: 1. The defensive player normally positioned directly in front of the goal. Specially equipped with a goalie mask, chest pad, padded leg guards, a large padded blocking glove (with which an enlarged stick with a long wide blade is held), and a catching glove (with which the puck may legally be caught), the goaltender is responsible for preventing the other team from scoring by blocking, catching, or deflecting the puck before it enters the net. The goaltender may not be checked while he is in the crease, and when assessed a minor, major, or misconduct penalty, is allowed to remain in the goal while another member of his team serves the penalty. If assessed a match, or a game, or gross misconduct penalty, a goaltender must leave the ice. also *goaler, goalie, goalkeeper, man between the pipes, netminder, puckstopper.* 2. The position played by a goaltender. also *goal, goaler, goalie, goalkeeper, man between the pipes, netminder, puckstopper.*

goaltending: The action of defending the goal. also *goalkeeping, netminding.*

goon: A particularly rough or violent player, one who is noted more for fighting than for hockey skills. also *hatchetman, headhunter.* compare *enforcer, policeman.*

goon it up: To fight, or play in an extremely rough or aggressive manner.

green light: A green-colored signal light set up behind each goal at the end of the rink and linked with the game clock to light automatically at the end of a period or the game. A goal cannot be scored when the green lights are on.

gross misconduct: A penalty in which a player, manager, coach, or trainer is suspended for the balance of a game for "gross misconduct" of any kind. Ten minutes is charged in the records against a player who incurs a gross misconduct (and an automatic fine is assessed in the NHL), but a substitute may immediately replace the offending player. compare *game misconduct, match penalty.*

gunner: A player noted for his skill at shooting the puck. also *sniper.*

Hall of Fame: see *Hockey Hall of Fame, United States Hockey Hall of Fame.*

handcuff the goalie: To place a shot so that the goalie is unable to try to make a save because of his position or the position of his stick or his glove hand. (handcuffed the goalie with a quick wrist shot high on his stick side)

hand pass: An illegal play in which the puck is deliberately thrown, batted or deflected toward a teammate, resulting in a minor penalty. A player is permitted to stop or bat a puck in the air with his open hand, or push it along the ice with his hand so long as he doesn't deliberately direct the puck to a teammate. In the case of a hand pass, play is stopped and the puck is faced off at the spot where offense occurred.

hanger: see *floater.*

Hart Memorial Trophy: The annual award given to the NHL player judged to be the most valuable to his team, as selected by the Professional Hockey Writers' Association. The Hart Memorial trophy was presented by the NHL in 1960 after the original Hart Trophy, named after Cecil Hart, former manager-coach of the Montreal Canadiens, was retired to the Hockey Hall of Fame. Frank Nighbor of the Ottawa Senators won the first Hart Trophy in 1924. also *Hart Trophy.*

Hart Trophy: see *Hart Memorial Trophy.*

hatchetman: see *goon.*

hat trick: Three goals by the same player in a single game. From the game of cricket in the late 1800s in England, when a hat was given to a bowler who took three wickets with successive deliveries. The expression appeared in hockey in the early 1900s and was originally used only to describe three successive goals by a player with no one scoring in between (now called a "pure hat trick"). Often when a hockey player scores three goals in a game, spectators will shower the ice with hats in celebration.

●●Three successive, identical accomplishments by the same individual, such as scoring three goals in a single soccer game, or three related accomplishments, such as hitting for the cycle (a single, double, and triple) in baseball, three consecutive wins in different horse races, or winning a particular race for three consecutive years.

headhunter: see *goon.*

head man, head man the puck: To pass the puck ahead to a player who is closer to the opponents' goal on a line rush. (head mans it to the center, who shoots from the blue line and scores)

heel: The part of a hockey stick where the blade is attached to the shaft.

helmet: A plastic or hard composition protective covering for the head, cushioned inside by webbing or padding. Helmets are mandatory both in international amateur hockey and in the NHL (players who signed an NHL contract before June 1, 1979 may be exempted from the rule requiring a helmet).

high-stick: To illegally hit an opponent with a stick held above shoulder level. (high-sticked him and got sent to the penalty box) see *high sticking.*

high stick: A stick carried so that the blade is illegally above a maximum allowed height (4 feet in amateur play and shoulder level in professional play). A goal cannot be scored with a high stick. see *high sticking.*

high sticking: The act or an instance of carrying a high stick or of hitting a player with a high stick, resulting in a minor or major penalty, depending on the severity and consequences of the infraction.

1. hip check: A check in which the puckhandler is bumped with the hip, usually while trying to skate around a defenseman who is backing up. (wedged him

against the boards with a perfect hip check)

2. hip check: To execute a hip check. (stopped a breakaway by hip checking him off the puck)

1. hit: To physically check an opponent, such as with a body check or hip check. (hit him and stood him up at the blue line)

2. hit: A check, especially a hard check with the body or hip. (somehow held on to the puck in spite of the hit)

hitter: A player known for his skill at checking, particularly one who is known for delivering especially hard checks. also *body checker, checker.*

hockey: see *ice hockey.*

Hockey Hall of Fame: The institution that honors distinguished players, referees, and executives in the sport of amateur and professional hockey. Candidates are selected by the Hockey Hall of Fame Governing Committee on the basis of playing ability, integrity, character, and their contributions to their team and the game of hockey in general. The Hockey Hall of Fame was officially opened in 1961 in Toronto, Canada.

Hockey Night in Canada: The traditional weekly (or twice weekly) Canadian radio and television broadcast of hockey games. First broadcast from the then new Maple Leaf Gardens in 1931 with Foster Hewitt at the microphone, Hockey Night in Canada is considered the longest-running program in the history of broadcasting. The program received its present name in 1935 and was first seen on television in 1952.

hockey pants: Loose thigh-length pants with pads inserted to protect the hips and upper legs of a hockey player. For the 1981-82 season, the Philadelphia Flyers became the first NHL team to replace the traditional pants with regular-length long padded pants.

hockey skate: A relatively flat-bladed skate, shorter than a speed skate and without the toe picks of a figure skate, with a sturdy leather or semi-hard plastic boot that extends high to both support and protect the ankle and Achilles tendon. also *skate.*

hockey stick: A stick (usually wood, though other shaft materials are beginning to be approved) no more than 58 inches long, with a blade no longer than 12-

1/2 inches long and 3 inches wide (no less than 2 inches). There may be up to 1/2-inch curvature in the blade of a stick to help control the puck. A goaltender's stick is slightly larger, with a widened portion extending 26 inches up the shaft from the heel, and the blade no more than 15-1/2 inches in length by 3-1/2 inches in width, except at the heel, where it may not exceed 4-1/2 inches. A player with a broken stick may continue to play provided he drops the broken portion (an infraction results in a minor penalty). A player whose stick is broken may not receive a stick thrown on the ice from any part of the rink or from a teammate, but must skate to the players' bench for a replacement. A goaltender whose stick is broken may not receive a stick thrown on the ice from any part of the rink, but must receive his stick from a teammate, on the ice or at the bench. A

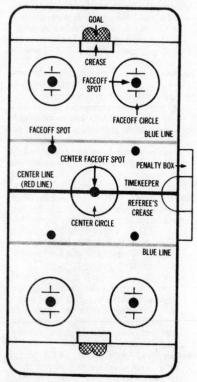

GOAL

CREASE

FACEOFF SPOT

FACEOFF CIRCLE

FACEOFF SPOT

BLUE LINE

CENTER FACEOFF SPOT

PENALTY BOX

CENTER LINE (RED LINE)

TIMEKEEPER

REFEREE'S CREASE

CENTER CIRCLE

BLUE LINE

player or goaltender who receives a stick illegally is assessed a minor penalty. also *stick*.

hockey stop: A technique for stopping in which both skates are quickly turned ninety degrees to one side, spraying ice as the parallel blades scrape, stopping the skater.

hold: To illegally grab or cling to an opponent in order to hinder his movement. see *holding*.

hold a check: see *finish off a check*.

holding: The act of grasping or interfering with an opponent's movement with either the hands or stick, a violation that results in a minor penalty.

hook: To illegally hold an opponent back with the stick. see *hooking*.

1. hook check: A stick check in which the player lays the stick on the ice in front of the puck, forming a "hook" to trap the puck. A hook check is often executed from behind and from the side, as the puck carrier attempts to skate around the defenseman. (takes the puck away at the blue line with a hook check)

2. hook check: To execute a hook check.

hooking: The act or an instance of illegally using the stick to hold back an opponent, resulting in a minor or major penalty at the discretion of the referee.

ice: 1. The playing area of a hockey game. (penalized for too many men on the ice) 2. To illegally shoot or direct the puck from behind the center red line (or from the defensive zone in amateur play) across the opponent's goal line. see *icing*.

ice hockey: A game played between two teams of six players on an ice rink ideally measuring 200 feet long by 85 feet wide (up to 100 feet wide in international amateur play), and enclosed by a 4-foot-high wall with an unbreakable glass or metal screen attached to the top to protect spectators from an errant puck. Players wear ice skates, and attempt to move a hard vulcanized rubber puck, using thin-bladed sticks, into the 6-foot-wide by 4-foot-high net-draped goal (one at each end of the rink) defended by the opposing team. A team is comprised of a goaltender, usually positioned just in front of the goal and responsible for blocking shots into his goal, two defensemen responsible for thwarting attacks and gaining possession of the puck, and three forwards (a left wing, right wing, and a center) responsible for moving the puck into the opponents' end of the ice and shooting at their goal. Players may not catch or direct the puck toward a teammate or the goal with the hands, but may knock the puck to the ice with their hands in order to play it with the stick. A player with the puck or contending for the puck may be checked (bumped) with the upper body or hip, but may not be charged, held, or tripped by an opposing player. A player who commits an infraction or foul is sent off the ice to a designated penalty box and a replacement may not be sent in for the duration of the penalty (usually two to five minutes, but variable according to the severity of the offence). A game is divided into three twenty-minute periods. To begin play at the start of a period, after a goal, after a foul, or after the puck is hit out of the playing area, the puck is dropped or thrown to the ice by the referee or a linesman between two opposing players in a faceoff. Teams may substitute freely at any time during a game so long as each team has no more than six players on the ice at one time. No player is permitted to enter the attacking zone (marked by rink-wide blue lines 60 feet out from each goal) ahead of the puck. An infraction of this rule (offside) results in a faceoff in the neutral zone between the two blue lines.

iceman: A hockey player.

ice time: The amount of time a player is on the ice. (giving his new players more ice time every game)

icing: An infraction in which a player shoots or directs the puck from behind the center red line (or from the defensive zone in amateur play) across the opposing team's goal line, where it is then touched first by an opposing player other than the goaltender. Icing is not called if the puck is played (or, in the judgement of the officials, could be played) by an opposing player before it crosses the goal line, if it is first touched by the defending goaltender, if it is played first by a teammate (who is not offside) of the player who directed or shot the puck into the zone, if it is driven into the zone directly from a faceoff, if the team sending the puck into the zone is playing shorthanded, or if the

puck enters the goal for a score. When icing is called, play is resumed with a faceoff in the offending team's defensive zone.

IIHF: The International Ice Hockey Federation.

illegal curve: Curvature of a stick blade that exceeds the maximum 1/2-inch allowed, resulting in a minor penalty (and an automatic fine in professional hockey). see *illegal stick*.

illegal stick: A hockey stick that deviates from the allowed rules for length, width, or curvature. A player using an illegal stick is assessed a minor penalty (and is subject to a fine in professional hockey).

in goal: see *in the nets*.

in hand: Being one or more games that remain on the schedule for one team, but that have already been played by a division, conference, or league rival. A game in hand is an opportunity to gain ground in the standings on a rival team that has already played that game in the schedule. (one point behind in the standings, but they have two games in hand)

interference: An infraction in which a player impedes the progress of an opponent who is not in possession of or in contention for the puck, deliberately knocks a stick out of an opponent's hand or prevents a player from regaining possession of a dropped stick, interferes with the movement of the puck or an opponent on the ice from the player's bench, stands in the crease when the

HOLDING

231

puck is elsewhere, impedes the movements of a goaltender by physical contact while the goaltender is inside the crease, runs ''interference'' for the puck carrier against a checker, or makes a drop pass and follows through to make bodily contact with an opposing player. Interference results in a minor penalty.

International Ice Hockey Federation: The governing body of international amateur hockey, headquartered in Vienna, Austria. Founded in 1920, the International Ice Hockey Federation is responsible for sanctioning and supervising World Championship and Olympic ice hockey competition. also *IIHF.*

in the nets: Playing goal. (whoever is in the nets tonight will be busy against this sharpshooting team) also *between the pipes, in goal.*

Jack Adams Award: The annual award presented by the National Hockey League Broadcasters' Association to the NHL coach judged to have contributed the most to his team's success. Named in memory of J.J. "Jack" Adams, longtime coach and general manager of the Detroit Red Wings, the award was first presented in 1974 to Fred Shero, then coach of the Philadelphia Flyers.

LINESMAN

James Norris Memorial Trophy: The annual award given to the best all-round defense player in the NHL, as selected by the Professional Hockey Writers' Association. Named in memory of James Norris, former owner-president of the Detroit Red Wings, the award was first given to Red Kelly of the Detroit Red Wings in 1954. also *Norris Trophy.*

keep one's head up: To maneuver with the puck or play without looking down toward the ice, to stay alert so as to be able to anticipate an opponent's check. (was knocked sprawling a few times before he learned to keep his head up)

●●To stay alert and on guard. (an exciting part of town to see at night as long as you keep your head up)

kick save: A save in which the goaltender stops or deflects the puck with an extended leg or skate. compare *blocking glove save, glove save, stick save.*

kill a penalty: To successfully prevent the opposing team from scoring a goal during the time one's team is shorthanded due to one or more players serving penalties. To "kill a penalty," a team concentrates on defense and deliberate, time-consuming puck control whenever possible. (managed to kill the penalty and hold on to the lead)

Lady Byng Memorial Trophy: The annual award given to the NHL player judged to have exhibited the best type of sportsmanship and gentlemanly conduct combined with a high standard of playing ability, as selected by the Professional Hockey Writers' Association. The first Lady Byng Trophy, named after the wife of Canada's Governor General at the time, was given to Frank Nighbor of the Ottawa Senators in 1926. After Frank Boucher of the New York Rangers won the award seven times in eight seasons, he was given the original trophy to keep in 1935 and Lady Byng donated another trophy for the following year. After her death in 1949, the NHL presented a new trophy, changing the name to the Lady Byng Memorial Trophy.

leave the puck: To make a drop pass to a teammate.

left wing: 1. The offensive player who lines up and operates primarily on the left side of the ice. The left wing is normally involved in any attack, and helps to move the puck into the offensive zone where he may shoot, or pass to a teammate for a shot on goal. The left wing is also responsible for digging the puck out of the corner on the left side of the goal. 2. The position played by a left wing.

Lester Patrick Trophy: The annual award given for outstanding service to hockey in the United States. The winner (a player, coach, executive, or referee) is selected by an award committee consisting of the President of the NHL, an NHL Governor, a hockey writer from a United States national news service, a nationally syndicated sports columnist, an ex-player in the Hockey Hall of Fame, and a sports director of a United States national radio-TV network. Named in memory of longtime general manager and coach of the New York Rangers, Lester Patrick, the award was first presented in 1966 to J.J. "Jack" Adams, former coach and general manager of the Detroit Red Wings. also *Patrick Trophy*.

lie: The angle at which the shaft of a hockey stick meets the blade.

line: see *forward line*.

line change: The substitution of one line or group of forwards for another during a game. Line changes normally occur every several minutes in order to keep a fresh, rested group of forwards on the ice at all times. A team may change lines on the fly or wait for a stoppage of play.

linemate: A teammate who plays on the same line. (normally functions as the digger, while his linemates are the shooters)

line rush: An offensive attack in which the forwards skate from the defensive or neutral zone toward the attacking zone with the puck. (got caught up ice after a line rush)

linesman: Either of two officials who are primarily responsible for determining icing and offside violations, stopping play when the puck leaves the playing area, conducting faceoffs, watching for too many men on the ice, breaking up altercations, and reporting fouls to the referee.

loose puck: A puck that is in play but not controlled by either team, such as a rebound from the goalkeeper's stick or

pads or from the boards. (scrambling for a loose puck in front of the net)

major: see *major penalty*.

major penalty: A five-minute penalty assessed for certain serious infractions (such as fighting, spearing, butt-ending, etc.) and some lesser infractions (such as boarding, cross-checking, elbowing, charging, etc.) if they have been committed with violence or caused an injury. In the NHL, a player who receives three major penalties in one game is suspended for the balance of the game and subject to an automatic fine. also *major*. compare *minor penalty*.

man advantage: A numerical advantage on the ice (as in a power play) when the opposing team has one or more players in the penalty box. (had a good opportunity to score with the man advantage)

man between the pipes: see *goaltender*.

Masterton Trophy: see *Bill Masterton Memorial Trophy*.

match penalty: A penalty assessed for a serious infraction (such as a deliberate attempt to injure an opponent) in which the penalized player is suspended for the balance of the game. In a match penalty, the penalized player may be replaced with a substitute after ten minutes playing time (if an injury resulted from the foul) or five minutes playing time (if there was intent to injure but no injury resulted). compare *game misconduct, gross misconduct*.

mind the nets: see *tend goal*.

minor: see *minor penalty*.

minor official: Any of six off-ice officials (two goal judges, a penalty timekeeper, an official scorer, a game timekeeper, and a statistician) chosen by each home team from the local community and approved by the league.

minor penalty: A two-minute penalty assessed for certain lesser infractions (such as delaying the game, disputing an official's ruling, playing with illegal equipment, etc.) and certain other infractions (such as boarding, charging, cross-checking, elbowing, etc.) if they are not committed with violence and cause no injury. A player assessed a minor penalty must proceed immediately to the penalty box and may not rejoin the game nor be replaced by a teammate before the two-minute penalty is served. If, however, the opposing team scores a goal while a team is short-handed because of one or more minor penalties, the first minor penalty is automatically terminated. also *minor.* compare *major penalty.*

minutes played: The statistic that reflects a goaltender's total playing time in minutes (as in a game, season, or career), and that is used to determine his ''goals against average.''

misconduct: see *misconduct penalty.*

misconduct penalty: A ten-minute penalty for certain unacceptable behavior (such as abusive language, failure to proceed to the penalty box, prolonged fighting, etc.), accompanied by an automatic fine in the NHL. A player assessed a misconduct penalty must remain in the penalty box until the first stoppage of play after the penalty has expired, but may be replaced on the ice by a substitute while the penalty is being served. compare *game misconduct, gross misconduct, match penalty.*

mucking: Digging, or contending for the puck in the corners.

National Hockey League: The major professional hockey league in North America. Organized in Montreal, Canada in 1917, the National Hockey League is comprised of two conferences, the Clarence S. Campbell Conference and the Prince of Wales Conference, each with two divisions. The Clarence S. Campbell Conference is comprised of the five-team Norris and Smythe Divisions. The Prince of Wales Conference is comprised of the five-team Adams Division and the six-team Patrick Division. Conference champions (determined by divisional playoffs) meet annually for the league championship in the best-of-seven Stanley Cup Championship Series. also *NHL.*

net: 1. The white nylon mesh netting draped over the top, sides, and back of each goal. 2. see *goal.*

nets: see *goal.*

netminder: 1. see *goaltender.* 2. The position played by a goaltender.

netminding: see *goaltending.*

neutral zone: The central portion of the playing area between the two blue lines and bisected by the center line. compare *attacking zone, defensive zone.*

NHL: The National Hockey League.

Norris Division: One of the two divisions

of the Clarence S. Campbell Conference, comprised of the Chicago Black Hawks, the Detroit Red Wings, the Minnesota North Stars, the St. Louis Blues, and the Toronto Maple Leafs. The Norris Division was named in honor of James Norris, former owner-president of the Detroit Red Wings. compare *Smythe Division.*

Norris Trophy: The James Norris Memorial Trophy.

offensive zone: see *attacking zone.*

official scorer: A minor official whose responsibilities include securing a list of all eligible players, the starting lineup of each team, and the name of the captain (and making this information known to the opposing team before the start of the game), keeping a record of the goals scored, the scorers, and the players to whom assists have been credited, recording the time of entry into the game of any substitute goaltender, and noting any goal scored when the goaltender has been removed from the ice.

offside: 1. A situation in which a player is in the attacking zone (both skates entirely over the blue line) when the puck crosses the blue line. If during an attack the puck is cleared or accidentally tipped out of the attacking zone, all attacking players must leave the attacking zone before the puck can re-enter to prevent an offside violation. When a player is called offside, play stops and a faceoff is held in the neutral zone at the faceoff spot nearest the attacking zone. also *offsides.* 2. A situation in which a player is entirely over the center line (on the side closest to the attacking zone) and receiving an offside pass. see *offside pass.*

offside pass: 1. A pass made by a player in the neutral zone to a teammate in the attacking zone, resulting in a stoppage of play and a faceoff in the neutral zone at the faceoff spot nearest the attacking zone. 2. A pass made by a player in the defensive zone to a teammate past the center line, resulting in the stoppage of play and a faceoff from the point from which the pass was made. also *two-line pass.*

offsides: Slang for offside.

off wing: Either of the two wing positions when played by a winger who shoots from the side opposite that used normally by a player on that wing. A left winger normally shoots left-handed (right hand on top and the left hand underneath), with the stick blade held on the side close to the boards. A left winger who shoots right-handed (stick blade held on the side away from the boards) is said to play the "off wing."

one man back: Having a single defenseman between the goaltender and the attackers. (caught with only one man back on a line rush)

open ice: An unguarded area of the ice. (hit his teammate's stick with a perfect pass into open ice)

open net: see *empty net.*

open net goal: see *empty net goal.*

out of the net: Away from the normal goaltender's position in front of the net, either to gather or clear the puck, to cut down the angle against a shooter, or to skate to the bench to make room for an extra attacking player on a delayed penalty or in the last minutes of a game when behind by one goal.

overskate the puck: To lose control of the puck while skating with it or fail to gain control of a loose puck or a pass by skating past it. (saw the rebound in front of an open net but he overskated the puck)

overtime: An extra twenty-minute period of play used in the NHL to decide a Stanley Cup playoff game tied at the end of regulation play. An overtime begins with a faceoff at center ice, and ends when one team scores or when time runs out. If neither team is able to score in the overtime period, twenty-minute periods continue to be played (with intermissions in between) until one team scores. The longest NHL overtime game (and the longest game in Stanley Cup history) was played in 1936, between the Detroit Red Wings and the Montreal Maroons, ending after 16 minutes, 30 seconds of the sixth overtime period (for a record total of 116 minutes and 30 seconds of overtime) when the Red Wing's "Mud" Bruneteau scored to give Detroit the win. The shortest overtime game in the history of the NHL was played in 1975 between the New York Islanders and the New York Rangers, ending 11 seconds after the start of the first overtime period, when Jean-Paul Parise scored for the Islanders. also *sudden death overtime.*

pad save: A save made with one of the large leg pads worn by a goaltender. compare *blocking glove save, glove save, kick save, stick save.*

1. pass: To direct or deflect the puck to or toward a teammate with the stick.

2. pass: A puck directed or deflected to or toward a player from the stick of a teammate.

Patrick Division: One of the two divisions of the Prince of Wales Conference, comprised of the New Jersey Devils (formerly the Colorado Rockies), the New York Islanders, the New York Rangers, the Philadelphia Flyers, the Pittsburgh Penguins and the Washington Capitals. The Patrick Division was named in honor of Lester Patrick, long-time general manager and coach of the New York Rangers. compare *Adams Division.*

Patrick Trophy: see *Lester Patrick Trophy.*

penalty: 1. The removal of a player from participation in a game for a specified time (assessed in two-minute, five-minute, and ten-minute increments), or for the balance of the game for an infraction of the rules. see *minor penalty, major penalty, match penalty, misconduct penalty, game misconduct, gross misconduct.* 2. A foul or infraction of the rules for which a play-

PENALTY BOX

er was, will be, or should be assessed a penalty. (playing with an illegal stick is a penalty) 3. Short for penalty shot.

penalty bench: see *penalty box.*

penalty box: Either of two separate designated areas in which a penalized player must remain for the duration of a penalty. Penalty boxes are usually located adjacent to the ice on either side of the game timekeeper's area across the ice from the player's benches. Also *box, penalty bench, sin bin.*

penalty killer: Any player on the ice to prevent the opposing team from scoring a goal during the time his team plays shorthanded due to one or more players being in the penalty box. see *penalty killing.*

penalty killing: The act of preventing the opposing team from scoring a goal during the time one's team is shorthanded due to one or more players being in the penalty box. Penalty killing involves defense, time-consuming puck control, and icing the puck when necessary.

penalty killing percentage: A statistic that reflects the percentage of times a team has successfully killed a penalty, determined by dividing the difference between the number of times a team was shorthanded and goals allowed while shorthanded by the number of times a team was shorthanded.

penalty minutes: A statistic that reflects the cumulative total of penalty time (expressed in minutes) charged against a player, team, or two teams in a specified period of time (such as a game, series, season, or career). The NHL record for the most penalty minutes for both teams in a single game was set February 26, 1981, at Boston, when the Boston Bruins and the Minnesota North Stars were assessed eighty-four penalties, totalling 406 penalty minutes. The one-season NHL record for penalty minutes was set in 1974-75 by Philadelphia Flyers player Dave "The Hammer" Schultz (472 penalty minutes). In 1981-82, Dave "Tiger" Williams (Toronto Maple Leafs, Vancouver Canucks) became the all-time career penalty minutes leader, amassing 2,422 penalty minutes in his first eight NHL seasons.

penalty shot: A shot at the goal defended only by the goaltender, awarded to a player or team for certain infractions committed by a member or members of the opposing team, such as interfering with a player on a breakaway by throwing a stick or any object, or tripping or fouling him from behind, throwing a stick or any other object at the puck in the defensive zone, picking up or falling on a puck in the crease (except if done by the goaltender), deliberately displacing a goal post, or making a deliberate illegal substitution with insufficient playing time remaining (to serve the penalty). On a signal from the referee, the fouled player (or, in some circumstances, a player selected by the team captain from those on the ice at the time of the foul) takes the puck from the center faceoff spot (or at the penalized team's blue line in college play) and attempts to score on the goaltender, keeping the puck moving forward toward the opponent's goal line once it crosses the blue line. The goaltender must remain in his crease until the player taking the penalty shot has touched the puck, and all other players must withdraw to the sides of the rink and beyond the center line. Once a shot is taken or the puck crosses the goal line, play is stopped (no goal can be scored on a rebound). Play is resumed by a faceoff at center ice if a goal is scored on the penalty shot, or at either of the end faceoff spots near the goal if the penalty shot was unsuccessful. The penalty shot rule was introduced in the NHL in 1934, and first invoked at Toronto on November 10, 1934, when Armand Mondou of the Montreal Canadiens took the first penalty shot against Maple Leaf goaltender George Hainsworth. Hainsworth stopped that first attempt, and the first goal from a penalty shot was scored three nights later when Ralph Bowman of the St. Louis Eagles beat goaltender Alex Connell of the Montreal Maroons. A study in the early 1980s revealed that since 1934, goals have been scored on 35.6 percent of all penalty shot attempts (28.3 percent since the NHL's 1967 expansion). also *penalty.*

penalty timekeeper: The minor official located between the two penalty boxes adjacent to the referee's crease, and who is responsible for recording and timing each penalty.

period: A unit of playing time. There are

three twenty-minute periods in a regulation hockey game, with extra or overtime periods played under certain circumstances.

pine, pines: The bench, or benches. (rode the pines a lot in his rookie season)

pipe: A goal post. also *post*.

playmaker: A player known for causing or initiating plays, one who regularly makes critical passes and sets up linemates.

plus-minus: A statistic used to measure a player's value, determined by establishing either the percentage or number of his team's goals, for and against, for which the player is on the ice with both teams even (power play goals and shorthanded goals are not considered). If a player is on the ice for a higher percentage or number of goals by his team, he has a "plus", if for a higher percentage or number against his team, he has a "minus." For instance, a player who was on the ice for 51.4 percent or 51 of his team's even-strength goals over a season and 34.4 percent or 34 of the even-strength goals scored against his team would be considered "plus 17" for the season.

point: 1. The basic scoring unit of a hockey game, with a team being awarded one point for each goal scored. 2. A scoring unit credited to a player's records, with one point awarded for each goal and each assist. 3. A scoring unit used to determine division and league standings, with two points awarded to a team for each win, one point for a tie, and no points for a loss. 4. The area on either side of the ice close to the boards and just inside the blue line of the attacking zone. Defensemen attempt to keep the puck in the offensive zone and support an attack from the points. 5. The position played by a point man.

point man: A player (usually a defenseman) who takes an offensive position at the point, as during a power play.

poke check: A stick check in which a defender attempts to dislodge or "poke" the puck away from the puckhandler by jabbing his stick blade at the puck.

poke-check: To execute a poke check. (poke-checked the puck away)

policeman: A tough or physically intimidating player who is known for retaliating when unnecessary roughness is used against a teammate by an opponent. (have to worry less about goons now that their six-foot four-inch defenseman is known around the league as a policeman) also *enforcer*. compare *goon*.

pond hockey: Informal outdoor hockey, played on a frozen lake or pond.

post: Short for goal post. (hit the post with a wrist shot) also *pipe*.

power play: A situation in which a team has more players on the ice while one or more members of the opposing team are serving penalties. Because the opponents are outnumbered, a team on a power play has a greater opportunity to score a goal. also *man advantage*.

power play goal: A goal scored by a team on a power play. Phil Esposito of the Boston Bruins set the NHL record for the most power play goals in one season, scoring twenty-eight power play goals in the seventy-eight games of the 1971-72 season. Esposito's record was tied by Mike Bossy of the New York Islanders in the 1980-81 season, when he scored twenty-eight power play goals in eighty games. compare *shorthanded goal*.

power play goal percentage: A statistic that reflects the percentage of times a team scores a goal while on a power play, determined by dividing the number of power play goals scored by a team by the number of power plays.

power skating: A skating technique that maximizes speed and efficiency by utilizing the full power of the legs to push off on each stride. Skating teacher and author Laura Stamm brought national attention to the technique of power skating in 1978-79 when she became the first woman ever to serve as a coach in the NHL (for the Atlanta Flames).

Prince of Wales Conference: One of two NHL conferences, each comprised of two divisions. The Prince of Wales Conference, named in honor of His Royal Highness, the Prince of Wales (who, in 1924, donated a trophy to the NHL to be given in his name), includes five teams from the Adams Division and six teams from the Patrick Division. see *Adams Division, Patrick Division*. compare *Clarence S. Campbell Conference*.

Prince of Wales Trophy: The award presented annually to the team finishing with the most points in the Prince of Wales Conference at the end of the regular championship schedule. Named in honor of His Royal Highness, the Prince of Wales, who donated the trophy to the NHL in 1924, the award was presented to the team finishing first in the American Division of the NHL from the 1927-28 through 1937-38 seasons. From 1938-39, when the NHL reverted to one section, to 1966-67, it was presented to the team winning the NHL championship. With expansion in 1967-68, the award again became a divisional trophy until 1974-75, when it was first awarded to the winner of the Prince of Wales Conference.

puck: The vulcanized rubber disk, 3 inches in diameter and 1 inch thick, weighing between 5-1/2 ounces and 6 ounces, and used as the object both teams attempt to drive into the goal defended by the opposing team. To insure uniformity, NHL regulations stipulate that pucks to be used in a game must be kept in a frozen condition.

puck carrier: The player in control of and moving with the puck. (will try to check the puck carrier at the blue line) also *puckhandler.*

puckhandler: 1. One who is able to maneuver and control the puck with his stick. also *stickhandler.* 2. The puck carrier.

pull the goalie: To call the goalie to the bench in order to make room on the ice for an extra attacker in the case of a delayed penalty or an attempt to score in the closing minutes of a game when behind by one or two goals. In the latter circumstance, a team will pull the goalie when in possession of the puck in the attacking zone, risking the possibility of an empty net goal (should the opposing team gain control of the puck) in the hopes that an extra forward will lead to a score that ties the game.

PUCK

238

pure hat trick: A hat trick in which a player scores three consecutive goals, with no goals from either team being scored in between. see *hat trick.*

rag the puck: To keep control of the puck for an extended period of time, as by clever stickhandling. (did a good job of ragging the puck to kill the penalty)

rebound: 1. A puck that bounces off the goalie, the crossbar, a goal post, or the boards behind the goal and remains in play. (stood planted in front of the crease, looking for a rebound) 2. A goal scored off a rebound.

red light: A red light above and behind each goal, activated by the goal judge to signify the scoring of a goal.

red line: The 1-foot-wide red line that extends from one side of the rink to the other (and continues vertically up the sideboards), dividing the ice in half. The red line is used to determine icing and offside passes. The red line was introduced in the NHL in 1943, at the same time forward passing was first allowed up to mid-ice, opening up the game and beginning the modern era of hockey. also *center line.* see *icing, offside pass.*

1. referee: The official responsible for supervising the conduct of a professional hockey game (or, in amateur hockey, either of two supervising officials), with full authority over all players and game officials while a game is in progress. The referee is responsible for checking all clothing and equipment used, conducting faceoffs, assessing penalties for rules infractions and fouls, and awarding goals. The referee orders the teams on the ice at the appointed time to begin a game and at the commencement of each period, and presides over all stoppages of play. In case of any dispute, the referee's decision is final (as in the case of a disputed goal, where a referee may overrule the goal judge).

2. referee: To act as the referee for a game.

referee's crease: An area marked on the surface of the ice directly in front of the penalty timekeeper in the shape of a semicircle with a 10-foot radius. While the referee is reporting penalties to the penalty timekeeper, no player is permitted inside the referee's crease.

restraining circle: A faceoff circle.

ride off the puck: see *skate off the puck.*

rink: The playing area for a hockey game, an ice surface in the shape of a rounded-off rectangle, ideally measuring 200 feet long by 85 feet wide (up to 100 feet wide in international amateur play), and enclosed by a 4-foot-high wall with an unbreakable glass or metal screen attached to the top to protect spectators. Ten feet from and parallel to each end of the rink, a goal line is drawn across the ice (and vertically up the sideboards), at the middle of which is a goal. An 8-foot-wide, 4-foot-deep rectangular goal crease (or a 6-foot-radius semicircle for college play) is marked in front of each goal. Two 12-inch-wide blue lines extend across the rink (and continue vertically up the sideboards) 60 feet out from and parallel to the goal lines, dividing the rink into a neutral zone (between the two blue lines) and two end zones (between the blue lines and the ends of the rink). A 12-inch-wide red center line (the "red line") is marked across the middle of the rink (and up the sideboards), dividing the ice in half. Two faceoff spots, surrounded by 15-foot-radius restraining circles, are marked in each end zone. Five faceoff spots are marked in the neutral zone, one in the middle of the center line with a 15-foot-radius restraining circle. see *blue line, faceoff spot, goal, goal line, red line.*

rocker: The slight upward curve of the bottom edge of a skate blade. Hockey skates have a relatively flat blade with only a slight rocker.

roughing: 1. The act or an instance of excessive or unwarranted roughness against an opponent, as in checking. Roughing results in a minor penalty. also *unnecessary roughness.* 2. The penalty that results from the use of excessive or unwarranted roughness.

1. rush: 1. The movement of the puck by one or more players into the attacking zone. 2. A line rush.

2. rush: To carry the puck forward into the attacking zone.

rushing defenseman: A defenseman who is adept at carrying the puck out of the defensive zone into an attack. The prototype for the modern rushing defenseman was the phenomenal Bobby Orr of the Boston Bruins (1966-67 through 1975) and the Chicago Black Hawks

(1976-77 through 1978-79). Orr holds the NHL career records for the highest points-per-game average (1.393, with 270 goals and 645 assists), as well as the record for the most goals scored in one season by a defenseman (46 in eighty games, Boston Bruins, 1974-75), and the records for the most assists (102) and the most points (139) in one season by a defenseman (in seventy-eight games for the Boston Bruins, 1970-71).

1. save: To prevent a goal by catching, blocking, or deflecting the puck before it crosses the goal line.

2. save: The act or an instance of preventing a goal by catching, blocking, or deflecting the puck before it crosses the goal line. Each save is credited to a goaltender's statistical records. also *stop.*

1. screen: To deliberately or inadvertently take a position between the goalie and the player shooting the puck, thereby blocking the goalie's vision when the puck is shot. (was screened on the scoring shot from the point)

REFEREE—ROUGHING CALL

2. screen: The act or an instance of screening. (stood in front of the net to act as a screen)

screen shot: A shot made when the goalie is screened, most often made around a defender who is trying to prevent the shot, inadvertently screening the goaltender.

Selke Trophy: see *Frank J. Selke Trophy.*

serve a penalty: To proceed to the penalty box and remain for the duration of a penalty assessed because of a foul or an infraction of the rules. see *major penalty, minor penalty, bench minor penalty, misconduct.*

1. shadow: To follow and closely guard a particular opponent (usually the leading scorer of the opposing team) throughout the game, whether or not he is in possession of the puck.

2. shadow: A player who shadows the opposing team's leading scorer. (had little effect on the game because he couldn't get away from his shadow)

shin guard: A padded (usually hard plastic) protective covering for the front of the leg, extending up from the ankle to above the knee, and held on by straps.

shinny: 1. An informal game resembling hockey, played in the street or a vacant lot with curved sticks and a ball or some another object as the puck. 2. Unskilled, sloppy, or disorganized play. (only one team was playing hockey, the other played shinny)

short a man: see *down a man.*

shorthanded: Outnumbered on the ice due to one or more players serving penalties in the penalty box. see *kill a penalty.*

shorthanded goal: A goal scored by a team that has one or two fewer players on the ice than the opponents, due to penalties being served. The NHL record for the most shorthanded goals in one season (ten) was set in 1974-75 by Marcel Dionne, then of the Detroit Red Wings. compare *power play goal.*

short side: 1. The side of the goal on which the goaltender is playing, presenting the least amount of space between him and the goal post. 2. The side of the goal closest to a shooter approaching from an angle.

shot on goal: Any shot or deflection that results or would result in a goal if not for the intervention of a defensive player or a save by the goaltender. A goal

scored counts as a shot on goal, but a shot that hits the post, or one that goes wide of the net (though handled by the goalie) does not count as a shot on goal. Shots on goal are recorded in statistical records.

shoulder pads: The protective covering for the collarbone and shoulder area of a hockey player, comprised of a hard outer surface (such as molded plastic) on top and a foam cushion layer underneath.

shutout: A game in which the opposing team is held scoreless. A shutout is credited in the statistical records of a goaltender. The NHL career record for shutouts is held by Terry Sawchuk, who in 971 games played over twenty-one seasons from 1949 through 1970, earned 103 shutouts, playing for the Detroit Red Wings, the Boston Bruins, the Toronto Maple Leafs, the Los Angeles Kings, and the New York Rangers. The NHL record for the most shutouts in a single season was set in 1928-29 by George Hainsworth of the Montreal Canadiens, who recorded a phenomenal 22 shutouts in 44 games.

shut out: To hold the opposing team scoreless. (shut them out for the first two periods)

sideboards: The section of the boards between the goal lines on both sides of a rink.

sin bin: Slang for the penalty box. also *box, penalty bench.*

sixth attacker: see *extra attacker.*

1. skate: see *hockey skate.*

2. skate: 1. To move along the surface of the ice on ice skates. 2. To carry the puck, controlling it with the stick while moving along the surface of the ice. (skated the puck into the attacking zone)

skate off the puck: To lean into the puck carrier or an opponent going for a loose puck while moving along the ice beside him in order to push him away from the puck. (skated off the puck by the defenseman) also *ride off the puck.*

skate save: A save in which the puck is blocked or deflected with the goaltender's skate.

slapper: A slapshot.

slapshot: A powerful shot in which a player winds up with a full backswing and follows through, driving the puck at speeds of up to 110 miles per hour.

Chicago Black Hawks star Bobby Hull developed and popularized the slapshot in the early 1960s. also *slapper*.

1. slash: To illegally strike or attempt to strike an opposing player with the stick, or swing the stick at an opposing player, regardless of whether contact is made. see *slashing*.

2. slash: The act or an instance of striking or attempting to strike an opposing player with the stick, or swinging the stick at an opponent; slashing. see *slashing*.

slashing: The act or an instance of an illegal slash. Slashing results in a minor or major penalty, depending on the severity and consequences of the infraction. also *slash*.

sleeper: see *floater*.

slot: An imaginary area approximately the width of the goal and extending about 10 yards out from the crease. The slot is considered the most advantageous area from which to score a goal.

slow ice: A soft or mushy ice surface, the result of improper preparation and freezing. Slow ice affects the speed of a shot or passed puck, as well as skating speed.

slow whistle: 1. see *delayed penalty*. 2. see *delayed offside*.

smother the puck: To deliberately fall on or over the puck in order to stop play. A goaltender may legally smother the puck in the crease if he is being challenged or checked by an opponent. In such a case, play is resumed with a faceoff at one of the faceoff spots in the end zone of the defended goal. A minor penalty is assessed to a goalie who deliberately falls on the puck in the crease without being challenged or checked, and to any player (including the goaltender) who deliberately falls on the puck anywhere else on the ice.

Smythe Division: One of the two divisions of the Clarence S. Campbell Conference, comprised of the Calgary Flames, the Edmonton Oilers, the Los Angeles Kings, the Vancouver Canucks, and the Winnipeg Jets. The Smythe Division was named in honor of Conn Smythe, former coach, manager, president and owner-governor of the Toronto Maple Leafs. compare *Norris Division*.

snap pass: A quick pass in which the puck is propelled forward with a quick snap of the wrists, using no backswing.

SLAPSHOT

snap shot: A wrist shot. also *wrister*.

soft goal: A goal scored that should have been stopped by the goalie. (lost on a soft goal after making big saves all through the game)

sniper: A player noted for his skill at shooting the puck. also *gunner*.

spear: To illegally poke or stab an opponent, or attempt to poke or stab, an opponent with the tip of the stick blade. see *spearing*.

spearing: The act or an instance of illegally poking or stabbing or attempting to poke or stab an opponent with the tip of the stick blade. Spearing results in a major penalty (and in the NHL, an automatic fine) and can result in a match penalty if, in the referee's judgement, there was a deliberate attempt to injure.

split the defense: To maneuver between the defenders into the attacking zone with the puck.

spot: Short for faceoff spot.

stand up: To check an opponent from the front, stopping his forward progress. (an aggressive defenseman who often stands opposing forwards up at the blue line)

standup goalie: A goaltender who makes most saves standing up, rather than flopping to the ice. compare *flopper*.

Stanley Cup: 1. The trophy awarded annually to the NHL champion, the winner of the best-of-seven Stanley Cup Championship Series between the Prince of Wales Conference champions and the Clarence S. Campbell Conference champions. The oldest trophy competed

SPEARING

for by professional athletes in North America, the Stanley Cup was donated by and named after Frederick Arthur, Lord Stanley of Preston and son of the Earl of Derby, in 1893. Presented to Canada's amateur hockey champions at first, the trophy has been the symbol of professional hockey supremacy since 1910, when the National Hockey Association took possession. The Stanley Cup has been competed for only by NHL teams since 1926 and has been under the exclusive control of the NHL since 1946. The Montreal A.A.A. was the first winner of the Stanley Cup in 1893. 2. The best-of-seven Stanley Cup Championship Series between the Prince of Wales Conference champions and the Clarence S. Campbell Conference champions.

stick: see *hockey stick*.

stick-check: To execute a stick check. (stick-checked the puck away)

stick check: The act or an instance of knocking or taking the puck away from an opponent with the stick. see *hook check, poke check, sweep check*.

stick handle: To maneuver the puck with the stick, especially while moving between or among opponents. (stick handled past the defenseman at the blue line)

stickhandler: One who is able to deftly maneuver and control the puck with his stick. also *puckhandler*.

stick save: A save made with the goaltender's stick. compare *blocking glove save, glove save, pad save*.

stick side: The side on which a goaltender holds the stick. (scored high on the stick side to tie the game) compare *glove side*.

stone: To stop (save) the opposing team's shots. (stoned them in the final game for a shutout)

stop: A save. (ended the period with a great stop on a breakaway)

street hockey: An informal hockeylike game played on pavement (as in the streets) by players who wear sneakers and use hockey sticks and a plastic puck or a small ball (often a tennis ball).

sudden death overtime: see *overtime*.

sweep-check: To execute a sweep check.

sweep check: A stick check in which the stick is "swept" in a circular motion along the ice in order to knock the puck away from an opponent.

take a penalty: To commit an infraction for which a penalty is assessed. In some game situations, a player will intentionally take a penalty, as to prevent a breakaway or a dangerous scoring opportunity. Such an infraction would be considered a "good penalty" if the consequences of the penalty are less dangerous than the activity that the infraction prevented. A "bad penalty" would be a needless infraction that prevents no danger, but puts the offending player's team in danger for whatever time they must skate shorthanded. (took a bad penalty near the end of the third period, and it cost them the game)

take a run at: To deliberately and violently charge into or check an opponent. To take a run at an opponent usually involves an infraction such as charging, roughing, boarding, etc., and results in a minor or major penalty, depending on the nature and severity of the infraction.

take the body: 1. To physically check an opponent or opponents, or to emphasize a checking style of play. (were more effective when they started to take the body in the second period) 2. To adopt the strategy of checking the puck carrier off the puck and out of the play, attempting to check or "take the body" of the puck carrier while a second defenseman goes after the puck. also *take the man.*

take the man: see *take the body.*

tend goal: To play goal. (was injured, and unable to tend goal for the third period) also *mind the nets.*

third man in: The third player to become involved in an altercation, or the first to intervene in an altercation already in progress. The third man in receives an automatic game misconduct penalty.

three star selection: The selection of a game's three most effective players by local sportswriters and sports broadcasters, traditionally announced at the conclusion of most NHL games.

thrown out of the circle: Removed from the faceoff circle by the referee or a linesman for failing to take the proper position for a faceoff. In such a case, no penalty is assessed, but a teammate must take the place of the player thrown out of the circle for the faceoff.

tie up: 1. To check or hold the puck carrier against the boards, usually resulting in a faceoff. 2. To check and momentarily delay an opponent in order to take him out of the play.

tight checking: see *close checking.*

time of the goal: The exact minute and second of elapsed time in a specified period that a goal is scored. (scored the winning goal at 19:59 of the third period)

time of the penalty: The exact minute and second of elapsed time in a specified period that a penalty is recorded. A penalty recorded in the last few minutes of the first or second period continues into the following period, and one that is recorded in the last few minutes of the third period is continued in case of an overtime, but does not carry over to the next game.

time out: A thirty-second stoppage of play allowed to each team once per game in the NHL, to be taken only during a normal stoppage of play.

tip in, tip-in: A goal scored by a player positioned close to the opposing team's goal, by tapping in a teammate's pass or shot.

too many men on the ice: More than the number of players a team is allowed to have on the ice at any time during a game (six unless one or more players are serving penalties), an infraction that results in a bench minor penalty being assessed to the offending team. If, due

STICKHANDLER

243

to insufficient playing time remaining, such a bench minor penalty cannot be served in its entirety within the legal playing time, a penalty shot is awarded against the offending team.

top shelf: see *upstairs.*

toy department: see *upstairs.*

trailer: A trailing teammate, one who skates behind the puck carrier in position for a drop pass, rebound, etc.

triangle: A defensive formation employed when a team must skate shorthanded by two players, in which the three remaining players form a triangle in front of their goaltender, with two players in front of and to either side of the goal, and the third player deep in the slot to guard the points.

tripping: The act or an instance of a player placing his stick, knee, foot, arm, hand, or elbow in such a manner as to cause an opponent to trip or fall. Trip-

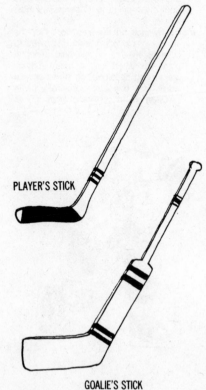

PLAYER'S STICK

GOALIE'S STICK

ping is illegal and results in a minor penalty. If, during a breakaway, the puck carrier is tripped from behind, a penalty shot is awarded against the offending team. If a player on a breakaway is tripped from behind, while the opposing team's goalie is off the ice, thus preventing a reasonable scoring opportunity, a goal is awarded to the attacking team.

two-line pass: An illegal pass made by a player in the defensive zone to a teammate past the center line (crossing two lines, the blue line and the center line), resulting in a stoppage of play and a faceoff from the point from which the pass was made. also *offside pass.*

two-way player: A player who plays well both offensively and defensively.

up and down the wing: Back and forth between the attacking and defensive zones in an imaginary lane on both sides of the ice where a wing is supposed to skate in the traditional or classic style of hockey (as opposed to the constant circling and crossing first popularized in European and international amateur hockey).

up ice: To or toward a team's attacking zone or the goal a team is attacking. (almost gave up a breakaway by being caught up ice)

upstairs: Player's slang for the upper part of a goal. (beat the goalie with a shot upstairs) also *top shelf, toy department.*

use one's edges: To take full advantage or be able to take full advantage of the ability of ice skates to turn, change directions, start fast, and stop short. A good skater is one who uses his edges.

Vezina Trophy: An annual award given to the NHL goaltender or goaltenders having played a minimum twenty-five games for the team with the fewest goals scored against it in regular season play. Named in memory of Georges Vezina, an outstanding goaltender of the Montreal Canadiens who collapsed during a game in 1925 and died of tuberculosis a few months later, the Vezina Trophy was presented to the National Hockey League in 1926-27 by former Montreal Canadiens owners Leo Dandurand, Louis Letourneau, and Joe Cattarinich. The first Vezina Trophy was given to Montreal Canadiens goalie George Hainsworth in 1927. Hainsworth also won the award in 1928 and 1929. Jacques Plante won the Vezina Trophy a record seven times, six while playing for the Montreal Canadiens (1956, 1957, 1958, 1959, 1960, 1962) and once for playing for the St. Louis Blues (1969).

washout: 1. A signal given by a referee or linesman in which both arms are swung laterally across the body with the palms down (similar to the "safe" sign in baseball). When used by the referee, a washout signifies a disallowed goal (because the puck has been illegally kicked into the goal, batted in with a high stick, etc.). When used by a linesman, a washout signifies that no icing or offside is being called, or that the puck has not been illegally batted or passed with a high stick. 2. A disallowed goal.

1. whistle: 1. A stoppage of play (as for a penalty, an injury, or equipment repair), signified by the referee blowing a whistle. 2. The police-type whistle carried by a referee (usually attached to a two-finger ring or bracelet on one hand) and used to signal a stoppage of play.

2. whistle: 1. To stop play (by blowing the whistle) for a penalty, an injury, or equipment repair. 2. To assess a penalty for a foul or rules infraction. (got whistled for roughing near the end of the second period)

wing: 1. Either of two players who flank the center at the outside positions on the forward line. Normally playing along the side portion of the ice, a wing is responsible for helping move the puck into the offensive zone, shooting or passing to a teammate, digging for the puck in the corner, and helping out on defense when the opposing team gains control of the puck. also _winger, wingman._ 2. The position played by a winger. (will play at left wing tonight) 3. The area on either side of the ice near the sideboards.

winger: A player who plays one of the wing positions on the forward line. also _wing, wingman._

wingman: A player who plays on one of the wing positions on the forward line. also _wing, winger._

World Championships: The international tournament held annually (except in Olympic years) to determine a world champion among amateur teams representing participating nations. The round-robin competition is at three different levels, determined by prior international competition. The lowest level (the ten-team "C" Pool) and second level (the eight-team "B" Pool) compete in March for separate championships, with the top two "C" Pool finishers exchanging pools with the bottom two "B" Pool finishers for the next competition. The eight teams in the highest level "A" Pool compete in April, with the last place finisher exchanging pools with the winner of the "B" Pool Championship

TRIPPING

for the next competition. The first World Championships were held in 1930 in Chamonix, France, and Berlin, Germany, and won by the team representing Canada.

wrist shot: A quick shot in which the puck is propelled off the stick blade with a quick snap of the wrists, using no backswing. also *snap shot, wrister.*

wrister: A wrist shot. also *snap shot.*

Zamboni: A special vehicle used to clean and resurface the ice between the periods of a game. The Zamboni was introduced in 1949 by Frank J. Zamboni, a rink manager in California.

zebra: A nickname for a referee or linesman, because of their black-and-white striped shirts.

zone: One of the three areas of the ice (a central or neutral zone, and two end zones), divided by the blue lines. (cleared the puck out of the zone)

SOCCER

Man has been "playing ball" since the first pebble was kicked along the ground, and in many early cultures, contests evolved in which a sphere was directed at, over, or through some kind of goal. Such ancestors to soccer, or football as it is known around the world, were played centuries before Christ in the Orient and Europe, and, surprisingly, date back as far as 1000 B.C. in the Americas.

Terra-cotta figurines of ball players from that period found in Xochipala in Guerrero, Mexico, are evidence of a game played in various forms by Indians all throughout Mesoamerica and the Caribbean Islands. Early in the sixteenth century, astonished Spanish conquistadores discovered the Aztec version of the game. Called *ullamaliztli*, it was played in a large walled court (*tlachtli*) in the shape of a short, broad capital "H," with vertical rings mounted as goals at the midpoint of the high sidewalls bordering the central section, about ten feet off the ground. Two teams of two or three players attempted to score points by propelling a solid rubber ball with the hip or knees against or over the low walls at each end of the court, or to end the game outright by putting the ball through one of the rings. In other versions, the ball was played with the head and feet. Reliefs from the Maya-Toltec era (960-1200 A.D.) depict the sacrifice of a player. It is believed that in certain contests, the losing players may have been killed as an offering to the rain gods.

Though the Spaniards ultimately demolished all the Aztec tlachtlis and prohibited the game because of its "heathen" religious aspects, they were fascinated by the rubber ball (Christopher Columbus had brought one to Europe in the late 1400s), and by the skill and dexterity of the players, and in 1528, Indians brought to Spain by Hernan Cortes put on a demonstration at the court of Charles V.

Reports of warriors playing "football" games in China date back as far as the Spring and Autumn period (c. 772-481 B.C.), and some believe that simple ball games may have been played as early as the Shang Dynasty (c. 1766-1122 B.C.). *Tactics of the Warring States: The Tactics of the Qi Kingdom,* written about the period between 475 and 221 B.C., mentions that kicking a ball around was a favorite sport of the citizens of Linzi, the capital of Qi in Northeast China. The father of Liu Bang, founder and first emperor of the Han Dynasty (c. 206 B.C.-220 A.D.), is said to have enjoyed the pastime. Records from the Western Han Dynasty (206 B.C.-24A.D.) mention that famous Han generals Wei Qing (died 106 B.C.) and Huo Qubing (died 117 B.C.) were enthusiasts of a competitive game played by soldiers and using a leather-covered ball stuffed with feathers.

Inflated leather balls were introduced toward the end of the Tang Dynasty (618-907A.D.) and large-scale football competitions were featured entertainments during the reign of Emperor Hui Zong (1082-1135). In these games, two teams of eleven players, wearing turbans and jackets of red silk for one side and black for the other and captained by a distinctively turbaned leader, attempted to kick a ball through a 20-inch hole in the upper part of a curtain hung in the middle of the playing area from a 30-foot high frame festooned with colorful streamers. The winners of a game were awarded such prizes as silver bowls and lengths of silk, while the captain of the losing team was whipped.

Soccer's European foundations were much less sophisticated than either the ancient Chinese or Mesoamerican examples. Among the earliest European ball games is one mentioned in Homer's *Odyssey* as being played by the Greeks in the twelfth century B.C. It is believed to be the Spartan game *episkyros,* or *epikoinos*, meaning "team game" which was played on a field with a center line, and in which players from two teams attempted to throw, push, kick, or wrestle a small ball past the opponent's goal line. A relief unearthed in Athens in 1922 shows six players engaged in such a game, with three on each side of a midline, one behind the other, somewhat suggesting the concept of defenders, midfielders, and forwards.

Caesar himself is said to have enjoyed the rough-and-tumble Greek and Roman game of *harpastum*, in which players attempted to win possession of a small, hard, hair-stuffed ball from the opponents. Other ball games developed, predating the medieval Italian game *calcio*, in which an inflated ball was kicked between players, but it was harpastum that the Roman legions spread throughout Europe and Britain.

Within Britain itself, there are conflicting ideas about the exact origin of football. Most accounts center around Shrove Tuesday, including the centuries-old legend that the first football was the head of a captive Dane (or a dug-up Danish skull) kicked through the streets of Chester by a group of boys.

Glover's *History of Derby* mentions football contests played between church districts from 217, the year that local fighters are said to have vanquished a cohort of Roman legionaires. It is alleged in Derby that the first Shrove Tuesday contest (and thus, the first soccer game) was a celebration of that battle. However records show that similar brawling contests in which a ball was kicked through the streets or over the countryside, occurred at about the same time in towns and villages throughout Britain. The memory of these early contests is still celebrated every Shrove Tuesday in Ashbourne, Derbyshire, in a ceremonial game played through the city streets between one side of the town and the other.

By the Middle Ages, the crude and often violent form of "mob football" (so called initially because it was played on foot rather than on horseback) had gained enough popularity in Britain to incur the displeasure of royalty and the church. In 1314, Edward II of England banned the game as a breach of the peace "forasmuch as there is great noise in the city caused by hustling over large balls from which many evils might arise which God forbid." The pastime was seen by Edward III as no less than a threat to the security of the nation, taking thousands of young men away from archery and other martial training. In 1349, he too ordered the game suppressed, as did Richard II in 1389 in a statute which forbade "all playing at tenise, football, and other games." Henry IV, Henry VIII, and Queen Elizabeth all issued reenforcing prohibitions during their reigns, but interest in the game continued through the seventeenth century. Even Oliver Cromwell was an avid player, mentioning it frequently in his letters.

During the Industrial Revolution, former artisans, farmers, and merchants found less time for leisure activities such as football as their work conditions changed. By now, however, the game had become popular with the sons of the educated classes, and as the working man's interest waned, football flourished in the "civilized" atmosphere of England's public schools.

By the early nineteenth century, some form of football was being played at the best of these institutions, each school evolving its own style with various basic and sometimes conflicting playing rules. Charterhouse and Westminster played twenty men to a side and permitted no handling of the ball, while Harrow limited a team to eleven. Eton played its version of the game alongside a wall on a 120-yard long pitch which was only 6 yards wide (still played today as the traditional Eton Wall Game) and was first to recognize offside (called "sneaking"), though the actual term "offside" came later from Cheltenham, as did the first crossbar and throw-in from "touch."

In 1823, an incident occurred that would ultimately divide football into two distinctly different games. During a match at Rugby School (where the ball could be handled as long as the player didn't move his feet), one participant, William Webb Ellis, suddenly picked up the ball in frustration and carried it across the opponent's goal line. Although Ellis's act was controversial at the time, the practice soon became accepted and was identified with the school as the "Rugby game."

In 1848, in the first effort to arrive at a uniform code that would allow competition among schools, fourteen Cambridge University students, among them a Rugby graduate, finally agreed on rules that allowed handling, but no running with the ball, and prohibited kicking, tripping, or grabbing an opponent. Passing forward was allowed as long as three opponents were between the receiver and the goal. To score, the ball had to be kicked between two posts and under a connecting tape.

Football thrived with the new rules and soon was being played outside of school by specially formed clubs. The first of these was created in the northern industrial city of Sheffield sometime in 1854, and, as Sheffield United, it remains today the oldest football club in existence. Some of the clubs that followed preferred a version of football dubbed "The Simplest Game," developed at Uppingham School, and still others the Rugby game.

In a historic series of meetings in 1863 between representatives of various local clubs at London's Freemasons' Tavern, England's Football Association (FA) was born and, after long and heated arguments, a uniform set of rules was adopted that once and for all separated "rugby football" from the sport of "association football." Soon after, Charles Wreford-Brown, an Association committee member and player, was asked if he would like a game of "rugger," a nickname for rugby. "No, soccer," he replied, creating a similar word play on the abbreviation "assoc" for association football. Oddly, the term "soccer" would be widely used only later in the United States and Canada.

The 1863 rules were in fact just basic guidelines, but they did set the maximum dimensions for the pitch (200 yards by 100 yards) and goals (initially, two posts 8 feet apart, with no connecting tape), and specify the method of scoring (by kicking the ball through or over the space between the posts), offside rules (no player was to be closer to the opoent's goal than his teammate at the moment he kicked the ball), throw-in rules (at a right angle to the touch line, by any method), and initial regulations for kickoffs, free kicks, etc. They permitted catching the ball, and throwing or passing it if the ball was caught on the first bounce or with a "fair catch."

A specific playing code gradually evolved, and the game of "soccer" began to assume its eventual worldwide form. Handling the ball was abolished after 1866, and an upper limit for the goals was marked with tape. In 1867, the offside rule was changed back to the 1848 version, calling for three opposing players closer to the goal. Goal kicks were introduced in 1869, and in 1870, the number of players on a team was fixed at eleven, and separate playing rules were instituted for the goalkeepers. In 1872, corner kicks were introduced, as were umpires in 1874. Two innovations made their appearance in 1878: Floodlights were used to illuminate the first night game at Sheffield, and referees began using whistles when an infraction occurred.

Late in 1882, representatives of the English, Scottish, Welsh, and Irish Associations standardized the size of the ball, made crossbars mandatory, and agreed upon a version of the Scottish two-handed throw-in.

Though adjustments would continue for some time, the major laws of soccer were in place by 1891. By the early 1900s, the game that had been shaped in the British Isles had spread all through Europe and across the Atlantic to North and South America. England won the first Olympic soccer competition in 1900, though a gold medal was not awarded until Canada won at the St. Louis Olympics in 1904. That same year, representatives from Belgium, France, Holland, Spain, Sweden, and Switzerland persuaded the English Football Association to join in forming the Federation of International Football Associations (FIFA) to govern what was already becoming a true world sport.

Football was brought to the United States some time in the early nineteenth century, long before the 1863 Football Association rules were framed, though surprised Pilgrims had watched American Indians in the New England area play a native game in the early 1600s called *pasuckquakkohowog*, meaning roughly, "gather to play football." In it, a small wooden or deerskin ball (about 2 inches in diameter) was kicked along the beach between goals set about a mile apart with a line marked halfway between them. Accounts say that teams ranged anywhere from thirty to over a thousand on each side when neighboring villages or tribes competed.

Though crude forms of football were played at Harvard and Yale as early as the 1820s (sometimes as a means of hazing freshmen) and were subsequently banned at both schools in the 1830s, the first recorded soccer team in the United States was the Oneida Football Club of Boston. Comprised of boys from three local high schools, the Oneidas were organized and captained by fifteen-year-old Gerrit Smith Miller in 1860 and used a modified version of the 1848 Cambridge University rules. It was nine years before the first intecollegiate game was played, in which Princeton and Rutgers met in 1869, with twenty-five players on each team. Rutgers won the first game 6-4, in spite of a tactic employed by Princeton. At strategic moments during the match, the Princeton players all gave out with a startling scream. Unfortunately, the tactic backfired, serving mostly to wind the players, so for the rematch a week later, they were joined in the yells by a group of Princeton students on the sidelines and won 8-0. This is believed to be the origin of formal sideline cheers which were to become a tradition at later American football games.

Yale, Cornell, Columbia, and Michigan also formed "football" teams, and, in 1873, an attempt was made at Yale to create an intercollegiate association for the sport. Harvard (having developed its own "Boston Game," in which an inflated rubber ball could be picked up and run with) declined to join, a decision which ultimately resulted in the creation of American football and diverted the attentions of many of the country's finest athletes away from soccer in its critical formative years in the United States. Consequently, soccer developed more slowly in America than in other countries and would for many decades be regarded as a foreign game, played for the most part by immigrants and the sons of immigrants. Despite this, the sport did continue to grow.

In 1884, the American Football Association was formed, and two years later, it sent a team selected from clubs in New Jersey to play a series of games in Canada against a Canadian all-star team in what are believed to be the first international matches played by an American team. In 1890, Kensington F.C. of St. Louis became the first all American-born soccer team in the United States. The first college-level soccer organization was formed in 1905, the Intercollegiate Association Football League, comprised of Cornell, Columbia, Haverford, Pennsylvania, and Harvard. The same year, the University of Pennsylvania met Toronto in Philadelphia in the first international college soccer game. That year also saw the first indoor soccer game with abbreviated sides, played in New York's Madison Square Garden, and in 1909, a touring English team, the Pilgrims, defeated the Cincinnati All-Stars 10-0 in the first night game, under the artificial lights at Cincinnati's baseball park.

A milestone in American soccer was reached in 1913 with the forming of the United States Football Association (later the USSF), and the first national competition for the U.S. Challenge Cup, donated by the noted British sportsman, Sir Thomas R. Dewar. The Challenge Cup, which became open to both professional and amateur teams after the first year, remains today the most prestigious soccer competition in the United States.

In 1921, the American Soccer League was formed, the first professional soccer league in the Americas. Disbanded in 1933, the league was reorganized the following year and is still operating under the same name.

The sport continued to grow after World War I, and by the 1924 Paris Olympics, twenty-two nations were represented in the soccer competition. In 1930, the first World Cup tournament was hosted and won by Uruguay. Thirteen national teams participated, including the United States team (led by Hall of Famer Billy Gonsalves) and four European teams. The U.S. reached the semifinals before losing a controversially rough match to Argentina.

Outside the United States, soccer was becoming more popular, and international matches began to take on an added significance with national pride at stake. Nowhere was this more evident than at the World Cup. Italy won the second and third World Cups, the first at home in 1934, where Mussolini watched as the Italians crushed the United States team 7-1 in the opening round, and the second in Paris in 1938, as the dark clouds of war hung over Europe. The stars of soccer included the legendary Stanley Matthews, Spain's brilliant goalkeeper, Zamora, and the acrobatic Brazilian, Leonidas, who first showed his spectacular bicycle kick in Paris in 1938.

Uruguay won the 1950 World Cup, defeating Brazil in front of 220,000 spectators in Rio's Maracana Stadium. But the most stunning upset in international soccer occurred when England's first World Cup bid ended with a 1-0 loss to the United States. Haitian-born Joe Gaetjens headed in the game's only goal on a perfect cross from fellow Hall of Famer Walter Bahr.

The dominant club of the 1950s was undoubtedly Spain's Real Madrid, who won the first European Cup in 1956, and, with Argentine great Alfredo di Stephano and Puskas from Hungary, Real Madrid went on to win the next four.

The 1958 World Cup in Sweden was won by Brazil in a tournament that marked the debut of the seventeen-year-old Brazilian "phenom," Pele.

Known as "The Black Pearl," "God of the Stadiums," or simply "El Rey," Pele reigned as the undisputed king of soccer and the most popular athlete in the world for over twenty years, scoring a record total of 1,251 goals in international or first division play (101 for Brazil, 1090 for Santos and 60 for the New York Cosmos), and 33 more in exhibition and All-Star games. He led Brazil to an unprecedented three World Cups, winning again in Chile in 1962, and in Mexico in 1970 (England won at home in 1966, the year Pele was carried off the field and unable to return after being brutally fouled in a game with Portugal). It is a tribute to his mastery that other great modern goalscorers, dribblers, and playmakers have been and continue to be measured against Pele, among them Portugal's Eusebio, George Best of Northern Ireland, Peru's Teofilo Cubillas, Franz Beckenbauer and Karl-Heinz Rummenigge of West Germany, Holland's Johan Cruyff, Kevin Keegan of Great Britain, Russia's Oleg Blokhin, Michel Platini of France, Italy's Paulo Rossi, Diego Maradona of Argentino, and Brazil's own Zico, known in that country as "The White Pele." Even defensive stars like England's Bobby Moore and goalkeeper Gordon Banks are often remembered by a particular effort against Pele.

Soccer in the 1960s fell into a negative, goal-stifling era in which mass defense was emphasized, with relentless man-to-man marking. The Italian *catenaccio* ("big chain" of defenders), with its extra back (*livero*) playing behind four fullbacks, served as the widely copied model for this style of play, epitomized by Italian coach Helenio Herrera's Inter-Milan team, winner of the European Cup in 1964 and 1965. Cup victories in 1967 by Scotland's attack-minded Glasgow Celtic, and in 1968 by Manchester United (with outstanding performances by George Best and Bobby Charlton) offered the first ray of hope.

Brazil's convincing win in the 1970 Mexico World Cup final over the conservative Italians marked the end of the defensive era. But it was Rinus Michels's energetic Ajax team from Holland, led by the brilliant Johan Cruyff, which introduced the first tactical innovation of soccer's new era, "total football" (or "total soccer"). European Cup winners in 1971, 1972, and 1973, Ajax employed a strategy in which players constantly exchanged positions during the course of play, moving freely between offense and defense as needed, as opposed to being restricted to a certain role or area of the field.

Soccer began to take hold with the youth of America in the 1970s (organized youth soccer participants outnumbered Little League players in many states by 1976). When Pele came out of retirement to join the New York Cosmos in 1975, the sport was given a much-needed boost at the professional level. Suddenly the record crowds attracted by the legendary Brazilian enabled the NASL, founded in 1968, to take its place among the country's established major sports leagues.

Soon, other soccer greats followed Pele to the United States to play. World-class players like Eusebio, George Best, Bobby Moore, Rodney Marsh, Giorgio Chinaglia (who would shatter every NASL scoring record), Teofilo Cubillas, Gordon Banks, Franz Beckenbauer, Trevor Francis, Johan Neeskins, Gordon Hill, Gerd Mueller, Carlos Alberto, and Johan Cruyff brought their varied styles of international soccer to the American game, lifting the level of play and giving America's budding stars the opportunity to learn from the best. Top-level coaches also came, among them Germany's Hennes Weisweiler, Brazilian Claudio Coutinho, and Holland's Rinus Michels.

After leading the Cosmos to the NASL championship over Seattle at the 1977 Soccer Bowl, Pele retired from active competition, scoring his last goal in front of 76,000 rain-soaked fans (and millions more over national television) in an emotional farewell exhibition match between the only clubs he ever played for, the Cosmos and Santos of Brazil. During Pele's three-year stay, NASL attendance had more than tripled, and, at the time of his retirement, another professional league was formed, the Major Indoor Soccer League, devoted solely to the fast, high-scoring indoor version of the sport.

With continued interest in the sport at the youth, high school, and college levels, more home-grown soccer players will follow in the footsteps of American pro stars such as Bob Rigby (holder of the NASL record for the lowest one-season goals-against average, and the first soccer player ever on the cover of Sports Illustrated), Kyle Rote Jr., Al Trost, Shep Messing, Arnold Mausser, Ricky Davis, and Steve Moyers. It now seems possible that before the end of the decade, an American team will once again compete at the World Cup.

advantage: Short for advantage rule.

advantage rule: A clause in the rules of soccer which enables the referee to allow play to continue after a foul if a stoppage of play would take away an advantage held by the fouled player or his team. If the foul committed is serious or violent, the offending player may still be warned, cautioned, or ejected, even though the advantage rule is applied. also *advantage*.

air ball: A ball in flight, or in the air.

American Soccer League: The oldest professional soccer league in the United

States, headquartered in Bethlehem, Pennsylvania. Founded in 1934, the American Soccer League announced a six-team alignment in 1983, comprised of the Carolina Lightnin, the Dallas Americans, the Detroit Express, the Jacksonville Tea Men, the Oklahoma City Slickers, and the Pennsylvania Stoners. also *ASL*.

American Youth Soccer Organization: The largest youth soccer organization in the United States. Founded in 1964, the American Youth Soccer Organization conducts programs in twenty-eight states for boys and girls between the ages of five and eighteen. Special rules require balanced competition and specify that every player on a team must play at least one half of each game. The American Youth Soccer Organization is headquartered in Torrance, California. also *AYSO*.

area: The penalty area. also *box*.

ASL: The American Soccer League.

assistant referee: The official positioned by the side of the playing area of an indoor soccer game, who is primarily responsible for assisting the referee in the control of the game in accordance with the Laws. An assistant referee controls the bench and penalty box areas, indicates illegal substitutions and three-line violations, supervises the timekeeper, and keeps a written record of the game and time penalties.

association football: A British term for soccer, originally used to differentiate the kicking sport from rugby, also known as "football." The term refers to the type of football approved by the London Football Association, the first real governing body of soccer, founded in 1863. see *soccer*.

attacking zone: The part of the playing area in indoor soccer which contains the goal at which a team shoots, bounded by the nearest red line. compare *defensive zone, neutral zone*.

AYSO: The American Youth Soccer Organization.

back: A fullback or defender.

back four: The four fullbacks in a formation which uses four defensive players.

1. back heel: To kick the ball backward with the heel. (back heeled the ball to a trailing teammate)

2. back heel: The act or an instance of using the heel to make a backward pass.

back pass: A pass backward, made either with the heel or by rolling the ball with the bottom of the foot.

ball boy, ball girl: One of a number of boys or girls positioned around the perimeter of the playing area, responsible for retrieving the ball when it is kicked out of play.

banana kick: A kick in which the ball is hit off center to make it spin and thus curve or bend in flight (as around a wall of defenders) before dropping suddenly. Among the first to popularize the technique in the 1950s was the Brazilian Didi (Vvaldyr Pereira), whose special shot was called the *folha seca* (Portuguese for "dry leaf") because it dropped like a dry or dead leaf from a tree. Other internationals who have been known for the banana kick (a name popularized in Germany) are Eusebio of Portugal, Ireland's George Best, Bobby Collins of Scotland, England's Bobby Charlton, Franz Beckenbauer of Germany, and Brazil's incomparable Pele.

banjoed: Players' slang for having been kicked in the groin.

beat: 1. To gain a momentary advantage over an opponent, or to get past an opponent. (beat his man and sent a cross into the middle) 2. To score with

BICYCLE KICK

a shot past the goalkeeper. (beat the keeper with a little chip shot)

bench penalty: A penalty assessed in indoor soccer against a coach, trainer, or player on the bench for delaying the game or for ungentlemanly or violent conduct. A bench penalty results in a time penalty (the length of which depends on the nature and severity of the offense) to be served by a player designated by the coach and during which the offending side must play shorthanded. If the offense is severe, the offending coach, trainer, or player may be cautioned or ejected. After a bench penalty, play is restarted with a drop ball.

bend: To make the ball curve in flight by kicking it off center so that it spins. (bent the ball in by the far post) also *curl.*

bicycle, bicycle kick: An overhead kick in which a player leaps almost upside down to volley the ball with a scissors-like leg motion. When properly executed, the bicycle kick is a powerful shot and one of the most spectacular plays in soccer, whether used to score by a forward with his back to the goal, or to clear or even save the ball by a defender facing the goal. Most often associated with the legendary Brazilian player Pele, the bicycle kick was introduced in the 1930s by another Brazilian international, Leonidas da Silva, after whose nickname, "the Black Diamond," a candy bar was named. Because the leg motion is similar to that used in the horizontal scissors volley or scissors kick, the bicycle kick is sometimes referred to as a scissors kick. also *double kick, hitch kick, overhead volley, reverse kick.*

bite: To go for the ball in an attempt to

BOOTS

tackle it away from an opponent, to commit to tackling the ball. (will lay the ball off to the side as soon as a defender bites) also *challenge.*

blind-side run: An advance, unseen by defenders, by a player without the ball into an attacking space on the side of the field opposite that where the ball is.

block tackle: The act or an instance of blocking the ball with the foot or body at the moment an opponent attempts to kick it. also *front block tackle.*

1. blue card: A small blue card shown by the referee in MISL games to indicate that a player is being assessed a time penalty. see *time penalty.*

2. blue card: To show a blue card.

board: To illegally force or push an opponent into the boards which surround the playing area in indoor soccer. (injured his knee when he was boarded) see *boarding.*

boarding: The act or an instance of illegally forcing or pushing an opponent into the boards surrounding the playing area in indoor soccer. Boarding results in a direct free kick for the offended team and, if the infraction is serious, a two-minute penalty for the offending player.

boards: The 4-foot-high wooden wall which surrounds and forms the perimeter of the playing area in indoor soccer. Attached to the top of the boards (except in front of the players' benches) is an unbreakable glass screen to protect spectators from the ball. also *dasher boards, perimeter wall, woodwork.*

book: To issue a yellow card (or less frequently, a red card) to a player for a serious foul or unsportsmanlike conduct, and to record the name of the guilty player or players. All serious fouls and instances of unsportsmanlike conduct are reported by the referee to the league or sanctioning body for possible further disciplinary action should the guilty player repeat such offenses in future games. *see caution, ejection.*

booking: The act or an instance of issuing a yellow card (or less frequently, a red card) to a player guilty of a serious foul or unsportsmanlike conduct.

boots: The traditional name for cleated soccer shoes. Soccer boots normally have low-cut soft leather uppers (sometimes padded slightly to protect the Achilles tendon) with tough plastic or composition soles and one of three types of cleats or studs, depending upon the playing surface. For thick grass and/or wet or muddy ground, boots with six (or occasionally eight) screw-in replaceable studs (not more than 3/4 of an inch long, nor less than 1/2 inch in diameter) are used. Such studs are made of leather, rubber, aluminum, or plastic, and must be solid. For normal grass or dry or hard ground, boots with ten or more molded cleats (3/8 of an inch minimum diameter) on the sole are used. For artificial turf, boots with many small (approximately 1/4 inch in diameter and 1/4 inch long) molded rubber cleats are used.

bounce ball: see *drop ball.*

box: 1. Slang for the penalty area. (sent a crossing pass into the box) also *area.* 2. Short for the penalty box in indoor soccer. also *sin bin.*

bring down: To cause an opponent to trip or fall down, as with an illegal or late tackle. A foul which results in a direct free kick by the opposing team at the spot of the offense, or if committed by a defender in his penalty area, a penalty kick. In indoor soccer, the offending player may also be assessed a two-minute time penalty. If, in the opinion of the referee, the foul is serious or violent, the offending player may be cautioned (an automatic two-minute time penalty in indoor soccer) or sent off (an automatic five-minute time penalty in indoor soccer, to be served by the ejected player's substitute). also *take down.*

bring the ball down: To trap and control an air ball until it reaches the ground so that it can be dribbled, passed, or shot. (brought the ball down, turned, and chipped it over the diving goalkeeper)

build up: The process of incorporating a number of players into the launching and supporting of an attack. A player who intercepts the ball at midfield will often pass back or laterally in order to allow time for a proper build up for an attack.

bully: A scramble by players from both teams to control a loose ball, especially in front of the goal.

by-line: The goal line. also *endline.*

capped: Having participated as a member of a national team in international matches. (capped six times before he reached the age of twenty) see *caps.*

caps: A term of merit awarded to players who participate as members of a national team in international matches. From the custom in some countries of giving a ceremonial tassled cap to each player for every international match.

1. card: To show a yellow card. see *caution.*

2. card: A yellow card. see *caution.*

catch the defense flat: To momentarily catch the opposing defenders lined up laterally across the field, with no one trailing behind to guard against a through pass. (caught the defense flat and quickly put the ball through into the area for the center forward) also *catch the defense square.*

catch the defense square: see *catch the defense flat.*

catenaccio: A system of play first popularized in Italy in the 1950s and 1960s, utilizing a *livero* or "free man" to cover any place behind a line of three or four fullbacks. Primarily a defensive system, the catenaccio (Italian for "big chain" of defenders) was adapted from the Swiss *verrou* or "bolt" system pioneered in 1931 by Karl Rappan, a former Austrian international player who coached the Servette-Geneva team in Switzerland. In 1947, in order to counter the scoring threat of some of the wealthier Italian first division teams, Nereo Rocco, manager of a small club, Triestina, used the deeply positioned back from the defensive mode of the *verrou* system to anchor his catenaccio. After Triestina's impressive climb from last place to second at the end of the season, other Italian clubs adopted the system, among them, Helenio Herrera's Inter-Milan, European Cup winners in 1964 and 1965. The catenaccio dominated Italian soccer for almost twenty years and served as the prototype for soccer's goal-stifling era of mass defense and relentless man-to-man marking.

1. caution: An official warning to a player guilty of a serious offense such as a deliberate or dangerous foul, persistent infringement of the Laws, dissent, dangerous play (at the option of the referee), entry to or exit from the field without permission, deliberate time wasting, infractions during a penalty kick, intentionally moving a corner flag, upright, or crossbar, ungentlemanly conduct, or in indoor soccer, to a player who is assessed a two-minute penalty more than once in a game for a penal offense. A player who receives a caution is automatically assessed a two-minute penalty in indoor soccer. also *card, yellow card.*

2. caution: To show the yellow card and issue an official caution. also *book, card, yellow card.*

1. center: To kick or play the ball toward attacking players in the center of the field, such as into the penalty area in front of the goal, from the side or sideline area. also *cross.*

2. center: A ball which is centered. also *cross.*

center back: 1. The central defender (or, less frequently, either of two central defenders). Normally positioned directly in front of the goal, the center back is responsible for man-to-man coverage of the opposing center forward and must be strong enough and tall enough to beat opponents on the ground and in the air. The center back was created in 1925 to counter the new-found freedom of forwards because of the change in the offside rule that year (only two, instead of three, defensive players had to be between an offensive player and the goal line when the ball was played). Herbert Chapman's Arsenal team featured a center back when he introduced the W-M formation, in which the old center half was moved back between the two fullbacks. Because of this, and the then-popular custom of numbering positions rather than players, the new central defender was still called a "center half" or "center halfback" (and remains so today for some British traditionalists). Arsenal's first center back was Jack Butler, but he was soon replaced by Herbie Roberts, a tall and able policeman who served as a prototype for all those who followed. also *center full, center fullback, policeman, stopper.* 2. The position played by a center back. (still called "center half" or "center halfback" by some British traditionalists). also *center full, center fullback, policeman, stopper.*

center circle: A circle with a 10-yard radius (10-foot radius in indoor soccer) marked around the actual center of the playing field and bisected by the halfway line. A kickoff is taken from the spot (center spot) in the middle of the center circle at the beginning of each half and overtime period and after each goal. On a kickoff, no player from the defending team may enter the center circle until the ball has been played. also *kickoff circle.*

center forward: 1. The central attacking player on the forward line, normally the player positioned closest to the opponent's goal. The center forward must be skilled enough on the ground to be able to turn and shoot with either foot when being closely marked, and good enough in the air to head in balls crossed into the area from the wings. also *spearhead, striker.* 2. The position played by a center forward. also *spearhead, striker.*

center full: see *center back.*

center fullback: see *center back.*

center half, center halfback: 1. The central midfield player in any formation with three midfielders. The center half has both offensive and defensive responsibilities (the extent of which vary with different formations and styles of play), and must be able to pressure opposing forwards and midfielders in the central portion of the field, to drop back to help out when the defense is outnumbered in the penalty area, and to serve as a link between the defense and offense, bringing the ball forward and distributing it to attacking players, as well as backing up and supporting an attack in progress. see *pyramid.* 2. The position in the midfield played by a center half. see *pyramid.* 3. The central defensive player.

center line: The halfway line, especially in indoor soccer. see *halfway line.*

center spot: The spot marked at the middle of the halfway line within the center circle, and from which kickoffs are made at the start of each half or overtime period and after each goal.

1. challenge: To confront an opposing player with the ball and attempt to tackle it away from him. also *bite.*

2. challenge: The act or an instance of challenging an opponent.

chance: An opportunity to score or shoot at the goal.

change: To pass the ball from one side of

the field to a teammate on the other side. also *switch*.

change on the fly: To substitute a player or players in indoor soccer while the game is in progress rather than waiting for a stoppage in play. A legal tactic as long as the player or players substituted for arrive at the bench (off the field or in contact with the sideboard in the bench area) before the replacement or replacements enter the field of play. When an infraction occurs (too many men on the ice), the offending player or players are assessed a two-minute penalty, and the opposing team is awarded an indirect free kick from where the ball was when play was stopped.

1. charge: To run into or make contact with an opposing player, legal only if contact is made with the shoulder (a "fair charge" or "shoulder charge") when contending for a ball within playing distance (3 to 4 feet). see *charging*.

2. charge: The act or an instance of running into or making contact with an opposing player. see *charging*.

charging: The act or an instance of an illegal charge. If the charge is made from behind the opponent (unless the opponent is deliberately obstructing) or made in a violent or dangerous manner, a direct free kick is awarded to the offended side from the place where the infraction occurred, or a penalty kick is awarded to the offended team if the infraction is committed by a defending player inside the penalty area. In indoor soccer, the offending player may also be assessed a two-minute time penalty. If, in the opinion of the referee, the foul is particularly serious or violent, the offending player may be cautioned (an automatic two-minute time penalty in indoor soccer) or sent off (an automatic five-minute time penalty in indoor soccer, to be served by the ejected player's substitute). If a fair charge is made with the shoulder when the ball is not within playing distance, or if no attempt is being made to play the ball, or if the goalkeeper is illegally charged, an indirect free kick is awarded to the offended team at the place where the infraction occurred.

chest: To trap and control an air ball with the chest. (chested the ball down to his

thigh, gave it a little bounce, then turned and volleyed it into the net)

chest trap: The act or an instance of stopping and controlling an air ball with the chest. compare *foot trap, head trap, sole trap, sweep trap, thigh trap*.

1. chip: To kick under and lift the ball off the ground into a high lobbing arc, usually for a short distance (such as over one or more defenders). also *flight, loft*. compare *lob*.

2. chip: A pass or a shot which is lofted or chipped. (a set play which called for him to run onto a little chip over the wall) compare *lob*.

chippy: Unnecessarily rough, as of one or more fouls, the play of one or more individuals or a team, or of a game in general. (cautioned for a particularly chippy foul)

chop: see *hack*.

clear: To kick or head the ball away from in front of the goal, out of danger. (gave up the goal when his defenders failed to clear the ball)

clearance: The act or an instance of clearing the ball.

clear off the line: To clear a ball out of danger just before it entirely crosses the goal line.

close down: 1. To thwart or successfully defend against an opposing player or team, whether by aggressive individual marking or teamwork and strategy. (able to close down their center forward) 2. To defensively seal off an area of the field.

combination passes, combination play: A series of short, low passes between two or more players to advance the ball toward the opponent's goal. Combination play was introduced in the early 1970s by Queen's Park of Scotland, replacing the traditional English dribbling game and revolutionizing soccer.

convert a corner: To score a goal from a corner kick.

convert a penalty: To score a goal from a penalty kick.

Copa Libertadores: An annual tournament to determine the top club team in South America. The competition is open to the league champion and runner-up in all South American countries. The Copa Libertadores was first won in 1960 by Penarol of Uruguay.

corner: Short for corner kick.

corner area: The area within the corner kick arc marked inside each corner of the playing field. Corner kicks may be taken from anywhere within the corner area. also *quarter circle*.

corner flag: 1. A small flag atop a post not less than 5 feet high (and having a non-pointed top) placed at each corner of the playing field. The corner flag (including the post) may not be moved in order to take a corner kick. 2. A small flag atop a post raised 3 feet above the level of the perimeter wall in indoor soccer at each corner of the playing area, at the point where an undrawn extension of the goal area line meets the perimeter wall.

corner kick: 1. A direct free kick awarded to the attacking team when a defender is the last to touch a ball that crosses entirely over the goal line (outside the goal) out of play, taken from anywhere within the corner area on the side of the field on which the ball crossed the goal line. A corner kick is a dangerous scoring opportunity for the attacking team. Though a goal may be scored directly from a corner kick by "bending" the ball into the goal behind the goalkeeper (at one time a favorite technique of Irish soccer great George Best), the ball is usually lofted into the penalty area where it can be headed toward the goal by a teammate. Opposing players may be no closer than 10 yards from the ball until it is in play (travels the distance of its own circumference). The corner kick was first introduced in 1872 by the Football Association in England. also *corner*. compare *goal kick*. 2. A direct free kick awarded to the attacking team in indoor soccer when a defender is the last to touch a ball which leaves the playing area (passing over the perimeter wall between the corner flags in the zone), taken from the corner kick spot on the side of the goal on which the ball left the playing area. Opposing players may be no closer than 10 feet from the ball until it is in play (travels half the distance of its own circumference). also *corner*.

corner kick arc: The 1-yard radius quarter circle marked inside each corner of the playing field, enclosing the corner area from which corner kicks are taken. also *quarter circle*.

corner kick spot: A 19-inch dot marked at each corner of the playing area in indoor soccer at the intersection of the touchline and an undrawn extension of the goal area line. Corner kicks are taken from the corner kick spot. also *corner mark*.

corner mark: see *corner kick spot*.

cover: To take a defensive position behind a defending teammate, freeing him to challenge the player with the ball without fear of being beaten or of the player passing the ball through for an attacking teammate to run on to. A basic and essential tactic in soccer.

crease: The rectangular area marked in front of each goal in indoor soccer, measuring 16 feet wide (2 feet wider than the goal on each side) and 5 feet deep. The term is taken from hockey's similar "goal crease." also *goal area*.

create space: To cause the opponents to momentarily leave a strategic area of the field unguarded, such as by drawing defenders away with the ball, or with a dummy run or pass. (drew the defender out toward the wing, creating a space in the penalty area) also *make space*.

1. cross: To center the ball from the side or sideline area into the penalty area. also *center*.

2. cross: The act or an instance of centering the ball from the side or sideline area toward the middle of the field, especially in front of the opponent's goal. also *center*.

crossbar: The horizontal bar which marks the top of the goal, extending 8 yards between the goal posts 8 feet above the ground. First used at the Cheltenham public school in England, the crossbar was made obligatory by the Football Association in 1882. In indoor soccer, the crossbar extends 12 feet between the goal posts 6-1/2 feet above the ground.

curl: see *bend*.

cut down the angle: To move out from the goal line toward an attacking player with the ball so that he will be able to see less of the goal, and be forced to shoot from farther away. also *narrow the angle*.

cut the ball out: To tackle the ball away from an opponent.

dangerous play: Any action by a player which is dangerous or likely to cause injury to the player, a teammate, or an opponent. The most frequent instances of a dangerous play are kicking a ball near one or more other players which is high enough to normally head, or heading a ball near one or more other players which is low enough to normally kick. A dangerous play results in an indirect free kick by the opposing team from the spot of the offense.

dasher boards: see *boards*.

dead ball: 1. A ball that is out of play, such as when the ball crosses the goal line or a sideline or after a stoppage of play. 2. A ball placed anywhere within the playing area by the referee, such as for a kickoff or a direct or indirect kick. 3. A ball resting on the ground.

dead space: Areas of the playing field occupied by opposing players. compare *drop zone, space*.

defender: A fullback, one of the players on the back line whose main responsibility is to prevent the opposing team from scoring a goal. also *back*.

defense kick: see *goal kick*.

defensive zone: The part of the playing area in indoor soccer which contains the goal defended by a team, bounded by the nearest red line. compare *attacking zone, neutral zone*.

delay of game penalty: 1. An indirect free kick awarded to the opposing team when a player or players, in the opinion of the referee, indulge in tactics to hold up the game or waste time. 2. In indoor soccer, a two-minute penalty assessed to the goalkeeper (to be served by another player) when the ball is passed back into the defensive zone by a teammate from any other zone and is then handled by the goalkeeper (an indirect free kick is awarded to the opposing team from point of the infraction); or a two-minute penalty assessed to a player who intentionally kicks or heads the ball outside the playing area (an indirect free kick is awarded to the opposing team from the point of the infraction).

direct free kick: A free kick which is awarded to the opposing team at the point of the offense when a serious foul (such as pushing, holding or kicking an opponent) or infraction (such as intentionally handling the ball) is committed by a player, and from which a goal

may be scored directly against the offending team (should a ball be miskicked into a team's own goal, no goal results). When a direct free kick is taken, no opposing player may be closer than 10 yards from the ball (10 feet in indoor soccer) until it is played, unless the opposing player or players are standing on their own goal line between the goal posts. When a direct free kick is taken by a player from within his own penalty area, no opposing player may be inside the area or closer than 10 yards (10 feet in indoor soccer) until the ball is played. The ball must be stationary when a direct free kick is taken, and is in play when it has traveled the distance (or half the distance in indoor soccer) of its circumference (and is beyond the penalty area, if the kick is taken by a player from within his own area). The kicker may not play the ball a second time until it has been touched or played by another player. compare *indirect free kick*.

dissent: The act or an instance of vocally and persistently disagreeing with the decision of a referee, which can result in an indirect free kick being awarded to the opposing team from the point where the infraction occurred and in a yellow card (or in indoor soccer, a two-minute penalty) for the offending player.

dive: A faked or exaggerated fall to call the referee's attention to an alleged foul (such as at the time of a charge or tackle) in the hopes that a foul will be called against an opponent.

division: A group of competing teams at a specified level of play. In most countries, soccer competition is arranged by divisions, with the highest level being the "premiere" or "first" division, the next highest level being the "second" division, and so on. The English Football League, the first and prototype league for all that followed, added a second division in 1892. Each division is comprised of a given number of teams, with the highest finishers (usually two or three) of the previous season in each division below the first division moving up to the next higher division, and the last two or three finishers in each division suffering relegation to the division below for the next season. This automatic promotion system, pioneered by the Football League in 1899, provides incentive for teams in the lower divisions not only to win within their division, but to attempt to advance to a higher and more prestigious division, and for teams in the higher divisions to avoid relegation.

double minor: Two two-minute time penalties (minor penalties) assessed against a player (such as for unsportsmanlike conduct which does not warrant a caution) to be served consecutively. When a player is assessed a double minor and a goal is scored against his team during the first two-minute segment, the balance of the first segment is voided and the player remains in the penalty box for the second two-minute segment only. compare *major penalty, minor penalty*.

double pass: see *give-and-go*.

double kick: A bicycle kick.

drag the ball back: To suddenly move the ball closer with the foot, such as to protect it from an approaching defender.

1. dribble: To maneuver with or advance the ball using the feet to guide and control it with a series of light taps. (dribbled through the two fullbacks and shot)

2. dribble: The act or an instance of dribbling the ball.

dribbler: One who dribbles or is adept at dribbling the ball. Great Britain's beknighted winger, Sir Stanley Matthews (who played from the 1930s through the 1950s), Brazil's sensational winger of the 1950s, Garrincha (Manoel Francisco dos Santos), Ireland's magician with the ball, George Best (who burst into international prominence with Manchester United in the late 1960s and early 1970s), and, of course, Brazil's legendary Pele are regarded as some of soccer's greatest dribblers.

drop ball: A method of restarting play which has been stopped for a reason other than a foul (such as a serious injury, too many men on the field, or an outside influence) in which the referee drops the ball between two opposing players. The ball may not be touched or kicked by either player until it touches the ground. also *bounce ball, faceoff*.

dropkick: 1. A goalkeeper's technique in which the ball is dropped and kicked

just as it bounces up from the ground. 2. A half volley.

drop-kick: 1. To drop the ball and kick it just as it bounces up from the ground, legal for a goalkeeper when he is within the penalty area. 2. To half volley the ball.

drop pass: A pass in which the player in control of the ball, while moving forward, steps over the ball and rolls it, taps it (as with a back heel), or simply leaves it for a trailing teammate, and continues without breaking stride in the hopes of drawing away a defender.

drop zone: An area of the field unguarded by players of the opposing team, into which the ball is played to link up with an oncoming teammate.

dummy: A fake or feint intended to momentarily deceive an opponent. (went for the dummy and broke up the wall before the ball was kicked) see *sell the dummy*.

ejection: The expulsion of a player from a game for a serious or dangerous foul, persistent dissent, unsportsmanlike conduct, for a second caution during a game (or in indoor soccer, for his third two-minute time penalty for a penal offense), and which is signaled by the referee showing a red card to the guilty player. An ejected player may not be replaced by a substitute for the remainder of that game (except in indoor soccer, when the substitute must first serve a five-minute time penalty) and is usually suspended from playing in at least one future game. also *red card*.

eleven: A soccer team. (the most talented eleven in the country) also *side*.

encroach: To move closer to the ball than the 10-yard limit (10 feet in indoor soccer) on a kickoff, free kick, or corner kick (or on a kick-in in indoor soccer), to interfere with a throw-in or with the movement of a goalkeeper, or to enter the penalty area or move closer than the 10-yard limit (10 feet in indoor soccer) on a penalty kick. see *encroachment*.

encroachment: The act or an instance of encroaching, resulting in a caution for the guilty player and ejection if the infraction is repeated. In indoor soccer, encroachment results in a two-minute time penalty and a caution if the infraction is repeated.

end line: The goal line. also *by-line.*

equalize: To score a game-tying goal. (equalized in the final minute) also *knot.*

equalizer: A game-tying goal.

European Championship: The European Football Championship.

European Championship Clubs' Cup: A prestigious annual competition between the national champions of all European nations, commonly known as the European Cup. Proposed in 1954 by Gabriel Hanot, editor of the French sports paper *L'Equipe,* the European Cup was played first in 1956, with sixteen clubs participating. Real Madrid of Spain won the first European Cup, defeating Reims in the final played in Paris, France. With great foreign players such as Argentinian Alfredo di Stefano and Hungarian Ferenc Puskas, Real Madrid went on to win the next four European Cups (through 1960).

European Cup: The European Championship Clubs' Cup.

European Cup Winners' Cup: An annual tournament between cup winners from European nations (as opposed to national or league champions). The first competition was held in 1960, with Fiorentina of Italy winning in the final over Scotland's Glasgow Rangers.

European Football Championship: A quadrennial competition between national teams held midway between World Cup years. Originally called the European Nations Cup, the first European football Championship final was held in Paris in 1960, with Russia defeating Yugoslavia in extra time. also *European Championship.*

extra time: Playing time added to the end of a half to make up for delays because of injuries ("injury time"), a lost or difficult-to-recover ball or one in need of replacement, deliberate time-wasting by either team, or penalty kicks. The referee records all such delays to determine the amount of extra time to be added to each forty-five-minute half. The concept of extra time was introduced shortly after a controversial incident at the conclusion of a match in 1891 in England between Aston Villa and Stoke. With just over a minute left in the game, Stoke, down 1-0, was awarded a penalty shot. But Villa's wily goalkeeper grabbed the ball and kicked it as far as he could, over the

startled spectators and completely out of the playing grounds. Before it could be found and returned, the referee had whistled the end of the game.

face: Short for "face the goal" or "face the play," called out to teammates who have momentarily turned their backs on play, such as when players return after an unsuccessful attack or corner kick. "Face," then, is a warning to pay attention, so that the opposing team cannot gain a quick advantage when the ball is put back in play.

faceoff: Slang for a drop ball in indoor soccer. also *bounce ball.*

face off: To participate as one of the two players involved in a drop ball.

FA Cup: The Football Association Cup, the annual postseason elimination tournament and trophy for the championship of the British Football Association. The oldest continuous major sports competition, the FA Cup was the idea of British football (soccer) pioneer, Charles W. Alcock and was held first in 1872, with fifteen teams competing. In the first final, played in London before 2,000 spectators, the Wanderers defeated the favored Royal Engineers. The last amateur club to win the FA Cup was the Old Etonians in 1882. In 1894, Notts County defeated Bolton to become the first second division club to win the competition.

fair charge: A legal shoulder charge. see *charging, shoulder charge.*

far post: The goal post farthest from where the ball is being played. compare *near post.*

Federation Internationale de Football Association: The Federation of International Football Associations (FIFA), the international governing body of soccer. Founded in 1904, FIFA is headquartered in Zurich, Switzerland, with a membership of 154 nations.

field player: A player other than a goalkeeper.

FIFA: The Federation Internationale de Football Association.

fifty-fifty ball: A free ball in play that opposing players have an equal chance of controlling or playing. (an aggressive midfielder who wins most fifty-fifty balls)

1. finish: To shoot at the goal.

2. finish: A shot at the goal, as after a solo run, or after combination play approaching the goal.

finisher: One who shoots the goal. (looks awkward, but he's a great finisher)

1. **first time:** Played on the initial touch, without first trapping or controlling, as of a ball approaching on the ground or in the air. also *one touch.*

2. **first time:** Of or pertaining to a ball played on the initial touch, without trapping or controlling it first. (scored with a first time volley) also *one touch.*

fist: To punch a dangerous air ball away from the goal with the hand clenched, legal for a goalkeeper anywhere within the penalty area. (fisted the cross away to prevent a goal)

five-second rule: A rule in indoor soccer which prohibits a goalkeeper in full possession of the ball from delaying the release of the ball from his hands by more than five seconds. An infraction of the five-second rule results in the awarding of an indirect free kick to the opposing team from the place where the infraction occurred.

1. **flag:** A small, colored (usually bright yellow or red) flag on a short pole carried by linesmen and used to signal an offside, or the side entitled to a corner kick, goal kick, or throw-in when the ball leaves the playing area. (appealed to the linesman for the offside flag)

2. **flag:** To signify an offside by raising the flag. (flagged the offside to nullify the goal)

1. **flick:** 1. To pass or shoot the ball with the outside of the foot, quickly snapping the foot outward to propel the ball. (flicked the return pass into the goal first time) 2. To head the ball (usually a short distance) toward the goal or a teammate. also *nod.*

2. **flick:** A short pass or shot made by flicking the ball with the foot or head toward a teammate or the goal.

flick kick: A jabbing kick in which the ball is flicked with the outside of the foot. also *jab kick.*

flick on: To head an air ball in such a way as to keep it moving in or near its original direction. (flicked the ball on, just over the defender)

flick-on header: A header in which the ball is flicked on, in, or near its original direction.

flight: see *chip.*

football: 1. The international name for soccer. also *association football.* 2. A soccer ball.

footballer: A soccer player.

foot trap: A trap in which the foot is used to null and control a ball in the air, or a moving ball on the ground (such as with a sole trap or sweep trap). compare *chest trap, head trap, thigh trap.*

forward: A primarily attacking player on the front line. The center forward, strikers and/or wings are all considered forwards, as are the inside left and inside right in formations where these positions are utilized. Forwards are primarily responsible for maneuvering the ball close to the opponent's goal and taking shots. In some modern formations, all the forwards are called strikers. see *pyramid.*

1. **foul:** A violation of the rules which involves physical interference with an opponent (such as kicking, tripping, jumping at, charging, striking, spitting, holding, pushing and, in indoor soccer, boarding), intentionally handling the ball, dangerous play, or unsportsmanlike conduct, penalized by awarding a free kick to the opposing team (a direct free kick, indirect free kick, or penalty kick, depending on the location and severity of the foul) and assessing a yellow or red card (and in indoor soccer, a time penalty) to the offending player if the foul is considered serious or violent.

2. **foul:** 1. To commit a foul. 2. To commit a foul against a particular opponent. (fouled him when he took him down from behind)

4-4-2: A formation which employs four defenders, four midfielders, and two forwards. The 4-4-2 formation became popular in England in the 1970s, an outgrowth of the 4-3-3 formation first used

DEFENDERS

MIDFIELD

FORWARDS

4-4-2

by the victorious Brazilians at the 1962 World Cup in Chile, and then by the English national team, World Cup winners in 1966. compare *4-3-3, 4-2-4, pyramid, 3-4-3, W-M.*

4-3-3: A formation which employs four defenders, three midfielders, and three forwards. The 4-3-3 formation was introduced in 1962 by Brazil, World Cup winners that year in Chile, and used successfully again four years later at the 1966 World Cup by team manager Alf Francis's victorious English national team. compare *4-4-2, 4-2-4, pyramid, 3-4-3, W-M.*

4-2-4: A formation which employs four defenders, two midfielders, and four forwards. Though a somewhat similar system had been shown by the talented Hungarian team of the early 1950s, the 4-2-4 was introduced in 1958 at the World Cup in Sweden by the victorious Brazilian national team. compare *4-4-2, 4-3-3, pyramid, 3-4-3, W-M.*

freeback: see *sweeper.*

free kick: An unhindered placekick which is awarded to the opposing team at the point of the offense when a foul or infraction is committed by a player. When a free kick is taken, no opposing player may be closer than 10 yards from the ball (10 feet in indoor soccer) until it is played, unless the opposing player or players are standing on their own goal line between the goal posts. Depending upon the severity of the foul or infraction, a free kick may be either a direct free kick (from which a goal may be scored directly against the offending team) or an indirect free kick (from which a goal cannot be scored until the ball has first touched another player). In indoor soccer, a free kick must be taken within five seconds of the referee's signal. An infraction results in a two-minute time penalty for the kicker, and play is restarted with the original free kick. Free kicks were first introduced by the English Football Association in 1873. see *direct free kick, indirect free kick.*

friendly: A friendly match outside of regular league or international championship play. (will play a series of friendlies before their World Cup elimination matches)

front block tackle: see *block tackle.*

front man: see *target man.*

fullback: 1. A primarily defensive player on the back line who normally plays closest to the goal defended by his team. Fullbacks are primarily responsible for preventing opposing forwards from shooting at the goal, and for gaining possession of the ball, either to clear it away from the area in front of the goal, or to pass it to a teammate upfield. Depending on the style of play used, fullbacks may occasionally move forward to support or take part in an attack. also *back, defender.* see *overlap, pyramid.* 2. The position played by a fullback. see *pyramid.*

full time: The end of regulation time for a match, not including injury or extra time. A British expression.

funnel back: To, as a part of a deliberate strategy, fall back defensively in such a way as to "funnel" attacking opponents into a sealed-off central area.

get tight: see *mark up.*

ghost: To deliberately play in such a way as to go unnoticed by the opposing team (either momentarily, or for an extended period of time) in the hopes of being undefended at some critical point in a game or series of games.

give and go: To execute a give-and-go.

give-and-go: A play in which the player with the ball makes a short pass to a teammate, then breaks past a defender or defenders into an open space for a quick return pass. The give-and-go is one of the most effective and frequently used tactics in soccer. also *double pass, one-two, wall pass.*

give away a corner: To cause a corner kick to be awarded to the opposing team either deliberately or accidentally by being the last to touch the ball

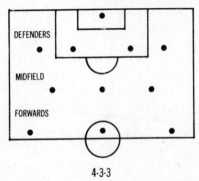

4-3-3

before it crosses out of play over one's own end line. When outnumbered or in danger in the penalty area (as when the goalkeeper is down or out of position), a defender will frequently kick or deflect the ball over the end line and "give away a corner" in order to give the defense time to regroup.

give some stick: To play rough, especially to physically punish a particular opponent. A British expression, applied both to rugby and soccer. compare *take some stick*.

●●To razz or give someone a hard time. (gave him some stick about showing up late)

goal: 1. The structure centered on each end line into which the ball must be played in order to score. A goal consists of a rectangular wood or metal (or other FIFA-approved material) frame, with two upright goal posts 24 feet apart, joined 8 feet above the ground by a horizontal crossbar. The goal posts and crossbar may be no more than 5 inches thick, and must be the same. A mesh net is attached to the goal posts and crossbar and the ground behind (back far enough to allow the goalkeeper room to maneuver) to completely enclose the top, back and sides of the structure. The first modern rules regulating goals were adopted at Cambridge in England in 1848, calling for two vertical posts with a string or tape stretched between them. In 1863, the English Football Association called for two posts 8 yards apart, adopting Cambridge's connecting tape in 1866. The crossbar, first used at Cheltenham public school, was made obligatory in 1882, with nets being added in 1891.

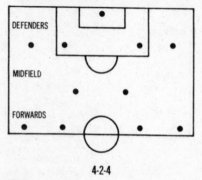

4-2-4

also *net*. 2. The structure in the middle of the perimeter wall at each end of the playing area in indoor soccer, into which the ball must be played in order to score. A goal consists of a rectangular wood or metal (or other FIFA-approved material) frame, with two upright goal posts 12 feet apart, joined 6 feet, 6 inches above the ground by a horizontal crossbar. The goal posts and crossbar may be no more than 5 inches thick, and must be the same. A mesh net is attached to the goal posts and crossbar and the ground behind (to a suggested depth of 5 feet) to completely enclose the top, back and sides of the structure. also *net, nets*. 3. A point scored as a result of the ball being played (off of any part of the goalkeeper, or any part of a field player except for the arms and hands) completely over the goal line between the goal posts and under the crossbar. A goal is credited in the scoring records to the player who propels the ball into the opponent's goal. The legendary Pele is the greatest goal scorer in the history of soccer, netting an incredible 1,251 goals in first division or international competition in his 21-year career (1956-1977), not counting 33 goals scored in exhibition and All-Star games. Pele scored 1,090 goals for the Brazilian club, Santos, 101 goals for the national team of Brazil (14 in World Cup competition), and 60 goals for the New York Cosmos of the North American Soccer League. Giorgio Chinaglia, the NASL all-time goal scoring champion, set the single season record in 1978, scoring 34 goals in thirty games. In indoor soccer, the MISL all-time goal scoring champion, Steve Zungul of the New York Arrows, set the single season record in 1981-82, scoring 103 goals in forty games. also *marker, tally*.

goal area: A rectangular area marked in front of and centered on each goal, 20 yards wide and 6 yards deep (16 feet wide and 5 feet deep in indoor soccer), and from which goal kicks are taken. see *crease*.

goal area line: 1. A 20-foot line centered on each goal, marked 6 yards out from and parallel to the goal line, and serving as the front boundary of the goal area. 2. A 16-foot line centered on each goal in indoor soccer, marked 5 feet out from and parallel to the goal line, and serving as the front boundary of the goal area or crease. see *corner flag, corner kick spot.*

goal difference: A statistic which reflects the difference between the number of goals a team scores and the number of goals a team gives up during a particular period (as in a tournament or season).

goalie: Slang for a goalkeeper.

goal judge: Either of two officials positioned behind the goals in indoor soccer who decide whether or not the ball has passed wholly over the goal line for a goal, and who signify the scoring of a goal by switching on the red goal light (or by holding up a flag). The referee may overrule a goal judge's decision to allow or disallow a goal.

goalkeeper: 1. The defensive player normally positioned in front of the goal who is responsible for blocking shots and keeping the ball from going into the goal. The goalkeeper is the one player allowed to use his hands to catch or to deflect or punch the ball away, provided he is within the penalty area. He may not take more than four steps while holding, bouncing, or tossing the ball up in the air to himself, but may roll or dribble the ball, though it may then be contested for by opposing players. (In indoor soccer, the goalkeeper must release and distribute the ball within five seconds.) A goalkeeper must wear colors which distinguish him from the other players and the referee. The special rules which govern goalkeepers were introduced in 1870 by the English Football Association. also *goalie, keeper.* 2. The position played by a goalkeeper. also *goalie, keeper.*

goal kick: An indirect free kick awarded to the defensive team when an attacker is the last to touch a ball that crosses entirely over the goal line (or the perimeter wall between the corner flags in indoor soccer) outside the goal and out of play, taken from within the half of the goal area on the side of the field on which the ball left the playing area. A goal kick must clear the penalty area and may not be played again by the

kicker until it has been touched by another player, nor may it be kicked into the goalkeeper's hands until it has first left the area. Opposing players must remain outside the penalty area until the kick is taken. The goal kick was introduced in 1869 by the English Football Association. compare *corner kick.*

goal light: A red light located behind the goals in indoor soccer, activated by the goal judge when a goal has been scored.

goal line: The boundary line marked at each end of the playing area, extending the width of the field between the touchlines, and in the center of which is located the goal (in indoor soccer, the goal line is marked only between the goal posts, with the perimeter wall between the corner flags marking the end boundary). When a ball crosses entirely over the vertical plane of the goal line between the goal posts and under the crossbar, a goal is scored. When a ball crosses entirely over the vertical plane of the goal line outside the goal (or the perimeter wall between the corner flags in indoor soccer), the result is a corner kick (if the ball was last touched by a defender) or a goal kick (if the ball was last touched by an attacker). also *by-line, end line.*

goal post, goalpost: Either of two square, rectangular, round, half-round or elliptical poles or posts, 24 feet apart (12 feet in indoor soccer) and connected by the crossbar 8 feet above the ground (6 feet, 6 inches in indoor soccer), and which serve as the side boundaries of the goal. also *post, upright.* see *goal.*

goals against: The total number of goals allowed by a goalkeeper or team within a specified time (such as a game, tournament, or season). In 1973, goalkeeper Bob Rigby (then of the Philadelphia Atoms) set the NASL record for the fewest goals against in a season, allowing only eight goals in 1,157 minutes played.

goals against average: The statistic reflecting the average number of goals allowed by a goalkeeper in one ninety-minute game, computed by multiplying the total number of goals against by ninety, then dividing by the total number of minutes played, usually carried two decimal places (a goalkeeper who has played a total of 2,880 minutes and given up forty-five goals has a goals against average of 1.41). Goalkeeper Bob Rigby holds the NASL record for the best goals against average for a season, 0.62 (Philadelphia Atoms, 1973).

good in the air: Adept at heading the ball.

graft: British slang for hard work and persistence on the playing field, especially in attempts to tackle and win the ball from opponents.

grafter: British slang for a player known for hard work and persistence on the playing field, especially in attempts to tackle and win the ball from opponents.

ground: 1. A stadium or playing field and environs. A British term. (aspires to play at Wembley, one of soccer's most hallowed grounds) also *grounds*. 2. A British term for a playing field. also *grounds, pitch*.

grounds: see *ground*.

hack: To kick an opponent, a foul which results in the awarding of a direct free kick to the offended team at the spot of the offense, or if within the penalty area of the defending team, a penalty kick. In indoor soccer, the offending player may also be assessed a two-minute time penalty. If, in the opinion of the referee, the foul is serious or violent, the offending player may be cautioned (an automatic two-minute time penalty in indoor soccer) or sent off (an automatic five-minute time penalty in indoor soccer, to be served by the ejected player's substitute). The prohibition of hacking in the first rules adopted by the English Football Association in 1863 was one of the provisions which separated soccer from rugby. also *chop*.

hacker: A derogatory name for a rough player, usually a defender, who often kicks or physically fouls opponents.

half: 1. Short for halfback. 2. The position played by a halfback. (a great playmaker at left half) 3. Either of the two halves of the field, from the midfield line to the goal line. (couldn't get the ball out of their own half) 4. Either of the two forty-five-minute periods of play in a game (plus any extra time added by the referee). 5. The end of the first forty-five-minute period of play in a game (plus any extra time added by the referee).

halfback: 1. A midfielder. see *pyramid*. 2. The position played by a halfback. see *pyramid*.

1. **half volley:** A powerful kick in which the ball is contacted just as it bounces up from the ground. also *dropkick*. compare *volley*.

2. **half volley:** To kick the ball just as it bounces up from the ground. (half volleyed the low cross for a goal) also *drop-kick*. compare *volley*.

halfway line: A line marked across the center of the playing area (touchline to touchline, or side perimeter wall to side perimeter wall in indoor soccer) parallel to the goal lines. The center spot, from which kickoffs are taken, and the surrounding center circle are marked in the middle of the halfway line. also *center line, midfield line*.

handball: The act or an instance of illegally handling the ball, a foul which results in the awarding of a direct free kick to the opposing team at the spot of the offense, and if the foul is committed by a defensive player (other than the goalkeeper) in his penalty area, a penalty kick. In indoor soccer, the offending player may also be assessed a two-minute time penalty. No handball is called if a goalkeeper handles the ball within his penalty area, if the player's hand is in a natural position and contact is unintentional, or if the player moves his hands in the path of the ball to protect his face or groin (or a woman to protect her breasts). also *hands*.

handle: To carry, strike, or propel the ball with any part of the hand or arm, a foul (except in the case of a goalkeeper within the penalty area). England's Football Association abolished the rugby-inspired fair catch and thus, handling, in 1870, permitting only goalkeepers to play the ball with the hands thereafter. see *handball*.

hands: see *handball*.

hat trick: Three goals by the same player in a single game. Though the expression is commonly used in connection with hockey, baseball, and horse racing, "hat trick" was originally from the game of cricket. In England in the late 1800s, a cap or hat was given to a "bowler" who took three "wickets" with successive deliveries. Soccer's greatest goal scorer, the legendary

Pele, scored ninety-three hat tricks in his remarkable twenty-one-year career (1956-1977).

head: To shoot, pass, or clear an air ball out of danger by propelling it with the head. Although there is evidence to show that the head was used in ancient Chinese and Mesoamerican "football" games, it is believed that a Lieutenant Sim of southern England's Royal Engineers team (FA Cup winners in 1875) was the first to use heading as an intentional tactic. also *flick, nod.*

header: A shot, pass or clearance which is propelled with the head. In a properly timed and executed header, contact is made with the forehead, and the ball may be accurately driven, using the neck muscles for power, or delicately lobbed toward the intended target.

head trap: A trap in which the head is used to null and control an air ball. compare *chest trap, foot trap, sole trap, sweep trap, thigh trap.*

heavy pitch: A slow, soft playing surface, as one in which the turf is wet or not closely cut.

heel kick: A backward pass made by stepping over the ball and kicking it with the heel.

Hermann Trophy: The annual award given to the outstanding college soccer player in America, as selected by college coaches, sports editors, and soccer writers. The equivalent to college football's Heisman Trophy, the Hermann Trophy was created in 1967 by soccer patron Robert Hermann of St. Louis, Missouri, owner of the former NASL St. Louis Stars. The Hermann Trophy was first awarded in 1967 to Don Markus of Long Island University in New York.

hitch kick: A bicycle kick.

hold: To illegally grab or grasp an opponent or the uniform of an opponent. Holding is a foul which results in the awarding of a direct free kick to the opposing team at the spot of the offense, or if the foul is committed by a defender in his penalty area, a penalty kick.

home: Into the goal for a score. (drove the equalizer home in extra time)

human pinball: A facetious name for indoor soccer because of the speed of the game and the way the ball is made to carom off the boards.

indirect free kick: A free kick which is awarded to the opposing team at the point of the offense when an infraction (such as a dangerous play, a fair charge when the ball is not within playing distance, obstruction, etc.) is committed by a player, or after a player is cautioned (as for illegally leaving or entering the field, dissent, or ungentlemanly conduct), and from which a goal cannot be scored until after the ball has been touched by another player. When an indirect free kick is taken, no opposing player may be closer than 10 yards from the ball (10 feet in indoor soccer) until it is played, unless the opposing player or players are standing on their own goal line between the goal posts. When an indirect free kick is taken by a player from within his own penalty area, no opposing player may be inside the area or closer than 10 yards (10 feet in indoor soccer) until the ball is played. The ball must be stationary when an indirect free kick is taken, and is in play when it has travelled the dis-

HEADER

267

tance (or half the distance in indoor soccer) of its circumference (and is beyond the penalty area, if the kick is taken by a player from within his own area). The kicker may not play the ball a second time until it has been touched or played by another player. compare *direct free kick.*

indoor soccer: A version of soccer played indoors on artificial turf between teams of six players (a goalkeeper and five field players) on a hockey-rinklike playing area approximately 200 feet long by 85 feet wide, and enclosed by an unbreakable glass-topped wall (to protect spectators) with 12-foot wide by 6-1/2-foot high goals centered on each end. The playing field is marked with goal and penalty areas, penalty spots, a center line and circle, four corner kick spots, and touchlines 3 feet from and parallel to the sideboards. Two red lines are marked 30 feet on either side of and parallel to the center line, dividing the playing area into three parts. Indoor soccer is played by international soccer rules with the following exceptions: a game is divided into four fifteen-minute quarters, and the clock is stopped when the referee blows his whistle to stop play or the ball goes out of play; unlimited substitution is allowed during a game, provided no more than six players a side are on the field at one time; kick-ins from the touchlines replace throw-ins when the ball goes out of bounds (over the sideboards);

corner kicks are taken from the corner kick spots; indirect free kicks are awarded to the opposing team when a ball is played in the air across the three lines (the center line and both red lines); on kickoffs, kick-ins, corner kicks, and all free kicks, opposing players must remain 10 feet from the ball until it is played; and two and five-minute time penalties are assessed for fouls, during which the guilty player must wait in a penalty box while his team plays shorthanded (as in hockey). Though an indoor game with abbreviated teams was played in the United States as early as 1905 in New York's Madison Square Garden, professional indoor soccer (as played by the MISL) was the result of a popular series of exhibition games between NASL teams and the Soviet Union's Moscow Dynamo and Zenit-Leningrad in 1974. see *kick-in, Major Indoor Soccer League, North American Soccer League, three line pass.*

injury time: Extra time added by the referee at the end of a half to make up for playing time lost because of an injury to one or more players.

inside forward: Either of two attacking players (inside left or inside right) who normally play on the forward line between the wings and the center forward in the classic pyramid formation. see *pyramid.*

inside left, inside right: The inside forward on the left or right side of the field in

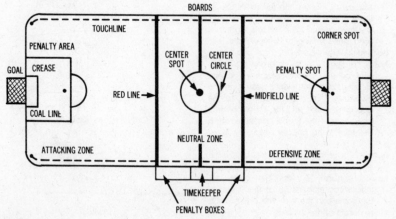

the classic pyramid formation. see *pyramid*.

instep kick: A powerful kick in which the ball is struck with the shoelace area of the boot.

inswinger: A corner kick (or kick from the wing area near the end line) which bends or curves in toward the goal. compare *outswinger*.

interfere: To illegally obstruct or physically impede the play of an opponent, a foul which results in the awarding of an indirect free kick to the opposing team from the spot of the offense.

international: 1. A match between national teams. The first international soccer match was between Scottish and English select teams in 1972, a 0-0 draw in front of 4,000 spectators at the West of Scotland Cricket Club in Partick. 2. A player who is a member of a national team and takes part in international matches.

in to touch: Completely over the touchline and out of bounds. (couldn't get to the ball before it rolled in to touch) see *touch*.

jab kick: see *flick kick*.

jockeying: Strategically giving ground while marking the player with the ball in such a way as to lead him to a less dangerous or more securely defended area of the field. also *shepherding*.

juggle: To keep the ball in the air and under control by bouncing it with the feet, knees, or head.

keeper: Short for goalkeeper.

kick-in: The method of restarting play in indoor soccer when the ball goes out of bounds (passing completely over the perimeter wall) along either touchline. A kick-in is an indirect free kick awarded to the opposite team of the player who last touched the ball, and taken from the point where the ball crossed the touchline. A kick-in is the indoor equivalent to a throw-in. Ironically, in the 1860s and 1870s, some teams in the Sheffield area of northern England used a kick-in instead of a throw-in.

kickoff: The method of starting play at the beginning of a half (or a quarter in indoor soccer) and after a goal. A kickoff is a placekick taken from the center spot with the players positioned in their own half of the field. No opposing player may be closer than 10 yards

from the ball (10 feet in indoor soccer) until it has been kicked off. The ball must be kicked into the opposing half and is in play when it has traveled the distance (half the distance in indoor soccer) of its own circumference. The kicker may not play the ball a second time until it has been touched by another player. A goal cannot be scored directly from a kickoff. The rules which govern a kickoff were established in 1863 in England by the Football Association.

●●Of or pertaining to the beginning of something, especially an introductory occurrence. (began the cruise with a kickoff party)

kick off: To execute a kickoff.

●●To begin something. (will kick off the annual clearance sale with a full-page ad in the newspapers)

kickoff circle: The center circle.

kill a penalty: To use up the time one's team must play shorthanded while a teammate is in the penalty box without allowing a goal. A team attempting to kill a penalty emphasizes defense and deliberate, time-consuming ball control.

kill the ball: To null or trap and control a moving ball, especially an air ball.

knot: To tie the score of a game with a goal. (knotted the game with a header) also *equalize*.

late tackle: A sliding tackle made after the ball is clearly out of the defender's reach, and usually resulting in physical contact. A foul which results in a direct free kick by the opposing team at the spot of the offense, and if committed by a defender in his own penalty area, a penalty kick. In indoor soccer, the offending player may also be assessed a two-minute time penalty. If, in the opinion of the referee, the foul is serious or violent, the offending player may be cautioned (an automatic two-minute time penalty in indoor soccer) or sent off (an automatic five-minute time penalty in indoor soccer, to be served by the ejected player's substitute).

Laws: The international rules of soccer, controlled and interpreted by FIFA, the world-governing body of soccer. The Laws of soccer stem from the playing rules adopted in 1863 by England's Football Association, which in turn were heavily influenced by a code formulated in 1848 at Cambridge University.

libero: see *sweeper.*

linesman: Either of two officials just outside the touchlines who assist the referee by indicating offside violations and when and where the ball goes out of bounds and the team that last touched it by raising and pointing a small flag, and who call attention to fouls that might not have been seen by the referee. One linesman patrols each touchline in one half of the field, moving between the center line and the goal line as play dictates. A linesman's decision may be overruled by the referee. Linesmen replaced umpires and were given their present responsibilities in 1891, when the referee was moved to the field and given full control of the game by the Football Association in England.

linkman: 1. A midfielder, so-called because midfielders serve as a "link" between defensive and offensive players. 2. The position played by a linkman.

1. lob: 1. To kick a ball (stationary or moving on the ground or in the air) in a gentle high arc. compare *chip.* 2. To kick a ball in a gentle high arc over one or more players. (lobbed the diving keeper to score)

2. lob: The act or an instance of lobbing a ball. compare *chip.*

loft: see *chip.*

Major Indoor Soccer League: The youngest of the professional soccer leagues in the United States, and the only one to conduct its entire schedule indoors. Established in 1978, the Major Indoor Soccer League (MISL) began operating with six teams for the 1978-79 season, with the New York Arrows defeating the Philadelphia Fever to become the first MISL champion. For the 1982-83 season, the MISL announced a forty-eight-game schedule (twenty-four home, twenty-four away), and an alignment comprised of fourteen teams split into two divisions: The Eastern Division, with the Baltimore Blast, the Buffalo Stallions, the Chicago Sting, the Cleveland Force, the Memphis Americans, the New York Arrows, and the Pittsburgh Spirit; and the Western Division, with the Golden Bay Earthquakes, the Kansas City Comets, the Los Angeles Lazers, the Phoenix Inferno, the San Diego Sockers, the St. Louis Steamers, and the Wichita Wings. The MISL league championship is decided in a best-of-five championship series between divisional playoff winners.

major penalty: A five-minute time penalty assessed against a player (or a coach, manager, or trainer on the bench) who receives a second caution during a game or is sent off (as for a serious or violent foul or abusive language). In such a case, the guilty player (or coach, manager, or trainer) must return immediately to the dressing room, and the five-minute time penalty is served by a designated substitute. The offending team must play shorthanded for the duration of a major penalty. compare *double minor, minor penalty.*

make space: see *create space.*

man advantage: A numerical advantage on the field in indoor soccer (as during a power play) when the opposing team has one or more players in the penalty box. compare *shorthanded.*

man-advantage goal: A power play goal. compare *shorthanded goal.*

man down: see *man short.*

man in the middle: Slang for the referee. also *ref.*

man short: Lacking one player on the field, usually because of an ejection. also *man down.*

mark: To guard an opponent. (closely marked for the entire game)

marker: 1. One who guards or is in the process of guarding an opponent. 2. A goal. (got his second marker with a diving header) also *tally.*

mark up: To guard an opponent, especially to move closer and guard an oppo-

CENTER BACK OR CENTER HALF   GOALKEEPER

RIGHT BACK   LEFT BACK

MIDFIELDERS

CENTER FORWARD

RIGHT WING   LEFT WING

STRIKERS

3-4-3 OR W-M

nent. (allowed the winning goal because they failed to mark up on a corner kick) also *get tight*.

M formation: An attacking configuration (not to be confused with the defensive M of the more common W-M) in which two inside forwards play closest to the opposing goal, with three more forwards (attacking midfielders) playing further back, one in the center and one on each flank. Imaginary lines connecting them would appear like the letter M from above. compare *W formation, W-M*.

midfield: 1. The area in the middle of the field (roughly the central third) between the two goal lines. 2. The position played by a midfielder. also *half, halfback, linkman*. 3. The midfielders. (a strong, hard-working midfield)

midfielder: One of several players (the number varies with different formations) who function in the central part of the field, and whose responsibilities include moving the ball from the defensive area up to the forwards (and sometimes, depending on the style of play, supporting and participating in attacks), attempting to win the ball from opponents in the midfield, and falling back to help defend when the fullbacks are outnumbered in and around the penalty area. Usually, among a team's midfielders, different players emphasize the defending, playmaking, and attacking aspects of play. also *half, halfback, linkman*.

midfield line: The halfway line. also *center line*.

minor penalty: A two-minute time penalty in indoor soccer, assessed against a player (or bench personnel) guilty of an intentional penal or technical offense, or unsportsmanlike conduct. compare *double minor, major penalty*.

MISL: The Major Indoor Soccer League.

narrow the angle: see *cut down the angle*.

NASL: The North American Soccer League.

National Amateur Challenge Cup: The annual national competition for the "Amateur Cup," open to all amateur teams under the jurisdiction of the United States Soccer Federation. A knockout competition instituted in 1923, the National Amateur Challenge Cup was first won in 1924 by Fleisher Yarn F.C. of Philadelphia, Pennsylvania.

National Challenge Cup: The annual national competition for the "Open Cup," open to all amateur and professional teams under the jurisdiction of the United States Soccer Federation. The oldest soccer competition in the United States, the National Challenge Cup was first won in 1914 by the Brooklyn Field Club of Brooklyn, New York. also *National Open*.

National Open: The National Challenge Cup.

near post: The goal post nearest to where the ball is being played. compare *far post*.

1. net: 1. The hemp, jute, or nylon mesh netting attached to the goal posts and crossbar, and which covers the top, sides and back of a goal. see *goal*. 2. The goal. also *nets*.

2. net: To score a goal. (netted the equalizer in injury time)

nets: The goal. also *net*.

neutral zone: The central area of the playing field in indoor soccer, between the two red lines. compare *attacking zone, defensive zone*.

nod: see *flick*.

North American Soccer League: The premier professional soccer league in the United States and Canada. The North American Soccer League (NASL) was founded in 1968 when two one-year old professional soccer leagues merged, the United Soccer Association and the National Professional Soccer League. Seventeen teams participated in the NASL's initial season in 1968, with the Atlanta Chiefs emerging as the first league champions. For the 1983 season, in addition to the eleven regular league teams (the Golden Bay Earthquakes, the San Diego Sockers, the Seattle Sounders, the Vancouver Whitecaps, the Chicago Sting, the Montreal Manic, the New York Cosmos, the Toronto Blizzard, the Fort Lauderdale Strikers, the Tampa Bay Rowdies, and the Tulsa Roughnecks), the NASL and USSF announced the creation of an innovative new franchise, Team America, comprised exclusively of American players drawn from the NASL, MISL, and ASL. Based in Washington, D.C., Team America is functionally the nucleus of the United States national team and plays international matches as well as a full 30-game schedule against other NASL teams in competition for a playoff berth and the opportunity to play for the league championship in the Soccer Bowl.

nutmeg: To kick the ball through a defender's legs, then run past him to recover it and continue. Defenders consider being "nutmegged" a particularly humiliating way of being beaten by an opponent.

obstruct: To illegally hamper or impede the movement of an opponent (such as by stepping in front of an opponent or between an opponent and the ball when it is not within playing distance, or stepping in front of the goalkeeper to prevent him from putting the ball in play). see *obstruction*. compare *screen*.

obstruction: The act or an instance of illegally obstructing an opponent, a foul which results in the awarding of an indirect free kick to the opposing team at the spot of the offense.

official time: The actual time of a game, kept by the referee alone in all games played under international rules. In high school and college games, and in indoor soccer, a timekeeper keeps the official time.

off one's line: Away from the goal line and toward the shooter in order to narrow the angle, as of a goalkeeper. (came off his line quickly and made the save) see *cut down the angle, narrow the angle.*

1. offside: Being ahead of the ball in the opposing half of the field when there are less than two opponents (including the goalkeeper) nearer the goal at the moment the ball is played by a team-

OFFSIDE TRAP

mate, an infraction which results in the awarding of an indirect free kick to the opposing team at the spot of the infringement. An offside player is not penalized if, in the opinion of the referee, he is not interfering with the play or with an opponent, or not seeking to gain an advantage. Like most of the early rugby-soccer rules, the concept of offside, first called "sneaking," originated at one of England's public schools (Eton) in the mid-1800s, as did the name "offside" (Cheltenham). Initially, any player ahead of the ball when it was kicked anywhere on the field was offside. In the code adopted by the English Football Association in 1866, a player was offside if less than three defenders were nearer the goal when the ball was kicked. By the 1920s, the offense-stifling offside trap began to dominate the game. As a result, in 1925, the offside rule was changed to require only two defenders nearer the goal. In the following season, the number of goals increased by over 40 percent in the English Football League, but new tactics and formations (such as the W-M) were developed to both exploit and defend against the new freedom of attacking players. see *offside trap, W-M.*

2. offside: 1. The act or an instance of being offside. 2. The infraction which results when a player is offside.

offside trap: A defensive tactic in which one or more defenders move toward the halfway line to pull even with or pass one or more attacking players in an attempt to put them offside before a teammate plays the ball. The offside trap is an effective method of nullifying an attack, but risky because of the possibility of misjudging or mistiming, or of the referee and linesman not detecting the momentary offside. It was the development of the offside trap and its offense-stifling effect on the game which caused the offside rule to be changed in 1925, reducing the number of defensive players required to be between an attacking player and the goal from three to two.

offside violation: A three-line pass in indoor soccer. also *red line violation, three-line violation.*

off the ball: Away from the ball. (made the

goal possible with his off the ball running) compare *on the ball*.

1. one touch: Played first time. see *first time*.

2. one touch: Of or pertaining to a ball played first time. see *first time*.

one-two: A wall pass or give-and-go. also *double pass*.

on the ball: In possession or control of the ball, dribbling. compare *off the ball*.

on the turn: Turning to face or shoot at the goal, especially while being closely marked in the penalty area. (a strong center forward who is good on the turn)

open net: A goal left unguarded, as when a goalkeeper falls down, or is beaten or out of position, or when the goalkeeper has been pulled in indoor soccer.

opposing half: The half of the field that contains the goal defended by the opposing team. compare *own half*.

outlet pass: A quick pass from the goalkeeper or a defender to a teammate closer to the opposing team's goal, especially in indoor soccer to start an attack.

outside forward: 1. Either of two attacking players (outside left or outside right) who normally play near the touchlines in the classic pyramid formation. see *pyramid*. 2. The position played by an outside forward. see *pyramid*.

outside half: 1. Either of two midfielders who normally play on the flanks of a central halfback. see *pyramid*. 2. The position played by an outside half. see *pyramid*.

outside left, outside right: 1. The outside forward on the left or right side of the field. see *pyramid*. 2. The position played by an outside left or outside right. see *pyramid*.

outswinger: A corner kick (or kick from the wing area near the end line) that bends or curves out from the goal. compare *inswinger*.

overhead volley: A bicycle kick.

1. overlap: To move forward from a defensive position (with or without the ball) in order to take part in an attack.

2. overlap: The act or an instance of a defender overlapping.

over the top: A situation in which a player tackles over the ball in such a way as to kick or make physical contact with

an opponent's legs. A foul that results in a direct free kick for the opposing team at the spot of the offense, and if committed by a defender in his own penalty area, a penalty kick. In indoor soccer, the offending player may also be assessed a two-minute time penalty. If, in the opinion of the referee, the foul is serious or violent, the offending player may be cautioned (an automatic two-minute time penalty in indoor soccer) or sent off (a five-minute time penalty in indoor soccer, to be served by the ejected player's substitute).

overtime: One or more extra periods of play to decide a game tied at the end of regulation play. In the NASL, two seven and one-half minute sudden death periods are played, after which a shootout takes place if there is no winner. In the MISL, one fifteen-minute sudden death period is played, after which a shootout takes place if there is no winner. In college play, two ten-minute overtime periods may be played.

own goal: A goal that results when a member of the defending team accidentally knocks the ball into his own goal.

own half: In the half of the playing field that contains the goal defended by one's team. compare *opposing half*.

pace: 1. The speed of a moving ball. 2. The speed with which a game is played (whether by one or more players, or by one or both teams).

1. pass: To kick, head, or deflect (first time) the ball toward a teammate, or toward a space into which a teammate is moving.

2. pass: The act or an instance of passing the ball.

penal offense: Any of nine offenses (ten in indoor soccer) which, if committed intentionally, result in a direct free kick or (if committed by a defender within his penalty area) a penalty kick for the opposing team. In indoor soccer, the offending player may also be assessed a two-minute time penalty. Penal offenses include kicking or attempting to kick an opponent, tripping or attempting to trip or throw an opponent down, jumping at an opponent, charging an opponent in a violent or dangerous manner, charging an opponent from behind (unless the opponent is obstructing), striking or attempting to strike an an opponent, or handling the ball (not applicable to the goalkeeper within his own penalty area). In indoor soccer, boarding (charging an opponent into the perimeter wall) is also a penal offense. A player is automatically cautioned for a second penal offense during a game in indoor soccer, and sent off for a third. compare *technical offense*.

penalty: 1. Short for penalty kick. also *spot kick*. 2. see *time penalty*.

penalty arc: The arc marked outside each penalty area with a 10-yard radius (10-foot radius in indoor soccer) from the penalty spot. At the time of a penalty kick, no player other than the kicker is allowed inside the penalty arc until the ball is kicked. The penalty arc was added in 1937 to help enforce the 10-yard rule on penalty kicks. also *restraining arc*.

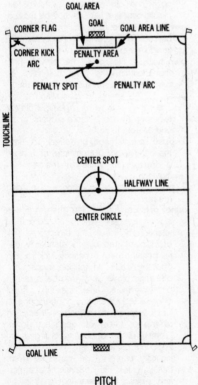

PITCH

penalty area: The rectangular area (44 yards wide by 18 yards deep, or in indoor soccer, 30 feet wide by 24 feet deep) marked in front of each goal, inside which the goalkeeper may handle the ball. A serious foul (any "penal offense") against an attacking player within the penalty area results in a penalty kick. The modern configuration for the penalty area was adopted in 1902 by the English Football Association. also *area, box*.

penalty box: Either of two enclosed areas (one for each team) within which a penalized player must remain for the duration of a time penalty in indoor soccer. Penalty boxes are located adjacent to the middle of the playing area across from the team benches, usually on either side of the area used by the timekeeper and assistant referee. also *box, sin bin*.

penalty box attendant: An official seated between the two penalty boxes in indoor soccer (sometimes one attendant is seated in each penalty box), who is responsible for the proper administration of time penalties in cooperation with the timekeeper.

penalty kick: A direct free kick taken from the penalty spot, awarded to the attacking team when a major foul (any "penal offense") is committed by a defender within the penalty area. When a penalty kick is taken, all players other than the kicker must remain outside the penalty area and at least 10 yards from the penalty mark (10 feet in indoor soccer), and the goalkeeper must stand (without moving his feet) on his own goal line, between the goal posts, until the ball is kicked. The ball must be kicked forward and may not be played a second time until it has been touched by another player. The penalty kick rule was adopted by the English Football Association in 1891, although the goalkeeper was not specifically prohibited from moving off his line until 1927. also *spot kick*.

penalty kick mark: The penalty spot.

penalty killer: Any player sent onto the field while one or more teammates are in the penalty box and the opposing team is on a power play. see *kill a penalty, power play*.

penalty mark: The penalty spot.

penalty spot: A spot in the penalty area marked 12 yards (8 yards in indoor soccer) out from the mid-point of the goal line, from which penalty kicks are taken. also *penalty kick mark, penalty mark, spot, 12-yard mark, 12-yard spot.* see *penalty kick.*

perimeter wall: see *boards.*

pitch: The traditional British name for the playing area, which must be rectangular and measure between 100 and 130 yards long by 50 to 100 yards (length must exceed width). also *ground, grounds.*

placekick: A kick taken when the ball has been placed on the ground, as for a kickoff, goal kick, corner kick, free kick, or penalty kick (and, in indoor soccer, a kick-in).

play on: A verbal signal to continue play, called out by the referee at a point when play could be stopped, such as after an infraction when the advantage is being applied.

play the ball: To cause the ball to move, stop or change directions with any part of the body. (played the ball back to the goalkeeper)

point: 1. The area on either side of the playing field close to the boards and just inside the red line of the attacking zone in indoor soccer. From the similar hockey usage. 2. The position of a player stationed at the point, especially on a power play.

policeman: 1. The central defender, a center back. see *center back.* 2. The position played by a center back.

post: 1. Short for goal post. 2. In indoor soccer, a position in or near the penalty area in front of the goal in the attacking zone, often occupied by a forward who acts as a targetman, receiving and relaying passes, and always a threat to turn and shoot. Similar to basketball's post position in the free throw lane, from where the term originates.

power play: A temporary numerical advantage on the playing field in indoor soccer while one or more members of the opposing team are serving time penalties. Because the opponents are outnumbered, a team on a power play has a greater opportunity to score a goal. also *man advantage.* compare *shorthanded.*

power play goal: A goal scored by a team on a power play. also *man-*

advantage goal. compare *shorthanded goal.*

professional foul: see *tactical foul.*

promotion: The automatic advancement to the next higher league division of the highest finishing teams (usually two or three) of the previous season in the division below. Conversely, the two or three lowest finishing teams in the higher divisions suffer relegation to the division below for the next season. Pioneered by the English Football League in 1899, the system of automatic promotion and relegation is now in use in many countries.

pull the ball back: To pass the ball from near the goal line on one side of the goal defended by the opponents back to a teammate in front of the goal. (was able to pull the ball back before it crossed the goal line)

pull the goalkeeper: To replace the goalkeeper with an extra field player in an attempt to score in the closing minutes of a game when behind by one or two goals. A desperate and risky tactic which is attempted by a team only when in control of the ball (should the opposing team gain control of the ball, an easy open net goal often results).

punch: To save, clear or deflect an air ball with a clenched fist. (punched away the centering pass before the striker could get to it) also *fist.*

punch save: A save made by punching an air ball out of danger

1. punt: A goalkeeper's technique for kicking the ball a long distance, executed with an instep kick of a ball released from the hands.

2. punt: To execute a punt.

push: 1. To shove the ball forward (as for a short pass) with the inside of the foot. 2. To shove an opponent with the hands or arms. A foul which results in a direct free kick by the opposing team at the spot of the offense, or if committed by a defender in his penalty area, a penalty kick. In indoor soccer, the offending player may also be assessed a two-minute time penalty. If, in the opinion of the referee, the foul is serious or violent, the offending player may be cautioned (an automatic two-minute time penalty in indoor soccer) or sent off (an automatic five-minute time penalty in indoor soccer, to be served by the ejected player's substitute).

push off: To push or shove an opponent while jumping to contend for an air ball, considered a pushing foul. see *push.*

push out: To move away from the goal one is defending toward the midfield line in order to force opposing-players to back up or be offside. also *push up.*

push pass: A short pass shoved or "pushed" forward with the inside of the foot.

push up: 1. see *push out.* 2. To move forward from a defensive position in order to take part in an attack.

pyramid: The original and classic tactical formation, in use from the 1880s until the W-M or 3-4-3 was introduced in 1925. Many position names originated from the pyramid formation, which used two defenders (fullbacks), three midfield players (halfbacks or halfs, including a center halfback or center half and two flanking wing halfbacks or wing halfs, sometimes called outside halfs) and five attacking players on the front line (forwards, including a center forward, two inside forwards on either side of him, the inside left and inside right, and two outside forwards, the outside left and outside right, or wings). The formation's name came from the pyramid or trianglelike appearance of the 2-3-5 configuration. compare *4-4-2, 4-3-3, 4-2-4, 3-4-3, W-M.*

quarter: One of four fifteen-minute periods of play in indoor soccer (or eighteen-minute periods in some high school leagues).

quarter circle: 1. The corner area. 2. The corner kick arc.

rate: 1. To estimate and consider the abili-ty of a player or team. 2. To attribute a certain amount of skill or ability. A British expression. (supposed to be a good player, but the coach didn't rate him after the tryout)

1. red card: 1. A small red card displayed by the referee when a player is being sent off, or ejected from a game. 2. The ejection of a player from a game. (forced to play a man down after the red card) see *ejection.*

2. red card: To show a red card or eject a player from a game. (got red carded with twenty minutes left to play in the game) also *send off.*

red line: One of two red-colored lines marked across the playing area (and vertically to the top of the perimeter walls) in indoor soccer, 30 feet on either side of and parallel to the center line. The red lines divide the playing area into the attacking, defensive, and neutral zones, and are used to determine three-line violations. see *attacking zone, defensive zone, neutral zone, three-line violation.*

red line violation: see *three-line violation.*

1. ref: Short for referee. also *man in the middle.*

2. ref: To serve as the referee. also *referee, run the middle.*

1. referee: The official (or either of two officials in MISL indoor soccer) in charge of a match, assisted by two linesmen (or in indoor soccer, an assistant referee). The referee is responsible for enforcing the Laws of soccer, acting as timekeeper and recording all time lost because of injuries, a lost or not easily recovered ball, deliberate time wasting by either team, or a penalty kick to be added as extra time at the end of the period (in indoor, college, and high school soccer, the referee works in conjunction with an official timekeeper), starting and stopping play or terminating a game because of the elements, spectator interference, or an emergency, calling and penalizing infractions or fouls by awarding direct, indirect, and penalty kicks (and in indoor soccer, time penalties), cautioning and, if necessary, ejecting players guilty of serious, ungentlemanly, or violent misconduct, awarding or disallowing goals, and recording all goals and incidents of misconduct which warrant a caution or ejection. Originally, two

GOALKEEPER

DEFENDERS

RIGHT BACK   LEFT BACK

MIDFIELD

RIGHT HALF   CENTER HALF   LEFT HALF

FORWARDS   CENTER FORWARD

INSIDE RIGHT   OUTSIDE LEFT

OUTSIDE RIGHT   INSIDE LEFT

2-3-5 OR PYRAMID

shield

umpires (one furnished by each team) officiated from the touchlines. In 1871, a neutral referee was added to settle disputes between the umpires, whose method of stopping play was the waving of handkerchiefs until 1878, when whistles were used for the first time in a game between Nottingham Forest and Sheffield Norfolk. In 1891, the umpires were changed to linesmen, and the referee was moved to the field and given control of the game, although until 1894, he could only give a decision if appealed to. also *man in the middle, ref.*

2. referee: To serve as the referee. also *ref, run the middle.*

referee's crease: The area within a semicircle with a 10-foot radius marked at the middle of the playing field against the perimeter wall in front of the timekeeper in indoor soccer. No player is permitted inside the referee's crease while the referee reports a time penalty to the official timekeeper. An infraction results in the assessment of a two-minute penalty to the guilty player, and if continued or repeated, a caution.

relegation: The automatic demotion to the next lower league division of the lowest finishing teams (usually two or three) of the previous season in the division above. see *promotion.*

1. restart: To resume play after a stoppage, as with a drop ball or free kick.

2. restart: The act or an instance of resuming play after a stoppage, as with a drop ball or a free kick.

restraining arc: The penalty arc.

reverse kick: A bicycle kick.

ride a tackle: To maintain control of the ball in spite of a tackle.

run: A clever or opportunistic advance (with or without the ball) to a position near the opponent's goal, as a blindside run into the penalty area for a through pass, or a dribble through several defenders.

run on to: To catch up to a lead pass or a ball played into an open space by a teammate. (ran on to a little chip over the wall)

run the line: To serve as a linesman. compare *run the middle.*

run the middle: To serve as the referee. compare *run the line.*

1. save: To prevent a goal by catching, blocking, deflecting, or clearing the ball out of danger before it crosses the goal line.

2. save: The act or an instance of making a save.

scissors kick: 1. A scissors volley. 2. see *bicycle kick.*

scissors volley: 1. A leaping horizontal volley in which a scissorslike leg motion is used to kick the ball. A spectacular and powerful shot when properly executed. also *scissors kick.* 2. see *bicycle kick.*

screen: To interpose the body between the ball and a defender, legal as long as the ball is being played (as opposed to just obstructing the opponent). also *shield.*

sell the dummy: To momentarily deceive an opponent with a fake or feint. (sold the dummy and broke into the penalty area alone)

send off: To eject a player from a game, as for a serious or violent foul, foul language or gestures, or for persistent misconduct after having received a caution. also *red card.* see *ejection.*

Senior Bowl: The Senior Bowl Soccer Classic, an annual East-West all-star game for outstanding players in their senior year of college, sponsored by the Intercollegiate Soccer Association of America (ISAA). Thirty-two participants are chosen after recommendation by their respective coach or athletic director by the ISAA National Selection Committee. The Senior Bowl was initiated in 1972 by Wayne Sunderland, then president of the ISAA.

service: Passes sent into the penalty area for strikers, such as centering passes or crosses.

set piece, set-piece play: A prearranged team strategy with specific assignments for certain players, such as for drop ball, free kick, corner kick and throw-in (or in indoor soccer, kick-in) situations.

1. shadow: To closely mark a particular opponent throughout a game. also *shadow mark.*

2. shadow: A defender assigned to closely mark a particular opponent throughout a game.

shadow mark: To shadow an opponent.

shepherding: see *jockeying.*

shield: To screen the ball with the body, legal as long as the ball is being played (as opposed to just obstructing the opponent).

shinguards: Small protective pads for the shins, worn under a player's socks, usually constructed of a high-density foam rubber or light plastic with a thin layer of foam rubber underneath. Shinguards were introduced in 1874, and are normally the only protective pads worn by soccer players.

shoot: To kick, head, or deflect (first time) the ball toward the goal in an attempt to score.

shootout: The method used in the NASL and MISL to decide the outcome of a game that is tied at the end of overtime. Beginning with the visiting team and alternating after each attempt, five players from each side individually challenge the opposing goalkeeper. Starting from a spot in the center of the field 35 yards from the goal line (or in the MISL, starting from the center of the nearest red line), at a signal from the referee, each player has five seconds to dribble and shoot (in the NASL, only one shot may be taken; in the MISL, any number of shots may be taken within the five seconds). There are no restrictions on the movement of the goalkeeper once the five-second period begins. The match is decided and attempts are ended when one team achieves an insurmountable advantage (such as scoring on the first three attempts while the opponents miss their first three). If the teams remain tied after five attempts each, alternate players continue to shoot until one team scores more times than the other in an equal number of attempts. Only those players who were playing at the end of overtime are eligible to participate in the shootout (except in the MISL, where all players dressed for the game are eligible), and no player may shoot twice until all eligible teammates have made one attempt. In the MISL, any foul committed by the goalkeeper outside of the penalty area results in a penalty kick. The shootout was pioneered by the North American Soccer League in 1977.

shorthanded: Outnumbered on the playing field due to one or more teammates serving penalties in the penalty box. see *kill a penalty.* compare *man advantage, power play.*

shorthanded goal: A goal scored by a team that has one or two less players on the field than the opponents, due to penalties being served. compare *man-advantage goal, power play goal.*

1. shoulder charge: To use the shoulder to lean or push against the shoulder of an opponent while contending for a ball, legal as long as the ball is within playing distance (3 to 4 feet). see *charging.*

2. shoulder charge: The act or an instance of leaning or pushing with the shoulder against the shoulder of an opponent while contending for a ball, legal (a fair charge) as long as the ball is within playing distance (3 to 4 feet). see *charging.*

show the ball: To tempt a defender to challenge or tackle by displaying the ball in a seemingly vulnerable position. A favorite tactic of great dribblers such as England's now beknighted Sir Stanley Matthews, Garrincha of the Brazilian national team in the 1950s, and Ireland's George Best, to lure a defender into committing to a course of action.

side block tackle: The act or an instance of blocking the ball with the foot from the side at the moment an opponent attempts to kick it.

side-foot: To pass or shoot the ball with the side of the foot.

sideline: Either of the two side boundaries of the playing area, more commonly known as the touchlines. see *touchline.*

sitter: An easy goal, or the opportunity for an easy goal (as close in front of an open goal).

sin bin: Slang for the penalty box in indoor soccer. also *box.*

sky: To miskick a ball in such a way as to direct it much higher than intended, as over the goal.

1. slide tackle: To execute a slide tackle.

2. slide tackle: The act or an instance of sliding into the ball feetfirst (as a base runner slides in baseball) in order to dislodge or kick the ball away from an opponent. A slide tackle can be executed from the front, rear, or side, and is legal even though contact is made that causes the opponent to trip or fall, as long as the ball is played first and the contact with the opponent is the result of a natural follow through (and not violent or intentional). also *sliding tackle.*

sliding tackle: A slide tackle.

slot: 1. To kick the ball into the goal, especially with a shot that travels along a narrow, ideal path or "slot" (as between defenders or just outside the reach of the goalkeeper). (slots the ball just inside the post for a goal) 2. An imaginary area in front of the goal inside the penalty area in indoor soccer. From hockey.

soccer: A game played between two teams of eleven players on a rectangular field measuring 100 to 130 yards long by 50 to 100 yards wide (length must exceed width) and having a 24-foot-wide by 8-foot-high net-draped goal at each end. The object of the game is to propel an inflated ball into the goal defended by the opposing team. A team is comprised of a goalkeeper, usually positioned just in front of the goal, and varying numbers of defenders, midfield players, and forwards, depending upon the formation and system of play used. The ball is most often kicked, but may be propelled with the head or any part of the body except the hands and arms. Only the goalkeeper is permitted to catch or play the ball with the hands, and then only when he is within the penalty area, a rectangular area 44 yards wide and 18 yards deep marked in front of the goal. Players are not permitted to kick, trip, jump at, charge (except for shoulder-to-shoulder contact when contending for a ball within playing distance), strike, hold or push an opponent. Such fouls, if intentionally committed, result in a direct free kick (an unhindered placekick from which a goal may be scored directly) for the opposing team at the point of the offense, or if the foul is committed by a defender in his own penalty area, a penalty kick (an unhindered placekick directly at the goal, from a point 12 yards in front of the center of the goal line, during which the goalkeeper must remain on the goal line, without moving his feet, until the ball is kicked). For unintentional fouls and other infractions, an indirect free kick (an unhindered placekick from which a goal may not be scored until the ball touches another player) is awarded to the opposing team from the spot of the offense. At the beginning of a period of play and

SLIDE TACKLE

after each goal, play is started by a kickoff (an unhindered placekick into the opponent's half of the field from the center of the midfield line). When the ball crosses over the touchline, it is put into play by the team opposing that of the last player to touch it with a throw-in. When the ball crosses over the goal line (outside the goal) last touched by the defending team, it is put into play by the attacking team with a corner kick (a direct free kick taken from the corner on the side of the field the ball crossed over the goal line). When the ball crosses over the goal line (outside the goal) last touched by the attacking team, it is put into play by the defending team with a goal kick (an indirect free kick taken from the goal area). Soccer is played in two forty-five-minute halves (or in high school play, two thirty-five-minute halves or four eighteen-minute quarters) and play is continuous, stopping only in the case of a serious injury, a lost ball, or deliberate time-wasting by either team (in college soccer, play is also stopped after a goal and for a penalty kick; in high school soccer, play is also stopped after a goal and to administer a caution, warning, or ejection). Two substitutions are allowed during a game (unlimited substitution in high school soccer, unlimited substitution from among five designated substitutes in college soccer). The international name for soccer, association football, came from England's Football Association, formed in 1863 to separate soccer from the other football game, rugby. Association committee member and amateur

player Charles Wreford-Brown is reported to have created the term "soccer" as a word play on the abbreviation "assoc." When asked at Oxford if he would like a game of "rugger" (rugby), he facetiously replied, "no, soccer." In countries other than the United States and Canada, the game is still known as association football, or football. see *indoor soccer.*

soccer ball: An inflated (9 to 10-1/2 pounds per square inch) leather or approved simulated leather-covered sphere with a circumference of 27 to 28 inches, and weighing 14 to 16 ounces at the start of a match. The size of the ball was fixed at a meeting in 1882 of representatives of the English, Scottish, Welsh, and Irish Football Associations. English football pioneer and mid-1920s Arsenal manager Herbert Chapman is credited with introducing the white soccer ball.

Soccer Bowl: The annual post-season game between Divisional Playoff winners for the North American Soccer League championship. Although the first NASL championship game was played in 1968 (won by the Atlanta Chiefs, led by player-coach Phil Woosnam—later NASL Commissioner), the name Soccer Bowl was first used in 1975, when the Tampa Bay Rowdies defeated the Portland Timber 2-0.

Soccer Hall of Fame: The honor roll of outstanding players and administrators who have made a contribution to American soccer. The Hall of Fame was originated by the Oldtimers' Soccer Association of Philadelphia in 1950, and by mutual agreement, taken under the guardianship of the United States Soccer Federation in 1953. Final selections for membership are made by the Soccer Hall of Fame Committee (former USSF presidents) from nominations made by affiliated state associations, the North American Soccer League, the Major Indoor Soccer League, the American Soccer League, the National Soccer Coaches Association, a special Veterans' Committee, and various intercollegiate groups.

sole trap: A trap made with the sole of the shoe, wedging the ball against the ground. compare *chest trap, head trap, sweep trap, thigh trap.*

GOALKEEPER

RIGHT BACK   LEFT BACK
SWEEPER
CENTER BACK   CENTER BACK

MIDFIELDERS

STRIKER   STRIKER

SWEEPER

space: An open or unguarded area of the playing field that can be exploited by the attacking team.

spearhead: see *center forward.*

spot: Short for penalty spot.

spot kick: A penalty kick.

spread the defense: An offensive strategy in which attacking players attempt to draw defenders away from the middle of the penalty area toward the flanks.

1. square: 1. Laterally or directly to the side, roughly parallel to the goal line. (played the ball square into the middle) 2. Lined up laterally, roughly parallel to the goal line.

2. square: To pass the ball square.

square ball, square pass: A pass that is played square.

step over the ball: To attempt to momentarily deceive a defender by shifting the body as if to move one way with the ball, but instead, stepping over it, then quickly moving the ball in the opposite direction.

stopper: 1. The center back, originally, the player assigned to "stop" the opposing center forward in the W-M formation popularized in England by football pioneer Herbert Chapman's Arsenal team in 1925. 2. The position played by a center back.

striker: 1. The center forward 2. The position played by a center forward. 3. A forward.

strip: A team uniform. A British expression.

sweep: To play as a sweeper.

sweeper: 1. A roaming defender normally positioned just behind or in front of the back line, where he can move laterally across the field to cover or help out the other defenders. The origin of the sweeper dates back to 1931, when the Servette-Geneva team of Switzerland, coached by Karl Rappan, introduced the Swiss *verrou* or " bolt," so called because the deeply positioned back in the defensive mode of the system was likened to a boltlock against opponents. In 1947, Nereo Rocco, coach of a struggling Italian first division team, Triestina, introduced the *catenaccio* ("big chain" of defenders) anchored by a *livero,* a permanent deep fullback inspired by Rappan's earlier system. Eventually, the Italian "free man" became the *libero* and "sweeper" or "freeback" in Spanish and English-speaking countries, and by the 1966 World Cup, most teams employed a sweeper. A sweeper's role can be primarily defensive like that of hard-tackling Nobby Stiles of England's victorious 1966 World Cup team, or creative and offense-inspiring, like those created by Franz Beckenbauer and Carlos Alberto (later, both players for the New York Cosmos). also *freeback, libero, sweeper back.* 2. The position played by a sweeper. also *freeback, libero, sweeper back.*

sweeper back: 1. A sweeper. also *freeback, libero.*

sweep trap: A technique in which a moving ball is trapped against the ground with a sole trap, but immediately rolled in a desired direction with the bottom of the foot rather than stopped. compare *chest trap, head trap, thigh trap.*

switch: To pass the ball from one side of the field to a teammate on the other side. also *change.*

table: A British expression for a schedule of league standings. (a good team, currently third in the table)

1. tackle: To use the feet to block, dislodge or win control of the ball from an opponent. see *block tackle, slide tackle.*

2. tackle: The act or an instance of blocking, dislodging, or winning control of the ball from an opponent. (took the ball away with a perfect tackle). see *block tackle, slide tackle.*

tackle through the ball: To tackle with such speed or power that physical contact with the opponent's legs is assured after the ball is played, most often resulting in a fall, and sometimes, injury to the opponent. A foul, if intentional, that results in a direct free kick by the opposing team at the spot of the offense or, if committed by a defender in his penalty area, a penalty kick. In indoor soccer, the offending player may also be assessed a two-minute time penalty. If, in the opinion of the referee, the foul is serious or violent, the offending player may be cautioned (an automatic two-minute time penalty in indoor soccer) or sent off (an automatic five-minute time penalty in indoor soccer, to be served by the ejected player's substitute).

tactical foul: An intentional foul committed when the consequences of the foul are less damaging than if play is allowed to continue, as in the case of bringing down an attacker who is about to break through into the penalty area when the goal is unguarded because the keeper is down or out of position. By the time the resulting direct free kick is taken, the goalkeeper and a wall of defenders can be in position. Always questionable in terms of sportsmanship, the tactical foul was used in its most blatant and violent form to intimidate and injure key players like Brazil's Pele in the 1966 World Cup finals in England. also *professional foul.*

take down: see *bring down.*

take one's number: To note the jersey number or identity of a player who intentionally fouls or is unnecessarily rough so as to be able to retaliate later in the game (when the referee isn't looking). A common practice among professional players, although against the rules.

take some stick: To be the object of rough play, especially to be kicked. A British expression applied both to rugby and soccer. compare *give some stick.*

●●To be razzed or given a hard time. (took some stick about his political views)

1. tally: To score a goal. (tallied with a header to knot the game)

2. tally: A goal. also *marker.*

targetman: 1. The central striker positioned close to the opponent's goal to receive long or centering passes in order to relay the ball to other attacking teammates, or to turn and shoot. also *frontman.* 2. A centrally positioned midfielder to whom outlet passes are directed for distribution to attacking teammates. also *frontman.*

technical offense: An infraction of the rules or foul which does not involve physical contact in indoor soccer, such as playing the ball twice on a kickoff, kick-in, free kick or goal kick before it is touched by another player (outside the penalty area on a goal kick), an illegal substitution, a three-line violation, delaying the game, hitting the superstructure of the arena with the ball, penalty kick violations, and violations of the restrictions placed on goalkeepers. A technical offense results in a two-minute time penalty which does not count in the accumulation of total time

TACKLE

penalties for the purposes of ejection, unless a caution is administered for ungentlemanly conduct for persistent infringement of the laws. compare *penal offense.*

thigh trap: A trap in which an air ball is stopped and controlled on the thigh. compare *chest trap, foot trap, head trap, sole trap, sweep trap.*

3-4-3: see *W-M.*

three-line pass: see *three-line violation.*

three-line violation: A violation in which a ball is passed across three lines (the two red lines and the center line) in the air, toward the opponent's goal line, without touching another player or the perimeter wall. When a three-line violation is committed, an indirect free kick is awarded to the opposing team at the point where the ball crossed the first line. When a team is playing shorthanded by two players, a three-line violation by any player on that team except the goalkeeper is not penalized (at no time may a goalkeeper throw, punch, punt, or drop-kick over the three lines). also *offside violation, red line violation, three-line pass.*

through: Into an open space between the last line of defenders and the goalkeeper.

through ball, through pass: A ball passed into an open space between the last line of defenders and the goalkeeper for an attacking teammate to run on to. (caught the defense square with a beautiful through pass)

throw-in: The method by which the ball is put back into play when it crosses entirely over a touchline, taken from out of bounds at that point by the team opposing that of the last player to touch the ball before it leaves the playing field. At the moment a throw-in is taken, the thrower must be facing the field from no more than one meter away and have part of both feet on or outside the touchline and on the ground (the ball may not be thrown while running). A throw-in must be made with both hands moving simultaneously with equal force, and the ball must be delivered from behind and over the thrower's head. There is no offside nor can a goal be scored directly from a throw-in (a goal kick results if the ball is thrown into the opponent's goal). An opponent may stand on the touchline in front of the thrower, but no attempt may be made to distract or impede him (an infraction results in a caution for the guilty player). Like many of soccer's rules, the concept of a throw-in from the touchline originated in the mid-1800s at one of England's public schools, Cheltenham, though it was delivered one-handed at right angles to the line, and by the first player to touch the ball out of bounds (thus, "touch" and "touchline"). By 1877, the throw-in was allowed to be taken in any direction by the team opposing the last player to touch the ball. The Scots favored a two-handed throw-in, and, at a meeting in 1882 of the English, Scottish, Welsh, and Irish Football Associations, it became the agreed method, largely because of England and Notts County cricket and football player, William Gunn, who could throw the ball one-handed 60 yards in the air, farther than most of his contemporaries could kick it. Other rule changes followed in 1920 (no offside), 1925 (both feet on the ground), and 1931 (throw-in to the opposing team for an illegal throw). In recent years, the long throw-in has

THIGH TRAP

emerged as an offensive weapon, with the ability of some players to deliver a centering pass-like throw from the touchline into the penalty area. compare *kick-in*.

throw in: To put the ball in play with a throw-in.

timekeeper: 1. The official responsible for keeping the time of a game and supervising the serving of time penalties under the jurisdiction of the referee in indoor soccer. The timekeeper is situated in an area adjacent to the playing field at the center line, between the penalty boxes. 2. The official responsible for keeping the time of a game in conjunction with the referee in high school and college soccer (one timer to be provided by each school).

time out: A one-minute interruption in play allowed to each team once during each half in indoor soccer, to be taken only at a normal stoppage of play when that team is in possession of the ball or when the ball is in full possession of the goalkeeper. No time outs are permitted in an overtime period.

THROW-IN

time penalty: A two-minute or five-minute penalty (or two consecutive two-minute penalties) assessed against a player or bench personnel for certain fouls and rule infractions in indoor soccer. For the duration of a time penalty, the guilty player (or a designated substitute in the case of an ejection or a penalty assessed a goalkeeper or bench personnel) must remain within the penalty box, and his team must play short-handed. see *double minor, major penalty, minor penalty*.

toe-kick: To miskick the ball with the toe instead of the instep.

toe kick: The act or an instance of miskicking the ball with the toe instead of the instep.

toe-poke: To push or poke the ball with a toe.

toe poke: The act of toe-poking the ball.

total football, total soccer: The name coined for the style of play developed by Rinus Michels's energetic Ajax team from Holland, European Cup winners in 1971, 1972, and 1973, and popularized by Holland (coached by Michels) at the 1974 World Cup finals in Germany. Total football or total soccer is a system in which the movement of players is constant and fluid, with few restrictions placed on any one position. Forwards exchange with midfielders, dropping all the way back to their penalty area when needed, and defenders frequently move forward to attack, confident that their defensive responsibilities will be taken up by teammates. Total football requires a high level of technical skills from all the players (not just the forwards), tremendous fitness, and equally important, understanding and teamwork. The 1974 Dutch side had all these, with gifted players like Ruud Krol, Wim Suurbier, Wim van Hanegem, Rob Rensenbrink, Johnnie Rep, Wim Rijsbergen, Johan Neeskens, and the brilliant Johan Cruyff. Playing the most exciting and creative soccer in the tournament, Holland defeated Uruguay, Sweden, Argentina, East Germany, and Brazil without giving up a goal, before losing 2-1 in the final to Helmut Schoen's West German team, who practiced their own, more disciplined, if less inspirational, form of total football.

touch: The out of bounds area along the sidelines, up to but not including the touchlines. The first rules governing a ball out of bounds on the sideline were adopted in the mid-1800s at the English public school, Cheltenham, and called for a throw-in to be taken by the first player who touched the ball after it crossed the sideline. Thus, out of bounds became the "touch area," later "touch," and the sidelines became the "touchlines."

touchline: 1. One of the two boundary lines on each side of the playing area between and perpendicular to the goal lines. A ball is not out of bounds until it has wholly crossed a touchline. also *sideline.* see *throw-in, touch.* 2. One of two broken lines (6-inch segments separated by one-inch spaces) marked 3 feet from and parallel to the side perimeter walls between the corner marks in indoor soccer, and from which kick-ins are taken. see *kick-in.*

1. trap: To stop and control a ball moving on the ground or in the air, as with the head, chest, leg, or foot. also *kill the ball.*

2. trap: The act or an instance of trapping a ball.

turn a defender: To make a defender turn one way with a fake, then quickly take the ball around him the other way. (was able to sell the dummy and turn the defender to break into the area)

12-yard mark, 12-yard spot: The penalty spot.

UEFA Cup: The Union of European Football Associations Cup, an annual competition played over five rounds of home-and-away pairings, in which the winner is determined by aggregate score (if a tie results, away goals count double). Sixty-four teams participate, selected from among the runners-up to league champions in European countries. The number of teams a country can enter is determined by points accrued in the competition over a five-year period. The competition began in 1955 as the Inter-Cities Fairs Cup, and was open only to cities staging international trade fairs. The first tournament took three years to complete, with FC Barcelona defeating a London side assembled with players from several teams. The Fairs Cup became known as the "Fouls Cup" because of unfortunate incidents of rough play and violence in the first years. In 1971, the competition

was taken over by the Union of European Football Associations, and the first UEFA Cup was won by Tottenham Hotspur. Because of the number of games played by the many entrants, the UEFA Cup is considered a good barometer of the relative strength of the European leagues.

United States Soccer Federation: The national governing body of soccer in the United States, an affiliate member of the Federation Internationale de Football Association. The United States Soccer Federation is responsible for conducting regional and national youth, amateur, and open competitions, and for the development and sponsorship of the various national teams (Youth Team, Olympic Team, and the National Team). Founded in 1913, the United States Soccer Federation is headquartered in New York. also *USSF.*

unmarked: Not guarded by a defender. (ghosted through unmarked)

unsighted: Blocked or unable to see, as of a goalkeeper. A British expression. (unsighted for the second goal)

upright: A goal post. also *post.*

USSF: The United States Soccer Federation.

1. volley: A powerful kick in which an air ball is kicked first time, without trapping or controlling it first. compare *half volley.*

2. volley: To execute a volley. compare *half volley.*

wall: A number of defenders (usually three or more) standing side-by-side to act as a human barrier in order to block a part of the goal when a free kick is awarded to the opposing team near the defenders' goal, legal as long as the wall is formed no closer than the minimum 10 yards.

wall pass: A give-and-go. The teammate who makes the return pass acts as a "wall" off which the first player bounces the ball, as though passing it to himself. also *double pass, one-two.*

W formation: The attacking half (three forwards, two midfielders) of the W-M formation. see *W-M.*

wing: 1. Either of two attacking players (left wing and right wing) who normally play on the outside or flanks of the front line. also *outside forward, outside left, outside right, winger.* see *pyramid.* 2. The position played by a wing. also *outside forward, outside left, outside right, winger*. see *pyramid*. 3. The area of the playing field close to the touchlines.

winger: see *wing*.

wing half: 1. Either of two midfielders who normally play on the flanks of a central midfielder in the classic pyramid formation. also *outside half, wing halfback*. see *pyramid*. 2. The position played by a wing half. also *outside half, wing halfback*. see *pyramid*.

wing halfback: see *wing half*.

win a corner: To be awarded a corner kick in the opposing half because the defending team, by an accidental deflection or an intentional play, last touches the ball before it crosses entirely over the goal line outside the goal. compare *give away a corner*.

win the ball: To gain possession of the ball by taking it away from an opponent, intercepting a pass or cross played to an opponent, first reaching and controlling a loose ball, or by playing it off an opponent in such a way as to win a corner kick or throw-in. (a good tackler who can also win the ball in the air)

withdrawn forward: An attacking player who normally operates from a central position behind the forward line. In modern formations, a withdrawn forward is considered an attacking midfielder, but the first withdrawn forwards were nominally center forwards, moved back to draw the opposing cen-

ter back out of position. At Wembley in 1953, Hungary used a withdrawn forward to hand England its first defeat ever at home. With the English stopper Harry Johnston confused and drawn out of position to cover the withdrawn Hungarian center forward, Nandor Kidegkuti, Hungary's gifted strikers Sandor Kocsis and Ferenc Puskas were able to break through repeatedly in front of the English net. The result was a lopsided 6-3 win for Hungary.

W-M: A formation which employs three defenders, four midfielders, and three forwards. The W-M (so called because imaginary lines connecting the two front midfielders and three forwards would appear from above like the letter W, and similar lines between the two rear midfielders and three defenders, like an M) resulted from the 1925 change in the offside rule, reducing the number of defenders required to be between an attacking player without the ball and the goal from three to two. With the offside trap made more difficult and risky by the new rule, scoring opportunities increased greatly (the number of goals scored in the English Football League rose by over 40 percent in the first year of the change). To counter this, English football pioneer Herbert Chapman, just made manager of Arsenal, together with inside forward Charlie Buchan, devised the W-M, in which the old attacking center half was repo-

VOLLEY

sitioned between the two regular full-backs to become a center back or stopper, and the two inside forwards moved back to the midfield. The W-M was an immediate success and became the standard of soccer in England (and, consequently, much of the world) for twenty years. also *3-4-3*. compare *4-4-2, 4-3-3, 4-2-4, pyramid*.

woodwork: 1. Slang for the goal posts or crossbar. (caromed in off the woodwork) 2. Slang for the boards in indoor soccer.

work-rate: A term applied to the amount of running a player or team does or is able to do during a game. The expression originated in England in the mid-1960s, when a high work-rate became a basic tenet of English soccer. (known more for his work-rate than skill)

world-class: Having sufficient skill or merit to be able to compete at the highest level of international competition. (will get their first look at the new acquisition, a world-class midfielder)

●●Being of the highest caliber. (feasted on a world-class meal)

World Club Championship, World Club Cup: An annual competition between winners of the European Cup (European Championship Clubs' Cup) and the South American Copa Libertadores. The World Club Cup (originally called the Intercontinental Cup) was first held in 1960, with Real Madrid of Spain defeating Penarol of Uruguay.

World Cup: The prestigious quadrennial competition between teams representing 24 countries from among the over 150 member nations of FIFA. With the host country and defending World Cup champion automatically qualified, the remaining twenty-two finalists are determined by qualifying rounds played within five geographical elimination groups; Europe, South America, CONCACAF (North and Central America and the Caribbean Zone), Africa, and Asia/Oceania. Through the efforts of FIFA president Jules Rimet, after whom the original World Cup trophy was named, the first competition was hosted and won by Uruguay in 1930. In 1970 in Mexico, Brazil, led by the incomparable Pele, won the World Cup for an unprecedented third time. The Jules Rimet trophy was retired and given permanently to Brazil. The present trophy, the FIFA World Cup (which cannot be won outright), was first presented to winner West Germany at the 1974 competition. It is estimated that over 1-1/2 billion people (roughly one-third of the world's population) watched the telecast of the 1982 World Cup Final (Italy 3, West Germany 1), the largest television audience ever to watch a sporting event.

1. **yellow card:** 1. A small yellow card displayed by the referee when a player is cautioned. see *caution*. 2. A caution, the act or an instance of a player being cautioned. see *caution*.

2. **yellow card:** To show a yellow card; to caution a player. (got yellow carded for arguing with the referee) also *book, card*. see *caution*.

Though some basic elements of tennis have been borrowed from early Arab, Greek, and Roman pastimes involving a bat or racket and a ball, the modern game of tennis is a direct descendant of a game that became popular in France in the Middle Ages. As its name *jeu de paume*, literally "play of palm," suggests, this was originally a hand game in which a small, tightly bound cloth or leather-stuffed ball was hit back and forth over an obstruction (later a net) and around the walls and cloisters of outdoor courtyards within twelfth-century monasteries. French clerics were certainly the first enthusiasts of the sport of court tennis. In Northern France, the Archbishop of Rouen became so alarmed by his priests' preoccupation with the game that he banned the playing of it in 1245. There is even evidence of a specially built indoor court fifteen years earlier in central France, owned by a Peter Garnier in Poitiers.

By the fourteenth century, royalty had taken a particular interest in the game, which had already spread to England and many parts of Europe. Louis X of France is said to have died in 1316 from a chill contracted by drinking cold water after a tennis match.

Now being played with small paddles or *battoirs* instead of bare or gloved hands, court tennis had gained enough popularity by the late 1300s to make its first appearances in Western literature, both in Chaucer's *Troylus and Creseda* ("but canstow playen racket to and fro. . ."), and in Donato Velluti's lines about invading French knights playing the game in his *Chronicles of Florence* ("at this time was the beginning in these parts of playing at tenes"). This was the earliest mention of any form of the word "tennis," which is believed to have come from the French *tenez*, meaning "take heed" or "play."

The first rules of court tennis were written in France in 1592 by Forbet, and published in 1599. In 1632, these rules were expanded and republished under the title *Le Jeu de la Paulme* by Forbet's countryman, Charles Hulpeau. They describe a complex, scientific game that remains much the same today (as court tennis in the United States or real tennis in Great Britain) as it was in the days of Henry VIII.

The seventeenth century brought court tennis across the seas to the New World, even as its popularity began to decline in England and France. England's civil war during the reign of Charles I virtually brought an end to the sport, as did the French Revolution in that country in the eighteenth century. Though there were revivals in the ninteenth century when, once again, royalty and the gentry embraced the game, court tennis would never again be a popular sport.

Although court tennis had been played outdoors within walled courtyards and reports tell of some kind of "field tennis" played on a close-cut grass field in Battersea Fields near Ranelagh in 1767, no successful outdoor version of grass tennis was possible until the mid-1800s when a rubber ball was invented that would bounce on a surface other than flagstones.

In 1858, Major Harry Gem and Jean-Baptiste Perera marked out a tennis court on grass in Edgbaston (Birmingham, England) and played the first recorded "lawn tennis" game with the rackets, net, and court markings of court tennis. In 1872, Major Gem founded the Leamington Lawn Tennis Club, the first outdoor tennis club.

An English army major and court tennis player, Walter Clopton Wingfield, first tried the outdoor game at a lawn party at his Lansdowne House in London in 1869. In 1874, Major Wingfield patented a version of the game, marketing a set including balls, racquets, a net, and an instruction booklet. Claiming that tennis came from an ancient Greek sport, Wingfield called his game "sphairistike," which was soon contracted to "sticky" and finally replaced by "lawn tennis."

A popular and commercial success, Wingfield's game featured a strange 60-foot-long, hourglass-shaped court, 30 feet wide at the baselines and 21 feet wide at the 4-foot, 8-inch-high net. Oddly, service was from a small diamond marked in the middle of one side of the court only, and delivered to a service court which was between the service line and the baseline.

Lawn tennis had been taken to Bermuda by a British officer the year before Wingfield's patent. It was seen and admired there by an American girl, Mary Ewing Outerbridge, who brought rackets and a few tennis balls home with her in March of 1874, and a couple of months later, set up what is believed to be the first tennis court in the United States at the edge of a cricket field on the grounds of the Staten Island Cricket and Baseball Club. Tennis pioneer and five-time United States doubles champion Dr. James Dwight also set up a court in Boston the same year, where he and a friend, Fred Sears, taught the game to Sears's younger brother, Richard, later the United States singles champion seven times and U.S. doubles champion six times (five with Dr. Dwight).

A more stimulating game than croquet, the only other outdoor sport that could be played by men and women, the "new" tennis quickly gained popularity in both countries. In 1875, the Marylebone Cricket Club, England's accepted governing body of court tennis and rackets, published a unified code of rules.

Wingfield's hourglass-shaped court was retained, though widened at the slightly higher net and lengthened to its present 78 feet. The service court extended 26 feet from the net, rather than being marked from the baseline. Only the server could score, keeping the serve until losing a rally. Scoring was derived from rackets, with a game being fifteen points.

In 1875, in order to increase diminishing revenues, the All England Croquet Club expanded to include tennis at the urging of one of its founders, Henry Jones. Facing another financial difficulty in 1877, the club (now named the All England Croquet and Lawn Tennis Club) decided to sponsor an all-comers tennis tournament, the first Wimbledon Championship. Wimbledon remains today the most important, as well as the oldest, competition in tennis. Jones, who suggested the event, also participated in framing the rules for it, most of which were adopted around the world and remain virtually the same today.

Among Jones's contributions was the change from rackets scoring back to the "clock" system originally used in court tennis, with the four points being fifteen, thirty, forty-five, and game. The Wimbledon court was rectangular with the same outer dimensions as the modern singles court, though the net was 5 feet high at the posts and 3 feet, 3 inches at the middle.

An accomplished cricket player, Spencer W. Gore, introducing his somewhat controversial volley shot, won the first Wimbledon, a men's singles event only. The first men's doubles championship was held in Scotland in 1878, and the first women's singles championship, the following year in Ireland. The first "open" competition (in which other than club members could participate) in the United States was staged in 1880 at the Staten Island Croquet and Baseball Club, with O.E. Woodhouse, a British player who is believed to have introduced the smash, winning the "Championship of America."

In 1881, the United States National Lawn Tennis Association (later the USTA) was formed, becoming the world's first national governing body of tennis. That same year, the new organization adopted the All England Club's Wimbledon rules and staged the first official United States Championships at the Newport Casino in Newport, Rhode Island. Richard Sears won the singles championship in straight sets, the first of his remarkable seven singles titles. Though the inaugural men's doubles event was won by Clarence Clark and Fred Taylor, Sears went on to take the next six doubles championships. Meanwhile, in England, the Renshaw twins, William and Ernest, had introduced their aggressive and exciting style of play that would popularize tennis as a spectator sport and dominate Wimbledon for a decade. From 1880 to 1890, the Renshaws won eight singles titles, losing in the finals on two other occasions, and seven doubles titles.

The first National Men's Inter-Collegiate Championships were held in 1883, with the fall leg won by Harvard's Howard Taylor and the spring leg by teammate Joseph Clark. The same year, Clark and his brother Clarence, with the permission of current United States doubles champions Dwight and Sears, journeyed to England to represent the United States against the British team of Reggie and Laurie Doherty in the first international tennis match. The Dohertys won and, in 1884, added fuel to the growing rivalry between tennis enthusiasts in the United States and Great Britain by defeating Dwight and Sears in the semifinals of Wimbledon's first men's doubles championship. The same year, Maud Watson, the nineteen-year-old daughter of an English vicar, defeated her older sister Lilian to become the first ever Wimbledon women's singles champion.

The first women's singles championship in the United States was staged in 1887 at the Philadelphia Cricket Club and won by Ellen Hansell. The USNLTA was reluctant to sponsor an official women's championship until 1889, but then recognized the two previous events retroactively. When the first modern Olympics were held in Athens in 1896, a tennis competition was included. J.P. Boland won the gold medal in men's singles.

In 1900, American player Dwight Davis donated the International Tennis Challenge Trophy for the first team competition between nations, known thereafter as the Davis Cup, the most prestigious international tennis competition. Behind the big serve of team captain Davis and the particularly baffling American twist and reverse twist serves introduced by teammates Holcombe Ward and Malcolm Whiteman respectively, the Americans soundly defeated the British team in the first tournament. In 1903, Britain won the Davis Cup with a two-man team of the incredible Doherty brothers, Reggie and Laurie, who from 1897 to 1906 won nine Wimbledon singles and doubles titles. In 1902, they won the United States doubles championship, and in 1903, Laurie Doherty became the first foreigner to win the United States singles title.

By the early 1900s, tennis had become a true international sport. Six nations entered the Davis Cup in 1905, won by Great Britain, and for the first time, an overseas player won a Wimbledon Championship when American May Sutton (ironically, born in Great Britain) took the women's singles title. The same year, the first Australian Championships were staged, with R.W. Heath winning in singles and T. Tachell and R. Lycett taking the doubles event.

The dominant players of the time were William Larned, who matched Dick Sears's record, winning the United States singles championship seven times, the last in 1911 when he was thirty-eight; Australian lefthander Norman Brookes, the first overseas player to win the Wimbledon men's singles championship in 1907; New Zealand great Tony Wilding, four-time Wimbledon singles and doubles champion; and Maurice McLoughlin (the "California Comet"), the two-time United States singles and three-time doubles champion, whose blistering serve at Wimbledon in 1913 was the first to be called a "cannonball."

In Paris in 1913, with representatives present from Australia, Austria, Belgium, the British Isles, Denmark, France, Germany, Holland, Russia, South Africa, Sweden, and Switzerland, the International Lawn Tennis Federation was founded. The United States was reluctant to join, primarily because of the number of so-called "world championships" which were allocated, and would remain outside and independent of the ILTF (ultimately, the ITF) until these so-called championship titles were eliminated after World War I.

Three of the greatest players of all time quickly established the popularity of tennis after the war: the magnetic and almost invincible Frenchwoman, Suzanne Lenglen; and two Americans, Helen Wills (later Moody), Lenglen's equally dominant successor, and the incomparable William Tatem Tilden II.

Lenglen burst into the tennis world at Wimbledon at the age of twenty in 1919, wearing a revealing calf-length dress with short sleeves at a time when women played only in high-necked, long-sleeved, ankle-length dresses with petticoats. Sipping brandy between sets, she stunned seven-time singles champion Dorothea Lambert Chambers in the final round, taking the title in what is now regarded as one of the classic matches in tennis. An emotional player with exceptional athletic ability and accuracy, Lenglen won both the singles and doubles titles at Wimbledon every year between 1919 and 1925 (except when illness forced a withdrawal in 1924) and proved to be tennis's greatest drawing card. In 1926, Lenglen became the first true tennis professional and toured the United States under the management of sports entrepreneur C.C. Pyle.

Wills was entirely different from Lenglen, both in personality and style. Nicknamed "Little Miss Poker Face," Wills showed little emotion, basing her game on power and tactics rather than speed and mobility. She won the United States singles championships seven times and the Wimbledon singles title a record eight times in nine tries. Lenglen defeated Wills the only time they met, at a much celebrated match in Cannes in 1926, but Wills's supporters are quick to point out that at nineteen, she had not yet reached her peak, and that a year later, the game might have had a different result. From 1927 through 1932, Wills won seven United States and five Wimbledon singles championships without losing a single set.

Bill Tilden first won the United States and Wimbledon singles championships when he was twenty-seven in 1920. A tall and graceful athlete, Tilden was the master of all strokes, as well as a brilliant tactician, competitor, and showman. He dominated tennis from 1920 through 1926 and was practically unbeatable. Tilden won more United States men's titles (sixteen) than any other player. He also played in Davis Cup matches for a record eleven years, and his record of sixteen consecutive singles match wins still stands. He won his second Wimbledon singles championship in 1930 at the age of thirty-seven, and finally turned pro in 1931 after years of feuding with the USLTA about his amateur standing. Tilden gave credibility to professional tennis, and, partnered with promoter Bill O'Brien, launched the first men's pro tour in 1932 and 1933.

New amateur stars emerged in the 1930s, among them the twenty-one-year-old American Ellsworth Vines, who, with his 121 mile-per-hour cannonball, scored a phenomenal thirty service aces in the singles finals to win at Wimbledon in 1932; three-time United

States and Wimbledon singles champion Fred Perry, considered England's greatest player; American Donald Budge, who, in 1938, became the first player ever to win the four major championships in one year, namely, the United States, Australian, French, and Wimbledon Championships, a feat known thereafter as the "Grand Slam"; and American Bobby Riggs, the 1939 United States and Wimbledon singles winner. Typical of the crafty Riggs, he reportedly took English bookies for over $100,000 by betting he would win the singles, doubles, and mixed doubles events. He did, becoming the only man other than Budge to win a Wimbledon "triple." Starting with Vines in 1934, all these players followed Tilden's example and turned professional by the start of World War II, breathing new life into the young pro tour. Though the United States Championships continued uninterrupted through the 1940s, international play ceased until after the war.

The postwar era saw a tremendous upsurge in the popularity of tennis in the United States, particularly on the West Coast, where scores of new low-maintenance concrete courts were constructed to keep up with the increasing number of new enthusiasts.

In tournament play, American players dominated the 1940s behind the "big game" of Robert Falkenburg, Jack Kramer, Ted Schroeder, and Pancho Gonzales. American women were equally strong, winning every singles and doubles title in the United States, French, and Wimbledon championships, as well as the Wightman Cup for almost a decade after the war.

Australia's victory in the 1950 Davis Cup, led by Frank Sedgman, signaled a changing of the guard in men's tennis. Australian players, among them Sedgman, Ken Rosewall, Lew Hoad, Roy Emerson, Neale Fraser, Fred Stolle, and Rod Laver, were to take most of the major championships for nearly two decades and win fourteen of the next seventeen Davis Cup matches, losing only to United States teams led by Tony Trabert and Vic Seixas in 1954, Alex Olmeda in 1958, and Dennis Ralston in 1963.

The 1950s and 1960s produced some of the game's great women players, such as America's Maureen "Little Mo" Connolly, who, in 1953, became the first woman to score a Grand Slam, and whose brilliant career was cut short in 1954 by a leg injury when she was hit by a truck while riding a horse; Althea Gibson, two-time United States and Wimbledon champion and winner of eleven major titles, also the first black player to win a major championship; Maria Bueno of Brazil, winner of twenty Big Four titles and regarded as one of the game's great stylists; Margaret Court, holder of the all-time record for the most Big Four singles (twenty-four) and overall (sixty-two) titles, and who achieved the Grand Slam in 1970; and the incomparable Billie Jean King, second only to Court in overall Big Four titles (thirty-eight) and winner of more Wimbledon Championships (twenty) than any player in history.

By the late 1960s, tennis was at a crossroads. New stars were emerging from all over the world, including Australia's John Newcombe and Tony Roche, South Africa's Cliff Drysdale, Manuel Santana of Spain, Holland's Tom Okker, Jan Kodes from Czechoslovakia, Romania's Ilie Nastase, and Americans Arthur Ashe and Stan Smith, but more and more of the best players were becoming professionals. The problem was that the best tournaments were still amateur, or allegedly so. In fact, since the 1920s, ever increasing amounts of under-the-table money had been paid at major tournaments, giving rise to the character-ization of tennis amateurs as "shamateurs." Finally, the ILTF relented, and, in 1968, the modern era of "open tennis" arrived. Professionals as well as amateurs could now compete in major tournaments.

Tennis was at last a big-time, big-money sport, and, in the 1970s and 1980s, millions of new enthusiasts watched on television as new superstars Jimmy Connors, Guillermo Vilas, Bjorn Borg, John McEnroe, Jose Luis Clerc, and Ivan Lendl rose to prominence. Due in no small part to the efforts of Billie Jean King (including her widely publicized "Battle of the Sexes" victory over fifty-seven-year-old Bobby Riggs in 1973, watched in person by a record crowd of 30,472 and by over 50 million on national television), women's professional tennis also flourished, showcasing the talents of players like Evonne Goolagong, Virginia Wade, Chris Evert, Martina Navratilova, and Tracy Austin. Austin, who in 1977 at the age of fourteen became the youngest player ever to compete at Wimbledon, was the first of a succession of female pro prodigies who followed in the 1980s.

1. **ace:** An unreturnable serve that the receiver is unable to hit, or a point won with such a serve. From the Latin and later the French *as* meaning a single spot or "one" in dice games, then card games, then tennis and other games. Originally, an ace could be any single winning stroke, but by 1800, popular use narrowed the meaning to an unreturnable serve. also *ace on service, service ace.*

2. **ace:** To serve an ace. (aced him at match point to take the singles trophy)
   ●● To get the better of, as by a decisive move or action. (kicked hard and aced him at the finish line)

ace on service: see *ace.*

ad: Short for advantage.

ad court: Short for advantage court.

ad in: Short for advantage in.

ad out: Short for advantage out.

advantage: 1. A point won by a player after deuce. If the same player wins the next point, he wins the game; if he loses the next point, the score returns to deuce. From the French *avant* meaning "ahead." also *ad, vantage.* 2. The score for a point won by a player after deuce. (advantage Smith) also *ad, vantage.*

advantage court: The receiver's left service court, into which the ball is served from the baseline behind the server's left court on an advantage point. also *ad court, backhand court, left-hander's court, second court.* compare *deuce court, first court, forehand court, right court.*

advantage in: The server's advantage. also *ad in, advantage server.* compare *ad out, advantage out, advantage receiver.*

advantage out: The receiver's advantage. also *ad out, advantage receiver.* compare *ad in, advantage in, advantage server.*

advantage receiver: see *advantage out.*

advantage server: see *advantage in.*

advantage set: A set tied after ten games. In order to win the set, one side must win two consecutive games. This principle was introduced at the 1878 Wimbledon Championships and stood until only recently. In 1967 at the Newport Casino Invitational, Dick Leach and Dick Dell defeated Tom Mozur and Len Schloss in what is believed to be the longest advantage set ever played in a major tournament, ending finally at forty-nine games to forty-seven. To prevent such marathon events, tie-breakers and sudden death began to come into use after 1970 as a way of ending tied sets. also *deuce set, games-all.*

alert position: The position assumed by a player waiting for a serve or a return. also *anticipatory position, readiness position, waiting position.*

all: Each; apiece, as for an equal number of points in a game or games in a set. compare *games-all.*

all-around play: Both a good ground game and a good net game. compare *all-court game.*

all-court game: The ability to play all kinds of strokes from anywhere on the court. compare *all-around play.*

all-court player: A player with the ability to play all kinds of strokes from any part of the court.

alley: Either of the two 4-1/2-foot-wide areas on the sides of the singles court that are used to make the court wider for doubles play and that are out of bounds in singles play. The use of the term "alley" was popularized in America and taken from the sport of bowling. From the French *alee,* meaning "walkway." also *tramline, tramlines.*

American formation: see *Australian formation.*

American twist: A serve in which topspin is imparted with an upward and outward motion of the racket as the ball is struck, causing it to bounce high and to the receiver's left (with a right-handed server) when it hits the ground. The American twist first came to prominence at the 1900 Davis Cup competition in Boston, when Holcombe Ward of the victorious American team bewildered his British opponents with the technique. also *kicker, kick serve, twist.* compare *reverse twist.*

1. angle: To hit the ball diagonally across the court.

2. angle: A stroke hit diagonally across the court.

angle game: A style of play which emphasizes short angle crosscourt shots which land in the forecourt or midcourt near the sideline.

anticipatory position: see *alert position.*

approach shot: A hard, forcing shot usually hit from the midcourt deep into the opponent's court after which a player moves to the net. A well-placed approach shot puts the opponent on the defensive and allows a player to move in to position to attempt to win the point with a volley.

around the post: A stroke hit from the area wide of the court which does not pass over the net, but lands fairly in the opposing court. A rare occurrence, but

BACKHAND

legal even if the ball is low enough to be stopped by the the net.

Association of Tennis Professionals: A service organization for male professional tennis players. Founded in 1972, the Association of Tennis Professionals (ATP) functions as the representative of touring professionals in matters regarding tournament play and provides a computer ranking service (based on performance) for all professional players. To qualify for membership in the Association of Tennis Professionals, a player must be ranked among the top 200 players in the world according to the ATP computer. see *computer rankings.*

ATP: The Association of Tennis Professionals.

attacking game: A strategy in which a player attempts to keep the opponent off balance and on the defensive, as by aggressive net play utilizing the volley and smash.

attack the net: To move toward the net in order to be in position to volley or kill the ball for a winner. (likes to serve and attack the net) also *rush the net, take the net.*

Australian Championships: One of the Big Four or Grand Slam tournaments, along with the French, United States, and Wimbledon Championships. The Australian Championships were first held in 1905, with Rodney Heath winning the men's singles and Tom Tachell and Randolph Lycett winning the men's doubles event. Women first competed in 1922, with Mal Molesworth winning the first women's singles, Esna Boyd and M. Mountain the first women's doubles, and Esna Boyd and John Hawkes the first mixed doubles event. The Australian Championships became open to both amateurs and professionals in 1968. Since 1980, the Australian Championships for men and women have been held separately. also *Australian Open.*

Australian doubles: see *Australian formation.*

Australian formation: An unorthodox doubles formation in which the server's partner stands on the same side of the court as (or directly in front of) the server. In Australia, the formation is known as the "American formation." also *Australian doubles, I formation, tandem formation.*

Australian Open: The Australian Championships.

backboard: A wall against which the ball is hit for practice, usually marked with a net-high horizontal line.

backcourt: The area of the court from the service line to the baseline, between the sidelines. also *deep court, no-man's land.* compare *forecourt, midcourt.*

1. backhand: A stroke hit from the side of the body opposite the racket hand, with the playing arm extended across the body. The term "backhand" refers to having the back of the racket hand toward the net when the ball is hit. Among the first exponents of the backhand was 1902-1906 Wimbledon and 1903 United States singles champion H. L. "Laurie" Doherty of England, but the player credited with changing the backhand from a defensive stroke into an attacking stroke was 1938 Grand Slam winner Don Budge, who is reputed to have had the greatest backhand in the history of tennis. compare *forehand, overhead.*

2. backhand: Of or pertaining to a stroke hit from the side of the body opposite the racket hand and made with the playing arm extended across the body. compare *forehand, overhead.*

3. backhand: To hit a backhand stroke.

backhand court: The left service court, on the backhand side for most (right-handed) receivers. see *advantage court.*

backhand grip: A method of holding the racket for a backhand stroke in which, with the racket held across the body (strings square to the net), the V between the thumb and forefinger is placed over the near bevel on top of the handle, and the thumb wrapped around extended diagonally across or straight up the back surface of the handle. also *Eastern backhand grip.* see *Continental grip, two-handed backhanded grip, Western grip.*

back room: see *runback.*

backspin: see *underspin.*

backstop: The fence or obstruction behind the ends of a court to keep the ball from rolling away.

backswing: The taking back of a racket just before a stroke is made.

1. bagel: Slang for a set won in six straight games. Coined in the early 1970s by popular American professional Eddie

Dibbs, who likened the loser's score, a zero, to a bagel. also *bagel job, love set.*

2. bagel: To win a set in six straight games.

bagel job: see *bagel.*

ball boy, ball girl: A boy or a girl who keeps the playing area clear by retrieving balls for the players during a tournament or match.

band: The canvas strip attached to the top of the net.

baseball grip: An unorthodox method of holding the racket for a two-handed forehand, in which the dominant hand is placed on the racket handle just above the other hand, as in gripping a baseball bat. see *two-handed player.* compare *chopper grip, Continental grip, Eastern grip, shake-hands grip, service grip, Western grip.*

baseline: Either of the end boundary lines or back lines of a court, extending between the sidelines, and behind which a player stands to serve.

baseline game: 1. A style of play in which ground strokes are played from near the baseline, with the player seldom moving to the net. The 1925 Wimbledon singles champion, Jean-Rene ("the Alligator") Lacoste, one of France's legendary "Four Musketeers," was the last great exponent of the baseline game. compare *net game.* 2. Ground strokes played from near the

BALL BOYS

baseline. compare *net game, net play.*

baseline judge: Either of two linesmen or lineswomen responsible for watching the baseline and calling when a ball goes out of play, positioned on a line with the baselines on the same side of the court as the umpire. also *baselinesman.*

baseliner: A player who stays near the baseline to play groundstrokes, seldom moving to the net. The 1925 Wimbledon singles champion, Jean-Rene ("the Alligator") Lacoste, one of France's legendary "Four Musketeers," was the last great baseliner. compare *net rusher, power player, retriever, shotmaker, touch player.*

baselinesman: see *baseline judge.*

beaten by the ball: Arriving too late to be able to make a good stroke, being passed or almost passed.

1. Big Four: The four "Grand Slam" events: the Australian Championships, the French Championships, the Wimbledon Championships, and the United States Championships. The countries sponsoring these championships were the most powerful or "Big Four" of tennis, whose supremacy at the Davis Cup was unchallenged until 1974, 1975, and 1976, when the competition was won by South Africa, Sweden, and Italy, respectively. see *Grand Slam.*

2. Big Four: Of or pertaining to the four "Grand Slam" events: the Australian Championships, the French Championships, the Wimbledon Championships, and the United States Championships. (will only play in Big Four events this year) also *Grand Slam.*

big game: A style of play which emphasizes a powerful serve and aggressive net play. Though the birth of the "big game" or "serve-and-volley" game is most often associated with the post-World War II American Davis Cup teams featuring Jack Kramer, Ted Schroeder, and Pancho Gonzalez, the same style of play was demonstrated as early as the 1914 Davis Cup Challenge Round between Maurice McLoughlin, the "California Comet," and Australian Norman Brookes, and later in 1932, by United States and Wimbledon Champion Ellsworth Vines. also *power game, power tennis.*

big serve: A powerful serve. also *cannonball.*

big server: A player with a powerful serve. also *fireballer.*

Big W: Slang for Wimbledon, the site of the British National Championships.

bisque: A bonus or handicap occasionally given in a friendly or informal game. As in golf, a bisque may be taken at any time during a game. Originally from the medieval game of court tennis.

blanket the net: To play at the net. (likes to blanket the net after his serve)

1. blitz: 1. A succession of quick, powerful shots to keep an opponent on the defensive. 2. A game with four straight points. also *love game.*

2. blitz: 1. To make a succession of quick, powerful shots to keep an opponent off balance. 2. To win a game with four straight points.

blocked ball: A ball returned with the racket held stationary, often resulting in a stop volley. see *stop volley.*

body shot: A serve or stroke hit directly at or close to an opponent, often resulting in a weak or clumsy return.

1. break: To win a game against the server. To be "broken" means to lose the game one is serving. (will lose the set if he is broken again) also *break service.*

2. break: 1. A service break. 2. see *kick.*

break back: To, immediately after being broken, break the opponent's serve on the next game.

break point: 1. A situation in which the next point to be played could result in a service break for the receiver if the point is won by the receiver. A break point score can be love-40, 15-40, 30-40, or ad out. (forced the game to break point before losing to the server) 2. The point which caused a service break.

break service: see *break.*

British National Championships: The Wimbledon Championships.

bullet: A hard-hit ball.

butt: The end of the racket handle.

bye: The right to, having been assigned no opponent, automatically advance to the next round of a competition without playing a match. Byes are necessary in the first round in order to achieve the correct number of players in the second when the number of entries in a draw is not exactly two, four, eight, sixteen, thirty-two, sixty-four, or a higher power of two.

The number of byes necessary in the first round can be determined by subtracting the number of entries from the next higher power of two. If, for example, there are twenty-seven entries, there will be five byes in the first round (thirty-two is the next higher power to two; thirty-two minus twenty-seven equals five). In some major competitions, byes are used to insure that seeded players or nations are not eliminated by each other in early rounds. The term "bye" comes from the Old English *bi*, meaning "near to," and probably derives from the fact that a player who has drawn a bye is left to stand by (or "near to" the competition) until the next round is played. also *walk-in*. see *draw, seed*.

1. call: To make and/or announce an official ruling or judgment on a play. (called a foot fault on the server)

2. call: 1. A ruling or judgment made by an official. 2. The score at any given time during a match.

cannonball: An extremely fast serve. The term was coined at Wimbledon in 1913 to describe the serve of Californian Maurice McLoughlin, nicknamed the "California Comet." Other players who were noted for a cannonball serve were the great Bill Tilden, 1932 Wimbledon champion Ellsworth Vines (who scored a remarkable thirty aces in the final round with his 121 mph serve), Pancho Gonzales (118 mph), and English professional Michael Sangster (154 mph). In the 1970s and early 1980s, left-hander Roscoe Tanner became known for having the fastest serve in tennis, clocked at over 155 mph. also *big serve*.

1. carry: To intentionally hold or carry a ball in play on the racket. An infraction which results in the loss of the point.

2. carry: The act or an instance of intentionally holding or carrying a ball in play on the racket. An infraction which results in the loss of the point.

center court: The main court in any tennis arena. After Wimbledon's famous Centre Court in England.

●●At the center of attention. (stood there arguing at center court, right in the middle of the dance floor)

center line: see *center service line*.

center line judge: Either of two linesmen or lineswomen, responsible for watching the center line on serves in tournament play and calling when a ball lands outside the service court. Center line judges are positioned in line with the center service lines behind the baselines.

center mark: A line (4 inches long and 2 inches wide) extending inward from and perpendicular to the baseline at its midpoint. A player serving must stay behind the baseline and between an imaginary extension of the center mark and the sideline on the side from which the serve is taken.

center service line: A line parallel to the sidelines which extends from the middle of the net to the midpoint of the service line, separating and serving as a boundary for the left and right service courts. also *center line, half-court line*.

center strap, center strop: A 2-inch-wide piece of canvas that runs down the middle of the net and is anchored to the court on some surfaces to secure the bottom of the net and to keep the top of the net at the proper height.

Centre Court: The hallowed main court at Wimbledon, used only for the Wimbledon Championships (with the exception of one professional tournament in 1967) since the 1936 Davis Cup Challenge Round. Opened in 1922, the Centre Court seats just under 12,000, with standing room for almost 3,000 additional spectators.

chair umpire: see *umpire*.

chalk: 1. The powdered white substance used to mark the lines on some tennis surfaces. In arguing about a ball called out by a line judge, players often claim to have "seen chalk," in reference to the puff of white dust raised when a ball hits a chalk-marked line. 2. A boundary line.

changeover: The one-minute period after every odd game in a set, during which players refresh themselves and change to opposite sides of the net. Players also change sides after the end of each set, unless the number of games played in a set is even, in which case the change is made at the end of the first game of the next set.

cheat: To move toward one side of the court in anticipation of a stroke.

1. chip: see *dink*.

2. chip: To execute a chip. see *dink*.

1. chop: 1. A slicing stroke in which a pronounced underspin is imparted to the ball (bottom of the ball rotates in the direction of flight) made by striking or "chopping" down with the racket and causing the ball to skid low, stop, or even recoil slightly, depending on the type and condition of the playing surface and the amount of underspin applied. compare *chip, cut, cut shot, cut stroke, dink, slice.* 2. Underspin. (a lot of chop on the ball) also *backspin, reverse spin.* compare *curl, cut, overspin, sidespin, topspin, twist.*

2. **chop:** To hit a ball with a "chopping" downward stroke (racket face open) in order to impart underspin. compare *chip, cut, dink, slice, undercut.*

chopper grip: The Continental grip. also *English grip, service grip.*

circuit: A scheduled series of professional tournaments. also *tour.*

clay: 1. The natural clay or claylike material used to form the surface of a clay court. see *clay court.* 2. Short for clay court. (prefers the clay for her baseline game) 3. Slang for a tennis court. (soft-spoken in person, but a fierce competitor on the clay)

clay court: A tennis court with a surface constructed on any of a number of kinds of natural clay or claylike loose material bound together by watering and rolling. Clay courts have a firm, smooth surface, are slower than grass, and favor touch players, retrievers, and baseliners, rather than power players. Among the earliest clay courts was one built in the late 1890s at the Hotel Beau in Cannes. In 1909, a new kind of court made from a blend of burned and finely crushed clay was built in Leicestershire, England, at the home of Commander Hillyard, R. N., captain of the English Tennis Team. It was inspired by the crushed and rolled termite ant-heap courts Hillyard had played on while touring South Africa. Because of the constant maintenance they require, clay courts have become less popular in recent years, although the French National Championships are still played on clay. In most of the world, a clay court is considered a hard court (in the United States, hard court refers only to concrete and asphalt surfaces). also *clay.*

clean winner: A winning stroke that is untouched by the opponent. also *placement.*

close: To move close to the net in doubles play to be in position to volley.

closed grip: A grip that makes the racket face tilt downward toward the ground, as with the Western grip. compare *open grip.*

closed racket, closed racket face: A racket held so that the racket face is tilted downward toward the ground. compare *flat racket, flat racket face, open racket, open racket face.*

club player: An individual who plays at one or more clubs rather than on a professional tour. Also commonly used as a somewhat pejorative reference to a player of less-than-professional skill.

computer rankings: Any of three computer rating systems (ATP, Nixdorf, and WTA) for professional players. Based on performance over a twelve-month period, computer rankings are issued periodically to determine tournament entries and seedings worldwide. ATP computer rankings are based on the performance of male players in Grand Prix tournaments (excluding the Volvo Masters). Nixdorf computer rankings are based on the performance of male players in Grand Prix tournaments (including the Volvo Masters), WCT tournaments, and major international team competitions (Davis Cup, ATP Team Championship, World Team Cup). WTA computer rankings are based on the performance of women players in WTA-approved tournaments.

concrete court: A tennis court with a surface constructed of a porous or nonporous mixture of concrete. Concrete provides a smooth, hard, and relatively fast surface, one that provides a firm foothold and favors power players rather than touch players, retrievers, or baseliners. Porous concrete courts require virtually no maintenance and have enjoyed increasing popularity since their introduction in the mid-1950s. The first concrete tennis court was constructed in 1879 in Santa Monica, California. compare *clay court, grass court, synthetic court.*

Continental grip: One of the two most popular methods of grasping the racket, in which, with the racket pointed at the net and held parallel to the ground (short strings pointing up and down), the palm of the hand rests near the top of the handle, with the V formed by the thumb and index finger (of a right-handed player) over the left bevel, leaving the racket face slightly open. Though difficult for beginners, the Continental grip is used by most high-level players for the serve and overhead volley and can be used for the backhand. Originally used in England in the early 1900s (and called the English grip), the grip soon became popular throughout "continental" Europe, where the low-bounce clay courts favored its open racket face, as did England's grass courts. also *chopper grip, service grip.* compare *baseball grip, Eastern grip, shake-hands grip, Western grip.*

court: 1. The rectangular playing area for the sport of tennis, 78 feet long by 27 feet wide for singles play (36 feet wide for doubles play) divided across the middle by a net, 3 feet high at the center, suspended from 3-foot, 6-inch-high posts, the centers of which are 3 feet outside the court on each side. Service lines, which extend between the singles sidelines, are marked 21 feet from each side of the net and parallel to it. On each side of the net, the space bounded by the service line and singles sidelines is divided into two equal parts called the service courts by the center service line, marked halfway between and parallel to the sidelines. A 4-inch-long perpendicular line, the center mark, extends into the court from the middle of each end boundary line or baseline. The center service line and the center mark are 2 inches wide. All other lines must be between 1 inch and 2 inches in width, except the baseline which may be 4 inches in width. All measurements are made to the outside of the lines. The playing surface of a court may be made of grass, clay, or claylike materials, concrete or asphalt, wood, or of synthetic materials, and, in championship play, must extend a minimum of 21 feet behind each baseline and 12 feet outside of the sidelines. The Marylebone Cricket Club's 1875 code of rules for lawn tennis called for an hourglass-shaped court that was wider at the "baseline" than at the net, as had been suggested by tennis pioneer Walter Clopton Wingfield. Regulations stipulating a rectangular court were adopted for the inaugural Wimbledon Championship in 1877. The word "court" comes from the old French *cort* (derived from the Latin *cohors*), meaning a yard or enclosure. also *tennis court.* see *fast court, hard court, slow court.* 2. The playing area and environs, including adjacent stands and backstops or side barriers. 3. Short for service court. also *service box.*

courtside: The area or seating area immediately adjacent to the perimeter of a tennis court.

cover: 1. To move into or be in position to return an opponent's shot. 2. To close the racket face or turn it downward in

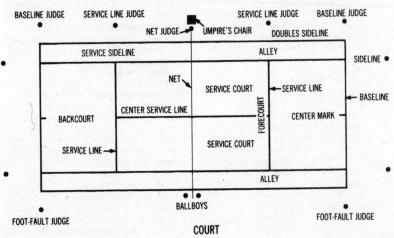

COURT

BASELINE JUDGE   SERVICE LINE JUDGE   SERVICE LINE JUDGE   BASELINE JUDGE

NET JUDGE →   UMPIRE'S CHAIR   DOUBLES SIDELINE

SERVICE SIDELINE   ALLEY   SIDELINE

NET   SERVICE COURT   ← SERVICE LINE   ← BASELINE

CENTER SERVICE LINE   FORECOURT   CENTER MARK →

BACKCOURT

SERVICE LINE →   SERVICE COURT

ALLEY

BALLBOYS

FOOT-FAULT JUDGE   FOOT-FAULT JUDGE order to impart topspin to the ball.

covered court: An English expression for an indoor court, usually with a wood or synthetic playing surface. Though tennis had been played indoors for some time, specially designed "covered courts" with wood floors began to be constructed in Scandinavian countries at the turn of the century. In recent years, large inflatable plastic coverings which can be taken down in warm weather have become popular in Scandinavia and other cold winter locations.

1. crosscourt: Diagonally across the court. (volleyed crosscourt for a winner)

2. crosscourt: To or toward the diagonally opposite court. (ended the rally with a crosscourt backhand)

curl: see *cut.*

1. cut: 1. see *cut stroke.* 2. The amount of spin on a ball resulting from a cut stroke (usually a combination of underspin and sidespin). also *curl.* compare *backspin, chop, overspin, reverse spin, sidespin, topspin, twist, underspin.*

2. cut: To hit the ball with a short slicing motion and an open racket face. compare *chip, chop, dink, slice, undercut.*

cut shot: see *cut stroke.*

cut stroke: A stroke in which underspin and sidespin are imparted to the ball with a short slicing motion as the open racket face "cuts" under and inside or outside of the ball to make contact. The cut stroke was a refinement of early slicing strokes used in the forerunner of modern tennis, court tennis. In 1920 at Wimbledon, all-time tennis great Bill Tilden used a devastating cut stroke to defeat the defending champion, Australian Gerald Patterson, in the final. also *cut, cut shot.* compare *chip, chop, dink, slice.*

daisy cutter: A stroke in which the ball skids along the ground or bounces very low when it lands. A difficult shot to return unless it can be volleyed.

Davis Cup: An annual international tournament contested by two or three-man national teams (plus alternates) for singles and doubles competition. A total of sixteen teams compete for the Davis Cup, the twelve top teams from the previous tournament (seeded on the basis of results), and the winners of four zonal competitions held during the year. The Davis Cup (named after its donor,

Dwight F. Davis of St. Louis) was first offered in 1900 at the initial International Lawn Tennis Championship, played at the Longwood Cricket Club in Boston. A team from the British Isles was the only challenger in the first competition, which was won handily by the American team comprised of Dwight Davis, Holcombe Ward, and American champion M.D. Whitman. The tournament became a true international competition at Wembley in 1904, when Belgium and France first took part (ironically, the United States did not field a team that year).

dead: Slang for out of play, as for a ball which has bounced out of bounds, bounced twice on the court, hit the net, or which has been "killed" on a winning stroke.

dead rubber: A match that remains to be played in a team competition when one side already has a winning lead (such as 3-0 or 3-1 in the Davis Cup).

deep: Far into the backcourt near the baseline. (caught her offguard with a deep lob) compare *long, short, wide.*

deep court: The backcourt.

1. default: The failure of a player or side to take part in or complete a game, set, or match, resulting in a walkover, an automatic victory for the opponent.

2. default: To lose a game, set, or match because of failure to take part in or complete it.

defensive lob: A ball hit high in the air so as to give a player enough time to properly position himself for the next stroke. compare *offensive lob.*

defensive volley: A return that can only be made by a volley, usually in desperation from below the level of the net. also *low volley.* compare *high volley, offensive volley.*

delivery: A serve.

designated tournament, designation: One of twelve tournaments (including Grand Slam events) in which a professional player must take part in one year in order to participate in the Volvo Grand Prix competition and Masters tournament. Designations are chosen by a special committee of the Men's International Professional Tennis Council from a list of preferences made up by each player according to guidelines established by the player's performance in the previous Masters tournament or ATP computer ranking. A player who fails to participate in a designated tournament is subject to an action that may include fines, designation to additional Grand Prix tournaments, loss of bonus points in the Grand Prix bonus pool, and ineligibility to participate in the Masters competition.

deuce: 1. A tie in a game after six points have been played (each side having a score of forty). At deuce, one side must score two consecutive points to win the game. The point scored after deuce is called advantage (either to the server or receiver). If the side with the advantage scores the next point, that side wins that game; if the opposing side wins the point, the score reverts to deuce, and does so indefinitely until one side wins two consecutive points. Deuce, from the French tennis expression *a deux de jeu*, meaning "at two to play" (or that two points must be won), was introduced in the rules adopted in 1875 by the Marylebone Cricket Club, then the governing body of cricket, tennis, and rackets. At the time, rackets scoring was used, with the first side to reach fifteen winning, unless the score was 14-all ("deuce"), in which case two consecutive points were necessary to win. 2. A tie after ten games of play in a set (five games for each side). To win the set, one side must win two consecutive games.

deuce court: The receiver's right service court, into which the ball is served (from the baseline behind the server's right court) whenever the score is deuce. see *first court.*

deuce set: see *advantage set.*

die: To not bounce or scarcely bounce, as of a ball with underspin. (hit in the forecourt and died)

1. dink: A softly sliced return intended to fall between the net and the service line in front of an opponent. also *chip, softie.* compare *chop, cut, cut shot, cut stroke, slice.*

2. dink: 1. To execute a dink. also *chip.* compare *chop, cut, slice, undercut.* 2. To hit a dink against a particular opponent. (dinked him to keep him off balance)

double-fault: To commit two consecutive faults while serving from the same court, resulting in the loss of the point. see *fault.*

double fault: The act or an instance of committing two consecutive faults while serving from the same court, resulting in the loss of the point. see *fault.*

DINK

double-fisted player: see *two-handed player*.

double-handed player: see *two-handed player*.

double hit: The act or an instance of striking the ball twice during the same stroke. If done intentionally, an infraction that results in the loss of the point.

doubles: A game between teams of two players or "pairs," played on a court slightly wider than in singles, utilizing the two 4-1/2-foot alleys and baseline extensions normally marked outside the sidelines of a singles court. Rules for doubles play specify that service is alternated between the pairs with all four players serving in turn, and that the players receiving service must receive from the same court throughout a set (the order of service or the court from which either partner receives may be changed at the end of each set). All other rules of singles play apply to doubles. Doubles is categorized into men's doubles, women's doubles, and mixed doubles. The first recorded doubles championship (men's doubles) was held in Scotland in 1878.

doubles court: The 78-foot-long by 36-foot-wide rectangular playing area for doubles. A doubles court is slightly wider than that used for singles, and includes the two 4-1/2-foot alleys and baseline extensions normally marked outside the sidelines of a singles court. The portions of the singles sidelines that lie between the service lines are called the service sidelines on a doubles court.

doubles sideline: One of the two side boundaries for a doubles court, drawn 4-1/2 feet outside the singles sidelines and extending between the baselines.

double-strung racket: A racket strung with two sets of vertical (long) strings and only five or six widely spaced cross strings, wrapped at the junctions with various bracing materials (among them, a plastic tubing known as spaghetti, the source of the racket's other name, the spaghetti racket). A West German, Werner Fisher, invented the double-strung racket, which was used in several major tournaments in 1977 with startling results. The extremely low-tensioned strings virtually catapulted the ball off the racket, at the same time imparting an unnatural amount of topspin. Within the year, the double-strung racket was banned by the ITF.

down the line: Parallel and close to the sideline.

down the T: Down the middle of the court along the center service line, which forms a "T" where it intersects with the service line.

1. draw: 1. The method by which match-ups and the playing order of a tournament are determined. Except for seeded players who are scheduled before the draw, the names of entered players are drawn blindly from a hat or container and placed in the order drawn on a draw sheet that indicates match-ups. see *seed*. 2. The arrangement in the order drawn of match-ups on a draw sheet.

2. draw: 1. To randomly pick the names of players entered in a tournament to determine match-ups and playing order for a draw sheet. 2. To be matched against a particular opponent or be assigned a particular position in the schedule in a draw.

draw sheet: An official schedule of the match-ups and playing order for a tournament based on the results of a draw.

1. drive: A hard groundstroke (forehand or backhand), hit either flat or with topspin, usually from near the baseline. The drive is the most frequently used shot in tennis.

2. drive: To hit a drive with the forehand or backhand.

drive volley: A hard volleying stroke played from the backcourt in the manner of a drive.

drop: Short for drop shot.

drop shot: A softly hit forehand or backhand stroke (usually hit with underspin) in which the ball barely clears the net and "drops." A drop shot is used to catch a retreating or deep-playing opponent off guard, or to pull an opponent out of position for a subsequent passing shot or lob. also *drop*.

drop the ball: To execute a drop shot.

drop volley: A drop shot hit on the volley.

early ball: 1. A volley made by rushing the net, rather than waiting for the ball to arrive. 2. A half volley.

Eastern backhand grip: see *backhand grip*.

Eastern grip: The most popular method of holding a racket for the forehand drive, in which the player "shakes hands" with the racket (held on edge), resting the palm on the back side of the handle, with the fingers and thumb closed naturally around it. With the Eastern grip (so-called because it was first used by East Coast American players), the racket face is neither open nor closed, but flat or vertical. also *shake-hands grip*. compare *baseball grip, chopper grip, Continental grip, service grip, Western grip*.

elbow: A slang term for a case of nerves suffered by a player at a crucial point in a match. Possibly an allusion to tightening or contracting the elbow and, thereby, restricting the swing when feeling stress. (fighting the elbow at match point)

end: Either of the two halves of a court occupied by one player or a side.

English grip: see *Continental grip*.

error: A mishit and failed attempt to make a return, resulting in the loss of the point. see *forced error, unforced error*.

face: The flat surface formed by the strings on either side of a racket. also *strings*.

fall: To bounce twice without being returned, as of a shot.

fast court: A court with a surface that allows the ball to skid, promoting a fast, low bounce. Fast courts favor a big serve and serve-and-volley game, and, consequently, are preferred by power players. Grass, wood, smooth concrete and asphalt, and most synthetic surfaces tend to make fast courts (the bounce and speed characteristics of synthetic surfaces can be varied). compare *slow court*.

1. fault: The failure to complete a legal serve, either by serving into the net or beyond the boundaries of the proper service court, swinging at and missing the ball altogether, or by serving from a position other than behind the baseline and between an imaginary extension of the center line and the proper sideline. One fault is allowed for each serve, but two faults on a serve result in a lost point. The term "fault" comes from the Old French *faute*, meaning "mistake." see *double fault, foot fault*.

2. fault: To commit a fault while serving.

Federation Cup: An international tournament played annually between national teams and consisting of singles and doubles competition for women. Compar-

able to the Davis Cup for men, the Federation Cup competition was first held at the Queen's Club in London in 1963, where the United States team of Billie Jean King Moffitt (later King) and Darlene Hard defeated the Australian team of Margaret Court and Lesley Bowrey.

fifteen: The first point scored in a game for either player or side. see *point*.

fireballer: A player with a cannonball serve. also *big server*.

first court: The receiver's right service court. Called "first court" because each game begins with a serve delivered from the baseline behind the server's right court to the receiver's right court. also *deuce court, forehand court, right court*. compare *ad court, advantage court, backhand court, left court, left-hander's court, second court*.

first serve: The first service delivery of a point, usually the server's hardest and best serve. If a fault is made on the first serve, the second delivery is usually made more carefully in order to prevent a second fault and the loss of the point. compare *second serve*.

flat: Fast and straight with little or no spin, as of a stroke or serve.

flat racket, flat racket face: A racket held so that the racket face is vertical or perpendicular to the ground. also *square racket, square racket face*. compare *closed racket, closed racket face, open racket, open racket face*.

1. foot fault: A fault committed by the server in which a serve is delivered while walking or running, or from a position other than behind the baseline and between an imaginary extension of

EASTERN GRIP

the center line and the proper sideline. Stepping on or over the baseline before making contact with the ball is the most common foot fault. A second foot fault on a serve or a foot fault that follows any other kind of fault results in a lost point. see *fault, double fault*.

2. foot fault: To commit a foot fault while serving.

foot-fault judge: The official responsible for calling foot faults, positioned on a line with the server's baseline on the side of the court opposite the baseline judge. see *foot fault*.

force: To apply pressure by putting an opponent on the defensive, off balance, or out of position with one or more shots.

forced error: An error or point lost by a player because of a good shot made by the opponent (rather than because of a mistake). compare *unforced error*.

forcing shot: A shot that puts an opponent on the defensive off balance or out of position for the next shot.

forecourt: The area between the service line and the net, between the sidelines. compare *backcourt, midcourt*.

1. forehand: A stroke hit from the same side of the body as the racket hand, with the palm of the hand facing the direction of movement. compare *backhand, overhead*.

2. forehand: Of or pertaining to a stroke

FOREHAND

hit from the same side of the body as the racket hand, with the palm facing the direction of movement. (won the point with a forehand volley) compare *backhand, overhead*.

forehand court: The right service court, on the forehand side for most (right-handed) receivers. see *deuce court*.

forehand grip: Any of several methods of holding the racket for a forehand stroke. Forehand grips include the Eastern grip, the Continental grip, or chopper grip, the Western grip, and the two-handed baseball grip. see *baseball grip, chopper grip, Continental grip, Eastern grip, English grip, Western grip*.

forty: The third point made in a game by a player or side. When both players or sides reach forty, it is called deuce. see *deuce, point*.

French Championships: The French International Championships, an international tournament held annually at the Stade Roland Garros, one of the prestigious "Big Four" or "Grand Slam" events, and considered the unofficial world championships on clay courts. The French Championships were first held in 1891 and open only to French citizens. That year, the men's singles competition was won by J. Briggs, with B. Desjoyau and Legrand winning in doubles. Women's singles was added in 1897 and won by Cecelia Masson. In 1925, mixed and women's doubles were played, and for the first time, the tournament was opened to non-French citizens. The competition was dominated by French players, however, with two of the famous "Four Musketeers" winning the men's singles (Jean-Rene Lacoste, the "Alligator") and doubles (Lacoste and Jean Borotra, the "Bounding Basque") and a third, Jacques Brugnan, teamed with one of the game's all-time great woman players, Suzanne Lenglen, won the mixed doubles. Lenglen also won the women's singles and, with Diddi Vlasto, the women's doubles. also *French Open*.

French Open: see *French Championships*.

gallery: 1. The area for spectators at the sides and ends of a court. In the medieval game of court tennis, the indoor ancestor of modern tennis, galleries were netted openings in the side wall on one side of the court, and a ball played into them figured in the scoring. 2. The spectators at a match.

gallery play: 1. A showy or elaborate shot made for the benefit of the spectators. 2. A sensational get or shot.

game: 1. A single contest throughout which one player or side serves, and that ends when either player or side scores four points if the opponent has scored two points or less, or when either player or side scores two consecutive points if both have scored three points (deuce). compare *match, rubber, set, tie.* 2. The final or game-winning point, as the fourth point scored by either player or side when the opponent has scored two points or less, or the second consecutive point scored by either player or side after both have scored three points (deuce). see *game-set, game-set-match.*

game point: The point that, if won by the leading player or side, wins a game. compare *match point, set point.*

games-all: see *advantage set.*

game-set: The game-winning point in a set-winning game. compare *game-set-match.*

game-set-match: The game-winning point in a game that wins a set that wins a match. compare *game-set.*

garbage: A lob, dink, or other softly hit shot.

get: A successful return of a difficult shot. (saved the point with an incredible get on the low volley) also *retrieve.*

Ginny Circuit: A series of eight or more professional tournaments for new or developing women players, with a year-end championship tournament for the winner and runnerup in each event. Effectively a minor league for the Virginia Slims World Championship Series.

Grand Master: A former major championship winner over forty-five years old who participates in the professional Grand Masters tournament circuit. see *Grand Masters.*

Grand Masters: A professional tournament circuit for players over forty-five years old who have won a major championship. The Grand Masters circuit was inaugurated by Cincinnati businessman Al Bunis in 1973.

Grand Prix: see *Volvo Grand Prix.*

1. Grand Slam: The winning of the four major tennis championships in one year (the United States, French, Australian, and Wimbledon Championships). The expression "Grand Slam" was coined by American Don Budge after he became the first to accomplish this rare feat in 1938. Only three other players have won the Grand Slam: Maureen "Little Mo" Connolly of the United States in 1953, and Australians Rod Laver in 1962 and 1969 and Margaret Court in 1970. In 1951, Frank Sedgman and Ken McGregor of Australia achieved the first Grand Slam in doubles.

2. Grand Slam: Of or pertaining to the four major tennis championships (the United States, French, Australian, and Wimbledon Championships). Australia's Margaret Court won more Grand Slam titles than any player in tennis history (sixty-two, including singles, doubles, and mixed doubles championships). Fellow Australian, Roy Emerson, holds the men's record with twenty-eight Grand Slam titles (twelve singles, sixteen doubles). also *Big Four.*

grass: Short for grass court. (has been unbeatable on grass).

grass court: A tennis court with a grass surface, which, unless damp or soft, usually provides a relatively fast surface which favors power players rather than touch players, retrievers, or baseliners. The first tennis courts were laid out on the lawns of Victorian England (hence, the name "lawn tennis"), with the oldest on record dating back to 1858 at Edgbaston, near Birmingham. Because of the amount of maintenance required for grass courts, alternative surfaces were already in use by the 1900s. Today, grass courts are comparatively rare. The oldest and most famous competition in tennis, however, is still played on the grass courts at Wimbledon. also *grass.* compare *clay court, concrete court, synthetic court.*

groove: To repeat a stroke with little effort because of practice and familiarity. (will try to move his opponent around so that he can't groove his returns)

ground game: A style of play which emphasizes groundstrokes.

groundie: Slang for a groundstroke.

groundstroke: A stroke made by hitting the ball after it has bounced (as a forehand or backhand drive). Groundstrokes are hit from the backcourt or behind the baseline. also *groundie*. compare *volley*.

hack: To make an awkward or poor swing at the ball.

hacker: An ordinary or, by professional standards, poor player. Popularized by 1966 United States Championships winner Fred Stolle of Australia, who humorously referred to himself as an "old hacker" after his victory from an unseeded position.

half court: The service court.

half-court line: The center service line. also *center line*.

1. half volley: A stroke in which the ball is hit just as it bounces up from the ground. also *early ball, pickup shot*. compare *volley*.

2. half volley: To hit the ball just as it bounces up from the ground. compare *volley*.

Hall of Fame: The International Tennis Hall of Fame.

hard court: 1. In the United States, a concrete or asphalt surface court (or a rarely seen wood surface court). 2. In Europe, Australia, and most of the world, a concrete, asphalt, or clay surface court (or a rarely seen wood surface court).

Har-Tru: A particular brand of synthetic clay surface popularized in the United States in the mid-1970s.

heavy ball: A ball that travels through the air at great speed and drops suddenly because of topspin. (doesn't look strong, but hits a surprisingly heavy ball)

high volley: see *offensive volley*.

hold one's serve: To win a game one is serving. (held her serve again to take the set) also *hold service*. compare *break, break service*.

hold service: see *hold one's serve*.

I formation: see *Australian formation*.

impervious surface: A smooth, non-porous playing surface such as sealed concrete or asphalt. A relatively inexpensive, virtually no-maintenance surface popularized in the United States (particularly on the West Coast) after World War II. compare *pervious surface*.

International Tennis Federation: The world governing body of tennis and guardian of the official rules of tennis. The International Tennis Federation (ITF) now recognizes twelve official tennis championships (including the four Grand Slam competitions), authorizes all major professional tournaments, and organizes and manages the Davis Cup and Federation Cup International Team Championships. Founded in 1913 as the International Lawn Tennis Federation, with thirteen affiliated nations (the United States joined in 1924), the ITF is headquartered in London, England.

International Tennis Hall of Fame: The institution that honors all-time tennis greats and outstanding contributors to the game. From 1954 when it was founded, through 1974, only American players were enshrined in the National Lawn Tennis Hall of Fame. In 1975, the present name was adopted and British tennis great Fred Perry became the first foreigner to be inducted. The International Tennis Hall of Fame is located at the Newport Casino in Newport, Rhode Island. also *Hall of Fame*.

ITF: The International Tennis Federation.

jag: To hit the ball in any manner necessary to get it over the net, regardless of style or form. Australian slang.

jam: To serve or drive the ball directly toward or close to an opponent in order to force a weak or clumsy return.

kick: The bounce of a hit ball, or the speed, height, or change of direction of a hit ball as it bounces off the ground, especially from a cut or twist stroke. also *break*.

kicker: An American twist serve.

kick serve: An American twist serve.

1. kill: To slam the ball past the opponent or to a place on the court from which it cannot be returned, most often with an overhead. (killed the lob for a winner) also *put away, slam, smash*.

2. kill: A kill shot.

kill shot: A slammed shot that is virtually unreturnable. (ended the long rally with a kill shot) also *kill, put-away, slam, smash*.

lawn tennis: The traditional name for tennis, adopted in England in the late 1850s to separate the new game (played on grass) from the older game court tennis.

left court: The service court to the left of the center service line on the server's side of the net, and the service court diagonally opposite it (the receiver's left service court). see *advantage court*.

left-hander's court: The left service court. Called "left-hander's court" because it is on the usually favored (forehand) side for left-handers. see *advantage court*.

let: 1. A serve which hits the top of the net before landing in the proper service court. When this occurs, the serve does not count and is replayed. also *let cord, net*. 2. The signal or call by a net judge or umpire indicating that an otherwise legal serve has hit the top of the net and must be retaken. also *net*. 3. A stroke which does not count and must be replayed, as when a serve is delivered before the receiver is ready, when a linesman's decision is doubted, disputed, or reversed by the umpire, or when play is interrupted (as by an animal running through the court, etc.). When a let occurs, the whole point is replayed (including both services, unless the let involves the second serve itself, in which case only the second serve is retaken). 4. The signal or call by an umpire when a stroke does not count and must be replayed.

let cord: see *let*.

line ball: A ball that lands on or touches a line and is, therefore, good. also *liner*.

line judge: see *linesman, lineswoman*.

liner: A line ball.

linesman, lineswoman: One of ten officials in championship play who judge whether or not the ball is good (whether or not it has landed in or out of the court). Each linesman or lineswoman is responsible for one boundary line on his or her side of the net. Three are positioned behind the baselines in line with the sidelines (sideline judges) and the center line (center line judges). Two are positioned parallel to the sideline (on the umpire's side of the court) on each side of the net, in line with the service line (service line judges) and the baseline (baseline judges). The judgment of a linesman or a lineswoman may be appealed to and overturned by the umpire. also *line judge, line umpire*.

line umpire: see *linesman, lineswoman*.

lingering death: A form of tie-breaker officially approved by the ITF in 1976 which may be invoked if a set is tied after twelve or sixteen games. One additional game is played, with the winner being the first player or side to reach seven points, provided there is a two-point margin. Often called the "twelve-point tie-breaker," but "lingering death" is more appropriate because

of the possibility of a drawn out game if the score reaches 6-6. compare *sudden death*.

1. lob: A stroke in which the ball is hit into a high arc either to allow a player time to get back into position (defensive lob), or to loop the ball over an opponent at the net (offensive lob). Wimbledon winner (1878) P. Frank Hadow introduced the lob. see *defensive lob, offensive lob*.

2. lob: 1. To hit the ball into a high arc. 2. To hit a lob over a particular opponent. (lobbed him as he rushed the net)

long: Out because of landing behind the service line on a serve or behind the baseline on a stroke, resulting in a lost point (or on a first serve, a fault). compare *deep, short, wide*.

love: A score of zero for a player or side. A popular theory holds that "love" is a corruption of the French *l'oeuf*, meaning "egg," because of the resemblance of an egg to a zero. It is more probable that the present use equates "love" with "nothing," as in the expression "a labor of love," meaning a task performed for nothing (but love).

love game: A game in which the losing player or side scores no points. also *blitz*.

love set: A set in which the losing player or side fails to win a game. also *bagel, bagel job*. 2. A set in which the winning player or side wins six straight games (regardless of whether the opponent wins one or more games). A British usage.

low volley: see *defensive volley*.

Masters: see *Volvo Masters*.

match: A contest between two players or sides, usually decided over the best of

three sets, or over one set in informal play. Men's singles and doubles matches are decided over the best of five sets in major tournaments and championship play. also *rubber.*

match point: 1. A point that, if won by the player or side leading, will decide the match in favor of that player or side. compare *game point, set point.* 2. A situation in which the leading player or side can win a match by winning the next point. compare *game point, set point.*

Men's International Professional Tennis Council: The governing body of men's professional tennis, with nine members representing players, the International Tennis Federation, and tournament directors. Formed in 1974 by the ATP and ITF, and expanded a year later to include tournament directors, the Men's International Professional Tennis Council administers the Grand Prix circuit and is responsible for matters regarding tournament applications, scheduling, player conduct, and conditions of play. also *MIPTC, Pro Council.*

midcourt: The part of the court near the service line. compare *backcourt, forecourt.*

MIPTC: The Men's International Professional Tennis Council.

mixed doubles: Doubles competition between teams comprised of one male and one female. The first recorded mixed doubles championship event was played in 1879 at the Irish Championships.

1. net: 1. The webbed barrier stretched across the middle of the court over which the ball is hit. The net is suspended from a cord or metal cable from two 3-1/2-foot-high posts (the center of which are located 3 feet outside the sidelines) and slopes to a height of 3 feet at the center, held taut by a center strap, a 2-inch-wide piece of canvas that runs down the middle of the net and is anchored to the court. A 2 to 2-1/2-inch-wide tape band covers the cord or metal cable at the top of the net. English tennis pioneer Walter Clopton Wingfield's 1874 rules called for the net to be 4 feet, 8 inches high at the center, attached to 7-foot-high posts on either side of the court, then 21 feet wide. The 1875 Marylebone Cricket Club rules widened the court to 24 feet

and made the net 5 feet high at the posts and 4 feet at the center. At the first Wimbledon Championships in 1877, 4-foot, 9-inch posts were used to support a net that measured 3 feet, 3 inches high at the center. The net posts were lowered to 4 feet in 1880, and to the present height in 1882. 2. see *let.*

2. net: To hit the ball into the net, resulting in the loss of the point. (netted what should have been an easy return)

net cord: 1. A shot that hits the top of the net then drops into the opponent's court. 2. The cord or metal cable that supports a net.

net-cord judge: see *net judge.*

net game: 1. A style of play in which a player stays close to the net whenever possible in order to volley the ball. compare *baseline game.* 2. Strokes (usually volleys) played from the forecourt close to the net. also *net play.* compare *baseline game.*

net judge: An official seated at one end of the net (below the umpire's chair) who is responsible for detecting and calling lets on a serve. When the ball is being served the net judge rests a hand on top of the net in order to be able to feel whether the ball hits the net. If a let is called, the serve is retaken. also *net-cord judge.*

netman: Slang for a tennis player.

net man: The partner in doubles who plays close to the net while his teammate serves.

net play: see *net game.*

net rusher: A player who regularly attacks the net after serving and whenever possible during a rally to be in position to volley. compare *baseliner, power player, retriever, shotmaker, touch player.*

no-ad: A method of scoring pioneered by tennis innovator Jimmy Van Alen in which the traditional love, fifteen, thirty, forty are replaced with one, two, three, four. Deuce is eliminated, the first player or side to reach four wins (when the score is tied at 3-3, the receiver is given the choice of courts for game point). No-ad scoring is presently used by Team Tennis. also *VASSS.*

no-man's land: Slang for the backcourt, or between the service line and the baseline. Called no-man's land because players standing there are usually too far forward to play groundstrokes and too far back from the net for offensive volleys, and frequently are forced to make awkward shots when the ball bounces at or near their feet. also *deep court.*

not up: Not playable. Called when a player hits the ball just as or after it bounces for the second time, or half volleys the ball down to the ground from where it then bounces over the net. The net judge (or the offending player if there are no officials) usually makes the call, which results in the loss of the point.

offensive lob: A lob hit deep into the backcourt, over the head of an opponent at the net. In 1878, P. Frank Hadow introduced the offensive lob to defeat the volleying of Spencer W. Gore at Wimbledon for the singles championship. compare *defensive lob.*

offensive volley: A volley that is made (usually from above the level of the net) in order to catch the opponent off guard by means of speed or placement. also *high volley.* compare *defensive volley, low volley.*

open: For both amateurs and professionals, as of a tournament. In the early days of tennis, professionals were always barred from competing. At that time, "open" meant that a competition was not restricted to the members of a club or the residents of a certain city, state, or country. The first such "open" on record was the inaugural Wimbledon Championship in 1877. The first "open" tournament in the modern sense of the word was the 1968 British Hard Court Championships, in which Ken Rosewall defeated Rod Laver in men's singles and Virginia Wade defeated Winnie Shaw to win the women's singles title. All major championship tournaments are now open competitions.

open grip: A grip that makes the racket face tilt upwards toward the sky, as with the chopper or Continental grip. compare *closed grip.*

open racket, open racket face: A racket held so that the racket face is tilted upwards toward the sky. compare *closed racket, closed racket face, flat racket, flat racket face.*

open up the court: 1. To draw an opponent away from a part of the court which is then left unguarded for the next shot. (opened up the backcourt with a little chip just over the net) 2. To

move to one part of the court and thus, leave another area unguarded.

overdrive: To hit the ball too hard and drive it over the opponent's baseline, resulting in the loss of the point.

1. overhead: A stroke (most often a smash) hit from above the head, much like a serve. Among the early players noted for the overhead were Maurice McLoughlin, the "California Comet," whose cannonball serves and overheads stunned the 1913 Wimbledon spectators, and 1932 Wimbledon singles champion Ellsworth Vines, also feared for his serves and overheads. compare *backhand, forehand.*

2. overhead: Of or pertaining to a stroke hit over the head, as of a smash or volley. (ended the rally with an overhead smash) compare *backhand, forehand.*

overspin: see *topspin.*

1. pace: The speed of a hit ball. A British term used first in billiards, cricket, and football (soccer), and derived from the Latin *passus,* meaning "rate of movement."

2. pace: To hit the ball at a controlled speed. (a highly paced first serve)

pair: A doubles team.

partner: A teammate on a doubles team.

1. pass: A passing shot.

2. pass: To make a passing shot against a particular opponent.

passing shot: A ball driven past and beyond the reach of an opponent in the forecourt or midcourt area. also *pass, pass shot.*

pass shot: A passing shot.

pervious surface: A porous court surface that permits water to filter through. compare *impervious surface.*

pickup shot: A half volley.

place: To hit a ball so that it goes precisely where intended. (fooled him with a well-placed drop shot)

placement: 1. A perfectly placed shot that the opponent cannot reach, a clean winner. 2. The placing of a shot or shots.

1. poach: To cross in front of a doubles partner to volley a ball that would normally be played by the partner. An aggressive tactic that can backfire if the volley is returned to the part of the court left undefended by the poaching player. The term "poach" is from the Old French *pochier,* meaning originally "to put into a bag" and, in later usage, "to trespass" or "to steal." Poaching was used first by male partners in mixed doubles matches in the late 1870s.

2. poach: The act or an instance of poaching. (angled the winner with a courageous poach)

point: The basic scoring unit, with a game being won by the first player or side to win four points, unless both sides reach three points ("deuce") after which the game is won by the first to win two consecutive points. In the traditional method of scoring tennis, the first point is "fifteen," the second, "thirty," the third, "forty," and the fourth, "game" (except after "deuce," after which the first point won by either side is "advantage," and the second consecutive point, "game"). Scoring by fifteens ("forty" was shortened from "forty-five") began in the Middle Ages with the original French indoor tennis game, *jeu de paume* which was sixty points divided into four parts of fifteen. This was probably due to the medieval importance of the sexagesimal system, prevalent in weights and measures, money, and, of course, time (sixty sec-

onds in a minute, sixty minutes in an hour). When lawn tennis was first played in 1858, variations of rackets scoring were used, and this practice was maintained in the 1874 rules published by tennis pioneer Major Walter Clopton Wingfield and in the first official rules published a year later by the Marylebone Cricket Club. Finally, in 1877, at the urging of cofounder Henry Jones, the All England Croquet and Lawn Tennis Club initiated the clock system for the inaugural Wimbledon Championship; fifteen (minutes) for the first point, thirty (minutes) for the second, forty-five (minutes)—later changed to forty, possibly because it was easier to say or to hear when called out—for the third, and game at one hour. see *VASSS*.

point penalty: A penalty of one point assessed by the umpire against a player for conduct violations such as delaying the game, throwing or kicking the racket or ball, verbal or physical abuse, or obscenities. Pioneered by the men's professional Grand Prix circuit in 1976, the penalty point provision allows the umpire to assess penalties of a point or a game, depending on the gravity or frequency of violations.

post: One of the 3-1/2 foot uprights that support the net.

power game: see *big game*.

power player: A player whose style of play emphasizes a big serve and powerful strokes, together with aggressive net play. Though the term was coined much later, the first great power player was 1912 United States Championships singles winner Maurice McLoughlin. The 1932 Wimbledon singles champion, Ellsworth Vines, was another early example, but the term "power player" is most often associated with America's post-World War II Davis Cup teams which featured Jack Kramer, Ted Schroeder, and Pancho Gonzalez. compare *baseliner, net rusher, retriever, shotmaker, touch player*.

power tennis: see *big game*.

Pro Council: The Men's International Professional Tennis Council.

puddler: Slang for a player who regularly chips shots just over the net, forcing opponents to stoop forward to retrieve them, as from a puddle.

put away: To hit a kill shot. (was able to

RACKET

310

put away his opponent's defensive lob) also *kill, slam, smash.*

put-away: A kill shot. also *kill, slam, smash.*

racket: The implement with which the ball is struck, an oval frame strung with crossing gut (lamb intestines) or nylon strings, and a long, straight handle. Modern racket frames may be constructed of wood, steel, aluminum, fiberglass or graphite. There are no rules that govern the exact size or shape of a racket, but most are between 25 and 27 inches long and weigh between 12-1/2 and 16-1/2 ounces. The word "racket" is from the Arabic *rahah*, meaning "palm of the hand" and was probably brought back to France from the Crusades. In the medieval French version of tennis, the palm of the hand itself was used to hit the ball, thus the name *jeu de paume*, literally "play of palm." Gloves and crude wooden paddles followed, and early in the sixteenth century, small strung *racquettes* were introduced. Larger rackets with a longer handle became popular in the eighteenth century, and by the late 1800s, the racket had evolved into the basic size and configuration that remains the standard today, although after steel rackets were introduced in 1967, other new frame materials such as aluminum, fiberglass, and graphite began to find favor. In 1976, rackets with "oversized" heads appeared. With approximately the same weight and balance as conventional models, these revolutionary rackets have twice the hitting area.

1. rally: An exchange of shots by opponents until one side fails to make a good return.

2. rally: 1. To engage in a rally. (rallied from the backcourt until he could move to the net) 2. To warm up before a game by exchanging practice strokes with one's opponent.

readiness position: see *alert position.*

receiver: The player to whom the ball is served. compare *server.*

1. referee: The official in charge of a tournament. Though not involved with the actual conduct of individual matches, the referee may be asked to come to the court in order to interpret a rule.

2. referee: To act as a referee for a tournament.

1. retrieve: To return a shot that is diffi-

cult to handle or reach. (had to get back in position after retrieving the lob)

2. retrieve: The act or an instance of returning a shot that is difficult to handle or reach. also *get.*

retriever: A player who emphasizes a defensive style of play, relying on the ability to retrieve whatever strokes are played by the opponent, rather than aggressive tactics like serve-and-volley. compare *baseliner, net rusher, power player, shotmaker, touch player.*

1. return: To hit a ball played by an opponent back over the net.

2. return: The act or an instance of hitting a ball played by an opponent back over the net.

reverse spin: see *underspin.*

reverse twist: An unorthodox serve in which topspin is imparted with an upward and inward motion of the racket as the ball is struck, causing it to bounce high and to the receiver's right side when it hits the ground. Malcolm D. Whitman introduced the reverse twist to the tennis world at the 1900 Davis Cup competition in Boston, where the unconventional and awkward delivery bewildered his British opponents and played an important part in the American team's victory. compare *American twist.*

right court: The service court to the right of the center service line on the server's side of the net, and the service court diagonally opposite it (the receiver's right service court). see *first court.*

round: A stage in an elimination tournament consisting of a series of matches, the winners of which advance to the next stage.

round robin: A tournament in which every player or side meets every other player or side in turn, with the final standings determined by the overall won-lost records. Originally, a "round robin" was a written complaint with the names of its signers arranged in a circle to disguise the order in which they signed.

rubber: A British expression for match.

run around the backhand: To avoid one's backhand, to position oneself or move so as to insure a stroke will be played on one's forehand side.

runback: The area at either end of the court between the baseline and the backstop. also *back room.*

run down: To run after and return a shot

hit to another part of the court. (ran down the crosscourt drive to save the point)

run out a set: To win all of the remaining games in a set.

rush the net: see *attack the net.*

second court: The receiver's left service court. Called "second court" because the ball is delivered from the baseline behind the server's left court to the receiver's left court on the second service turn in a game. see *advantage court.*

second serve: A serve made after a fault has been declared on the first serve. Usually a more conservative delivery, with more emphasis given to placement than power to prevent a second fault and the loss of the point. compare *first serve.*

1. seed: 1. To schedule top players within a draw to insure that they won't meet before the later rounds of a tournament. In major tournaments, professional players are seeded according to computer rankings and performance records. Some seeding was first tried at Wimbledon in 1924, with the singles events being completely seeded in 1927. From the Old English *saed,* meaning in agriculture "to separate or select from a group." 2. To rank players for a tournament. A seeded player is a player who is ranked.

2. seed: A player who has been seeded in a tournament. (will face the top seed in the final)

1. serve: 1. To put the ball in play with a serve. Derived from the Old French *servir,* meaning "to work as a servant" and originally, the Latin *servus,* meaning "slave." In the medieval game of court tennis, the serve was merely a convenient way of starting a rally, and often the ball was served by someone other than a player, as by a servant. 2. To act as the server for a particular game. (will serve the first game)

2. serve: 1. The method or act of putting the ball in play at the beginning of each point. In a serve, the ball is thrown into the air and hit (usually with an overhead stroke) over the net into the service court diagonally opposite the server (beginning with the right court and alternating with each point). To deliver a serve, the server must stand with both feet at rest behind the baseline in back

SERVICE

of the proper service court between an imaginary extension of the center line and the sideline (inside sideline for singles, outside for doubles). The ball must be thrown into the air and struck before it hits the ground (a player with one arm may project the ball into the air with the racket). The server may not walk or run, nor touch any area with either foot outside the prescribed area until the ball is struck ("foot fault"). If the rules of service are broken on a serve, or if the serve fails to reach the proper service court on the first delivery ("first serve"), a fault is declared and the server is given a second opportunity ("second serve"). If a fault occurs on the second serve, the point is lost. If an otherwise legal serve hits the top of the net before landing in the proper service court, or if a serve is delivered before the receiver is ready, a let is called, and the serve is retaken (regardless of whether it occurs on the first or second serve). Only one player serves in a game. In singles, players alternate as the server throughout the games of a match. In doubles, service is alternated between the pairs with all four players serving in turn, and with the receivers receiving from the same court throughout a set. (The order of service or the court from which either partner receives may be changed at the end of each set.) also *delivery, service.* 2. The turn or right of a player or side to serve. (will spin the racket to determine whose serve it is) also *service.* 3. A stroke made with a service. (aced him with a hard, flat serve) also *delivery, service.*

serve-and-volley: A style of play in which the server rushes the net after each serve in order to be in position to volley. also *serve-volley.*

serve and volley: To rush the net after serving, to play a serve-and-volley style of game.

server: The player who serves or whose turn it is to serve.

serve-volley: see *serve-and-volley.*

service: see *serve.*

service ace: see *ace.*

service box: Slang for a service court.

service break: The act or an instance of a player winning a game against the server. also *break.*

service court: Either of two 13-1/2-foot-wide by 21-foot-deep rectangular areas on each side of the court, bounded by the net, the service sideline, the service line and the center line (which separates them). In order to be legal, a serve must be delivered into the proper service court. also *court, service box.* see *left court, right court.*

service grip: The Continental grip. also *chopper grip, English grip.*

service line: The line on either side of the court that extends between the singles sidelines parallel to and 21 feet from the net, and which marks the rear boundary of the two service courts. The service line was originally drawn 26 feet from the net for the first Wimbledon Championship in 1877, and was changed to the present 21 feet for the 1880 event.

service line judge: Either of two linesmen or lineswomen responsible for watching the service line on serves in tournament play and calling when a ball lands outside the proper service court. Service line judges are positioned on a line with the service lines on the same side of the court as the umpire.

service sideline: The portion of the singles sideline that lies between the net and the service line, and that marks the outside boundary of the service court.

service winner: A serve that the receiver hits but is unable to return. compare *ace, ace on service, service ace.*

set: 1. The next to highest scoring unit, a group of games that is won by the first player or side to win at least six games with a two-game margin, or by a tie-breaker. "Set" is from the Old French *sette* meaning "sequence." see *tie-breaker.* compare *game, match, rubber, tie.* 2. The next to highest scoring unit, a group of games that is won by the first player or side to win thirty-one points in a tournament using VASSS single point scoring, or if the score is tied at 30-30, the first to win a tie-breaker. see *tie-breaker, VASSS.*

set point: 1. A point that, if won by the player or side leading, will decide the set in favor of that player or side. compare *game point, match point.* 2. A situation in which the leading player or side can win a set by winning the next point. compare *game point, match point.*

setter: A match with a specified number of sets. (will play a three-setter)

setup: A soft shot, often a high lob hit to the forecourt, that can be easily put away. also *sitter*.

shake-hands grip: The Eastern grip.

short: In the front part of the forecourt near the net. (dinked the ball short) compare *deep, long, wide*.

short ball: A ball hit short to the forecourt, especially when the opponent is playing deep.

shot: The act or an instance of hitting the ball toward the opposing court with the racket. also *stroke*.

shotmaker: A player whose style of play emphasizes placement and a variety of accurate rather than powerful strokes. also *touch player*. compare *baseliner, net rusher, power player*.

sideline: A side boundary, either for the singles court or the doubles court, extending between the baselines (27 feet apart for singles, 36 feet apart for doubles). Between the net and the service line, the singles sidelines serve as the side boundaries of the service courts ("service sidelines").

sideline judge: Any of four linesmen or lineswomen (two at each end of the court) who are responsible for watching the sidelines in tournament play and calling when a ball lands outside the court. Sideline judges are positioned in line with the sidelines behind the baselines.

sidespin: Spin around a vertical or near vertical axis imparted to the ball by brushing the racket face across the ball at the moment of contact, as with a slicing or cutting stroke. Sidespin causes the ball to curve in flight and to bounce or break to the side on landing (which side depends on the direction of the spin). compare *backspin, chop, curl, overspin, reverse spin, topspin, twist, underspin*.

singles: A game or match between two players, played on a singles court that does not utilize the two 4-1/2-foot alleys and baseline extensions normally marked outside the sidelines for doubles play. The first men's singles championship tournament was at Wimbledon in 1877, and won by S.W. Gore. The first women's singles championship was held in Ireland in 1879, and won by May Langrishe.

singles court: The 78-foot-long by 27-foot-wide rectangular playing area for singles, not including the two 4-1/2-foot alleys and baseline extensions normally marked outside the sidelines of a singles court. The present outside dimensions for a singles court were adopted in 1877 by the All England Croquet and Lawn Tennis Club for the inaugural Wimbledon Championship.

singles sideline: One of the two side boundaries for a singles court, 27 feet apart and extending between the baselines. Between the service lines, the singles sidelines are the side boundaries of the service courts (service sidelines).

sissy game: A derisive description of a game or a style of play characterized by soft lobs, slices, and weak groundstrokes, and by a lack of hard shots and aggressive play.

sitter: see *setup*.

1. slam: A smash.

2. slam: To execute a smash.

1. slice: 1. A stroke in which underspin and sidespin are imparted to the ball by hitting under and across it with an open racket face. With a slice, the ball curves in flight and bounces low and to the side on landing (which side depends on the direction of the sidespin). "Slice" is from the Old French *esclice* meaning "splinter." 2. Short for slice serve.

2. slice: 1. To hit a ball with a slicing motion of the racket to impart underspin and sidespin. 2. To hit or serve a slice.

slice serve: A serve hit with a slicing motion to impart underspin and sidespin. A slice serve curves in flight and bounces low and to the side (which side depends on the direction of the sidespin), and is often used for a second serve. also *slice*.

slowball: To use soft shots such as lobs, chips, slices, and drop shots against an opponent. (changed his tactics and slowballed him in the second game)

slow court: A court with a surface that produces a high bounce, such as clay or claylike surfaces. Slow courts favor shotmakers and touch players rather than serve-and-volley or power players. compare *fast court*.

slow court game: 1. A style of play that emphasizes lobs, sliced and chipped strokes, and a strong and steady baseline game. 2. The lobs, chips, slices, drop shots, and accurate groundstrokes that are most effective on a slow court.

1. smash: A hard overhead stroke in which the ball is hit down at the opposing court, often for a winner. It is believed that Englishman O.E. Woodhouse, winner of the title "Champion of America" at the first open tournament in the United States held at the Staten Island Cricket and Baseball Club in 1880, introduced the smash. also *kill, kill shot, put-away, slam.*

2. smash: To execute a smash. also *kill, put away, slam.*

softie: A dink. also *chip.*

spaghetti racket: see *double-strung racket.*

1. spin: Rotation imparted to the ball to affect its line of flight and the way it bounces. see *sidespin, topspin, underspin.*

2. spin: To hit a shot with spin on the ball. (spun her return crosscourt)

spin it in: To deliver a serve with spin (as a slice serve) rather than trying to hit it hard.

square racket, square racket face: see *flat racket, flat racket face.*

steelie: Slang for a steel frame racket. The steel racket was introduced in 1967 by Wilson Sporting Goods from a design by former French tennis great Rene Lacoste. Used at the United States Championships at Forest Hills that year by women's singles winner Billie Jean King among others, the steel frame racket was the first of a succession of revolutionary racket designs featuring new materials such as aluminum, fiber glass, and graphite.

stop volley: A soft volley in which the ball drops just over the net, used when the opponent is in the backcourt.

straight sets: Without losing a set, consecutive victories. (won the match in straight sets)

1. string: One of the nylon or gut (lamb intestines) cords that are woven in the head of a racket to provide a hitting surface.

2. string: To put strings in a racket, to weave and properly tension the strings in the head of a racket.

strings: The flat hitting surface. also *face.*

stroke: 1. A swing of the racket that is intended to hit the ball. (a slicing stroke) 2. A shot that results from hitting the ball with the racket.

sudden death: A tie-breaker of a specified length that may be invoked if a set is tied after twelve or sixteen games. One form, pioneered by tennis scoring innovator Jimmy Van Alen, is the nine-point sudden death, in which a single extra game is played, with the first player or side to reach five points winning. Another is the thirteen-point sudden death, in which the winner is the first player or side to reach seven points in the extra game. compare *lingering death.*

Supreme Court: A particular brand of synthetic carpet playing surface used in many professional indoor tournaments.

sweet spot: The optimum hitting area in the middle of the racket face, variable according to the size and design of the racket head and the gauge and tension of the strings. An enlarged sweet spot is the main advantage of the rackets with "oversized" heads introduced in 1976.

take the net: see *attack the net.*

tandem formation: see *Australian formation.*

tape: 1. The 2 to 2-1/2-inch-wide band of tape (usually canvas) that covers the net cord at the top of the net. 2. Slang for a boundary line because of the occasional use of tape to mark the boundary lines on clay courts. also *chalk.*

team tennis: A tennis competition between teams of players (usually two men and two women), with a match consisting of single sets in men's singles, women's singles, men's doubles, women's doubles, and mixed doubles. The winner of the match is the side that wins the most games.

Team Tennis: A one-month series of professional matches between teams of four players (two men and two women) consisting of single sets in men's singles, women's singles, men's doubles, women's doubles, and mixed doubles. No-ad scoring is used, and a tied set is decided by a nine-point tie-breaker, or, if the game decides the match, by a thirteen-point tie-breaker. A reorganization of the World Team Tennis circuit of the mid-1970s, Team Tennis began operating in 1981 with four teams and increased to eight teams in 1982. Headed by tennis entrepreneur Larry King, Team Tennis scheduled a twelve-team circuit for the 1983 season. see *no-ad, tie-breaker.*

tennis: A game between two players

(singles) or two teams of two players (doubles) played on a rectangular court (78 feet long by 27 feet wide for singles, or 36 feet wide for doubles), and in which players in each half of the court, using strung rackets, hit a small inflated felt-covered rubber ball over a net across the middle of the court until one side wins a point by hitting a stroke that lands within the opponent's court and cannot be returned. On each point play begins with a serve, a stroke hit from a stationary position behind the baseline in which the ball is thrown into the air and hit to the diagonally opposite service court. If the serve fails to land in the proper service court, or if any of the rules of service are broken, a fault is declared and the server is given another chance to serve. A second fault (double fault) results in the loss of the point. One player serves each game with service alternating between players in successive games (in doubles, service alternates between sides with all four players serving in turn). The first player or side to reach four points (traditionally called "fifteen," "thirty," "forty," and "game," or in no-ad scoring, "one," "two," "three," and "four") wins a game, provided there is a two-point margin. If each side reaches three points ("deuce"), the first side to score two consecutive points thereafter wins the game (in no-ad scoring, deuce is eliminated, and a 3-3 tie is decided by the next point). Groups of games are arranged in sets, with the first player or side to win six games winning the set, providing there is a two-game margin. If a set is tied after twelve games, extra games are played until one side or the other wins by a two-game margin (or the set is decided by a single tie-breaker game). A match is decided on the basis of the best of three sets, or in men's singles and doubles events in major tournaments (or if the VASSS single point scoring system is used, on the basis of total points won, with the first side to win thirty-one points the winner, or if the score is 30-30, the side that wins a tiebreaker). Though a number of theories have been put forward regarding the origin of the word "tennis," some alluding to the ancient Greek game of

phennis or a reported Roman game *teniludius*, or to the single early mention of a *tenes* game in western literature in the fourteenth century *Chronicles of Florence* by Italy's Donato Velluti, the most popular belief is that the French *tenez*, meaning roughly "take heed," was called out at the beginning of a game, and eventually came to represent the game. also *lawn tennis.*

tennis ball: A pressurized rubber sphere between 2-1/2 and 2-5/8 inches in diameter and weighing between 2 and 2-1/16 ounces, covered with a nap of wool and nylon (usually white or yellow). Though specific regulations govern the bounce and compression characteristics to insure a certain amount of uniformity, differences exist between the balls used in Europe and the United States. The American ball has more pressure, favoring the power game more than the softer European ball. In critical tournament play, the nap thickness of the ball varies according to the court surface in use, with hard courts calling for a thick nap, grass, a thin nap, and clay, in between. Early court tennis balls were made of thin leather or cloth stuffed with feathers, hair, or meal. Later, cloth centers were used, tightly bound with string and covered with flannel. The invention of a rubber ball (which would bounce on grass) made lawn tennis possible in the nineteenth century. The first regulations for a tennis ball were adopted in 1877 for the inaugural Wimbledon Championship and called for a ball between 2-1/4 and 2-5/8 inches in diameter and weighing between 1-1/4 and 1-1/2 ounces. In 1924, the first stitchless ball with cemented seams appeared. The result was an increase in speed and a lessening of the effects of spin. A pressure increase in 1931 was the last major change in the ball.

tennis court: see *court.*

tennis elbow: Pain and inflammation in the tendons around the elbow, the result of the excessive twisting motions of the hand and the jars and strains sustained while playing tennis.

thirty: The second point made in a game by a player or side. see *point.*

throat: The thin part of a racket between the head and handle.

tie: A British and European expression for a

team match between countries (such as the Davis Cup and Federation Cup). compare *game, match, rubber, set.*

tie-break: A tie-breaker.

tie-breaker: One of several methods of ending a set tied after twelve or sixteen games by playing one extra game instead of the traditional deuce or advantage set. Tie-breakers are either sudden death, in which the extra game ends with a sudden death point when the score is 4-4 in a nine-point sudden death or 6-6 in a thirteen-point sudden death, or lingering death, in which the extra game is extended until one side wins by a margin of two points. also *tie-break.* see *lingering death, sudden death.*

top: To impart topspin to the ball on a stroke.

top seed: The player judged by a tournament committee to be the favorite to win a tournament based on performance records and computer rankings and scheduled within the draw so as not to meet other favorites until the later rounds of the competition.

topspin: Forward spin around a horizontal axis imparted to the ball by brushing the racket face upward and over the ball at the moment of contact. Topspin causes the ball to drop deceptively and bounce high on landing. also *overspin.* compare *backspin, chop, curl, reverse spin, sidespin, twist, underspin.*

touch: Subtle and precise control in the placement of strokes. (may have lost a step with age, but he still has great touch)

touch player: A player whose style of play emphasizes precise control, placement, and a variety of accurate rather than powerful strokes. also *shotmaker.* compare *baseliner, net rusher, power player.*

tour: A scheduled series of professional tournaments. also *circuit.*

tramline, tramlines: British slang for alley. see *alley.*

triple: The winning of the singles, doubles, and mixed doubles events at a tournament.

twist: The combination of topspin and sidespin imparted to a ball, as with an American twist or reverse twist serve. Twist causes the ball to drop sharply and bounce high and to one side on landing (which side depends on the direction of the sidespin). compare *backspin, chop, curl, overspin, reverse spin, sidespin, topspin, underspin.*

two-handed backhand: A backhand stroke in which the racket hand is positioned normally with the other hand placed above it on the handle in a forehand grip. The strength and control of the backhand are improved with the two-handed shot, but reach and mobility may be somewhat restricted. Vivian B. McGrath, 1937 Australian men's singles champion, was the first world-class player to use a two-handed backhand.

two-handed player: A player who grips the racket with two hands to make forehand or backhand strokes, or both. Though two-handed players can be more vulnerable to angles and passing shots due to restricted reach and mobility, strength and control are considerably improved on the two-hand side. The first successful two-handed player was Australian Vivian B. McGrath, who defeated his countryman John Bromwich, another exponent of the two-hand technique, to become the 1937 Australian men's singles champion. McGrath, Bromwich, and fellow Australian Geoff Brown all played their backhand as a two-handed stroke, but in the post-World War II years, a two-hand forehand was first seen with the rise to prominence of popular Pancho Segura of Ecuador. In the 1970s, the two-handed technique was spotlighted again with the emergence of Jimmy Connors and Chris Evert (later Lloyd). also *double-fisted player, double-handed player.*

1. **umpire:** The official in charge of a match, positioned in a raised chair at one end of the net. The umpire keeps and calls out the score and is the final arbiter on questions of fact and judgment. An umpire may reverse the decision of a linesman or judge on appeal and is empowered to default a player for bad conduct. (In men's Grand Prix events, the umpire may also impose point penalties for rules infractions.) The first umpire was used at the inaugural Wimbledon Championship in 1877. To give him an overview of the match, the umpire's chair was placed on top of a table, the origin of today's raised chair. also *chair umpire.*

2. umpire: To act as an umpire for a match.

underspin: Backward rotation around a horizontal axis (bottom of the ball rotates in the direction of flight) imparted to a ball by brushing the racket face downward and under the ball at the moment of contact, as with a chop. Underspin slows the flight of a ball and can cause it to skid low, stop, or even recoil slightly on landing, depending on the type and condition of the playing surface and the amount of underspin applied. also *chop, backspin, reverse spin.* compare *curl, overspin, topspin, twist.*

unforced error: A point lost because of a mistake (such as hitting the ball out, or into the net) rather than a good shot by the opponent. compare *forced error.*

United States Championships: An international tournament held annually at the USTA National Tennis Center in Flushing Meadow Park, New York, one of the prestigious "Big Four" or "Grand Slam" events. The first United States Championships were held on the grass courts of the Newport Casino in Newport, Rhode Island, in 1881, with Richard D. Sears winning the men's singles competition in straight sets, and C.M. Clark and F.W. Taylor winning the men's doubles title. From 1915 through 1920, the Championships were held at the West Side Tennis Club in Forest Hills, New York. After three years at the Germantown Cricket Club in Philadelphia, the event was moved back to Forest Hills, where it stayed until moving to its present location in 1978. The first United States women's singles championship was held in 1887 at the Philadelphia Cricket Club and won by Miss Ellen Hansell. Miss Ellen Roosevelt and Miss Grace W. Roosevelt won the first women's doubles championship in 1890. The first mixed doubles championship was won by C. Hobart and Miss M.E. Cahill in 1892. All five events have been played at one location since the first open tournament in 1968. also *United States Open, United States Open Championships.*

United States Open, United States Open Championships: The United States Championships.

United States Tennis Association: The national governing body for amateur tennis in the United States. Formed in 1881, the then United States National Lawn Tennis Association was the world's first national governing body for tennis. In 1920, the word "national" was dropped from the name, and in 1924, the United States body became a member of the International Tennis Federation (then called the International Lawn Tennis Federation). In 1975, the name was officially changed to the United States Tennis Association (USTA). The USTA has conducted the United States Championships (which became the United States Open in 1968) since 1881.

up and back: A popular doubles strategy in which one partner plays close to the net while the other plays in the backcourt.

USTA: The United States Tennis Association.

Van Alen Streamlined Scoring System: see *VASSS.*

vantage: see *advantage.*

VASSS: The Van Alen Streamlined Scoring System. Any of several simplified methods of scoring pioneered by tennis innovator Jimmy Van Alen, all of which eliminate the provision of deuce in a game or set (advantage set), and therefore, prevent the marathon matches that sometimes occur with traditional scoring methods. Van Alen's no-ad system substitutes "zero," "one," "two," "three," and "four" for the more complicated "love," "fifteen," "thirty," "forty," and "game," with the winner being the first player or side to win four points. His sudden death nine-point tie-breaker replaces advantage sets with a single game, the winner of which is the first player or side to reach five. Under Van Alen's tournament scoring system, the first player or side to reach thirty-one points wins the set, with a tie-breaker to settle a 30-30 tie. see *no-ad, sudden death, tie-breaker.*

Virginia Slims World Championships: The season-ending championship tournament for the top twelve singles and six doubles finishers of the Virginia Slims World Championship Series. Along with Wimbledon and the United States Open, the Virginia Slims World Championships ranks as one of the three most important professional tournaments for women players.

Virginia Slims World Championship Series: A women's professional tennis series that links the most prestigious tennis tournaments (including the Grand Slam events) in a year-long worldwide circuit on which players earn points as well as prize money for their performance in each event. These points go toward a spot in the Virginia Slims World Championships (held at the end of the season) and toward a share in a bonus pool of prize money, distributed among the circuit's leading point-winning singles and doubles players at the conclusion of the series. To be eligible for the bonus pool, a player must agree to play in at least eleven WTA-approved major tournaments, not including Grand Slam events. The Virginia Slims World Championship Series is administered by the Women's International Professional Tennis Council. see *Virginia Slims World Championships.*

1. volley: A stroke in which the ball is hit in the air before it bounces. The word "volley" is from the Middle French *volee,* meaning "flight," and originally, the Latin *volare,* meaning "to fly." The volley was introduced in the finals of the inaugural Wimbledon Championship in 1877 by singles winner Spencer W. Gore. Other early volley exponents were 1881 United States singles champion Richard Sears, England's famous Renshaw twins of the 1880s, William and Ernest, and 1907 Wimbledon singles champion, the Australian left-hander, Norman Brooks. see *early ball.* compare *half volley, pickup shot.*

2. volley: To hit a ball in the air before it bounces. compare *half volley.*

Volvo Grand Prix: A men's professional tennis circuit that links the most prestigious tennis tournaments in a year-long worldwide circuit on which players earn points as well as prize money for their performance in each event. These points go toward a spot in the year-end Volvo Masters and toward a share in a bonus pool of prize money, distributed among the circuit's leading point-winning singles and doubles players at the conclusion of the Grand Prix year. To be eligible to compete in the Grand Prix, a player must agree to play in twelve designated tournaments during the year in the highest classification of tournament for which his ranking makes

him eligible. The four Grand Slam events make up the first or highest classification group, followed in descending order by the Super Series tournaments and Regular Series tournaments, which differ in the amount of prize money offered. Now administrated by the Men's International Professional Tennis Council, the Grand Prix circuit was initiated in 1970 through the efforts of former tennis great Jack Kramer. see *computer rankings, designated tournament, designations, Volvo Masters.*

Volvo Masters: The championship tournament of the Volvo Grand Prix circuit, played annually at Madison Square Garden in New York between the circuit's eight top singles players and the four top doubles teams. The first Masters Tournament, then called the Grand Prix Masters, was played in 1970 in Tokyo, with Stan Smith winning both the singles championship and, teamed with Ken Rosewall, the doubles title. also *Masters.*

waiting position: see *alert position.*

walk-in: see *bye.*

walkover: 1. A game, set, or match in which a winner is declared because the opponent defaults. 2. Slang for a particularly one-sided game, set, or match.

WCT: World Championship Tennis. A year-long worldwide series of twenty men's professional tournaments, divided into seasonal circuits of fall, winter, and spring, each concluding with an eight-man championship final. Players earn points as well as prize money for their performance in each WCT event, and for the United States, French, and Wimbledon Championships. These points go toward a spot in the season-ending WCT finals in Dallas in May, and toward a share of a bonus pool distributed there. In 1980, WCT introduced a new player rating system (Nixdorf computer ranking) and a new tournament format to begin the following year, in which the seasonal circuits are replaced by three separate "surface" circuits (hard court, clay court, and indoor carpet surfaces), each concluding with its own championship. A combination of twelve-tournament winners, high points scorers, and exempted ranked past winners meet in Dallas for the annual WCT Finals (first won by Ken Rosewall,

1971). WCT also sponsors the annual Tournament of Champions at Forest Hills in New York, open to all winners of major tournaments (first won by Harold Solomon, 1977). WCT was founded in 1967 by sports entrepreneurs Lamar Hunt and Dave Dickson (the latter was bought shortly therafter by WCT president Al Hill, Jr.) see *computer rankings.*

Western grip: A not often used method of holding a racket in which the player, with the racket held on edge, rests the palm of the hand near the bottom side of the handle. With the Western grip (so called because it was developed on California's lively concrete tennis courts), the racket face is closed, making the grip suitable for high volleys and high-bouncing groundstrokes. Some early exponents of the Western grip simply turned the racket over for a backhand stroke rather than making the necessary large change in grips, but in recent years, some players have used the Western grip as one half of a two-handed grip for backhand strokes. compare *chopper grip, Continental grip, Eastern grip, English grip, service grip.*

wide: Out because of landing beyond the service sideline on a serve or beyond the sideline on a stroke, resulting in a lost point (or on a first serve, a fault). compare *deep, long, short.*

Wightman Cup: An annual women's competition between the United States and Great Britain, consisting of five singles and two doubles matches. The trophy, actually inscribed the "Women's Lawn Tennis Team Championship between Great Britain and the United States," was donated by and later named for United States tennis great Mrs. Hazel Hotchkiss Wightman, who captained the winning side in the first event in 1923.

wild card: A player included in the draw (and sometimes seeded) at the sole discretion of the tournament committee rather than on the basis of a qualifying competition or computer rankings.

Wimbledon: 1. The All England Club in Church Road, Wimbledon, England, home of the Wimbledon Championships, the oldest and most famous competition in tennis. The original Wimbledon, abandoned for the present

facilities in 1922, was also the site of the first recorded international match in 1883 when C.M. and J.S. Clark (with permission from the United States doubles champions at that time, James Dwight and Richard Sears) represented the United States and were defeated by England's famous Renshaw twins, William and Ernest. 2. The Wimbledon Championships.

Wimbledon Championships: An international tournament held annually at the All England Club in Church Road, Wimbledon, England, one of the prestigious "Big Four" or "Grand Slam" events, and the oldest and most famous competition in tennis. The first Wimbledon Championship, for which many of the basic rules of modern tennis were drafted, was held in 1877, with S.W. Gore winning the only event, men's singles. Men's doubles were added in 1879 (won by L.R. Erskine and H.F. Lawford), women's singles in 1884 (won by Miss M. Watson) and women's doubles (won by Mrs. R.J. McNair and Miss D.P. Boothby) and mixed doubles (won by H. Crisp and Mrs. C.O. Tuckey) in 1913. Wimbledon became an "open" competition in 1968. also *British National Championships, Wimbledon.*

winner: A shot that wins a point, a winning stroke.

WIPTC: The Women's International Professional Tennis Council.

Women's International Professional Tennis Council: The governing body of women's professional tennis, comprised of representatives of players, the International Tennis Federation, the Women's Tennis Association, and tournament directors. Formed in 1975, the Women's International Professional Tennis Council is responsible for matters regarding tournament applications, scheduling, player conduct, and conditions of play. also *WIPTC.*

Women's Tennis Association: A service organization for women professional tennis players. Founded in 1973 through the efforts of first president Billie Jean King, the Women's Tennis Association (WTA) functions as the representative of touring professionals in matters regarding tournament play and provides a computer ranking service (based on performance) for professional players.

wood shot: A shot accidentally hit with the frame of the racket.

wristy: Having a lot of spin, as of a stroke or serve.

wrong-foot: To hit a shot to one side of an opponent who is leaning or moving in the opposite direction, or on the "wrong foot." (wrong-footed him to take the last point)

WTA: The Women's Tennis Association.

WORLD ALMANAC PUBLICATIONS
200 Park Avenue
Department B
New York, New York 10166

Please send me, postpaid, the books checked below:

☐ THE WORLD ALMANAC® AND BOOK OF FACTS 1984 . . . . . . $4.95
☐ THE WORLD ALMANAC BOOK OF WORLD WAR II $10.95
☐ 101 LISTS: HOW TO DO PRACTICALLY EVERYTHING FASTER,
    EASIER, & CHEAPER $4.95
☐ THE WORLD ALMANAC DICTIONARY OF DATES. $8.95
☐ THE SNOOPY COLLECTION $9.95
☐ THE LAST TIME WHEN $8.95
☐ WORLD DATA $9.95
☐ THE CIVIL WAR ALMANAC $10.95
☐ THE OMNI FUTURE ALMANAC $8.95
☐ THE LANGUAGE OF SPORT $7.95
☐ THE COOK'S ALMANAC. $8.95
☐ THE GREAT JOHN L $3.95
    WORLD OF INFORMATION:
☐ MIDDLE EAST REVIEW 1983. . . . . $24.95
☐ ASIA & PACIFIC 1983 . . . . $24.95
☐ LATIN AMERICA & CARIBBEAN. $24.95
☐ AFRICA GUIDE 1983. $24.95

(Add $1 postage and handling for the first book, plus 50 cents for each additional book ordered.)

Enclosed is my check or money order for $_____

NAME_____

ADDRESS_____

CITY_____ STATE_____ ZIP_____